Forty-Eight Minutes: A Night in the Life of the NBA
(with Bob Ryan)

Tark: College Basketball's Winningest Coach
(with Jerry Tarkanian)

Bull Session: An Up-Close Look
at Michael Jordan and Courtside Stories About the Chicago Bulls
(with Johnny "Red" Kerr)

You Could Argue But You'd Be Wrong
(with Pete Franklin)

Sixty-One: The Team, the Record, the Men
(with Tony Kubek)

A Baseball Winter: The Off-Season Life of the Summer Game
(with Jeff Neuman)

Earl of Baltimore: The Earl Weaver Story

Super Joe
(with Burt Graeff and Joe Charboneau)

The Greatest Summer:
The Remarkable Story of Jim Bouton's Comeback to MLB

LOOSE BALLS

The Short, Wild Life of the
American Basketball Association
—As Told by the Players,
Coaches, and Movers
and Shakers Who Made It Happen

TERRY PLUTO

SIMON & SCHUSTER PAPERBACKS
New York   London   Toronto   Sydney

SIMON & SCHUSTER PAPERBACKS
Rockefeller Center
1230 Avenue of the Americas
New York, NY 10020

First Simon & Schuster paperback edition 2007

SIMON & SCHUSTER PAPERBACKS and colophon are registered
trademarks of Simon & Schuster, Inc.

For information regarding special discounts for bulk
purchases, please contact Simon & Schuster Special Sales
at 1-800-456-6798 or business@simonandschuster.com

Manufactured in the United States of America

6 8 10 9 7

Photo Credits:
AP/Wide World Photo, 48; *The Courier-Journal*, 33, 39, 51;
The Denver Post, 13, 14; *The Greensboro News & Record*, 36 (Jimmie Jeffries),
7, 35 (John Page), 19 (Larry Tucker); Al Hall, 17, 28, 42, 57; Indiana Pacers, 16,
20, 21, 22, 23, 24, 25, 26, 27, 31, 40, 50; Robert Pavuchak/*Pittsburgh Press*, 15;
San Antonio Spurs, 54, 55; Collection of Jon Singer, 2, 3, 8 ,10, 11, 12, 18, 43,
44, 45, 46, 52, 53; *The Sporting News*, 1, 4, 5, 9, 29, 32, 34, 38, 49, 56

To Karen and Tony Stastny

*and to Gene Littles, Steve Jones, Dave Twardzik, Mel Daniels,
Terry Stembridge, Mack Calvin, Mike Storen, Dick Tinkham,
Harry Weltman, Carl Scheer, Billy Keller, Ron Grinker
and all the rest who lived the ABA.*

Acknowledgments

The reason for this book is that so many people felt it had to be written. There were those who wanted to write the book themselves but never got around to it, yet the stories of the ABA lived on inside them, waiting—maybe even demanding—to be told. So this book is really their book in their voices. The hardest part of this project was choosing what should stay in, not finding enough stories to fill it. The original manuscript was nearly a thousand pages; I trust that the stories that didn't make it will eventually be heard. The book was originally the idea of Simon & Schuster editor Jeff Neuman, who went far beyond the call of duty in shaping the material. Roberta Pluto and Pat McCubbin transcribed more than 150 hours of tapes. Others behind the scenes who made significant contributions to this work were Faith Hamlin, Dale Ratermann, Wayne Witt, Mark Patrick, Warner Fusselle, Jon Singer and Alan Spatrick. I thank them all.

—Terry Pluto

Contents

Part I:
OPENING GAMBITS

Part II:
MIDDLE GAME

Part III:
ENDGAME

LOOSE BALLS

Introduction

The old American Basketball Association . . .

Most fans remember it for the quirky red, white and blue basketball. Or perhaps as the league that made famous the 3-point shot. Maybe some fans know that the ABA gave birth to the Slam Dunk Contest. Astute basketball fans think of it as the league that gave us Julius Erving, Larry Brown, Doug Moe and Connie Hawkins, as well as Moses Malone and a couple of other high school kids who went straight to the pros. Some even remember that it was the birthplace of the San Antonio Spurs, the Denver Nuggets, the New Jersey Nets and the Indiana Pacers.

Ever hear of a guy named Bob Costas? His first radio gig was in the ABA as the voice of the Spirits of St. Louis, where he tried to explain to the world—or at least the good part of it reached by KMOX's booming 50,000-watt signal—that star Marvin Barnes had missed yet another team flight, this one from Louisville to St. Louis that was scheduled to depart at 8 A.M. eastern time and arrive at 7:59 central.

Why did Barnes miss the flight?

Because, as Barnes explained, he "didn't want to get in no time machine."

Then again, Barnes seldom made any flight before noon, regardless of the time zone. After missing one flight, he hired a private jet to take him to a road game, then forgot to pay the pilot. At the end of the first quarter, the pilot showed up at the arena wanting his money. During the next timeout, Barnes, in uniform, went into the dressing room, came out with his checkbook and paid the man.

True story . . . we think.

Barnes also had 13 telephones in his house, but that's another story. Is it true? Maybe. When asked about it, Barnes counted up to seven phones in his house, then started laughing so hard he quit counting.

Hardcore basketball fans think about Marvin Barnes as much as they think about Julius Erving when it comes to the ABA. It's like Barnes was the bad angel on one shoulder, Erving the good angel on the other.

Erving was the league statesman, the spokesman, the player who could outdo anyone on any playground with his soaring dunks and double pumps under the basket. And in the boardroom, Erving could sound like one of the league's owners, selling the ABA as a real alternative to the NBA—and how if the NBA were smart, they'd merge the two leagues right now. Dr. J's on-court aerobatics made the case as persuasively as any economic argument could.

If Marvin Barnes had been smart, he'd have listened a little more to players like Erving. Of course, it would have helped if Barnes had just shown up with his teammates. Too often, he wandered in about 30 minutes before tip-off, sometimes with a bag of burgers and fries from McDonald's, then sat on the trainer's table getting his ankles taped as he chowed down a Big Mac. Then went out and scored 40.

True story . . . or at least that's how some remember it.

But that's what the ABA was about: stories, myths and legends—including the stories about the guy named John Brisker, who brought a gun to the dressing room; who once stomped a player's head on the court; who later was killed in Uganda while doing some diamond business with Idi Amin.

True stories? Who knows?

But they're all a part of the ABA, the most storied league of them all.

Keep this in mind: The ABA never should have been started, much less have lasted from 1967–76 while changing the entire structure of pro basketball in the process. The Indiana Pacers, New Jersey Nets, San Antonio Spurs and Denver Nuggets never should have played a single game, much less moved from the ABA to the NBA. The 3-point shot should be nothing more than a piece of long-forgotten basketball history, much like the center jump made after each basket.

That's because when Dennis Murphy came up with the idea of the

ABA in the 1960s—he's not sure exactly when—it was supposed to have been a second pro football league, only the American Football League had already beaten Murphy and his friends to the idea.

Murphy was the mayor of Buena Park, California. He had assembled some money people for his proposed football league. When that concept fell through, he did some serious marketing research and came up with the idea of the ABA. That research consisted of one thing: counting the number of NBA teams. "There was only one hockey and one basketball league," Murphy said. "So why not have another? Since I knew nothing about hockey, but basketball was my favorite sport, I figured I'd pursue the idea of a basketball league. I saw that the NBA had 12 [teams]. It seemed like there should be more teams. Why? I don't know. What the hell, it was worth a shot."

It's hard today to imagine the pro sports landscape of the middle 1960s. There was no cable TV, no internet. There was no tremendous love for pro basketball, even the NBA variety, in most cities. The Boston Celtics were winning world titles every year, but they seldom sold out and usually were outdrawn by the National Hockey League's Boston Bruins. Yes, the NBA had only a dozen teams, but close to half of them consistently lost money. There were only three channels available on most black-and-white TVs, and the networks often recorded higher ratings for bowling and boxing than for NBA playoff games. Had Murphy actually studied the situation with some people who could realistically assess the utter lack of interest in pro basketball, the experts would have told him that pro sports was like this: Baseball was still king, but football was ascending to the throne: pro football was the emerging as the sport of the 1960s. Pro basketball was a distant third in most cities. In some places it was fourth, behind either boxing or college basketball.

There already had been a second pro basketball league in the early 1960s, the American Basketball League. It folded despite the presence of an owner named George Steinbrenner and a coach named Bill Sharman, who was a Hall of Fame player for the Boston Celtics and would win NBA and ABA championships later in his career. Remember, more people wanted to watch bowling than the NBA. Another pro basketball league? Been there, done that and here's the red ink on the bank statements to prove it.

Murphy and his buddies didn't worry about that. In fact, they didn't even think about it. They wanted a piece of the pro sports action—almost any piece of any sport. They had seen the upstart AFL force a lucrative merger with the established National Football League, and they figured they could get in on some of that action in another arena. They were dreamers, schemers and sometimes liars. Often, the biggest whoppers they told were to themselves, just to keep the league alive. They were driven more out of desperation than inspiration.

Dick Tinkham was one of the early owners in the league, putting together the Indiana Pacers. Tinkham said, "We had no plan. None. We wanted to start a second basketball league and force the NBA to merge with us. That was a goal. But a plan? We had none. We went by the seat of our pants and made it up as we went along. If a rule didn't fit with something we wanted to do, we just changed it or ignored it. If someone had an idea, no matter how lame-brained, usually someone tried it."

Which brings us to the red, white and blue basketball.

It was the brainchild of George Mikan, the man voted the NBA's best player for the first 50 years of the 20th century. He was 6-foot-10 in an era when that made him look 7-foot-10. He was Chamberlain and Shaq before there were Chamberlain and Shaq. When Dennis Murphy and the boys were hunting for a commissioner of the new league, they found Mikan in Minneapolis, where he owned a travel agency and practiced a little law.

Once again, this was the result of in-depth research: "I think Dennis Murphy read an article about me in *Sport* magazine which said I'd make a good commissioner of the NBA because I had a law degree."

The new owners of the new league that had yet to play a game, sign a player or even buy a basketball approached the NBA's first real star and offered him the keys to the ABA. Of course, there were no buildings, either.

But the guys did seem to have some money, and Mikan convinced them to pay him $50,000 annually for three years.

That was a lot of money in 1967, more money than Mikan had ever made as a player.

The new owners wanted the ABA office to be in New York.

Mikan said it had to be in Minneapolis, because his travel agency was in Minneapolis and he wasn't moving.

So they headquartered the ABA in Minneapolis, which was not exactly the media capital of America. Of course, Mikan could have said Siberia, and the owners would have invested in sled dogs and snowshoes to make him happy. Having Mikan gave them legitimacy. He was a real basketball name, one of the all-time greats, a Hall of Famer. He was everything the founders of the ABA were not—he was Mr. Pro Basketball.

What does this have to do with the red, white and blue ball?

"The ABA had a red, white and blue ball because I said it would have one," said Mikan.

Most of the owners stared up at the monstrous Mikan as he if had just lost his mind, but no one was about to look him in the eye and tell him that. How could they, unless they stood on a ladder?

Besides, they wanted Mikan. And Mikan—who wore glasses—said he had trouble seeing the brown ball when he watched basketball games. If Mikan had had better eyesight, would the ABA also have had a brown ball? Who knows? Mikan just said the league was the *American* Basketball Association, and *America's* colors are red, white and blue. You can see a red, white and blue ball.

"The owners acted like I wanted to burn the flag when I said to forget the brown ball," said Mikan.

Once again, no marketing surveys, no firms hired to determine the viability of a red, white and blue ball. George Mikan wanted a red, white and blue ball, so the ABA had a red, white and blue ball.

Something else Mikan added: We will have a 3-point shot.

OK, said the owners. Why not? If we have a 3-colored ball, why not a 3-point shot?

True stories, for real.

That's why it's so easy to fall in love with the ABA—especially when looking at it in the nostalgic tint of life's rear-view mirror. You hear these stories and realize there will never be anything quite like this again.

•   •   •

That's also why people have been reading *Loose Balls* since it was first published in 1990. It's the story of some of basketball's biggest names: Julius Erving, Rick Barry, Billy Cunningham and Spencer Haywood. Even Wilt Chamberlain passed through the ABA. But it's the guys like Dennis Murphy who make the story irresistible. They were making it up as they went along. It's as if a bunch of neighborhood kids got together, decided to put on a little show with some music in their garage and came up with *Oklahoma!* or *Cats.*

It just never should have happened . . . but it did.

This book is much like the league. The Dennis Murphy of the project was a former Simon & Schuster editor named Jeff Neuman. He had grown up an ABA fan, watching Julius Erving and the New York Nets. He proposed the idea of an ABA book to me. I had grown up in Cleveland and had never seen an ABA game, although my mother used to buy me a red, white and blue basketball every Christmas. Just like George Mikan, she liked the colors better than the standard drab brown of the NBA.

I knew nothing about the ABA. As I began to research the league, I discovered there was little actually written about it. Nor did much film remain. All that lived on were the people involved and their memories. Or, as Bob Costas told me, "Virtually everything that is known about it comes by word of mouth, as if it happened centuries ago."

Neuman told me to write it that way: Just write what they said.

This reminds me of what frustrated reporters sometimes admit in private: "We don't write the truth. We just write what people say is the truth."

Forget about not being able to handle the truth, as Jack Nicholson screams in *A Few Good Men.* When it comes to the ABA, it's really impossible to know the truth, the whole truth and nothing but the truth.

What you have are incredible stories that seem even more amazing with the passing of time.

I started much like Murphy did with the real ABA. I talked to one person from the league. Then another. And another. They'd tell me that I needed to contact this guy, who knew the real scoop. They gave me names and phone numbers of people whom I'd never heard of, despite being a veteran pro basketball writer at the time. Virtually everyone—big name or obscure front-office worker—wanted to tell their story about the ABA.

They loved the league. They wanted to make the book work. They trusted me with their time, stories and in some cases pieces of their heart and a good chunk of their youth.

It's what people said that forms the truth about the ABA, or as much truth as we know or need. Sometimes, memories were fuzzy. Other times, accounts didn't match up. In some cases, they seemed so outrageous, I couldn't believe they were true—but I put them in the book anyway, especially when several sources told me the same story. The book is pure oral history, as if you were sitting at a table with Larry Brown, Doug Moe, Bob Costas and so many others—listening to them tell the story of the ABA.

That idea also was Neuman's, and the concept was completely foreign and incredibly scary to me, despite the fact that I had already written eight books. It was our version of the red, white and blue ball. We knew some people would be put off by the format, but others would be fascinated by it. The idea was to make it easy to read, free flowing, sometimes wild, usually unusual.

Part of what made the book popular is the hip style that reflected how the game was played in the old ABA.

As veteran agent Ron Grinker said, "The NBA was a symphony, the ABA was jazz."

And the tunes matched the times.

Which brings us to the Slam Dunk Contest.

This was vintage ABA. The year was 1976. The war between the ABA and the NBA had lasted nine long years. The ABA was down to seven teams and one division. How can you have an All-Star game with seven teams? That was the question facing ABA executives (or what was left of them). Three teams had folded since the start of training camp. The game would be in Denver, because Denver had a strong fan base, a great coach in Larry Brown and a superstar in David Thompson. Why not have the Nuggets play a group of All-Stars from the other six teams?

Why not, indeed?

Done.

(In fact, this was what the National Hockey League had done during its many years as a six-team league—play an All-Star game between the Stanley Cup Champions and the top players from the other five teams. Of course, the Denver Nuggets weren't the reigning ABA champions—the Kentucky Colonels were—but nobody was going to let that stand in the way of a good promotion.)

They wanted something special for halftime. They had already imported Glen Campbell and Charlie Rich to do a concert around the game. Hey, this was 1976. Denver was the West. Campbell and Rich were still hot in country music. But they wanted something else, something funky, something that could catch the attention of the country.

A guy named Jim Bukata, a former ABA public relations man, said, "Let's have a Slam Dunk Contest."

Everyone at the table said, "Hey, that sounds great, a Slam Dunk Contest."

Then silence struck.

How do you have a Slam Dunk Contest? As far as any of them knew, there had never been a dunking contest. So like everything else in the ABA, they began to just make it up. And it ended with Julius Erving winning it when he drove the length of the court, took off from the foul line, flew 15 feet in the air—and dunked!

True story . . . almost.

His foot went a little bit over the foul line—we actually do have film of this—but it was close enough! Give him 14 feet, 10 inches and a dunk for the ages.

Here were the competitors in the contest: David Thompson, George Gervin, Larry Kenon, Artis Gilmore and Erving. Now there's a starting five that would have won a few games in any league.

And when the NBA finally brought four teams into the NBA for the 1976–77 season (Indiana, San Antonio, Denver and the New York—soon to be New Jersey—Nets), the world discovered something ABA fans had known for the last nine years following the red, white and blue bouncing ball: These guys could really play!

In that first year after the merger, four of the NBA's top 10 scorers had played in the ABA. Five of the 10 starters in the NBA finals between Portland and Philadelphia had played in the ABA. Denver won the Midwest Division. Ten former ABA players made the All-Star teams.

But more important, the ABA brought its loose, improvisational style to the NBA, a new approach to everything from playing to coaching to marketing. The dance teams that you see in virtually every NBA arena? The ABA had them first, or something like them. There were these girls in Miami who sat under the baskets, gave officials water during timeouts and jiggled for the fans. They wore bikinis. Or as one Miami Floridians operative said, "We are talking about a very brief bikini situation." They were much more honest than many of today's "dance teams." They skipped the dancing part and just strutted their stuff. Let's be truthful, the NBA has incorporated every major ABA innovation except for the red, white and blue ball. And with the league's quest to sell merchandise, who knows? Maybe one day that tricolored ball will show up at an NBA arena near you. It's already featured in the 3-point shooting contest at the All-Star weekend. The last ball of each rack, which counts double and is called "the money ball," is red, white and blue.

True story.

—Terry Pluto,
October 2006

Cast of Characters

STEVE ALBERT: Broadcast the New York Nets in their final championship season and now does the same for the New Jersey Nets.

STEVE ARNOLD: The agent for Julius Erving and others, now in private business in California.

RICK BARRY: First NBA player to jump to the ABA. A member of the Hall of Fame and a broadcaster of NBA games for the TNT network.

BOB BASS: A coach of several ABA teams, now general manager of the San Antonio Spurs.

ZELMO BEATY: All-Star center for Utah, now a stockbroker in Seattle.

AL BIANCHI: Former coach of the Virginia Squires, now the general manager of the New York Knicks.

LEONARD BLOOM: Former owner of the San Diego franchise, now in private business in California.

ROY BOE: Former owner of the New York Nets, now a restaurant owner in Long Island, New York.

PAT BOONE: Former owner of the Oakland Oaks, still singing and playing pickup basketball in Los Angeles.

HUBIE BROWN: Former coach of Kentucky, now analyst for CBS.

LARRY BROWN: Former coach of Denver and Carolina, now coach of the San Antonio Spurs.

ROGER BROWN: All-Star forward with Indiana, now lives in Indianapolis and operates several small businesses.

JIM BUKATA: Former ABA public relations man, now works for International Management Group.

13

MACK CALVIN: All-Star guard with several ABA teams, now an assistant coach with the Milwaukee Bucks.

DON CHANEY: Spent one year with St. Louis, now coach of the Houston Rockets.

JIM CHONES: Former center with New York and Carolina, now a broadcaster for the Cleveland Cavaliers.

BOB COSTAS: Former broadcaster with St. Louis, now works for NBC.

DAVE CRAIG: Still trainer of the Indiana Pacers.

LARRY CREGER: Former assistant to Bill Sharman in L.A. and Utah, now operates the L.A. summer pro league.

BILLY CUNNINGHAM: Former member of the Carolina Cougars, now executive vice president of the Miami Heat.

MEL DANIELS: Former All-Star center with Indiana, now works for the Pacers as a scout.

JEFF DENBERG: Former New York sportswriter, now covers the Atlanta Hawks.

LARRY DONALD: Editor of *Basketball Times.*

ANGELO DROSSOS: Former owner of the San Antonio Spurs, now an investment broker in San Antonio.

NORM DRUCKER: Former ABA official, now works with the World Basketball League as chief of its officials.

WAYNE EMBRY: Former general manager of the Milwaukee Bucks, now general manager with the Cleveland Cavaliers.

JULIUS ERVING: Greatest player in ABA history, now has a variety of business interests in Philadelphia.

COTTON FITZSIMMONS: Veteran NBA coach, now with Phoenix.

EARL FOREMAN: Former owner of the Virginia Squires, now commissioner of the Major Indoor Soccer League.

WARNER FUSSELLE: Former broadcaster in Virginia, now works for Major League Baseball, Inc.

MIKE GOLDBERG: Former ABA legal counsel, now represents several NBA coaches.

RON GRINKER: Still an attorney and players' agent.

JOE GUSHUE: Former ABA official, now in private business.

ALEX HANNUM: Former coach of Oakland and Denver, now lives in California and is in the construction business.

JERRY HARKNESS: Former Indiana Pacer, now lives in Indianapolis and is in private business.

DEL HARRIS: Former assistant in Utah, now head coach of the Milwaukee Bucks.

GEORGE IRVINE: Veteran ABA player, now player personnel director of the Indiana Pacers.

DAN ISSEL: Former ABA star center and forward, now broadcasts the Denver Nuggets games.

STEVE JONES: Played with seven different ABA teams, now lives in Portland and broadcasts the NBA on the TNT network.

BILLY KELLER: Former Pacer guard, now lives in Indiana and runs basketball clinics for the Pacers.

JOHNNY KERR: Former general manager of Virginia, now a broadcaster for the Chicago Bulls.

BILLY KNIGHT: Former Pacer star, now works in the team's front office.

BARNEY KREMENKO: Former Nets public relations director.

SLICK LEONARD: Former Pacer coach, now a broadcaster for the team.

GENE LITTLES: Veteran ABA guard, now coach of the Charlotte Hornets.

JOHN LOPEZ: Texas sportswriter who grew up in San Antonio.

KEVIN LOUGHERY: Former Nets coach, now a broadcaster for the Atlanta Hawks.

BOB MACKINNON: Former coach of St. Louis, now player personnel director for the New Jersey Nets.

RUDY MARTZKE: Former public relations man in Miami and general manager in St. Louis, now writes for *USA Today.*

LEE MEADE: First ABA public relations man, now public relations man for a professional volleyball league.

TOM MESCHERY: Former coach of Carolina, now teaches high school in Reno.

GEORGE MIKAN: First ABA commissioner, now a businessman in Minneapolis.

DOUG MOE: Veteran ABA player and coach, now coaching Denver.

JOE MULLANEY: Veteran pro and college coach.

TEDD MUNCHAK: Former owner of the Cougars and ABA commissioner, now in private business in Atlanta.

DENNIS MURPHY: Founder of the ABA, now trying to start a Global Hockey League.

BOB NETOLICKY: Former Pacer forward, now works at the Indianapolis Auto Auction.

PETE NEWELL: Veteran NBA general manager, now a scout with the Cleveland Cavaliers.

TOM NISSALKE: Former coach of Dallas, San Antonio, and Utah, now coach of the Memphis Rockers of the WBL.

JIM O'BRIEN: Covered the ABA for *The Sporting News,* now editor of *Street and Smith's Basketball Magazine.*

DAVE ROBISCH: Veteran ABA player, coaches in the World Basketball League.

BOB RYAN: Writes for the *Boston Globe.*

CARL SCHEER: Former general manager in Carolina and Denver, now general manager of the Denver Nuggets for a second time.

SAM SMITH: Former Floridians broadcaster, now broadcasts Miami Heat games.

LARRY STAVERMAN: First Pacer coach, now works for the Cleveland Stadium Corporation.

TERRY STEMBRIDGE: Former Spurs broadcaster, now in the oil business in Kilgore, Texas.

JOHN STERLING: Former Nets broadcaster, now works in broadcasting in New York.

MIKE STOREN: Former ABA executive, now in public relations.

ROD THORN: Former ABA coach, now director of operations for the NBA.

JOE TAIT: Veteran NBA announcer with the Cleveland Cavaliers.

DICK TINKHAM: Former legal counsel with Indiana, now a lawyer in Indianapolis.

DAVE TWARDZIK: Former Virginia guard, now an assistant with the L.A. Clippers.

JOHN VANAK: Former ABA official, now a private detective.

DAVE VANCE: Former Kentucky general manager, now a racetrack manager in Oklahoma City.

VAN VANCE: Former Kentucky broadcaster, now broadcasts University of Louisville basketball games.

HARRY WELTMAN: Former president of the St. Louis Spirits.

LENNY WILKENS: Veteran NBA player and coach.

CHARLIE WILLIAMS: Former ABA guard, now a sales representative for a steel company in Cleveland.

MAX WILLIAMS: Former Dallas general manager and coach, now in the oil business with Terry Stembridge in Kilgore, Texas.

WAYNE WITT: Public relations man for the San Antonio Spurs.

Year-by-Year Standings and Franchise Shifts

For each team, the history of the franchise can be traced by reading across. Won-lost records and standings (for each division) are listed below each team. Superscripts refer to logos and nicknames, overleaf. Asterisks indicate the league champions.

Year 1 1967–68	Year 2 1968–69	Year 3 1969–70	Year 4 1970–71	Year 5 1971–72
PIT[1] 54–24, 1E*	MIN[2] 36–42, 4E	PIT[2] 29–55, 5E	PIT[3] 36–48, 5E	PIT[4] 25–59, 6E
MIN[1] 50–28, 2E	MIA[1] 43–35, 2E	MIA[1] 23–61, 6E	FLA[1] 37–47, 4E	FLA[2] 36–48, 4E
IND[1] 38–40, 3E	IND[1] 44–34, 1E	IND[1] 59–25, 1E*	IND[1] 58–26, 1W	IND[1] 47–37, 2W*
KY[1] 37–42, 4E	KY[1] 42–36, 3E	KY[1] 45–39, 2E	KY[2] 44–40, 2E	KY[2] 68–16, 1E
NJ[1] 36–43, 5E	NY[1] 17–61, 5E	NY[1] 39–45, 4E	NY[1] 40–44, 3E	NY[1] 44–40, 3E
NO[1] 48–30, 1W	NO[1] 46–32, 2W	NO[2] 42–42, 5W	MEM[1] 41–43, 3W	MEM[2] 26–58, 5W
DAL[1] 46–32, 2W	DAL[1] 41–37, 4W	DAL[1] 45–39, 2W	TEX[1] 30–54, 4W	DAL[2] 42–42, 3W
DEN[1] 45–33, 3W	DEN[1] 44–34, 3W	DEN[1] 51–33, 1W	DEN[1] 30–54, 5W	DEN[2] 34–50, 4W
HOU[1] 29–49, 4W	HOU[1] 23–55, 6W	CAR[1] 42–42, 3E	CAR[2] 34–50, 6E	CAR[2] 35–49, 5E
ANA[1] 25–53, 5W	LA[1] 33–45, 5W	LA[2] 43–41, 4W	UTAH[1] 57–27, 2W*	UTAH[1] 60–24, 1W
OAK[1] 22–56, 6W	OAK[1] 60–16, 1W*	WAS[1] 44–40, 3W	VIR[1] 55–29, 1E	VIR[2] 45–39, 2E

Year 6 1972–73	Year 7 1973–74	Year 8 1974–75	Year 9 1975–76
IND[1] 51–33, 2W*	IND[1] 46–38, 2W	IND[1] 45–39, 3W	IND[1] 39–45, 5
KY[2] 56–28, 2E	KY[2] 53–31, 2E	KY[2] 58–26, 1E*	KY[2] 46–38, 4
NY[2] 30–54, 4E	NY[2] 55–29, 1E*	NY[2] 58–26, 2E	NY[2] 55–29, 2*
MEM[3] 24–60, 5E	MEM[3] 21–63, 5E	MEM[4] 27–57, 4E	BAL[1]
DAL[2] 28–56, 5W	SA[1] 45–39, 3W	SA[1] 51–33, 2W	SA[1] 50–34, 3
DEN[2] 47–37, 3W	DEN[2] 37–47, 4W	DEN[3] 65–19, 1W	DEN[3] 60–24, 1
CAR[2] 57–27, 1E	CAR[2] 47–37, 3E	STL[1] 32–52, 3E	STL[1] 35–49, 6
UTAH[1] 55–29, 1W	UTAH[1] 51–33, 1W	UTAH[1] 38–46, 4W	UTAH[1] 4–12,
VIR[2] 42–42, 3E	VIR[3] 28–56, 4E	VIR[4] 15–69, 5E	VIR[4] 15–68, 7
SD[1] 30–54, 4W	SD[1] 36–47, 5W	SD[1] 31–53, 5W	SD[2] 3–9,

ABA Team Logos

The following are the team logos, as reproduced in
The Sporting News' ABA Guides and team programs.

ANA[1]
Year 1

| DAL[2] | DEN[1] | DEN[2] | DEN[3] |
| Years 5–6 | Years 1–4 | Years 5–7 | Years 8–9 |

| KY[1] | KY[2] | LA[1] | LA[2] |
| Years 1–3 | Years 4–9 | Year 2 | Year 3 |

| MIA[1] | MIN[1] | MIN[2] | NJ[1] |
| Years 2–3 | Year 1 | Year 2 | Year 1 |

| OAK[1] | PIT[1] | PIT[2] | PIT[3] |
| Years 1–2 | Year 1 | Year 3 | Year 4 |

| SD[2] | TEX[1] | UTAH[1] | VIR[1] |
| Year 9 | Year 4 | Years 4–9 | Year 4 |

BAL[1]
Year 9

CAR[1]
Year 3

CAR[2]
Years 4–7

DAL[1]
Years 1–3

FLA[1]
Year 4

FLA[2]
Year 5

HOU[1]
Years 1–2

IND[1]
Years 1–9

MEM[1]
Year 4

MEM[2]
Year 5

MEM[3]
Years 6–7

MEM[4]
Year 8

NO[1]
Years 1–2

NO[2]
Year 3

NY[1]
Years 2–5

NY[2]
Years 6–9

PIT[4]
Year 5

STL[1]
Years 8–9

SA[1]
Years 7–9

SD[1]
Years 6–8

VIR[2]
Years 5–6

VIR[3]
Year 7

VIR[4]
Years 8–9

WAS[1]
Year 3

In an era where sports is overexposed and overtelevised, the ABA is the last significant sports venture that has any mystery about it. Julius Erving symbolizes the ABA, and the mystique that exists about Julius to this day is there because he began his career in "the other league." How many people really saw Julius with the Virginia Squires? And the ABA lasted from 1967 to '76, so it wasn't in the dark ages, yet there was no national television contract, no cable deal, not even ESPN or CNN to show you what was happening in the ABA. Virtually everything that is known about it comes by word of mouth, as if it happened centuries ago. The ABA was like basketball's Wild West, and Julius Erving, George Gervin, James Silas and all the other ABA stars were the gunfighters. They are men of legend known to millions, but whose actual deeds were seen by few.

—Bob Costas

Prologue

The first Slam Dunk Contest was like most things in the ABA—an act of desperation designed to get a few more fans to walk through the doors. Sports Illustrated called it "the best halftime invention since the rest room." There were five contestants—Julius Erving, Larry Kenon, Artis Gilmore, David Thompson and George Gervin. Erving asked coach Kevin Loughery if it might not be a bad idea for a white player to be in the dunking contest; Loughery agreed, but neither Loughery nor Erving could come up with a white guy whose dunking was worthy of display. There was a sellout crowd of 15,021 on hand at McNichols Arena to see a pregame show of Glen Campbell and Charlie Rich, the dunkers, and, oh yes, the league's All-Star Game.

CARL SCHEER: When it was decided that the 1976 All-Star Game would be held in Denver, frankly, I was scared to death. I wanted our franchise to look good, especially since we all believed that a merger was inevitable and we wanted to get into the NBA. But I was worried that we wouldn't sell out just with the game. I knew we needed more than the game—we needed entertainment. Glen Campbell and Charlie Rich were very popular back then, so we lined them up for pregame entertainment. But I wanted more than just singers. That was when Jim Bukata and I sat down and said, "What else can we do?"

JIM BUKATA: You have to understand where the ABA was at this point. Baltimore had folded before the end of training camp. Utah and San Diego went down early in the season. How could we even have an All-Star Game when we had only seven teams and one division?

The game was already set for Denver. We decided that the team in first place would play the All-Stars from the six remaining teams, and we prayed that the Nuggets would have the best record by the All-Star break so they could not only be the host city, but the host team. Thank God, that happened.

So we had a meeting to discuss some kind of basketball-related entertainment. The game was going to be on national television and we wanted a very strong gimmick for halftime. Throwing out ideas were Carl Scheer, *(ABA financial director)* Jim Keeler and myself. We talked about what the ABA was known for—its athletes and its dunking.

Then I said, "Hey, let's have a Slam Dunk Contest."

Everybody said, "Great."

Then we all said, "Okay, how do you have a Slam Dunk Contest?"

There had never been a dunking contest before, or at least none of us knew of one. We had no idea about rules or anything like that. So we simply made it up as we went along.

DAN ISSEL: The Slam Dunk Contest went right to the heart of the old ABA. The dunk was a bigger play in the ABA than it is in today's NBA; it was a statement of your manhood and your talent. The dunk was so important to the ABA that the pregame warm-ups became a show. The Nets had a guy named Ollie Taylor who would just go off in pregame. He would windmill, do reverse dunks, everything you could think of, and the fans would get pumped up before the game even began. The contest was an inevitable extension of that.

JIM BUKATA: Once we decided to have a contest, we had to figure out whom to invite.

To save money, we decided to only have guys who were going to be at the game already—guys from Denver or the All-Stars. Why bother to fly in anybody else? We didn't think this would be that big a deal. We picked the guys we thought would put on the best show and came up with Gilmore, Gervin, Thompson, Kenon and Doctor J. The winner was to receive $1,000 and a stereo system.

CARL SCHEER: We had five guys in the contest, but we knew that it would be a contest between Erving and David Thompson.

JULIUS ERVING: When the idea of a Slam Dunk Contest was presented, it concerned me some, because I had never been in one before. I always considered myself a very good dunker, and I wanted to win, but my best dunks were always done in the game. I didn't think about them, I just did them.

The other thing about the contest was that it would be held at halftime, so we would all have been playing and our legs would be a little tired. Now the Slam Dunk Contest is held on a different day than the All-Star Game and the guys have fresher legs. Really, none of us did much preparing for the contest; we all sort of winged it.

GEORGE IRVINE: One dunk that Julius planned to do was to run the length of the court, take off from the foul line and slam it. In his usual obnoxious way, Doug Moe said that Julius would never be able to dunk taking off 15 feet from the basket. That wasn't a knock on Julius; Doug talked endlessly about how great Julius was, but he didn't think even Julius could dunk from 15 feet away. Most of the other players said he could and they swore they had seen him do it during games. So we started making side bets. Some guys said Julius could do it, others said he couldn't.

JIM BUKATA: Before the contest, Doug Moe and Julius were talking about the foul-line dunk. Supposedly, Jumping Jackie Jackson, a New York playground legend, was the first guy to do it. Jumping Jackie also was the guy who supposedly jumped up and took a quarter off the top of the backboard. Both guys being from New York, Doug and Julius were talking about Jackson and some other playground guys. Julius said he could dunk from the foul line, Doug said no way. They made a side bet on it.

CARL SCHEER: Since the game was in Denver, David Thompson was the favorite of the fans. And really, Thompson and Julius were far above the other guys—it was a two-man duel.

JIM BUKATA: Probably the most spectacular dunk of the night didn't even count. In the practice session, Thompson did this cradle dunk where he cradled the ball in his left arm and then leaped over the rim and punched the ball down through his arm into the rim. He really was dunking the ball with his fist.

DAN ISSEL: Everybody was pumped up about the contest. They told us that we didn't have to stay around during halftime, that we could go into the dressing room, but everyone stayed on the court and we sat on the floor, sort of in a semicircle around the basket. When a guy would make a good dunk, you'd see the other players cheering, giving each other high fives. It was like we all were back on the playground, watching this shootout to see who really was the master of the dunk.

JIM BUKATA: The first dunks weren't that special. It looked as if George Gervin was going to do something great: he had a basketball in each hand and he was going to dunk them both, one after the other, in windmill fashion. But at the last second, he threw one of the balls away and then just did a regular windmill dunk. Artis looked like he was trying to tear the rim off with his dunks. His thing was power.

JULIUS ERVING: As the contest began, I had a plan.

For my dunk from the left side, I did what I call the Iron Cross. I'd jump by the basket, spread my arms as if I were flying and then dunk the ball behind me without ever looking at the rim.

For my standstill dunk under the basket, I took a basketball in each hand and then slammed one after the other.

For my dunk from the right side, I drove under the basket, grabbed the rim with my right arm and slammed the ball with my left.

JIM BUKATA: I thought that Julius's dunk where he swung on the rim after coming out of the right corner was the best, most imaginative dunk of the day. No one had ever seen anybody try that.

JULIUS ERVING: My favorite dunk was by David Thompson. He came out of the corner, spun 360 degrees in the air and slammed it. That was a 50 by anyone's standards.

Thompson also had an amazing reverse dunk from the stand-still position under the basket, but he missed when he attempted to throw the ball off the backboard, catch it and slam.

CARL SCHEER: The fans were going crazy all during the contest, as if they were seeing something they'd want to tell their grandchildren about. And for the people watching on the court, the tension was building, because we were all waiting for Julius's long dunk.

GEORGE IRVINE: When Julius got ready for his long dunk, I went to one side of the floor even with the foul line and Doug Moe was at the opposite side. We wanted to be sure that we knew where Julius took off from. We were sort of like net judges in tennis.

JULIUS ERVING: I had dunked in practice from behind the foul line, so I knew I could do it. But I had to get my stride just right. Everything had to be perfect for it to work.

CARL SCHEER: Julius went to the foul line, turned, and started pacing off in the opposite direction from the basket. He cradled the ball in his hand as if it were a baseball—it looked that small. As he paced off, the crowd started screaming. Then, when he got to about three-quarters court and turned and faced the basket, there was silence. The crowd knew it was going to see something special.

Julius stared at the basket for a moment. Then he took off with his long, majestic strides. The arena was so quiet you could hear his every step as his shoes touched the floor. I can still see that long, galloping stride as if he were an antelope, so graceful he was. Then he was off, in the air, and he brought the ball back from behind himself somewhere as if he were a helicopter. He rammed it through the rim, and only when the ball hit the floor did the crowd react. People just went crazy.

JIM BUKATA: If you watch the tape of the dunk, you'll see Doug Moe pointing to the foul line, indicating that Julius's foot was on the line.

JULIUS ERVING: I did step on the line, as Doug Moe was quick to point out.

I said to Doug, "Look, I'm not doing that again. No one else can dunk from anywhere near as far out as I just did."

Then we all laughed.

O O O

HUBIE BROWN: I go around the country giving coaching clinics and people ask me about the best team I ever coached. I say, "It's not even close—the 1975 Kentucky Colonels." Then half the people in the audience look at me as if I were talking about something from outer space. We had a front line of Dan Issel, Artis Gilmore and Wil Jones. You'd have to admit that Issel and Gilmore went on to have monster careers in the NBA. Those guys played forever. In the backcourt we had Louie Dampier and Teddy "Hound Dog" McClain. People say, "Who?" I say that Louie Dampier was as good a clutch player as I have ever seen. He was phenomenal when it came to taking and *making* the shot when the game was on the line. In the last couple years of the ABA, think about some of the other forwards—Julius Erving, George McGinnis, David Thompson, Bobby Jones, George Gervin, Larry Kenon, Caldwell Jones, Maurice Lucas, Marvin Barnes, Danny Roundfield, Billy Knight, Moses Malone—I'm talking about great talent, better talent than you'd find in the NBA. The ABA also gave a chance to Doug Moe, Connie Hawkins and Roger Brown, who were banned from the NBA and then went on to have tremendous pro careers.

We were ahead of the NBA in so many different ways. We had the 3-point play. The NBA said it was a gimmick; now it's one of the most exciting parts of the pro game. We used pressing and trapping defenses, something you never saw in the NBA. We had All-Star weekends, Slam Dunk Contests, and we even had the best officials because we had raided guys like John Vanak, Jack Madden, Norm Drucker and Ed Rush from the NBA. About everything we did in the ABA they do now in the NBA, except they didn't take our red, white and blue ball.

LARRY BROWN: I loved that red, white and blue ball and I loved the ABA. The league was the greatest thing that ever happened to me and to everyone connected with it. The ABA gave me a chance to play when the NBA said I was too small. It gave me a chance to coach on the pro level, and that probably never would have happened if it weren't for the ABA. Think about the coaches who got their start in that league—Hubie Brown, Doug Moe, Kevin Loughery, Al Bianchi, K. C. Jones, Tom Nissalke and Stan Albeck—these were men who went on to have significant and long careers in the NBA. How many of them would have gotten that chance without the ABA?

BILLY CUNNINGHAM: I played in both leagues, and I can say without a doubt that the ABA had a huge impact on the NBA. The ABA players and coaches forced a faster pace of the game, they pushed the ball up the court, they created a more exciting brand of basketball, the kind of basketball you see in most of the NBA today. When the Knicks were pressing and shooting 3-pointers and all of that under Rick Pitino, people acted as if that was something new. Hey, half the teams in the ABA played like that.

RON GRINKER: The difference between the two leagues is this: The standard of excellence in the NBA was the Boston Celtics, who were the masters of fundamental basketball. Those guys would pick-and-roll you to death. They played right out of the textbook. The ABA was Julius Erving, it was glitzy, get the ball out and let's run and jump and play above the rim and we'll make things up as we go along. The NBA was a symphony, it was scripted; the ABA was jazz. People weren't sure exactly what they did even after they did it. They felt something and they tried it.

BOB COSTAS: The players, their fashions and lifestyles were a reflection of the times, from the huge Afros to the beards, bell-bottom pants and platform shoes. I remember Larry Brown coaching while wearing farmer's overalls. But the real flair was on the court.

JULIUS ERVING: In some respects we were a maverick league, but so what? What was wrong with a red, white and blue ball? What was wrong with the 3-point shot or creating a faster tempo so that the little man would have an opportunity to play? What's wrong with a little experimentation and encouraging an individual to excel in a team sport?

When I signed with the Virginia Squires in 1971, I was under the impression that there would soon be a merger, no more than a year or two away. But merger or no merger, I was 21, out of the college environment and on my own for the first time. And I loved every minute of it. Basketball was truly a game, there were few hassles, and on the court we were freewheeling. The guys were playing to win, but also playing for fun and playing to entertain, pretty much how it is in the NBA now.

Underneath all that was the feeling that we were all in this great struggle together, fighting for survival and respect. When the NBA or anyone else criticized us, it just brought us closer together. We were stigmatized because we weren't the NBA, but wait a minute. Didn't we come from the same college basketball system as the NBA players? Didn't we play against the NBA guys in college and then later in summer leagues and All-Star Games? There was no difference between the players in the NBA and those in the last few years of the ABA.

What really upset a lot of us was the NBA's condescending attitude toward ABA players after the merger. But then ABA teams like Denver and San Antonio went out and won their divisions, beating out the established NBA teams.

Listen, the ABA gave the NBA a wakeup call. We were the first league that really knew how to promote its teams and its stars. What the NBA now does with Michael Jordan, Larry Bird and Magic Johnson, the ABA was doing with players such as George McGinnis, George Gervin and myself.

In my mind, the NBA has just become a bigger version of the ABA. They play the style of game that we did. They sell their stars like we did. The only difference is that they have more resources and can do it on a much grander scale than we in the ABA ever could.

BOB COSTAS: The ABA tried to promote Julius Erving, and even though he spent the last three years of his ABA career in New York, he never received the respect he deserved. Julius made moves that were truly astonishing, moves that had never been seen before. You know that play Julius made against the Lakers in the fifth game of the 1980 playoffs, where he went under Kareem Abdul-Jabbar and then under the basket and then hit that incredible reverse layup? I saw him make plays that good or better several times just in my two seasons covering the ABA. But there was no ESPN or CNN or SportsChannel to bring Julius into the nation's living room, even for a 10-second tease. Julius and the rest of the ABA stars performed in this netherworld of pro basketball that really wasn't pro basketball because the NBA didn't sanction it. It was almost as if the ABA players were a bunch of unappreciated artists

saying, "We may die impoverished, but one day our work will hang in
the Louvre."

DAVE TWARDZIK: We felt as if we were in the shadows. You'd pick up
The Sporting News and there would be NBA articles all over the place
and maybe one column with ABA news. You'd go through Chicago and
pick up a newspaper at the airport and you'd be lucky if they ran the
ABA standings or the box scores. In the ABA cities, our coverage was
usually very good, but just go a little outside that area . . . forget it. It
was as though we didn't exist.

GENE LITTLES: We had this immense pride that, right or not, we were
as good if not better than the NBA. The difference was that they had
television and we didn't. We never felt inferior, because guys from the
NBA would jump to the ABA and they didn't tear up the league. The
adversity kept us together and, like old foxhole buddies from the Army,
we still help each other. My first pro coaching job was with the Utah Jazz
as Tom Nissalke's assistant, and Tom knew me from when we both were
in the ABA. I now work as coach of the Charlotte Hornets and I was
hired by Carl Scheer, who was the general manager of the Carolina
Cougars when I played there. Harry Weltman was the GM in New
Jersey. He had that same job with the St. Louis Spirits and Bob MacKinnon was his coach. Later MacKinnon became Harry's assistant in New
Jersey. ABA guys are very loyal to each other.

BILLY CUNNINGHAM: I went from Philadelphia of the NBA to Carolina
of the ABA and had two of the most enjoyable years of my pro career.
The ABA people were so much closer than the guys in the NBA. They
really looked out for each other. When I played for the Cougars under
Larry Brown and Doug Moe and with guys such as Gene Littles and Ed
Manning, I felt like I was back in college. It was that kind of atmosphere.
I would have finished my career in the ABA, despite the crummy travel,
if I had thought the league had a chance to survive.

TOM MESCHERY: When I coached Carolina *(in 1971–72),* we had a
stretch where we played 21 games in 31 days and we finished it off by
playing Virginia three days in a row in three different towns. You usually
played three days in a row on weekends—Friday, Saturday and Sunday—because those were the days you drew the best. So you really
needed a lot of depth because of all the games, but for most of the years
in the ABA, while you could carry 12 players on your roster, you only
took 10 on the road to save travel expenses. I had come from the NBA,

where we flew first class and went to major markets. In the ABA, we flew coach and we went to places like Salt Lake and San Antonio—places where you had to go somewhere else before you could get there. A two- or three-stop flight was the norm. But very few guys complained. They just scrunched their big bodies into those coach seats and made the best of it, because they wanted to play.

BILLY CUNNINGHAM: When I played for the Cougars, our home base was Carolina and we always had to fly to Atlanta first, then catch a connection to where we went next. I felt like I had a second home at the Atlanta airport.

JOE TAIT: When I traveled with the Cleveland Cavaliers as their radio broadcaster, we often ran into ABA teams in the Atlanta airport. Many of the guys would have that blank, almost haunted look about them, as if they had been on too many airplanes in too few days. They would tell you these harrowing tales of trying to get from Salt Lake to Norfolk with four stops in between. They always had 5 A.M. wakeup calls. To us in the NBA, it was amazing that those guys could still stand up, much less play.

DICK TINKHAM: I was with Indiana from the beginning of the ABA until the final season. We get a lot of credit from some people for being bright and innovative, and I guess we were. But if there is one message I'd like to get across about the ABA, it was that we had *no plan.* Sure, we wanted to merge with the NBA. That was a goal. But a plan? We had none. We went by the seat of our pants and made it up as we went along. If a rule didn't fit with something we wanted to do, we just changed it or ignored it. If someone had an idea, no matter how lame-brained, usually someone tried it.

AL BIANCHI: We'd hold a draft at the drop of a hat. We drafted every-one—college kids, high school kids, underclassmen, NBA guys. We had a great time drafting people. If you still wanted a guy and a draft was over, you could put him on your draft list anyway. In Virginia, we developed a track record of finding pretty good players no one knew about, like Julius Erving and George Gervin. The NBA started drafting people we had taken, figuring that maybe we knew something. So we would draft guys we knew couldn't play just to see if the NBA would take them, and sure enough, some of those names would show up on an NBA draft list and we'd just laugh.

DOUG MOE: One of the biggest disappointments in my life was going into the NBA after the merger. The NBA was a rinky-dink league—listen, I'm very serious about this. The league was run like garbage. There was no camaraderie; a lot of the NBA guys were aloof and thought they were too good to practice or play hard. The NBA All-Star Games were nothing—guys didn't even want to play in them and the fans could care less about the games.

It wasn't until the 1980s, when David Stern became commissioner, that the NBA figured out what the hell they were doing, and what they did was a lot of the stuff we had in the ABA—from the 3-point shot to All-Star weekend to the show biz stuff. Now the NBA is like the old ABA. Guys play hard, they show their enthusiasm and there is a closeness in the league. Hell, the ABA might have lost the battle, but we won the war. The NBA now plays our kind of basketball.

BOB COSTAS: I just wish that some of the great ABA players, such as Willie Wise, Mel Daniels, Roger Brown, Louie Dampier and the rest, could have played against NBA competition in their primes. No one will ever know how great James Silas could have been in the NBA, because he blew out his knee right before the merger. He played after that, but he wasn't the same. Freddie Lewis was a terrific player, but his best days were in the ABA. That's another aspect about the ABA—the mystique of the guys who never got a chance in the NBA.

LARRY DONALD: Those who lived through the ABA get a warm feeling thinking about those times. It's what it must have been like to have been on the Confederate side during the Civil War. They were charging up the hill, outmanned, outgunned and outfinanced. But they had enough General Lees to keep it interesting. If you're a basketball fan and have a drop of nonconformist blood in your veins, then you had to like the ABA.

HUBIE BROWN: It was Doctor J who said it all when he received the trophy as the NBA's most popular player in 1977. He held the trophy over his head as only he could and said, "I accept this award on behalf of all the players who played in the ABA but aren't here today." It was a very moving gesture.

JULIUS ERVING: I was in the ABA from 1971 to '76. It was the first third of my career, sort of a bridge from being an amateur to a professional, and I loved the ABA very much. I remember being at the first

All-Star Game after the merger, looking around and seeing that 10 of the 24 players had been in the ABA. I said, "Just looking at the people here, I guess that should answer any questions you have about parity between the NBA and the ABA."

Part I

OPENING GAMBITS

Birth Pangs

The patron saint of the ABA was Dennis Murphy, who later would be among the founders of the World Football League, the World Hockey Association, World Team Tennis, and the 6-foot-5-and-under World Basketball League. Now, he is putting together the Global Hockey League. As veteran official John Vanak said, "If they ever put any kind of league on the moon, Dennis Murphy probably will start it." In the early years of the ABA, Murphy was either a general manager or public relations man—sometimes both—for the Oakland Oaks, Minnesota Muskies, Denver Rockets and Miami Floridians.

DENNIS MURPHY: The ABA began as a football league. It was in 1965, and the American and National Football Leagues were in a major war. I was the mayor of Buena Park, California; I had always been a sports nut and I was a USC fan. I was close to Jim Hardy, the former USC quarterback who played for the St. Louis Cardinals. Our idea was to put together a group to get an AFL franchise for Anaheim. We wanted to get some money people interested in bringing football to Orange County, for a couple of reasons. We knew that a merger between the two leagues was coming and we figured if we could get a team in Anaheim, we'd either end up with an NFL franchise or they would have to buy us out. Either way, we'd win. We even sponsored an AFL football doubleheader in Anaheim. But the two football leagues merged a few weeks later, so we were finished; we knew there was no way the L.A. Rams would want us to have a team in their territory. Jim Hardy and I had put a lot of work into this and we were pretty disappointed about ending up with zilch. I kept thinking about it, how we had a pretty good group of money people who loved sports and we should do *something.*

I thought, "There's only one basketball league and one hockey league, so why not have another?" Since I knew nothing about hockey, but basketball was my favorite sport, I figured I'd pursue the idea of a basketball league. That was the reasoning—I liked basketball better than hockey. No surveys or anything like they'd do today. The NBA had only 12 teams in 1966. It seemed like there should be more teams. Why? I

39

don't know. It was worth a shot. What the hell, the AFL had worked, hadn't it? They got a merger. Maybe we could force a merger with the NBA.

I knew Bill Sharman from my connections to USC. At the time, Sharman had just left as coach at Cal State–Los Angeles. He had coached Long Beach in the old American Basketball League *(1961–62)*, which had folded, so he knew what we would be facing if we tried another league. It was Bill and I who came up with the name ABA, or American Basketball Association. For a while, I thought Bill would be our front man, our basketball guy who had a name and credibility, because he had been a fine player in the NBA, but Bill had to drop out because he was offered the San Francisco Warriors coaching job *(for the 1966–67 season)*. Bill suggested that we use the 3-point play, which was a part of the old ABL. He also encouraged us to keep pressing ahead with putting together a league. He suggested that I call George Mikan, who was probably the biggest name in basketball—the Basketball Player of the First Half-Century, in fact. Bill thought that Mikan could get the league some attention. I thought about it and talked about it for a few weeks. One day I mentioned Mikan to my neighbor, Bill Goff, who said, "I know George from the insurance business. I talk to him a lot. Let me call George for you."

So that was how the first contact was made with Mikan. Goff called George, then Bill told me to call. I talked to George and he said something that surprised me: "I just got a call from this guy in New York, Connie Seredin, who said he was putting together a new basketball league. He's a real promoter type, lots of hype." I wrote down Seredin's name and called him. He was an advertising man in New York. I said since we both wanted the same thing, we should join forces. He agreed to a meeting. I kept talking to people and got some interest from people such as John McShane, a local radio DJ. I talked to people, they talked to other people, and soon Roland Speth, Larry Shields, Art Kim, Gary Davidson and Don Regan became involved. Seredin and I met in L.A. and we got along all right. I could tell that Connie's head was a little in the clouds, but I thought things would be okay. He said he had all these money people back East, so we set up another meeting, this one in New York, between my group and his group.

The New York meeting was an absolute fiasco. I had the impression that Connie would have all these people there, but there were only about four of us. They didn't seem very far along at all. It was nothing like Connie had led me to believe. But Connie and I did agree to merge; I would handle the organization and he would take care of the publicity.

We set up another meeting in California, this one at the Beverly Wilshire Hotel. Now I was getting really worried, because the only person of substance Connie had was Gabe Rubin. That was when McShane and I realized that we really had to take this thing over. We each put in $10,000 and we asked Connie for $10,000. He said that was a stumbling block, and I think he put in about $3,000. By this time, there was a lot of suspicion between my group and Seredin's group. But we did have the common bond that we wanted a basketball league. We had yet another meeting and pretty much ironed things out. McShane and I opened up an office on Fall Street in Orange County, we hired a secretary, and the ABA was in business. We put out some brochures, and it was at this point that Gary Davidson, a young lawyer, got involved. Gary has been credited with being a founder of the ABA, but he wasn't. *(Davidson admitted as much in his book,* Breaking the Game Wide Open.) Gary's real role was with the people putting together the Dallas franchise.

We kept having meetings. The only people with any basketball experience were Art Kim and Gabe Rubin; Rubin had been with the Pittsburgh Pipers of the ABL, and Kim was involved with the Washington Generals, the team that played the Globetrotters. But we kept pushing, kept meeting, kept talking to people and in the end we got a group together that would form the ABA. We went back to Mikan several times, but he said, "I've got a great reputation. I get asked to do things 100 times a day and I'm not going off half-cocked. Get the thing moving. Get the money; I just don't want to hear a lot of talk. Then maybe I'll work with you. But I'm not about to jeopardize my situation with a lot of B.S."

DICK TINKHAM: There were a lot of guys around trying to start basketball leagues in the 1960s. I was a lawyer and a friend of the DeVoe family in Indianapolis. John DeVoe had played basketball at Princeton, and DeVoe and I had been involved in an indoor racquet club in Indianapolis. One day we got a call from a guy in Louisville; the name escapes me. He was talking about something called "The Lively League," with no players over 6-foot-4. Connie Seredin was the East Coast promoter putting it together. The guy from Louisville said that he would go in if we went in. But John, his brother Chuck and I talked it over. Indiana was a basketball-crazy place on the high school and college level. But who wanted to see a bunch of little guys play basketball? Then we heard from Dennis Murphy. The 6-foot-4 was gone, it was just a regular pro league. That was something that interested us. Given the basketball climate in Indiana, it just seemed that a pro team would be a natural. A local group had gone to the NBA about an expansion team, but the NBA wasn't very enthusiastic and they talked about $1.5 million to get in. That sounds like pennies in today's market, but was a lot of money in the middle 1960s. We heard that there would be an ABA investors meeting in New York. You brought a check for $5,000 and you were in—not just in the meeting, but the league! So we got the five grand and we were in. There were a lot of people like us in the sense that they liked basketball, but they didn't want to pay $1.5 million to get into the NBA.

MIKE STOREN: Here is how Dennis Murphy operated. I was the business manager for the Cincinnati Royals of the NBA and I was a very close friend of Dick Tinkham's. One day I heard from Tinkham, who asked about this Dennis Murphy and the new basketball league. I guess Murphy wanted $25,000 to get into the league. I told him not to give Murphy a cent, to wait and see what developed. And sure enough, the price went down *(to $5,000)*.

CARL SCHEER: I was working as Walter Kennedy's assistant in the NBA office when I heard this talk about starting another basketball league. Frankly, I couldn't figure out why they wanted to do it. The ABL had died. The NBA was not exactly going great guns. Common sense back then would have told you that those guys had no chance to survive.

MIKE STOREN: The NBA was still trying to present itself as a viable third pro league—after baseball and football. The television contract was weak. There was a Sunday afternoon game and either Bill Russell or Wilt Chamberlain played. Ideally, it was Russell *vs.* Chamberlain. The NBA was a very distant third in the eyes of the sports fan. In my mind, the ABA had a snowball's chance in hell of becoming a viable pro basketball league.

DICK TINKHAM: The early meetings for the ABA were incredible. We went to one in New York where some guys said they each had four or five franchises. We from Indiana felt like we were in the minority, because we only had one. But to the everlasting credit of Arthur Brown from ABC Freight in New York, he stood up in the middle of this insane meeting and said, "Now we'll each put up a $50,000 performance bond and then we'll go ahead with this venture." There was an adjournment and a lot of the people—many who thought they owned five franchises—didn't come back. The $50,000 bond scared them off, and the people left were serious and had a few bucks.

DENNIS MURPHY: All during this time, we were talking to George Mikan, trying to get him as the first commissioner. The league was starting to take shape. We had people of substance such as Art Kim (Anaheim), Arthur Brown (New York), the DeVoe Family (Indiana), Gabe Rubin (Pittsburgh), T. C. Morrow (Houston), Joe Gregory (Kentucky), Ken Davidson (Oakland), Charlie Smither (New Orleans), Bob Folsom (Dallas), and Larry Shields (Minnesota). So we were in the position to get Mikan.

GEORGE MIKAN: I think Dennis or someone had read an article about me in *Sport* magazine that said I would make a good commissioner of the NBA because I had played the game and also had a law degree. The ABA owners were very impressed with the fact that I was an attorney, and that probably closed the deal. Once we settled on the money and I got them to put it into escrow, we were ready to go.

DENNIS MURPHY: George didn't agree to be commissioner until 10 minutes before the start of the press conference we had set up at the Summit Hotel in New York to introduce the league to the media. George wanted a three-year deal at $50,000 a year and he was hanging tough. Some of the owners felt that he put a gun to their heads about the money. He also made it clear that he didn't need us. He lived in Minneapolis, where he was an attorney and had a travel agency. We wanted him to move to New York for the first league office, but George said he wasn't moving; if we wanted him, the league office had to be in Minnesota. In the end, George got what he wanted. And to George's credit, he saved that first press conference. We had about 50 media people there. I had arranged press conferences before because I had worked in various political campaigns in California, but I had never seen anything like this. The press conference was Connie Seredin's idea and it was heavy on schmaltz. We had stars like Frank Gifford there. We had girls in hot pants handing out drinks and press releases. We gave away red, white and blue basketballs. But the thing also started to look like a zoo, and we probably were going to get ripped in the press. *(The press conference cost a reported $35,000 as the whiskey flowed.)* George sensed we could be in trouble. He said, "This is all a bunch of crap. I'm gonna get up there and run this show." That's exactly what he did. He explained the idea behind the league, why there would be a red, white and blue ball and why the league could make it. I know some of the owners didn't like George, but he was the reason the ABA got off of the ground. I'm convinced that we would have died at that first press conference without him. Let's face it, when a guy who was the greatest basketball player of his era, a guy who is a successful businessman and a guy who was 6-foot-10 with the charisma of Mikan stood up and spoke, people listened.

MIKE STOREN: If there was no George Mikan, there would have been no ABA. The league was always looking for fresh money and new investors. George Mikan could go into any major city in the country and get meetings with the high rollers, even the mayor, because they all wanted a chance to shake George's hand. A guy may be a busy, millionaire businessman, but if he was a basketball fan it was pretty tough to turn down a chance to have lunch with George Mikan. If four guys named Joe came to town to talk about a new basketball league, fat chance that they would ever get through the door at city hall. His credibility was something you couldn't buy. Later on, he had real problems running the league. But he was the ideal guy to get it off the ground.

The Ball

GEORGE MIKAN: The ABA had a red, white and blue ball because I said it would have one. It was that simple. We wanted our own identity, and the ball is the symbol of basketball, isn't it? To this day, you hear ABA and people talk about the ball.

I admit that I had a personal beef about the brown ball. I remember sitting up in the balcony at some NBA games and I just couldn't see the darn thing that well. The arenas were darker then than they are now, and the ball just sort of blended into the background. When you watched a basketball game on television, that dirty brown ball didn't show up very well.

Okay, so I wanted a different color for our new league. Then I said, "What's the name of the league?"

The American Basketball Association.

What's America's colors?

Red, white and blue.

So why not a red, white and blue ball?

LEE MEADE: George loved that ball. He'd say, "When people see our ball, they'll stand up," the implication being that the ball was like the flag.

GEORGE MIKAN: The owners acted like I wanted to burn the flag when I said forget the brown ball. I had to prove to them that there was nothing sacred about the brown ball. I did a lot of research and showed them that there were over 50 different shades of brown used over the years in college and pro. Hell, the original NBA ball was the color of cowhide, it was off-white. And there was nothing "natural" about the color, as some owners said—it was *dyed* brown. I said let's be creative and dye the damn thing red, white and blue. That was something you could see from the balcony, you could see it on television. When you shot it, it left a red, white and blue streak—like a rainbow.

DENNIS MURPHY: In our first meeting with George to seriously discuss what the ABA should do, he brought up the colored ball. I loved it. I saw it as an incredible gimmick, something so easy to promote, but the other owners didn't like it.

BOB BASS: While George never said it, you had a feeling he wouldn't have stayed as commissioner unless we approved the colored ball and the 3-point play. He was passionate about those two things.

MIKE STOREN: To this day, only George Mikan knows why he even thought of a red, white and blue ball. You ask him about it, and he just says he liked it and that was that. At first, I argued vehemently against the ball. I thought it would make us look like buffoons. But once we adopted it, the benefits of the ball became clear to me. When people in the early ABA talked about dropping it, I told them they were fools. This was a great marketing tool. In Indiana, one of our first and most successful promotions was with Standard Oil and we gave away a half-million of those basketballs. Kids just loved them.

ALEX HANNUM: I believe I was the first one to say that the ABA ball belonged on the nose of a seal. I was coaching in the NBA at the time and it looked like a beach ball to me, but when I went to Oakland and then Denver and had a chance to coach with it, I liked the ball. It was a good ball to teach shooting with because it made it easy to see the rotation.

MEL DANIELS: When I signed with the Minnesota Muskies out of New Mexico, I had no idea that they were going to use a red, white and blue ball in the ABA. In fact, when I signed they gave me a standard brown ball that said "Mustangs." Then I showed up for training camp and there they were, using the red, white and blue ball. I said, "What the hell is that?" They said, "It's our ball." I couldn't believe it, but then I started to use it and it seemed like any other ball to me. In fact, there was something about the seams—they sort of locked your hand to the ball, made it easier to palm.

LEE MEADE: Right after we introduced the ball, we were bombarded with complaints. Players said it was too slippery; others said it was too big. I called the Rawlings Company and told them that the players were saying the ball was too slippery. There was a long silence on the other end of the phone. Then the guy from Rawlings said, "Would it make a difference if we could show you that the color pigmentation we use for your ball is the same that we use for the NBA's ball?" There was no difference in the amount of dye in either ball; the only difference was the color of the dye. We put out a press release about that and it got pretty good play around the country.

BOB BASS: While I was coaching Denver, we had our first preseason game in Tucson and no one had a red, white and blue ball. We couldn't play with a brown ball, because this was the first game in the history of the Denver franchise, even if it was an exhibition. So some genius got the idea of taking a brown ball and spray-painting it red, white and blue. Let's just say that made the ball a little slick. There were 44 turnovers—just in the first half!

MAX WILLIAMS: In Dallas, our first coach was Cliff Hagan. He had come over from the NBA and he just hated the ABA ball. He complained and complained, and soon the players were complaining, too. Finally, we told Cliff that the red, white and blue ball was our ball, it wasn't going away, so just shut up about it. He got used to it and by midseason, no one said a word.

MIKE STOREN: In Indiana, I was hearing all kinds of crazy things. One player told me that the ball was heavier, then the next day a guy said it was lighter. On and on it went. Finally, I called a team meeting and I held the ball in my hand. I said, "Here is our ball. I've been to the factory and there is no difference between this ball and the NBA's ball. It's not lighter, it's not heavier, it's not slipperier. The only thing different about it is that this ball photographs better and shows up on television better. Is that understood?"

I still could see some doubters out there.

Then I said, "If that's not understood, this should be: from now on, anyone associated with the franchise who says anything derogatory about the ball will be fined."

That was the end of the moaning.

STEVE JONES: When the league began, the ABA balls *were* far more slippery than the kind we were used to, for a very obvious reason—*they were new.* All new balls, regardless of the color, are slippery. That's why in games they use balls that have been in action for a while. But since there never was a red, white and blue ball before, you couldn't have any used ones. With Oakland, our first exhibition game was in Phoenix. There was no air-conditioning in the place and it was over 100 degrees inside. We had the new ABA balls—which were slippery—and they went off our sweaty hands. It was awful. Guys were swearing at the ball, blaming the colors. But once the balls were used for a few months, they weren't slippery anymore.

GENE LITTLES: I do think there was a difference between the two balls. The NBA ball had wider seams, which made it easier for guys to palm, easier to handle. The ABA ball had smaller seams and that made it seem slicker. But it was the same size, weight and all that. As a guard, what I liked about the ABA ball was the color. It was a special feeling to take a long shot and watch those colors rotate in the air and then see the ball with all those colors nestle into the net. It made your heart beat just a little faster when you hit a 25-footer with the ABA ball.

DAVE TWARDZIK: As a shooter, what I liked about the ABA ball was when you hit a jumper and that ball would take that last little spin while in the net. You'd see those colors turn . . . it just was neat. It's a shooter's ball. If you don't think so, then why do they use the red, white and blue ball in the NBA 3-point contest as the ball that counts double? Because there is something special about watching it go into the basket.

JOHN STERLING: When I broadcast the New York Nets games, some people gave me flak about the ball—they were Knicks fans. But the thing about the ball was that it made the game much easier to watch for the novice fan. That's why kids were attracted to it. The colors were almost mesmerizing.

ROGER BROWN: I developed a one-on-one move that was strictly for the ABA. It had to do with the red, white and blue ball. When you watched that thing spin in the air, there was something mesmerizing about the colors. So I'd get the ball and sort of spin it before I made my move. Some defenders' eyes went right to the ball, to the colors spinning. It was hypnotic, and that one second that they stared at the ball was enough for me to get by them.

JOHNNY KERR: Given *(NBA Commissioner)* David Stern's marketing background, you'd think he'd want the red, white and blue ball. When the ABA was around, you saw those balls everywhere. *(Various reports say that over 30 million red, white and blue balls have been sold.)* Can you imagine the money the NBA would make if the league switched to that ball? You use that thing on national television and every kid in America would want one. Then you license it and collect the royalties. With the way salaries are going in the NBA, you'd think the league would jump at a chance like this to rake in the bucks.

LEE MEADE: The most colossal marketing blunder of all time was that no one from the league licensed the red, white and blue ball. You could drive by any playground in the country and see kids using that ball, but the ABA never got anything out of it. We just never thought about things like licensing. If we did, we might still be around today.

DENNIS MURPHY: We never could get our act together on patenting the ball. We had several different guys say they were going to do it for the league, and there was a lot of bickering and confusion. In the end, no one got it done. Mike Storen probably came as close to getting the rights as anyone.

MIKE STOREN: We did a test where we put a bunch of 9-year-olds in a sporting goods store and told them they could either have the brown ball or the ABA ball. Every kid picked the ABA ball. I mean, every single one, and I'm talking about hundreds of kids. So I tried to patent the thing if the league couldn't do it, but what I found out was that you can't patent a color scheme, just a logo. So I got the patent on the red, white and blue ball with the ABA logo on it, and I still have it. A lot of good that does me today, right?

The First Jumper

DICK TINKHAM: We did some crazy things before that first season. All the owners got together one day and we drafted all the NBA players. It was like dealing baseball cards. In Indiana, we wanted both Van Arsdales, Dick and Tom, but another team took Tom, so we traded two of the Boston Celtics we had for Van Arsdale. We were very serious about it. We hadn't played a game, but we were deluding ourselves into thinking that all these NBA guys would jump leagues and we'd better have their rights. The college draft didn't even interest us that much, because we thought we'd get our talent by raiding the NBA. Of course, it didn't take long for reality to set in. The ABA made some offers to NBA guys and got absolutely nowhere, except with Rick Barry, which was a special case because of his father-in-law.

DENNIS MURPHY: As one of the founders of the league, I was going to get a franchise, and it was supposed to be Oakland, but Ken Davidson wanted Oakland and said he could get Pat Boone involved so we *(the league)* let him have it. Pat Boone was a basketball nut. I think he still plays full-court basketball today, and he's no kid anymore. Then Ken Davidson asked me to be his general manager. We wanted to make a splash, and we wanted to get a name player. The biggest name in the Bay Area was Rick Barry with the San Francisco Warriors, so one of the first things we talked about was how to get Barry. That led us to go after Bruce Hale as our first coach. Bruce was Barry's father in-law, and he had coached Rick in college at Miami (Fla.). We gave Bruce about $35,000 to be coach and then set our sights on Barry.

PAT BOONE: I had known Ken Davidson for years; we went to the same church in Inglewood, California. He knew I loved basketball, and he wanted to know if I would be involved in this new basketball franchise that was going to play in Oakland. I told him that I wasn't interested in being an investor, but Ken said, "Oh, no, we don't need your money. I've got other people putting up the money and I'm putting in some money. We'd like you to be involved as a co-owner, lend your name to it." Davidson said he would give me a small piece of the franchise *(about 5 percent)* just so he could correctly say that I was an owner. I wished the team would play closer to L.A., but I went along with it.

Later, they set up a press conference to announce the formation of the franchise and Ken told me, "By the way, we've issued a press release that says you're going to be president of the team." I said, "If I'm the president, then I should get more than 5 percent of the team." Ken asked what I wanted, and I said a president should have at least 10 percent. He said, "Okay, you've got 10 percent." I said, "Okay, I'm in."

At that first press conference, we had a demonstration of the 3-point shot and introduced a couple of the players we had signed, although I can't recall who. We then had a shooting contest for 3-pointers and I won, which I guess should have told me we were in real trouble. Actually, the players weren't used to shooting from 25 feet and I like to shoot out there with a one-handed set shot, because I was never tall enough to go inside. The whole thing was a lot of fun.

George Mikan took an active part in starting some of the franchises, and I think it was his idea to get Bruce Hale. Obviously, the fact that Bruce was Barry's father-in-law had a bearing on our decision, but he also was a qualified, experienced coach and a gentleman.

RICK BARRY: When Bruce was hired by the Oaks, it naturally got my attention. He was like a second father to me, and the idea of playing for him again had so much appeal. I loved playing for Bruce in college.

At the time, I was 23 and had just finished my second year with the Warriors *(leading the NBA in scoring at 35 points in 1966–67)*. We also had made the NBA finals, but despite all that, for the first time in my life the game wasn't fun for me. I was playing for Bill Sharman, a man I respect tremendously on a personal level, but Bill was very set in his ways. I just didn't enjoy basketball under him. The money was a factor, but not an overwhelming one. I made $30,000 with the Warriors and had gotten a $15,000 bonus that brought it to $45,000. My contract with the Warriors was up, or at least I was led to believe it was. I was supposed to be tied to the Warriors for another year after my contract was up by the "reserve clause," a clause that said every player had to play an extra year for his team after his contract was up. *(This also was known as the option clause.)* But it was never challenged in court, and the lawyers I talked to didn't think it would hold up. So when the Oaks called, I was willing to listen, because I thought I could change leagues without missing a year.

PAT BOONE: I was appearing at the Golden Nugget in Sparks, which is just outside of Reno. Rick was playing in a golf tournament there and we set up a meeting. Rick told me that he loved the Warriors, liked *(owner)* Franklin Mieuli and that his future was secure. If he was going to come over to a new league, Rick said he needed something very solid.

Ken Davidson was at the meeting and he said, "Rick, what if we were to make you a part owner? How does that sound?"

I think this was the first time in the history of sports that a player was offered a chance to become a part-owner. We offered him 15 percent of the team, and I think that was really what convinced Rick to make the jump.

RICK BARRY: I told the Oaks, "Give me your best shot and then I'm going to go to the Warriors and say the same thing. I'm not going to switch back and forth. I'm going to take the two offers and pick the one I like best."

Oakland offered me $75,000 for three years and 15 percent of the team. I loved the Bay Area and didn't want to move if the team did. I got a verbal agreement from Oakland that I would never have to leave with the team, but there was never anything in writing. That was my fault. I took their word and it came back to haunt me.

The Warriors offered me $45,000 with various bonuses worth $30,000 that could bring it to $75,000. I took Oakland's offer. I went back to Franklin to tell him that I was leaving. Franklin then pulled out a contract worth a straight $75,000 from his desk drawer, but I said it was too late.

Franklin was a man who talked about loyalty. Well, I believe in loyalty, too. I cared about Franklin and the Warriors, but I cared about Bruce Hale and my family more. Money wasn't the overriding point to all this. I made the jump for $30,000 a year and a piece of a fledgling franchise that may not have been worth anything, and it turned out it wasn't worth a dime to me. That was not a real smart business decision. I could have gone back and forth several times to both sides, jacking up the price, if all I wanted was the money. That's why it was stupid to say I was money-hungry. Then there were people who said I signed with Oakland because Pat Boone promised to get me into the movies. That was just a bunch of bull and it was stupid to say that, too. The main thing was my family, sharing basketball again with Bruce Hale.

PAT BOONE: Rick was interested in the movies and broadcasting. We talked about it. He even took some acting lessons, and I said I would help him down the line if I could, but no promises were made. Rick signed with us because of Bruce Hale and because we made him a good financial deal.

GEORGE MIKAN: I wanted every team to do what Oakland did—sign an NBA star. Then we could have filed a class-action suit on behalf of all the players to get the option clause revoked. But Oakland was the only team that took my advice.

PAT BOONE: Our opinion in the Rick Barry case was that the reserve clause was a restraint of trade and that made it illegal, so we could ignore it. Our attorneys said that Rick would be free and clear to play, but Franklin Mieuli took us to court, got an injunction, and later a San Francisco judge ruled in Franklin's favor, saying that the reserve clause was binding and either Rick played for the Warriors or he had to sit out. Since Rick was a 15 percent owner of the Oaks, it made no sense for him to play for the Warriors, so he decided to sit out the season and do commentary on our TV games.

RICK BARRY: I spent that first year doing TV work and playing for the KYA radio basketball team. We were the Radio Wonders. I played point guard and fed Johnny Holliday, who took about 40 shots a game. Holliday has done well in radio since, as has another guy on our team, Steve Sommers, who is with WFAN in New York. You could say I played very well against some of the best high school faculties in the Bay Area.

The Shakeout Begins

DICK TINKHAM: Not long before we actually started to play, there was a shakeout among the owners. By that, I mean we found out who had some money and who didn't. The guys who started the league, such as Dennis Murphy, Gary Davidson, Roland Speth—they gave themselves franchises but they didn't have the capital to run them. So they sold out for a few bucks to the guys who would really become the owners.

DENNIS MURPHY: The only money I made in the ABA was when I sold my piece of the Oakland franchise to Ken Davidson and Pat Boone. Gary Davidson sold his piece of Dallas, Don Regan sold his piece of Kentucky. Gary Davidson wanted to stay active in the league and he came up with the idea that George Mikan would be commissioner of the ABA, but he'd be president. George would be in charge of everyone while Gary would be president of just the owners. I liked Gary and I helped him get elected, but he and George Mikan never got along.

Once, Mikan threatened to suspend Gary Davidson and Davidson then threatened to suspend Mikan. There was nothing in the ABA bylaws about this type of conflict and no suspensions were issued.

LEE MEADE: Gary Davidson really made his reputation in the World Football League. He was a major player there. But in the ABA, he just wasn't important, even if he was the first president. He got that position before Mikan became commissioner. After George took over, he didn't want Gary around.

DICK TINKHAM: Gary Davidson appeared at one of the early league meetings. First, he wanted to be commissioner. Then he ended up being president somehow. None of us *(owners)* could figure out why we had to listen to Gary Davidson. Who was he?

At one league meeting, Joe Geary, who was a big money guy from Dallas, asked me, "Does Gary own any part of Indiana?"

I said he didn't.

Geary said, "That's what I thought."

Geary had been checking with everyone in the room, trying to figure out why Davidson was acting like he owned the league. Geary called for a recess and asked Davidson to step out of the room. When the meeting resumed, Gary Davidson was gone, and that was the last any of us saw of him in the ABA.

o o o

MAX WILLIAMS: I had been a fairly well-known basketball player at Southern Methodist University and I was a member of the All-Sports Association in Dallas. Roland Speth was our first contact with the ABA. He was a friend of Dennis Murphy's and Gary Davidson's, and Speth said that there was this new basketball league and he had the Dallas franchise.

At first, Speth indicated that he and Gary Davidson had enough money to run the franchise, but it soon became clear that they didn't. I liked the idea of pro basketball in Dallas, and I got together with some people I knew, people who had real money, such as Bob Folsom, who later would become mayor of Dallas. I also talked to some SMU boosters I knew. Anyway, we put together 30 investors and raised $300,000. When the ABA began, we were the best-financed team in the league.

LEE MEADE: I remember a league meeting where the various owners were saying what their net worth was. Guys were saying a few million; maybe one guy said $10 million. Bob Folsom's group was worth $480 million.

TERRY STEMBRIDGE: For better or worse, I was with the Dallas/San Antonio franchise from the start to the end of the ABA. In February of 1967, I was a high school history teacher in Kilgore, Texas, and I also did play-by-play on the local radio station for the high school team. My goal was to do play-by-play in pro sports, and I really thought I could jump from Kilgore to the big leagues. I was working for a station that you couldn't hear nine miles out of town, which shows you how naive I was. I read an article in the newspaper that the ABA had been formed and Dallas was one of the franchises. I thought, "Okay, here's my chance." I called the sports staff of the *Dallas Morning News;* I didn't ask for anyone in particular, because I didn't know anyone. I talked to a guy named Bob St. John, and he told me that Roland Speth was running the team. I made some more calls and I got in touch with Speth. The guy later became the manager of the Monkees, and he was sort of far out in left field to be in pro basketball. Roland was a real fast talker. He said for me to send him some tapes and he'd meet with me when he was in Dallas. I sent the tapes and followed up with a phone call a little later. I think it was in May of 1967 when I got ahold of Speth in California and he was telling me, "Hey, everything is going great. We're putting together a great team, we're getting great investors . . ."

I asked him about my tapes.

He said, "Oh, yeah, I heard the tapes. Let's talk when I get to Dallas."

In Dallas, I went to see Speth in his hotel room. He acted real receptive and he was talking a great game, but all he really was saying was that he would listen to my tapes and get back to me. That surprised me, since he'd led me to believe he had already heard the tapes, or why would he agree to meet with me? I went home to Kilgore, waited a week or so, then called Speth. He told me, "I've made a decision—you're our new announcer. I'll get to you within a week or so about a contract."

One week went by, then two weeks and then three weeks. I didn't hear a thing. You can imagine what I was going through. I kept calling Speth and I couldn't get in touch with him. Finally, someone in the front office told me, "Speth is out and the new guy in town is Michael O'Hara. He seems to be running the team."

I called Mike O'Hara and he didn't have the slightest idea who I was or what I was talking about. I told him that Roland Speth had promised me the job, and O'Hara got a little nervous. By now, the team was in the process of changing hands from Speth and O'Hara to the real owners—Bob Folsom and his group. Eventually, I was asked to come to Dallas for another meeting. I thought it would be more of the same, but it turned out that I went in front of the board of investors. O'Hara was now the GM, Max Williams was operations manager, and I was interviewed. They said they didn't even know if they were going to have a radio contract, but if they did, I could be the broadcaster. What they really wanted to know was if I was willing to work in the front office and help get the team off the ground.

I said I would be glad to. They asked me to step outside. A few minutes later, Bob Folsom came out and asked me to go to lunch with him at the Hilton. He bought me a chicken sandwich and then offered me the job for $9,500 with the understanding that I would work with Max Williams in the front office.

It turned out that Folsom had never heard my tapes. Neither had Max Williams, Mike O'Hara or Roland Speth. Heaven only knows where my tapes were, but they hired me anyway. They asked me what title I wanted, and I said I didn't care. They said, "Let's make you public relations director," which was a mistake because I ended up doing a lot of work with press releases and all that in addition to broadcasting the games. It also turned out that Max Williams and I *were* the front office. There were four of us in the office—Max, myself, a secretary and a ticket manager, and it seemed that the ticket manager was quitting every week and we had to hire a new one.

MAX WILLIAMS: When I say that Terry Stembridge and I did everything that first year, I mean everything—we even had to put the 3-point line down on the floor when we played exhibition games around Texas. We sold the tickets before the games, swept up after and did everything in between.

TERRY STEMBRIDGE: I always thought we had one of the best nicknames in pro sports—the Chaparrals. But there was no great thought given to what to name the team. One of the early investors meetings was held at the Chaparral Room in the Dallas Sheraton. At the time, that was one of the best private clubs in Dallas, and one of the investors was looking at a napkin with the chaparral *(a roadrunner)* on it when he suggested that Chaparrals would make a good name for the team.

MAX WILLIAMS: When it came to putting a team together, we were a little behind, because we messed up the college draft. In a sense, this tells you a lot about what was going on when Roland Speth was in charge. The draft was coming up and I made some calls to coaches I knew, did some checking around, got all the basketball magazines I could and put together a draft list. I gave it to Speth and figured we'd talk about it in a few days.

One day, Speth said to me, "Well, we had our draft."

I said, "What are you talking about?"

He said, "It happened so quickly. They just said the draft was tomorrow. I couldn't find you so I went to New York and I took your list along and I did the draft."

Of course, the reason he went to the draft by himself was that Speth didn't want to spend the money to take me, too.

I said, "You should have taken me. You don't know anything about players."

He said, "I got the first five guys on your list."

I said, "That wasn't a *talent* list. That was a list of players in *alphabetical order.*"

He said, "Oh."

That was it—"Oh."

So the first draft pick in the history of the Dallas franchise was Matt Aitch from Michigan State, because his last name began with "A."

Look at our draft:

1. Matt Aitch.
2. Jim Burns.
3. Gary Gray.
4. Pat Riley.
5. Jim Thompson.

Then in the supplemental rounds it went:

1. Paul Brateris.
2. Jeff Fitch.
3. Ted Manning.
4. Duane Heckman.
5. Gilbert McDowell.
6. Jerry Southwood.
7. Tom Storm.

The only guy out of alphabetical order was Heckman, and my guess is that Speth probably just looked at the list wrong. I couldn't believe it. It was going to be hard enough putting together a team without a stunt like this. I was really glad when Speth and those guys got out and the Texas people took over.

o   o   o

LEE MEADE: Before I was named the ABA's PR director, I was sports editor of the *Denver Post,* so I was very familiar with that franchise. It was originally owned by James Trindle, who was a friend of Dennis Murphy's. Trindle wanted to put the team in Kansas City, but couldn't get enough playing dates at the arena, so he came to Denver. Before the team even played its first game, Trindle sold out to Bill Ringsby. I had never heard of Bill Ringsby, and I asked the managing editor of our paper if Ringsby had enough money to buy the team. I was told, "He has enough to buy the whole league." The team was named the Rockets, after Ringsby's business—Rocket Truck Lines. Because Ringsby was a man of substance, his presence meant that the local papers had to pay attention to the team. Dennis Murphy had been the general manager under Trindle and he stayed on for a while to work for Ringsby. Dennis will never admit it, but before Ringsby named the team after his trucking company, Dennis wanted to call it the Colorado Lark Buntings, after the state bird of Colorado. You may not have thought much about naming the team after Bill Ringsby's trucking company, but it was a lot better than Dennis's idea.

BOB BASS: The characters among the owners were something. I was the first coach in Denver, and there was a league meeting in Denver, so I went. Kentucky's Joe Gregory was there—with his dog. A $10,000 dog. That dog was worth more than a lot of the players. But can you imagine sitting at a league meeting and looking right across from you and seeing a damn dog?

VAN VANCE: The dog's name was Ziggy and they even had its picture in the first Kentucky Colonels program. That dog was all over the Colonels' promotional material. The Gregorys took Ziggy to the games with them. I even recall seeing the dog in one of the team pictures. The Gregorys went from dog show to dog show in one of those big vans, so I guess they thought you're supposed to take that dog everywhere.

TERRY STEMBRIDGE: Joe Gregory had married a woman who had a lot of money and was a dog-show judge. I was Dallas's broadcaster and I remember getting on an airplane and seeing that dog in first class with the Gregorys. They told me they had bought Ziggy a seat. Ziggy was a Brussels griffon, some kind of rare breed. His real name was Gaystock Monsignor and he won more than 150 of those Best of the Breed titles in his career. He was Top Griffon in both 1966 and 1967. Don't ask me why I remember all that.

MAX WILLIAMS: The Gregorys had a lot of dogs. We had a player in Dallas whose name Gregory loved so much that he gave one of his dogs the same name—Manny Leaks.

BOB BASS: There was a league meeting where Anaheim's Art Kim and Pittsburgh's Gabe Rubin got into one of the damnedest arguments I had ever seen. These guys were yelling, screaming and then they wanted to kill each other. Rubin said that Kim was an idiot, Kim said he was a karate expert and he was going to break Rubin in half. During the whole thing, the little dog was just sitting there, watching it. Even the dog was wondering what the hell was going on. Finally, big George Mikan stepped in there and picked up Kim with one hand, Rubin with the other and separated them. He told them to cut it out and he wasn't going to put them back down until they did. Of course they did cool down, but stuff like this made our league meetings more fun than some of the games.

Finding Players

STEVE JONES: I remember walking into a tryout for the Oakland Oaks at St. Mary's College and there were 100 guys there. I had some friends who had recommended me to the Oakland owners and Bruce Hale, so I had an advantage in that Bruce knew who I was. You could tell that there was a division at the camp between guys who were supposed to be able to play and guys basically off the street. I had played at Oregon and been drafted by the Warriors and had been to two of their training camps, so I was one of the guys who could play. But I still couldn't believe that mass of humanity in the gym. The coaches seemed overwhelmed. They started having 3-on-3 games for 15 minutes. If you didn't show much in that 15 minutes, you were outta there, so you can imagine that there was a lot of passing going on, right? They cut 60 guys the first day. I think back on that as the "Hundred Rifles" camp, because you had 100 guys doing nothing but shooting.

Most of the guys who eventually made the team had played either in AAU ball or the Eastern League and had at least been to an NBA camp. Guys like Ira Harge, Jim Hadnot, Levern Tart, Wes Bialosuknia. We sort of looked at ourselves as pioneers. All we wanted was a shot at pro basketball. We figured if we didn't make it in Oakland, we could go to another ABA team and make it there. Everything was pretty wide open.

BOB BASS: Obviously, you had to be a bit of a gambler to get involved with the ABA. I had coached great NAIA teams at Oklahoma Baptist. We were national champs in 1966, runners-up in 1965 and 1967. I could have stayed there comfortably forever or gone on to another major-college coaching job. I had a good player in Al Tucker, and Bruce Hale came down to talk to me about Tucker. Bruce had just been hired by Oakland, and he asked me if I was interested in getting into the ABA. I told him that I had no idea, I really hadn't thought about it. We pretty much let it drop after that.

Two days later, I got a call from Dennis Murphy, who was then the general manager in Denver. Murphy offered me $20,000 to coach the team, which was pretty good, since most of the players were making $8,000. I took it.

When I got to Denver, the college draft was over and they had done things like draft Walt Frazier and Bob Rule, who had signed with the

NBA. I had no players. We put together a tryout camp at Pacific University. We had about 100 guys in the gym and it got real hot, so we opened the doors. But it was so smoggy outside that the smog rolled in and it got so bad that we had to call off practice, because we couldn't see. Besides, an open tryout like that wasn't going to do us much good, anyway.

The most important thing we did was sign Wayne Hightower, who had played in the NBA.

Hightower had the perfect name for a 6-foot-9 rebounder/shot blocker. In four NBA seasons with Baltimore and San Francisco, he averaged 9.4 points and 7.1 rebounds, but shot only 36 percent.

LEE MEADE: Even though Hightower probably would have had a hard time finding another NBA job, it still was a big deal when he signed with Denver. I mean, at least the hard-core fans had heard of him.

BOB BASS: I took the NBA rosters from 1965 to '67 and looked for the names of guys no longer in the league. Then I tried to track them down, figuring if they were good enough at one time to play in the NBA, then they should be good enough for our league. Actually, none of us really knew what would be good enough, since there was nothing to compare it to.

Another talent source was the AAU leagues. Teams such as the Akron Goodyears *(Larry Brown)*, the Phillips 66ers *(Darel Carrier)* and Jamiaco Saints *(Steve Jones and Levern Tart)* sent us a lot of players. But the ABA effectively put the AAU out of business by taking its best players, and that league had some pretty good ones, guys who just missed out on making the NBA.

One of the guys we did find was Tommy Bowens, who was 6-foot-8 from Grambling. He was one of the more amazing leapers I had ever seen. He could dunk from two feet *behind* the foul line. I know no one believes me when I tell them Bowens did that, but I saw it in practice. He could dunk from much farther out than Julius Erving. He could break the high-jump and long-jump records all at the same time. He was just a raw talent who really couldn't do much with the basketball, but how he could jump.

Bowens's ABA career, in which he averaged 5.4 points, spanned three teams in three years.

LEE MEADE: Bob Bass was desperate for players. He signed Byron Beck out of the University of Denver, which was a great move because he was a terrific player for Denver during all nine years of the ABA. He signed Willie Murrell out of the Eastern League, and Willie became the subject of perhaps the first of about a million lawsuits about players in the ABA. The Eastern League sued Denver for signing Murrell, but the ABA countersued. I don't remember how it was exactly resolved, but Willie played for Denver *(and averaged 16.4 points).*

LARRY BROWN: The guy I still kid Bob Bass about is Lefty Thomas. We *(New Orleans)* played Denver early in the season and they had this guy, Lefty Thomas. He went for 20 points against us, but he shot it every time he touched it. That wasn't that unusual, but Lefty was the first player I had ever seen who wore a ring on every finger. I still ask Bob if he has signed any more guys who wear 10 rings.

BOB BASS: Thomas had 39 points for us in our opener, but he was totally out of control. I just couldn't handle the guy. Every time he got the ball, he went left and then he shot it. He had played for the Harlem Clowns and some of those other teams that played against the Globetrotters. After a few weeks, I let him go and Anaheim picked him up, maybe because he had the 39 points against them. But he didn't last there, either.

A 6-foot-2 guard, Thomas played 62 games and had 55 assists, so "pass" wasn't in his vocabulary. He averaged 9.1 points and shot 44 percent.

MAX WILLIAMS: Our biggest job was to find players. I got a lot of letters and calls. One guy wrote me from the state penitentiary in Oklahoma. He said if he could produce a contract, they'd let him out to play ball for Dallas. I passed on that one. We had an open tryout and drew about 100 guys. That was just a zoo, people killing each other, but we didn't find anyone of significance.

TERRY STEMBRIDGE: I don't remember seeing any real players at those tryouts; it was just a bunch of guys running around. The players we ended up with were guys that Max found. One of my favorites was Maurice "Toothpick" McHartley. He was a 6-foot-3 guard who came from the Wilmington Blue Bombers of the Eastern League. Maurice had to have a toothpick in the corner of his mouth or he wouldn't play. He was ahead of everybody when it came to fashion, because he was the first guy on the team wearing bell-bottoms and stuff like that. He worked hard at being Mr. Cool. I remember him shooting the ball a lot, but I don't remember it going in that often.

(Toothpick averaged 15.3 points, but shot only 40 percent for Dallas. He played for four teams in the first four years of the ABA, averaging 12 points on 41 percent from the field.)

Another one of my favorite guys was A.W. Holt, a kid from Jackson State, a left-handed shooter. He went into Max's office to sign a contract and they talked for a while. When they came out, Max asked me to take Holt to the airport because he was going home. In the car, I said, "A.W., did you sign?"

He said, "No, man, I didn't sign that contract."

I said, "Why not?"

He said, "I made up my mind before I came here that unless I got a $1,000 bonus, I wasn't going to sign. But all they offered me was fifteen hundred dollars."

I started to laugh, but I realized that A.W. was serious. He didn't get it and that was sad. Anyway, he eventually did sign, but he didn't make the team.

STEVE JONES: When the guys in AAU ball heard that the ABA was forming, we said, "It will never last." Then we said, "Where do we go to try out?" So like a lot of guys, I went for it, and it felt great when Oakland signed me for $10,000 that first year. We turned out to have a terrible team, but we didn't know it at the time. Who could? No one had any idea what would be good enough to win in a league that had never existed before.

LARRY STAVERMAN: I was the first coach of the Indiana Pacers, and in the summer before that first season, we announced that we would have our first practice, which was really a tryout. We held it at the Jewish Community Center, which had room for about 400 people, but 1,500 showed up. We turned fans away to see a glorified tryout! That was amazing when you consider that there was no team, no league, nothing but a dream at that point.

Our big tryout was held at the Fairgrounds Coliseum. We had a couple of hundred guys trying out and about 7,000 fans there to watch. I stepped out on the court to start the tryout and guess what—*no basketballs.* My GM had forgotten to get us some balls. I had to figure out what to do with all these people. I had the guys run sprints, then I had them run a passing drill, a Figure-8, pretending they had a ball. I cut some guys before they even touched a ball because it was obvious they couldn't run and had no idea what the most basic Figure-8 drill was all about. Over the course of the various tryouts we had, we must have looked at a thousand guys. We did get one player out of it who we didn't have a line on originally—that was Bobby Joe Edmonds, and he averaged eight points for us that first year.

JERRY HARKNESS: A lot of the players in the early ABA were like myself, good college players who never got a chance in the NBA. I had played for the 1963 Loyola of Chicago team that won a national title. I was drafted by the New York Knicks and was cut. I got my college degree and went to work for the Quaker Oats Company and I had a good job. I figured that was it for my basketball career. But then I read about the ABA starting and I kept thinking, "Maybe I should try it once more. If I don't try it, I'll always wonder."

My wife hated the idea. She thought I was crazy to throw a good job away, but I had to try, even if it made no sense financially. So I quit and went to a Pacer tryout camp. There were at least 50 guards there. Notice I said *guards,* not players. There were over 100 players. Larry Staverman was running the practice and Slick Leonard was helping out. Staverman and Slick remembered that I had played at Loyola four years before, so they gave me a break, and I needed it. After running a bunch of sprints, I found out I wasn't even close to basketball condition and I threw up. Staverman was great. He told me to work myself into shape. I was rooming with some guys who would practice all day and then go out on the town all night. I just stayed in my room, concentrated on my conditioning, and after three weeks of practices, I was beating everyone in sprints. I had to take it seriously. I had quit Quaker Oats, my wife thought I was doing something really dumb and I was out of shape. I had to make sure I didn't get cut, and I was just so relieved to make the final roster.

MIKE STOREN: We at Indiana were looking for anyone with a little experience. When I was with Cincinnati, Freddie Lewis sat on the bench. He never played, but I figured if he was good enough to make the Royals team, he had to be good enough to play for us.

DICK TINKHAM: We signed Lewis for $15,000. We agreed on the money pretty fast, but he also wanted a new refrigerator in the deal; his was shot. So we compromised and we gave Freddie a used one and he signed.

MEL DANIELS: I was an All-American center at the University of New Mexico. The ABA wasn't even around during my senior year, and the NBA had very little visibility. Even though I was big and strong *(6-foot-9, 225 pounds)* and a damn good player, I didn't even think about being a pro until my senior year. My father lived in Detroit and worked at the Chevy plant for $92 a week, and I figured that after college I'd go home and he'd get me a job in the factory, too. After my senior year, I was a first-round pick by the Cincinnati Royals in the NBA. Then I found out that I also was drafted by the ABA, by this new team in Minnesota. Minnesota got to me first and they offered me a $12,000 bonus plus a $14,000 salary. I wasn't getting a dime at New Mexico, so I was going from zero to $26,000. And then I thought, there was my father busting his ass all those years for $92 a week, I better pay some attention.

I was invited up to Minneapolis. George Mikan met with me, took me to the gym and showed me a hook shot, which was something I didn't have until then. Jim Pollard was coaching the team and he took me around the town. Minnesota made it known that they wanted me badly and they upped their offer to a $12,000 bonus and a $24,000 salary, making it $36,000. To me, that seemed like $3 million, especially since I hadn't had any serious talks with Cincinnati. Finally, the Royals offered me $14,000. I signed with Minnesota. I took that $12,000 bonus, bought a 1955 Buick and gave the rest to my parents. That's how I became the first No. 1 draft choice to pass up the NBA for the ABA. I did it for the money and because I figured if the league did go under, I could always play in the NBA.

No one was making any money in either league back then. Connie Hawkins was getting only $15,000 from Pittsburgh. Most guys were under $10,000. Charlie Williams was all-ABA that first year with Pittsburgh and he made $7,500. One of my Minnesota teammates was Sam Smith, and he signed a blank contract just for a chance to play. He told the team to pay him what they wanted and they gave him $6,000. So me making $36,000 that first year—I felt like a king.

Opening Tip

DOUG MOE: Larry Brown and I had several conversations after we signed with New Orleans and through much of that first year. We wondered if the league would get through a whole season. We figured if it did, it would be a miracle. We'd go to Minnesota and there would be more people on the floor than in the stands, then we'd go to Houston and it would be even worse than Minnesota. Anaheim, that was nothing but a joke. In New Orleans, we were okay. The only teams really doing

any kind of job at the gate were Indiana and Kentucky. By the end of
the season, we were still playing, and the unbelievable thing was that no
one had folded.

LARRY BROWN: In one of the early practices in New Orleans, guys were
told to brown-bag it so they would have something to eat. The team wasn't
paying meal money and it sure wasn't going to supply food. When you
went on the road, your trainer didn't go with you. So when you got to a
place like Denver, it was up to Denver to supply a trainer you could use
that night. In Denver, the trainer they gave us taped my ankle so tight that
it ended up bleeding. I went into the shower and cut the tape off and I saw
other guys doing the same thing. So I went up to the trainer and asked him
what he did in real life—I couldn't imagine that he did this for a living.
The guy hesitated for a moment and said, "Well, I'm a poultry farmer."

The teams did anything they could to save money. We flew those
three-stoppers because the airline tickets cost less. We had 12 players at
home, but only traveled 10 to save on the airline, meal and hotel bills.
Really, it was a struggle. That first year, the best thing about the league
was the players, because there was a lot of untapped basketball talent out
there with only 12 NBA teams.

MIKE STOREN: Indiana played an exhibition game against Anaheim at
the San Jose Civic Arena. There weren't 150 people in the stands. We
were broadcasting the game back to Indiana on radio, and you could
hear the announcer's account all through the stands. Later in the season,
we played a game in Minneapolis that was being televised. We got the
few fans who were there to all sit on one side of the arena, then we put
the camera on the other side so it would look like we had a decent crowd.

TERRY STEMBRIDGE: Anaheim's owner was Art Kim, and he got the
brainstorm to play as many games on the road early in the season as he
could. He wanted to be everyone's home opening opponent because the
owners were splitting the gate revenues and he figured that he could
make some money that way. So the Amigos opened the season with a
six-game, thirteen-day trip that went from Oakland to Denver to Dallas
to Indiana to Kentucky to Minnesota. Three of those games were openers, and the Amigos lost the first five, won at Minnesota, then opened
at home and lost again. They were running players in and out so much
that they wouldn't give the guys the meal money for the whole trip, just
day-to-day. That way, if they cut a guy, he wouldn't make off with an
extra week of expense money. They were so cheap that at the end of the
year, they ran out of players and didn't want to sign anyone new so they
activated Dick Lee, who worked in their public relations department. If

you check the first-year stats, you'll see that he played two minutes and appeared in two games, getting one rebound and one assist.

LEE MEADE: As PR director of the league, I remember getting a report of a game where Anaheim played somebody in Fresno and the attendance was 98. That wasn't what we wrote press releases about.

BOB BASS: We didn't have money problems in Denver, because our owner was Bill Ringsby, who was very wealthy and owned Rocket Truck Lines. In fact, the rocket logo on our uniforms was the same as on the side of his trucks. But a team like Anaheim would come into Denver and the hotel wouldn't take them because they still hadn't paid their bills from the last trip, so we looked around town to find another hotel that would take them.

MEL DANIELS: Our meal money was $7 a day, and the big thing was to get a hotel near a McDonald's, a Kentucky Fried Chicken, or a White Castle hamburger joint.

BOB BASS: Bill Ringsby also owned Aspen Airlines, so we had our own plane. That sounds great until you find out that it was a DC-3 built in 1941. I actually saw the plate in the cockpit that said, "Manufactured in 1941." Our pilot had flown in the German air force and we called him the Red Baron. Actually, he did a pretty good job with that old plane.

CHARLIE WILLIAMS: It was an adventure every night. I was with Pittsburgh, and our first exhibition game was against the New Jersey Americans. New Jersey's uniforms never showed up and they played in white T-shirts with numbers written on the back in Magic Marker. They also wore shorts or sweat pants that didn't match. Never in my life was I so grateful to have my own uniform.

Later, we played a game in New Orleans that was held up for a half hour because something happened to the electricity. *(A possum got into the wiring.)* But for me, it was exciting. I wanted to play basketball and that was what I was doing.

LEE MEADE: When the ABA began, I was amazed at how little preparation went into it. One day I talked to some people I knew in the ABA office and asked them what they were going to do about stats. They said they hadn't thought about it. I said the league was getting ready to start in a couple of weeks and someone should do something. Finally, I said, "I'd really like to see this league go. If you need someone to help with the stats, I'll help."

About a week later I got a call from Don Carr, a friend of George Mikan's who was handling the ABA's PR for a while. Carr asked me how much I wanted to do the stats for the league. I had no idea how much to charge for that. Finally, I said, "I'll do it for $1,000 a team and you pay all the postage. I'll also need $1,000 to get started."

Carr didn't say anything. I don't think he knew how much you were supposed to pay for stats. He said he'd get back to me and he did. He called back and said, "Congratulations, you're our new statistician. The season starts in 10 days—can you come up with a scorecard and stats forms right away?"

I had a lot to think about. I wanted the ABA stats to be different, because the league was going to be different, with the ball and the 3-point play. I also wanted to do something with numbers that would get the league some attention. I thought about when I had covered basketball games, how I liked to keep track of blocked shots, individual turnovers, and break down rebounds into offensive ones and defensive ones. I made a list of things that ideally would be part of a complete basketball box score if I could have my own, because that was what I was getting the chance to do—design my own box score.

I came up with the following that was new:

1. Rebounds—offensive and defensive. The NBA just kept total rebounds, no breakdown.
2. Individual turnovers. We called them "errors." The NBA didn't keep this stat.
3. Steals. The NBA didn't keep it.
4. Blocked shots. The NBA didn't keep it.
5. Team rebounds. The NCAA used it, but the NBA didn't.

Now steals, blocks, turnovers are all standard at almost any level of basketball. But it was revolutionary back then, and a lot of the teams didn't want to go to the trouble of keeping all those numbers. The NBA didn't do it, they said, so why should we? Of course, the fact that the NBA didn't do it was exactly why we should do it.

That first year, the stats were a problem. Some teams didn't complete all the categories on the scorecard. Occasionally, a team wouldn't send in any box scores. I kept the stats by projections. I took the games and stats I did have and projected them out over the course of the season. So I wouldn't put much faith in those early ABA stats.

MEL DANIELS: To survive the ABA that first year, you really had to be pretty tough. In my case, it was 78 games and 78 fights. In my very first pro game, I got thrown out right after the half for fighting with Kentucky's Bobby Rascoe. I had 19 points and 17 rebounds in the first half, and obviously Kentucky was tired of me kicking their ass on the boards. On the first play of the third quarter, I got a rebound and Rascoe hit me from behind in the back of my head. I turned around and slapped him and that started it. Soon, we both were gone. It came down to the fact that guys were playing for their lives. Intimidation was a big part of it. If you were a man and had any pride in yourself and wanted to be respected, you had to fight. It was that simple, especially if you played under the basket like I did.

TERRY STEMBRIDGE: One day Dallas was playing at Denver in that small auditorium of theirs *(6,800 seats)* where the fans were right on top of the players. Denver had an AAU team and the fans knew a lot about basketball and they liked physical basketball, which was what the AAU and the early ABA were all about. There was a fight; I don't remember who started it. But I saw Dallas coach Cliff Hagan go over to Bob Bass. Cliff is about a foot taller than Bass and Cliff said, "Get out of here, you little shrimp, before someone throws you across the floor." Bass is a tough guy, but that time he sort of backed out of the way, because he probably knew that Hagan would be that someone who would throw him around the gym. Los Angeles columnist Jim Murray summed up that first year in the ABA when he wrote, "You almost had to present your X rays to get a free throw."

Off the court, Cliff Hagan was a gentleman. He was soft-spoken, well-dressed and very handsome. He carried himself with a lot of pride. He collected antiques and especially liked crystal and cut glass. He had a lovely wife named Martha, two well-behaved daughters and a young son when he came to Dallas. He was a class act all the way.

But something happened to Cliff when he put on that uniform. He was the toughest player I've ever seen. He simply gave no quarter. One night, we were playing in Pittsburgh and the Pipers had a 15-game winning streak. Hagan was matched up against Art Heyman, who was a flaky guy. He also did something that wasn't real smart. As the opening jump ball went up, Heyman started elbowing Hagan, and that really got Cliff mad. Cliff just reached back and slapped Heyman right across the face. I had never seen anything like that. Naturally, it scared Heyman to death and he spent the rest of the night trying to shake Cliff's hand and apologize.

MAX WILLIAMS: Cliff was the same way, regardless of the game. I used to play in summer pickup games with him and before every game Cliff would say, "Let's play this one for blood," which would have been funny, except he meant it. I went in once for a layup that would have won the game, except Cliff drilled me right into the wall. I was knocked out for a minute and when I came to, I looked at the floor and saw my blood dripping down.

Hagan asked me if I was okay and I said, "Sort of."

Then Cliff left me there, bleeding. Remember, I was his boss, the general manager. I ended up driving myself to the hospital to get some stitches over my eye.

ALEX HANNUM: Cliff Hagan's locker room lectures were legendary. He'd get his players in the room and yell at them forever. The guys all talk about how Cliff burned their ears.

MAX WILLIAMS: To hear Cliff in the dressing room, you'd never believe it was the same guy you saw at the Baptist church, or anywhere else but on the court. He was so foul-mouthed that it was truly something to behold. I asked him about it and Cliff said, "Max, I had eight coaches in the pros. I liked six of them and hated the other two. The only guys we won with were the guys I hated." Well, Cliff managed to get the players to hate him. They respected him as a player and a person, but they hated him as a coach.

MIKE STOREN: During one game at Indiana, Cliff asked one of our ballboys for a key to get something out of the dressing room. It was the ballboy's job to lock up the room before the start of the game and then open it up for the half. But this time, Cliff borrowed the key. When he went into the room for the half, all the windows were open and it was freezing in there. He went into a frenzy about "the goddamn bush-league treatment they're giving us in Indiana. They're trying to freeze us out." On and on it went. I'm convinced that Cliff went back into the room and opened those windows himself so he'd have something to get his team riled up about. That was the kind of stuff he liked to do.

MAX WILLIAMS: Denver had Byron Beck (a 6-foot-9, 240-pound center), and he'd just as soon run over your rear end as look at you. He was always causing problems out there, and I picked up the phone to complain to George Mikan about him, but then I thought to myself, "Wait a minute, I can't say anything about Beck. I've got Hagan and he's even worse than Beck."

TERRY STEMBRIDGE: The one incident that shook up some people was when we had a Kids' Day game on a Sunday afternoon at home. We were playing Minnesota with Mel Daniels and Les Hunter and they were one of the best teams in the league. We had our biggest crowd of the season, about 7,000, and most of them were kids. Early in the game, Hunter elbowed Cliff. I thought, "Oh no, he shouldn't have done that." Les Hunter's nickname was "Big Game," and he was a big, strapping guy, 6-foot-7 and 235 pounds, from Loyola of Chicago. Well, after Hunter elbowed Hagan, they had words, and I figured Cliff told him don't try it again. Anyway, next time down the floor, Hunter elbowed Hagan again. Without a word, Hagan turned, faced Hunter and *bam, bam, bam.* It was an unbelievable right-left-right combination and Cliff just flattened Hunter.

Mel Daniels went crazy and he grabbed Hagan. I can still see the big bloody streak on Hagan's face—Daniels got him with a fingernail. The officials stepped in and threw everybody out of the game and that was the end of it, but it was pretty scary, because it wasn't your usual basketball fight where guys just push each other around—there was a real streak of violence in it. I ran into Hunter a few years later in a hotel bar and we talked about that fight. He told me, "I'm telling you, I never knew what hit me. I never saw it coming and I've never been hit that hard in my life."

MAX WILLIAMS: Hagan just cold-cocked Hunter. There's no other way to put it. He knocked Hunter right out and he did it 30 seconds into the game with all these kids watching. I knew the front office wasn't going to like this.

TERRY STEMBRIDGE: The Dallas owners were just horrified. These were gentlemen and they came to a nice Sunday afternoon basketball game with their kids. The owners never heard a coach curse like Hagan and they never saw a fight like that on the court before. So the owners were unhappy about that, and they were unhappy because we lost our coach and our best player after 30 seconds and that was a good way to lose the game.

MAX WILLIAMS: After Kids' Day, Bob Folsom was really upset and he said that we had to do something to calm Hagan down. One way to get to him was through his wallet, so we told Cliff, "If you get thrown out again, it will cost you $2,500."

Cliff said, "Max, if I can't fight, I can't play."

I said, "If you fight and get thrown out, we have no coach and our best player is gone and then I have to come out of the stands and coach the team. *(No one in the early ABA had assistants.)* I don't want to coach. I hired you to coach."

We talked some more and I suggested that he coach the team, but not play. Maybe that would keep him out of trouble. So Cliff would dress for the games wearing his jersey and his warm-up pants, but no basketball shorts, just a jockstrap. That way he wouldn't be tempted to put himself in the game and that would keep him from getting in fights.

We went on a West Coast trip with the team and I was at a game in Anaheim against the Amigos. One of the players said to me, "Hey, Max, tonight Cliff has his shorts on."

I started to worry.

But the game went on and on and Cliff didn't put himself in. With 40 seconds left, the score was tied and I saw Cliff rip off his warm-ups and put himself into the game. Cliff cut across the lane, caught a pass and made that great hook shot of his. Then one of the Anaheim players jumped on his back and rode Cliff right to the floor. Cliff stood up, looked at the guy and cold-cocked him.

I thought, "He's only been in the game for five seconds and he already punched somebody."

The amazing thing was that neither official saw it. Hagan stayed in the game and saved himself $2,500.

The 3-Pointer

DENNIS MURPHY: Unlike the red, white and blue ball, which was George Mikan's idea and really came to the league late in the development process, the 3-point play was going to be a part of our league from the beginning. Everybody involved in putting together the ABA liked the idea because it was good for the little man—it had to be exciting. The 3-point shot was exactly what our league was supposed to be about: something a little wild, a little out of the ordinary basketball they played in the NBA.

GEORGE MIKAN: We called it the home run, because the 3-pointer was exactly that. It brought the fans out of their seats. It was first used by Abe Saperstein in the old ABL, and we adopted the rule and their distances.

The shot was called a 25-footer from the key area, 22 feet from the corners. Later, measuring from the middle of the rim, it was determined that it was 22 feet in the corners, but actually 23 feet, 9 inches from beyond the key. The same distance is used today in the NBA.

ALEX HANNUM: In the NBA, we just clogged up the middle and dared teams to shoot from the outside. Nobody bothered to guard anyone 20 feet from the basket, but the 3-point play really did open up the middle. A guy starts hitting jumpers for three points instead of two and the coach has to change his thinking—and his defense. No other rule made the game more wide open and more fun to watch.

HUBIE BROWN: For a coach, the 3-point play is a form of mental gymnastics. All your life, you've been trained that a basket is worth two points. That was how you always played the game, how the game was always played, until the ABA made the 3-point play popular. So a guy makes two field goals, you figure that's four points. But in the ABA, it could be six points and that can shake you up as a coach. It makes you constantly check the scoreboard. You have to adjust. You have to tell your players to remember who the shooters are and when those guys are 25 feet from the basket, get in their jocks and guard them. Don't give them the 25-footer, which is something players had been conditioned to do all their lives. And as a coach, if you have a shooter with range, you have to give him the freedom to take the 25-footer, which is a philosophy that goes against what you learned as a young coach—namely, pound the ball inside. The 3-point play forced ABA coaches to be more creative and to give their players more freedom.

BOB BASS: I don't think anyone knew what to make of the 3-pointer. A few of the first ABA guys had played with it in the old ABL, but none of the coaches had. It was certainly a totally new concept for me. I was hired as Denver's first coach after being at Oklahoma Baptist, an NAIA school. I had no experience with the shot and I only used it when we were desperate, down by a lot of points at the end of the game and needed to come back quickly. *(Bass's Denver team took 149 3-pointers that first year and shot an underwhelming 17 percent.)*

TERRY STEMBRIDGE: To show how unfamiliar we were with the 3-pointer that first year, I was broadcasting a game between Dallas and Indiana on November 13, 1967. The game was in Dallas and we had a 118–116 lead with one second left. There were about 2,500 people in the stands and Indiana had the ball out-of-bounds under its own basket. The Pacers threw the ball in to Jerry Harkness, and he was 92 feet from the basket. He uncorked this high, arching hook shot that banged against the backboard and went in. At first we were stunned, then we figured—okay, overtime. But what we forgot was that we had a two-point lead and

Harkness's shot was a 3-pointer. I was one of many people who didn't realize at first that the game was over.

JERRY HARKNESS: I was the Pacers' third guard that season and the only reason I was in the game was that Freddie Lewis had a sprained ankle. Dallas's Charles Beasley hit a jumper to put them ahead by two points with two seconds left. We got the ball out under our basket and Oliver Darden threw it to me. I was not quite all the way in the corner, but I was on the baseline and behind the backboard, but just barely inbounds. Bob Netolicky was up the court and he was yelling at me to pass the ball to him. I knew I didn't have time to do that. The crowd was small, but really loud. I can still hear them screaming. There was no choice—I had to shoot it, so I sort of hooked it over my head. When I let the ball go, it just kept rising and the people were screaming. It was like everything was in slow motion. Then the ball went in and there was this total silence, except for my teammates, who mobbed me. But they thought it was a 2-point basket and we had overtime coming up. We were running off the floor to huddle up for the overtime when the official, Joe Belmont, came up to me and said, "Jerry, it's over. That was a 3-pointer." I said, "I forgot all about that. A 3-pointer." Then we were celebrating again, because we found out that we won the game. The shot became known as the longest in basketball history—92 feet.

The irony is that I wasn't much of an outside shooter. In fact, that was the only 3-pointer I made that season.

The Dallas Chaparrals painted the ABA logo on the spot on the floor where Harkness made the shot, and it was the first real publicity the league received for something that happened on the court, something that wasn't a new-colored basketball or a lawsuit involving Rick Barry.

CHARLIE WILLIAMS: The 3-point shot helped make our league special, but you had to be careful, because it could be addicting. It was like we all had found a new toy. My first year with Pittsburgh, I really was enamored of the shot. I took about two 3-pointers a game, but my teammate, Chico Vaughn, took about five a game. He really loved it. But the epitome of the ABA's 3-point shooters that first year was Les Selvage. All he did was shoot the 3-pointer. I never saw a guy like that before or since.

BOB BASS: One night, we ran into the Anaheim Amigos and Les Selvage. Louis Dampier and Darel Carrier of Kentucky would really become the guys who made the 3-pointer famous, the guys who knew how to use the shot more than anyone and use it right. But Les Selvage was a legend in the first year of the ABA. He was a 6-foot-3 guard who was in love with the 3-point line. He acted like if he stepped over it, he was going to get killed or something. He didn't just shoot 25-footers —he took 30-footers. I am not exaggerating. And he did it at any time in the game. He'd be on the wing on a fast break, stop a good step behind the 3-point line and cut loose. And the guy had strong arms and wrists—he didn't take a set shot from 30 feet, he took a normal jumper. The game that made him famous came against us at the Denver Coliseum. He got on a roll in the third quarter and hit six 3-pointers against us. Then he drove to the basket, made a layup and we fouled him. He made the foul shot and finished the quarter with 21 points—six 3-pointers and then a 3-point play. By the end of that game, we were running four guys at him, begging him to take a layup, but he just kept shooting from farther and farther out.

In retrospect, Les wasn't much of a basketball player, he was just a shooter. Anaheim found him playing in some amateur league and he didn't last long in the ABA. All he could do was shoot, and he shot too much. But when he was hot, he was unlike anything I had ever seen. In that game, which we won, he just scared the hell out of me.

Selvage went to Kirksville State in Missouri, then played AAU ball for the Phi Beta Sigs of the Interfraternity League in Los Angeles at night while working as a shipping clerk at Douglas Aircraft during the day. Then he tried out with the Amigos, making both the team and some headlines. During the ABA's first season, Selvage fired away from 3-point range 461 times, not just more than any other ABA player but more than any other ABA team but Pittsburgh. But Anaheim's 25–53 record made it "a season of three and sympathy," according to Frank Deford. After the first third of the season, Selvage was shooting much better from 3-point range (42 percent) than on 2-pointers (32 percent). He ended up making 32 percent of his 3-pointers, sixth best in the league. Kentucky's Darel Carrier was tops at 36 percent and Minnesota's Ron Perry was next at 35 percent. Selvage's 10-for-26 on 3-pointers in that game against Denver would remain the ABA record, but Louis Dampier would pass Selvage's season record for attempts and conversions when he was 199-for-552 (36 percent) in 1968–69. Selvage's ABA career totaled 82 games and he averaged 13.2 points.

MIKE STOREN: Selvage was more of a novelty act. The guys who made the 3-point play a viable weapon were Kentucky's guards—Dampier and Carrier.

HUBIE BROWN: When I had Dampier, I set up a play for him to take the 3-pointer off the fast break. He would fill a lane and instead of going to the basket for a layup, I wanted Louie to pull up from 25 feet and take the shot—his percentage was that good, especially on a play like that where he wasn't forcing it and had time to get himself set. We had plays for Dampier to take 3-pointers off out-of-bounds situations. He was a remarkable shooter.

GENE LITTLES: Dampier was only 6-foot and not that fast. When you guarded him, you didn't think he was that tough. But he had a great jumper with a lot of range and a quick release. A lot of the time, he'd have the ball 25 feet or so from the basket and you'd think, "He won't shoot from that far out." All he needed to do was see you relax for a second and he got the shot off.

DAVE VANCE: I was the assistant general manager in Kentucky when we had Carrier and Dampier. Louie had played for Adolph Rupp at Kentucky, and Coach Rupp had called Dampier the greatest shooter he had ever seen, which is the ultimate tribute. Every year, they would talk about this kid or that kid coming into training camp who was supposed to take Dampier's job, but none of them could. Part of the reason was that none of them could shoot like Louie.

One of the real treats was watching Carrier and Dampier play 3-point H-O-R-S-E. These guys would be taking shots from two full steps behind the line—legitimate 30-footers—and making them. Seeing that red, white and blue ball rotating in the air and going in for three points really did give you the effect of a home run. If you were a basketball fan, it had to make your heart beat a little faster.

The difference between Dampier and Carrier was that Louie was a better all-around player than Darel. When we got Dan Issel and Artis Gilmore, Louie was able to go from a shooter to a playmaker whose main job was to get the ball inside. He still could make the jumper, but he looked for the pass first.

Dampier and Denver's Byron Beck were the only ABA players to go from the beginning to the end of the ABA with the same team. Dampier averaged 19 points and shot 46 percent from the field, which was very high for a guard in the 1970s. For his career, he was a 36 percent 3-point shooter and averaged three bombs per game. Dampier also was the ABA's all-time assist leader and durable—he missed only 13 games in nine years despite being the "little guard from Pee Wee, Kentucky." Pee Wee was where he lived for a time. Dampier also was a terrific foul

*shooter, setting a record for both the ABA and NBA when he made 57
in a row in 1970–71, which stood until Rick Barry hit 60 straight for
Golden State in 1976. The current NBA record is 78 in a row by Calvin
Murphy in 1980–81.*

HUBIE BROWN: Louie Dampier was a good player who used the
3-pointer to make himself great. He was one of those guys who would
be a Mark Price type today, the smart 6-foot guard who could beat you
with the shot or the pass. It was just too bad that he spent his whole
career in the ABA, because very few people now appreciate him for what
he accomplished.

ANGELO DROSSOS: When the leagues merged, the NBA moguls didn't
want the 3-point shot. Red Auerbach hated it and said the Celtics would
never go along with it. He had everybody up in arms against the play.
Of course, a few years later Red drafted Larry Bird and suddenly he was
all for it. And suddenly one of the bigger attractions at the All-Star Game
is the 3-point shootout.

Larry and Doug

BOB BASS: In the first year of the ABA, Larry Brown and Doug Moe
were the New Orleans Buccaneers. The team had some other good
players and they had a great coach in Babe McCarthy, but when you
thought of New Orleans, you thought of Larry and Doug. Off the court,
they were like twins. If you saw one, you saw the other. It's hard to
believe that two guys would be together like that—everywhere. On the
court, it was like they were operating from the same brain. Larry was
the point guard and he'd bring the ball up the court, then Doug would
cut backdoor and catch a perfect pass from Larry for a layup. They made
the kind of plays guys can only make when they've played together for
years.

GENE LITTLES: I played under Larry and Doug when they were coaching the Carolina Cougars, but you could tell that here were two guys who
knew each other forever. Everything would be quiet, then one of them
would start yelling and the other would scream back, "That's bullshit,
that will never work." They'd start a fight, call each other all kinds of
names and then 15 minutes later, they were back to being the best

buddies in the world. They grew up together in Brooklyn and played together from the time they were kids. They both went to North Carolina and played under Dean Smith, and Dean's boys are a very close-knit fraternity.

LARRY BROWN: The reason I played in the ABA was Doug and the reason he played was me. I was an assistant coach under Dean Smith at North Carolina when I got a call from Babe McCarthy telling me about the ABA being formed. Babe was a very respected college coach and he said that he had been hired by the New Orleans franchise and needed players. What he really wanted to talk about was finding Doug Moe, who was playing in Italy. We got in touch with Doug, who said he knew nothing about the ABA but would play if I would play. I told that to Babe McCarthy, who said that he would be glad to have both of us. Doug and I flew to New Orleans to meet with somebody about a contract. We expected to go into an office building with a big marquee that said, "New Orleans Buccaneers," but it was just a regular office building, no sign about the basketball team.

We were led into an office and there was Morton Downey, or Sean Downey Jr. as he was known back then. He had one of those signs on his desk that you can flip over. On one side it said, "American Can Corp., Vice President of Sales." But when he saw us in the office, he flipped it to the side that said, "Sean Downey Jr., President New Orleans Buccaneers."

So we started to talk contract, and Downey offered Doug $22,000 and he offered me $12,000. I was happy because $12,000 was more than I expected. But Doug said, "What if Larry starts?"

Downey said, "I'll give him another $2,500."

That sounded pretty good to me, but Doug kept trying to get me more money. Then Downey said, "Larry, I know you've been a coach, so why don't you move to New Orleans now and start giving clinics for kids? If you do that, I'll give you another $8,000."

That really sounded good. Then I started to add it all up—I had $12,000 as a base salary, $8,000 for the clinics and $2,500 if I started. That was $22,500, which was more than Doug would make.

Then Downey wrote us each bonus checks—$5,000 for Doug and $2,500 for me. We walked out of the Bucs office looking at those checks and thinking that they would bounce, the whole league was a sham and we'd never play pro ball. The first thing we did was rush to the bank and cash those checks, and we were amazed when they didn't bounce.

Doug loved it. He said, "Look, we're money ahead already."

DOUG MOE: To me, that was the key—when the bank cashed the first check. That told me the league was for real. Then the next thing was that we wanted to at least make it one year.

LARRY BROWN: One of the last things Morton Downey did with New Orleans was sign us. He really didn't last long at all, but he used to go around town handing out these gold passes, which were lifetime passes to Bucs games. We'd have 350 people in the stands, and they all got in on those gold passes.

The guy who really ran the team besides Babe McCarthy was Charlie Smither, who was the principal owner. After games, I recall seeing Mr. Smither carrying the gate receipts out of the building in a shoe box.

ALEX HANNUM: The only reason Larry Brown didn't play in the NBA was that the 1960s was the era of the big guard. Little guys didn't get a chance, and if you were under 6-foot, forget it. Now, you see guys like Spud Webb, Tyrone Bogues and Mark Price in the NBA. We would have thought that they were too small. I thought Larry Brown was too small until I coached him in Oakland—then I knew he was an NBA point guard. He was obsessed with the game of basketball, always talking about it and thinking about it. He was well-schooled from being under Dean Smith. It's a cliche, but Larry Brown was the kind of little point guard who made your team better, the classic coach on the floor. As for Doug, he was a 6-foot-5 forward and an NBA player all the way.

Along with Connie Hawkins and Roger Brown, Moe was banned by the NBA because of his alleged connection to a point-fixing scandal, a connection that was never established in court.

BOB BASS: The ABA was made for Doug and Larry. It was a wide-open league, a league that ran the fast break and didn't have a lot of big men clogging the middle. That was why little guards such as Larry and Mack Calvin bloomed in that league; the accent was on speed and finesse, while the NBA played walk the ball up the court and jam it down your throat.

STEVE JONES: Larry and Doug had definite ideas of what they wanted to do on the court. In New Orleans, Babe McCarthy would draw up a play and then Doug and Larry would come out of the huddle. Doug would say to Larry, "Larry, forget all that crap, just get the ball to me and I'll take it to the hole." Doug had a terrific first step to the basket. Although he's right-handed, he could shoot with either hand as he drove, which made him especially tough. His shooting range was about 17 feet in. Doug has always been the same. We *(Oakland)* played them one night and were getting creamed. By the end of the game, Doug was shooting 15-footers against us—left-handed.

GEORGE IRVINE: Doug was a very streaky shooter and his game was almost chaotic. If he wasn't shooting well right-handed, he was liable to switch to left-handed in the middle of a game, and I've never seen anyone else do that. His speciality was defense. He just wouldn't give you a free shot. He certainly wasn't fast, but his anticipation was amazing. He would guess where you were going and then beat you to the spot.

Later in his career, Doug developed knee problems. It started to bother him in the 1971–72 season, even before training camp. We were playing 2-on-2 against Willie Sojourner and somebody else. Doug's knee started to bother him, but he kept playing. We won the first game easily; then they beat us in the second game, but it was very close. Now it was time to play the rubber game, and I wanted to play, but I could see that Doug's knee was killing him. He said, "Ah, let's play the thing." He wanted to win a 2-on-2 game.

As the year went on, his knee got worse and worse. I was his roommate, so I knew how much it was hurting him. He started wearing a knee brace. I used to help him put it on and take it off, because he had trouble bending his knee to do it. One day, I wasn't around and he tried and tried to get the brace off. Finally, he did and he heard something pop in his knee. I went to the doctor with him and watched him get his knee drained. It was sickening. But Doug kept playing with it. He would go out there on a bad knee and guard a guy like Dan Issel one night and Julius Erving the next. He obviously couldn't run with those guys, but he got on them and almost tore their skin off, he guarded them so close.

EARL FOREMAN: No one in the ABA guarded Rick Barry better than Doug Moe. He would scratch and claw Rick to death; it almost killed Rick. Doug truly hated it when the man he guarded scored against him.

LARRY BROWN: Doug was fearless on the court, but he was scared to death of flying. When he was my assistant with the Carolina Cougars, sometimes he wouldn't fly to a road game with the team. He would drive and meet us there, because he hated to fly that much.

GENE LITTLES: Doug would look at some of those little commuter planes we'd take and say, "I'm not going up in that thing." Then he'd walk right out of the airport, get in his car and drive to the city where we were playing. When he was on the plane, he'd be all hyper, walking up and down the aisles, driving everyone crazy. Whenever there was a bump, he thought the plane was going down.

GEORGE IRVINE: Doug Moe seldom drinks. He always was and still is a coffee-shop guy. But when we flew and it wasn't a game day, he'd drink. He'd get in a part of the plane where he could pull down all the shades, then he'd have a couple of Scotches. At first, seeing Doug so nervous on the airlines was sort of funny. But then it got to me: here was the toughest guy I knew and he had absolute fear in his eyes. I started to think, "Maybe he knows something." Pretty soon, I didn't get as bad as Doug, but I didn't like to fly, either. I still don't.

The Hawk

Connie Hawkins was a playground legend from New York City who led Brooklyn's Boys High to two consecutive city titles. He grew up in the Bedford-Stuyvesant section of Brooklyn. His mother was blind and on welfare. After an intense recruiting battle, he signed with the University of Iowa, but never played a varsity game. After his freshman year, he was banned from college competition because of his alleged association with gamblers. While he never was convicted of anything, he also was banned from playing in the NBA and even the Eastern League, which was a forerunner to the CBA. He played in 1961–62 for the Pittsburgh Rens of the old American Basketball League, where he averaged 27 points and 13 rebounds. He was the league's Most Valuable Player at the age of 19 and he made $5,000. The ABL folded 14 games into the 1962–63 season. He then played for a while with the Harlem Globetrotters, but didn't enjoy it. When the ABA began, the 6-foot-8, 215-pound Hawkins was 27 years old and he needed work. So he jumped at a chance to sign with the Pipers, who gave him a $5,000 bonus, a $15,000 salary for the first year and a $25,000 salary for the second, with the option of becoming a total free agent at the end of the second season. Obviously, Hawkins had a lawyer masterminding this deal; it was David Litman, who also was suing to have Hawkins reinstated by the NBA.

JIM O'BRIEN: I was a sportswriter in Pittsburgh when the ABA and the Pipers started. A gravelly voice called me on the phone one day and said his name was Gabe Rubin. I knew Rubin as a guy who owned a movie theatre in Pittsburgh called the Nixon. Let's see—you could say that the

Nixon Theatre featured "adult art films." I knew the Nixon as a place I wasn't allowed to go as a teenager.

Rubin's voice on the phone was so low, so gravelly, that I wondered if it was an obscene call. He said, "Hello, Jimmy. I understand that you know a lot about basketball."

So I talked with Gabe and I gave him some names of players. I even interviewed a few guys for him, such as Craig Raymond from Brigham Young.

But the move that made the franchise that first year was signing Connie Hawkins. Connie had played for the Pittsburgh Rens, but after the ABL went under, Connie was hanging around Pittsburgh. He was playing in an industrial league at the Young Men's and Women's Hebrew Association (a team called the Porky Chedwicks) and admission was 50 cents a night. In the summer of 1967, Connie had no money. He was living in a row house on Charles Street on the north side of Pittsburgh. The place was in pretty bad shape. Connie was married, had a couple of kids and also was looking after his wife's brother, who was mentally retarded. He had just about hit bottom.

JERRY HARKNESS: I can recall seeing Connie while still in high school play against a team of pros that included Wilt Chamberlain, and Connie held his own. In high school he was already the greatest talent I had ever seen. When he played with kids his own age, it was ridiculous. He just toyed with them. He was already as good as the pros when he was 16. He had those huge hands and he could do anything he wanted with the basketball. Then came the scandal and suddenly he had no place to play—no place until the ABA came around. Then it was the same thing, like it was when he played against the high school kids on the playground—he was so great, he could just control the game without breaking a sweat. Everyone who knew basketball knew about The Hawk, and they knew it galled him not to play in the NBA.

RON GRINKER: I had a friend named Barry Kramer, who was a star basketball player from New York, and he played briefly with the Nets in 1969–70. I went to see him at a summer game at Roosevelt Field in New Jersey; there was an outdoor basketball court near a baseball field. Word was that Connie Hawkins would play, but the game began and he wasn't there. It was getting dark, and late in the first quarter, Connie came out of one of the baseball dugouts. He didn't even have his basketball shoes on. He sat down in the on-deck circle to put on his tennis shoes, and the people hanging around started chanting, "Hawk, Hawk, Hawk." There were a lot of legends in the game, like Roger Brown. Just looking at Connie, I had a feeling that he had had a few drinks and he obviously wasn't thinking only about basketball, because he had shown up late. But he got in the game and the first three times he touched the ball, he went coast-to-coast and then executed three different dunks. The court was getting a little wet because of the night dew, but he seemed to glide over it and slam. People watching it were going crazy, calling his name. It was one of those experiences I only had heard about, the kind of thing that made Connie Hawkins a legend.

GEORGE MIKAN: One of the first things I did as ABA commissioner was to let Roger Brown, Tony Jackson, Connie Hawkins, Charlie Williams and Doug Moe play. I investigated the situation and they seemed all right to me. I figured they deserved a second chance. They said they were sorry if they did anything wrong. Hey, anybody can make a mistake, and look what happened after we gave those guys a second chance. I'm proud to say that I'm the guy who brought Doug Moe, Roger Brown, Connie Hawkins and those other guys back into pro basketball.

STEVE JONES: The Hawk gave our league instant credibility and brought us a lot of attention. For years, everyone had heard how great the guy was, but very, very few people saw him play. Well, the ABA became his first stage. And the thing was that because Pittsburgh had a lot of talent, Connie just cruised during much of the regular season. He was maybe three levels above everyone else, so he could take it easy and still get his 25–30 points and 10–12 rebounds every night. He was good people. He just wanted to play ball and to get along with the other guys. He was doing things with the basketball, with those huge hands of his, that people had never seen before. Just about all the stuff Julius Erving did palming the ball, Connie did first. So that first year, I don't think The Hawk ever let himself go until the playoffs; then he showed that he really knew how to carry the load of a team on his back.

BOB BASS: One night, Pittsburgh coach Vince Cazzetta was sick and he asked Connie to coach the team. I was coaching Denver and I was very interested to see what Connie would do. Well, he took it very seriously, probably too seriously. He concentrated so much on coaching that he hardly played himself. This was during the time when a team came to town for a two-game series, so Pittsburgh played in Denver on Friday and Saturday. We won both games *(by scores of 119–99 and 112–99)* and I told my players, "Let's just be thankful that The Hawk felt more like coaching than playing."

CHARLIE WILLIAMS: Connie deserved a lot of the credit for making us into a team. Let's face it, he was a tremendous, overwhelming talent. He could have decided he was going to average 50 points a game and been able to do it. But he loved and understood team basketball. He would get on Chico Vaughn and myself not to shoot so much from the outside. But he wouldn't say, "Get me the ball." He'd say, "Let's move the ball around. Let everyone touch it." People wanted Connie to shoot the ball more. I know George Mikan told him to do that.

(Mikan would have liked for Hawkins to average 50 points because it would have meant more publicity for the ABA. Mikan also said he liked Hawkins because Connie would stand at attention with his hand over his heart during the National Anthem. "He's a real patriot," Mikan told friends.)

No matter what Mikan or anyone wanted, Connie knew how the game was supposed to be played and he talked a lot about passing and defense. He was a true student of the game. He'd say to me, "Hey Charlie, watch me close tonight. See if you can find something to make me better." When a guy of Connie's ability says that to you, it makes you look at your game in the mirror, too. He really was a leader, and by the end of the year, guys got the message. Tom Washington was our center and he knew he was there to rebound, so he went after every rebound and then threw the outlet pass to the guards. Chico Vaughn was hitting from the outside. Art Heyman would come off the bench and not just shoot, but he was passing, too. In the first round of the playoffs, we blew out Indiana in three straight. Then we faced Minnesota in the second round and took four of five from them.

In the finals, we had to play New Orleans. Those guys were good—with Doug Moe, Larry Brown and Jimmy Jones—and they got up 3–2 on us, with a chance to win the title in Game 6 in New Orleans. I was matched up with Larry Brown, who at 5-foot-9 was the only guard in the league smaller than I was. I started posting Larry up and Connie took over the game. He just wouldn't let us lose. I had 32 points and 10 assists, which was really gratifying to me because Larry Brown had been the MVP in the All-Star Game and some people thought he was the league's best point guard. Connie had 41 points, and we won 118–112. He did it against Doug Moe, who was the best defensive forward in the league. To win on the road like that, before a sellout crowd in that little gym at Loyola of New Orleans, really was amazing.

After that game, a crazy thing happened with Art Heyman. This fan had spit on Art and he punched the guy. Art was in our locker room changing his clothes when the New Orleans police came in and arrested him. We were all staring at Art, wondering how could this guy get in trouble with the cops in the middle of a championship playoff. It turned out that the fan had some sort of physical problem and he didn't intentionally spit on Art, and when Art decked him a complaint was filed. Art apologized and patched things up, so the charges were dropped.

So we went home for Game 7. Art was out of trouble and I just knew that we'd win. We had won the series in Game 6 in New Orleans when we didn't fold. When we took the floor, we couldn't believe all the fans in the stands. Most of the time, we had been playing before 2,000 at home. But we had a sellout *(11,457)*. The fans were noisy and we jumped out early and stayed in control the whole game.

(Pittsburgh won 122–113. Williams had 21 points in the first half, Tom Washington had 27 rebounds and Hawkins had 20 points, 16 rebounds and nine assists.)

After the game was over, it was very emotional in the dressing room. Remember, we were guys who were cut by the NBA, or guys denied the chance to play in the NBA, or guys who had been branded head-cases. In one way or another, all of us had been rejected, and we had gone out and won a championship. Tom Washington was so happy that he just broke down and cried. He was leaning on Connie's shoulder, crying like a baby. A number of us sat there saying, "We did it," over and over. It was something special, to be the first champions in a new league. They gave us each a little trophy, and our winner's cut of the playoff money was $2,200.

MEL DANIELS: Connie Hawkins was our first true star, in the sense that he was a great player whose style attracted a lot of attention, yet he also played an all-around game. The guy who didn't know basketball that well could look at Connie for 15 minutes and know that Connie was great. Then a guy who was a basketball person could watch Connie and see the subtle things—his passing, how he blocked shots and rebounded and knew how to help out his teammates on defense. I am convinced that the Connie Hawkins that led Pittsburgh to that first title could play in the NBA and be on the same level as Magic Johnson, Larry Bird and Michael Jordan are today. The Connie Hawkins that eventually got into the NBA was nearly 30, he had a couple of knee problems—it wasn't the same guy.

BOB BASS: Those who say that Connie was the first player to really show what it meant to have huge hands and palm the ball are right. He'd get a rebound, hold it in one hand and then throw it the length of the floor. The basketball looked like a softball in his hands. He and Charlie Williams had a great play. Connie would get a rebound and Sweet Charlie—that was Williams's nickname—would be on the wing. Connie would fake a pass to Charlie—I'm talking about a one-handed pump fake like a quarterback—and Charlie would run downcourt, catch a long pass from Connie and make a layup. Name one guy who can execute a fast-break pass like that today.

CHARLIE WILLIAMS: Connie would hold that red, white and blue ball in one hand and start waving it around. He told me that it was one of his old Globetrotter routines. His hands, his sense of style, and that red, white and blue basketball were made for each other.

GENE LITTLES: When I came into the ABA, Connie had already jumped to the NBA. He was rich. He had his new contract from the Suns, his court settlement with the NBA. I played on a summer barnstorming team with him, and Connie always kept a $100 bill balled up in his pocket. Right before he'd go on the floor, he'd give the crumpled-up bill to the coach and tell him to keep it until the game was over. I guess Connie figured no matter what happened, he'd always have $100. Probably that was how you thought if you came from Brooklyn and went through all that Connie did.

Bad Times in Oakland

PAT BOONE: Even without Rick Barry, I was hopeful at the start. For the opener, I had James Gardner with me and I thought he might become a co-owner with us. I was feeling very secure, because I had a 10 percent piece of the team and it didn't cost me anything. Ken Davidson had a good relationship with Bank of America, which was lending him the money necessary to run the team. I also know that Ken's mother-in-law was worth several million dollars. More than once Ken told me, "We put up the family jewels; we're in this all the way." I even had a personal letter of indemnification from Ken keeping from me from any financial or legal harm (and liability). I figured I was in good shape.

RICK BARRY: Poor Bruce Hale just didn't have much talent on the Oaks, and he really took a beating. I felt for him. His best player probably was Levern "Jelly" Tart. I liked Jelly. He carried a gun in his car, and

I'm serious about that. But I'm also serious when I said I liked Jelly, because he was a 6-foot-3 guard who could score *(he averaged 27 points and shot 43 percent in his 42 games with the Oaks before being traded to New Jersey for Barry Leibowitz).* I've always liked scorers, and he could fire it up.

PAT BOONE: That first year, Tart was our best player. He made some truly phenomenal shots, the kind only a great player can. But he did shoot the ball quite a bit.

STEVE JONES: Jelly was our dominant player and personality. He was a tremendous competitor who hated losing, no matter if it was a pickup game with college kids in the Bay Area, in practice with the Oaks or in the ABA. Levern wanted to win and if you were on his team and didn't win, you heard about it in no uncertain terms from him. If he passed you the ball and you fumbled it, that just might be the last pass you'd see from him. He'd rather take a bad shot than give you the ball again.

Now he sounds very selfish, but there were two different Tarts. On the floor was this competitive guy who would kill his mother to win a game. Off the court was a guy who was courteous, polite, the whole thing. He loved to go to charity events for kids and the elderly. He did more of that than anyone I've ever met.

TERRY STEMBRIDGE: Bob Bass told me that once Byron Beck and Tart got into a fight and Beck was chasing Jelly toward the dressing room. Somebody grabbed Beck and said, "Don't follow him in there—Tart's got a gun in his locker." I don't know if that was true, but those were the stories. There were a million Jelly Tart stories and none of them were good and he made a lot of stops in the ABA. *(Tart played with six teams in four seasons, averaging 19.4 points.)* So I was worried when I had to room with the guy one night when he was with the Chaparrals, but he was one of the nicest guys I've ever been around. He was reading his fan mail and showed me some of it. You'll never believe this, but Jelly Tart was corresponding with people in rest homes, with nuns.

STEVE JONES: I never knew what would happen to Tart. You'd put him in shorts and sneakers and he became almost suicidal to a team. He was a nightmare for Hale to deal with. Hale had no idea how to cope with a street-smart guy like Tart. One day I was in a car with Hale and he said, "That Jelly, he's one tough guy. I'd hate to meet up with him in a dark alley." Here was the coach talking about one of his players and he also was talking about trying to get control of the team.

It came to a head in Minnesota when Jelly had one of his 30-point first halves. Donnie Freeman was with Minnesota and I said, "Donnie, Jelly might get 60 tonight."

Donnie said, "Steve, he'll be lucky to get three more baskets."

I said, "No way, the man's on fire."

Well, Minnesota started double- and triple-teaming Tart every time he touched the ball. At first, Tart threw a few passes to guys who were open, but they missed the shots. Then Tart said, "That's it," and he started firing it up and missing.

During a time-out, Hale said, "Levern, you're forcing it."

Tart said, "Forcing it? I'm not forcing nothing. They're just playing good defense."

Hale said to Andy Anderson, "Andy, go in for Levern."

But the time-out ended and Tart took the ball and went on the court. He grabbed the ball before Andy could get in the game. So Andy went to the scorer's table to wait for a dead-ball situation. He went into the game and said, "Jelly, I'm in for you."

Tart said, "No, you're in for someone else."

Andy looked at the bench and said, "Coach, he won't come out."

Hale stood there and said, "He won't come out? What do you mean he won't come out?"

Andy said, "He won't come out, that's what he said."

Hale said, "Go back there and tell him that he's out of the game."

Tart said, "I told you, you've got someone else. I ain't coming out, got that?"

Andy went back to Hale, then back to Tart for a third time, trying to get him out of the game. Tart had his fist all balled up and he said, "If you're coming for me, you're coming for the wrong guy."

Eventually, Tart left that game. And Freeman was right: I think he ended up with something like 36, so they shut him down in the second half. But that was the end between Hale and Tart and that led to Tart being traded to New Jersey. We really were bad and lost 17 straight to end the season *(and 25 of their last 28 to end the season as the ABA's worst team, at 22–56).*

About all Bruce Hale could do was to say to himself, "Wait until Rick gets here next year."

PAT BOONE: We lost about a million dollars that first year. We averaged about 2,500 fans at the Oakland Coliseum. I spent a lot of time talking to Bruce Hale about what we could do—trying to get companies like Kaiser Industries involved and other community support. In the meantime, I still had my season tickets for the Laker games and I heard from

(Lakers owner) Jack Kent Cooke that he wanted to meet with me. I went to see him and he said that I should get out of the ABA while I could. He said he had friends who were involved in the old American Basketball League and they were still paying off their debts. He seemed like he was talking to me as a friend. I went back to Ken Davidson and George Mikan and told them that I wanted out of the ABA. They said, "Cooke is the NBA, why would he want you to stay in the ABA? All we're doing is causing trouble for them. If he gets you out, he weakens our league."

I agreed with Davidson and Mikan. I figured that we got the first year out of the way and things couldn't get any worse, and Rick Barry was coming back. We decided to make a coaching change and hired Alex Hannum, who was a great coach in the NBA. We pulled a super trade, getting Larry Brown and Doug Moe from New Orleans for Steve Jones. So I hung in there to see what happened.

RICK BARRY: I was disappointed when they pushed Bruce Hale out of coaching and into the front office, but I knew and liked Alex Hannum and had played for him in my first year with the Warriors. I didn't feel as though I was deceived. Bruce was still with the Oaks *(as general manager)*. Actually, the first year was so brutal on Bruce that maybe it was best that he didn't coach again. It really tore him up, losing all those games. He was still in Oakland and our families were together, and I couldn't wait to play.

First-Year Notebook: 1967–68

The first ABA game was played on October 13, 1967—as in Friday The 13th of October 1967—when the Oakland Oaks defeated the Anaheim Amigos 132–129 before 4,828 fans at the Oakland Coliseum. Oakland's Willie Porter scored the league's first points on a tip-in 64 seconds into the game. The Oaks slapped a 70-point first half on the scoreboard. Andy Anderson had 33 points and Jim Hadnot had 21 rebounds for Oakland. Anaheim's Les Selvage drilled four 3-pointers . . . At Indianapolis, a standing-room crowd of 10,835 watched the Pacers beat Kentucky 117–95. There were 1,700 SRO tickets sold at a dollar each. GM Mike Storen said the Pacers turned away 2,000 fans on the advice of the fire marshal. Roger Brown led the Pacers with 24 points on 9-for-18 from the field. Right before the opening tip-off, a high school band played "Mame," in honor of Colonels owner Mamie Gregory, who was celebrating a birthday . . . Denver opened its home season with a 110–105 victory over Anaheim. About 5,000 fans saw Denver's Willis "Lefty" Thomas score 39 points on 19-for-31 from the field. The 6-foot-2 Thomas came straight to the Rockets from the Harlem Clowns, where he said he once scored 55 while on a European tour. The Amigos had an ABA first as they shot better from 3-point range (50 percent on 7-for-14) than they did from 2-point range (32-for-81 for 40 percent). Les Selvage had four of those 3-pointers and finished with 26 points. Pregame entertainment was a 35-minute clarinet concert by Peanuts Hucko and his quartet . . . In Dallas, 3,800 fans saw the Chaparrals beat—who else?—the Anaheim Amigos 129–124. The Amigos may have set some sort of record by losing four openers—three on the road and one at home. The Chaparrals had a mascot, Miss Tall Texan. Her real name was Miss Brenda Darney and she said she was 6-foot-7 or so, "give or take a few inches for my hairdo." *Dallas Times-Herald* columnist Blackie Sherrod noted, "The team's battle cry was supposed to be like the TV cartoon roadrunner noise— something like beep-beep, *barrrooom*. It was supposed to go off whenever the home team made a 3-pointer, but it bleated sporadically during the game and sounded like the mating call of a kazoo" . . . The sanctioned ABA official's uniform was a red shirt, white pants, a blue belt and blue shoes. The officials also had their names on the back of their shirts, a first in pro basketball. File this comment under the heading of No Kidding: "We feel the colorful uniforms will set the officials apart from the players," said Assistant ABA Commissioner Thurlo McCready . . . Kentucky became the first ABA team to fire a coach when the axe fell on John Givens after a 5–12 start and he was replaced by Gene Rhodes, who went 31–30 . . . A novel coaching move was made by Anaheim when it canned Al Brightman after a 13–24 start. Well, Brightman actually wasn't "fired"—he was "promoted" to public relations director, according to the Amigos' press release. Was that release written by new PR man Brightman? No one knows. Owner Art Kim just said, "Coach Brightman has been our most effective public relations man, so why not make him the public relations man?" Taking Brightman's place was assistant Harry Dinnell, whose record was 13–29 . . . Denver's Larry Jones became the first ABA player to score 50 points in a game (52, to be exact) as he shot 20-for-28 against Oakland. The prior ABA scoring record was 49, held by Levern Tart. Asked why he had such a hot night, Jones first said he was lucky, then credited eating oatmeal for breakfast. Jones had been a teammate of Tart's with the Wilkes-Barre Barons of the Eastern Basketball League before the ABA was formed. He also had spent 23 games with the Philadelphia 76ers, averaging 5.7 points in 1964–65 . . . Kentucky's Louis Dampier later passed Jones's mark when he threw

in 54 points against Indiana. Dampier was 19-for-36 from the field
. . . Mikan surprised more than a few people with his reply to this
question: "When do you think the ABA will reach parity with the
NBA?" Mikan said, "In our first year. . . . How long does it take to train
a basketball player? You're only talking about five men. What did the
Cleveland Browns do when they came from a defunct league to the
NFL?" . . . ABA PR Director Lee Meade created the Bialosuknia Line.
Oakland's Wes Bialosuknia had the longest last name in the league—11
letters. So Meade made the league stats sheets long enough to accommodate players with 11-letter last names. At the University of Connecticut,
Wes was known as "The Typographical Terror." He also had a 3.0 GPA
in economics. As a pro, he set an ABA record by hitting nine consecutive
3-pointers and made 29 of 73 3-point attempts for the season (40 percent), which would have been the league's best, but he didn't have the
100 attempts to qualify for the leadership . . . Pittsburgh became the first
ABA team to protest a defeat, claiming that a game it played against
Indiana in Shelbyville, Indiana, was on a floor that was only 84 feet long
instead of the required 94 feet. Mikan did not grant the protest . . . No
ABA player was traded more in the first year than Barry Leibowitz. He
started the season with Pittsburgh, then was traded to the New Jersey
Americans for Art Heyman. Then Leibowitz went to Oakland for Levern
Tart. That made three teams in the first four months of the season. He
averaged 11 points in his only ABA season . . . Dallas and Pittsburgh
had to delay a game for 20 minutes when both teams' uniforms were lost
at the cleaners . . . Anaheim's Ben Warley made 16 consecutive field
goals in the Amigos' 145–142 victory over Houston. Warley finished
with 43 points. More significantly, the 6-foot-8 Warley was on his seventh pro basketball team in three different leagues, which was believed
to be some sort of record. He was with the Cleveland Pipers and the Long
Beach Chiefs of the old American Basketball League. Then came stops
with three different NBA teams and two ABA teams . . . New Jersey and
Kentucky finished in a fourth-place tie for the last playoff berth. A
sudden-death playoff game was scheduled. First, it was to be at New
Jersey's regular home, the Teaneck Armory, but that was booked by the
circus, so the game was moved to Commack Arena on Long Island. But
when the teams arrived, the floor was a shambles, with pieces of wood
sticking out and loose nuts and bolts all over the place. Both teams called
Mikan for a ruling, since the floor was unplayable. He forfeited the game
to Kentucky, putting the Colonels in the playoffs. Then—only in the
ABA would this happen—next season, the New Jersey Americans became the New York Nets and played their games at—you guessed it—
Commack Arena . . . Pittsburgh started the season with an 11–12 record.

Then the Pipers got hot after trading Leibowitz (who else?) for Art Heyman and won 15 games in a row. Heyman averaged 20.9 points during the winning streak. Pittsburgh finished the season at 54 –24 (the most regular-season victories in the ABA) and then defeated New Orleans in the playoffs to win the first ABA title . . . The Pipers' Connie Hawkins led the league in scoring at 26.7 and was the league's MVP. He was voted the ABA's best forward, yet he spent far more time at center. Meanwhile, Minnesota's Mel Daniels was voted all-ABA as a center, but he spent more time at power forward. Other members of the all-ABA team were Pittsburgh's Charlie Williams and Denver's Larry Jones at the guards and New Orleans's Doug Moe at forward . . . New Orleans's Larry Brown was the All-Star Game MVP and led the league in assists . . . The ABA claimed to draw 1,200,439 fans for an average of 2,804 per game, which by all accounts was wildly overstated. Indiana led the league in attendance at 5,965, followed by Denver at 4,100 . . . The league claimed to finish $2.5 million in the red. The biggest losers were Oakland at $750,000 and Anaheim at $500,000 . . . Franchises were made available to anyone who could produce a certified $50,000 check against a purchase price of $650,000.

The $1.3 Million Glass Ring: An ABA "Success" Story

DOUG MOE: When Oakland traded for me and Larry *(Brown)* and only gave up Steve Jones, this had to be the most lopsided trade in the history of professional sports, bar none. With Steve Jones, Oakland won only 22 games, while Larry and I got New Orleans into the ABA finals. Then Steve goes to New Orleans and they end up in the tank *(actually, New Orleans was 46–32)* and then Larry and I are on an Oakland team that wins the title. Every time I tell that to Steve Jones, it pisses him off. But it was an unbelievable trade. I think New Orleans didn't think it had the money to pay Larry and me. When I tell that to Steve, he gets even madder. He doesn't want to sound like some guy dragged out of a bargain basement.

ALEX HANNUM: Bruce Hale made the Moe deal, and that turned our team around as much as signing Barry.

DOUG MOE: After I got to Oakland, I had trouble with Alex Hannum. He wouldn't give me a guaranteed contract worth $30,000. I wanted a guarantee. I had a good year in New Orleans *(24 points, 10 rebounds).* I was second in the league in scoring and the MVP voting. That should have been good for something.

Alex said, "You don't have any bargaining power."

I said, "Hey, I had a good year."

Alex said, "You're getting old."

I said, "Old? I'm 28."

Alex said, "When I say something, I mean it."

I said, "Listen Alex, I have as much bargaining power as I need. If I never get on another airplane and fly again, that will be fine with me."

That was how it ended. Larry *(Brown)* eventually signed a nonguaranteed contract, but I wouldn't. Coach *(Dean)* Smith *(a close friend of Moe's)* didn't like how this was going and he got involved. He asked me if I'd take some money up front as a bonus instead of a no-cut. I said that sounded pretty good to me.

Coach Smith called Alex and said, "Give Doug a $5,000 bonus and the $30,000 you offered him and he'll sign."

Alex agreed.

All of that really sounds pretty boring; I got $35,000, big deal, right?

But at the end of the season, I got another check for $5,000—they paid me the $5,000 bonus twice. I told the Oaks they paid me $5,000 too much, but they said they didn't. I had my wife Jane check our finances, and she said they paid us $5,000 too much. So Jane and I drove to the Oaks office and tried to give them the money back for a second time, but they wouldn't take it.

I got back into the car with the check in my hand, but then I said to Jane, "We can't keep this, it's not right." So I went back into the office and talked to Alex Hannum's wife, who was handling the books. I tried to give her the $5,000 but she wouldn't take it. Here the team was losing a million dollars and I wanted to give them money, but they still didn't take it. I walked back to the car and told Jane, "Three strikes, they're out. Let's cash this," and we did and the check didn't even bounce.

ALEX HANNUM: Once we got Doug and everyone signed, it was time for training camp. I believe in a lot of running and a lot of drills. If you missed a layup at any time during practice, you ran laps. No one should miss an open layup anytime; that's how I felt. If you missed, you weren't concentrating. If you weren't in shape for my training camps, you regretted it for a month, because it would be the worst month of your life.

STEVE JONES: I later played for Alex in Denver, and he may have had the toughest training camp ever. We had to climb up and down this ladder he had set up in the gym, and you had to do it in 24 seconds or you did it again. He had a length-of-the-floor layup drill that was a killer. If you missed, you ran laps. Guys ran a lot of laps. He also had a drill where you always had to throw a bounce pass; if you screwed that up, you ran more laps.

When you ran laps, he put a clock on you and he wanted them done in a certain time. If they weren't, you ran some more until they were. Then after the laps were done, you'd scrimmage.

TOM MESCHERY: Rick Barry and I played for Alex with the Warriors. When I think of Alex's training camps, I think of guys throwing up.

ALEX HANNUM: When I coached Wilt Chamberlain, he only went to one of my training camps. After that, he just decided it was easier to hold out in training camp and then sign right as the season started.

At the end of each practice, we had a game to five baskets. For the winning team, there was a prize—no running. The losers ran—a lot. You could say that those games were pretty intense. We had a few fights.

DOUG MOE: Fights? Guys were ready to kill each other. Alex worked you to death, but in Oakland, with guys such as Larry *(Brown)*, Rick *(Barry)* and myself, we liked the work. He pushed us and pushed us and pushed us, but we could take it, and in a way we liked it.

STEVE JONES: An Alex Hannum team was always the best-conditioned in basketball. You were so tough that you just wouldn't get tired. His toughness and single-mindedness carried over to the players.

DOUG MOE: The only time Alex ever lost his cool in camp with Oakland was when Jim Hadnot just fell to the floor while we were doing sprints. He was rolling around saying, "Alex, I can't breathe."

Alex said, "What's wrong?"

Hadnot said, "Alex, you won't believe this, but I'm breathing through my ears."

Alex just lost it. He laughed so hard that he even stopped the sprints—for a minute, anyway.

STEVE JONES: Alex went against the attitude that most pro coaches had. The idea was that once a player went from college to the pros, he had time to work himself into shape. You didn't push yourself hard from day one. But Alex was different, because Alex had a personality that was larger than life. He had been the only guy to break in and win a title when the Celtics had their dynasty going. He was the one guy who got the most out of Wilt Chamberlain. He also had the attitude that players liked— Alex didn't like management. Of course, that was because Alex wanted to *be* management. In Oakland, he and his wife really ran the front office with Bruce Hale. Later, in Denver, Alex was GM and coach. He liked complete control. But he was good with players. He could push them harder than probably any other coach without having a rebellion, because there was something about Alex that made you trust him. There were no stories about Alex screwing anybody. All you ever heard was that Alex Hannum was a fair guy.

WAYNE EMBRY: Alex created what is now known as the double-pick and also the double–low post offense. For years, virtually every team in the NBA was running Alex Hannum's plays, only they called them something else. He was more than a disciplinarian—he was an innovator.

STEVE JONES: All you had to do was look at Alex's Oakland team to see why the players liked him. They averaged 126 points a game. They ran for 48 minutes, played tough defense and had a lot of offensive freedom. Not only were they the best team in the league talent-wise, they were the hardest-working and best-conditioned and they had Barry, who was sensational. They talk about Larry Bird today as a guy with great ability to pass and hit the outside shot. But Rick Barry brought those same things to the ABA. He was 6-foot-8 and could run like a deer. Okay, he didn't have any conscience about putting the ball in the air, but he'd pass and he rebounded very well for a small forward. Watching this guy, you never would have believed that he sat out a year.

ALEX HANNUM: Rick was under a lot of pressure from the opening tip, but it never bothered him. He was a great player and he was great right away. Just check how he played in his first few games.

(Barry opened the season with 36 points at Indiana, then 46 at Kentucky, hitting 31-for-54 from the field and perfect on 20 free throws. At Kentucky, he had 14 rebounds; at Indiana, 12 assists. Indianapolis had a sellout while Kentucky drew what was then the ABA's largest crowd of 13,067.)

Rick's one fear was injury. He always worried that someone would undercut him, and that was exactly what happened and it knocked him out for the season.

Rick Barry: We were playing New York at Commack and I was going for a layup when Ken Wilburn blindsided me. He just clobbered me, and in the air our legs got tangled up. When I came down, my left knee was bent wrong, and right away I knew I was in deep trouble. I was so frustrated, because I had sat out a year and was playing really well *(averaging 34 points and nine rebounds and shooting 51 percent in 34 games).*

Doug Moe: When Rick blew out his knee, I think that Alex thought we were in big trouble.

Larry Brown: The day after Barry's injury, we played in Indiana. Alex was in the dressing room and you could tell by the tone of his voice that he had real doubts about the game. Indiana was a terrific team and almost unbeatable at home. I was watching Doug during Alex's talk and he was getting pissed. As we walked out on the floor, Doug had that look about him. He wanted to prove Alex wrong, and it spread to the whole team. We won that game, then we won nine in a row without Rick; that's how good we were. We made a shambles of the whole league *(finishing at 60–18).*

Pat Boone: We had a 16-game winning streak at one point. It was a great feeling. Then we went on and won the championship without Rick. It really was an amazing team and I was pretty caught up in it. Later on, that would cost me. But at the time, I didn't know what was coming.

Rick Barry: When I was healthy, we could have played against the best NBA teams and held our own, and I could say that from the perspective of a guy who played in both leagues. The only teams that might have given us problems were the few with All-Star centers. We had Ira Harge in the middle and he was a hard-working guy on the boards, but he was only 6-foot-8 and scored just eight points a game. Our other key players were NBA caliber. You can't tell me that Larry Brown couldn't have been a good NBA point guard, but no one would give him a chance, because he was 5-foot-9. The guy was the ideal point guard, because he really ran the offense. Doug Moe was a Dave DeBusschere type, only he was better because he could score more. I'm very sincere when I say that you take Moe and DeBusschere in their primes and Moe was a better player.

Doug Moe: We can talk all we want about how good that Oakland team was and no one will believe us. They just would say, "You guys were in the ABA," and that's it, end of discussion. We were better than the Warriors, for instance, but that's reality and people don't like to face reality and give the ABA credit.

LARRY BROWN: On that Oakland team we had only 10 guys—and one was our trainer. That was fine with us, because it meant we could split our playoff money just 10 ways, and that meant more for each guy *(about $4,500 for winning the championship).*

RICK BARRY: The best thing about the early ABA was the players. So many other things were Mickey Mouse. One of my most vivid memories is from the finals with Oakland. We finally had a big crowd, about 7,000, and there was George Mikan before the game, telling our fans, "It sure is nice to be here in Oklahoma."

PAT BOONE: Today, I look at my ABA championship ring and think that it only cost me about $1.3 million. I want to show it to Elizabeth Taylor. She has some expensive stuff, but even she never paid $1.3 million for a ring. And actually, the team's losses for the two years were over $2.5 million. And our ring is just glass—green glass and some heavy lettering.

To this day, I'm amazed at how I ended up losing all that money when being in the ABA wasn't supposed to cost me a thing.

It started when Ken Davidson brought me a Bank of America check that he wanted me to sign. I said, "There is no amount written on this check."

He said the check would be for about $250,000 to pay off the current debt. He said he couldn't remember the amount, it would be either $245,000 or $251,000. We both needed to sign it and that would take care of it. I called my business manager and he said I had indemnification. I had a signed statement from Ken Davidson to that effect. Besides, I had known Davidson for all these years, he was my partner, and if worse came to worst, I figured I could pay it off.

So what I signed was really a blank check.

Later, my lawyer went to the bank and said I was disassociating myself from the whole thing and I wanted out. The banker showed my lawyer the blank check, which was now filled in for $1.3 million! And it had my signature on the bottom. The amount had been written in by the banker.

My lawyer asked me why I had signed a check for $1.3 million. I said I hadn't, and then I remembered the blank check. I called Ken Davidson about it and he said he gave the check to the bank blank because he couldn't remember the figure.

I said, "Ken, that check now says $1.3 million! I've got to invoke that right of indemnification real quick."

Then Ken said he wanted out. He said that he was busted, his mother-in-law wouldn't put in any more money. He also said that he had been able to get the bank to lend us over $2 million, just based on our signatures.

Suddenly, I had a $2 million debt dumped in my lap. I was in for $2 million and somehow Ken had been about to finagle out of it. The banker also had gotten so caught up in the ABA and the idea that the Oakland franchise would succeed that he probably went farther than he should have in approving things without actual collateral. From what I understand, someone at the bank put the $1.3 million on the blank check to protect himself. I wanted to go to court, but my lawyer said, "You can't fight Bank of America. Besides, how can you prove that the check was blank when you signed it?"

I said we'd also have Ken Davidson's word, but the lawyer said it was our word against the bank's and that wasn't good enough. Somehow, Ken had turned the whole team over to me, so I was the sole owner. That also meant my letter of indemnification meant nothing.

DICK TINKHAM: For a long time, Ken Davidson was writing checks left and right, giving the league a lot of money. We figured he was loaded.

PAT BOONE: When the season ended and it became apparent that salaries were escalating like crazy, that our debt was out of control and that we had no more buyers on the horizon, I was in deep trouble. It was a Wednesday and I had gotten a letter from Bank of America demanding $1.3 million by Friday or the bank would take "swift and appropriate action." My attorney said that meant the bank would attach everything I had. Although I had enough assets to cover the debt, not enough of them were liquid and I'd probably end up having to sell my house.

Meanwhile, my career had suffered because I had spent so much time on basketball and my other business ventures. My wife Shirley and I told our advisors, "We're out of answers. There's nothing we can do but pray. We really need some sort of miracle, and we're going to pray for one."

Later, my advisors said that they looked at us and thought, "Well, Pat and Shirley have flipped out this time. Maybe they're so out of touch with reality that they'll handle this disaster better than we thought they would."

I said something about it all being in the hands of God and a sharp businessman I know said, "No, Pat, it's in the hands of Bank of America."

The debt had risen to over $2 million. If something miraculous didn't happen, I was going to lose my home and be held up to public ridicule. That's where we stood on Wednesday, with the Friday deadline bearing down on us. On Thursday, nothing happened, except that Shirley and I prayed a lot.

On Friday, there was a meeting at the Bank of America and when I walked in, a fellow by the name of Earl Foreman was there, and he had a banker with him. I had never met either of these gentlemen.

Earl Foreman said, "Pat, I want to buy the Oakland Oaks. How much?"

I couldn't believe it. My miracle was standing in front of me. I stammered a bit and said, "$2.5 million."

Foreman said, "I'll take it now. I want to move the team to Washington. I want to establish an $18 million line of credit, because we're building a sports syndicate in the Washington area."

All the bankers and lawyers went to work and hammered out a deal.

DICK TINKHAM: Ken Davidson and Pat Boone were going under fast in Oakland. *(Denver owner)* Bill Ringsby and I went to the Bank of America to see what we could do to keep the franchise alive. We also had been talking to Earl Foreman, who wanted to get into the ABA with a team in Washington.

The kicker was that the NBA's Baltimore Bullets were in the same territory and we were in the middle of the never-ending merger talks. Abe Pollin owned the Bullets and he said he'd never go for a merger if the ABA put a team in Washington.

I talked to Boone and he told me, "I have a partner I met from church and I've signed these checks and we're way overextended. . . . I've had some oil wells that have gone bad. . . . If my wife ever finds out, I'll be in such bad trouble that you won't believe it."

He poured his heart out and I never met a guy I liked better than Pat Boone.

EARL FOREMAN: I was vacationing in Maine when a business associate of mine called and said, "The Oakland Oaks can be bought." I flew to San Francisco to meet with the banks and with Pat Boone. Pat had guaranteed a lot of notes and he just wanted to get the hell out. I never knew exactly how much the Oaks lost in their first two years, but it was millions. I was made an offer that I couldn't refuse; in effect, I was paid in hard bucks and credit to take over the team. I took on some of the debt for tax purposes. It was a great business deal; it didn't cost me a cent and I got a lot of things in return.

DICK TINKHAM: We didn't want Foreman to take the team to Washington because of the merger talks, but he pulled an Al Davis. He and the bank just said, "We got a deal, we're going and there's nothing you can do about it."

EARL FOREMAN: You get into the pro sports business either for ego or for money. In my case, you could say it was primarily greed. As I've said, getting the Oaks was a helluva business deal. For example, the tax arrangement for Rick Barry's contract was equal to the purchase price of the team. There was over a $500,000 write-off for me from Rick's contract, when you figured in depreciation. In the end, they said the purchase price of the team was a half-million dollars. Then the tax lawyers went to work and it was nothing.

PAT BOONE: After all the deals were done between Earl Foreman and the Bank of America, the ABA ended up costing me about $1.5 million. I had to pay $700,000 for the moves that Ken Davidson made and another $600,000 of the debt. There also was another $160,000 that came when *(Warriors owner)* Franklin Mieuli took Ken Davidson and me to court in the Rick Barry case. He sued for a million and we settled for $160,000—I paid him $16,000 a year for 10 years.

After the case, I set up a meeting with Franklin and told him, "I want to apologize and ask your forgiveness. Even though our attorneys told us that the reserve clause wasn't binding and we were operating within our own legal boundaries to do what we did, I had a moral lapse, which I am confessing to you privately. I overlooked the fact that Rick had made a personal commitment to you. I should have encouraged Rick to go ahead and keep his word to you. If I had a million to pay you, I'd pay you a million. We're settling for $160,000, but I feel bad about it."

Franklin didn't seem to understand what I was talking about. He still had blood in his eyes and he kept saying, "I want to get the whole." He kept repeating that phrase. That meant he wanted Barry back for his team to be together again.

When I apologized, he didn't say, "I forgive you."

Instead, Franklin stared hard at me and said, "I want you to know that the scruffy little Italian was right and Mr. All-American was wrong."

I wrote him letters, sent him a Bible to read, just so he could understand where I was coming from. I acknowledged that we had been wrong, but none of that seemed to change Franklin's heart.

After I talked to Franklin, I went to see Ken Davidson and said, "Ken, can you help me a little? Can you pay $200, even $100 a month toward the $160,000?"

Ken refused. He was still selling insurance, still living in his same house and still driving a big car. He obviously had no plans to pay anything. There is a part in the Bible that says if you've been given much, you also should forgive. One day, I asked Ken to come over to our home. Shirley and I took out the letter of indemnification, gave it back to him and said, "Okay, you don't owe us a thing. But if you are ever able to pay me, please do so."

I had to pay off the full amount by myself. I had to accept a lot more engagements and work a lot harder than I would have liked. I feel good that I was able to meet all the debts, and we've come back nicely. I'm just thankful that Earl Foreman came along or I would have been in the hole for $2.5 million. All I know is that professional sports can make you act irrationally, because you become so wrapped up in it.

The funny thing is that some years later I was asked to become involved in the expansion franchise in Dallas, the Dallas Mavericks of the NBA. I said, "No way. I'm a player, not an owner. I never want to own a team again." So I passed up a chance to be in with Donald Carter and those guys and own a very successful and valuable NBA team. I guess I never could figure out the basketball business.

The Leaders Crumble

CHARLIE WILLIAMS: After that first year in Pittsburgh, we knew that Connie Hawkins would eventually end up in the NBA. He had a lawyer working on his case and he had gotten a lot of publicity from being on a championship team in the ABA. People were starting to see what a crime it was to deny a man of his ability the chance to play in the NBA, and we knew that the NBA was what he really wanted. The NBA was the one place that wouldn't let him play and that bothered him, although he never said much about it.

When I think back on it, none of it made much sense. There was no reason for the NBA to deny guys like Connie and myself a chance to play. Then we went to Pittsburgh and won more games than anyone in the league and no one paid attention to us until the final game. Then we packed in the fans and the town started to talk about the Pipers and Connie Hawkins. You would think that would be something to build on—we were the defending champs, and Connie lived in Pittsburgh year-round. We should have been ready for a big second season at the gate and on the court.

Then I heard that Gabe Rubin had moved the team to Minnesota. I said, "Minnesota?" I mean, Minnesota just had a team and it moved to Florida because it didn't draw, and Minnesota had the second-best record in the league *(50–28)* with guys like Mel Daniels on the team. If the people didn't go see that team, why would they go see us?

MIKE STOREN: The real reason for the move was that George Mikan was putting on the pressure for an ABA team to be in Minnesota after the Muskies went to Florida. Mikan and the ABA league offices were in Minneapolis, so it would look bad if there wasn't a team there, too, especially since Mikan had been criticized for not having the league office in New York. Did any of that make sense? Of course not. But that was how Mikan sometimes did business.

CHARLIE WILLIAMS: So whether we liked it or not, we were going to Minnesota. Vince Cazzetta really didn't want to move his family to Minnesota. He had about six kids in school, as I remember. Anyway, Vince went in and figured that if he had to move, he at least deserved a new contract. He coached us to the championship, he was the ABA Coach of the Year. Gabe didn't want to pay, so, in effect, he fired Cazzetta. He started knocking Vince in the press.

(Rubin was quoted as saying, "Cazzetta was overrated. He was a lousy coach. The Pipers won in spite of him.")

Vince's personality was why the guys on the team pulled together and won a championship. The guys liked and trusted him. We had a lot of guys who had been around and had pro experience. We didn't need a heavy coaching hand. Vince knew that. The guy who replaced him—Jim Harding—didn't.

In a textbook example of how a good team can shoot itself in the foot, the Pittsburgh-turned-Minnesota Pipers made one error after another, moving being just the first. The biggest blunder was hiring Jim Harding as coach. Harding had no pro experience. He had coached at Loyola of New Orleans, LaSalle and Gannon, and he claimed never to have lost three games in a row. When he blew the whistle, he expected everyone to freeze. He took one look at Connie Hawkins and reportedly mumbled, "So that's the best player in the ABA?" Later, he tried to change the form on Hawkins's jumper. In the second game of the season, Hawkins played all 48 minutes as Harding used only six players.

CHARLIE WILLIAMS: The players called Harding "The Maniac." While Vince was a soothing father-type coach, this guy was a screamer. He wanted us all to wear white shirts and ties on the road. He said that was what his college teams did. Connie talked him out of that. His training camp was brutal, absolutely brutal. We didn't have double-sessions, we had triple-sessions. We practiced in the morning, had lunch, practiced in the afternoon, ate again, and then practiced at night. And we always went full tilt. Guys started breaking down, pulling muscles, twisting ankles, things like that. First Connie hurt his knee, then I pulled a hamstring, then Chico Vaughn got hurt, but he wouldn't let any of us rest. He wouldn't even take us out. Some of us played 48 minutes a night.

When we lost an exhibition game, he'd act like the world ended. He was playing the starters over 40 minutes *in preseason*. We started the season fast because we had great talent, but soon we were breaking down. We went into the All-Star break in first place *(20 –12)*, but that was when Harding went just one step too far.

RICK BARRY: One of my vivid ABA memories was the 1969 All-Star banquet when Gabe Rubin and Jim Harding got into a fight. It was the epitome of Mickey Mouse. These guys were ripping each other's sports coats off, clawing at each other. I thought they had lost their minds.

CHARLIE WILLIAMS: Connie Hawkins had been picked for the All-Star team, but he didn't go because of his knee injury. Tom Washington and I were picked and there was confusion about the banquet the night before the game. Anyway, Tom and I weren't there when they introduced us at the banquet. It wasn't intentional, we just had the wrong time. Well, Harding went crazy when our names were called and we weren't there. Gabe Rubin defended us, saying that we were good guys and something must have happened for us to be late.

Harding screamed at Rubin, "These guys won't be able to pick up their paychecks with a spoon when I get through with them."

It was sort of a strange thing to say, because it meant that Harding was going to lay some heavy fines on us.

Then Harding and Rubin got into a fight right there in the middle of the party, and Rubin fired Harding right on the spot in front of everybody. That party we just heard about. When Tom and I did get to the lobby, we saw Rubin coming out of the banquet room with a big scratch on his face from where Harding had got him.

BOB BASS: That whole Pittsburgh-Minnesota operation was a mess. I can still see Gabe Rubin at the 1969 draft, sitting there with a basketball magazine from 1968. He was looking at the magazine and drafting guys who were already playing in the NBA.

The Pipers finished at 36 – 42 and were knocked out of the playoffs in the first round by Miami, which ironically had played in Minnesota the season before. They averaged 2,263 fans in Minnesota. A knee injury limited Hawkins to 47 games. Charlie Williams limped through most of his 68 games as his hamstring injury was never given time to heal. Williams averaged 18.7 points, but shot only 38 percent. After the season, in which the Pipers reportedly lost over $250,000, Gabe Rubin's Minnesota investors gave the team right back to him.

CHARLIE WILLIAMS: Think about this for a minute. After a year in Minnesota, Gabe had no idea what to do with the team, so he moved it back to *Pittsburgh.* Only now, our name was changed from the Pipers to the Condors, as if that was going to make a difference or make people forget that this was the team that moved out of town the year before. I had people come up to me and ask, "What are you guys doing back in town?" I really didn't have a good answer for them. Why should I? None of it made any sense.

The only good thing was that the NBA agreed to let Connie Hawkins play and he didn't have to come back to Pittsburgh. I was so happy for him, as were the rest of the guys. It was like he was one of our honor graduates.

Hawkins signed a five-year, $410,000 guaranteed contract with the Phoenix Suns. He received a $250,000 bonus, $35,000 for his legal fees and a $600,000 annuity paying him $30,000 annually starting at age 45.

STEVE JONES: After that team went back to Pittsburgh, it became the Devil's Island of the ABA. A player's worst nightmare was to be traded there. We all did jokes saying that if Pittsburgh wasn't basketball's end of the world, you could see it from there. They talk about the Ted Stepien days in Cleveland with the Cavaliers in the early 1980s being bad, but the Condors were worse. There was no money, a lot of dumb ideas, and people running the show who had no idea what they were doing.

CHARLIE WILLIAMS: We were so desperate for players that we were trying anything. One day Charlie "Helicopter" Hentz from Arkansas AM&N showed up. He was 6-foot-6, 230 pounds and could jump higher than anyone I had ever seen. He'd jump after every rebound, but he had absolutely no timing. He jumped too soon or too late. He jumped on guys' backs and he got a lot of rebounds that way, but the officials would just take the ball away from him because he fouled someone.

But Helicopter did have his move. One game he went up for a dunk and just ripped the rim right off. We all stood there and just looked at the rim on the floor. Breaking rims and backboards are normal today, but they never happened back then. The Helicopter just stood there smiling.

JOHN VANAK: The game was in Raleigh—Pittsburgh against the Carolina Cougars. The Helicopter went up for a slam and just tore the rim right off. I mean, you'd have thought the whole arena was coming down. He had a powerful one-handed tomahawk slam. It really was a sight. The first time it happened—yes, I said the first time—was late in the first half and they held up the game for an hour, but eventually found another rim and backboard. But in the second half, the same damn thing happened again. Helicopter went up for a dunk and I said to myself, "Oh, no, not again." Sure enough, he broke another backboard. Now I knew we were in real trouble. Where were we going to find another backboard? It was about 11 at night. *(Cougars GM)* Carl Scheer wanted to call off the game and then replay it with a big promotion—Broken Backboard Night or some such thing. Jack McMahon was coaching Pittsburgh and he said he didn't care if we had to wait until 3 A.M., we were going to finish the game. They brought in a wooden backboard from a local high school and we did finish, probably about 3 A.M. I had worked in the NBA since 1960 and I had never seen one backboard smashed, and the Helicopter did it twice in a night. Of course, a month later Pittsburgh cut Helicopter and he was playing in the Eastern League, so it was probably good he did break those backboards or else no one would remember the guy.

Hentz averaged 6.0 points and 6.3 rebounds in 57 games with Pittsburgh in 1970–71.

DAVE VANCE: The Condors had a publicity director named Fred Cranwell, who was a Rodney Dangerfield–type guy, a terrific sense of humor. In that job, he needed it. I was the assistant GM in Kentucky when I first met Fred. I asked him about the exhibition game the Condors played in Scranton.

"You want to know about the crowd?" he asked me. "I'll tell you about the crowd. After the game, we sent them home all in the same yellow cab."

Then he'd wait for the laugh.

"I've decided to be a ticket taker in Scranton when I retire," he said. "There's a job where you do no work."

Then Fred started telling stories. They had cupcake night in Pittsburgh and gave away 1,000 cupcakes to a fan. The problem was that the guy who won it was a diabetic. Making matters worse was that the guy said he was diabetic when he was introduced at halftime and the crowd booed.

I was there one night when they were giving away Condors wrist-watches. The PA man said, "And now for the winners of the Condors wristwatches," and the people booed.

Then Fred Cranwell leaned over to me and said, "Did you hear about the break-in we had last night at our office? It was our last season ticket holder giving back his seats."

VAN VANCE: I was broadcasting the Kentucky games and one night they wouldn't let me into the arena in Pittsburgh. They wanted $50 if you were in radio, $200 for each television camera you brought in. Apparently the team wasn't paying the rent and the arena was trying to get cash any way it could. Every time you'd come to Pittsburgh, you'd broadcast a game from a different location, because they kept moving the phone lines around the arena. I guess they weren't paying their phone bills either, so when the phone company shut off one line, they'd open up another.

One night I was ready to go on the air and a guy from the arena came up to me and said, "As soon as you say, 'Good evening,' I'm going to rip this phone line right out unless you pay me fifty dollars."

The Pittsburgh GM was Mark Binstein, and he came running over and said, "Van, don't worry about a thing. You'll be able to broadcast the game if I have to hold a gun to this guy's head all night."

As I went on the air, Binstein and these guys were screaming at each other and you could hear it all over the air. What a mess, but at least I stayed on the air all night.

The best thing the ABA did was just fold that team *(after the 1971–72 season)*. In their last year, the Condors were playing "home games" in places like Tucson and Birmingham, Alabama. Supposedly they were checking out where they might move, but I guess no one would have them.

MEANWHILE, DOWN IN NEW ORLEANS . . .

STEVE JONES: People still talk about the trade that sent me to New Orleans for Doug Moe and Larry Brown, because Doug likes to talk to people about it. Then if Larry is around, Doug gets Larry talking about it, and they say things like it was the most lopsided deal ever made and all that. All I know is that after the trade, my career took off. The new

Oakland coach was Alex Hannum, who had cut me with the San Francisco Warriors, so getting traded was more than fine with me. Babe McCarthy got ahold of me and moved me from small forward to shooting guard—I'm 6-foot-5 and I was not going to be one of those "piss-ant guards" that Babe hated. I went from scoring 10 a game in Oakland to a shade under 20 in New Orleans, so leaving Oakland was fine with me.

LARRY BROWN: I loved Babe McCarthy, but he had a thing about small guards. He used to call me "the little piss-ant."

STEVE JONES: When we played a team with small guards, Babe would say, "Boys, all they got out there is a couple of little piss-ants. We got to take those piss-ants down low, boys. That's what we'll do, we'll post those piss-ants up under the basket."

The guy who exemplified Babe's attitude toward little guards was Mike Butler, a 6-footer from Memphis State who was supposed to be our point guard after Larry Brown was traded to Oakland. But Butler wasn't a ballhandler. He was a pure shooter. In practice, you could tell him to hit a certain spot on the rim and he'd do it 10 times in a row. He could bank in 3-pointers from any angle. Now when you put somebody on him, it was a whole other game for Butler. He had real problems and he wasn't playing much.

One day we were in Denver and Larry Jones was hot. He was just killing us and Butler was bugging Babe to put him in the game to stop Larry Jones. Finally, Babe did and Larry went for 12 points in about six minutes. Babe took Butler out and said, "That's why you're just a damn little piss-ant guard and I don't want you to bother me anymore about playing."

BOB RYAN: Even though I worked for the *Boston Globe* and was an NBA guy through and through, I had respect for Babe McCarthy. He had great teams at Mississippi State with Bailey Howell, and he was the first coach in the deep South to let his team play against a team with blacks in the NCAA tournament. He had to sneak his team out of Starkville, Mississippi, in the middle of the night to go to the tournament game. He was defying the segregation laws. This guy was special. He had that wonderful Southern accent that made him sound like Charles Laughton in *Advise and Consent.*

LARRY DONALD: Babe's nickname was Old Magnolia Mouth. He loved to talk and tell stories. When he coached at Kentucky, he had a suite at the Executive Inn, which was across from the arena. After games, he'd invite the reporters over, open up a bottle of Jack Daniel's and then talk until the light of day, so long as there was someone around to listen.

STEVE JONES: In the dressing room, he was hilarious. He'd say, "Tonight we've got to get after them like a biting sow."

I'd be sitting there, biting my lip so I didn't laugh. He'd see me and say, "Steve, you never heard that one before? Hey, Jimmy, tell Steve what I'm talking about."

Another of his favorite expressions was "We're gonna cloud up and rain all over them."

DOUG MOE: Babe knew better than to take practice too seriously. There were times when he worked us hard, but other times he sensed that what we needed most was to take the day off. A couple of times, he brought us to the gym and then said, "Boys, the door is locked and I don't have a key. Why don't we just take it easy today?" If a guy was going bad, he'd say, "We've got to get this boy loose." He'd leave for a while and then come back with two ladies, one on each arm. Babe then would say to the player who was struggling, "Here's a couple of ladies who would like to make your acquaintance."

TOM NISSALKE: I was scouting an ABA game in Memphis when Babe was coaching there, and poor Babe, he had a terrible team, no talent. After the game, Babe and I were standing in the parking lot, talking. He was telling some story like always when all of a sudden somebody backs right out of a parking spot and right into Babe. Babe went right up on the trunk. I asked him if he was hurt and Babe said, "Bad enough that I have to coach this outfit here in Memphis, now somebody's trying to run me over in the damn parking lot."

o   o   o

STEVE JONES: My biggest concern was about being a black in New Orleans in 1968. There still were sit-ins, marches and other racial upheaval, which was not something I was used to. I was born in Alexandria, Louisiana, but I grew up in Portland, Oregon, and then played in Oakland. Race just wasn't much of an issue on the West Coast.

I called Babe McCarthy after the trade and said, "I'm happy to be coming down there, but will there be any problems in terms of housing?"

Babe said, "Don't worry about it, son. You just come on down. Hell, we've got damn integrated housing. No problem."

I went to New Orleans a few weeks before training camp, because I had a gut feeling that it would be tough to get an apartment. I found out that there were only two decent places that would take blacks. I can't remember the name of the first, but the second was in Algiers, Mississippi, and I wasn't about to stay in Algiers, Mississippi. I spent the first four months in the Sheraton Hotel on Canal Street, going out most days to look at apartments, seeing a "Vacancy" sign in the window, then being told there were no vacancies. It was constant rejection, something I had never encountered before. I went apartment hunting every day, got rejected every day, and was unhappy every day.

Babe McCarthy suggested that Gerald Govan and I should live together. Govan was from New Jersey and he was in his second season with the Bucs, but he had lived with a black family in town, as a lot of the black players did. He had already spent a year in New Orleans and he didn't know any more about how to find a place than I did.

I called a place on Lake Pontchartrain and the guy said, "Hey, come on down, bring your money, we'll take you." But when Govan and I showed up with our money, they had no vacancies, even though it was a new complex and there were open apartments everywhere.

I asked the guy what happened and he said, "I didn't know y'all were single."

I said, "I told you there were two of us yesterday and I told you that we were single yesterday and we're still single today."

But it didn't matter. He wasn't going to rent us a place.

I complained about the hassles, and the Bucs front office told me, "Well, you should have been here five years ago. Hey, five years ago they wouldn't even let you walk down Bourbon Street."

I said, "I don't care about five years ago, I just want to know when the hell I'm gonna get a place to live. If I don't get an apartment, I'm outta here. You traded for me easy enough, so you can just go ahead and trade me away."

I even went on television and said how I couldn't find a place to live. There was a girl at one apartment complex who was fired for trying to help me. I finally found a place with the help of a black construction guy.

I know it wasn't anything personal. I know that even most Southern whites knew in their hearts that not renting apartments to blacks was wrong, but the thought of change paralyzed them. Intellectually I understand what was going on, but that doesn't deny the fact that it hurt me and the other black players deeply.

The saving grace was that Babe McCarthy was a great guy and that we were all getting a chance to play basketball, which is what we wanted. Also, no matter what Doug Moe says, our team wasn't bad at all after he and Larry left.

The Bucs were 46–32, finishing the season with a 13-game winning streak and then losing to Moe's Oakland team in the second round of the ABA playoffs.

Second-Year Notebook: 1968–69

Like the first year, the ABA had 11 franchises, but four of them moved—
the Anaheim Amigos became the Los Angeles Stars, the New Jersey
Americans became the New York Nets, the Pittsburgh Pipers became
the Minnesota Pipers and the Minnesota Muskies became the Miami
Floridians . . . When the season began, the NBA raised its minimum
salaries to $10,000 for rookies and $12,000 for veterans. The ABA minimum was $7,500 for everybody . . . The ABA's most-traded player in
the first year, Barry Leibowitz, refused to report to his latest team—New
Orleans. Instead, he signed to play in Israel. Leibowitz averaged 10.9
points for three ABA teams in 1967–68 . . . The ABA changed the refs'
uniforms, removing their names from the back of their jerseys. Instead,
there were just numerals. The officials wore red shirts, royal-blue pants
and white shoes. The year before, they wore red shirts, white pants and
blue shoes . . . Early in the season, four ABA officials resigned: Joe
Belmont, Tom Miller, Ralph Stout and Doug Harvey. Miller and Stout
went back to college officiating, saying the conditions were better at that
level. Belmont went to work in the front office of the Denver Rockets.
Harvey, also a National League umpire, quit because the ABA dumped
Ed (brother of George) Mikan as chief of ABA officials. Veteran NBA
official Sid Borgia was hired to replace Ed Mikan . . . Indiana Pacers
president John DeVoe died of a heart attack while watching his team
play Houston on December 14, 1968 . . . The Kentucky Colonels lost a
bidding war for Louisville star Wes Unseld, who signed with the NBA's
Baltimore Bullets for $400,000 over four years. The Colonels' original
offer was $500,000 for four years, but when Unseld began to talk seri-
ously with the ABA, the real dollars turned out to be $210,000 for four
years and Unseld said good-bye to the ABA . . . In their first year, the
Nets (actually the Americans) averaged only 2,008 fans and lost a reported $500,000 in New Jersey. They moved to Commack Arena where,
a month into the season, Levern Tart ran off the court, hit some ice, fell
down and fractured his cheekbone . . . Indiana became the first team in
Year II to fire a coach, as Larry Staverman was replaced by Slick
Leonard after a 2–7 start . . . Early in the season, Mel Daniels broke his
nose, refused to sit out, and scored 30 points in two of his next three
games. He also had a 56-point, 31-rebound game against New York.
Daniels averaged 24 points and 16.5 rebounds and was named the

league's MVP . . . The ABA's first league media guide came out two months into Year II. Price was $1.25 . . . In a game against the New York Nets, Houston went 36-for-36 from the foul line. According to ABA PR director Lee Meade, that was the first time a pro team was perfect from the foul line in a game where it took more than 10 shots. Tony Jackson was 15-for-15 and Stew Johnson was 10-for-10 . . . New York's Bob Lloyd set an ABA record by making 49 consecutive free throws over 13 games . . . Denver's Larry Jones had 23 straight games in which he scored at least 30 points . . . Oakland's Warren Jabali was suspended for 15 days and fined $250 for stomping the Stars' Jim Jarvis in the face . . . Pipers coach Jim Harding was fired by Pipers owner Gabe Rubin at the All-Star banquet. In the game itself, the West defeated the East 133–127 as Dallas's John Beasley was the MVP with 19 points and 14 rebounds. It was a delight only if you like foul shots—there were 94 of them. Only 5,407 showed up in Louisville to watch it . . . Indiana's Roger Brown had a league-record 21 consecutive field goals over three games . . . The Pacers defeated Los Angeles 174–141. They had a 90-point half and a 51-point quarter . . . For the last two months of the season, Minnesota tried to attract fans by selling every ticket for $2. It didn't work. The Pipers lost $400,000 in their year in Minnesota . . . The ABA held its "secret draft" on February 15, 1969, which was news because word leaked out and the draft took place before the end of the college season, something that the NCAA considered a serious breach of conduct. The draft rights to Lew Alcindor went to the New York Nets . . . The ABA filed an antitrust suit against the NBA in federal court. The ABA claimed the NBA was blacklisting players and coaches who went to the ABA . . . The Houston franchise was purchased by a group headed by Jim Gardner, who planned to move the team to North Carolina for Year III . . . Indiana's Slick Leonard was named Coach of the Year. His record was 42–27 after he took over the Pacers. Indiana made it to the ABA finals, losing to Oakland . . . After winning the ABA title, Oakland coach Alex Hannum wired Celtics president Red Auerbach a challenge for the two teams to meet in a basketball World Series. Auerbach wasn't interested . . . Warren Jabali was voted Rookie of the Year . . . The all-ABA team was Denver's Larry Jones, New Orleans's Jimmy Jones, Indiana's Mel Daniels, Minnesota's Connie Hawkins and Oakland's Rick Barry . . . The ABA averaged 2,981 fans per game. Indiana led the league with 288,678 fans (a 5,864 average), which was 100,000 more than any other ABA team. Houston and New York failed to draw 50,000 for the season.

Saved from the Brink

DENNIS MURPHY: When the ABA began, Houston's T. C. Morrow was one of our wealthiest owners. We're talking about very big money, one of the richest men in the country. Then a crazy thing happened. He came to one of our league meetings at the Disneyland Hotel in Anaheim and he met a girl working at the registration desk. Morrow was probably in his 50s and he fell in love with this girl and married her. He had hired Slater Martin to coach the team and Slater was really running everything. One day, George Mikan got a telegram from Morrow saying that he was getting married and that his new wife "wasn't basketball-oriented." He wanted out of the league.

DICK TINKHAM: It was early in the second season of the ABA when Morrow said that he was finished. Morrow called to say that he was on his way to his favorite duck blind. He said, "I can't sign Elvin Hayes *(from the University of Houston),* I can't find a buyer for the team. I've had enough. I'm folding the team and going duck hunting."

We wanted to know about the $150,000 performance bond that any owner was expected to pay if he dropped out of the league without selling his team.

Morrow told us, "Try to get it from me."

I was at the league meeting in Indianapolis and I was representing the Pacers. We had been having one crisis after another and this seemed pretty serious. *(Denver owner)* Bill Ringsby had heard enough. He turned to his son and said, "Donnie, call our private plane and tell them not to move from the airport. I'm not paying for one more road trip for the team. This league is out of business."

Denver had a game at Minneapolis that night. I didn't like the sound of any of this. I knew that if we lost Morrow and Ringsby, two of our wealthiest owners, in one day, we were finished.

It was 8:30 in the morning and I said to Ringsby, "Bill, let's go get a drink."

You need to know this about Ringsby: he was a guy who loved to stand up at league meetings, slam his first, scream and curse. He also liked to drink a bit, so having a drink at 8:30 in the morning had a certain appeal to him. Meanwhile, I guess you'd say I'm a two-fisted Chablis drinker, but there I was by 9 A.M., looking at a bottle of Old Fashion with

Ringsby. At this point, Donnie showed up and told his father that the team had already left for Minneapolis.

That was great news to me. I am convinced that the ABA would have died that morning had Ringsby stopped the plane. If he had quit, a lot of other guys would have followed. But since the plane had left, there was time to keep talking. So we had downed a few Old Fashions and I said, "Bill, I bet you a hundred bucks that your team can't beat Minnesota tonight."

Ringsby said, "You don't have a hundred bucks."

Think about this for a minute. Here's two ABA owners getting sloshed on Old Fashion at nine in the morning talking about betting on a game.

Then we started talking some more and I mentioned to Ringsby that there were these guys from North Carolina who wanted to get an expansion team. It was Jim Gardner *(a former congressman and a multimillionaire from the Hardee's restaurant chain)* and his group.

I said, "Bill, don't you see what we can do? We'll sell these North Carolina guys Morrow's franchise."

A few days later, there was an ABA Executive Board meeting in Minneapolis with George Mikan, Oakland's Ken Davidson, Bill Ringsby and myself.

Gardner and these guys started telling us what a great state North Carolina was, how much the people loved basketball and how it would be a perfect spot for an ABA team. They were trying to sell us on North Carolina and were worried that we wouldn't take them. Meanwhile, we would have thought the North Pole was a great spot for an ABA franchise if there was an Eskimo who could buy one.

At that point, I stood up and said to Gardner's group, "All of this sounds very impressive, but obviously it's too late to expand this year. As you're well aware, the NBA is charging $1.5 million for an expansion team, but we are offering franchises next year for $500,000."

Suddenly, Ringsby stood up, cleared his throat and asked for a recess.

Ringsby and I went outside and he screamed, "How can you ask for $500,000 for an expansion team when we've got this thing in Houston we can't even give away?"

I said, "Bill, those guys don't know we're on the verge of going out of business. If they did, they wouldn't want to be in the league."

He sort of grunted.

I said, "Let's establish a price and see what happens."

We went back into the room and I said, "The price for an expansion team is $500,000, but there is a way you can get into the league for less than that. You can buy the Houston franchise for $350,000 if you agree to finish out the season down there. Then you can move it to North Carolina for next year."

Gardner thought it was a great idea and went for it.

LEE MEADE: I am convinced that Jim Gardner saved the ABA. T. C. Morrow was nothing but one problem after another for the league. He was our weakest link and there was a real danger that we wouldn't make that second season until Gardner came along. When he bought Houston, it seemed to give everyone a more positive attitude. We thought, "Here's a young, aggressive, imaginative guy with money. Let's see what he can do with this team in North Carolina; let's go for a third year."

RICK BARRY: The ABA just had to do something with Houston. In that second year, there were more guys on the floor, on the benches and sitting at the scorer's table than there were people in the stands. I know, because I counted everybody. Moving that mess to Carolina did a lot for the image of the league.

ABA legend has it that Houston had the smallest crowd ever for a game—89. In two years, Houston's record was 52–104. In Carolina, the owners made an immediate attempt to appeal to the local fans by signing and trading for area players. The Cougars had three North Carolina Tar Heels on the roster—Doug Moe, Bill Bunting and Larry Miller. They had Bob Verga from Duke, Randy Mahaffey from Clemson, George Lehmann from Campbell, which is in the southern part of the state, and Gene Littles from High Point College, which is 25 miles from Greensboro. The coach was Horace "Bones" McKinney, the legendary Atlantic Coast Conference coach from Wake Forest. The Cougars were 42–42 in 1969–70 and Gardner became a force in the league. He signed two NBA players to contracts—Billy Cunningham and Luke Jackson. Jackson never did jump leagues and stayed with the Philadelphia 76ers. Cunningham wanted to go back to the Sixers, but the courts ruled that he had to play for Carolina, though not until the 1972–73 season. Gardner also convinced four of the NBA's officials to jump leagues: Earl Strom, John Vanak, Joe Gushue and Norm Drucker.

Washington: First in War, First in Peace, and Third in the *Western* Division?

RICK BARRY: I had a verbal agreement with Pat Boone and Ken Davidson that I'd never have to leave the Bay Area if Oakland moved. I know I should have gotten it in writing, but I guess I just didn't expect the team to go broke and for someone else to buy it and move it to Washington. Not real smart on my part. Bruce Hale told me that he was going with the team to Washington in order to fulfill his contract. Alex Hannum had it in his deal that he wouldn't have to go if the team moved, so Alex was out.

At this point, I had made $75,000 a year for the season I sat out and the season I played. I still had two years left on my contract plus my option year, because the first season I sat out didn't count, even though I was paid. So that meant three more years in the ABA. During this time, *(Seattle owner)* Sam Schulman approached me in behalf of Franklin Mieuli, who wanted to sign me back with the Warriors. We worked out a five-year deal worth $1 million. I even went to training camp with the Warriors. I felt no obligation to go to Washington, because of the verbal agreement. Also, I never received a dime when the team was sold, and supposedly I was a 15 percent owner.

EARL FOREMAN: Rick wanted to play for the Warriors, but I still had a valid contract with him and I took him to court and won. Rick's contract with the Warriors couldn't start until he was done with his ABA contract. I give Rick a lot of credit. His attitude was, "I'd like to get out of this contract, but if I can't, I'll be there and show up."

When Rick lost, he got into his car and drove cross-country. He pulled up in front of my Washington office and announced himself. In my mind, he was a consummate pro. He did what he had to do. While the Barry case was going on, I had to put together a team and find a coach, because Hannum wouldn't leave the West Coast.

AL BIANCHI: I had been a head coach in Seattle for two years *(1967–69)* and I had a year to go on my contract when I did a dumb thing—I quit.

The Seattle management was trying to tell me who to draft and not draft and I got pissed off and walked out on a contract without having another job. I also was having some family problems at that time and I probably wasn't in the best frame of mind to make a good decision. I quit in June of 1969 and I was just floating around, not getting paid, hoping something would break. That came in August when Earl Foreman moved the Oaks to Washington and needed a coach. I was glad to get a job, but we didn't have any offices or anything. For the first week of the season, I didn't even have a trainer. I taped the guys' ankles. And as for having an assistant—you gotta be dreaming.

EARL FOREMAN: The league put us in an impossible situation. We had moved the team from Oakland to Washington and changed the nickname from the Oaks to the Capitols, but they made us play a Western Division schedule even though we were on the East Coast.

AL BIANCHI: It was a suicide schedule. This was back when the ABA was playing a lot of doubleheaders and we always seemed to be the team in the first game, always on the road. We only played 27 actual home games, 57 on the road. Rick Barry got hurt early; the whole thing was a mess.

EARL FOREMAN: I had never seen an ABA game before I bought the Caps. We didn't have a big crowd for our opener and I remember sitting there saying to myself, "What have I gotten into?" I had these terrible cold chills, this awful feeling that I had really made a mistake.

Our home court, the Washington Coliseum, was a sardine box, an ancient assembly hall in the worst neighborhood in town. For the opener, I had new arc lights installed on the streets. I hired motorcycle police to protect the fans. It looked like "Storm Troopers of America." But it had the opposite reaction to what I wanted. Instead of making people feel they were safe, it scared the hell out of everybody. I had friends who bought season tickets and then said, "But you know, Earl, we won't go to the games in that neighborhood!"

I even had minibuses running from the parking lot to the front door of the arena. But one day, I was alone on a minibus and it stalled about halfway to the arena. It was then I realized that I had to walk out there alone, at night. I thought to myself, "Now I know what my friends have been talking about." To put it mildly, this was not conducive to getting fans to the games.

AL BIANCHI: The schedule was so brutal. We went on road trips for weeks at a time. We played games in cities like Wichita and Albuquerque. I felt like we were a damn traveling circus. Sometimes, it got so bad that I was just happy we still had Larry Brown *(Doug Moe had been traded to Carolina)*. Anyway, when I got really fed up, I'd tell Larry, "I'm going scouting for a few days, you coach the team."

Larry would say, "Where you going, Coach?"

I'd say, "Larry, I don't know. I'm just getting the hell out of here before I go crazy. You got it. This will be good training for you. You want to coach, here's a chance."

Then I'd leave and come back feeling better.

EARL FOREMAN: At the end of the season *(1969–70)*, it looked like there really would be a merger. A committee from both leagues had worked out a tentative agreement. There was a bill in Congress to take care of the antitrust problems and everything. But I was a problem. Both leagues wanted me to move and to get out of the Baltimore Bullets' and Abe Pollin's territory. But I wasn't going to move, or at least that's what I said. I sensed this was a chance to really get a good deal. Inside, I knew there was no way I could go back to Washington, not in that arena and not after how lousy we drew. I'd die if I stayed in Washington, but I kept saying I wasn't going to budge because if I showed any weakness, I was finished. There was a big meeting of owners from both leagues trying to figure out what the hell to do with me.

For two days, nothing happened. Then *(Seattle owner)* Sam Schulman said, "Okay, you don't want to move, but what would it take to get you to move . . . theoretically?"

I hesitated for a moment, then said, "Okay, a million dollars in cash and a free franchise in the new merged league."

At that point, *(New York Knicks owner)* Ned Irish ran into the bathroom mumbling and cussing. All you could hear was the toilet flushing over and over. He had gone absolutely bananas because he was part of the old guard who was against the merger to begin with.

To make a long story short, I got an agreement for a free franchise and moving costs to go into any open territory I wanted. I was rolling, but then the merger fell through and that was it.

Now I had to move the team anyway. I couldn't go back to Washington again. I did a survey and decided on Virginia because there were three new arenas in Richmond, Hampton Rhodes and Norfolk. Also, the team would still be close to my home, and I did get some money from the ABA to move my team so the Washington/Baltimore thing wouldn't be a problem in future merger talks. I came out all right, but it could have been great.

RICK BARRY: When Earl moved the team to Virginia, I thought, "This is it, the end of the line." I didn't want any part of Virginia and was going to do all I could to get back to the Warriors, or at least out of Virginia.

EARL FOREMAN: I knew that Rick was being interviewed by *Sports Illustrated* and that he was having his picture taken, which he did in a new Virginia Squires uniform. This would be a big deal for us. We had Rick Barry in *Sports Illustrated* in a Virginia uniform. The league heard about it and was happy. The fans in Virginia were looking forward to the story. Then the story came out and Rick was quoted as saying, "I don't want my kids growing up and saying, 'Hi, y'all, Dad.' " People resented it, and they should have. I don't know if Rick was being cunning or if he was just being Rick and saying what was in his head, but he got an incredible negative reaction.

RICK BARRY: When I made the "Hi, y'all, Dad" comment, I figured that would force Earl's hand. I knew that it would upset enough people that he'd get me out of Virginia. My wife and kids had stayed on the West Coast and I was alone in Washington. That was no good for any family. I even offered to buy back my own contract from Earl *(for $100,000)* so I could go to the NBA and play for the Warriors, but he refused.

EARL FOREMAN: Rick was being his usual pragmatic self. He wouldn't play for the Squires and told me, "I'll only play in California or New York, and you don't have a team in either place." Then he hung up the phone.

I got to thinking about the situation and talked to Al Bianchi. We had signed Charlie Scott out of North Carolina and Al told me, "I'd love to have Rick, but I can live without him."

My main concern was keeping Rick in our league and away from the NBA. I called Rick back and said, "We do have a team in New York—the Nets. They play on Long Island, but you'll still get all the publicity, endorsements and notoriety from being a New York player." He didn't say no, so I went to work on *(Nets owner)* Roy Boe. I almost had to twist Roy's arm, beating him up to take Barry. He was scared to death that Barry's contract was too high, that his partners wouldn't go for the deal. They were not real experienced at the time.

I ended up getting nearly zilch for Rick—$25,000. I think it was half now and half later, like if I catch up with them. *(The deal was announced as $200,000.)* The main thing was that Rick remained in the ABA. We set up a New York press conference for Rick at "21"; it got great press and what the hell, I was now out from under Rick's contract and I'd get all the money at the gate when he came to Virginia and all the fans came out to boo him. Not a bad deal at all.

AL BIANCHI: I was always amused when Rick said he didn't want his kids saying, "y'all." I told Rick, "Yeah, take your kids to New York where they'll grow up saying, 'youse guys.' "

ROY BOE: I got a call from Earl Foreman and he told me about his troubles with Rick Barry, how he couldn't take Barry with him to Virginia because of the *Sports Illustrated* story. I don't remember any hesitation on my part or anything. We talked about the price and it ended up being something like $75,000 and a draft pick, which meant nothing in those days because ABA teams could pretty much sign who they wanted. It was a pretty straight deal.

RICK BARRY: If Earl Foreman really only got $25,000 for me, he blew it, because I offered him a lot more than that myself to buy back my own contract. It's not like Earl to make a bad financial deal. I guess if he really did sell me for $25,000, then he was trying to do something good for the league. All I cared about was that I was out of Virginia and in New York.

After my two years in New York, the second contract I had signed with the Warriors went into effect and I was supposed to go back to the NBA. I did talk to Roy Boe about staying in New York and we came very close to making a deal that would keep me with the Nets, but to do that I would have had to sit out another year. I couldn't stand the thought of not playing for a second year. Roy was great about it; he said he understood why I couldn't sit out, and I went back to the Warriors *(for 1972–73)* with no hard feelings.

STEVE JONES: When Rick was in the ABA, it was sort of like he wasn't one of us, almost as if he was doing us a favor. One year, we were at the All-Star Game and we were talking about striking to get official recognition for our new ABA Players Association. Different players were speaking their minds about what we should do, then Rick said, "I'll tell you what I would do if I were you guys . . ."

Rick *was* one of us, but he didn't see himself that way, because he thought he always had the option of going back to the NBA. It was like he was there, yet he wasn't there.

On the court, no complaints. Rick was truly a great player. What I really admired is that when he faced a defender who was giving him a hard time, he would just foul the guy out. In one game, Goo Kennedy was pushing and shoving Rick and Rick got mad. He told Kennedy,

"You're history. I'm gonna foul you out." Then Rick started head-faking, going to the basket and Kennedy got four fouls in about four minutes while Rick was on his way to a 30-point night.

DAN ISSEL: Rick was a little arrogant, like most of the players who jumped from the NBA to the ABA. But he was a scoring machine. I once heard him say that he expected to score 30 a night. He had it all figured out: he'd take 20 shots, make 12, and then he'd get to the foul line six or eight times to pick up the rest. He talked about it like anyone could do it.

RICK BARRY: I was always an easy target. I was one of the first athletes not to play the dumb-jock role, and a lot of writers resented that. I also think that writers were going through a stage where they resented all the big money that was going to the players, especially since sportswriters thought their jobs were more important and meaningful than shooting baskets. I think the fact that I was a player with a brain and some semblance of intelligence just didn't sit well with some people.

I didn't set out to be a pioneer. I was sure that other guys would jump, and they did—later on. Since I was the first, I caught all the heat. I took the lead for all the guys who came behind me, and I got raked over the coals for it. I was money-hungry, back-stabbing, self-centered and a guy who didn't give a damn about anyone but himself, a guy just after the buck.

But I never played one league against the other. Guys like Billy Cunningham, they played one side against the other. But did they get criticized? No, it was, "Hey, guy, get it while you can. Strike while the iron is hot."

I don't hold that against those players, it just bothers me that I was destroyed in the press and I didn't do half the stuff that some guys did. And playing in the ABA probably hurt my basketball reputation, because I was in a league that didn't receive that much exposure. But so what? Decisions had to be made and I made them as best I could. If people didn't like it, there was nothing I could do to change the situation.

Sideshow in Miami

The Floridians began life as the Minnesota Muskies, a franchise so well financed that after achieving a 50–28 record in the ABA's first season, it packed up and moved to Miami, where it put in four unremarkable years before mercifully folding at the end of the 1971–72 season. The Floridians never did much on the court, but the weather was nice and the ballgirls were nicer.

RUDY MARTZKE: Florida was a franchise with its own special lore. I don't know if it was the warm weather and people feeling like they could do anything they wanted, but there were a lot of crazy stories coming out of there, even by ABA standards. At one time, Florida had eight owners and one of the owners would go around saying, "Has Sidney dumped his 25 grand in yet? We going to make the payroll this week?" There really were stories in the newspaper saying, "The Floridians met the payroll so they'll play tonight."

One of the owners decided to trade for Art Heyman from Pittsburgh without telling anyone else. Heyman showed up in Miami without half the people in the front office knowing he was coming. Bob Halloran from TV-4 in Miami spotted Heyman and interviewed him.

Heyman asked Bob, "Does this go out to Miami Beach?"

Bob said it did.

Heyman said, "Hello, Jews out there! Your boy is here!"

On and on it goes.

Levern Tart was from West Palm Beach, so they were going to have a Levern Tart Night. Hey, maybe they would bring in 50 extra people, who knows? So they publicized Levern Tart Night, but the day before the game he got traded and it was to a team that didn't play in Florida again for the rest of the year.

They even played some games at a place in Coconut Grove where there were so many cockroaches in the dressing rooms that the visiting teams just changed at the hotel. I found out that being Miami's PR man was no bargain, especially since pro football owned the town. One Sunday afternoon, we had a home game scheduled against Utah while the Dolphins were playing Baltimore in the AFC playoffs at the Orange Bowl. By the time we realized that our game would go off at the same time as the Dolphins game, it was too late to change it. Not one press guy showed up for the game—no one from the wire services, nobody from anywhere. There were 500 people in the stands—maybe.

(Marketing director) Kenny Small and I were talking and we decided to announce an attendance of 2,000. Who would know the difference? We settled on 1,650, which was still one of the bigger crowds of the season, and that was what ran under the box score. The next day we had press guys calling and saying, "Hey, that was a helluva crowd with the Dolphins playing and all." And I said, "Yeah, you should have been here."

STEVE JONES: In my mind, I always had this picture of Miami—sandy beaches, palm trees, beautiful girls in bikinis. But all we saw were these retirement communities—I guess that's a nice way of saying it. What it really was was all the old guys on one side of the street and the old ladies on the other side. I kept thinking, "This is all there is to Miami Beach?"

GENE LITTLES: It didn't get any better once you got to the arena, which was nothing more than an old auditorium on Miami Beach. They had the kind of baskets you just roll out there, they'd throw down the floor and then you'd play—before about 200.

DAN ISSEL: One time I came to Miami with Kentucky, and the Ice Capades was going in the other part of the building. I got my ankles taped and, in uniform, I walked over to watch the show. They had about 8,000 for the ice show and about 1,500 for our game.

STEVE JONES: The walls in the dressing rooms were so thin and the two teams' rooms were next to each other, so everybody could hear everything. I was in there with New Orleans and we were up by about 20 points at the half. *(New Orleans coach)* Babe McCarthy said, "Shush up, fellas. I want y'all ta lissen ta what's going on next door." *(Miami coach)* Hal Blitman was going nuts, screaming and cussing everyone out. Babe was biting his lip to keep from laughing and we were doing the same thing—we didn't want them to hear us. As we walked out on the floor, all Babe said was, "That's what I'm gonna sound like after the game if we blow this one." Florida was the only place in the league where you could hear the other team's halftime talk.

DAN ISSEL: Going to play at Miami was like taking a vacation. Their teams were so pitiful that you could lie around on the beach all day and then go out there and beat them at night even if you weren't really with it. All you had to do was make sure that Mack Calvin didn't go crazy, and since they drew so lousy, they had virtually no home-court advantage.

VAN VANCE: I remember broadcasting a Kentucky game in Miami and I asked a fan why the Floridians never drew. The guy told me, "If they put betting windows in here, the joint would be packed."

GENE LITTLES: No matter what you say about the Floridians, they had the greatest cheerleaders in the world. They were big league all the way, in their looks, their dance routines and their outfits. They got more attention than the team and that was how it should have been, considering the kind of teams they had down there.

VAN VANCE: The ballgirls were great-looking. I really mean that. They had long, tanned legs and super figures, all packed into those bikinis. During one game, perhaps the best-looking one came up to me and sat right on my lap while I was broadcasting the game. I just kept doing the game, and the girl turned to someone at the press table and said, "I don't get it. This guy just talks and talks, but he won't talk to me."

RUDY MARTZKE: As for the girls' outfits, they were pretty brief. Real brief. We're talking about a brief-bikini situation. We had four of them out there for every game. They sat under the basket, threw the ball out on the floor, served refreshments at halftime and generally looked very good.

FROM THE FLORIDIANS' PROGRAM: There is little question that the Floridians boast the five prettiest "ball-boys" in all basketball-dom. The quintet were chosen in a bikini contest held last August. . . . All five girls are highly talented. For instance, two of the girls, Sandy and Cindy Acker, are twins and majorettes at Norland High School. Vi Lloyd sings and dances professionally and already owns a pilot's license. Pinky White is a student at Miami's Central High School and aspires to become an actress. Janie Orman, a student at Miami-Dade North, is the outdoor type—she likes to ride horses, sail and play tennis.

If the innovation catches on, there is a likelihood that spectators will attend ABA contests as much to appreciate feminine pulchritude as good basketball.

RUDY MARTZKE: The big event for the girls came when we took them to New York for a Madison Square Garden all-ABA doubleheader. It was right before Christmas, we had a press conference with the girls, got a big turnout and naturally pictures of the girls in the papers. It was like a Hollywood opening, with photographers pushing and shoving to get into position to take pictures of the girls. Rick Barry was with the Nets and we had a promotion in Grand Central Station with Barry playing Al Albert in this gimmicky basketball game while the girls in their bikinis tried to lure people over to watch. It was pure schlock.

The doubleheader drew about 8,500 at the Garden and about 8,000 of the fans showed up to see the girls, because I bet they couldn't name three guys who played that night.

SAM SMITH: After the game in New York, I was with Bob Bass and we were looking at the *Sports Illustrated* story about it. The whole thing centered on the Floridian ballgirls and it sort of ended by saying, "Oh, by the way, there was a basketball game . . ."

Bob Bass looked at the article, sadly shook his head and said, "So this is what we've come to in the ABA."

RUDY MARTZKE: From a promotion standpoint, we tried everything. We had the ballgirls, we had giveaways of every type, 2-for-1 nights, ABA ball nights, ice cream nights.

(The Floridians even had their own song, "Get That Ball." It featured this lyric: "Go on and get that ball, Floridians, gotta get that ball before we score! Defense! Rebound! That's the way to win! Go till we're No. 1!")

You tell me, what else could we do? Tickets were cheap *(a season box seat was $100, daily prices were $5, $4 and $3)*. Our owner, Ned Doyle, was with Doyle Dane Bernbach, one of the country's largest advertising agencies. We pulled out all the stops, but nothing worked.

SAM SMITH: The last straw was when the ABA had one of its secret drafts *(in 1971)* and we lost the rights to Artis Gilmore to Kentucky somehow. Losing a player of that magnitude finished us, because he could have made us a winner. Artis was a quality center from Florida *(Jacksonville University)*, the kind you build a franchise around.

RUDY MARTZKE: With about a month left in the season, we got the word from Ned Doyle that we were dead in Florida. If we were going to survive, it would be in another city. Bob Bass and I sat down and talked about the cities that had expressed an interest in the ABA—San Diego, Omaha and Albuquerque. In a period of 10 days, I visited all three of those towns.

In New Mexico, I met a state legislator and even talked to the governor for 15 minutes. They said things like, "Bring that team here. Boy, do we need a major league franchise in this state." But there was nothing concrete, just a lot of talk.

In San Diego, there were three guys who had the money to buy the team, but they had trouble getting dates from the San Diego Sports Arena.

In Omaha, I met a guy from the Omaha Auditorium and he pulled out a folder with all these commitments for season tickets, 3,000 of them. So I went back to Miami and told people that we had to move to Omaha.

Everybody was happy for a few days, then one of Doyle's money men said, "You can't just move the team, you should sell it."

I called Omaha back and said we had to sell the team. The people from Omaha said, "No problem, we have an owner." It was supposed to be Peter Swanson from Swanson Foods. So I went back to Doyle and his people and said that we had a buyer for the team, but then Doyle's money men come back and say, "It's better just to fold it and take the tax write-off than sell it." I couldn't believe it, but that's how the Floridians came to an end: they were a write-off for Uncle Sam.

SAM SMITH: My wife and I had just picked out a home in Fort Lauderdale and Bob Bass had just moved into a home in North Miami Beach when we got word that the team had folded. Bob Bass called me and said, "Mr. Doyle wants to have a meeting with us, and it doesn't sound good."

It was late May and Mr. Doyle called what was left of the front office together and said, "I've spent all the money I'm going to spend on this. I've fought all the wars. I can't get a new arena built. I've been through a lot of battles, but this is it."

And that was it. I understand that Mr. Doyle lost $3 million over four years, and that was a lot of money in the early 1970s. So we folded and so did Pittsburgh.

RUDY MARTZKE: In one of our final days in business, Bob Bass said to me, "Rudy, before you do anything else, can you clean out your desk?"

"What do you mean?" I said. I wondered, was I fired or what?

"I just sold your desk to some guys in the office downstairs," Bass said. "They'll be up about noon and can you help them move it down there?"

What could I do? I cleaned it out, and about noon a long-haired guy came up. I helped him take the desk downstairs.

That night, I went home, watched the TV news and there was the guy who had my desk. It was Jerry Rubin! He was opening up an office to protest the 1972 Democratic Convention in Miami Beach.

FLORIDIANS FINAL INVENTORY

2,928   Promotional Balls

Office Furniture & Fixtures

1	Remington Typewriter—Manual	4	IBM Electric Typewriters
1	Royal Typewriter—Manual	1	Olivetti Calculator

1 Pitney-Bowes Postage Machine	1 Executive Desk
1 Gestetner Mimeograph Machine	2 Secretarial Desks
1 A.B. Dick "670" Copier (20	3 Secretarial Posture Chairs
Rolls of Copy Paper)	2 Green Guest Chairs
1 Hercules Fireproff *(sic)* File-Safe	5 Side Chairs (Metal Base)
1 Gestetner Folding Machine	4 Side Chairs (Wood Base)
1 Scriptomatic Addressograph	1 Tape Player-Receiver
2 Four-Drawer Metal File Cabinets	1 Paymaster Checkwriter
1 Metal Storage Cabinet	Miscellaneous Office Supplies &
7 Metal Six-Drawer Ticket	Equipment
Cabinets	1 Chevrolet Panel Truck (1969)
1 Folding Utility Table	Various Training & Player
6 Blue Leather Conference Chairs	Equipment
1 Bell & Howell Projector &	
Screen	

Inventory—3/2/72

T-Shirts

Men's Sizes	X-Large	27	
	Large	105	
	Medium	113	
	Small	79	
		324 @ $1.39	$ 450.36
Boys' Sizes	4	59	
	6	58	
	8	100	
	10	52	
	12	86	
	14	34	
	16	83	
		472 @ $ .71	$ 335.12
		796—Total	

Pro Basketball Guides	114 @ $ .75	$ 85.50
ABA All-Star Guides	218 @ $ .30	$ 65.40
Records—"Get That Ball . . ."	295 @ $ .50	$ 147.50
Sheet Music—"Get That Ball . . ."	65 @ $ .50	$ 32.50
License Plates	168 @ $ .35	$ 58.80

| Patches | 500 @ $ .26 | $ 130.00 |
| Buttons | 11 @ $ .19 | $ 2.09 |

Button Paks

Eastern Division	95 @ $ .52	$ 49.50
Western Division	47 @ $ .45	$ 21.15
		$1,377.92

| ABA Guides | 219 | |

Third-Year Notebook: 1969–70

A lot of big ABA names disappeared before the opening tap. Connie Hawkins told Pittsburgh-turned-Minnesota-turned-Pittsburgh to take a hike as he ran to the Phoenix Suns for big money in the NBA. Lew Alcindor said he would take only one bid from the NBA and the ABA. He listened to an offer by Commissioner George Mikan on behalf of the New York Nets and then he listened to the Milwaukee Bucks of the NBA. He picked the Bucks, as in those from Milwaukee. After failing to sign Alcindor, Mikan "resigned." The ABA owners were tired of the league office being in Minneapolis and Mikan wouldn't move to New York. Also, Mikan's popularity among the owners had greatly eroded. Jim Gardner was appointed interim commissioner until Jack Dolph was hired to do the job full-time. Dolph was the former head of CBS Sports and his sole purpose was to get the ABA on national television . . . Teams also moved. The Oakland Oaks became the Washington Capitols, but competed in the Western Division under Oakland's old schedule, which made for a traveling nightmare for new coach Al Bianchi . . . Alex Hannum left the Oaks for San Diego of the NBA . . . The Nets were purchased by Roy Boe, who moved them to the Island Garden while the Nassau Coliseum was being built. Boe also owned the NHL New York Islanders . . . The Pittsburgh Pipers had a contest to change their nickname and the winner was the "Pioneers." The winner had to write an essay in 25 words or less why he wanted the team to adopt his nickname. A woman sued Pittsburgh, claiming that the winning entry did not stay within the 25-word limit. Also, a local NAIA college, Point Park, threatened to sue the ABA because Point Park's nickname was the Pioneers. Finally, Pittsburgh settled on the Condors . . . The ABA did find some new stars. Spencer Haywood left the University of Detroit after his sophomore year to sign with Denver, becoming basketball's first "hardship case," an underclassman leaving school early for the pros ... The L.A. Stars signed Atlanta Hawks All-Star center Zelmo Beaty, but Beaty had to sit out a year before he could jump leagues. At midseason, the Hawks were willing to let Beaty play in the ABA for $75,000, but the Stars were losing money and didn't have the cash ... Boe signed Lou Carnesecca to be the Nets' coach and GM, but Carnesecca had a year left on his contract with St. John's, so York Larese kept the coaching chair warm for a year until Carnesecca could arrive ... In May of 1969, Larry Brown agreed to become the coach of Davidson College, replacing Lefty Driesell, who went to Maryland. But in July, Brown resigned to continue his playing career in the ABA ... Larry Cannon, Chicago's first-round choice, signed with the ABA's Floridians ... The Carolina Cougars announced they had signed Billy Cunningham, but Cunningham had to play another season with Philadelphia of the NBA before he could jump leagues ... The new commissioner, Jack Dolph, proclaimed in December of 1969 that the ABA "doesn't need a merger with the NBA." The feeling from the NBA was mutual ... The Indiana Pacers got off to a 14–2 start. Stars coach Bill Sharman said that the Pacers "could beat half the teams in the NBA. In fact, if games could be arranged, I'd bet my salary on that" ... In December, the ABA assigned draft rights to top college players. Among the notables: Indiana picked Rick Mount, Carolina picked Pete Maravich and Miami took Dave Cowens. Dan Issel was picked by Dallas, but his rights were sold to Kentucky for $25,000 ... For the first time in their 2½-year history, the Nets drew 4,000 fans for a game ... Miami fired Coach Jim Pollard and replaced him with Hal Blitman ... In Dallas, Cliff Hagan was canned in favor of Max Williams ... In Pittsburgh, John Clark was fired and GM Buddy Jeannette took over ... After a 9–19 start, Denver fired John McLendon and replaced him with Joe Belmont, a former ABA official who had been working in the Rockets' marketing department. Belmont's only coaching experience was with the Duke freshman team. His first move was to take Spencer Haywood out of the pivot and play him at power forward. Byron Beck was the new center and the team responded by winning 12 of 14 games, including 11 in a row ... Dolph finally got a TV deal for the ABA, albeit very limited. CBS agreed to broadcast the All-Star Game, which had been scheduled for Tuesday, January 27, 1970, at Charlotte. But CBS wanted the game on Sunday, January 25. Charlotte Coliseum was booked on January 25 with a Davidson-Princeton college game, so the ABA switched the site of its All-Star Game to Indianapolis to appease CBS. It was the second time in three years that the Pacers hosted the game. Haywood was the MVP with 23 points, 19 rebounds and seven blocked shots. He was given a 1970 Dodge Challenger and a $2,000 RCA color television set. Denver teammate Larry Jones had 30 points as the West bombed the East 128–98. The game was worked by ex-NBA officials Earl Strom and John Vanak. The crowd was 11,932, which was 2,821 over capacity. Ticket prices for the game were $6, $4, $3 and $2. The game nearly wasn't played as the players threatened to strike unless their newly formed union was recognized by the league. The issue was settled 45 minutes before the game and the ABA Players Association became a reality . . . In what was believed to be an ABA first, tickets were being scalped for more than face value as Denver's $4 box seats were being bought for up to $10 . . . The Pacers didn't lose two games in a row until the 49th and 50th games of the season, when Mel Daniels was out with a bruised knee . . . Indiana finished the season with a 59–25 record and defeated the L.A. Stars in six games to win the ABA title. Denver was 51–33, 42–14 under Joe Belmont . . . Haywood was voted both Rookie of the Year and MVP as he averaged 30 points and 19.5 rebounds. Along with Haywood, other members of the all-ABA team were Rick Barry, Larry Jones, Bob Verga and Mel Daniels . . . The Stars' Bill Sharman was Coach of the Year . . . For the third straight year, Larry Brown led the ABA in assists . . . Denver had 23 sellouts in its 7,000-seat building. Indiana averaged 8,500 fans to lead the league. The average ABA game drew 3,950.

Raiding the Refs

In one of its most creative moves, the ABA wounded the NBA in a very unusual place—by luring away some of the senior league's top officials. Late in the summer of 1969, Commissioner Jim Gardner signed Earl Strom, Norm Drucker, Joe Gushue and John Vanak to work in the ABA. Before the 1973–74 season, Jack Madden and Ed Rush jumped from the NBA to the ABA. In the meantime, Gushue and Strom had returned to the NBA. Drucker, Vanak, Madden and Rush went back to the NBA after the merger.

JOHN VANAK: The idea for the NBA to raid the ABA's officials came from Ralph Dolgoff, inventor of the Dolgoff Plan. Dolgoff was a neighbor of Norm Drucker's. Because he was one of the ABA's top money guys, he went to all their meetings. One day, the ABA was talking about how they could hurt the NBA. They talked about getting players to jump and all that. Then one owner said, "Too bad we couldn't get some of their officials. The NBA has some great refs and we need help."

Dolgoff said, "Did you guys ever talk to their officials?"

No one said they had. Then Dolgoff had a conversation with Norm Drucker and he found out that we weren't making much money. He told that to Jim Gardner and suddenly we became a hot item. The other league wanted us.

You have to understand something about the refs who started in the early 1960s: we just didn't make any money and we had no clout. They paid us by the game, something like $120 a game, so we would work over 125 games a year, counting exhibitions and playoffs. Before I got into basketball, I had been a police sergeant making $4,200 a year. I worked in the old American Basketball League in 1961 and then went over to the NBA.

Look at the other guys who jumped: Joe Gushue was a carpenter. Earl Strom worked for General Electric. Norm Drucker was a school guidance counselor. And Mendy Rudolph, who almost jumped with us, was in charge of sales for television station WGN in Chicago. Most of us worked these jobs in the off-season. When we jumped leagues, the NBA said we were making $22,000. But it was much less than that, because the $22,000 included our expenses. It was much closer to $15,000 for me, and that was after eight years as an NBA official.

JOE GUSHUE: I started in the NBA in 1960–61 making $5,000, and I was up to $13,000 when I was asked to jump leagues in 1969.

NORM DRUCKER: The ABA approached me first and said they wanted to get five of us to jump—Vanak, Gushue, Strom, Mendy Rudolph and myself. They offered us a $25,000 bonus to jump and $25,000 a year. That was more than doubling our salaries.

JOHN VANAK: Drucker approached all four of us, including Rudolph, and asked if we were willing to talk to the ABA. The five of us had all worked in the 1969 NBA finals. We were the best the NBA had.

We met clandestinely at Washington's National Airport. Drucker, Strom, Gushue and I were there, but Mendy didn't show. That was the first hint we had that Mendy might not be going along with us. We were dealing with a lawyer named Shelly Bendit, but we jokingly called him Shelly Bandit. He was from North Carolina and knew Billy Cunningham well. The ABA guys behind the deal were Jim Gardner, Dick Tinkham and Mike Storen. Tinkham was very active in this.

Really, these guys knew nothing about being an official. They didn't know the difference between a volleyball and a bowling ball.

We were meeting and the ABA guys said, "What do you want?"

We said, "Do you have an insurance policy for your officials?"

They said that they did. Businessmen always have insurance or they will get it because it generally doesn't cost that much.

We said, "What about expenses?"

They said, "Well, we'll fly you to the games."

We said, "That's nice, but what about a rental car when we get there? And how about per diem?"

They said, "Sure, you can have a car."

We mentioned the per diem again. "Hey, we have to eat, right?"

They said, "Oh, yeah, sure. How much do you want?"

We told them what we got in the NBA for expenses and said that was what we wanted. We talked some more about benefits and they sort of sat there with their mouths open. I don't think they had any idea what an official needed.

Finally, they said, "Look, if you guys jump leagues, we'll give you a bonus."

We said we liked the idea of a bonus.

They said, "How much do you want?"

We said, "$25,000 to $35,000."

They said, "All right, we'll give you $25,000."

We said that sounded all right.

They said, "What about salary?"

We said, "We need at least $25,000."

They said, "Fine . . . $25,000."

We also got $500 per playoff game and three-year contracts. By the time you added it all up, we were making between $60,000 and $75,000 a year. Hey, it was close to a $200,000 deal for three years, and I made $22,000 my last year in the NBA. And I had it in my contract with the ABA that no official in either league could earn more than I did or I automatically got a raise. I never made less than $60,000 in any season. The ABA changed my life around.

NORM DRUCKER: After we got the offer from the ABA, we went back to the NBA to try and meet with *(Commissioner)* Walter Kennedy. We just wanted the NBA to show that they appreciated us, that they wanted us to stay. They didn't have to match the ABA's offer, they just had to make some sort of gesture. But Kennedy wouldn't even meet with us. You know, I think if Walter had just said, "Look, we can't do anything for you this year, but next season we'll try this and that . . . ," just gave us the courtesy of hearing our side and made any sort of gesture, we would have stayed. But Kennedy didn't.

JOHN VANAK: In the pecking order of officials, Joe Gushue and I were considered "the two kids." So we stayed outside the building when Norm Drucker and Earl Strom went in to try and meet with Kennedy. Earl was going to put on a big show and say, "If you guys don't do this, we're history. We're jumping leagues." But he never got that chance, since Kennedy really wouldn't negotiate with them. When Drucker and Strom came out of the office, they told us, "Well, fellas, it's like this . . . basically, Kennedy threw us out of his office."

JOE GUSHUE: After we jumped, I got a two-page letter from Kennedy degrading me, saying he couldn't believe that I'd sell myself for so little money.

JOHN VANAK: The NBA never said they'd ban us, although we were worried that the ABA might fold and then the NBA wouldn't take us back. Then I got a five-page telegram from Walter Kennedy. It basically said, "You are an ungrateful young referee who had everything to live and work for. We had a five-year, unprecedented contract waiting for you to sign and you slapped us in the face and went to the other league . . ." Hey, they never said anything about a new contract to us. I later found out from Carl Scheer, who was Kennedy's assistant at the time, that no such contract existed. We caught them totally by surprise and they never believed that we'd jump. Their attitude was, "Who the hell are officials to think that they can just go and jump leagues?"

JOE GUSHUE: Why the NBA couldn't figure out that we were family men with children to feed—in my case, I had three kids—is beyond me. That is how it is with people; they don't think officials are people, too.

JOE GUSHUE: We really left the NBA in a bind. They had two experienced officials left—Mendy Rudolph and Richie Powers. Suddenly young guys such as Ed Rush, Jack Madden and Darell Garretson had to become lead officials, something they'd never done before, and that hurt the NBA for a few years until those guys learned what they were doing.

MAX WILLIAMS: One of the best moves we ever made was to get the NBA officials. The coaches and general managers just thought the officials in the early ABA were the worst. Guys like Monk Moyers, who

Commissioner George Mikan celebrates the ABA's first birthday, in front of a framed photo of his NBA champion Lakers, February 2, 1968.

Dennis Murphy, who would serve four different teams in various capacities, was the true founding father of the ABA.

Oakland owner Pat Boone, here with coach Bruce Hale, may have been smiling at the start, but that's hardly how he looked at the end.

Cliff Hagan brought his hook shot and fighting spirit to Dallas after a 10-year NBA career.

4

Finally given a chance to shine in the pros, Connie Hawkins (seen playing before a typical early ABA crowd) starred for two years before the NBA lifted its ban on him and he joined the Phoenix Suns.

From playing days in New Orleans to coaching in Denver, Larry Brown and Doug Moe were all but inseparable through the ABA's history. Larry, here with Virginia on a court of uncertain vintage, was the kind of smart, small point guard the NBA disdained then but cherishes now. Doug's tenacity, jump shot and fierce defense would have made him an All-Star in any league.

Rick Barry, the first player to jump leagues, averaged 30.5 points and displayed his flawless free-throw form over four seasons in Oakland, Washington and New York before returning to the NBA in 1972.

Alex Hannum brought a fierce, no-nonsense approach to Oakland, where he won an ABA title just two years after leading Philadelphia to an NBA championship.

10

Bill Sharman, an outstanding coach and innovator, first coached in the old ABL, then won championships in the ABA (with Utah) and the NBA (with the Lakers).

Looking something like a before-and-after picture of the Sixties, Steve Jones had an eight-year ABA odyssey that took him to Oakland, New Orleans *(left)*, Memphis, Dallas, Carolina, Denver and St. Louis *(right)*.

Spencer Haywood showed Denver some fancy moves and fancier clothes, but his fanciest move of all was his leap from college into the pros after his sophomore year at the University of Detroit.

Co-holders of the title "The Meanest Man in the ABA" were John Brisker (driving against New Orleans) and Warren Jabali (né Armstrong). Many tough players have frightened opponents; these two frightened their own teammates.

A small and uninterested gathering of fans and players watches as rookie Julius Erving shoots a free throw against the Pittsburgh Condors.

used to work the Globetrotters games, were calling our games. It was a total joke.

BOB BASS: Monk Moyers worked a game in Indianapolis where they had a stuffed referee hanging by the neck from a noose from the ceiling and the dummy had a sign that said "Moyers" across the chest. Monk didn't care. He called the whole game with the dummy hanging there.

TERRY STEMBRIDGE: There was an official named Pat Denoy. Poor Pat got so confused in one game that he called an illegal defense on a team and instead of giving the ball back to the offense out-of-bounds, he gave the offense two points. Nobody could figure out why he did it. The guy just made up a rule.

JOHN VANAK: My first ABA game was in Grambling, Louisiana, before about 600 people. Dallas was playing New Orleans. I called about 18 climbing-over-the-back fouls and about eight technicals. I think I wore out three whistles. Guys were killing each other and it was obvious that they weren't used to officials taking control of the game. The league had a real problem with fighting, because the officials were so inexperienced.

The next night, the same two teams were playing and I was working the game again. Both coaches came up to me and said, "We really like how you called that first game. Do it again. We need more guys like you to clean this league up."

NORM DRUCKER: The ABA was a different game than the NBA. The teams were smaller but quicker. The guards and especially the forwards dominated the league. Julius Erving, George Gervin, Willie Wise—I used to think, "Everybody should get a chance to see these guys play."

JOE GUSHUE: It was easier to call an ABA game because there wasn't as much dirty stuff under the basket. The ABA teams didn't just walk the ball up the court and pound it inside as most NBA teams did. The ABA was wide-open, streamlined and faster. It was much easier to see the action, because all the people weren't bunched up under the basket.

EARL FOREMAN: Earl Strom worked our first game in Washington after I bought the Oakland Oaks and moved them East. It was Earl's first ABA game and we had a terrible facility. The dressing rooms were like caves and the neighborhood around the place was dangerous. Earl and I were the last two people to leave the building. Earl knew me from my days in the NBA when I owned a piece of the Bullets. He said to me, "Mr. Foreman, tell me honestly, how is this league going to turn out?"

I put my arm around him, gave him a pep talk and told him that everything would be all right. But Earl was used to working games on national television, in Madison Square Garden, and you could tell he missed that so much.

SAM SMITH: I was broadcasting a Floridians game and we were playing Rick Barry and the Nets. Barry and Earl Strom had been jawing all night. Finally, Earl slapped Barry with a technical. Barry wouldn't shut up, so Earl gave him another T and threw Barry out of the game. In our league, no one threw Rick Barry out. He *was* the ABA in the early days. So Barry wouldn't leave. He'd take a few steps, turn around and scream at Earl, and Earl would signal another technical. By the time they finally got Barry off the court, Earl had called six technicals on him.

JOHN VANAK: At first, Earl was one of the strongest guys in favor of jumping leagues. I told him how hard it would be working in a new league, relating some of my experiences in the old American Basketball League. But Earl kept saying to me, "John, don't you want the money? Think of all that money they're offering us."

But from Day One, Earl had a rough time in the ABA. He was just despondent. He missed getting his name in the papers and being on television. He would call me every day and say, "Did you hear anything about a merger? Think we'll ever be back in the NBA?"

He was like a kid who was really homesick.

NORM DRUCKER: Earl Strom almost had a breakdown in the ABA. His ego demanded that he receive national attention and he wasn't getting it. John Vanak and I didn't have that problem, because our personalities were different from Earl's. He was an actor who missed center stage. He liked people to say, "There's Earl Strom, the great NBA official." In addition to working ABA games, I was the supervisor of ABA officials, and it's safe to say that I talked to Earl every day in the two years that he was in the ABA. I used to say that I was Earl's psychiatrist. After his first year, he wanted to give back all the money and go back to the NBA, but the ABA wouldn't let him out of his contract. If I had known he would react like that, I never would have let him jump leagues. He was much happier making $15,000 in the NBA than $50,000 in the ABA. So after two years, he quit the ABA. The NBA made him sit out a season before they took him back.

JOHN VANAK: The NBA made Earl do penance for a year in the Eastern League before they let him back in the league. But Earl did his time in purgatory. He would have done anything to get back into the NBA.

VAN VANCE: The officials paid a lot of dues in the ABA. I was broadcasting a Kentucky game and it was one of Jess Kersey's first games in the ABA. There was a hole in the roof and it was raining. Jess came running down the court after a play, hit a wet spot from the rain, fell down and severely pulled a groin or some muscle and was out for a couple of months.

MAX WILLIAMS: I was coaching Dallas and we were playing at Virginia. The game was being worked by some of the lesser officials—I can't recall who, but it wasn't the guys from the NBA. I decided to run on the court to get a technical, but they wouldn't hit me with one. On one play, Virginia took the ball out in front of my bench; I still wanted a technical, so I went out on the court to guard the Virginia player taking the ball out-of-bounds.

Still no technical.

All the officials did was blow the whistle and take the ball to the other side of the court, away from my bench, and give it to Virginia.

BOB BASS: For the most part, our officials were great. By the time I was their supervisor, Earl Strom had gone back to the NBA. But we still had Vanak and Gushue and we got Ed Rush and Jack Madden to jump from the NBA. Our officials were so much better than the NBA's, it wasn't even close.

JOHN VANAK: In 1973, Rush and Madden jumped to the ABA and word was that they got a $100,000 bonus to do it. That was another blow to the other league, and it just showed how the NBA didn't learn anything and still refused to pay the officials like they should.

NORM DRUCKER: Madden and Rush did get a $100,000 bonus and a salary of $25,000. While Earl Strom was gone, that still gave us five refs from the NBA. Then look at the other guys from our league who went on to work in the NBA—Jess Kersey, Walley Rooney, Ed Middleton, Mark Schlafman. That's a lot of quality.

HUBIE BROWN: When you think about it, the officiating at the end of the ABA was like the players—it was an incredible amount of talent, just staggering. And nobody knew it. The officials were even a bigger secret than the players.

The Indiana Pacers: The Boston Celtics of the ABA

No ABA team drew more fans, won more games, won more titles or had more stability than the Indiana Pacers. They won ABA titles in 1970, 1972 and 1973. They lost in the 1969 and 1975 finals, so they played for the title in five of the ABA's nine years. The Pacers also were unique in that they had only two coaches—Larry Staverman and Bobby "Slick" Leonard—and only two ownership groups. Since the merger, the Pacers have had only two winning seasons (1980–81) and have a 1–8 record in the playoffs. The franchise has retired only three uniforms—George McGinnis's No. 30, Mel Daniels's No. 34 and Roger Brown's No. 35. All three of those players come from the team's ABA days.

SLICK LEONARD: I coached the Pacers for basically eight years in the ABA, then the first four seasons after the merger. We had great teams in the late 1960s and early 1970s and great players who the country never saw because the ABA wasn't on television. I'm telling you that Mel Daniels, Roger Brown and Freddie Lewis were damn good players in any league. Bob Netolicky could have played in the NBA. I had played and coached in the NBA; I knew the talent they had and the talent we had, and our guys were terrific talents and terrific people. It was no accident that the Celtics won all those titles; it was more than having Bill Russell and all the great players, it was a sense of togetherness and purpose. We had the same thing with the Pacers.

MEL DANIELS: The Pacers were created and survived because a number of exceptional individuals came together in one place, and then they played together. From Day One of the ABA, Roger Brown, Bob Netolicky and Freddie Lewis were here. In the second year, the Pacers traded for me and hired Slick as coach. In 1971, we signed George McGinnis. I've worked for the Pacers as a scout and an assistant coach and I look around the dressing room and see guys today who have no idea what this uniform is about. They don't have the closeness we had. To this day, Roger Brown, Neto, McGinnis, Billy Keller and I all live in the Indianapolis area and we all stay in touch. No other ABA team can say that, and damn few NBA teams can, either.

BOB NETOLICKY: We were a unique group of guys. Ability was only one of the reasons we won. The rest was character. We didn't have all the white guys hanging out in one place and the black guys in another. We didn't have guys always whining about money, guys playing out their options and jumping to other teams or even to the other league. We didn't have a coach who sat in the ivory tower and wouldn't associate with the players. If you wanted to find Slick on the road, you just went to the hotel bar and there he was. He'd sit there, buy you a few drinks and if you and he got blasted once in a while, then you got blasted. It was no big deal.

In Indiana, basketball almost comes before church and family. You see more rims and basketball goals hanging up in some towns than there are people. When I signed with the Pacers back when they were just forming the ABA, *(Pacer legal counsel)* Dick Tinkham told me, "If you guys win, you'll be like gods in Indianapolis. This still is a small town. These people have been waiting for something like you guys to come along." I was from Iowa and had no idea what he was talking about, but he turned out to be right. It was an event if one of the veteran Pacers would show up at a grocery store. You'd spend a couple of hours talking to people and signing autographs. And you know what? I loved every minute of it.

DICK TINKHAM: When the ABA began, none of us had any idea what we were doing. We had 10 owners, the key guys being Chuck and John DeVoe. Our idea was that Indiana is great basketball country. There had never been a pro team of any type in Indianapolis and we had a chance to be the only show in town if we could win. Sounded good, but we had no idea how to do it. Our first choice to be GM was Bob Young, an Indianapolis guy, but he turned us down. We were racking our brains trying to think of someone who knew something about basketball, and I thought of Mike Storen. He and I had been in the Marine Corps together. He was the business manager of the Cincinnati Royals of the NBA and he had worked in the front office for the Baltimore Bullets. He had never been a coach or in the area of talent evaluation, but we had never been owners before, either, so we gave Mike a chance and we ended up as the best-organized team in the early ABA.

John DeVoe and I went to meet with Mike and he took the job for $15,000. Then Storen said, "Now I need a check."

I said, "What for?"

Mike said, "Just give me a check."

I gave him a check for $500.

Mike said, "I'm going to take this and sign our first player."

I said, "Who's that?"

Mike said, "You never heard of him, but his name is Roger Brown."

I said, "You're right. I never heard of the guy."

MIKE STOREN: It was late spring when I signed my contract with the Pacers at 10 A.M. on a Saturday in West Lafayette, Indiana. I took the check and drove right to Dayton, Ohio, to find Roger Brown, who was working in a factory. Oscar Robertson had told me that the two best players in America not in the NBA were Connie Hawkins and Roger Brown. He said both were all-pro material, and they had been involved in that point-shaving scandal and were banned by the NBA. I had never seen Roger Brown play; I just remembered what Oscar had said. Oscar had played against Brown in the summer. So I knew that Roger lived in Dayton and I went looking for him.

Roger was working at General Motors *(for $114 a week)* and playing some AAU basketball. I went in to talk with Roger, figuring he would jump at the first thing I offered him, but he held me up. He said he had a good job, that his wife was a nurse and she wasn't that anxious to move to Indianapolis. He ended up signing for $17,000, including a $2,000 bonus. We also gave him the use of a car for a year. We helped his wife get a job in Indianapolis. I felt like I had been outnegotiated by Roger, but I wanted him very badly.

ROGER BROWN: I was a little apprehensive about signing with the Pacers, because I had five years' seniority at GM. I wondered if the ABA would last any longer than the old American Basketball League *(which died in two years),* so I didn't want to throw a good job away for some fly-by-night league. But I was convinced that the ABA would at least make it through the first season and I figured this might be my last chance to play pro ball, so I took it.

MIKE STOREN: We signed Brown, which gave us a player. But we had no coach, no front office, even no office space. We rented an old jewelry store that was going to be our office, but the store had two more months on its lease and planned to stay in business, so for the first two months of their existence, the Pacers operated out of the back room of a jewelry store. The front office was my desk and a telephone. I remember going to a league meeting and hearing guys from other teams say they had these great front offices in place and they had already sold 2,000 season tickets, and I went home thinking, "Boy, we better get on the ball."

DICK TINKHAM: We needed a coach, and Johnny Dee at Notre Dame was an influential guy back then. His assistant was Larry Staverman.

Dee, who was an artist with words, convinced Storen that Staverman was ready "to move on to the pros." We offered him $15,000, but Staverman said he needed a station wagon for his family. So we got him for 15 grand and the use of a station wagon as his payment to be our first coach.

LARRY STAVERMAN: Actually, I got $13,500 to coach the Pacers. I was 29, had played for the Cincinnati Royals and had spent the last two years at Notre Dame under Johnny Dee. I was very excited about getting the job, because I knew there were enough players around to have a second pro league. I also knew Roger Brown. When I was with the Royals, Roger would come down from his home in Dayton to scrimmage with us. He held his own against Oscar Robertson, and Roger wasn't even in playing shape because he was working in a factory full-time. So I knew that Roger was a great guy to start the team with.

MIKE STOREN: The ABA had a college draft and we tried to prepare for it the same way you would today. We talked to college coaches, looked at films, got all the opinions we could. Our first pick was Jimmy Walker from Providence College, who was a helluva player, but he signed with the NBA. In the second round, we took Bob Netolicky from Drake. Even though he was just finishing college, he was 25 at the time and had spent most of school just screwing around. He had a reputation as a flake. His father was a wealthy surgeon and he actually kept a pet lion in his room at college. The thing slept in the bathtub. But I also heard that Neto was 6-foot-9 and could really play, so I didn't care what he kept for pets. Neto had also been drafted by the San Diego Rockets of the NBA in the second round, so this was the first time we were going head-to-head with the NBA.

We flew Neto into Indianapolis and he came in on his father's private plane. In fact, Neto flew the plane from Cedar Rapids to Indianapolis himself. He didn't need basketball to make money. He came from money, so when I picked him up in my beat-up old station wagon, he just laughed at me.

DICK TINKHAM: We met with Neto and his lawyer. The lawyer said, "What's your offer?"

I said, "$16,500."

Apparently that was higher than the lawyer expected, because I could tell he seemed pleased. Then he said to me, "Can I see you outside the room for a second?"

He and I went into the hallway and he said, "I think we can make a deal. I'm on my way to an important meeting in Florida and I don't have much time. Tell me, do you guys pay legal fees?"

I said, "Sure we do." I had no idea if you were supposed to or not, but I sensed that I could wrap this up in the hallway.

The lawyer said, "Does $250 sound like a lot of money to you?"

I said, "No, not if we have a deal for Bob for $16,500."

We shook hands and that was it. Then the lawyer called San Diego and told the Rockets that Netolicky was signing with the Pacers. The whole thing took about 10 minutes.

MIKE STOREN: While we were talking to Netolicky, he said he wanted a car as part of the deal. I said sure, we could let him use a car for a year.

Netolicky said, "I'd like a Corvette."

I said, "Fine . . . whatever." I was just happy he was signing with us instead of the NBA. I didn't know what a Corvette was. I thought it was some kind of Chevy. Later I found out that Neto really stuck it to us.

BOB NETOLICKY: I didn't sign with Indiana until my second trip to Indianapolis. The first time, they brought me to town, showed me around and offered me something like $15,000. I don't remember for sure, but I turned it down and went back to Drake. I figured I'd wait for the NBA draft and see what happened. Then the Rockets took Pat Riley first and me in the second round. The next morning, Dick Tinkham called me and screamed, "Don't do anything until we talk to you again."

I think he was worried that I'd think San Diego was a better place to live than Indianapolis, but I didn't look at it like that. The Pacers offered me more money than San Diego, I talked Storen into leasing me a Corvette for a year, and I bet he about died when he saw the insurance bill on that thing. Look, to me the money wasn't the point. I just wanted to play ball and play for the Pacers. I negotiated three contracts with Storen and each time I'd go to see him in his office, he gave me a beer, we talked a bit and made a deal.

Here is how I felt about the money: in 1971, Storen left and we got a new GM who didn't know his ass from a hole in the ground. He forgot to give me my option letter, which meant I was a free agent. It was about midnight and I was at the bar I owned. I called Dick Tinkham and said, "Guess what? I'm a free agent because you guys didn't give me my option letter in time." Then I hung up. Tinkham lived 30 minutes from my bar, but he was there in 15 minutes with that option letter in hand. If I had just kept my mouth shut, I could have become a free agent and made three times what the Pacers paid me. But I was making about 50 grand and I loved it in Indianapolis, so why leave?

DICK TINKHAM: We started the year really well. We opened the season at the Indianapolis Fairgrounds against Kentucky. I was driving to the game and there was a huge traffic jam. I figured it was the crowd from the fair, because they were having horse races and sprint-car events, things like that.

It never dawned on me that all these people were there for the game. But the place was packed. Police estimated that over 12,000 showed up, and the Fairgrounds seated only 9,111. We put in 10,835 and turned the rest away. As the game began, I started to worry. I said, "We have all these people here and what if we don't score a basket?"

I was thinking about George Peeples, who was our center. Poor George just couldn't score; he'd jump about 10 feet over the rim, and then try these outrageous slam dunks, banging the ball against the back of the rim and creating 20-foot rebounds. My nightmare was that Peeples would spend the whole game blowing dunks.

But we were fine. We beat Kentucky and won our first five games. We were in better shape than the other teams, because we had put together a team fast while the rest of the league was trying out everybody and their brother in-law. At one point, we were 18–7. Then the rest of the league caught up with us and we ended up 38–40.

MIKE STOREN: With about 30 games left in that first season, we were desperate for size. Our starting center was Bob Netolicky, who was really more of a forward. But it didn't matter what he was best suited to play, because Neto wasn't playing at all. He had the mumps. We sign a guy and he gets a child's disease. His backup was George Peeples, one of the all-time great guys, but his shooting range was about three inches and he shot only 40 percent from there, so we had to do something. I heard about Reggie Harding. You don't think about signing a guy like Reggie Harding unless you're desperate, and we were. Harding had been with several NBA teams and kept getting cut or traded, because the guy was a big problem. One GM told me he was "seven feet of trouble," but I needed a 7-footer and he was the only one available, and that was because he had just gotten out of jail.

We contacted Reggie and we were supposed to meet him at the Indianapolis airport at 5 A.M. Dick Tinkham and I were waiting for him and when he got off the plane, Reggie was wearing a long black coat that was about six sizes too small. He had a pair of tennis shoes slung over his shoulder, tied together by the laces. Tinkham and I were sitting there in our coats and ties, all proper, and Reggie was looking like a guy who just got out of jail. He was this huge creature, and at five in the morning it seemed like we were the only people in the airport. Our team was leaving on a road trip at 9:30 that morning, so we wanted to get Reggie signed fast and get him on the plane with the team.

DICK TINKHAM: Reggie Harding was the biggest guy I had ever seen. Most of our guys were 6-foot-8 or under; maybe only one or two guys in the league were really 7-foot. Getting off the plane, Reggie looked awful, as if he had just run the obstacle course at Parris Island. We sat down in a booth at the airport coffee shop. Storen was going on and on about what a great franchise we had, what a great basketball town Indianapolis was and how great the ABA was going to be. You know, you've heard it before—everything is great. Reggie was paying absolutely no attention. He was looking at the ceiling, staring at his fingernails, doing anything he could so he wouldn't have to listen to Storen.

Reggie said, "Man, when you get to the money, let me know, all right?"

I said, "Mike, I think he wants to hear the offer."

Mike said, "Half the season is over; we're prepared to give you $10,000 for the rest of the year."

Reggie said, "My man, if you wanted to buy a Cadillac, would you take just enough money to buy a Chevy?"

Reggie said he had a plane back to Detroit and he was going to get on it. I knew we had to do something. Netolicky had the mumps, we were getting our brains beaten out every night and if Reggie walked out, it was just going to get worse.

I said, "Mike, why don't you go see if you can hold Reggie's plane for a few minutes?"

Mike took the clue and left.

I said, "Reggie, take this pen and piece of paper and write down what you want for the rest of the year."

He took the paper and pen and wrote down $15,000.

I said, "Okay, here is how you can get that money. When you got off the plane, you said that we'd win the ABA title if we signed you."

Reggie said, "Piece a cake, man."

I said, "Here is what we'll do . . ."

We had 30 regular-season games left and about 20 in the playoffs if we were to win the title. I said that was 50 games. We'd pay him $300 a game and if the Pacers won it all, they'd play 50 games and Reggie would get his $15,000.

Reggie said, "Does that add up?"

I assured him that it did and he signed.

MIKE STOREN: The contract Tinkham gave Reggie was unbelievable. It was all incentives, based on how many games we played, how far we went in the playoffs. Nobody should ever agree to a contract like that. He just should have taken the 10 grand we offered him. So we got the deal done, then I sent Reggie out with our trainer. Our team all wore suits and ties on the road. Reggie said he didn't have one, so I sent our trainer out to buy him one. We got Reggie some clothes, got him on the plane. I told Larry Staverman, "If Reggie doesn't comply with the rules, he doesn't play."

That night about six, the phone rang in my kitchen. It was Staverman saying that Reggie refused to wear a coat and a tie to the game. He told Reggie that he wasn't going to play, but Reggie just put on his game uniform and said he was playing.

I said, "Larry, tell that son of a bitch that he's not playing. Go back in there and tell him!" I could see that Staverman was scared to death of Reggie Harding. It was just one problem after another with the guy. He wouldn't go to practice. He was late for team flights. Once he said that he had to leave the team to go to his daughter's funeral, which we fell for hook, line and sinker. Of course, he didn't have a daughter.

On the road, we had a roving-roommate system so cliques wouldn't form on the team. The Pacers were playing in New Orleans and one of our best shooters, Jim Rayl, went 1-for-14 from the field. I told my wife, "That damn Rayl was probably out all night in the French Quarter. When he gets home from this trip, I'm gonna kill him."

When the team got back, I called Rayl into my office and started to let him have it. Then he said, "Mike, you don't understand. I was rooming with Reggie."

Rayl was one of those high-energy guys who never stood still. The players called him "Tweetie Bird."

Rayl told me, "It was midnight and I was in bed and the lights were out. I heard Reggie come in and I heard him going around the room. It was still dark. Then I heard him close to me. He turned on the light and there was Reggie standing by my bed, holding a gun to my head. He said, 'Tweetie Bird, I hear you hate niggers.' "

Rayl said he didn't and he kept talking to Reggie and finally got Reggie to hand over the gun. When Reggie did, Rayl took all of the bullets out of the gun and said, "Reggie, let's go to bed now. We've got a game tomorrow."

Rayl turned out the lights and then he heard Reggie getting up and moving around the room. Rayl turned the lights back on and there was Reggie, again pointing the gun at Rayl.

Reggie said, "You didn't think I only had six shells, did you?"

Rayl grabbed some clothes, walked out of the room and spent the rest of the night sitting up in the hotel lobby.

"And that's why I was 1-for-14," Rayl told me.

It was always something, and by the end of the regular season, Reggie had been fined so much that he owed us about $4,000. We had suspended him for the playoffs. The final straw came when he was interviewed on television and he said that the Pacers would have won if he had played. Reggie also said, "And if I had a gun, I'd shoot Mike Storen." That got to me. I started thinking that if the guy really wanted to shoot me, he could; I knew damn well that he did have a gun. But he just disappeared and never played pro ball again. He later was shot in Detroit and I went to his funeral. I was one of only three white people there.

DICK TINKHAM: When the season was over, Mike and I sat down and said we had to get a center. A real center, not a Reggie Harding. At the time, the best big man in the league was Mel Daniels of Minnesota, which was having money problems.

At the end of one league meeting, Larry Shields from Minnesota came up to Storen and myself and said, "I need your help."

Both Storen and I got excited. We were going to approach Minnesota about Daniels, but it was even better that they came to us.

Shields said, "We're having cash-flow problems and we need money now so we can pay the league's $100,000 performance bond. We're $50,000 short."

What Shields wanted us to do was support his measure that the league lower the performance bond from $100,000 to $50,000.

I said, "To do that, you're going to have to give us some of your talent."

Shields said, "All right, we'll give you Smith."

Smith was Sam Smith, a 6-foot-7 forward who averaged about 10 points a game. He was nothing special.

I said, "We don't care about Smith, we want Mel Daniels."

Shields said, "No way can I do that. He's the franchise, the best center in the league."

Storen felt that not only was Daniels the best center in the league, he was the second-best player in the league that first year, Connie Hawkins being the first.

We talked some more and it was obvious that Shields was desperate for money. Finally, he said, "How much will you pay for Daniels?"

I said, "$150,000."

He said, "All right." Then we talked about giving them a couple of players, too. So we agreed to trade $150,000, Jimmy Dawson and Ron Kozlicki for Daniels. We wrote the deal out on a napkin and signed it.

MIKE STOREN: When Tinkham and I went back to our board of directors to tell them that we just committed the team to pay $150,000 for Daniels, they wanted no part of it. We lost about $70,000 that year and by the end of the season our crowds were in the 3,500 range. Tinkham and I found out that the fans liked basketball so long as it was winning basketball; when we started losing, there was a dramatic drop in the attendance.

My point was that Daniels would help us win, but the board didn't want to pay $150,000 for anyone.

After a while, we had to try something to get the deal done, so Tinkham and I said we would go to the bank ourselves, borrow the $150,000, buy Daniels and then *lease* him to the team. It was completely unprecedented and probably couldn't work, but that did get their attention.

DICK TINKHAM: We finally got the board to agree to pay $75,000 for Daniels. So I called Minnesota and told them all we could pay was $75,000. Naturally, they went crazy, screaming and calling me all kinds of names. But that was the best I could do, $75,000 and the two players, take it or leave it. The financial pressure was terrible, so they took it if we could get them the $75,000 right away, which we did.

Looking back, there were two moves that made the franchise. The first was signing Roger Brown, the second was getting Daniels. In a sense, Daniels was a pure accident. Yes, we had an interest in him, but Larry Shields came to us. If he had gone to one of the richer teams like Kentucky, Joe Gregory probably would have written them a $250,000 check on the spot for Daniels. Instead, we each signed a paper napkin to make the biggest trade in the history of the Indiana Pacers.

MEL DANIELS: At first, I was upset about being traded, but the Minnesota people explained to me that it was just business. They had no money. Mike Storen called me at our home in New Mexico. He flew my wife and me to Indianapolis, picked us up at the airport, took us out to a lot of nice places around town and made us feel wanted. Then he gave me a new contract for $35,000, which was huge money in those days. He talked about the good fan support in Indiana and said he wanted to make the Pacers the Boston Celtics of the ABA. Everything he did was first class.

When training camp started, I thought we'd have a good team. Roger Brown, Freddie Lewis, Netolicky and I were all quality players. But we opened the season with Larry Staverman as the coach and there was no chemistry. We just weren't playing together and we were losing.

MIKE STOREN: I don't want to say anything negative about Staverman, but he just wasn't ready to be a pro coach. I think he was too young and he had never been a head coach anywhere. We also had Slick Leonard around. I knew Slick from when I worked with the Bullets and he was coaching Baltimore. He was an emotional leader and we were a team that lacked fire. I thought that we needed his experience, so we had Slick take over for Staverman.

LARRY STAVERMAN: In my first season, we were 38–40 and we probably could have won more games, but I used the younger players I thought would develop. I was building for the future, not trying to win now. Then we started the second year at 1–7. The front office was unhappy with Roger Brown and wanted to trade him. They wondered if Netolicky could play and they were thinking about dealing him, too. I went to the wall for those two guys, telling Mike Storen to give them time and they'd be all right. I was asking for patience from a GM who had told the owners he had assembled enough talent to win a championship. That was not a good sign for me.

We were playing in Los Angeles and our record was 1–7 when Mike Storen asked me to go to breakfast with him. It was at a restaurant in sort of a run-down hotel in L.A. The name escapes me, but I can go out there today and find the place. In fact, when I am in L.A., I usually drive by it. It is sort of like seeing my personal Alamo, because what I heard that morning changed my life.

Storen told me, "I've made a decision to relieve you as coach of the Indiana Pacers."

He said it in exactly those terms, almost as if he were reading it from a press release. I was shocked. I had no idea it was coming.

Storen said, "What do you want to do about tonight's game?"

I had no assistant and we were playing the L.A. Stars.

I said, "I'll be on the bench."

We went out and beat the Stars that night. The players didn't know that I had been fired. When the game was over, I locked the dressing room and I yelled at them, praised them. I gave a very emotional talk. I told each guy what he needed to do to improve his game, to survive as a pro. Then I walked out of the dressing room and went to a secluded part of the arena where I knew that no one would see me crying.

I was 30 years old, and to be told you're not good enough to do the job you always wanted—it has to hurt. I was too young and not really prepared for life in the ABA. I also was naive and didn't look out for myself as well as I should have.

The thing that meant the most to me came when we went home after that game in L.A. The word of my firing wasn't released until I got to my house. Then I went out for a bike ride with my kid. When I got back, the entire Pacer starting team was waiting for me in my driveway. They came to say that they felt bad about me being fired and that it wasn't my fault, they had let me down. It was a tremendous gesture, because most of the time when a pro coach is fired, the players just shrug and wait for the next guy to take over. But these were quality people and I'll never forget pedaling into my driveway and seeing those players waiting for me.

ONE SLICK COACH

DICK TINKHAM: It would be nice to say that we all knew Slick Leonard would be perfect for this team and he'd take over and lead them to three titles. But there was no reason to think that. Slick had coached in the NBA and had a very unremarkable record *(13–29 with the Chicago Zephyrs in 1962, 31– 49 with Baltimore in 1963–64)*. But he went to Indiana University and was sort of an old local hero. Losing record notwithstanding, Slick at least had coached in the NBA, and that experience put him ahead of most guys in the league, so we went with him. Also, Storen had a good feeling about Slick.

MIKE STOREN: One of my main concerns was that we were nine games into the season and we weren't in shape under Staverman. We were getting tired at the end of the game, physically tired, and you could see it. That should never be the case. Slick knew it, too. He came in and ran a first practice that is still legendary among the Pacers who went through it.

BOB NETOLICKY: I had been out with Slick a couple of times during the summer after our first season and before he was named coach. We'd have a few beers, or maybe a few dozen beers, and he'd tell me that we were good enough to win but we just weren't playing together. He was right. We weren't organized or motivated.

When he took over, Slick called a team meeting and told us, "I want you to know that this is a whole new game and we're going to learn basketball all over again, the way it should be played. We are going to learn what it means to get along; this team will be a family and I don't ever want to hear any of this 'nigger' or 'honky' bullshit. We're all in this together. We win or lose together. When it gets rough, we stick together, because that is what families do."

MIKE STOREN: That first practice was brutal. He ran the guys up and down the court until they were about tripping on their tongues. He saw

Mel Daniels take a jump shot from outside the foul line, and he stopped practice and just screamed at Mel. Then Slick took a piece of chalk and drew a circle near the basket. "There," said Slick, pointing to the chalk mark. "That's where you're supposed to shoot from."

MEL DANIELS: Slick was screaming at me, "As long as I'm the coach, don't you ever even think about taking another 19-foot jump shot. You're paid to play under the basket, so get your ass under the basket."

He just came in and took charge. We were going to be his team, but he also understood ballplayers. He had lost in the NBA because he didn't have any talent, so he knew that talent was important. That sounds simple, but some coaches have such egos that they figure they'll win regardless of the talent. They think that it's the "system" that wins, but Slick knew it was the players that make any system successful. So he screamed at us and he worked us, but he also stuck with us. He did things to reward us. Before our first trip, he said that if we won five games we'd get a party and he'd pay for it. We won the five; he threw the party and celebrated with us.

SLICK LEONARD: After every game, I wanted the team to get together for a drink. It didn't matter what you drank, it could be apple juice or it could be a beer, I just wanted us together at least for a few minutes. That way we could talk about the game, develop relationships that extended beyond the court and the locker room. At first, it was awkward for the guys because they weren't used to that, but as time passed, they grew to like it, to want to get together.

BOB NETOLICKY: Slick sent very clear messages to the players. When we were winning, our practices were a piece of cake. He liked to practice at 7 P.M. We'd run through a few plays, shoot around and be out of there in an hour—that was when we won. When we lost and dogged it, he became the most miserable SOB on the face of the earth. He would run us until our feet fell off. When it was over you didn't want your children to see you because you felt like you died. It was almost like he was training Pavlov's dog: you win and you get a pat on the head, you lose and you get a boot in the behind that you'll never forget.

He also treated his players like men. He'd say, "I don't care what you guys do off the court, but you better be ready to play when you step on the court." I've walked down the street at midnight, dead drunk and arm-in-arm with Slick as we held each other up, knowing we had a game at 1 P.M. the next day. But he expected me to give 100 percent the next afternoon and I better not be hung over or he would have killed me. It was that simple.

SLICK LEONARD: When I took over the Pacers, I felt that the team was a lot better than 2–7, good enough to win a lot of games in the ABA. But someone had to take control and that meant kicking some butt. The guys seemed lost, without a sense of purpose. I don't think they valued winning. The reason you play the game on the pro level is to win. If you want rewards, you have to win—it's that simple.

DAVE CRAIG: I was the Pacers' trainer. I was a kid out of Purdue and Slick hired me. He took me to Sandy's Town Tavern and we sat there most of the night, drinking, eating and talking. He was very charismatic. He said that working for the Pacers would be the time of my life, that I would relish these moments. He said the team was a family and the trainer was a part of that. Then he offered me $10,000 and I jumped at the chance to take the job.

I got to know Slick very well. He was a guy with a huge heart who had grown up on the wrong side of the tracks. He grew up in Terre Haute, Indiana. He took me there once and we were driving along the railroad tracks. He stopped the car and pointed to a vacant lot near the tracks.

He said, "That's where I used to live."

I said, "Slick, there's nothing there."

He said, "Well, there used to be a house there, and every morning I would get up, go out on the tracks and pick up the coal that fell out of the train cars that came by that night. That was how we got coal for our stove."

There were stories of how Slick used to dribble a basketball a mile to catch a bus, then carry the ball on the bus, get off the bus and dribble some more. He even dribbled the ball up and down stairs. He talked about playing ball against guys who had just gotten back from the Korean War, guys who would just as soon slam you in the head as look at you. He went to Indiana University and was on that "Hurrying Hoosiers" team that won the NCAA title in 1953. He came from nothing and knew what basketball could mean. He loved the game with his heart and wanted his players to love it the same way.

DICK TINKHAM: One of the first things Slick did was leave Roger Brown home when the team took a road trip. He thought Roger wasn't putting out in practice, so he left him behind. At the time, we were talking about trading Roger. We offered him around the league, but no one wanted him. Two weeks later, everything was fine and Roger was playing great, but if we had gotten a call from someone, Roger Brown could very well have been traded. I know one thing—leaving Roger behind got the team's attention.

BOB NETOLICKY: In his third game as coach, Slick was upset at one of the officials. The guy had made a couple of terrible calls and Slick said, "If that guy blows another one, I'm gonna smack the hell out of him." Nobody on the bench who heard that thought much of it. Coaches say things like that all the time, but the ref blew another call, Slick went out on the court after the guy, and we almost had a riot.

MIKE STOREN: After that game, Slick went into the dressing room and he was hot. He screamed at his team, "Don't you clowns even know how to fight? When there's a fight out there, you don't hold your teammates back, you grab the guys on the other team and hold them down, got that? Don't you guys know anything?"

MEL DANIELS: Slick would go after anybody. One night, he even jumped on Warren Jabali. Lucky for him that there were guys all over the floor, because Jabali was as mean a guy as there was in the league. But Slick really didn't care who he fought.

GENE LITTLES: The Pacers were the bullies of the league, like the Detroit Pistons today. They were the champs and they figured they owned the ABA and could do whatever they wanted. If you got ahead of them, then Daniels or somebody would push you, the benches would empty and you'd have a fight. I remember a game where Bob Verga and Daniels got into a fight and the next thing I knew, Slick Leonard had jumped on Verga. That team fought so much that even their coach liked to fight. In my five years at Carolina, the only team I remember fighting with was Indiana.

DAVE CRAIG: Slick loved to work the officials. He threw bottles of rosin at the press table, and there would be a cloud of it hanging over the court.

SLICK LEONARD: One night, Ed Rush was working our game and we couldn't catch a break. After a while, I just couldn't watch it anymore and I threw the ball rack at him. There were 12 red, white and blue basketballs rolling all over the floor.

BOB BASS: I was the head of officials and Mike Storen was ABA commissioner when Slick threw the ball rack at Ed Rush. We had a meeting at the league office in New York—Storen, Slick, Dick Tinkham and myself.
Slick said, "Mike, forget the B.S.—what do you want to do?"
Storen said, "A thousand-dollar fine."
Slick said, "Fine. Let's go to the bar and have a drink."

SLICK LEONARD: That's right, except I also got suspended for two games. The funny thing was that I was kicking over chairs and throwing things long before Bobby Knight did, and people write a book about Knight and make a million dollars. I'm not sure what that means, but it is something I've thought about.

MIKE STOREN: It wasn't long before the team took on Slick's personality. Slick came in when we were 2–7 and we went 42–27 under him, making it to the finals, where we lost to Oakland, which had a helluva team. But that showed me what impact a coach could have on a team.

MEL DANIELS: Slick would never mince words. If he thought you were chickenshit, then he'd stand right in front of you and call you "chickenshit," challenging you to do something about it. He would get right in your face.

One day he got all over my butt when we were playing the Nets. Tom Hoover was their center, a bulky 6-foot-10 guy who had been a sparring partner for Muhammad Ali. I had the flu and was sick as a dog. Hoover was pushing me all over the place and Slick started cussing me out. He called me "chickenshit." He said it over and over and then he said, "You're an embarrassment to the uniform." I was cussing Hoover, cussing Slick, cussing everybody. Then I took my sick self out there and almost took Hoover's head off. But the point was that Slick got to me, he forced me to reach down and come up with that extra effort even if I was sick.

He would tell us, "I don't give a damn what you do off the court, but I want 48 minutes of total effort during the game. If you can't give me that 48 minutes, then you're cheating yourself and the team and you're outta here. I'll get rid of you."

DAVE CRAIG: In Slick's first few years as coach, if he thought there was a problem with a guy on the team he'd say, "Let's lock the clubhouse door. You don't like something? You guys want to fight about it? Okay, let's see who comes out of the room still standing."

Of course, there never was a fight. Slick would threaten one, but I think everybody knew that he was just talking. What he wanted to do was create some emotion. With the type of players he had, it was the perfect approach.

MEL DANIELS: If he thought we were dogging it, his face would turn red, his shirt would be unbuttoned halfway down his chest and you'd know all hell was about to break loose. Usually, it was the chalkboard.

He'd whack that thing and break it right in two pieces with one punch. The most famous incident was when he went after Neto with a hockey stick.

BOB NETOLICKY: We were playing in a hockey arena in Duluth and it was about 40 below zero outside. I think we were playing Pittsburgh and we were losing by about 20 at the half, really stinking up the joint. Slick got all over my ass about not hustling and it turned into a shouting match. He called me every kind of foul name you could think of, then he grabbed a hockey stick that was lying around and screamed, "I'm gonna kick your ass, Neto."

I didn't see him get the stick. I got sick of him yelling at me and I went into the bathroom and was sitting on the toilet. He was screaming, "Neto, where the hell are you? When I find you, I'm gonna kick your ass."

I was in the toilet stall and I yelled, "I'm in here."

He yelled, "You son of a bitch." Then Slick started beating against the bathroom door with the hockey stick. He was yelling, "I'm gonna kill you," and he beat the stick into a million pieces of wood.

I was still sitting on the toilet, laughing. The rest of the team was cracking up, too. When he had destroyed the hockey stick, he calmed down.

MEL DANIELS: In that hockey-stick game, we came back to win and Neto had 26 points and 19 rebounds, almost all of it in the second half. He jokes about it now, but Neto was scared out of his pants back then. His head was down, he was mumbling. Slick lit a fire under Neto's butt that night.

SLICK LEONARD: That night, Neto was screwing around. It was real cold in the arena and when we went on the floor for warm-ups, Neto was out there wearing gloves and his overcoat while shooting around. I didn't like that. His head wasn't in the game at the start, and by the half I had had enough of him. When I grabbed the hockey stick and swung at him, I was serious. I missed him and I hit the wall. He wasn't in the toilet stall; he was in the dressing room and he was frightened.

Look, I know that I did crazy things over the years. You have to be a little goofy to coach as long as I did. But my thing was winning. I would ask myself, "Why did Bear Bryant win? Or Vince Lombardi?" It came down to the same thing—they treated people like they would have wanted to be treated and they didn't ask their players to do something they wouldn't do. All great coaches had teams that were together and were physically and mentally tougher than the teams they were playing. So my practices weren't long, but they were demanding, as rough as I could make them. I ran the guys until they dropped, then I ran them some more. That was how they not only became strong mentally, but also physically. Then when a clutch situation came up, we were physically in condition to be strong at the end of the game and we were mentally strong enough not to panic. We believed in each other and that we'd win. When I took over the Pacers, Roger, Mel and the rest didn't suddenly become great players. They had the talent; I just helped them to bring it out. I made demands on them that no one else did.

All that X's and O's talk is garbage. Basketball isn't a complicated game. The coach's job is to keep the team together. I've never met a player in my life who didn't think he was better than he really was. A coach has to understand that most guys walk around wearing a sign that says, "Pat me on the back. Tell me I can play. Say something that will make me feel good." That's why I spent far more time teaching the guys to trust and respect each other than I did on all the technical stuff. I would tell the team on Day One of practice that they could do something spectacular if they decided to do it together. I told them that we were a special group, and that we had obligations to ourselves to play like that. The guys knew that and responded and pretty soon the whole team came together like a hand in a glove.

ROGER BROWN: Every year when we went to camp it was *expected* that we'd be in the ABA finals. It wasn't a dream or something that sounded good to talk about. Slick talked about it and made you live with it every day like he lived with it every day. We all were under the same pressure. What I loved about Slick is that it was never a situation where he'd say, "*We* won" but "*They* lost." On his teams, "we" did everything together, good or bad. And in his eight years in the ABA, five of his teams went to the finals and three won titles. No one in the ABA came even close to that record.

MEL DANIELS: One of the things I remember most about Slick is that he cared about people. It was not unusual to be walking down the street with Slick and see him come upon a bum, take the bum into a restaurant and buy him a meal. There was one incident where he ran into a bag lady who was such a pathetic case that Slick started to cry when he led her to a restaurant. He took us to hospitals where we saw crippled kids. He'd tell us, "You guys have a great gift, legs that enable you to run up and down the floor. Look at these kids. Think about what they would give just to be able to walk." He'd say and do things like that and thinking about it now, I still get a lump in my throat. How could you not love a guy like that?

BILLY KELLER: We used to go to a hospital ward for dying kids and you'd see them there, knowing that they were never going home . . . it just tore me up inside. A lot of us would walk out the door with tears in our eyes. Slick, too. He would say to us, "Look, guys, that is what real life can be about."

BILLY KNIGHT: Slick could always reach me when he dug down deep for one of his speeches. We'd be on the road and he'd say, "Tonight we will see what kind of men you are. We'll see if you have any guts, if you know how to accept a challenge. The only people who care about us in this building is us. Everyone else is against us—the fans, the other players, the officials, everybody. These guys think they are a physical team and I'm telling you right now, they are going to take the floor and try to beat us up. What I want to know is, what are we going to do about it? Are we just going to take it or do we fight back . . ."

I would be listening to that, my hands would ball up into fists and by the time he was done, I was ready to take on the world and I knew that Slick would be right behind me.

MEL DANIELS: You never knew what to expect from Slick. In the 1969 playoffs, we were down 3–1 to Kentucky in the first round. We had to win three games in a row or we were done. Slick had been screaming at us all year. It was his first season as coach and it was stormy because it took him a while to get the team to take on the personality he wanted. So we expected him to raise the roof when we were on the brink of elimination. Instead, he came in and said, "Basketball is a great game, but it's not the end of the world."

He was speaking very quietly, almost mellow.

He said, "All I'm asking out of you guys is 100 percent. Win or lose, you're still the Indiana Pacers, a helluva basketball team."

We were looking at each other saying, "Who is this guy and what are these soft words coming out of that dragon's mouth?"

He said, "If we lose, we lose. No one will kill you. There will be nothing to be ashamed of as long as you play like you can. Now just go out and play the game."

He caught us totally off-balance, and it worked. We came back to take three games from Kentucky. On that night, he sensed that we had been too uptight and he figured if he pushed us any harder, we would snap. So he eased off and let us take care of business.

BOB NETOLICKY: We knew if we kept the game close, Slick would come up with something that would win it for us. He was a great closer. I can't imagine a coach being better when the pressure is on. And we believed that Slick was the best coach in the world. We'd walk out of a huddle in a close game and look over at the other bench and know that we were better prepared than they were because we had a better coach.

ROGER: HE SCORED THE POINTS

When he was the first player signed by the Pacers in 1967, Roger Brown was 25 years old and had played for such AAU teams as Brothers Mortuaries while also working the night shift as an injection machine operator at the General Motors plant in Dayton. At Wingate High in Brooklyn, Brown was considered on the same level with a couple of other New York prep stars, Billy Cunningham and Connie Hawkins. With the Pacers, he was a 6-foot-5 small forward. He averaged 22 points from 1968 to 1971 and 17.4 for his eight-year ABA career. But where he really made his reputation was in the playoffs. When the Pacers won their first ABA title in 1970, Brown averaged 32.7 points and 10 rebounds in the finals against the L.A. Stars and Willie Wise, who also was an All-Star. In the last three games, he had 53, 39 and 45 points. In the final game, he drilled a league-record seven 3-pointers. Two years later, Brown went head-to-head with New York's Rick Barry in the 1972 finals and out-scored the Nets' star 32–23 in the final game as the Pacers won their second ABA title.

JERRY HARKNESS: I grew up with Roger Brown in New York. Like Connie Hawkins, he was a legend when he was in high school. He made 25-footers like most people made 10-footers and he had one of those bodies that was made for giving fakes. A quick turn of the head in one direction and he was gone. In New York, there were a million great 1-on-1 players, but he was as good as any of them. What made Roger so good on his 1-on-1 moves was that he'd fake you, then start to the basket, and you figured that since he was moving so fast, he was going all the way for the layup. But then he'd just stop and raise up with the jumper from 10 feet away. That was a killer move. I saw him beat guys on the playground with that move and I saw him take apart teams in the ABA finals doing the same thing. He was hurt by being banned from the NBA and I know that made him very suspicious of people. He is very reluctant to let anyone get close to him even today, and that comes from the things that happened to him as a kid. Imagine being 18 and knowing—as Roger did—that you were one of the best basketball players in the world and then being told that you couldn't be a pro, having your dream taken away. And the circumstances of that case were very shaky, as was shown later when the NBA had to allow Connie Hawkins to play in the NBA and they gave Roger the same chance, although he stayed with the Pacers and took a financial settlement.

MIKE STOREN: When Slick Leonard came in, it took a while for Roger and him to get on the same wavelength. Roger wasn't playing well *(averaging about 13 points)* and Slick left him home for that first road trip. But then they straightened everything out.

ROGER BROWN: I got a reputation for taking the big shot at the end of games, and Slick had a lot to do with that. The first time it happened was against Minnesota, which was Connie Hawkins's team. This was when there were rumors about me being traded to Minnesota for Steve Chubin. To this day, I'm not sure why Slick called my number, since he was thinking of getting rid of me, but he did. Maybe he wanted to see how I'd react under pressure, and if I folded, I was gone. He challenged me that day. He put the ball in my hands and said, "Win the game." I did, and the irony was that a little later, we did get Chubin, but we traded Mike Lewis for him.

MEL DANIELS: In that Minnesota game, Slick designed a play where we cleared out one side of the court and let Roger go 1-on-1.
   Slick said to Roger, "That's the play—can you do it?"
   Roger said, "Yeah."
   It was that simple. We gave Roger the ball, he beat his man and we won. By the end of the season, the Indiana fans would start to chant ROG-ER! ROG-ER! at the end of the games and it would pump him up.
   There was a game against Kentucky when we were down by two points with 17 seconds left. Freddie Lewis was bringing the ball up the court and Roger said real nonchalantly, "Clear it out, I'm going to win it." So we ran our clear-out play for Roger, getting him the ball on the wing. But this time, he made a step toward the basket like he was going to drive, his man backed off, Roger took a step backwards, and suddenly he was behind the 3-point line. He went up for the 25-footer and swished it and we won by a point. He was called "The Man with a Thousand Moves," and he had at least that many.

SLICK LEONARD: Roger was a complete basketball player. One-on-one, no man could guard him, like no man can guard Michael Jordan today.

In the 1972 finals, he went head-to-head with Rick Barry and no one could tell who was the better player. Today, everybody knows Rick Barry and no one knows Roger Brown, which is a shame. Roger was in the same class as Barry. He could do the same things—pass, go to the basket, and hit the 3-pointer.

ROGER BROWN: The ABA 3-point play was made for me. I took those same 25-footers over Billy Cunningham when we both were in high school, only they were worth just two points. I was very comfortable shooting from 25 feet.

The thing is that I have terrible eyesight. I never actually saw the rim when I took a jump shot. I just saw some orange on the backboard. I'd laugh when I'd hear guys say that they shoot for the front of the rim or the back or whatever. See the rim? Man, I had to ask my teammates to tell me how much time was left on the clock or what the score was, because I had trouble reading the scoreboard. There were some arenas where the guys complained that it was hard to shoot because it was so dark. It never mattered to me; I grew up on the New York playgrounds, where I had to wait until it was almost dark to get on a court and shoot. Even if I could see, playing at night meant all you saw was the outline of the rim as you shot the ball under a distant streetlight. That was life in New York, hanging around the playgrounds to get into a game. If they locked the playground on you, then you just climbed the fence and got in. You played into the night and got a beating from your mother when you got home because you missed supper. I learned to shoot in the dark, so it really didn't matter that my eyes were bad. I developed a high-arching soft shot and that is the key to being a good shooter, not the light.

BILLY KELLER: Having Roger Brown is great for a team's ego. To know that you're in a close game and all you have to do is get him the ball . . . I suppose that football teams felt the same way when they had Gale Sayers or Walter Payton and it was a third-down-and-one situation. You know you just give the guy the ball and he'd get the first down.

GENE LITTLES: Roger was the Larry Bird of the ABA. He had the all-around skills of Bird and he used that 3-point shot just like Bird—to break your back. Roger made the game look easy and he was a great forward in a league filled with great forwards. He made the game look so easy.

ROGER BROWN: The best thing that happened to me was signing with the Pacers and getting to play with Neto, Freddie Lewis and Mel Daniels. I loved Indianapolis and the Pacers and that was why I turned down a chance to jump to the NBA after the Connie Hawkins case. I never forgot that the NBA wouldn't let me play, but the ABA did. The NBA had to pay me quite a nice settlement from that case, but I had no desire to play in that league, not when I could stay with the Pacers and be a part of a great team. I still live in Indianapolis today, where I have several businesses. The Pacers and the town have been great to me.

MEL: HE GOT THE REBOUNDS

No ABA player got more rebounds than 6-foot-9 Mel Daniels. That is a fact. More facts are that Daniels was twice the league's MVP (1969 and 1971), won three rebounding titles (1968, 1969 and 1971) and retired with the league's best rebounding average (15.1 per game). In a March 18, 1969, game against New York, Daniels had 37 points and 26 rebounds—in the second half. He ended up with 56 points, the second most in Pacer history. He also was the only player to be picked to the all-ABA team in its first four seasons. But Daniels was much more than a collection of numbers, and that's a fact, too.

SLICK LEONARD: Mel Daniels was our emotional leader. I don't believe any player took losing harder than Mel. When we got beat, even I didn't want to get near him, and I was a pretty lousy loser myself. He was excitable, enthusiastic, a fierce competitor. He was not a man to back down from a fight.

ROGER BROWN: Back down from a fight? Mel would fight at the drop of a hat. I've heard him say that in his rookie year he was in 78 games and had 78 fights. Well, I say he started all 78 of them. He fought guys on the court, he tore up lockers in the dressing room. A couple of times, he got mad at Slick and went after his own coach and the guys had to step in between them. But Slick didn't care. Slick liked players such as Mel, because Slick was just like Mel. Slick wanted his players to have that emotional edge. Mel would get mad and cuss you out. In practice, we'd have fights, screaming matches, all that stuff. But an outsider had better not say a bad word about anyone on the Pacers. If they did they had to answer to Mel.

DAVE CRAIG: During a game, Mel would get so mad that he would stutter when he talked. Then the guys would get all over him about the stuttering, and it just made him madder and the stuttering worse. Finally, Mel would say, "You gu-gu-guys just cut it out before I ki-ki-kill you." By then, even Mel would be laughing.

BILLY KELLER: Mel Daniels was emotional, dramatic, hardworking and intense. As a coach, you can look at certain players and instantly know, "There's a guy who can help a team win."

Mel was that kind of guy.

He played a man's game inside. He set the picks, he got the rebounds, he blocked the shots and he was in the middle of every fight. He scared people out of driving the lane against the Pacers. If he went for the ball and ended up with someone's head in his hands, he was just as likely to put a headlock on the guy as let him go. If Artis Gilmore had had Mel's temperament, Artis would have been the greatest player in the history of the game. But Artis was just a quiet, nice guy. Mel would get right in his face and play the big fella even.

What impressed me about Mel was that he was very unselfish. When he got a defensive rebound, he immediately looked up-court to throw the long outlet pass and start the fast break. He didn't hold the ball like some big guys do, making the guard come back to get it so that the pace would be slower and the center could walk up the court and set up under the basket.

You'd also see that unselfishness on defense. If Neto's man drove around Neto, Mel would be there to pick him up. Mel got a lot of extra fouls that way, and he'd get mad at Neto for playing bad defense, but Mel was always there to clog the middle.

Offensively, he was not a graceful player. He used his size and strength to get second shots. But he did have one shot for which he was famous—he would catch the ball and fake as if he was going to drive the baseline, then shoot a soft, fadeaway jumper. That was an unstoppable move.

MEL DANIELS: I know it sounds vicious, but I loved to knock guys down. Freddie Lewis would come up the court and he would sort of slap his leg, which was a sign to get a certain player. It might be the guy guarding Freddie, and he would run the guy blind-sided into a pick I set. It was just how we played back then—we went with the contact and backed away from nothing and no one. When you went to the boards, you did it with your elbows out. If there was a fight, it wasn't just 1-on-1, it was 12-on-12. Hey, the fine for fighting was $25, so what the hell was that? What was 25 bucks? That wasn't going to stop any fights.

The guy who gave me the most problems was Zelmo Beaty from Utah. It wasn't as if I hated the guy—just the opposite; Zelmo is a great guy. But when he jumped to the ABA, I was the best center in the league and he was a guy who had been an All-Star in the NBA. Even before I saw him, there was a natural rivalry just because of who we were.

Zelmo knew exactly how to frustrate me. He would step on my foot or he would grab my shorts or he'd take his hand and lock it on my thigh so I couldn't move. I'd get so mad that I'd want to grab him and throw him down. If I tried that, I'd get called for a foul.

Then there was Zelmo's jump shot. I could block any center's shot but Zelmo's, and Zelmo didn't even get off the floor. He just took his turn-around jumper, letting it go right in my face, and I couldn't get it.

ZELMO BEATY: No doubt, Mel was the best center in the ABA's early years. He was the league's MVP when I came to Utah in 1970, and I think the fact that I was a good player in the NBA who moved into his turf became an ego thing with Mel. Every time we played, he wanted to put the NBA star in his place, but he wanted it too much.

I'd put my hand on Mel's hip, but unlike a lot of centers who rest their hands on their opponent's hip, I didn't *rest* my hand there, I would *squeeze* Mel's hip. So what would Mel do? Naturally, he'd slap my hand off. And the officials, what did they see? It's hard to see a squeeze, but you can see and hear a slap, so Mel would get called for the foul. That was a trick I used on all the young centers, not just Mel. But it was a move that worked very well against Mel because he was so high-strung.

It's nice to hear Mel say that he felt I got the best of him, because he was truly a great player. If I did have an advantage, it wasn't by much, believe me.

GENE LITTLES: I'm now the coach of the Charlotte Hornets and believe me, we'd pay a ton of money to get a young Mel Daniels to play center for us. In his prime, Mel would start for most of the NBA teams today, and I don't want to hear that he was only 6-foot-9 and would have to play forward. With Mel's attitude, he could have been a modern-day center.

NETO: HE POURED THE DRINKS

When ABA people talk about Bob Netolicky, they tend to forget that the 6-foot-9, 225-pound forward from Drake was a very good player— maybe not as good as he could have been, but good enough to average 16 points and 8.8 rebounds for his eight-year pro career. He was good enough to make four All-Star teams and to be on two of the Pacers' three championship teams and on four of the Indiana teams that went to the

ABA finals. The one season he was away from Indiana was 1972–73 when he was in Dallas, where he averaged 18.7 points and 10.1 rebounds while logging a career high of nearly 40 minutes a game. He was capable at both the center and power-forward positions. Netolicky could play and he also could play around; he saw himself as Indiana's Joe Namath, complete with his own nightclub, Neto's, for "swinging singles."

SLICK LEONARD: There is a lot to be said about Neto as a basketball player. He could run the fast break, he had a terrific hook shot and could really leap. But he also could go to sleep on you. Basketball wasn't the most important thing in his life. But he also was my favorite because through him, I could get to the rest of the team. When I wanted to scream at everybody, I'd start by screaming at Neto, because there usually was something to yell at Neto about.

BILLY KELLER: Neto sort of lived in another world and didn't worry about the same things the rest of us did. If he had been very dedicated, he could have extended his career. But that wasn't his nature. Neto just didn't worry about much. His father was a surgeon and he came from money, so he didn't have the same drive that the rest of us had. The guys would tease him about not brushing his teeth, or forgetting to take a bath or change his underwear. He'd say he changed his clothes. But knowing Neto, he probably pulled out what he thought was his new clothes from under a pile of dirty laundry he had in the corner of his room. He was just an easy target.

DAVE CRAIG: Neto established himself as a character even before he joined the Pacers, when he flew his own plane to town to sign his contract. He always had exotic pets. He had a wildcat, and the damn thing got out of his house and was running all over his neighborhood. It was on the radio and everything. The police were looking for Neto's wildcat. Once, Neto had a sprained ankle and I went to his apartment to treat it. He had been living there for three months and he never made the bed or did the laundry. His dirty clothes were stacked from the floor to the ceiling in one corner of his room. The place was a war zone.

BILLY KELLER: The other guys knew how to handle Neto. Freddie Lewis was our go-getter. He was very serious about the game. He would set up Roger for his shots on the wing. Then Freddie would get the ball to Mel under the basket and Freddie would talk to Neto, trying to keep Neto concentrating. It was funny; it was like Freddie started the whole thing. Not only was he the point guard, but he invariably took the first shot of the game. It was like we said, "Okay, Freddie got a basket, now we're ready." When I joined the team in 1969, it was like hopping on the bandwagon and letting these guys pull me along, because they were so tight with each other and had developed a winning system.

DAVE CRAIG: After McGinnis joined the team, you had a big five who hung out together—Brown, Daniels, Neto, Lewis and George. There was a trip to Dallas where we had a break in the schedule and were there for three days. I never saw those guys except at practice. Then I had to go to Neto's room, and these guys had a three-day card game going. They loved Kentucky Fried Chicken and that was all they ate for three days—I could tell because all the boxes were piled in one corner and Neto's clothes were in the other corner of the room.

BOB NETOLICKY: We just had a great time. We would tease Slick about his smoking, because he didn't want his wife to know that he smoked. Now, I don't know if any basketball players smoke. But back then, we didn't know how dangerous smoking really was. At halftime, you'd see Roger Brown, George McGinnis and Darnell Hillman almost in a frenzy looking for their cigarette packs. Right after a game, you'd almost always see McGinnis and Roger with a cigarette. And of course, Slick puffed away like a steam engine, then he begged us not to tell his wife.

BILLY KELLER: Neto saw himself as the Joe Namath of Indianapolis and he even started his own bar, Neto's, which was in the Meadows Shopping Area. For a couple of years, it became the place to go after a game. Most of the players from both teams would stop by and the place would be packed with fans, who knew that the players would be there. A couple of times, I saw James Garner there after a game. He was a very hot actor back then and he liked basketball, so he'd come see the Pacers. Neto wandered around, acted like he thought the owner should act and everybody had a great time. The bar expressed Neto's view of life.

DAVE CRAIG: Neto's bar was a perfect extension of Slick's rule that everybody get together for at least one drink after a game. Now we all had a place to go. When the team was winning, the fans would line up around the block to get in, but Neto would make a big show of letting the Pacers' people go right to the front of the line and up to the bar.

BOB NETOLICKY: The bar was a den of iniquity. It was sort of a psychedelic place patterned after Joe Namath's bar in New York. A couple of friends of mine wanted to get into the bar business and use my name, so we opened a place about four blocks from the old Fairgrounds Coliseum. Some fans would leave our games at the half and then walk the four blocks to get in line so they could get a good seat at the bar after the game. The building held about 300 people. We had a dance floor, a live band and a big basketball over the bar. We had a lot of red, white and blue basketballs and pictures of the players, race car drivers and other celebrities. It was really a nice little nightclub. For a few years about every girl in town came there, and that brought in a lot of guys.

DAVE CRAIG: When the Pacers were winning, the guys owned the town. Neto had the bar, Roger was elected to the city council, Slick made a lot of commercials and all the guys had so many requests for appearances that they had to turn down some of that extra money. Indiana loves its basketball players and that is why Slick, Billy Keller, Neto, Roger, Mel and McGinnis all still live there.

The more those teams won, the wilder some of the guys got. In the early 1970s, Daniels, Brown, McGinnis and some of the other guys started to think they were cowboys. Mel was from Detroit, but when he went to college in New Mexico, he got interested in horses. Then he bought a farm outside of Indianapolis and he had a bunch of the players out there, riding horses with him. Guys would come to practice all caked with dust and mud because they had been riding horses for a couple of hours. They rode through the rain, through rivers; they were crazy.

Then they started dressing like cowboys, and I'm not just talking about the hats and boots. They wore pistols and holsters like something out of "Gunsmoke." There were nights when they went out riding and didn't come back until daylight.

BILLY KELLER: We had a valuables bag where we stored our rings, watches, wallets and that kind of stuff. When those guys got on the cowboy kick, Dave Craig would open that valuables bag and you'd see a couple of holsters and 6-shooters right in there with all the wallets and watches. A couple of times, I walked into the dressing room and there were Mel and Roger, pulling pistols on each other like it was the O.K. Corral. They never shot at each other, but they waved the guns around, sometimes even wrestled with each other on the floor.

DAVE CRAIG: These guys were playing "Cowboys" as if they were kids. They would hide behind corners, or climb on top of the locker, draw their guns and do the "Bang, bang, you're dead" routine. Finally, I told Slick, "We've got to get these guns out of the dressing room before somebody gets hurt."

Slick thought the whole thing was pretty funny and said, "Nah, those guys are using guns that aren't loaded."

But one day, the guys were messing around and one of the guns went off. Thank God no one was hurt, but then we had to pass a rule that if you brought your gun to the game, you had to check it at the dressing room door.

BOB NETOLICKY: People who didn't know us thought our locker room was a little spooky, what with all the guns hanging on the wall. I mean, you'd walk into our dressing room and run into Mel Daniels holding a .45—it makes you wonder.

DICK TINKHAM: As owners of the team, we wondered if the guys were getting out of hand with all the cowboy stuff, but then we said, "Hey, we're winning. The fans love them. We don't care what they do as long as they play hard and don't shoot each other."

BILLY KELLER AND RICK MOUNT

Keller and Mount spent two years together in the backcourt at Purdue. Mount was the player everyone knew—Indiana's Mr. Basketball in 1966 and the first prep player ever to be on the cover of Sports Illustrated. *He was the 1969 Big Ten Player of the Year and averaged 33.3 points, second in the nation to Pete Maravich. Keller was the 5-foot-10, 180-pound guard at Purdue who threw Mount the ball. He was Nobody's All-American. The Pacers signed Keller in 1969, Mount a year later. Mount lasted only two years with the Pacers. Coach Slick Leonard was critical of Mount's defense and lack of speed. Mount then played for Kentucky, Utah and Memphis. Keller spent seven years in the ABA, all with Indiana. Ironically, Keller and Mount had the same career scoring average (11.8) and shooting percentage (43 percent). Keller was a 34 percent shooter from 3-point range and averaged three attempts a game, usually while serving as the Pacers' third guard. Mount averaged less than one 3-point attempt per game and shot 32 percent from that range. Keller's career came to an end because of a knee injury in 1976, when he averaged a career-high 14.2 points.*

DICK TINKHAM: The only reason we signed Billy Keller was as bait to hook Rick Mount a year later. Billy was considered Mount's best friend on the Purdue team; they played together in the backcourt and we wanted an edge so we could get to land Mount. Mike Storen had real doubts about Keller—he was only 5-foot-10, he was a fireplug-looking guy who seemed too slow. I said, "Forget that. Let's just sign him, keep him around for a year and we'll use him to help us with Mount." So we signed Billy for $12,500 and no one in the organization really thought he could play. But Billy came to training camp, worked hard, and Slick Leonard fell in love with him. Then the season came and the fans saw how Billy played all out, diving for loose balls and everything, and they loved him. Suddenly, for $12,500 we had our own Pete Rose, our "Charlie Hustle." He turned out to be a fabulous guy, a credit to the franchise and a damn good player. Who ever would have believed that Billy Keller would become a better player and a better 3-point shooter than Rick Mount?

BILLY KELLER: Rick Mount had a very positive effect on my career. He gave me an opportunity to be recognized and to get a tryout with the Pacers. I was drafted by Indiana and by Milwaukee of the NBA in the seventh round. I even talked to the Bucks, but I decided my best chance was with the Pacers because I was known in Indiana and that might work in my favor.

I was fortunate, because Slick Leonard liked me right from the start. When I came to my first training camp, I was in midseason physical condition and I was way ahead of everyone else, which helped me make a good immediate impression. I really didn't worry that much about making the team. No one expected much out of me, so whatever I did looked very good. It was the total opposite from what Rick went through a year later with the Pacers.

MIKE STOREN: As the years went on, Billy Keller became an alter ego for Rick Mount. By that, I mean that Billy was a Slick Leonard–type player who would fight you for every inch on the floor. He was the definition of "scrappy." Because he was so small, no one thought he could do anything, so when he made a good play, people said, "They can talk all they want about Mount, but the real player is Keller."

DICK TINKHAM: We thought that Mount would be perfect for our franchise. He was a local hero who became a national star, yet he wanted to stay home and play in Indiana. He also was a great shooter, which was something we needed.

We set out to get Mount even before his senior year, when we asked the league to hold a special draft.

The league asked why and we said we couldn't tell them. We said we wanted to have a draft for the guys who were going to become college seniors that season, even though the college season hadn't started.

The ABA loved to hold drafts for anything, because it was a good excuse for everyone to go to New York and then go drinking at "21" afterwards. So they called a meeting and we had a draft. We were the defending ABA champs, yet we got the first pick in the draft, which made no sense. But we got the first pick because we were the ones who wanted the draft—that was ABA logic.

So we got together for the draft. We stood up and said, "Indiana drafts Rick Mount."

All the other owners were there, nodding their heads and saying, "Listen to that; they must have Mount signed already. So that's why they wanted the draft."

We hadn't even talked to Mount. He had all these Purdue people shielding him from the pro teams and we couldn't get near him. It seemed like Mount had 18 guys around him keeping agents and pro teams away. We couldn't get through on the phone to him. The Purdue people told us that if we came on campus to talk to Mount, we'd be shot. All this was going on before Mount's senior season.

Nonetheless, we wanted everyone in the ABA to think we had signed Rick so that no other team would try to get the kid.

After Mike Storen and I picked Mount, we left the draft, because we had what we wanted. Then a huge fight broke out because several teams wanted the rights to Pete Maravich, and no one else even made a pick. So that was the end of what later was called "the Rick Mount draft."

We finally did meet with Mount after his senior season, and the thing that bothered me was that the kid couldn't express himself very well. I was involved in about 95 percent of the player signings during the history of the Pacers and if a player was so introverted that he couldn't talk, I didn't want to sign him. Tom Burleson of North Carolina State was a prime example. Tom just didn't have anything to say—nothing at all. He had about eight representatives and they all said, "How y'all doin'?" We got a bad feeling from all that and faded out, letting the NBA have him, and Burleson was a backup for most of his career.

Well, Mount didn't have much to say, either. But the kid averaged 35 points a game in college, the entire state was in love with him. We just had to sign him.

Mount signed what was announced as a "million-dollar deal for five years." In typical ABA fashion, it wasn't a million dollars at all. In real cash, he received $40,000 annually for five years, for a total of $200,000. He also had a Dolgoff Plan (see pages 177–78) that paid him $50,000 a year for 20 years, starting in 1991. Mount signed on March 9, 1971, two days after his last college game.

MIKE STOREN: Even though we were kept away from Mount until his last college game, we had gotten to know his high school coach, his family and his friends, and we already had Billy Keller on the team. We recruited him like a college would recruit a high school kid.

When he agreed to sign, we set it up so that he would sign the contract at 6 P.M., and it was televised live across the state on all the news shows. We played it for all the publicity we could get.

DAVE CRAIG: There was such a big deal made about Mount's signing that I know it bothered some of the players. In the two years before Rick, we made it to the ABA finals in 1969 and then won the title in 1970. The guys felt like they were a great team without Mount, so why should he be viewed as the franchise savior? The franchise already was in great shape. Also, much was made of his million-dollar contract or whatever, and I know some of the players were bothered by the fact that he was making more money than they were. So when he showed up, he got a very cold reception from a number of the veterans.

BILLY KELLER: I don't think that Mike Storen and Slick Leonard were on the same page when it came to Mount. Mount wasn't Slick's kind of player. Slick didn't look at Rick and say, "Here's a guy who is weak defensively, but he can really shoot it. Let's get him some plays where he can take shots." Slick saw no reason to change the offense of a championship team to accommodate anyone, and that made sense to me. But it also worked against Rick, because he needed the picks to get off his shots.

MIKE STOREN: When I saw Rick Mount at Purdue, he seemed like a natural for us. The 3-point play was made for him, because he had as much range on his jumper as anyone who has ever played this game. He also was an All-American boy, a genuinely good person, and the entire state worshipped him.

Then he came to Slick Leonard, who was probably considered the best outside shooter to ever come out of the state until the advent of Rick Mount. Leonard was a very proud, volatile, fiery guy. Rick was an introvert, whose personality needed to be handled with kid gloves. He was a fragile person, very sensitive and prone to going into a shell a little bit.

Well, Slick never liked Rick from the start and he never gave Rick a chance. He immediately labeled Mount a lousy defensive player and Slick wouldn't let up on it. Yes, Rick wasn't a good defensive player, but very few scorers are. In fact, Slick Leonard was never much of a defensive player in his career. Until Slick Leonard came along, no one had ever questioned Rick Mount's basketball ability. Instead of getting right in Slick's face, which is what most of the Pacers did when he challenged them, Rick withdrew. He was not the kind of person to go up to Slick and try to tear his head off.

DICK TINKHAM: I don't think Slick wanted Mount; Mike Storen just signed him. Then Mike left to take the job as GM in Kentucky and Slick was stuck with Mount. Slick was a hard-driving, two-fisted guy who coddled no one. In college, all Mount had to do was shoot. He couldn't play defense and he didn't fight, which is what it meant to be a Pacer under Slick Leonard.

BILLY KELLER: I was probably as close to Rick as anyone when he was at school, but I'm not sure how close we really were. With the exception of his wife, I don't know if anyone ever was close to Rick. He liked to hunt, to fish, and to be with Donna. The pro basketball environment, which consisted of a lot of travel and meeting and dealing with strangers, bothered him. He also had trouble socializing with the guys on the team, because it wasn't Rick's nature to go out. Some people thought it was because Rick considered himself "better" or "above" the rest of us, but that wasn't it at all. He was just plain shy.

SLICK LEONARD: Rick was under a lot of pressure because he was playing so close to home, and I think that was his biggest problem—dealing with unrealistic expectations.

MEL DANIELS: Rick was a loner and they roomed him with Neto, which was good for Rick because Neto made everybody have a good time. Rick did start to loosen up and played better in his second year with us, but I just think he was under too much pressure playing close to home. The fans expected him to score 35 a game like he did in college, and no one could come into the pros and do that. The fans almost loved him to death in college, then they felt he let them down as a pro. When the newspapers started knocking him, the fans booed. It was rough on the guy, but he was a player who was in the wrong place.

Mount averaged 6.6 points and shot 39 percent as a rookie in 1970–71, and raised those numbers to 14.2 points and 47 percent in his second season. Then the Pacers sold him to Kentucky.

MIKE STOREN: I always liked Rick and I kept getting him. I signed him when I was in Indiana. I traded for him when I was in Kentucky and then I traded for him again when I went to Memphis. His real problem was injuries. He was a tightly muscled guy who kept having hamstring and groin pulls. This was before we knew all about stretching exercises to prevent that sort of thing. He did a decent job for me in Kentucky *(14.5 points, 46 percent shooting in 1972–73).*

DAVE TWARDZIK: When a player like Mount becomes a pro, he discovers that he is put on a pedestal, just as he was in college, but the fans don't understand the difference between college and pro ball. Some guys are just destined to be great college players but ordinary pros, and Mount was one of them. But the fans who love the player so much have a tough time dealing with his failure. Instead of saying, "Well, he just reached his level," they blame the coach for not playing him more or using him right. Or they say the other guys on the team are jealous of him. That goes on for a while, then the fans begin to realize—our college star just isn't that good. That's when they turn on the player and it can be ugly. I've seen guys in that situation get crucified by the fans.

CHARLIE WILLIAMS: Mount was one of those guys who came into the league with a lot of hype. He was supposed to "make the ABA." Guys such as myself who had been in the league from the start felt that the ABA already was "made." We made the sacrifices to build the league. None of this was Rick's fault, but I know that it fired me up when I played him. It was natural to want to put the phenom in his place, and I bet every guy who guarded Rick in his first few years felt the same way. Also, Rick needed a pick to get open and we just made a point to switch men and jump out on Rick to take away his shot. Leave him alone and he never missed, but guard him and he was in big trouble.

TOM NISSALKE: By the time he was 28, Rick had had his fill of pro basketball. He just didn't want to play anymore. When I became the coach in Houston of the NBA after the merger, I tried to get Rick to play for me in 1976. For all his weaknesses, he remained a great shooter, and at 6-foot-4, he could get off a shot in the right system. He seemed interested in coming to camp with us and we had a ticket for him and everything, then he changed his mind and said he just didn't want to travel anymore. And that was it. He never played again.

MIKE STOREN: If you think about Mount's family, it's a remarkable story, truly a small-town Indiana basketball story. His father was a basketball star at Lebanon High and then Rick followed in his dad's footsteps at the same high school. Rick's dad was his mentor, and when

Rick beat his father in 1-on-1 for the first time, his dad supposedly went into the house and stayed there for two days. Then Rick's son became a star in Lebanon. Three generations of Mounts playing at the same high school; it's almost eerie. But when Rick got out of that environment, he had a hard time coping.

SLICK LEONARD: I don't mean to take anything away from Mount, but it didn't hurt Rick that he played on the same college team as Billy Keller. Billy was one of the most underrated college players ever and he became a damn good pro because he understood what it took to be a pro—he had heart, an overwhelming desire and toughness. God, he was a tough little player.

GENE LITTLES: As players, Mount and Keller were as different as they could be. Mount shied away from contact, but that Keller . . . he'd put that squat body of his on you and bump you with his chest with every step you took. He loved to body people. He also had a good 3-point shot and he fit in with the rest of the Pacers, because they were such a physical team.

BOB NETOLICKY: Billy Keller ended up filling the role that was supposed to go to Mount. Billy was the guy who took the heat off of our big guys or off Roger Brown when he was double-teamed. If I got the ball under the basket and the defense surrounded me, I knew that Billy was camped out there right behind the 3-point line. I'd throw him the ball and bingo, he'd drill the 3-pointer. Night in and night out, Billy kept defenses honest against us. Billy wasn't as tall or as talented as Rick, but he was tougher and he worked harder. Those are just the facts. And Billy was as wide as he was tall. He wasn't supposed to be a pro, but he became a damn good one. And the fans loved him, because he was so nice. He was the hometown kid who made good, and every mother wished she had Billy as a son or a son-in-law.

BIG GEORGE

The Pacers signed George McGinnis in 1971. He was a 20-year-old sophomore from Indiana University, and his signing by the Pacers was crucial to keeping the team on top. He joined the team in the fifth ABA season, when the core group of Pacers—Mel Daniels, Roger Brown, Freddie Lewis and Bob Netolicky—had started to show some age. At 6-foot-8 and 240 pounds, he not only rivaled Daniels in strength, but had graceful moves worthy of Roger Brown. He holds Pacers team records for points in a game (58), rebounds (37) and scoring average (29.8 in 1974–75). He was an Indiana Mr. Basketball at Washington High in Indianapolis in 1969. As a sophomore at Indiana, he led the Big Ten in scoring (29.9) and rebounding (14.4) before turning pro in 1971. In the 1975 playoffs, when McGinnis put the Pacers on his broad shoulders and carried them into the finals, he played in 18 postseason games and averaged 32 points, 16 rebounds and 8.2 assists. After four years with the Pacers, McGinnis jumped to Philadelphia of the NBA for the 1975–76 season. He returned to the Pacers in 1980. By then, he was 30, and his legs and skills were gone from all the minutes and the pounding he took on the court. He retired having averaged 24 points in four ABA seasons and 17 points in seven NBA seasons.

DICK TINKHAM: McGinnis wasn't the most difficult player we signed with the Pacers, but it was perhaps the trickiest signing we had. The problem was that George had just finished his sophomore year at IU, and while we were certain he wanted to turn pro, because he had told everyone that, we had to be careful. We couldn't make it look as if the local pro team was luring a player away from IU early, because that would have been terrible public relations for us.

At this time, IU had just hired a new basketball coach, Bobby Knight. At least a half-dozen times, we insisted to George that he talk to Knight before making any decision about the ABA. But George wouldn't do that. In fact, he got so sick of hearing us say, "Talk to Coach Knight," that George said, "If you don't sign me, I'm gonna sign with Kentucky or somebody else. I've got options."

At that point, we knew we had to make a move to get George signed, because it would have been an even bigger blunder to see McGinnis sign with Kentucky. We reached an agreement on a contract, then we told McGinnis, "Look, George, you're only 20. That means you're a minor. We signed your contract and we're going to give it to you. That is not a violation of NCAA rules. You have until training camp to decide what you want to do." George didn't sign the contract, but he had hired an agent, which basically made him a pro.

Meanwhile, people were coming to me and saying they were going to sue the Pacers because George had signed a contract while he was still an underclassman.

I said, "As far as I know, George McGinnis hasn't signed a contract with Indiana and he hasn't broken any NCAA rules."

Which was true. George had a Pacer contract, but he didn't sign it. Eventually, he signed with us and went to training camp, but it was his idea. I won't lie; sure, we encouraged him to sign. Our standard line was that a merger with the NBA is coming and when it does, you'll go into a common draft and you'll have to sign with the team that picks you. But if you sign now, you can pick the team you want. George was from Indianapolis and wanted to play for the Pacers. By signing, he could play where he wanted.

McGinnis signed a three-year deal for $50,000 annually. He got a $45,000 signing bonus and some perks, including $20,000 to buy three cars.

DAVE CRAIG: When McGinnis signed with us, he was 20 and making a lot of money, at least by the standards of that time. There was some initial resentment from people, because George was making more than a lot of guys on the team. But it wasn't long before George became one of the guys. He could really play, and the veterans sensed that. On the Pacers, the big thing was winning, and it was obvious that George would help them win. At heart, George McGinnis will always be a big kid, and he fit right in with Netolicky, Mel Daniels, Roger Brown and those guys.

BOB NETOLICKY: When George came to us, he was a pampered college star and really still a child in a man's body. But that body—for a basketball player, it was a superman's body. He was 6-foot-8, 240 pounds and could run faster and jump higher than anyone we had. He was as strong as Mel Daniels. While he was immature, he was a good guy and we all liked him. The Pacers liked anyone we thought had their heart in the right place and who was talented, even if it meant that he might take some of your playing time.

BILLY KELLER: George was smart in that he is a very social person, and that was a big difference between George and Rick Mount. He made a point to get along with the guys. And he was such a talent. There was no system that brought out the best in George, because George was best when there was no system, when he was left on his own to create things, to see some light and go to it. We would start to run a play, then George would go in a different direction when he saw some daylight, flash in that direction, get the ball and then go 1-on-1. Slick sensed this and he let George do pretty much what he liked on offense. George had his best years under Slick, because Slick knew how to get the most out of him.

SLICK LEONARD: Whenever you add a player who you expect to play a significant role, there is some anxiety on the part of the rest of the team, especially a team as close as the Pacers. It was, "Who is this new guy you're bringing into the family?" George had his weaknesses. His practice habits weren't the best, but he really played big in the playoffs. I never had any complaints about George McGinnis. I know what he meant to us and this franchise. You had to be patient with George and show him a lot of love, but if you did, he really responded.

TOM NISSALKE: It's hard to believe now, but there were serious arguments in the ABA about who was better—McGinnis or Julius Erving. That was the kind of talent a young McGinnis had. He was a forerunner to Karl Malone, the powerfully built big forward who had basketball skills, too. If anything, McGinnis had more basketball talent than Malone, but Malone has a much better work ethic.

GEORGE IRVINE: There was a natural rivalry between McGinnis and Erving, because they both came into the league in 1971. In fact, it seemed like there were games where George was trying to be like Julius, using all those one-handed passes, palming the ball and flashy stuff like that. But as George matured, he junked a lot of that one-handed garbage and began to play solid, physical basketball. I still don't think there was ever a player his size and that quick, and when he got everything together as he did in 1974–75, he was totally dominating. He became a monster, and that was when the McGinnis/Erving comparisons heated up, because they shared the 1975 MVP award. As great as Julius was, and I played with Julius in Virginia, in 1975 McGinnis had a better year.

Erving averaged 27.9 points, 10.8 rebounds, 5.1 assists and shot 50 percent. McGinnis averaged 29.8 points, 14.3 rebounds, 6.3 assists and shot 46 percent.

SLICK LEONARD: In 1975, George carried us into the finals against Kentucky. All the guys from our great teams were gone—Mel Daniels, Freddie Lewis, Bob Netolicky. Roger Brown was at the end of his career and coming off the bench. It was George, Billy Knight, Don Buse, Darnell Hillman and Len Elmore who made up the core of that team. But it really was just George in the playoffs. He wouldn't let us lose until we ran into that team Hubie Brown had in Kentucky. They just had too many weapons.

HUBIE BROWN: It's hard for me to imagine anyone having a better playoffs than George McGinnis did in the first two rounds of 1975. No one could do a thing with him. Night after night, he got 40 points and 20 rebounds. When we played the Pacers, we geared our whole defense to neutralize McGinnis. I'm not saying we stopped him—he scored in the 20s most games—but we kept him from single-handedly beating us.

SLICK LEONARD: After the 1975 season, George jumped to Philadelphia. We just didn't have the money to keep him, and that killed me because he was at his peak. I don't blame George—you do what you have to do to support your family—but I don't think he ever enjoyed basketball as much again after he left the Pacers. He had a couple of good years in Philly, then his game went down pretty fast.

ROD THORN: When George came to Philly (1975–76), they had an awful team and he played great. He led them to the playoffs and he was the big star. But then it changed when the Sixers signed Doctor J and everyone else. I think George had to be upset when Julius was signed. It wasn't personal. But when he was in the ABA, George was always compared with Doctor J. Then he jumped leagues and Julius ended up on his team. That just killed him, no matter how much Julius tried to get along with George. And after that, George's career went down quickly.

SLICK LEONARD: I think the fact that George didn't go 100 percent in practice caught up with him. When a player of his size who relies so much on his legs and athleticism starts to lose it, he can lose it fast. Everything goes all at once. I brought him back to the Pacers in 1980. He was only 30 years old and I thought if we were together again in Indiana, I could get a couple of good years out of George, but he had just lost it.

BILLY KELLER: It hurt to see George play at the end, because he had meant so much to the team. But he was playing for Jack McKinney, who ran a very structured offense—it was pick after pick after pick. That just wasn't for George, and poor George had trouble even making a foul shot. The shame is that the George McGinnis at the end of his career is the image many people have of him, and that wasn't George. For years, he carried this team like no other one player ever did before or after. That is how I'll always remember him.

o   o   o

BILLY KELLER: I never made a great deal of money in basketball. The last contract I signed was for three years—$60,000, $70,000 and $80,000. But most of the guys didn't make that much with the Pacers. I don't believe that the guys on those teams thought much about the money.

Instead, we came away with this tremendous feeling of love for each other and the fantastic support we received from the people of Indianapolis. You look at the situation—the franchise was strong, the coaching was strong, and the players were strong-willed, determined people. And the whole thing was a lot of fun. That's what I always think of when someone mentions the Pacers.

MEL DANIELS: While I was an assistant with the Pacers, I'd look at those guys and think that they had no idea what we went through so they could be in the NBA and have a beautiful place like Market Square Arena to play in. Now, they worry too much about money and not enough about pride. We won three championships and I believe our total playoff take for those three years combined was $11,000. I'm not going to dwell on the fact that the old days were better, but in the case of the Pacers, they were, because the fans could identify with the team and the players worked harder and cared more. We had an emotional attachment to the team and the league. We felt we were the Celtics of the ABA.

SLICK LEONARD: I used to tell the guys that when you are in a championship series and you walk down that tunnel from the dressing room to the court, it's almost as if you're walking down the "Tunnel of Life." The friendships you make, the camaraderie you feel, the things you accomplish—no one can ever take those away from you. It will be something that will bind you to your teammates for the rest of your life. In my eight years in the ABA, five times our teams went down that tunnel and three times we came back as winners. You talk to the guys from those teams and you know that something special happened to them, what I talked about in terms of the "Tunnel of Life" wasn't a bunch of crap. It's something we'll always share.

Part II

MIDDLE GAME

Star Wars

Not only did the ABA give us the 3-point shot, the Slam Dunk Contest and a faster-paced game, it gave us 21-year-old millionaires—even 19-year-old millionaires who left college before their four years of eligibility were up to turn pro. What the ABA did was bring big money into pro basketball. It was a fun time to be a college basketball star. As the late Pete Maravich said, "It's neat to talk to the ABA, because you can pick the team you want to play for."

MIKE STOREN: We were in a war with the NBA, and it was being fought on two fronts.

The first was for the kids coming out of college. The NBA had their draft and we had our drafts. I say "drafts," as in more than one draft, because we had secret drafts, drafts for underclassmen, drafts for seniors, drafts for everything and everybody imaginable. Until the ABA, the NBA had the college players in the palm of their hands. If you were drafted by the Boston Celtics, you signed with Boston or you didn't sign at all. Europe wasn't a factor as it is today. The NBA was the only game in town and they knew it.

The second front was with established players. We convinced NBA stars such as Rick Barry, Zelmo Beaty and Billy Cunningham to jump to our league, while they took Charlie Scott, John Brisker and guys like that from us.

The result of this fight for players was that the salaries went through the roof and a lot of guys hung out a shingle declaring themselves agents and got very rich.

RON GRINKER: The bidding wars brought on by the advent of the ABA showed just what selfish whores the owners were. In my mind, the people who were really stupid were the NBA owners. Those guys wouldn't share, as the ABA did. They were fighting the ABA and each other because they were so greedy. Yes, the ABA was the first to start throwing around the "big money." But the money really wasn't that big. It was paper money, annuities, the famed Dolgoff Plan.

177

I'll explain how the ABA did business, with Jim Ard as an example. Ard was a 6-foot-9 forward out of the University of Cincinnati who was a first-round pick by Seattle, the sixth pick in the entire 1970 draft. I represented Ard, and I talked to the Sonics and we were making some progress when Marty Blackman and Steve Arnold approached me. Blackman and Arnold were agents for the ABA. They went to individual players' agents on behalf of the ABA.

Marty told me, "We have a $1.4 million contract for Jim Ard. We don't know what ABA team will draft him, but the league will guarantee the contract for the $1.4 million. Just sign it and we'll figure out the team later."

In this case, we didn't agree to a deal until we knew what ABA team wanted Ard. It turned out to be the New York Nets. We got to talking and yes, the offer was worth $1.4 million—eventually.

Here was the deal:

Bonus: $25,000.
1970–71: $45,000.
1971–72: $50,000.
1972–73: $60,000.
1973–74: $70,000.

So the actual cash was $250,000 over four years. Ard also had a Nike shoe contract for $1,500.

How was it worth $1.4 million?

The Nets put $8,000 a year for 10 years in a Dolgoff Plan, which is really an annuity that Ard would collect from the age of 41 until he's 65. The remaining $1.15 million is paid out over 24 years starting in 1989, when Ard turned 41. Despite the fact that this was a long payout, the ABA paid Ard more in real cash than Seattle offered, so we took it.

But what happened was that the NBA saw numbers like $1.4 million to Jim Ard and they started paying in real cash, not in the long, deferred payouts the ABA used. It was the NBA that cut its own throat by offering real money when what Jim Ard really got was $250,000 and a Dolgoff Plan. The ABA paid in paper money, but the NBA responded to that by paying in real dollars, and it nearly bankrupted both leagues.

DICK TINKHAM: We in Indiana were the first to use the Dolgoff Plan, and we had it to ourselves for the first two years of the league before the rest of the ABA found out about it. The idea is very simple. You pick a mutual fund or any sort of growth fund. You pay into it for 10 years, then you wait more years and the player begins to collect on it from year

21 to year 40. You put $10,000 a year in for 10 years, and in 20 years the thing could be worth over $1 million. That's the nature of how money grows.

MIKE STOREN: The ABA has come under a lot of criticism for the Dolgoff Plan, but it's not fair. A lot of players are living off that money today. It is real money, albeit very stretched out. About every big-name ABA player was paid in this manner—Rick Mount, Dan Issel, Mike Pratt, Jim McDaniels.

PETE NEWELL: I never liked how the ABA did business, and it's not just sour grapes. I know that when I was general manager of the Lakers in the early 1970s, I offered players contracts worth more than the ABA was paying, yet some of them signed with the ABA. Why? I'm convinced that the ABA was paying agents under the table to send kids to their league. The players never knew they were being sold down the river, but they were.

WAYNE EMBRY: I know the ABA was paying off agents. They had to be for those kids to agree to some of the outrageous contracts that they did, contracts that were good for no one but the ABA and the agent. The kid wouldn't see most of his money for 30 years, if at all. I was offended by their business practices.

RON GRINKER: I think the NBA totally mishandled the competition from the ABA, but those who say that the ABA paid agents are right. I know of several cases where an agent double-dipped. By that, I mean the agent took his cut from the kid after doing the contract, then he took money on the side from the ABA to deliver the kid. I'm not saying all cases were like that, or even most, but it did happen sometimes.

STEVE ARNOLD: NBA people were always very sore losers. Their egotism wouldn't permit them to believe that a player would sign with the ABA, but players did because the ABA was far more organized. Instead of individual ABA teams trying to sign players, the ABA itself would sign the players and pool all of its resources to pay them. It would sign them to league contracts so that if a player signed with a franchise and that team went out of business, he would still be paid by the league. It gave the player more security. Also, if a player had a preference of where he wanted to play, the ABA could see to it that he played there. So Dan Issel went to the University of Kentucky and wanted to stay in Kentucky. Great; his rights go to the Colonels. It was just smart business.

We used the Dolgoff Plan a lot. You'd put $5,000 a year in a company like Prudential Insurance for 10 years, then wait 10 more years and that $50,000 you invested becomes something like $150,000. The NBA would say, "How do you know that the ABA will be around in 10 or 20 years?" I said that we didn't know, but we were sure that Prudential would, and we insured the contracts with them.

CARL SCHEER: The NBA was also signing players to league contracts. We would sign guys before our draft and then tell them that their contracts would be honored by the team that took them in the NBA draft. I'm not comfortable saying exactly who signed early like that, but I assure you that players did, and I know because I worked as an assistant to NBA Commissioner Walter Kennedy from 1968 to '70. Everything was cloak-and-dagger and we kept things very confidential. There were rumors that the ABA had infiltrated our league office, that we were being watched by spies who wanted to know what players we were after. We even had code names. Different players were assigned colors. I remember that we called Rudy Tomjanovich "Green."

I was in on the signing of Jo Jo White for the Celtics. We were going to meet with White's coach from Kansas, Ted Owens, in a motel room in Lawrence. After setting up the meeting, several of us were sitting in our NBA office in New York talking about Jo Jo White when some guys came in to paint the walls. We started interrogating the painter. We thought the guy was an ABA spy, but after about 10 minutes we decided the guy was all right, he was a painter. But that was how paranoid we were.

DENNIS MURPHY: We did have spies in the NBA office, guys who called us with information about what players the league wanted to sign. And they were spying on us. We actually found that our league meeting was bugged in Denver. We brought in a guy to sweep for bugs and he found one in a chandelier. Everybody wanted to know what everybody else was doing.

ROY BOE: When I came into the ABA in 1969, there were very few owners of any real substance. The Dallas and Kentucky teams had a lot of money behind them, but they didn't spend it. Indiana had some very creative guys, like Dick Tinkham, but they really weren't well off financially. You'd hear a lot of guys talk about knocking the NBA on its ass, but after they lost their million, they didn't want to be aggressive anymore. But you look at the teams that won, the teams that had good talent—San Antonio, Kentucky, Indiana, Denver and New York—and you'll see that we were very aggressive.

Memphis drafted Larry Kenon in 1973, but they didn't have the money to pay him. I told the league that I thought I could jump in there and sign Kenon with the Nets. The league said not to worry about Memphis; if I could sign Kenon, just sign him. Donald Dell was Kenon's agent. I spent a day with him and got the deal done. That was how it worked. You didn't pay much attention to who drafted a player. If you wanted a guy, you just signed him.

STEVE ARNOLD: The real breakthrough for the ABA came when we decided to sign underclassmen. One day, I said to the league, "What about going after guys who aren't seniors?"

They said, "How can you sign a kid if he's still in college?"

I said, "Suppose a kid goes to MIT. He's a genius and IBM wants him to work with them after his junior year. Does IBM say, 'Wait a year and then come to work for us'? No; they say, 'Here's the offer, come to work for us now and we'll pay you to go to school later on.' Why are athletes any different than that kid at MIT?"

They started talking about NCAA rules.

I said, "Are the NCAA rules legal? Will they hold up in a court of law? What we are talking about is equal opportunity. A kid plays basketball and wants to make some money and support himself and his family. That's illegal? We're not talking about wholesale signings, just the select few we know can come into the league and make it at a younger age."

We talked about it some more. Then I said, "Let's call it a Hardship Case. We'll make an exception and sign an underclassman if he's a poor kid who can show that he has to support his family. The kid has that right, and I think the courts will agree with us."

That was what set the stage for signing Spencer Haywood.

SPENCER HAYWOOD: THE HARDSHIP CASE

When Spencer Haywood signed with the Denver Rockets in the fall of 1969, the NBA was enraged, the NCAA was enraged and the ABA had one of college basketball's premier talents without having to outbid the NBA. The 6-foot-9 Haywood had been a star on the 1968 U.S. Olympic team and then played the 1968–69 season at the University of Detroit as a sophomore. Instead of following the NCAA's "Four-Year Rule," meaning a player couldn't turn pro until his four years of college eligibility were up, Haywood signed after his sophomore season. Of course, lawsuits followed, and as was often the case in the ABA, Haywood spent as much time in court as on it. But the courts eventually ruled in the spring of 1971 that Haywood could turn pro anytime he wished, that the

"Four-Year Rule" had no basis in law and that athletes had a right to earn a living the same as anyone else. Haywood played for the Denver Rockets in 1969–70, leading the league in scoring (30 points) and rebounding (19.5) and was named Rookie of the Year and MVP for both the season and the All-Star Game. With Haywood, Denver had the second-best regular-season record in the ABA at 51–33, and that came after a 9–19 start. Unhappy with the two contracts he signed with Denver, Haywood left the ABA and signed with Seattle of the NBA for the 1970–71 season.

STEVE ARNOLD: Spencer was the first undergraduate we approached on behalf of the ABA. He was unhappy at the University of Detroit and pretty much bored by college competition. He felt he was ready for the pros and wanted to make some money for his family. *(Haywood averaged 32 points and 22 rebounds as a sophomore.)* To Spencer, it made absolutely no sense that he had to wait two more years.

Marty Blackman and I showed Spencer what the NBA was paying for first-round draft picks and we showed him what the ABA would offer. Spencer had his high school coach, Will Robinson, as his advisor. It was an easy, clear-cut deal. Denver's Bill Ringsby was the one ABA owner willing to pay for Spencer, so the ABA gave Denver the rights to Haywood. No one talked about competitive balance. It was, "Ringsby, you think you can sign Haywood, he's yours."

We never were Spencer's agents. We never took a fee from Spencer. We were representing the ABA and our offer was in line with what the NBA was paying its first-rounders.

On paper, Haywood signed a three-year, $450,000 deal. But it really was $50,000 a year for three years. Then he was to receive $15,000 a year for 20 years starting at age 40. It was the famed Dolgoff Plan at work.

MIKE STOREN: When the ABA signed Haywood, we knew the whole basketball world was about to go crazy. There was a group of us—Bill Ringsby, Dick Tinkham, Scott Arnold, Jack Dolph and myself—and we were trying to figure out what we should say about this. I can't recall who first came up with the term "Hardship Case," but one of us did. There was no legal research or anything, we just invented the term. So we came out and said that Spencer was a special case, he had to take care of his mother and his nine brothers and sisters. He was the breadwinner in the family and the ABA was being a bunch of great guys by giving Haywood a chance to take care of his family.

BOB RYAN: When Haywood turned pro, my opinion was the same as Red Auerbach's and virtually everyone else's in the NBA: we thought it was un-American, that it would tear down the structure of sports and would lead to chaos. It had nothing to do with Haywood's ability—he averaged 30 points. Nor was the constitutional question about his right to earn a living under consideration. Rather, it was changing the system. The sports world was a simple, uncomplicated place until the ABA came along and screwed things up. That was the prevailing view and it was mine for a long time.

AL BIANCHI: The ABA got to the players first, when they were younger and before they had a chance to show their stuff in the postseason All-Star Games and all that. We hustled and scouted and beat the NBA to the punch. That was what the NBA didn't like. They would say that we were "dirty . . . those kids need their education."

Come on.

Earl Foreman and I took a lot of heat for signing guys like Julius Erving and George Gervin. Supposedly we were corrupting these kids by giving them money, as if none of the college stars were being paid at the big-name schools. I got tired of hearing the criticism. When a reporter would tell me that some athletic director was knocking us, I'd tell the reporter to go into that man's office and ask him what percentage of his basketball players had graduated in the last 10 years. We gave Julius Erving and all the other players a bonus if they finished their degree, which was more incentive than the colleges would give them. In Julius's contract, we said that since he was short one year of his degree, if he wanted to go back we'd pay for the classes and when he got his diploma we'd give him $10,000.

JOE MULLANEY: I was with Memphis when we drafted David Thompson in 1973. The ABA had a special undergraduate draft and we took Thompson after his freshman year at North Carolina State. We didn't make a serious attempt to sign David, we just wanted to control his rights for the future. I got a scathing letter from Thompson's coach, Norm Sloan. He blasted us, called us all kinds of names.

I was amused by Norm's attitude. If a kid leaves after high school and signs a minor league baseball contract, then everyone is happy for him. If a kid does the same thing to join the PGA Tour, then that's great. But if the kid leaves his college basketball team early, it's supposed to be a felony. Why?

You can't tell me that Norm Sloan was worried about David Thompson's academics. But Thompson leaving would cost Sloan and N.C. State a lot of money. What was good for the kid wasn't the point; the point was what was good for the program, and what's good for the program was David Thompson playing four years at N.C. State.

Sloan's actions weren't unusual. They were the typical response from colleges. But what if someone had offered Sloan a million bucks to go to the pros? He would have left the next day and no one would have said a word except "Congratulations." But if a kid left early for a million bucks, people said, "That's stupid." If it was your son who had the million-dollar offer, you'd say, "Take the money, son, and I'll be your agent. Norm Sloan can take care of himself."

STEVE ARNOLD: There was this silent partnership between the NBA and the NCAA. The NBA agreed not to touch the college players until their eligibility was up. That way, the colleges could make money off them. The colleges gave the NBA a free farm system so the players could develop their skills for four years and then there was an orderly way for those players to turn pro—the NBA draft—without the NBA having to worry about anyone competing for the players' services. And all of this was done under the guise of "educating the student-athlete." The hypocrisy was unending.

MAX WILLIAMS: After Haywood signed, the colleges were up in arms. Johnny Dee of Notre Dame was the head of the NCAA Basketball Coaches Association and he wrote letters to every major coach not to allow ABA people on campus as a protest of Haywood's signing. George Mikan contacted the general managers of every ABA team and he told us to ask the players what they got over and above their scholarships and books. So I went to our team and all but two guys with Dallas were getting extras—payoffs, cars, things like that. Mikan then contacted the NCAA Coaches Association and said he would make all this information public if they didn't back off and let the ABA people in their gyms. Right after that, the letter banning the ABA was withdrawn.

MACK CALVIN: From the moment Spencer came into the league at 19 years old, he was an incredible physical specimen. He was a highly skilled, fully developed player. He could score at ease and he got a lot of rebounds. But he wasn't a guy you physically feared, because his game was more finesse. He preferred to shoot from the perimeter. He was graceful rather than intimidating.

GENE LITTLES: When I was at Carolina, Doug Moe drew the assignment of guarding Spencer, and that was when Doug was at the end of his career and having knee problems. I felt sorry for Doug because Spencer was bigger, faster, and obviously a lot younger. It drove Doug crazy, because he wasn't used to a guy scoring on him like that. Spencer was very cocky. He drove a big black custom-made Caddy, and that was in 1969 when guys in the ABA drove Chevies and Buicks because the big-money era hadn't started yet. Spencer lived in this high-class town house in Denver, where you had to go through a security guard to get inside. Nobody had a security guard back then. He was living like some guy who had been a superstar in the NBA for 10 years, and he was really just a junior in college. He spent a lot of money early and then he found out that his contract wasn't what he thought it was when he signed, so they had to give him another contract after a couple of months.

Until Haywood arrived, Denver's highest-paid player was Larry Jones at $23,000. In the first two years of the league, Jones was first-team all-ABA and a 25-point scorer. Haywood had three contracts in his year with Denver. His third and last with the Rockets was for $1.9 million for six years. He was advanced a $50,000 bonus. His contract called for a salary of $50,000 for the first two years, and $75,000 for the last four. That came out to $400,000 in cash. The remaining $1.5 million was to be paid out in a Dolgoff Plan at $75,000 annually over 20 years, starting when Haywood reached 40. But a few months later, Haywood said this deal wasn't enough. He wanted the $1.9 million paid over five years and he had hired Al Ross as his agent. Ross pulled his usual trick of hiding a player, this time at the agent's home in Los Angeles, but Haywood blew the cover by running in a local park with a shirt that read, "Denver Rockets."

STEVE JONES: A couple of Spencer's contracts were the kind we called "April Fools." It was announced as $1.9 million and everybody was floored by that because it sounded so big. But guess again; it was to be paid out for a long, long time. When Spencer found that out, he said, "Hey, that's not right. When do I get my money?" So he hired Al Ross, who promised to get Spencer a great deal with the NBA.

RON GRINKER: The other agents called Ross "The Pirate." He came out of nowhere and all of a sudden he had all these clients—other people's clients. He was a sharp dresser who used to hang out at the L.A. Forum. He had Haywood, John Brisker, Jim McDaniels and Charlie Scott.

DICK TINKHAM: When it became apparent that the ABA was going to lose Haywood if something wasn't done, we had a league meeting. Bill

Ringsby had been screaming and pounding his fist on the table for about an hour, trying to talk the league into helping him pay Haywood's contract. Tedd Munchak had just bought the Carolina Cougars. Munchak got tired of listening to it and said, "Ringsby, meet me in the hall."

Those guys went out of the room and came back a few minutes later.

Munchak said, "I've solved the problem. I've just bought Bill's franchise."

There was a long silence, and then reality set in. Someone said, "Hey, you can't do that. You can't own two teams at once."

So that deal fell through. There were a lot of crazy things going on. *(Seattle owner)* Sam Schulman and I were on the merger committee and Sam told me that if the NBA teams wouldn't support our merger agreement, he was going to sign Haywood, move his franchise to Los Angeles and join the ABA! He told *(Lakers owner)* Jack Kent Cooke that this was what he planned to do. He said he would move right into Cooke's backyard if Cooke didn't back him. But like everything else that was talked about and threatened, nothing came of it.

LENNY WILKENS: I was a player-coach in Seattle when Sam Schulman signed Spencer. Sam mentioned that he had an interest in Haywood. It wasn't something we talked about at great length. The next thing I knew, he had signed Spencer. When Spencer joined the team, he was very engaging, but you knew right away he was also very young. He drove a Cadillac with a Rolls-Royce front, a leather top and some kind of grotesque hood ornament. When he came to Seattle, he was a little more sedate and switched to a Mercedes. He wore long coats, big hats and liked the Detroit Motown look. He was a tremendous talent who needed stability in his life, but he was with so many coaches and so many teams that I don't think he ever reached his potential.

Haywood signed a six-year, $1.5 million deal with Seattle, all cash and no Dolgoff Plan. He played in the NBA for 12 years with five different teams, averaging 19.2 points and 9.4 rebounds. He was a four-time NBA All-Star and later played two seasons in Italy (1980–82) before retiring.

JIM CHONES: A HARDSHIP CASE SPEAKS

Jim Chones signed with the New York Nets in 1972 after his junior year at Marquette. This was one of the few cases where a college coach didn't complain about losing a player early. In a January 11, 1972, issue of Basketball Weekly, Marquette coach Al McGuire said, "I recruited Chones to win basketball games. He's the best big man I've ever had.

He's my meal ticket. But Jim has the right to take the money and run. My stomach is full, but he has to worry about where his next meal is coming from. I've looked in his refrigerator and in mine. Mine was full, his was empty."

JIM CHONES: I grew up in Racine, Wisconsin, which is 25 miles south of Milwaukee. I was a very good high school player, 6-foot-11 although I was only 155 pounds. I was getting recruited by everyone in the country, everyone but the black schools. I guess they saw my name was "Chones," and that's usually a Greek name, so they stayed away. I was very interested in Grambling because they had a great tradition, but I never heard from Grambling. Bill Fitch, who would later coach me with the Cavs, was at the University of Minnesota and he was recruiting me hard, but I wasn't interested in Minnesota. I made a visit to Michigan State and I liked that. Fitch told me, "If you don't go to Minnesota, you should play for Al McGuire at Marquette." But I hadn't heard much of anything from Marquette, and I was only 25 miles away.

Late in the recruiting season, Al McGuire called me and said, "On Friday, I'm going to come down to Racine and see you." They came to see me in my beat-up old house with the vinyl floors torn up and looking like a map of the United States. There were roaches crawling on the walls, wood splinters coming off the walls. As we were talking, the roaches were falling off the walls and dropping onto people.

I was totally embarrassed for Al McGuire to see how we were living. Al McGuire sat next to me in a beat-up chair. He said, "Look, we want you to come to Marquette and I can talk about education and all the other good things we have to offer, but the real thing for you to know is that if you do what we tell you, you can be a pro and get the hell out of all this shit."

When Al left our house, my dad loved him and he told me, "I want you to play for Al McGuire." I had over 200 offers. I went to a Catholic high school and the people there wanted me to go to Marquette, although they tried not to put any pressure on me. Despite the fact that we were poor, I wasn't a street kid. I had five brothers and sisters, I used to have to be home at night and would baby-sit the younger kids in the family. We weren't allowed to swear at home. We went to church on Sundays.

But when I went to Marquette, I fell in with all these street kids from New York who Al had recruited, like Dean Meminger and George Thompson. I'd never met guys like these who stayed out all night and talked back to the coach. One day Al grabbed me and said, "Listen, you stay away from those New York guys. Get your ass back to your room and stay there. You can't run with those guys, you're not like them."

I listened to Al about that.

After my freshman year, my father died and my mother was working in a restaurant, making salads. I had a good sophomore season and then Virginia drafted me. Virginia approached a friend of Al's, Gene Smith, with an offer. Gene talked to Al and then Al told me about it.

Al said, "Virginia wants you to turn pro. They made an offer."

I said, "How much?"

He said, "A million for four years. I turned it down."

I said, "You turned it down? Coach, that's a lot of money. I know guys who work in the mills for $20,000 and they're dying in there with all the heat and smoke and hot iron."

I later learned that most of that offer was in deferred money. I don't even think it was worth $100,000 a year. The rest would be paid out in 20 or 30 years. That was how those hustlers and sharks operated in the ABA. I already had it in my mind that I would go pro early. I had paid attention to the Spencer Haywood case. I knew that it worked out for Spencer. I knew my family needed me. Actually, I was a good student at Marquette, a philosophy major. Unlike most basketball players, I enjoyed the academics. But I had to make some money.

I also didn't enjoy our style of ball at Marquette. We were a very conservative, slow-down team, and I didn't think that was helping to train me to become a pro. I felt it impeded my progress.

But when I asked Al why he turned down the offer from Virginia, he said, "Right now, the money isn't the issue. I promised your dad that I would get you ready to be a pro, and I'm going to keep that promise. Mentally, you're not ready for pro ball. We're going to win a lot of games with or without you, but I'm not going to let you go until you're ready to turn pro, and you need another year."

I had tremendous respect for Al, so I believed him and I stayed for my junior year. Around January, I had seen Nick Mileti, who owned the Cavaliers, and he was seeing if I was going to turn pro after my junior year and he also was feeling me out about money. He said that Cleveland, Buffalo or Portland would probably get my rights. Nick talked about $1.2 million for six years. Mileti had the long hair and gold chains and all that. I figured he'd get back to me, so I was stunned when he wrote out his offer on a napkin. This was in the middle of the season and I had a preliminary offer from an NBA team, so the NBA wasn't very innocent in all this stuff either.

About a month later, I got a call from Al to go see his attorney, Gene Smith. We had just beaten Jacksonville on national television. I saw Gene and he said, "We've gotten another offer for you, and it's substantial."

I was really ready for the pros and Al obviously thought so, too, or

he wouldn't have told me to see Gene Smith. Gene told me that the offer
came from the New York Nets. They offered $1.5 million for five years
plus a $500,000 interest-free loan. But I wouldn't see that $500,000 until
I was 32 years old, and then I was to get $39,500 a year for 15 years.
I know that doesn't exactly work out to $500,000, but it had to do with
taxes and things like that.

As for the $1.5 million, it was paid out for 10 years—so we were
talking about $150,000 a year for 10 years.

I went to the Nets. I played terribly; I was 20 years old, very immature,
and I got caught up in the New York City lifestyle. I didn't have an Al
McGuire there to keep on my case. I was playing with a bunch of guys
who had never made $25,000 in their lives and here I was with the
million-dollar contract. It didn't make me real popular. I needed stability
and found none. The league was new, the team was young, our coach
was Lou Carnesecca, who was new to the ABA and pro ball himself.
People said things like, "You make as much as Lew Alcindor; you should
be as good as him." I couldn't be that good; no one could. But I put all
this pressure on myself and that just made things worse. People in the
press were writing that I couldn't play at all.

I also wasn't very smart. I thought because I could shoot better, jump
higher and run faster than our other center, Billy Paultz, that I was better
than Billy. But I wasn't. Billy knew every trick in the book and all Billy
could do was help you win. I knew nothing. We had Jim Ard on that
team and he and I used to get into fights because he thought he was better
than me, but I was making more money. There was a lot of petty junk
like that. And I added fuel to the fire. I'd shoot off my mouth. If I felt
something, I just said it. I never thought about anything first and that
got me into a lot of trouble. I didn't want to hurt my teammates or coach,
but things came out wrong in the press. At Marquette, Al handled the
press and kept the heat off us. No one did that on the Nets. I remember
when I left school and Al made his comment about his refrigerator being
full and mine empty. That took a lot of pressure off me.

I was trying to deal with all the money, the leeches that come after
a young player who just got a bunch of money. I was with a bad agent
at the time (not Gene Smith) and Roy Boe came up to me one day and
said, "You know what that jerk of an agent of yours did? He asked me
for $50,000 of your money. Do you know that?"

I didn't. Then I started worrying that I would lose the money. Roy
Boe gave me a list of five respected agents to talk to and I hired one of
those, who helped me out. But all these things were going on and money
was a huge issue. I was driving a big car, other guys on the team were
in Volkswagens. The guys who were there when the ABA started were

hard-core guys from those old AAU and industrial leagues. Some of these guys, like Byron Beck, just went around beating up people. They grabbed you, elbowed you. It seemed like every team had at least two of those guys who wanted to do nothing but beat the hell out of a rookie like me. They liked to stick an elbow in your mouth, knock a tooth out, knock you over and then help you up. There were a lot of real fights, not these guys shoving each other and pointing like they do now, but fist-fights with guys wanting to put you in the hospital. I weighed only 190 pounds then and I couldn't bench-press 100 pounds. I was just a kid and these grown men were giving me my lunch every night. After that first year, I was traded to Carolina in the summer of 1973. I was labeled a head-case. We had a great team with Billy Cunningham, Joe Caldwell, Gene Littles, Steve Jones, Mack Calvin and all those guys with Larry Brown coaching. I was glad to get out of New York. I was embarrassed by my play. I was homesick. I used to call my mother every day while I was in school, but I didn't call her for six months because I felt so bad about how I was playing and how I was living off the court. Carolina was a better situation, because I wasn't expected to be the star.

But after my year in Carolina, the team was moving to St. Louis. Bill Fitch was coaching in Cleveland, and he had an interest in me. But the Lakers controlled my NBA rights. After the Cougars were sold, I was released from my ABA contract. Then a deal was cut and I ended up in Cleveland, which changed my life. By then, it was my third pro year but I was finally mature enough to be effective.

PETE NEWELL: I was the GM of the Lakers who set up the deal that got Chones to Cleveland. I'm convinced that it was the only ABA-NBA three-way trade ever. (Carolina GM) Carl Scheer called me and said that he couldn't afford to pay Chones's contract anymore and since I had his NBA rights, did I want Jim? I said I didn't, but I made some calls and Fitch wanted him. Carl just gave me Chones, because he wanted to dump the contract. I traded Jim to Cleveland for a first-round draft pick in 1975. This made Chones the only player ever to jump leagues without a lawsuit.

THE KEY BATTLES

The NBA and ABA fought for college players, for pro players, for anyone they thought could play anywhere. And the key word was fought, because this was clandestine war with millions of dollars at stake.

MIKE STOREN: We had a real chance to become a permanent second basketball league, or at least force a merger that would have been sooner and far more favorable to us, if we had signed Lew Alcindor *(Kareem Abdul-Jabbar)* in the summer of 1969. He wasn't just a franchise player to one team, he was the kind of player who could make a league, especially a league such as ours that was two years old. I was the GM in Indiana at this time and one of the leaders in the ABA when it came to signing players. We obviously knew what Alcindor could mean to us. He was far more than just a great 7-foot center from UCLA. He could have been our 7-foot symbol of legitimacy.

Dick Tinkham and I tried something very early in Alcindor's senior year. It didn't work, but it was interesting. We went to Las Vegas and had an idea for Howard Hughes. We wanted Hughes to put up $1 million to sign Alcindor, then we would put an ABA team in Los Angeles with Alcindor at center and give Hughes the right to televise the games on his Hughes Television Sports Network. We met with Robert Mayhew, who was the No. 1 guy in Hughes's organization. Tinkham and I stayed at the Desert Inn for three days as guests of Hughes while we talked about the proposal. Mayhew really liked it, but he said that he could never get a final answer out of Hughes, so it died.

Our next step was to design a strategy for signing Alcindor. We compiled a psychological profile: we had both industrial psychologists and professional psychiatrists prepare questions for Alcindor. Several different people interviewed Alcindor. We studied his activities at UCLA, talked to people from UCLA and people he knew from New York. We even hired a private detective to investigate him in California. We wanted to know who we had to get to in order to help Alcindor make the decision we wanted.

We called the whole thing "Operation Kingfish," and all the research didn't cost us that much, maybe $10,000.

From all the information, a profile emerged. Two key points were determined:

1. Alcindor would make the decision himself. It wouldn't be *(UCLA booster and Alcindor's agent)* Sam Gilbert. Nor would it be *(UCLA coach)* John Wooden, or Alcindor's parents, or a friend. Alcindor had enough confidence in himself to decide himself.

2. Once he made that decision, he would stick to it. He had a very strong strain of loyalty and you could place a lot of faith in what he said.

George Mikan was still the commissioner and he wanted to be in on the signing. New York had "earned the rights" to Alcindor. They earned it by having the worst team in the league. Also, Alcindor was from New York, so there was a hope that "going home" would be a factor.

Alcindor informed us, "I will be in New York on this date and I will take an offer from each team and then I'll make a decision. I will not spend a lot of time negotiating back and forth or meeting with different people. Give me one offer and one offer only—your best offer."

That fit with our profile.

Mikan wanted to be a part of the signing, as did Arthur Brown, who owned the Nets but made his money in the trucking business. Mikan and Brown decided they would handle the negotiations alone. Mikan viewed himself as a great businessman and all that. I wanted to get Dick Tinkham to go with them so at least one guy in there would have a brain, but they refused.

We drew up a certified check for one million dollars in the name of Lew Alcindor. Our research indicated that we should just go in there and lay the million-dollar check in front of Alcindor. That would be one way to cut through all the bull and get his attention. It would show that we weren't going to waste his time in needless negotiation.

That was the plan.

We were all huddled in a hotel suite. Brown and Mikan went down the hall to meet Alcindor and they were in there for three and a half hours. They came out and I said, "That check got us where we wanted to go, right?"

Mikan said, "We decided that it wasn't necessary to give him our best offer. We figure when he comes back to us, then we'll use the check for the second round of talks."

I screamed, *"You did what?"*

Mikan said, "Don't panic, we know that he's coming back. He's going to get the NBA's offer and he'll come back to us."

I said, "Is that what he said he would do?"

Mikan said, "Not exactly. The kid did say that he would make the decision."

I was really screaming. *"You dumb SOBs, why did we spend all that money to find out all this information if you're not going to use it? How could you guys not give him the check?"*

While I was talking to Mikan, Milwaukee was in there with Alcindor making their offer. It was better than Mikan's, but if we had used the check, we would have been higher. But how was Alcindor supposed to know that, since our guys neglected to tell him?

DICK TINKHAM: Our plan was to offer the million-dollar check and a mink coat to Alcindor as a signing bonus. Then we would work out the details of his yearly salary. Our research showed that the idea of becoming an instant millionaire was something that would appeal to Alcindor.

Also, his mother always wanted a mink coat. But Arthur Brown and Mikan just offered him $1 million for four years. Sam Gilbert asked if that was the ABA's final offer and Mikan said it was. When they told us that, I couldn't believe it.

MIKE STOREN: After thinking about the two offers, Alcindor met with a reporter from the Associated Press and some network radio people and gave them a story that he was signing with Milwaukee *(for $1.4 million for five years)*, which the reporters got on tape. We were calling around desperately to arrange another meeting. Alcindor wouldn't talk to us again. We found out that Alcindor and his father had a flight from New York to Los Angeles that night.

DICK TINKHAM: Guys went to the airport and found Alcindor and were telling him about the $1 million check and saying, "Let's talk again, we'll raise the offer." He just said that he had made a commitment to Milwaukee and that was it.

MIKE STOREN: I heard that when Alcindor's father was told about the $1 million, he wanted his son to sign with the ABA, but Alcindor refused. He had given his word to Milwaukee, he had given a statement to the press and that was that.

GEORGE MIKAN: I can't prove that Alcindor had a deal cut in advance with the NBA, but I think he did. We never really got a chance to negotiate. I know that Alcindor's parents had tears in their eyes when they saw that check and couldn't take it. In fact, I still have a copy of that million-dollar check.

DICK TINKHAM: The Alcindor fiasco finished Mikan as commissioner. Right or wrong, he was blamed for not signing Lew. The owners thought it was ridiculous to have the league office in Minneapolis when not one but two teams had failed in that city. Dallas pushed hard to get rid of Mikan and a lot of other teams joined in. Basically, it was a "what have you done for us lately?" attitude. Mikan was important when the league was beginning, but that was pretty much it.

ROY BOE: I bought the New York Nets in May of 1969, not long after the ABA lost Alcindor. I couldn't believe that the league office was connected to Mikan's travel agency in Minneapolis. It was stupid not to have the league office in New York, and I said so.

GEORGE MIKAN: I never understood the owners' fascination with New York. Why go right into the backyard of the NBA? Having an office in New York wouldn't get us more coverage, it would mean less, because we would get lost with everything else going on in New York. I told the owners that and they didn't believe me. When they said they were moving the office to New York, I said I wasn't going and that was that.

DICK TINKHAM: We hired Jack Dolph to replace Mikan because of Dolph's ties to CBS. We were convinced he would get us a national television contract. To Dolph's credit, he never promised anything and he even said he wasn't sure if it was possible to get a network deal. But at that point, we really weren't listening. We were saying things like, "Well, Jack can't tell us everything because that would blow the deal." But there was no deal. Dolph never said there was. And Dolph tried like hell to get something. Aside from getting the All-Star Game on and a couple of regular-season games, he just couldn't get it done.

LARRY DONALD: Dolph was involved in one of the ABA's biggest controversies when he left his briefcase open at the 1971 All-Star Game and several reporters saw that inside were contracts signed by Jim McDaniels and Howard Porter. Both guys were still playing for their respective schools, and in essence they were pros. Porter's Villanova team finished second in the NCAA tournament to UCLA and McDaniels's Western Kentucky team was fourth, and both of those schools had to forfeit their NCAA tournament money because these guys had signed early.

MIKE STOREN: Jack Dolph was a lot of fun to be with and he was a guy who liked to have a good time. He also was very forgetful. He got up and left his briefcase in the room with reporters. The reporters always claimed that the briefcase was open and that Jack wanted them to see the contracts. But I was told the briefcase was closed and that the reporters went through it. I do know that the league wanted to keep the deals with Porter and McDaniels quiet. Porter had signed with Pittsburgh and part of his bonus was a Chevy. When it came out that he had signed early, Porter got out of the Pittsburgh contract and signed with Chicago of the NBA. But the Chevy reverted back to Jack Dolph's office. When I became commissioner in 1973, Porter's Chevy was still property of the ABA. We promptly got rid of it. Porter was long gone, but his car stuck around for a couple of years.

JOHNNY KERR: When I took over as GM in Virginia, I went to the bank one day, and in the Squires' safety deposit box I found a contract signed by Bob McAdoo. It looked to me as if McAdoo had signed it while at North Carolina, but I couldn't be sure.

EARL FOREMAN: Charlie Scott *(then with Virginia)* talked Al Bianchi and me into going after McAdoo because they had played together at North Carolina. Al and I went out to see McAdoo play in a game at Maryland and Al's eyes lit up. He went bananas, telling me, "Earl, this is the guy I want."

Charlie set up a meeting between McAdoo and myself. McAdoo was going to be a huge coup for the ABA, because he was among the top three picks in the NBA draft. Well, we got McAdoo signed, but he was still in school. I think his team had just been eliminated from the NIT, but he was still enrolled as a student and was scared to death. I put the contract in a safe deposit box in Norfolk. I kept one key and gave the other to Charlie Scott. The idea was to keep the contract out of sight until McAdoo finished school that year, because the kid was frightened that someone would find out.

Now it got really strange.

Charlie Scott jumped to Phoenix, and he took the key with him. Meanwhile, there was talk about McAdoo playing in the 1972 Olympics. This was in the middle of the cutthroat, back-stabbing days of the ABA-NBA war when anything went on, so we all were pretty tolerant of the crazy things that happened. But even I was starting to worry; what if McAdoo went to the Olympics, the U.S. won a gold medal and then it was discovered that he had signed a contract and was a professional all along? All I could do was hope that McAdoo would remember he signed that contract and skip the Olympic trials, which he did.

So I thought we had McAdoo, but there were still problems.

No one but myself, Scott and McAdoo knew about the contract. The Buffalo Braves took McAdoo *(No. 2 in the 1972 draft)* and McAdoo decided he wanted to play for Buffalo. I suddenly realized that I probably couldn't keep McAdoo, for two reasons: first, he was under 21 when he signed the contract; second, the circumstances of the contract, signing it early and then hiding its existence, might cause me trouble in court.

(Also, the Squires never drafted McAdoo. No one can remember the Squires drafting McAdoo, nor does his name appear in any draft records as being taken by any ABA team.)

One day, I got a call from Paul Snyder, the Buffalo owner. He said, "We understand that there is a contract already signed by McAdoo."

I said, "I'm not saying there is or there isn't."

Snyder said, "We know there is."

I said, "That's fine."

Snyder said, "We don't like this situation. Let's settle."

He didn't like the situation. . . . I thought I was the guy who would end up with nothing. I would have taken a nickel for McAdoo, because I figured that was a nickel more than I'd get anyway.

Well, we talked some more and Snyder offered about $200,000 for the contract. I jumped at the offer and I told him about Charlie Scott having the key. They sent somebody to get the key from Charlie. Then Snyder came to see me and together we went to the bank to get the contract. I got it out of the safe deposit box, we went to my apartment and into the bathroom. Snyder lit the contract with a match and then dropped it into the toilet bowl. As it was burning, he handed me a certified check, then he flushed what was left of the contract down the toilet.

JOE MULLANEY: You can name just about any college star in the early 1970s and there is a war story about his signing. I was coaching at Kentucky and we were convinced that we would sign Ernie DiGregorio out of Providence. We had taken him in one of our infamous "secret drafts" in December, and of course everyone knew who was picked about 15 minutes after we walked out of the room. I went to see Ernie play at Providence and he saw me at the press table. He came by and said, "Coach, I heard I might be playing for you next year. That would be great."

I was convinced that we had a shot at the kid, because I had known him from his high school days. He needed to go to prep school to get his grades set in order to go to college, but any time Ernie left his home in North Providence, he was homesick. He went out of town to prep school, but called home and said he was going to quit. Ernie's parents called me, because I had coached at Providence College. They wanted me to talk to Ernie. So I went to see the kid and I said, "Ernie, do you really think you can play pro ball?"

Ernie said, "Ah, no problem."

I said, "If you leave prep school, that means no college and no pro ball."

Ernie's father was a sander. He worked on his hands and knees, sanding floors. It was hard, hot, sweaty work.

I said, "Ernie, do you want to spend the rest of your life on your hands and knees like your father? If you quit prep school, that's what is next."

We talked some more and he stayed.

I know that this incident made an impact on Ernie, because four years later when he was a senior at Providence, I was having dinner with him and his girlfriend and he told the girl the story. The dinner was to celebrate his signing with the Kentucky Colonels. Mike Storen and I were convinced we had a deal. Ernie thought so. Buffalo of the NBA had drafted him, but we had offered more money.

But I left Ernie and went to a friend's house and the first thing the friend said to me was, "Did you hear that Ernie D. signed with Buffalo?"

I couldn't believe it. I was just with the kid a half hour before. My friend insisted that he saw it on television. The friend said, "I saw Ernie being interviewed. He said, 'I just had dinner with Coach Mullaney and I know he'll be disappointed, but we have a deal with Buffalo.'"

It turned out that Larry Fleisher, Ernie's agent, had promised Buffalo that he would give them a chance to match our offer. Mike Storen had even sent a bonus check to Fleisher and Fleisher said he never expected Buffalo to match, but they did. Then Fleisher asked Ernie what he wanted to do, and Ernie said he preferred to play in the NBA if the money was the same, so we lost him.

MIKE STOREN: Our other big target was Bill Walton out of UCLA. He was Dallas's first pick in the 1972 draft, but Bill could have played for any ABA team he wanted. There even was some talk of putting an ABA team in L.A. and calling them the L.A. Bruins or something and trying to get all the old UCLA stars together. I don't know if that was serious or not. But on behalf of the ABA I did meet with Sam Gilbert, who was representing Walton.

Gilbert said, "We want Bill to be the highest-paid professional athlete in the history of mankind."

Then he paused and said, "We also want him to be on a great team surrounded by a lot of talent so that the responsibility for winning and losing does not fall directly on Bill. We don't want him to have to carry that burden around."

I was there with Gilbert, Walton's parents and some other people and they all were solemnly nodding their heads as Gilbert spoke.

I said, "Now wait a minute. Somebody has to bring some perspective on this. You want it both ways. You want your guy to be the highest-paid player in the history of the world, then you don't want him to be responsible for winning. If that's the case, what would we be paying him all that money for?"

We talked about the advantage of Bill playing in L.A. We pointed out that he probably wouldn't like Portland, which had his NBA rights. But our problem was that the L.A. Stars had just moved to Utah and we didn't have a team in L.A., although I insisted we'd move one there for Bill. They didn't go for it and I think Walton wanted to play in the NBA all along.

Dick Tinkham: Back then, there were intrigues and stories behind the stories and gamesmanship on both sides. The players used one league against the other. When Earl Monroe's contract was up with the Knicks, he started showing up in the stands to watch ABA games to create a stir that he might jump. That was a common tactic.

Lenny Wilkens: The ABA was the greatest thing that happened to the players. No one in the NBA objected when a player jumped to the ABA; the guy was just making a good deal for himself and it was also forcing the NBA to pay us more to keep us. For once we had leverage, because in the early years of the league getting a $5,000 raise after being an All-Star was a real struggle. So if a guy jumped, it was, "Good for him, now everybody will benefit."

SOME CONTRACTS

A random look at what various players signed for.

Len Elmore: A center out of Maryland who signed with Indiana in 1974 for $1,335,000 over six years. It broke down like this: $125,833 a year from 1974–75 to 1979–80; a $50,000 bonus; two autos for three years and one auto for the length of the contract. Deferred payments were as follows: $80,000 a year from 1980–81 to 1983–84, and $105,000 for 1984–85 and 1985–86.

Warren Davis: A 6-foot-6 forward who had been in the ABA for six seasons with five different teams and averaged 12.8 points. In 1972–73, he signed with the Memphis Tams for $30,000.

Nate Barnett: A 6-foot-3 rookie from Akron who signed with the Indiana Pacers in 1975. He received a $2,000 bonus, $35,000 for the first year and $40,000 for the second year. It was spelled out as a "cut contract," meaning only the $2,000 bonus was guaranteed. He played 12 games and was cut.

James Silas: An All-Star guard with the San Antonio Spurs. He signed an eight-year contract in 1975 for $180,000 a year: $100,000 paid annually and $80,000 deferred.

Ed Manning: The father of Danny Manning, he was a journeyman ABA player for six years with three different teams. Here is how his salary fluctuated: 1970–71: $30,000; 1971–72: $35,000; 1972–73: $37,000; 1973–74: $41,000; 1974–75: $45,000; 1975–76: $32,500.

George McGinnis: Signed with Indiana in 1971 at the age of 19 after his sophomore year at the University of Indiana. He received a bonus of $45,000; a $10,000 grant to finish college; $20,000 to buy three cars; $250 a month toward the rent of an apartment; $50,000 a year for three years; and a Dolgoff Plan that would pay him $40,000 a year for 20 years starting at the age of 41.

Bill Higgins: A guard from Ashland College who signed with Virginia in 1974. He received a $4,000 bonus, $25,000 for the first year and $30,000 for the second year, a $5,000 bonus if he was picked as the ABA Rookie of the Year and a $1,500 bonus if he was named to the ABA All-Rookie team. Higgins was cut after 15 games.

Artis Gilmore: All-America center from Jacksonville who signed with Kentucky in 1971 for $1,500,000 for 10 years.

The contract called for $150,000 a year in cash for 10 years, a $50,000 signing bonus, and the rest in deferred payments that started in 1981 and were for $40,000 a year for 20 years with a Dolgoff Plan.

Dan Issel: Signed a 10-year deal with Kentucky in 1970. It broke down like this: bonus of $72,000 paid out at $7,200 a year for 10 years; the use of a car; college tuition for Issel's children; a Dolgoff Plan paying him $12,000 a year for 10 years starting in 1989. His salary was spelled out in excruciating detail:

> 1970–71: $52,000 cash, another $40,000 deferred.
> 1971–72: $62,000 cash, another $50,000 deferred.
> 1972–73: $72,000 cash, another $60,000 deferred.
> 1973–74: $87,000 cash, another $75,000 deferred.
> 1974–75: $87,000 cash, another $75,000 deferred.
> 1975–76: $132,000 cash, another $100,000 deferred.
> 1976–77: $152,000 cash, another $100,000 deferred.
> 1977–78: $182,000 cash, another $100,000 deferred.
> 1978–79: $212,000 cash, another $100,000 deferred.
> 1979–80: $237,000 cash, another $100,000 deferred.

The deferred payments began in 1974 and ended in 1983. That was nine years covering 216 semimonthly payments.

Fourth-Year Notebook: 1970–71

As usual, ABA teams moved around. The L.A. Stars became the Utah Stars and took up residence in Salt Lake. The Washington Capitols became the Virginia Squires. New Orleans moved to Memphis. Both Dallas and Miami tried the regional franchise route, playing at several sites in their respective states . . . The ABA signed two big-name college players as the Colonels agreed to terms with Kentucky's Dan Issel and the Pacers signed Rick Mount from Purdue . . . The NBA owners voted 13–4 to work toward merger legislation with the ABA, but the NBA Players Association filed a suit, known as the Oscar Robertson suit, to prevent the two leagues from merging as a violation of antitrust laws. That suit effectively sacked serious merger talks . . . Rick Barry was sold by Virginia to New York . . . Denver's Larry Jones showed up at a game wearing a "railroad suit," claiming that was all he could afford. The three-time ABA All-Star was unhappy with all the money Spencer Haywood had received from the Rockets. Even though Haywood jumped to Seattle of the NBA, Jones couldn't get a new contract from Denver. Finally, Jones convinced Denver to trade him and the Rockets shipped Jones to Miami for Larry Cannon. Jones teamed with Mack Calvin in the Floridians' backcourt and the pair averaged 45 points a night . . . Denver signed Ralph Simpson, who had just finished his sophomore year at Michigan State under the "Hardship Rule." Commissioner Jack Dolph threatened not to approve the contract, as he was feeling pressure from the NCAA and the NBA not to sign underclassmen. Denver threatened to sue the league if Dolph stuck to his threat. In the end, Dolph relented and Simpson played for the Rockets, averaging 14 points as a 20-year-old rookie . . . North Carolina star Charlie Scott signed with Virginia . . . NBA stars Zelmo Beaty jumped to Utah and Joe Caldwell went to Carolina . . . From when the league began four years before, the only coach still with the same team was Babe McCarthy of Memphis, which was the old New Orleans franchise. The only GM in the same spot was Max Williams of Dallas. Only two officials—Tom Frangella and Bob Serafin—remained from the original crew . . . The TV pact for the All-Star Game and up to six other ABA games Dolph negotiated with CBS was worth only $10,000 to each team . . . Carl Scheer jumped from the NBA to become the GM of the Carolina Cougars . . . Mike Storen moved from his GM post in Indiana to handle the same job in Kentucky.

In a personality conflict, Storen fired Colonels coach Gene Rhodes, despite the fact that he had the team off to a 10–5 start. Rhodes was replaced by Frank Ramsey . . . After a 3–10 start, Denver fired Joe Belmont and replaced him with Stan Albeck . . . Max Williams stepped down as coach of Dallas after a 5–14 start. Williams remained as GM and named his assistant, Bill Blakely, head coach . . . After a 17–25 start, Carolina canned Bones McKinney and promoted assistant Jerry Steele . . . Pittsburgh's John Brisker had back-to-back scoring nights of 53 and 50 points . . . Dallas had its largest crowd of the season, 9,247, on a Kids' Night promotion, but the Chaparrals lost 113–112 to Memphis when Steve Jones threw in a 35-footer for three points at the buzzer. A week later, Jones scored the last five points of the game as Memphis upset Utah 116–115. Jones had 38 points . . . The Pacers won their first nine games of the season and rolled to a 58–26 record, the best regular-season mark in the ABA . . . Official Andy Hershock died of a heart attack in the first quarter of a Memphis–New York game. Hershock was a father of 11 . . . Official Earl Strom went into the stands after an irate fan during a game in Denver . . . Late time changes by ABA teams twice meant that officials showed up at night for games in the afternoon and the league had to scrounge up one whistle-blower so the games could be played . . . The East beat the West 126–122 in the All-Star Game before 14,407 in Greensboro. Mel Daniels was the MVP with 29 points and 13 rebounds in 30 minutes. At the All-Star Game, signed contracts by college stars Jim McDaniels and Howard Porter were found by reporters in Commissioner Jack Dolph's briefcase . . . An ABA doubleheader featuring New York, Indiana, Virginia and Denver drew 12,252 at Madison Square Garden as about 6,000 ABA balls were given away to children. The money at the gate was over $80,000, which was twice as much as any previous ABA gate . . . A veteran of four ABA teams in four years, Pittsburgh's Stew Johnson set the league scoring record with 62 points against the Floridians. Johnson was 25-for-44 from the field. He went into the game averaging 13 points and was scoreless on 0-for-7 shooting the night before his 62-point outburst. The ABA record had been 59 by Spencer Haywood . . . Led by Zelmo Beaty, Utah beat Kentucky in the ABA finals. Beaty had 36 points and 16 rebounds and Willie Wise had 22 points and 20 rebounds as Utah defeated Kentucky 131–121 in the final game. Dan Issel had 41 points for the Colonels . . . Making the all-ABA team were Mel Daniels and Roger Brown of Indiana, Virginia's Charlie Scott, New York's Rick Barry and Dallas's Donnie Freeman . . . Issel won the scoring championship, Daniels the rebounding title. Issel and Charlie Scott tied for Rookie of the Year . . . Virginia's Al Bianchi was Coach of the Year . . . Indiana led the league in attendance at 8,187. Kentucky was second (7,502), followed by Utah (6,245). At the bottom were Memphis and Pittsburgh, both at 2,900 . . . In a *Sports Illustrated* story that ranked all the pro teams 1-to-28, the first eight spots went to NBA teams, followed by Utah and Indiana at Nos. 9 and 10. Six of the top 20 spots went to ABA teams. Last was the NBA's Cleveland Cavaliers, just edging Carolina, Dallas and Denver of the ABA.

The Stars Rise in L.A., but Shine in Utah

The ABA desperately wanted to establish a team in Los Angeles. In the usual ABA fashion, the way to have a team in L.A. was to put a franchise in Anaheim, which the league did in its first year. The Anaheim Amigos came and went after one season and a 25–52 record. Other than the fact that Les Selvage averaged six 3-pointers a game, it was an utterly unre- markable and unmemorable team. In 1968–69, the Anaheim Amigos became the L.A. Stars, playing in the same L.A. Sports Arena that is now the home of the NBA Clippers. L.A. construction mogul Jim Kirst bought the team and hired Hall of Famer Bill Sharman to coach it. Sharman's Stars were 33–45 and didn't make the playoffs, but in 1969– 70, Sharman introduced two players to the ABA who would make major impacts on the league—Willie Wise and Mack Calvin. A 6-foot-6 small forward, Wise averaged 19.2 points in six ABA seasons and was consid- ered one of the league's best defensive forwards before his career was cut short by a knee injury. Mack Calvin was a 6-foot guard who averaged 19.9 points in seven ABA seasons. He was a five-time All-Star and considered one of the fastest guards in ABA history. With Calvin and Wise as rookies, the Stars won 17 of their last 21 games to finish at 43–41. Then they stayed hot in the playoffs, upsetting Dallas and Spencer Haywood's Denver team before losing to Indiana in six games in the ABA finals. But the Stars didn't draw. For one playoff game with Dallas, they had a gathering of 971, and that included 500 free tickets. At the end of the season, the Stars were purchased by Bill Daniels and moved to Utah for 1970–71.

MACK CALVIN: I was drafted by the Los Angeles Lakers in the 12th round in 1969. They took me just because I was a local guy. They had no interest in me as a player; the NBA was not going to give serious consideration to a 6-foot guard. They didn't realize what quickness meant. I think the Lakers offered me a Jerry West T-shirt and a free bus ticket to the L.A. Forum.

I was fortunate when Bill Sharman drafted me to play for the Stars. Bill had gone to Southern Cal; he knew me, knew my coach. I negotiated my own contract. I got $12,000 if I lasted the whole season, $3,000 if I made the team.

LARRY CREGER: Bill Sharman and I wanted Willie Wise going into the draft, but Jim Hardy, our GM, had seen Wise play and he decided that he didn't like Willie, so he overruled us. When the draft was over, both Bill and I were upset that we didn't draft Willie Wise, but no one else had, either. Bill had me get in touch with Willie and Willie told me, "Golden State drafted me, but they won't even pay my bus fare so I can go and try out."

We told Willie that we'd at least pay for his travel to try out with us and we'd give him a fair chance to make the team. We thought he'd have a chance to earn a spot on our bench, but I'd be lying if I said we had the slightest idea that he would become one of the best players in the history of the league.

MACK CALVIN: Willie Wise and I really came up together. We rode to training camp together every day. We were both sweating out being cut and we used to almost run out of the gym as soon as practice was over because that was when they would cut people. They'd see a rookie around after practice, call him over, and then he was gone. So Willie and I would blow out of there.

A lot of people thought Willie was strange, and I think that was why he wasn't drafted higher. He was with Drake during the 1969 Final Four and he said that he really didn't want to play pro basketball, he wanted to drive a truck for a living. He was a reborn Seventh-Day Adventist and people thought he might not play pro ball because of his religious convictions.

I roomed with him on the road for one trip. He would turn the heat up to 85, 90 degrees for a few hours, then he'd open all the windows. I don't know why he did it, but we'd joke that he was having hot flashes like a lady in menopause. A year later, when the team moved to Utah, Willie bought a motorcycle, which was considered a big deal and very antiestablishment back then.

But in that first training camp with the Stars, we were just a couple of scared kids, not knowing if we would be around the next day. We trained at Los Angeles Trade Tech, and they put Willie and me up at the Olympic Hotel, which was a real dump. We were the only two players in camp whose contracts weren't guaranteed. We were the first over to the gym so we could get in some extra practice early. We still were the first to leave, because we were afraid they would suddenly notice us there and then send us home.

For me, it was a legitimate fear, not making the team. There were six guards in camp and five of them had guaranteed contracts. I had players such as Merv Jackson, Larry Miller, Bobby Warren and George Lehmann in front of me. All of those guys would have solid ABA careers.

Willie and I were afraid that they would cut us before the first exhibition game. I had it in my head that if I made it to the exhibition games, I'd make the team. I knew if I got a chance to play in a few games, I'd show I was good enough.

When Willie and I got our uniforms for the exhibition game, we both broke down and cried. We thought we were all set.

But in the first game, I didn't play at all and Willie was out there for only five minutes. Right away, we thought we were going to be cut again.

The next night, we played Carolina and I got into the game with seven minutes and 20 seconds left in the first half. I scored seven points by halftime and then went crazy in the second half. I ended up with 33 points and nine assists. It was all adrenaline. I was playing out of fear. Willie got a chance to play that night and he did very well, too.

STEVE JONES: Willie Wise and Mack Calvin came out of nowhere. Nobody had heard about these guys.

Mack was amazing. After a made basket, he never took the ball in. He caught the first pass and then raced up the floor with it. He was one of those guys who was faster while dribbling the basketball than most guys were when they sprinted. On defense, he was all over you, contesting every dribble. He was so competitive, so fiery. He was one of those little guys who was always in your face. Mack's game really bloomed when he was traded to Florida the following year. That was when he and Larry Jones took most of their shots and Mack averaged 27 points a game. He went from being a nobody to one of the best guards in either league.

CHARLIE WILLIAMS: I was with Pittsburgh when the ABA began and I was considered the quickest player in the league. But all that changed when Mack Calvin came to the Stars. Not only was he like lightning, but he never got tired. It was amazing to see a little guy with that much stamina.

SAM SMITH: No matter where he played, Mack Calvin invariably became one of the team's most popular players. That was because he was a little guy who hustled so much, the fans identified with his size and his work ethic. He always had time to meet the fans and sign autographs. He was just a good person, the kind of guy you wanted to do well.

LARRY CREGER: Mack took one of those Stanford University tests that measure your desire, and he scored higher than anyone who had ever taken the test before. Somebody recently told me that Mack still has the highest score ever on that test, but that's not something I know for sure. If you saw Mack play at Southern Cal, you would have thought that he had a chance to make a pro team as a specialist, a little guy to come off the bench for a few minutes and shake things up. You never would have projected him as a star unless you got to know him and realized what a will he had to succeed.

ZELMO BEATY: I didn't play with the Stars until they moved to Utah, but I watched a lot of their games when they were in L.A., because I had to sit out a season. Mack Calvin and Willie Wise played with so much enthusiasm that it rubbed off on the rest of the team.

Every night, Willie Wise couldn't wait to get to the gym to play. His personality and love of the game were infectious. He also was a great defensive forward. The small-forward position probably had the most talent of any spot in the ABA—Julius Erving, Rick Barry, George Gervin, Roger Brown—and Willie could guard those people as well as anyone could. Willie would have been an All-Star in the NBA. He had a reliable jump shot from 15 feet and had a quick first step on his drive to the basket. Most nights, you'd put 20 points next to his name and you knew that he'd shoot 50 percent from the field. He was really consistent.

GEORGE IRVINE: When Willie Wise and Zelmo Beaty played together in Utah, Willie was dynamite because of Zelmo. Willie would come off a pick set by Zelmo and if you were guarding Willie and trying to fight your way through that pick, Zelmo would just knock your head off. But leave Willie open from 15 feet, he'd make the shot. He also guarded the small forwards such as Julius extremely well, at least until Willie hurt his knee late in his ABA career. Zelmo and Willie made a deadly combination.

LARRY CREGER: We kept stats on when a player got his rebounds, and Willie doubled his rebounds-per-minute in the fourth quarter. He'd get every loose ball and some balls that weren't loose. He was a great clutch rebounder. With Willie and Mack Calvin, we surprised the whole league by getting to the finals. We knew that the next year, we'd have a great team because we had signed Zelmo, but we didn't know where we'd be playing. We drew so poorly at the L.A. Sports Arena. Most of our crowds were under 1,000. We had a counter as part of the scoreboard. Whenever a fan went through a turnstile, it would record on the scoreboard. But at the end of the first quarter, you'd hear the scoreboard clicking like there were 500 people suddenly rushing through the gates. It turned out that our GM *(Jim Hardy)* would be cranking one of the turnstiles to jack up the attendance. Of course, no one was going in and it got to be a big joke, but that was how sad things were at the gate for us.

MACK CALVIN: One time, I remember that the crowd was 245 at the start of a game. At the end of the first quarter, it was 1,800, because somebody from the Stars had gone out there to crank up the turnstiles. We'd make bets on how small the crowd would be, then they'd cheat and mess with the counter. That led to arguments about what was the real count as far as our attendance pool was concerned.

Those were tough times, because we never knew if we'd get our next paycheck. The guy who wrote the checks was never in the office. If your check was due, you just wouldn't see the guy for a couple of days, until someone had deposited money in the bank. Then we'd get our checks and rush out and cash them. They always made payroll, but they often were late. It was inevitable that we'd have to move, but I think everybody was surprised that we ended up in Utah.

LARRY CREGER: Bill Daniels bought the Stars and he knew they would never make it in Los Angeles. He was from New Mexico and wanted to move the team to Albuquerque, and he almost moved the team there. Then he visited Salt Lake and came away very impressed, especially because the city had an excellent facility in the Salt Palace. He also knew that the Mormons in Utah loved basketball. It was the sport they played a lot in their recreation programs. In Albuquerque, New Mexico University had the facility tied up for many of the best dates and they had no other arena we could use, so we went to Utah. That decision was made before the playoffs were over.

MACK CALVIN: Utah turned out to be a great situation, but the tough thing was that while the Stars went to Utah and won an ABA title, they traded me to Miami for Donnie Freeman, who was a 6-foot-3 guard who scored about 25 points a game. I knew that Donnie was an excellent player, but the trade really broke my heart, because I loved Bill Sharman. We had just been to the ABA finals and I knew we would have a great team with Zelmo Beaty coming in the following year.

LARRY CREGER: It was nothing personal when we traded Mack, but he felt discarded. Secretly, he probably never will forgive us for the deal, but we felt that Freeman was a great player at the time, a shooting guard at the top of his game. It wasn't like we released Mack or anything—we traded him for an All-Star. In the long run, the deal worked out fine for Mack and fine for us, because we used Freeman to get Ron Boone, who was a super player for us.

ZELMO JUMPS

Zelmo Beaty was a 6-foot-9 center from Prairie View College who spent the first seven years of his pro career with the St. Louis–turned–Atlanta Hawks. He averaged 16 points and 12 rebounds in the NBA, being named to two All-Star teams. He signed with the L.A. Stars in 1969, but had to sit out a season as Rick Barry did when he jumped leagues because of the option clause in his contract. Beaty was 31 when he began his ABA career with Utah in 1970. He averaged 22.9 points and 15.7 rebounds while leading the Stars to the 1971 ABA title. He made three ABA All-Star teams and then returned to the NBA with Bill Sharman and the Los Angeles Lakers in 1974.

ZELMO BEATY: I had averaged 21 points in each of my last two seasons with the Hawks, and I was making $37,000. That doesn't sound like much after seven seasons, but I was the highest-paid player on the team. I felt I was worth a lot more than $37,000, but the Hawks were probably the cheapest team in the NBA. For years, they could get away with it by saying that if you didn't play for the Hawks, you couldn't play anywhere. But when the ABA came along, there was an alternative.

The Stars offered me about $250,000 a year for four years. The Hawks wouldn't even think about paying me $100,000. They didn't even want to pay me $50,000.

The Stars' offer was for $60,000 in cash annually and $190,000 deferred. So I had $760,000 deferred and it was supposed to be paid out over 10 years. Instead, it took them 15 years to pay all that I was owed and there was a lawsuit. It got all messed up when the Stars folded in 1975. For a while, I was even receiving checks from the St. Louis Spirits, even though I never played for them. It was pretty crazy.

I was only the second player to jump from the NBA to the ABA. Rick Barry was the first when he went from Golden State to the Oakland Oaks, and the courts made both of us sit out a season. The irony of all this was that the Hawks filed a lawsuit to keep me and said I was worth $4 million, yet they thought I was crazy when I asked for $100,000.

While the Stars had that great year when Mack Calvin and Willie Wise were rookies, I couldn't even practice with the team. I worked in a service department at a bank in L.A., handling accounts. At night, I went to the Stars games to watch as a fan. But something that always stuck with me happened when I was in the L.A. Stars dressing room after they were eliminated by Indiana in the finals. Bill Sharman talked to the team for a while, then looked at me and said, "Next year, we're gonna win it all with Zelmo."

That made me really want to play for that man.

LARRY CREGER: Zelmo was a terrific, underrated player. Wilt Chamberlain said that Zelmo gave him more trouble than anyone. At 6-foot-9, Zelmo was dwarfed by Wilt, but he was so strong. He knew how to spread himself out and get a lot of leverage from his legs. He also was an outstanding outside shooter, so he would draw the big men away from the basket to cover him. He had a tremendous attitude and worked so hard. He'd tell our young players, "We're going to play 84 games this season and if you're playing as hard as you should, you'll be sore after each of those games. So get used to the pain and being beat up." He wouldn't let guys say they were too sore to practice. He'd shame them into playing.

He also knew every little trick in the book. Players would complain that he held them, that he grabbed their trunks. He needed to do those things, because Zelmo just couldn't jump. The guys used to say that he couldn't dunk. Well, Zelmo could but he didn't like to. It took too much effort, too much out of his legs.

JIM CHONES: When I came to the ABA out of Marquette, they had some real hatchet men. Zelmo was as dirty as any player I've ever faced in either league, no doubt about it. He'd hit you with a quick elbow just as you were catching a pass, and he'd get you in the mouth. It was so fast that the officials seldom saw it. He'd step on your foot. He'd do anything. Then you'd push back and the officials would call the foul on you. I'd say, "Hey, this guy is trying to kill me and you're calling me for a foul?"

LARRY CREGER: The sad part of Zelmo's story with the Stars was that he had such bad knees. He had this debris floating in one of his knees.

Our team doctor looked at him and said, "Zelmo, if we go in to get it now, it will be a major operation. But one day that piece will float to the top of your knee and we can just take it out with a little hole. It will be no big deal. Should take five, 10 minutes."

After a game on a Wednesday night, that debris floated right up to where the doctor wanted it. I took Zelmo to the office. The doctor made the little hole and he went in there with some tweezers or whatever, and had the piece, but it slipped out. Now it went deep into Zelmo's knee.

Suddenly, the five-minute operation took an hour before he could get everything out, and it had to be really painful, but he never said a word.

Friday, we had a game, and guess who played? In fact, Zelmo played three games in four days, but then he broke the sutures and his knee started bleeding before the doctor made him rest for a week.

CHARLIE WILLIAMS: I roomed with Zelmo and I never saw a guy whose knees hurt him so much. He could barely get out of bed in the morning. He used to eat aspirin all day to deal with the pain, but he just kept playing.

ZELMO BEATY: Considering how bad my knees were, sitting out a year wasn't the worst thing that could happen to me. It let me rest my knees and I came back to have the best year of my career because my knees were in good shape. They started to break down after that, but I felt strong all during that championship season.

LARRY CREGER: We started Glenn Combs and Merv Jackson in the backcourt and we used Ron Boone as our sixth man. That was how strong we were—Boone was a great talent, but we could afford to bring him off the bench. Boone played shooting guard and small forward for us. He was only 6-foot-2, but he was athletically gifted enough to play small forward.

In his first seven years of pro ball, Ron Boone never missed one game because of an injury. In fact, he said that he never missed a game going back to junior high. He didn't get sick, he didn't get hurt, he didn't get tired.

HUBIE BROWN: In the ABA, Ron Boone was known as "The Legend." The guy just played and played and played. Physically, he was Superman. People were in awe of his body and how strong he was at 6-foot-2, 200 pounds. This guy was good enough to average 22 points for Kansas City the year after the merger.

ZELMO BEATY: Along with the money, a big reason I jumped from the NBA to the Stars was Bill Sharman. I had so much respect for the man.

He was more of a teacher than a coach and I never ran into a man quite like him before or after that. He would never yell at us. I mean, *never*. There were times when we knew he was mad, but he didn't start screaming.

Instead, he'd look at me, right in the eye, and say, "Zelmo, we've got to get those rebounds."

Or he'd stare right at Willie Wise and say, "Willie, you're rushing your shots. You're trying to shoot the ball before you even catch it."

He was always under control and trying to tell you something that would make you better. Not yelling at you and calling you names like some coaches, who thought that embarrassing you was coaching.

Bill never swore and about the strongest thing he'd say was, "Come on, we've got to get those buggers."

LARRY CREGER: Bill Sharman was more than a great coach, he really was a pioneer. Things we take for granted on the pro level—the shoot-around, preparation with films and in-depth scouting reports—can be traced back to Sharman. When he put them into place, they were considered revolutionary.

Bill was probably the first coach to consistently and effectively use films. He subscribed to the "a picture is worth 1,000 words" theory. You can tell a guy over and over that he doesn't box out when rebounding, or you can tell him that his left elbow is too far out when he shoots, and he might believe you or he might not. But if you show a film to the player where he can see that he isn't boxing out or that his elbow is too far out, it makes an impact. The player can't deny what he sees with his own eyes.

Before every game, you could walk into our dressing room and find a film of our opponent playing. The guys could watch it while they got dressed, or not. But Bill figured that if a television is on, most people will inevitably watch it. Now, you'll find a tape of the opponent in every dressing room in the NBA on game night, and that idea came from Bill.

MACK CALVIN: I owe a great deal of my success to Bill Sharman. In my 17 years in pro basketball as a player and an assistant coach, I've never been around a coach who brought more intangibles, who paid attention to more little things, than Sharman did.

When I was a rookie, Bill had me keep a notebook on all the guards I faced—how to defend them, which way they liked to go when they drove to the basket, right or left; how they played me, to the right or left. He wanted me to think about the game after it was over and then write down anything that struck me about the guys I played against that night. He said I was small and I needed every edge.

When I played for Bill, he was 43 years old and he'd get out there and scrimmage with us. He covered me and he'd knock me on my tail, level me with an elbow. He'd say, "Mack, if you don't start getting physical, these guys are going to run you out of the league."

So I started shoving him back, and he never said a word. That was what he was looking for. He was preparing me. That was why I made it as a pro, because Bill had an open mind about little guards and then he taught me the things I needed to know to survive.

ZELMO BEATY: Bill was a strong believer in the power of honey. In the dressing room, he had honey candy bars and honey and tea for us to drink. He also had chocolate bars. He believed that honey and chocolate gave you energy.

At first, I thought it was a little strange, but we were winning so I ate the honey bars and drank tea and honey. Bill had been a great NBA player and he was a successful coach. If he said honey helped, then I was willing to take his word for it. A lot of it was psychological—if you thought it made a difference, if you thought it gave you more energy than the guy you were playing against, then it did.

LARRY CREGER: Bill believed in psychology and diet. He brought in doctors and nutritionists to speak to the team. He settled into a plan of honey and hot water before the game, Hershey bars at halftime for the players. He didn't force the guys to eat the bars and drink the honey, but he kept saying how good it was for you and nearly all the guys followed his advice. I mean, how hard is it to drink honey and eat a chocolate bar?

MACK CALVIN: Bill developed an entire program for what he thought a player should do to improve. He gave us diet tips. We kept notes, we watched films and he had his own conditioning drills.

About 25 minutes before a game, he'd have us run in place. He'd yell, "Faster . . . slower"; he kept changing the pace. He said that you never ran the same pace during a game, so why wouldn't you prepare for the games by changing the pace? We'd get new guys on the team and they thought Bill was crazy. But they'd see the other players do it, so they'd fall in line.

The main thing was that we were winning. Did running in place make us win? No one knew for sure, but no one wanted to change anything.

ZELMO BEATY: When I came to the Stars, I couldn't believe the total approach to the game that Sharman had, especially the practice schedule. Sharman had instituted the morning shootaround on the day of the game. As far as I know, no other coach in either league was doing it. In the NBA, I'd stay up several hours after a night game and then sleep until about one in the afternoon.

At home, I couldn't believe that we had to go to the gym at 10 or 11 in the morning, then go back home for the afternoon, and then drive back to the arena that night. I thought, "I don't like this at all, but I don't want to say anything, because I just came over from the NBA, I sat out a year. I don't want to be a problem, but I wonder what he's doing."

But as the season went on, I started to like it. The morning practice made me go to bed earlier at night and it made me get out of bed earlier in the morning. When you lie around all day and then go to the gym at night, you sometimes feel like you're moving in slow motion in the first quarter. I would still be tired even though I'd slept until 1 P.M.

We had a lot of fun at the shootarounds. First, we went over the other team's plays and walked through any new plays that we may have put in—nothing very physical. Then we'd be free to just shoot around, and we'd play shooting games, making bets and stuff like that. It was a nice time, very relaxing, yet we were thinking basketball instead of lying around in bed.

LARRY CREGER: He was fanatical about practice. If we got into a town at 8 P.M., Bill would call a practice for 10 or 11 that same night. He wanted to get the guys in the gym, and more than once I had to call up the janitor, get him out of bed and down to a gym to let us in. We'd give the guy a good tip and then he'd be glad to do it again when we came back to town. Bill saw nothing wrong with taking the team straight from the airport to the gym.

ZELMO BEATY: Bill set up a system of fines and rewards.

If you shot over 80 percent from the foul line, you got a $100 bonus for every point over 80. Mike Butler shot 91 percent one season and that was worth an extra $1,100 to him at the end of the year.

If you blocked a shot, you got $5. If your man dribbled past you on the baseline, it cost you $5. If your man got an offensive rebound against you on a foul shot, that cost you $5. If you got an offensive rebound on a foul shot, you got the $5.

Larry Creger was in charge of keeping track of the fines and he paid the reward money at the end of the month. If you had to pay, it went into a pool.

Bill would read off the fine list in front of the whole team. He'd say, "Zelmo, you let your man go baseline six times; that's $30." Then all the guys would get on my butt. I'd get mad and promise myself that no one was going to drive the baseline on me again.

It became a pride thing on the team. No one wanted to hear their names on Bill's list. Bill thought it was human nature that a guy, no matter how much money he made, would rather pick up an extra $5 than pay out $5. The fines also made you concentrate harder in the game. Your man would beat you on the baseline and you'd think, "I'm down five bucks. I got to do something to get that back. I'll work a little harder to block a shot." It was Bill's way of teaching good habits.

○   ○   ○

After losing to Indiana in the 1970 finals, Stars coach Bill Sharman said he'd win a championship in 1971 with Zelmo Beaty, and he did. The Stars went 57–27 in the regular season, finishing one game behind Indiana in the Western Conference. They swept Dallas in the first round of the playoffs, then defeated Indiana in a grueling seven-game series. Finally, they defeated Kentucky in seven games to win the title. Beaty averaged 29.7 points and 16.4 rebounds in the finals. The Stars were an instant success at the gate, averaging over 6,246 fans in their first season in Salt Lake. That was the best attendance for a first-year team in either league up to that time. In the playoffs, they averaged 11,811 fans.

ZELMO BEATY: When the playoffs came, we knew that we'd have to get by Indiana to make the finals. In the first round, we faced Dallas; we were a much better team and we swept them. At the same time, Indiana swept Memphis in the first round.

So in the semifinals, it was the Pacers against us. A year before, Indiana had beaten us in the ABA finals when we were in L.A.

What was appealing about this series was the matchups:

Small forward, Roger Brown vs. Willie Wise;
Power forward, Bob Netolicky vs. Red Robbins;
Center, Mel Daniels vs. Zelmo Beaty;
Point guard, Freddie Lewis vs. Merv Jackson or Glen Combs;
Shooting guard, Billy Keller vs. Ron Boone.

I also liked to watch Slick Leonard coaching against Bill Sharman. When we played in Indiana and got a lead late in the game, Slick would do something to get kicked out. One night, he kicked over a chair. Another time, he threw the ball at an official really hard and then went over and pounded his fist on the scorer's table. When Slick was ejected, it seemed that his team always came back to win.

There was a lot of pride at stake. We felt that Willie Wise was the best small forward in the league, they said Roger Brown was. This was before Julius Erving came into the league.

At center, Mel Daniels was the MVP and I was the first center to come into the league who could physically deal with him. Some people were saying that I had passed Mel as the best center in the league, and Mel didn't like that. There was a lot of debate about who had the better backcourt.

The series naturally went seven games, and when we came out on top, I knew we'd win the title. Ours wasn't the kind of team that let down.

LARRY CREGER: The Indiana series was the key to the title. We had a 3–2 lead and then lost the sixth game in Salt Lake. That shocked everyone, because we seemed to always win at home. So it was 3–3 with the seventh game in Indianapolis, and everyone then assumed the Pacers would win. But Bill put together a great game plan; our guys had the look about them where it didn't matter if the game was in Indiana, Utah, or Slick Leonard's driveway, we were going to win, and we did. Bill Daniels was at the game, and afterwards he took us out to a party. He was throwing $100 bills around as tips, buying everybody food and drinks. But very early in the celebration, Bill Sharman came up to me and said, "Larry, let's go."

He didn't have to say anything more. I knew exactly what was next. He wanted to look at films of Kentucky. That's what we did. We went to Bill's hotel room, where he had set up a projector.

Kentucky took us seven games, but I knew we'd win. Zelmo, Willie Wise, Ron Boone—those guys just kept getting better and better the more they played together.

ZELMO BEATY: Throughout the playoffs, I kept thinking how Bill Sharman said, "Next year, we'll win it all with Zelmo," right after the previous year's finals. Those words were with me on the court every night. Bill never said them again, but he also knew that I'd never forget them. I never concentrated more and played better than I did that season. I was 30, experienced, and my knees hadn't totally given out. I was at my peak and I played for a great coach. That was my most satisfying year in basketball.

The Meanest Men in the ABA

In a league filled with tough guys and fighters, two stood out: Warren Jabali and John Brisker. Both could play—Jabali averaged 17.1 points per game in his seven ABA seasons, while Brisker averaged 26 with 9.1 rebounds in two and a half seasons before jumping to the NBA—but it's the fights and the controversy around them that everyone remembers. Jabali came out of Wichita State as Warren Armstrong, a 6-foot-2, 200-pound forward. He started out with Oakland, moved with the club to Washington, and traveled on to Indiana, Florida, Denver and San Diego before the string ran out. Brisker was a 6-foot-5, 215-pounder out of Detroit by way of the University of Toledo. He spent his ABA career with Pittsburgh before jumping to Seattle during the 1971–72 season. After basketball, rumors about what happened to Brisker were wild and frequent, the most prevalent one being that he became a mercenary, got involved with Uganda's president Idi Amin, and was killed. Few of his ABA opponents or even teammates would have been shocked by such an outcome.

STEVE JONES: In his first year with Oakland, Jabali was Warren Armstrong, because he hadn't become a Muslim yet and changed his last name. There was this great picture of him flying through the air—they called him Batman. Warren played a physically intimidating game. He'd drive on you to the basket, dunk it, then catch the ball and throw it into your face. He looked strong enough so that most people wouldn't mess with him, either.

This guy was a player. He could rebound in traffic with guys 6-foot-9. He could push the ball up the court like a guard and he was absolutely fearless going to the basket. People never appreciated Warren for the kind of player he was because of his politics and the things that happened around him. Remember that this was when black awareness was coming to the forefront—1969, 1970. Warren wanted little or nothing to do with anything that was white. If someone was in an accommodating state of mind toward the establishment, you always got an argument, and a strong one, from Warren.

I think what really changed Warren was the fight—well, don't call it a fight. He and Jim Jarvis got into something, Jarvis went down and, basically, Warren stomped him. There is no other way to say it, and after that, people around the league looked at Warren a little differently, to say the least.

PAT BOONE: I couldn't believe it when Warren stomped on that guy's head. Warren was running downcourt and he deliberately stepped on the guy's head, he really did. The game was on television and they played it over and over on the news. Jabali's response was that he learned to play basketball on the playgrounds and his instincts just came out. That was an explanation, I suppose, but not an excuse. I tell you, that incident really shook me up. I've played a lot of basketball in my life and when a guy is down, you go out of your way to avoid him, you don't step on him. The scary thing was that Jabali didn't seem sorry about it at all.

RUDY MARTZKE: I was the PR director in Florida when we got Warren *(1971–72)*. Okay, the ABA had sort of this semi-outlaw-league reputation, but Jabali was the real thing. He was just sinister. The only guy around who was as tough was John Brisker.

When we got Jabali, I asked *(Coach)* Bob Bass why he went out and did it.

Bass said, "Because all we had to give up was a second-rounder to Indiana for him."

I said, "Bob, I know he's good. I know we almost got him for nothing, but you know what kind of guy he is."

Bass said, "We got a bunch of weaklings on this team and we need a guy who'll stand up to Brisker. Brisker is always picking on our guys and I'm sick of it. Brisker doesn't mess with Jabali."

Hey, nobody messed with Jabali.

When he showed up for the first practice, he was heavy into the Muslim thing, his hair was all braided up. I went up to him and introduced myself. He just looked at me. Wouldn't say a word. I don't think he ever said a word to me. He gave you that look like he might strangle you or something. I just backed away, nodded, and that was it.

BILLY KNIGHT: Going to college at the University of Pittsburgh and playing on the team, I got to see a lot of ABA games and got to know guys like Connie Hawkins and John Brisker. Those guys used to work out with us at the Pitt field house. The first time I played a game against Brisker, he just turned toward me and busted me in the mouth. I mean, for no reason, he just punched me in the mouth and stood there waiting for me to do something about it. I didn't do anything. He just scared me.

MACK CALVIN: John Brisker scared everybody. Even the guys on his own team were frightened of the guy. He had a perpetual chip on his shoulder. But I was a guard, so he didn't pay much attention to me. He liked to pick on the big guys.

CHARLIE WILLIAMS: There was a real contradiction to Brisker. He was an exceptionally talented player with a good long-range jump shot, almost Downtown Freddie Brown–like range. He was vicious under the basket and got more rebounds than a 6-foot-5 guy should. He had good all-around basketball skills and really was an excellent player. But his personality was something else. Say something wrong to the guy—or at least that he thought was wrong—and you had this feeling that John would reach into his bag, take out a gun and shoot you. In training camp, if John sensed that there was a guy who might take his job, the rookie was in trouble. John would physically take that player apart. The guys on the other teams were just scared of him, and the guys on John's team were very leery of him.

DICK TINKHAM: The legendary Brisker story was that in one of its training camps, Pittsburgh brought in an ex–football player who was supposed to control Brisker. The football player was supposed to get into a scrimmage with Brisker and the first time Brisker stepped out of line, the football player was supposed to flatten him. Well, the two guys started going at it. Then the football player said, "The hell with you, I'm gonna get my gun." And Brisker said, "If you're getting a gun, then I'm gonna get *my* gun." Then the two guys ran off the court in different directions, presumably to get their guns. The coaches took one look at all that and called off practice before someone really did get killed.

JOHN VANAK: One time I was officiating a Pittsburgh game and Brisker was late coming onto the floor for the second half. Turned out that he had a fight in the dressing room with one of his own players.

VAN VANCE: Brisker intimidated the whole league. I was at the 1971 All-Star Game and after it was over, I saw Brisker wandering through the stands.

I said, "John, who are you looking for?"

He said, "Jack Dolph."

I said, "Why do you want the commissioner?"

He said, "I want my All-Star money right now."

Dolph came by just then and Brisker said, "I want my $300."

Dolph started to say something and Brisker repeated, "I played in the game. I get $300 for being in the game. I want my $300."

Brisker had that look about him. So Dolph just took out his wallet, peeled off three $100 bills and handed them over to Brisker.

TOM NISSALKE: When I was coaching at Dallas, we were on a nine-game losing streak and we went into Pittsburgh. Before the game, I got a telegram from our owner, Bob Folsom, and while I was opening it I was afraid that I was getting the "ziggy," as Dick Vitale likes to say. Instead, the telegram said, "Just want you to know that we're behind you and we think you'll get this thing turned around."

So I had a great feeling going into the game. The Dallas GM was Bob Briner and he used to let me keep a checkbook so if a guy played a great game, I could give him a couple hundred bucks as a bonus right on the spot.

So with all that going on, I wanted to do something dramatic to end our losing streak. Brisker had been just kicking our ass all year, I mean beating the hell out of us. So I told the team, "The first guy in this room who decks Brisker will get $500."

Lenny Chappell said, "How about starting me?"

I normally didn't start Lenny, but if he wanted to go out there and get a piece of Brisker, that was fine with me. I figured that Brisker would go up for a layup or a rebound and Lenny would nail him.

But as the ball went up for the opening jump ball, and everybody was looking up at the ball, Lenny Chappell just flattened Brisker. He punched him out during the jump ball. If you think about it, that's the best time to get a guy. No one expects it. Everybody is looking up, including the officials. No one even saw Brisker get hit. He was just out flat on the floor and guys were running over him. Nobody even saw what happened to call a foul.

After the game, I gave Chappell his $500 and we won the game.

From that point on, there was a $500 bounty on Brisker's head. If he ever started up talking or shoving somebody, the first player on my team to deck him would get $500. We never had any more trouble with Brisker.

DAN ISSEL: I played with Jabali later in his career in Kentucky and our whole team was scared to death of the guy because he was so mean. We were in the dressing room once and we had a black rookie on our team, I can't remember the kid's name. Anyway, Warren noticed that the kid was wearing cotton underwear. Jabali reached over and literally ripped the shorts right off the kid. Warren said, "Don't you know that our ancestors had to pick this cotton? Get yourself some slick drawers."

JOHN VANAK: I was officiating a game when Jabali was really working over the Virginia players. The Squires had a player named Neil Johnson, who was a pretty tough guy. He was warning Jabali to lay off, but Jabali kept bouncing guys around, doing the physical stuff he always did. He tried something on Johnson, but Johnson just reared back and belted him. Right at the foul line; it was a one-punch knockout. In 28 years of officiating, it was the most devastating punch I'd ever seen on the court. Jabali went down for the count and Johnson was standing over him, screaming for Jabali to get back up. And to tell you the truth, most people who saw what happened on both teams were glad that Jabali finally got his bell rung.

DAVE TWARDZIK: When you had guys like Jabali around, there were fights even in the exhibition games. I came to the Virginia Squires straight out of Old Dominion, and the basketball wasn't very physical at Old Dominion. The minute I got to practice, everybody was screaming, "Hand-check the guy," so I hand-checked, which led to a lot of slapping and grabbing. In my first exhibition game, we played Denver and they told me to go out there and hand-check a guard named Al Smith. So I did and *whap,* Smith just blindsided me. I never saw the punch coming. I thought, "Man, if this is an exhibition game I don't want to see the regular season." A week later, we were playing Jabali's team and he was shoving our guys around. He pushed Neil Johnson and Neil went down. He sat on the floor staring at Jabali. Then Neil got up and walked over to Jabali and belted him. I mean, *boom,* Jabali went down like a tree. He just coldcocked Jabali. It wasn't a sucker-punch because Jabali had to see it coming. Then Johnson stood over him and screamed, "Get up, you son-of-a-bitching racist, so I can really kick your ass." Here I was, 21, impressionable, and seeing that stuff. First Al Smith decks me, then Johnson almost kills Jabali. It scared the hell out of me, but the guys on my team were loving it because the whole league hated Jabali.

AL BIANCHI: I coached Jabali in Washington *(1969–70)* and I never really knew what was going on in his head, but I didn't care, either. And I know he did some dumb stuff early in his career, but I didn't worry about that. All I know is that when they put on the shorts and sneakers and threw up the ball, the man *played.* He may have been the toughest competitor I ever was around in a lifetime of basketball. I used him at forward—he was 6-foot-2. Imagine that, a 6-foot-2 forward! He would outrebound and outscore guys a half-foot taller. I have nothing but good memories about this guy, because he played so damn hard for me.

TOM NISSALKE: I ended up coaching Brisker in Seattle of the NBA. He asked if there really was a bounty on him—he had heard about it. He laughed. I think he felt honored.

By the time I got to Seattle, Brisker had started to really slip. We were playing in Portland and Brisker had missed the morning practice. I've always had a rule that if you didn't make the morning shootaround, you didn't play that night.

We played that night and it was a close game. I didn't use Brisker, and with three seconds left in the game, we were down by two points. I was drawing up a pick for someone to take a shot when Brisker said, "Tom, I'll hit that shot for you."

I looked at him. I thought maybe I'd show him up or whatever, but if he wanted to take the last shot of the game after having sat there all night, I'd let him. I put Brisker in and sure enough, he cranked it. He had that kind of ability and that kind of self-confidence.

But at this point, Brisker had started to get into drugs and it just messed up his whole career. One night he'd score 40 for me, the next he had nothing. That isn't an exaggeration. But when he was in the ABA, he was a helluva player.

Fifth-Year Notebook: 1971–72

An amazing thing happened to the ABA at the start of this season—every team was in the same location as it was a year ago, which was an ABA first. The league also signed several big names. Kentucky signed Artis Gilmore, Jim McDaniels went to Carolina, and John Roche went to New York. Then there were the Hardship Cases—Julius Erving to Virginia, George McGinnis to Indiana and Johnny Neumann to Memphis . . . Kentucky played a weekend doubleheader against New York and Milwaukee of the NBA. While the Colonels lost both games, the scores were close and the ABA was buoyant . . . The NBA and ABA players had a summer All-Star Game, with the NBA winning 125–120, despite the fact that Kareem Abdul-Jabbar didn't play. He was married that morning. New York's Walt Frazier was the MVP . . . After a stint with the San Diego Rockets of the NBA, Alex Hannum returned to the ABA as coach and GM in Denver . . . Villanova had to forfeit the $66,000 it received for finishing second in the 1971 NCAA tournament because Howard Porter had signed a contract with Pittsburgh while still playing in college . . . Former Milwaukee assistant Tom Nissalke was hired to coach Dallas. After leading the Chaparrals to a .500 season, Nissalke would be voted Coach of the Year . . . Other new ABA coaches were Carolina's Tom Meschery, Kentucky's Joe Mullaney and Utah's LaDell Andersen . . . According to Indiana legal counsel Dick Tinkham, the Dallas owners made this suggestion before the season: "They said, 'Let's not play the regular season,'" said Tinkham. "They said, 'Let's just skip it and by then we'll have the merger situation straightened out and we can hold the playoffs. We can save a lot of money by skipping the regular season'"... In three of his first four exhibition games, Julius Erving had 30 points. After watching one of Erving's dunks, Florida coach Bob Bass said, "He took the whole building through the net. He took off at the foul line, went into the stratosphere. Then he dunked the ball with so much force that he created such a vacuum that everyone's ears cracked"... Pittsburgh coach Jack McMahon missed a week of training camp when he hurt his back while picking up a box of shoes. McMahon became the first ABA coach fired that season when he was dumped after 11 games and replaced by GM Mark Binstein. One of Binstein's strategies was to practice two hours on game days, which didn't exactly make him Coach of the Year material... The Pacers' Roger Brown was elected to an at-large seat on the Indianapolis City Council. Brown also became the first ABA player to have a car phone, so he could conduct the business of politics while driving to and from practice... After watching Indiana's 20-year-old George McGinnis get 29 points and 15 rebounds against Carolina, former Cougars coach Bones McKinney said, "His arms are bigger than my legs when I played in the NBA"... When Utah signed Jimmy Jones as a free agent, Commissioner Jack Dolph ordered the Stars to give up a first-round draft choice to Memphis as compensation. This inspired Utah GM Vince Boryla to say, "Jack Dolph isn't qualified to run a kindergarten class"... Official Earl Strom was sued by a woman in Salt Lake who claimed that Strom made an obscene gesture at her during a game. Strom denied it. The case went to court and was dismissed... The ABA signed its smallest player in history—5-foot-6½ Jerry Dover of Memphis. He played in four games for a total of 13 minutes and scored eight points... The All-Star Game was held in Louisville before 15,738 at Freedom Hall. Dan Issel was the MVP with 21 points and nine rebounds, edging Jim McDaniels (24 points, 11 rebounds) by one vote. The East beat the West 142–115... A few days after the game, McDaniels jumped to Seattle of the NBA... Utah's Zelmo Beaty set a league record with 63 points against Pittsburgh... Larry Brown set a league record with 23 assists in a game. Brown retired after five years in the ABA as the league's all-time assist leader... Three weeks after Beaty scored 63, Carolina's Larry Miller scored 67 against Johnny Neumann. Miller averaged 16 points a game... Charlie Scott jumped from Virginia to Phoenix of the NBA in late March. Scott led the ABA in scoring with 34 points per game... Kentucky set an ABA mark with a 68–16 regular-season record, but the Colonels were upset in the first round of the playoffs by New York. The Nets were led by rookie John Roche, who averaged 32 points in the series, and the only reason Roche started was that veteran Bill Melchionni had a broken hand . . . Indiana defeated the Nets to win its second ABA title . . . Artis Gilmore was the MVP. The all-ABA team was Rick Barry and Melchionni of New York, Issel and Gilmore of Kentucky and Dallas's Donnie Freeman.

Enter the Doctor

AL BIANCHI: Julius Erving was hardly a household name when he was playing at the University of Massachusetts. I can't remember the first time I heard of him, I just recall someone saying something like, "There's this kid at UMass, up in New England, know what I mean? The kid's name is Julius Erving and he's something."

I said, "Julius Erving?"

He said, "Julius Erving . . . that's it."

So *(general manager)* Johnny Kerr and I tried to get a film of this Erving kid, and it was an NIT game between UMass and North Carolina. Julius got in foul trouble early and ended up fouling out. He didn't play that much, but we could tell that he was pretty damn good. Later, I ran into Bob Cousy and he knew about Julius. He liked Julius a lot.

JOHNNY KERR: You should have seen our film of Julius—it was an old grainy black and white. It was hard to see what was going on. But we did see enough to like Julius. I checked his stats and they were sensational *(27 points, 19 rebounds)*. Neither Al nor I ever saw Julius play in person until he signed with the Squires.

BOB RYAN: I often saw Julius Erving when he played at UMass. Back then, there was no Doctor J stuff, he was just Julius. Colleges had the "no dunk" rule, and I had no idea how much that would help him. I could sense that he was bored playing college ball, especially in the Yankee Conference. I thought he had a chance to be a dominant rebounder as a pro, but I never imagined that he'd become Doctor J, a guy who wasn't just a franchise player. He was the ABA itself.

JIM O'BRIEN: I was the editor of *Street & Smith's* magazine and I got a letter from Jack Leaman, who was Julius's coach at UMass. Jack was upset because we left Julius off our preseason All-American team before his junior year. I wrote Jack saying that it was hard to assess a guy who played in the Yankee Conference, because of the weak schedule. I said we'd keep an eye on him, but I'd never heard of Julius until his coach brought him to our attention. Later, Lou Carnesecca told me about Julius coming to his office, trying to sign with the New York Nets. Louie wouldn't sign him because he felt uncomfortable signing an underclassman.

JULIUS ERVING: Contrary to what has been written and said, I never attempted to sign with the New York Nets. In the spring of my junior year, I had been contacted by some agents—Steve Arnold and Marty Blackman—about turning pro early. I was close to my old assistant high school principal, Earl Mosley, and I told him about the agents. One day Earl came to my house and said, "Let's go see Lou Carnesecca at the Nets office." So I went along for the ride. But I never did get to see Lou, I only talked to one of his assistants. I know that Earl went into Lou's office and they talked behind closed doors, but I never talked to Lou. Nor do I know what was said between Lou and Earl Mosley. They were old friends, and that was the reason Earl took me down there.

EARL FOREMAN: I was sitting around with some people in a hotel suite in New York, and one of them was Lou Carnesecca. Louie said, "That Julius Erving is some player." Louie said something about talking to Julius earlier, but that hadn't worked out. The conversation went on for a while, then someone mentioned that Julius's agent was Steve Arnold. I knew Steve because he had dealt with the ABA before, and I filed all that away. The next day, I called Steve Arnold and set up a breakfast meeting. We talked about a few other players first, then I said, "Tell me about Julius Erving." Like any agent, Arnold made Julius sound like the greatest player who ever lived. On and on he went. I told Steve that we'd talk about it later.

Then I called my kid's camp counselor, who was an assistant football coach at Bates College in Maine. I asked the guy, "Did you ever hear of Julius Erving?"

He said, "Yeah, the basketball player."

I said, "What do you know about him?"

He said, "Forget Cousy, forget everybody. Julius Erving is the greatest basketball player ever to come out of New England."

I said, "Come on."

He said, "Earl, the guy is good."

That was it. I checked a Street & Smith's magazine and they had some

nice things to say about Julius. So that was our scouting system—
something mentioned at a party, an assistant football coach from Bates
College, and *Street & Smith's.*

STEVE ARNOLD: At one time, Marty Blackman and I had worked for
the ABA as agents, but when Julius came out of UMass, Marty and I
had severed our ties with the league and were on our own. I had seen
Julius play in the NIT and I thought he was a great talent. I talked to
him about turning pro after his junior year and he said that he'd love to
do it. I called every team in the ABA about Julius, and only Virginia and
Kentucky were interested, and Kentucky's interest was slight.

MIKE STOREN: I was the GM of Kentucky and I never heard about
Julius Erving until a league meeting. New York and Virginia got into this
heated discussion about this kid Julius Erving. I'd never heard of him,
but as the two sides talked, I learned he was from UMass. Finally, I
pounded the gavel and said, "Gentlemen, we have far more important
business to talk about than this kid. I will not have some junior from
UMass take up our whole meeting. I will take a 10-minute recess and
I want New York and Virginia to go out of the room and settle this.
When we come back, I want an answer." Well, they did go outside and
it ended up that Earl Foreman bought the rights to Julius Erving for
$10,000.

JULIUS ERVING: I felt I had accomplished all I could in college ball and
I was ready to turn pro. Virginia was interested in me and I was inter-
ested in talking to them, so we set up a meeting at a hotel near the
Philadelphia airport.

STEVE ARNOLD: I was Julius's agent. Julius's high school coach, Ray
Wilson, brought along another agent, Bob Woolf. As far as I was concerned, Woolf must have been Wilson's agent, because he sure wasn't
representing Julius. Woolf was telling Julius to stay in school for another
year, but Julius didn't want to do that. If he had been at a big-time
basketball program such as North Carolina, he may have wanted to play
his senior year to take a shot at the NCAA title, but that wasn't going
to happen at UMass.

EARL FOREMAN: When Johnny Kerr and I walked into that hotel room,
there were all kinds of people with Julius. He had two agents there—
Steve Arnold and Bob Woolf. This becomes important, because later on
Julius claimed he wasn't correctly represented. Anyway, we started talk-

ing about seven in the morning and we went into the night. It was a dawn-to-dusk negotiation. Later, I found out that the reason it was taking so long was that some of Julius's people were on the phone talking to *(NBA Commissioner)* Walter Kennedy, trying to see if there was any way to get Julius into the NBA.

JOHNNY KERR: During one of our breaks, Bob Woolf said, "Johnny, let's go get a cup of coffee." We did and Woolf told me, "You know that I'm advising Julius to stay in school for his senior season. If he waits another year, he'll be a surefire first-round NBA draft choice."

I said, "So why are you here?"

Woolf said, "If Julius does go against my advice and is determined to sign, then I want Julius to get the best contract possible."

Of course, Julius wanted to sign. Even at 20 years old, he was calm, mature and totally in control. He said his mother had some health problems and it was his turn to help support the family. He said his decision wasn't emotional, but purely economics. I still can see Julius sitting on the bed in that hotel room, surrounded by about seven people. It was his hands that I'll never forget. I never saw such long fingers. They were the fingers of a pianist or a surgeon.

EARL FOREMAN: After negotiating all day and night, the next morning I said, "The contract is typed, my secretary has flown up from Washington with a copy. Fish or cut bait, this is it." Julius signed it. *(It was for $500,000 for four years. Each year, Erving received $75,000 in cash and about $50,000 deferred to be paid out in seven years.)*

JULIUS ERVING: In my mind, that first contract with Virginia went pretty smoothly. The Squires were the only team I talked to. We negotiated all day, I slept on the offer that night and then signed the next morning.

AL BIANCHI: Even after we signed Doc, none of us really knew what we had. At the press conference we had, I remember telling the reporters that Julius could rebound and had big hands. I do know that at UMass, they still loved him, even though he only played two years. I spoke at a dinner there not long after we signed Julius and everybody kept telling me what a wonderful kid Julius Erving was.

GEORGE IRVINE: I read about the Squires signing this Julius Erving and naturally I was very curious about him. I was a forward and so was Erving, so I wanted to know what I was up against with this rookie coming in. I called my old college coach, Tex Winter, and he said, "Aw, that kid is really talented, but it's raw talent. Not a great shooter, not a real good ballhandler. But he is very explosive to the basket. He could end up being very good down the line."

Then he came to training camp and the first thing I noticed was his Afro. It was the biggest Afro I had ever seen. Like all rookies, Julius was very nervous. He was friendly but very quiet, trying to feel the situation out. For a while, he just sat and watched. Then he came in to play and I was guarding him. He started going around me—hell, jumping *over* me. This kid did things I had never seen before.

AL BIANCHI: Julius first played in a tryout camp in Richmond. We had a few veterans there, but mostly it was guys just trying to make the team. Julius was running up and down the court, dunking on people, and I was thinking, "Look what we found." Then Johnny Kerr came up to me and Johnny was as excited as he could be. He said, "Al, we better get that kid outta there before someone hurts him. The last thing we want is this kid getting undercut or something."

JOHNNY KERR: Julius was on the floor for a few minutes in that tryout camp and then a shot banged against the back of the rim and went straight up. It was one of those rebounds where it seems that all five players were jumping for it. Out of the middle of the pack came Julius . . . up . . . up . . . up. He cupped the rebound with one hand and then slammed it through the rim, all in one motion. The gym went silent. All the players just stopped for a few seconds. This was a tryout camp and I had just watched one of the best plays I had ever seen in my life. That's when I told Al to get Julius off the court. We had to save this kid. It wasn't long after that when I told some of the writers who covered the Squires, "You guys are going to think I'm crazy, but one day Julius Erving will be going into the Hall of Fame." I didn't know he'd become a living legend, but he had greatness about him that you could just sense.

EARL FOREMAN: I drove to that tryout camp in Richmond and I wanted to see Julius play. I hung around for a half hour and I didn't see anyone on the floor who even looked like Julius. Then practice ended and I asked Al Bianchi, "Jeez, where's this Erving kid? What do you think?"

Al said, "He's a player."

I said, "But I didn't even see him out there."

Johnny Kerr said, "Earl, we didn't want him to get hurt so we sent him home. He's that good, Earl."

Jim McDaniels, the much-heralded rookie 7-footer from Western Kentucky, personified the relaxed attitude toward contracts, signing a 6-year deal (including a 25-year payout) with Carolina and then jumping to Seattle after 58 games.

18

One of the few wholly happy moments for Joe Caldwell with the Carolina Cougars was the day he signed. Caldwell (with Carl Scheer) spent a stormy five seasons in the ABA, and the legal battles over his contract dragged on into the mid-1980s.

19

Baby-faced Johnny Neumann was a textbook case of too much too soon: a millionaire at 19, out of the game by 27.

20

The Indiana Pacers were the ABA's proudest franchise. *(Clockwise from above left)* Irresistible force Roger Brown, driving on immovable object Willie Wise, provided the scoring, particularly in the clutch; Mel Daniels was a force inside to go along with his soft turnaround jumper; coach Slick Leonard kept the team motivated through three league titles.

24

Billy Keller and Rick Mount were teammates at Purdue whose careers saw a major turnabout when they entered the pros. Keller (driving past Bobby Jones) was a hard-nosed scrapper who thrived under Leonard's coaching; Mount (shooting against Rick Barry) retreated into a shell and showed only brief flashes of his All-America form.

Bob Netolicky was an effective center-forward and certified flake whose Indianapolis bar, Neto's, became the postgame hangout for Pacers and their fans.

George McGinnis, pictured here as a rookie in 1971 and accepting the award as co-MVP in 1975, carried the scoring and rebounding load for Indiana, and almost single-handedly drove the Pacers into the '75 finals.

27

29

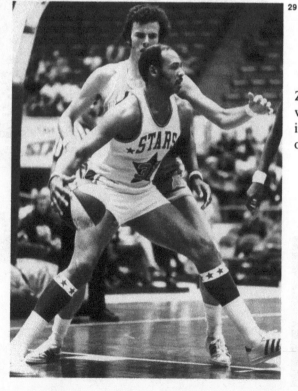

Zelmo Beaty brought a career's worth of tricks of the trade to Utah in 1970, and led the Stars to their only championship.

30

Among the many sideshow
attractions at ABA games were
the Miami Floridians ballgirls
and a cow-milking contest in
Indiana (Billy Keller is trying his
hands here).

31

The survivors: the only two players to last through all nine ABA seasons with the same team were *(left)* Byron Beck of Denver (and the University of Denver) and *(below)* Louie Dampier of Kentucky (and the University of Kentucky).

The Carolina Cougars' great 1972–73 season was fueled by the addition of Billy
Cunningham *(left)* from the Philadelphia '76ers, and the usual steady contribution
of guard Gene Littles *(right,* here going up against John Havlicek in an exhibition
game against Boston).

The Cougars were coached that
year by Larry Brown, in his first
head coaching job, and his able
assistant Doug Moe. (Hey, Doug,
is it the shoes? Is it the shoes?)

A brainstorm by San Diego owner Leonard Bloom put Wilt Chamberlain in a Conquistadors uniform, but a lawsuit by the Los Angeles Lakers restricted him to coaching duties. The photo of Chamberlain coaching here must have been taken late in the season, after the league ordered him to stop wearing sandals on the sidelines. Assistant Stan Albeck is seated behind Wilt, at far right.

37

38

Wendell Ladner was a crowd favorite everywhere he played, particularly among the ladies.

The biggest Afro in the ABA—no small accomplishment—belonged to Indiana's Darnell Hillman, here putting the squeeze on Caldwell Jones.

Lightning-quick guard Mack Calvin played for five ABA teams in seven years, averaging 20.1 points and 5.8 assists per game.

The quintessential Spirit of St. Louis was Marvin Barnes, here being kept away from Mel Bennett of Virginia by teammate Maurice Lucas in an unaccustomed role as peacemaker.

43 44

45 46

47

BOB COSTAS

"VOICE OF THE SPIRITS"

Among those who were part of the carnival that was the Spirits were *(top left and right)* Bob McKinnon and Rod Thorn, who tried to coach the club; *(middle left)* Fly Williams, New York playground legend whose game and mouth proved equally toothless; *(middle right)* assistant general manager Rudy Martzke, whose experience drove him all the way into journalism; and *(bottom)* broadcaster Bob Costas, about whom the Spirits media guide said, "He had as good a rookie year as Marvin Barnes."

48 Rookie Moses Malone marvels at his basket in the first quarter of his first pro game, October 18, 1974. While the body may not be recognizable, the mode of scoring is—a tap-in off an offensive rebound.

49

Mainstays of the powerful Kentucky Colonels team that won the 1975 ABA title were center Artis Gilmore *(left)*, enjoying a happy moment on the bench; forward Dan Issel (seen here with Denver, *right*), who combined with Artis to give the ABA its one great big-man tandem; and coach Hubie Brown *(below)*, making a point in his usual calm, reasoned way to Ron Thomas, Bird Averitt, and assistant coach Stan Albeck.

50

51

52   53

The rise of the San Antonio Spurs was due to the efforts of general manager
Angelo Drossos *(above left),* who swung the deals that brought in George Gervin,
Larry Kenon, Mike Gale and Billy Paultz; coach Bob Bass *(above right),* who
shifted the Spurs to an up-tempo, run-and-gun style of play; and Gervin *(below),*
the Iceman, who became one of pro basketball's greatest scoring machines when
Bass moved him from forward (at 6-foot-7, 170 pounds) to guard.

54

5

The Spurs' other major weapon was James Silas (shooting over Ron Boone of Utah), nicknamed Captain Late for his clutch end-of-game heroics. A knee injury suffered during the last ABA playoffs kept the NBA from seeing the real Silas.

David Thompson, the great leaper out of North Carolina State, joined Denver for the league's final season. He was the only player in the league whose acrobatics could match Dr. J's.

With two championships, three MVPs (one shared), four all-ABA selections and countless breathtaking moves, Julius Erving (hitting a reverse layup against Dan Issel and Claude Terry of Denver) personified the style and flair that was the ABA.

DAVE VANCE: I was the GM in Kentucky and I got a call from Al Bianchi in Virginia. He said, "Dave, I have a rookie you won't believe. We measured his hand from the base of the palm to the fingertips and it's 12 inches. When you measure his hand from the thumb to the little finger, it's 11 inches wide. No one has ever had hands that big."

I said, "Who is this guy?"

Al said, "He's Julius Erving and he's the most incredible player you will ever see."

AL BIANCHI: His hands. I was always overwhelmed by the size of Julius's hands. Then I saw all the things he did—the hanging in the air . . . it was amazing. Michael Jordan does much of the same stuff now and perhaps it's more dramatic because Michael is smaller, but Doc did it first. When I coached, I never had a bench that was more attentive than when Doc played for me, because the guys wanted to watch the game to see what he would do next.

GEORGE IRVINE: When the veterans started coming to training camp, I told them about Julius. I said, "I don't care if it was only rookie camp, this kid is something you've never seen before." George Carter had played a lot of small forward for us (averaging 21.4 points and making the 1971 All-Star team). Guys who hadn't seen Julius would say, "George will handle him. George is a veteran." But before training camp was over, George Carter had been shipped to Pittsburgh to open a lineup spot for Julius.

JOHNNY KERR: It was in training camp where Julius first got the nickname "Doctor." Willie Sojourner would say, "There's the doctor digging into his bag again," whenever Julius came up with a new dunk. Then he became Doctor J as the other players picked it up.

JOE MULLANEY: I was coaching Kentucky and we played the first exhibition game against Virginia after they signed Julius. Johnny Kerr was the Squires' GM and before the game he said to me, "Joe, wait till you see this guy."

I said, "What guy?"

He said, "Julius Erving."

I said, "Never heard of him."

He said, "Julius Erving from UMass."

I was good friends with Dave Gavitt from Providence College, and they had played UMass. Gavitt never said a word to me about Erving. So I really wondered just what Johnny Kerr was talking about.

But in that first game, oh my God, he did some things that I had never seen before. Early in the game, Julius just took the ball and dunked on Artis. He went right over 7-foot-2 Artis Gilmore and dunked on him. On another play, Julius drove the baseline, Artis came over for the block and Julius just floated past him in the air, under the basket, and then made a reverse layup.

VAN VANCE: I was Kentucky's radio broadcaster during Julius's first exhibition game. Early on, Julius got the ball on the break and it was just Artis Gilmore between him and the basket. Artis was 7-foot-2, the best shot-blocker in the league. Guys just didn't drive on Artis. Actually, Julius didn't drive on him either, he just soared over Artis and threw down a dunk.

WARNER FUSSELLE: Even Julius didn't know what to expect in his rookie year. He once told me that he knew he could rebound in the ABA, but he worried about his scoring.

GEORGE IRVINE: One time in warm-ups, Julius was doing this thing where he'd throw the ball off the backboard, grab it with one hand and dunk back over his head. It was a totally new dunk for him or anyone else. I said, "Doc, where did you come up with that one?"

He said, "Last night, I had a dream and I saw myself do it. I never tried it until today."

I thought, "Man, this guy even dreams about dunking." In the layup lines, no one wanted to go behind Doc. He'd do one of his indescribable dunks then I'd come along and do a little wimpy jam and the fans would get on me. After that happened once, I always made sure that I dunked in front of Julius.

EARL FOREMAN: Julius was a super young man. Both my wife Phyllis and I felt very close to Julius. He even stayed at our apartment for a time. Phyllis went bananas because all Julius was eating was SpaghettiOs. We went to his apartment and that was all we found in the pantry. Phyllis mother-henned Julius, and he was very affectionate and appreciative towards her.

JOHNNY KERR: We tried to promote Julius as much as possible. We had a Doctor Night where everyone with a medicine bag or a stethoscope got in for a buck. We dressed Julius like a doctor for a life-sized poster. The Doctor J nickname was a public relations man's dream.

GEORGE IRVINE: People always talk about two things when it comes to Julius. First, how gracious and classy he is. Second, everyone has a favorite Doctor J move. In Julius's rookie year, we were playing Indiana. He drove the baseline on the right side and went up. All of a sudden, Darnell Hillman went for the block. Julius just sort of brought the ball back and floated. He floated and floated, under the basket, and then saw that Mel Daniels was coming in for the block. He sort of ball-faked Daniels and was still floating when Roger Brown came in. Julius was now on the other side of the basket and the third Indiana player was after him while he was still in the air. He floated past Roger Brown and then put up a no-look reverse layup high off the glass on the left side of the basket with his right hand.

JOHNNY KERR: A young Julius Erving was like Thomas Edison. He was inventing something new every night.

GEORGE IRVINE: Julius was an incredible rebounder. He got 16 boards a game as a rookie, then averaged 20 a game in the playoffs. *(Erving also averaged 32 points and seven assists in 1972 postseason play.)* We knocked off Florida four straight in the first round. Then we drew New York in the second round and won the first two games on our home court. We were playing without Charlie Scott, who had jumped to Phoenix, while the Nets had Rick Barry, who was with us a year earlier. Game 3 was in New York, but we didn't play for nine days because the Nets couldn't get into their arena. Nassau Coliseum was booked and the ABA didn't want the games played at Island Garden, because it was a dump. Could you imagine the NBA playoffs today being held up for nine days because of problems getting a building? Anyway, the nine-day layoff took away our momentum. It also enabled the Nets to get Bill Melchionni back, because he had been out with a fairly serious ankle injury. During that layoff, both Doug Moe and I were injured in practice. New York ended up beating us in seven games. In the final game *(a 94–88 victory),* Barry hit a big shot in the last minute—a 3-pointer that he *banked in* from the top of the key. The neat thing was that we really had a playoff atmosphere *(five of the seven games drew at least 10,000 fans).* A lot of it had to do with Julius; he was turning people on.

AL BIANCHI: Julius was even better in his second year with us *(32 points, 12 rebounds, 50 percent shooting).* Now he was starting to get an idea how to play. But then all the stuff started with his contract and Atlanta.

STEVE ARNOLD: After his first year, it was obvious that Julius was grossly underpaid. I'm not blaming Earl Foreman or anyone else, because no one had any idea that he would be so great. But Julius naturally wanted his contract reworked since he had four years left, and Foreman said that a deal was a deal and all that. Then Irwin Weiner got involved and cut a deal with Atlanta and the whole thing ended up in court.

JULIUS ERVING: Following my rookie season, I went to Earl Foreman about my contract. I had four years left and I wanted some of the deferred money *($50,000 of his $125,000 annually was deferred)* moved up. I asked Bob Woolf to see if he could get my contract reworked, but he refused. So I went to Irwin Weiner. Irwin talked to Earl Foreman and Earl was willing to make some adjustments in my contract. Then I mentioned that I did not plan to spend my whole career with Virginia and would probably move elsewhere at the end of my contract. Earl got very upset and pulled the offer off the table.

Irwin started talking to the Atlanta Hawks *(who had lost Zelmo Beaty and Joe Caldwell to the ABA)* and he cut a deal for me to play with Atlanta. *(The contract reportedly was for five years, including a $250,000 signing bonus, a Jaguar and salaries of $200,000, $215,000, $230,000, $245,000 and $260,000.)*

I agreed to the deal with Atlanta before the 1972 NBA draft. I was eligible for the draft because my college class was graduating. On draft day, Atlanta didn't take me in the first round, because they didn't have a first-round pick. The Hawks already had a signed contract from me, so they thought that no one would bother to take me in the first round. It would be a wasted first pick. But Milwaukee did because the Bucks had two first-round picks and they used their second one on me. This caused a problem. I had signed with Atlanta, but my NBA draft rights went to Milwaukee. The NBA ruled in favor of the Bucks. That was a real problem.

WAYNE EMBRY: I was general manager of the Bucks when we got involved with Julius Erving. I knew Julius even before he went to UMass. When I played for the Celtics *(as a 6-foot-8, 275-pound backup center)*, I used to work a summer basketball camp in upstate New York. It was about four in the afternoon one day and I was going to shoot around for a while and then run a couple of miles. A coach at the camp said to me, "Would you like a little competition?"

I said, "I really don't think so. I'm just going to shoot a little bit."
The coach said, "I have this kid here and he'd really love to play you."
I said, "Is he a college player?"
The coach said, "No, he's just out of high school."
I said, "Nah, I don't think so."

But the coach kept talking to me and finally talked me into it. The kid came on the court and he was about 6-foot-5 and pretty skinny, but he had big hands. He introduced himself as Julius Erving, which meant nothing to me.

I said, "I won't shoot from inside the foul line."

Those were the rules. I had to shoot outside and the kid could do whatever he wanted, which is exactly what he did to me—whatever he wanted. He was absolutely phenomenal. I kept looking at him and couldn't believe he was a high school kid. His hands weren't just big, they were enormous.

We played another game, same rules, and I got my butt kicked again. For the third game I said, I'm going inside. I was going to muscle this skinny kid, but I couldn't catch him. He drove around me, he dunked over me. So that was it. I was an NBA center and I had lost to a high school kid. Later that day, Johnny Green wanted to play me. Johnny was also working the camp and he was a very good player for the Cincinnati Royals. By this time, Julius had worn me out and I told Johnny that I was tired. Then I said, "Johnny, I got somebody for you."

Green asked, "Who's that?"

I said, "Some kid out of high school."

Green said, "Man, I want some competition."

I said, "Just play this kid, will ya?"

So I got Julius and turned him loose on Jumping Johnny Green, as he was known back then. But Johnny found out who really could jump and Julius kicked his butt, too.

The next time I noticed Julius was when Marquette played UMass in the first round of the NIT. Al McGuire and Marquette really didn't believe that UMass could be any good. But UMass jumped out to a 12–0 lead and Julius had eight of those points. McGuire called time-out and said to *(assistant)* Hank Raymonds, "Who the hell is that kid out there?"

Raymonds said, "That's Julius, Coach."

McGuire said, "Julius who? What d'ya mean, Julius?"

By now, McGuire was ranting and raving, screaming, "Who's this Julius guy?" Remember, all this was going on during a time-out.

Raymonds said, "He's from New York."

Al screamed, "New York! New York! We get all the good players from New York. How come I didn't know about this guy?"

Then Al grabbed *(guard)* Dean Meminger, who was from New York, and screamed, "Dean, how come I don't know about this Julius guy?"

Al was really beside himself. He grabbed Gary Brell on the bench, shook him and said, "Go out there and don't let him score another point."

So both of those instants stuck in my mind. I had been aware of Julius for years before he signed with Virginia. In Milwaukee, we weren't in the business of signing underclassmen, but I followed him closely in the ABA. When Julius became eligible for the 1972 draft, we had the two picks and I told my owners, "I'm going to take Julius Erving with the second pick."

They said, "Who is this guy?"

I said, "He's the best player in the ABA."

They said, "How come we really don't know him if he's good?"

I said, "People said that same thing when he was at UMass."

They said, "You want to take him, even though he's in the ABA?"

I said, "Given all the problems they're having over there, you never know what will happen. So let's draft him and retain his rights." That's what we did. The guy was a great player, he *was* the ABA. We never did talk to anyone about signing Julius.

Anyway, Irwin Weiner cut a deal with Atlanta. We heard about it and couldn't believe it. I just dismissed it as one of the rumors you hear. How could Atlanta sign the guy when they didn't have his rights? But one night I was watching the news, and there was the announcement that Julius had signed with the Hawks. I got on the phone and called *(Atlanta GM)* Rich Guerin and asked, "What the hell is going on?"

He said, "We just signed Julius and we'll fight it out in court."

I said, "What the hell do you mean? You can't just sign this guy. What the hell is going on here?"

I got no satisfaction from Guerin, so we filed a complaint with the NBA. There was a hearing at the commissioner's office. They wanted us to take a settlement, but we wanted to fight to keep Erving's rights. We just refused to negotiate. The NBA board of governors ended up ruling in our favor. In the meantime, Julius even played two exhibition games with the Hawks and Julius had his own case in court so he could jump from the ABA to the NBA. It was a real mess.

EARL FOREMAN: When Julius said he was going to Atlanta, I said, "No you're not. We're going to fight it." We took the case to Federal Court and the judge ruled that we should go to arbitration to settle the dispute. In the meantime, Julius was to play for us in Virginia for his second year. I admired Julius's attitude. In effect, he lost. But he was a man about it, just as Rick Barry was when he tried to jump from the Oakland Oaks to the Warriors, but the courts said Rick had to play for me in Washington. Julius had a great second year for us while his case went to arbitration. The off-the-court stuff never bothered him. He was classy in every way.

WAYNE EMBRY: I knew that there was no way Atlanta would get away with signing Julius, and they didn't. The Hawks had to give us two second-round draft picks and $250,000 and we still retained the NBA rights to Julius.

JULIUS ERVING: I reported to the Hawks' training camp to challenge the issue. It turned out that the NBA fined Atlanta $25,000 for each of the two exhibition games that I played in. Cotton Fitzsimmons was the Hawks' coach and he had Lou Hudson and Pete Maravich. We could have been some team. Instead, I ended up in arbitration. I claimed that I hadn't been properly represented because Steve Arnold wasn't just my agent, he also was working for the ABA.

EARL FOREMAN: Irwin Weiner said that Julius was fraudulently induced to sign his contract, which was ridiculous. While they were talking to me, they also were trying to cut a deal with Walter Kennedy to get Julius to the NBA. He had agents, friends, everybody advising him in the hotel room. They had Bob Woolf, one of the best agents around. Bob Woolf flew in for the hearing and testified on behalf of the Squires, saying Julius was more than adequately represented, and Julius played his second season for us.

No one actually won the arbitration because before the ruling came out, we settled with Julius and I agreed to trade him to New York, where Roy Boe would give Julius a new contract. In my mind, everybody got what they wanted. We got a million dollars and George Carter *(who was traded by Virginia to New York two years before to clear a spot for Erving)*. New York got Erving, which it desperately needed, and Julius got the money he wanted. Even Milwaukee was paid off by Atlanta. From an economic viewpoint, we couldn't pay Julius any more money and the cash we received from New York helped us stay in business. We also kept Julius in the ABA, which was crucial. In my mind, this was a wonderful deal.

AL BIANCHI: Obviously, it broke my heart when we had to sell Julius to New York after his second year. But we didn't have the money to pay him and he was on the verge of going to Atlanta. The last thing we wanted was to lose him to the NBA. So I was glad he stayed in the league, even if it wasn't with me. It's fun to say that I saw Julius when he was a young colt in pro basketball, just getting his legs under him—and what legs they were! Unless you saw Julius in the ABA, you never really saw his high-wire act. He was a better overall basketball player later in his career, but he was more exciting with us and in his first few years with New York.

EARL FOREMAN: Roy Boe and the Nets desperately wanted Julius. They knew he had star quality and would be a terrific headliner for the entire league while playing in the New York market. When I mentioned that I had to sell Julius, Roy Boe couldn't write a check fast enough.

In the end, the final deal on August 1, 1973, was this:

- *Boe paid $500,000 to the Hawks.*
- *Boe sent $1 million and George Carter to Virginia for Erving and Willie Sojourner.*
- *Erving received $250,000 from the Hawks.*
- *Milwaukee received $250,000 and two second-rounders from the Hawks.*
- *Erving received a new five-year deal worth $2 million.*

JOHNNY KERR: Virginia selling Julius after his second year was like it would be if the Chicago Bulls sold Michael Jordan. Today, it is unimaginable. In the ABA, it was business. Hell, people were telling Earl Foreman what a great thing he did—he kept the Squires operating and he kept Julius in the ABA and he even got Julius to New York, where he could get the most publicity for the league.

From the Sublime to . . . Johnny Neumann

Perhaps no ABA player made less of more than Johnny Neumann. At least that was what Neumann's critics would say. His friends say he was a classic case of too much, too soon. He never worked hard because he never had to. He never achieved because he was a millionaire—at least on paper—by his 19th birthday. Neumann was a 6-foot-6 guard who had scored more points than any other prep player ever to come out of Tennessee when he was recruited to play at Ole Miss in 1966. A resident of Memphis, Neumann's choice of Ole Miss over nearby Memphis State was a source of controversy. As a sophomore, he led the nation in scoring with a 40.1 average. He went for 60 points against Baylor and 48 against Kentucky, and after that game Wildcat coach Adolph Rupp said, "Neumann is as good as a sophomore as Pete Maravich was as a senior." In high school and college, he often refused to go into his team's huddle during time-outs, preferring to stand off to the side, a gesture that in-

furiated coaches. He quit the Ole Miss team with two games left in his sophomore season to sign with the Memphis Pros in 1971—a five-year, $2 million contract, with much of the money deferred. Neumann said he left school early because his father had heart trouble and his family needed some immediate cash to pay medical bills. He went to Memphis, where he immediately feuded with coach Babe McCarthy. Neumann thought that McCarthy was overly critical of his mistakes. McCarthy thought it might be nice if Neumann played a little defense, showed up at practices on time and generally acted like a pro instead of an immature 19-year-old. In one game, McCarthy fined Neumann $100 and threw him off the bench in the third quarter. The players had severe doubts about Neumann for several reasons. McCarthy was a popular coach, a "players' coach." Neumann was cocky, abrasive and showed off his money. One of his favorite phrases was, "Paper (cash) means nothing to me." He bought a sports car in Indianapolis while the Memphis team was in town for a night game, then had to find someone to drive the car home. He said things such as, "To be honest, I was the biggest thing to ever come out of Memphis other than Elvis." He also drove a Pantera, "Just like the King does." His wife's nickname was "Slick." As a rookie, he averaged 18.3 points and shot 43 percent. The following season, 1972–73, he had his best year as a pro, averaging 19.3 points and shooting 48 percent under new Memphis coach Bob Bass. Early in the season, Neumann fought with Bass. Then Bass put him on waivers. Neumann returned somewhat humbled to the team when no other ABA team claimed him. Bass demanded that he pass the ball, and he had back-to-back games of 15 and 16 assists. But he never sustained that performance. He was continually out of shape, his weight moving from 200 to over 240 from year to year. He moved on to Utah to Virginia to Indiana to Kentucky back to Virginia to the L.A. Lakers of the NBA, and his career ended with Indiana in 1977–78 when he averaged 4.2 points in 20 games. He later played in Europe, then coached the Maine Lumberjacks of the CBA and coached in Europe.

TOM MESCHERY: You could take one look at Johnny Neumann and know he never should have left school early. Signing kids like that was one of the things the ABA did that was very destructive. Neumann had skills, and in terms of pure shooting he may have been better than Maravich and Rick Mount. He had the ability to be a great player, the athletic 6-foot-6 guard who could score and pass. But he was so immature and he never did grow up.

BOB RYAN: I saw Neumann play as a rookie and he had the worst case of acne I had ever seen on a pro. That just shows you how young he was.

He had an absolutely gorgeous jump shot, but with him it will always be a Paradise Lost story.

BOB BASS: I had Johnny in his second year and he owned seven cars. He also had a stock car with his name on it. He had blown nearly all of his money. Charlie Finley and I worked with him and got him down to three cars by the end of the season. He had a lot of friends and relatives around him and he was always giving them money, buying them things.

He was the kind of player who drives coaches crazy. He obviously was a scorer, but he didn't hold up his end on defense, nor would he create shots for his teammates. Everything was just for Johnny. I was all over him about this and one night he just got tired of hearing it. He went out and did nothing but pass—and he got 19 assists and we won the game. He showed me that he could flat-out pass, that he could be a great point guard if he felt like it. But the thing about Johnny Neumann was that he only felt like playing the game *his* way.

GENE LITTLES: Johnny was a flake and he seemed to work at it. He would do things such as reporting into a game with his jersey on backwards. He never took the game seriously and I never thought he was nearly as good as his reputation. Guys such as myself, ABA players with no national names, loved to guard Johnny, to press him and to frustrate him—and it was easy to do that. You liked to stick it to a guy like that because he seemed to be wasting so much of what he had while you were busting your butt for a few bucks.

JOE TAIT: The legendary Johnny Neumann story was that one night he was sitting on the bench and the coach called his name. Neumann stood up, tore off his warm-up pants, and all he was wearing underneath was his jockstrap.

JOE MULLANEY: I had Johnny in Utah. He wasn't playing that much and he didn't like it. We had practices as 11 A.M. He would get to the gym maybe around 10:30, but he wouldn't go out and shoot with the other guys. Instead, he'd sit under the basket until a minute before 11, then he would walk on the floor at the last possible second before he would get fined. He was a very hard person to understand.

DAVE TWARDZIK: The guy was the best practice passer I've ever seen. He really could see the floor and make the right pass to the right guy at the right time. It was amazing how well he handled the ball in our practices in Virginia. Then the striped shirts and whistles would come out and forget it—Johnny had tunnel vision on the court. Johnny wasn't thinking about anyone but Johnny during games. This was one of many contradictions with Johnny. He played hard most of the time, but he was out of shape for much of his career. He hated to work out in the off-season and he'd stay out really late during the season. The game always came easy for him, so he saw no reason to get in shape. He always could hit the jumper. And when someone criticized him or when he was traded, Johnny never sat back and thought, "I wonder why that happened?" He just said, "Screw it, that SOB just doesn't like me." It was never his fault. He was traded a million times, but that light bulb never went on, he never thought, "Maybe I'm doing something wrong."

GEORGE IRVINE: When Johnny was in Virginia, I lived two doors down from his town house. He had all these dogs and he had a Ferrari and Harley Davidson and he was always looking to have a good time. He was a classic case of a guy who never grew up. Generally, he wasn't very responsible, but if a friend asked him for a favor, he would be there for you. He'd make sure he did what you asked. That was the thing about Johnny—he knew how to do things right, he just didn't always do them. He actually was more responsible when it came to helping someone else than he was when it came to looking out for himself.

DAVE TWARDZIK: Johnny lived in the fast lane and he had the problems that a young guy has when his life is always going 100 miles per hour. He had nice clothes and fast cars. He had a Ferrari. He had a Harley Davidson motorcycle. In fact, I bought the Harley from him. He was going through a divorce and he had this girlfriend in Salt Lake City. He was continually flying out to see her; that was his champagne taste. So he was going through a lot of money between the divorce and the trips to Salt Lake. His wife in Memphis was going to keep his Jaguar and the house in Memphis, so Johnny needed some cash. One day he walked into the dressing room and was sort of auctioning off the Ferrari and Harley, seeing what anybody on the team might be willing to pay. I was into motorcycles and Johnny had a Harley 1200 which was a good one, so I bought it from him. I kept it for a while, did some work on it and sold it for a profit.

But I really blew it, because I should have bought the Ferrari. That was in 1974 and he wanted $19,000 for it. I thought, "Geez, 19 grand for a car." That car would be worth $170,000 today.

BILLY KELLER: When Johnny played with us in Indiana, he had this girlfriend in Salt Lake. He was flying out there a lot to see her, and that meant he was late getting back to practice, or he wouldn't make practice at all. He'd get fined. He would get benched. Slick Leonard would scream at him, but that never made an impression. He was so confident in his talent—I'd say he was overconfident—that he figured he could do anything he wanted and still produce on the court. The same was true of money. He always thought the big money would be there and he almost had a desire to go out and burn it. It wasn't Johnny's nature to give a thought to what tomorrow might bring.

WARNER FUSSELLE: Johnny Neumann will forever be one of those "what might have been" stories. It was almost like the fact that he was capable of greatness was enough for him, he didn't have to *be* great. There was a game where he had 38 points, but only three in the second half. It was like, "I had a 35-point half, what else do you want me to do?" He was likeable and the only guy he ever hurt was himself, but that bothered other people because of what he could have been.

HUBIE BROWN: I had Johnny in Kentucky for a while and he did a pretty good job for me. The problem with him was his legacy, being the next Pete Maravich and all that. What I liked about Johnny was that he understood the game and could see the floor, see plays developing. He loved the game and craved the ball. He was very good under pressure. When he got on a hot streak, the degree of difficulty of his shot was irrelevant. He would make everything, and as a coach you had to be smart enough just to ride his streak and let him take it, no matter how outrageous the shot. He was with me from February until the end of the season during the last year of the ABA, and I have no complaints. I liked the guy.

DAVE TWARDZIK: The game of basketball never came easy for me. I was a 6-foot guard and had to claw and work for everything. Johnny was 6-foot-6, the prototype big guard the pros love. The thing was that George Irvine and I got along great with Johnny. We really liked the guy. But it drove us crazy to watch a guy with his talent just waste it. Maybe it would have been different if I had averaged 40 points a game as a sophomore and if everyone had thrown all that money at me when I was 19. Or maybe things just came too easy for him, but it always bothered me that Johnny Neumann never was the player he should have been.

Memphis Follies

Memphis started as the New Orleans Buccaneers of Larry Brown, Doug Moe, Babe McCarthy and, for a fleeting moment, Morton Downey Jr. In the ABA's fourth season (1970–71), the Buccaneers moved to Memphis and became the Pros for the next two seasons. In 1972–73, they changed their name to the Memphis Tams for two years. In 1974–75, they were the Memphis Sounds. Then they moved to Baltimore in the fall of 1975, where they were the Baltimore Hustlers, then the Baltimore Claws, and then Baltimore was simply gone before ever playing an ABA game. Memphis was not known for winning or for even having a winning season. Nor was it known for its players, and certainly not for its fans, since there were none. In three different seasons, the Memphis franchise was taken over by the league, which paid the players' salaries. When the Bucs moved to Memphis, the owner was P. L. Blake, a friend of Coach Babe McCarthy's. There was trouble from the start. The move was made so late in the summer that there weren't enough open dates at the Memphis Mid-South Coliseum. The team had 42 home games, but the arena had only 31 open dates, so games were played in such places as Jackson, Tennessee, Greenville, Mississippi, and Jackson, Mississippi. One game in Jackson, Mississippi, had an announced crowd of 465. Three months into the 1970–71 season, Blake claimed to have lost $200,000 and put the team on the market, which led to Charlie Finley's first and last basketball venture.

BOB BASS: The first time I talked to Charlie Finley was when I was still the coach and general manager of the Floridians, right after the 1969–70 season. That was when our owner, Ned Doyle, told me that he either had to sell the Floridians or he would fold the team. At the end, the front office was my PR man, Rudy Martzke, and myself. We were trying to find a new owner for the team so we could keep our jobs.

One day Rudy said, "Look at this story in the paper on Charlie Finley. He owns a team in every sport but basketball."

I can't believe I did this, but right after Rudy said that, I picked up the phone and got in touch with Charlie Finley. He said to me, "Why in the hell would I want a damn basketball team?"

I said, "Charlie, you own everything else, you may as well have one of these, too."

I talked to Charlie Finley every day for 10 days. It turned out that Charlie was good friends with Dick Tinkham, who owned part of the Indiana Pacers. Tinkham told Charlie to forget about buying Florida and to buy Memphis because Memphis was cheaper and a better team.

DICK TINKHAM: I was one of the ABA owners who served as an unofficial ambassador of franchise sales. In other words, if a franchise was in trouble, I'd help them look for an owner. It was pure self-interest. The Indiana franchise was successful and the last thing we wanted was the league to fold, so we were continually looking for viable investors who were willing to buy into any team.

Charlie Finley was interested in the ABA just because he already had a baseball team and a hockey team. Charlie told me, "I'll buy it, you just tell me when."

I waited until the league had taken over the Memphis franchise and there was talk of folding it, then I told Charlie to make his move. He got the team for virtually nothing—he assumed the debts.

At a league meeting, I told what was left of the original group that owned Memphis that Finley was ready to buy the team. The Memphis people got so excited that they went down to a bar to celebrate, and they celebrated so well that they missed their flight to meet with Finley. Naturally, Charlie was livid when those guys didn't show up, so he made them wait for three days for another appointment. Then Charlie changed the terms of the deal, really putting the screws to the Memphis people.

BOB BASS: One day Charlie called me and said, "I just bought the Memphis team, why don't you come down there with me?"

I wasn't sure how serious Charlie was, but I was dead serious about getting a job because after the Floridians folded, I needed work. I think he hired me to be coach and general manager because I was one of the few basketball people he knew, and he knew me from my trying to sell him the Florida team.

We had a contest to change the nickname from the Pros to something else. There was a contest and Charlie picked the winner—the Memphis Tams. That's T-A-M-s as in Tennessee, Arkansas and Mississippi. We were going to draw fans from those three states, according to Charlie. Nobody else much liked the Tams nickname, but he owned the team so that was that.

Then he made Adolph Rupp president of the team. Coach Rupp had been retired from the University of Kentucky and Charlie just wanted his name associated with the Tams.

About once a month, Coach Rupp would fly to Memphis from Lexington, Kentucky. I'd pick him up at the airport and Coach Rupp would ask me, "What does Mr. Finley want me to do this time?"

I'd say, "What did he say to do?"

Coach Rupp said, "He never tells me anything, just says go to Memphis, so here I am."

My only orders from Charlie were, "You just get Adolph to sit at the press table during the games so everybody can see him."

Once in a while, I'd have Coach Rupp talk to our team. Sometimes I would take him with me to speak at luncheons and things like that. Mostly, he and I sat around, talking basketball. I loved to pick his brains.

RON GRINKER: Charlie Finley would have Adolph Rupp sit at the press table for a game. It was a $90 round-trip ticket from Lexington to Memphis, so it didn't cost Charlie much to bring in Adolph, and Charlie was always very big on saving money.

Once, I was on a flight with Rupp and sat with him in the first-class section. He had about six Kentucky bourbons in less than an hour and was about halfway to the wind. I told him that I was an attorney who represented some basketball players. Now, I had never met the man, and the first significant thing he said to me was, "The trouble with the ABA is that there are too many nigger boys in it now."

I sat there just stunned. That just killed my image of Adolph Rupp the great coach. Maybe it was because he had too much to drink, but even so . . . He asked me to sit with him during the game that night. I spent the first half with him and then left. I couldn't stand listening to him anymore.

MIKE STOREN: In my brief ownership of Memphis, Adolph Rupp was still around and he was very nice to me. He used to sit in my office and tell stories by the hour. He had time for everyone and wasn't one of those guys always looking at his watch. I liked him.

BOB BASS: After naming the team and hiring Coach Rupp, Charlie changed our team uniforms. We wore the same colors as his Oakland A's. One day we'd have white shorts and green and gold jerseys, then it would be green shorts and white tops the next day. We also could wear all-green or all-white uniforms, so we had four different looks, and Charlie loved having us change our uniforms around.

He brought me to Chicago and had his personal tailor make me six sports coats—but they were all the team colors, that bright green and gold. The buttons were etched with Charlie O—which was his mule, the mascot of the baseball team. He also bought me white shoes. By the time he got done with me, I was some sight.

DICK TINKHAM: From the moment he came into the ABA, Finley was a royal pain in the ass to the league. He'd go to a league meeting and drone on for two hours because we wouldn't let him draft a player he wanted to or something. We'd try to conduct league business, and he'd just butt in and take over. He always was behind on paying his league assessments and he'd spend hours at league meetings telling us why he shouldn't have to pay. Nobody could stand it once Charlie got up to say something because we all knew it would waste hours of our time.

CHARLIE WILLIAMS: Charlie should have stayed in baseball. He made us wear these crazy uniforms and seemed to have no interest in the team. The players all thought he wanted to move the franchise, but he never did.

I went to see him at his Chicago office about a new contract because he had invited me to lunch. I got there and Charlie said, "Let's eat." Then he walked over to the hot plate he kept in his office and turned it on. He took a couple of cans of soup off a shelf and put them on the hot plate.

I started to think, "Boy, things must be tough with the team when he can't even afford to go out for lunch."

In retrospect, I know now that Charlie wanted me to think just that. I walked into that office wanting to get $30,000. I ended up signing for $23,000 because Charlie conned me into thinking that was all he could pay.

BOB BASS: In December of 1972, I got a call from Charlie and he started the conversation by saying, "Bob, I'm quitting."

I said, "You're what?"

He said, "I'm through with basketball."

I said, "You can't quit. You just bought the team. We have fifty-some games left."

He said, "I'm telling you to just look out for yourself because I'm bailing out of this basketball thing as soon as I can."

Charlie ran into money problems when he bought the Oakland Seals of the National Hockey League. Right after that, the World Hockey League came into existence and ran up all the hockey salaries. That made Charlie mad at everybody—hockey, basketball, you name it.

LEONARD BLOOM: I owned San Diego and I was good friends with Charlie. He was going through hard times in hockey, in basketball, everywhere. He also was getting divorced. One day he said to me, "You want my baseball team?"

I said, "Why?"

He said, "You want the A's? Just sign your name on a piece of paper, it won't cost you a dime."

I said I didn't want to get involved with baseball.

He said, "Just take the team. You can turn around and sell it for a profit. I just don't want it anymore."

I turned him down, saying I didn't know anything about baseball and I was too involved with the ABA to do anything else. But he really was ready to give me his baseball team.

BOB BASS: That first year with Charlie was a disaster. Our record was 24–60 *(in 1972–73)*. Charlie made only one player move all season, and it was terrible. One day, he just sent me Luther Rackley, who had played for Cleveland and Cincinnati in the NBA and had been trouble everywhere.

Charlie said, "I've got a player for you."

I asked, "Who?"

He said, "Luther Rackley. He'll be getting in at three o'clock."

I said, "Oh no, Charlie, not Luther Rackley."

Charlie said, "If you don't like him, we'll pay him off."

Apparently, signing Luther was a favor for somebody. So I kept him around all year and he was a big pain in the butt. At the end of the season, we had to win our last game to make the playoffs, and we got beat. In the dressing room after that game, I walked by the showers and Luther was in there whistling "Taps."

I went crazy; I was screaming at him, threatening to fine him.

That's one of my worst memories in basketball, Luther whistling "Taps" after a 24–60 season. That whole year was a worst-case scenario.

In late April of 1973, Charlie called and said, "Disconnect all the phones and sell the furniture. We're finished."

Our trainer, Don Sparks, took care of that and for three months the Memphis Tams existed on paper, but didn't even have a phone. I had left to go to work for Mike Storen, who was named ABA commissioner. Mike hired me to be in charge of the league's officials.

When Charlie called Sparks in the fall of 1973 to say he was back in business, Sparky was the only guy left on the payroll. Then Charlie hired Butch van Breda Kolff as coach.

STEVE JONES: That second season with Finley *(1973–74 and a 21–63 record)* was a total joke, and I was just so happy to be out of there. That team's attitude was, "Who cares?" It was like, "Why should we bother to put out a game program when no one comes?"

MIKE STOREN: After the 1973–74 season, the league decided that two years of Finley was more than enough. The league had been more or less running the franchise anyway, because Charlie had stopped paying the bills. So for the 1974–75 season, the league took over Memphis from Charlie and I resigned as commissioner to move to Memphis and run the team. I figured a merger was only a year away and I wanted to get in on the settlement.

TEDD MUNCHAK: Mike Storen just hopped on a plane, went to Memphis and declared himself owner. Why not? Nobody else wanted it.

DICK TINKHAM: Mike Storen was a great commissioner. The press loved him and he got us a lot of publicity. Once a week, he was declaring war on the NBA or working with the league to sign a big name for one of the franchises. That was the perfect job for him.

Then Mike started talking about Memphis.

I told Mike that going to Memphis would be the dumbest thing he could do. He would go broke and could really mess up his life. He said he wanted to be an owner and he had some singers behind him and they were going to call the team the Memphis Sounds. I said I still thought it wouldn't work. Memphis had never worked for anybody. But he was determined. I guess it was just an ego thing with him.

MIKE STOREN: The league paid off Finley and turned the team over to me. I had a group consisting of Avron Fogelman, Kemmonis Wilson and Isaac Hayes. Fogelman later bought the Kansas City Royals. Wilson owned the Holiday Inn chain, and Hayes was hot with hits such as "Shaft."

It all started to fall apart when the bottom suddenly dropped out of the Holiday Inn stock. Wilson told me, "Mike, I know I agreed to go into this basketball team with you, but right now the only thing on my mind is if I should jump out of a window or not. I just can't extend myself anymore right now."

I couldn't blame the guy, but I also was getting very nervous.

Next, I went to Hayes. When you saw pictures of the guy, you figured he was about 6-foot-10, 240 pounds. On the screen, he looked big. But in person, he was about 5-foot-8, 130 pounds.

The first thing he said was, "I don't want to do anything unless I'm the major stockholder."

Hey, that was no problem. If Hayes had the money, he could be the guy, and I told him that.

Hayes said, "Come to my office, Sunday night, nine o'clock."

On Sunday at nine, I went to his office, and it was beautiful. Everything was white—the furniture, the walls, the rugs. He answered the door wearing a T-shirt, jeans, and a pistol shoved inside the belt holding up his jeans.

He was a wonderful guy. We got along great and he wanted to be an ABA owner. Then he handed me a bag full of money, I'd say about $50,000.

I said, "It's 10 o'clock on Sunday night. I can't walk out of here into the streets of downtown Memphis with $50,000 in a bag. You're going to have to write me a check."

He didn't want to write me a check. He said we'd talk about it later and we did, but he never did come across with a check. It was about that time when Hayes's Stax Records empire started to crumble.

So Wilson was out and Hayes was out. Fogelman said he would do what he could, but I couldn't ask him to be a major investor when I had no one else and when he clearly did not intend to be the sole owner of the team. In other words, we were in really big trouble, and in the last eight weeks of the franchise the league was paying all the bills. I did what I could. I hired Joe Mullaney to coach. I made some trades, but it was a no-win situation.

DICK TINKHAM: That last year in Memphis, Mike lost all of his common sense. He paid us $150,000 for Mel Daniels, Roger Brown and Freddie Lewis, and those guys were washed up.

MEL DANIELS: The idea was to put the old Pacers together in Memphis. I was hurt to be traded by Indiana, but I figured if I went anywhere, at least I would be with my friends. But that didn't last long. Storen traded Freddie Lewis to St. Louis and Roger Brown to Utah and I was by myself. I had to approve the deal to Memphis and I did, because Storen promised me more money and an apartment. Indiana had signed Len Elmore and he was supposed to be the Pacers' center of the future. So I went to Memphis to be with Freddie and Roger. But there wasn't any more money, Freddie and Roger were traded, the team was awful and it turned out to be the biggest mistake I've ever made.

MIKE STOREN: Roger Brown had some physical problems and he just wasn't Roger Brown anymore. He was 32 and his age was really showing.

Mel Daniels slipped in the bathtub and did something to his back. We needed some size, so we traded Lewis to St. Louis for Tom Owens.

Look, everything just went wrong.

Rick Mount got off to a great start for us. After the first month of the season, he was leading the league in scoring, then he broke his collarbone. We had Larry Finch from Memphis State, who was a great guy but too slow to be an effective pro. We had Jim O'Brien, who had wild red hair and looked like Bozo the Clown. Our best player was Stew Johnson, a guy who played nine years and never dove for a loose ball. He had four different spots on the floor where he could make shots and Joe Mullaney drew up plays where all Stew had to do was shoot from those spots. Joe did a helluva job with no talent. We went 27–57 and it was a miracle we won the 27 games. And that was the end of the line in Memphis.

Sixth-Year Notebook: 1972–73

Two ABA teams died mercifully as the Pittsburgh Condors and Miami Floridians folded when neither team was able to find a buyer. That reduced the ABA to nine teams, but then the expansion San Diego franchise—the Conquistadors, which was a headline writer's nightmare—was added to give the league 10 teams. The Qs, as they became known, hired K. C. Jones as their coach. Even though he set an ABA record with 67 points, Larry Miller was put in the expansion draft by Carolina and he was taken by the Qs. So was Stew Johnson, who once scored 62 points in a game . . . Jack Dolph quit as commissioner, probably before he was to be fired. Dolph never did get the ABA a significant national television contract. In his last speech, he claimed a merger with the NBA was imminent. He was wrong. Bob Carlson, the New York Nets' team legal counsel, took over for Dolph . . . Federal courts made an impact on the hardwood courts as Rick Barry was ordered away from the Nets and told to honor his contract and play for Golden State of the NBA. Billy Cunningham was told that he had to leave Philadelphia of the NBA and play for the Carolina Cougars . . . Larry Brown became coach of the Cougars and hired Doug Moe as his assistant. With Cunningham leading the way, Carolina was 57–27 after winning only 35 games in 1971–72. Brown became the first homegrown ABA player to serve as a head coach in the league . . . The Indiana Pacers traded Rick Mount to Kentucky as Mount never developed into the player they had hoped . . . Babe McCarthy left Memphis to coach Dallas and Bob Bass (of defunct Miami) was hired by Charlie Finley to coach the Memphis Tams . . . Because Qs owner Len Bloom had problems with the San Diego Sports Arena, Bloom's team played at 3,200-seat San Diego State. But the San Diego State team was able to cut a deal and play in the Sports Arena . . . The Qs passed on a chance to take troubled Joe Caldwell and his $220,000 contract in the expansion draft . . . Earl Strom returned to officiating in the NBA. Official Mark Schlafman also jumped from the ABA to the NBA . . . Carolina rookie Dennis Wuycik played eight minutes in his first ABA game—and fouled out . . . Without Rick Barry, the Nets stumbled to a 30–54 record after losing to Indiana in the 1972 ABA finals. Utah veteran Jimmy Jones said of the Nets, "Sometimes they stand around like they're waiting for Rick Barry to come back" . . . Denver's Julius Keye set an ABA record with 12 blocks. The old record was 10 by Artis Gilmore and Darnell Hillman . . . Indianapolis reporter Dave Overpeck gave San Diego GM Alex Groza the "Dennis Murphy Prize for Padding Attendance." Overpeck overheard Groza tell one of his staff members, "Oh, let's say the attendance is 1,764" . . . Thriving in Larry Brown's pressing defense, Carolina's Joe Caldwell set a league record with 10 steals in a game . . . Memphis cut Ron Franz on Christmas Eve and Merv Jackson on New Year's Eve. When the players went to see Charlie Finley for their last checks, they were told to turn in their team jackets, suitcases, duffel bags and tennis shoes. When Memphis center Randy Denton went to the front office to get some pictures to send to fans, Denton was told that Finley said he had to pay for them . . . In the All-Star Game, the West beat the East 123–111 in Salt Lake before 12,556. The players on the winning team received $500 each, the losers received $300. Warren Jabali was the MVP as he scored all 16 of his points in the second half. Jabali won a free airline ticket to anywhere in Europe, but the Muslim forward said, "I want to go to Africa instead. If they won't send me to Africa, I want the money instead of the ticket. Why should I go to Europe? I don't know anyone there" . . . Before their game with Utah, Pacers coach Bob Leonard promised the American Cancer Society that the team would donate $100 for every point in its margin of victory. The Pacers crushed Utah, 113–86, making the margin 27 points, or $2,700. Denver coach Alex Hannum, who wasn't a part of the game, claimed that Leonard was using the charity as an unfair motivational tool to run up the score against Utah . . . In March, Babe McCarthy quit Dallas to coach at the University of Georgia. He was the last of the original ABA coaches. Forty-two coaches came and went before McCarthy resigned . . . Indiana defeated Kentucky in the ABA finals, giving the Pacers their third ABA title in four years. The final score in Game 7 was 88–81 in Louisville, and George McGinnis had 27 of the winners' 88 points. McGinnis averaged 25 in the finals . . . Billy Cunningham was named MVP. Julius Erving won the scoring title (32 points), Artis Gilmore was tops in rebounding (17.5) and field goal percentage (56 percent). The all-ABA team was Jimmy Jones, Gilmore, Erving, Cunningham and Jabali.

Carolina: Where the Cougars Roamed

Sportswriters always have ideas, and they are good ideas, according to the sportswriters. The Carolina Cougars were the brainchild of Frank Deford, then of Sports Illustrated. A University of North Carolina graduate, Deford proposed in print on October 21, 1968, that a pro team be placed in the basketball-crazed state of North Carolina. While that state did not have one major city, it had several sizable areas such as Greensboro, Charlotte and Raleigh. Hence, the idea of the regional franchise was hatched; it would later spread to Virginia, Florida and Dallas. While it never worked anywhere for a long period, it was most successful in North Carolina.

After the first five ABA seasons, the Cougars (including their record as the Houston Mavericks) were the league's worst surviving franchise. They had never had a winning season, their best record being 42–42 in 1969–70. They had appeared in seven playoff games and lost them all. They wore out owners—Jim Gardner and the group that brought the club to Carolina sold out after just one season—and they wore out coaches. The last two coaches left totally soured on pro basketball. Jerry Steele, who took over when Bones McKinney was fired midway through the Cougars' second season, fled for the serenity of an NAIA program at High Point College. Tom Meschery left coaching altogether and enrolled in a writers' program at the University of Iowa. He now lives in Truckee, California, where he teaches high school.

Even their triumphs were disasters. The Cougars signed 7-footer Jim McDaniels, who led Western Kentucky to the Final Four in 1971. The school had to forfeit its NCAA tournament prize money when it was discovered that McDaniels had signed with Carolina in November 1970. McDaniels was expected to be the "franchise center," but he was never more than a 7-foot jump shooter whom Meschery described as "the worst defensive player I had ever seen." In his first 58 games, McDaniels averaged 27 points and 14 rebounds before jumping to Seattle of the

NBA. Instead of a center, new Carolina owner Tedd Munchak found himself with a pile of legal bills, and he ended up settling with Seattle for a reported $400,000.

Carolina's efforts to get NBA players to jump were only moderately more successful. They signed Billy Cunningham from the Philadelphia 76ers during the 1969–70 season, but a judge ruled that he could not play for them until the 1972–73 season. More disastrously, they signed Joe Caldwell from the Atlanta Hawks. Caldwell was one of the best defensive players in the NBA, but he had knee problems, and proved to be a major contractual thorn to Carolina management. His deal with the Cougars called for $150,000 a year in cash and $70,000 deferred, for a total of $220,000 a year in a five-year deal. A unique clause in the contract stipulated that Caldwell would be paid as a pension $600 a month multiplied by the number of years he played pro basketball. The pension would start at age 55. Since Caldwell turned out to be an 11-year pro, his monthly pension would be $6,600, or $79,200 a year. The Cougars claimed this was a typo in the contract, and that Caldwell should be paid in multiples of $60, not $600—even though $600 was spelled out in both numbers and letters according to Caldwell's attorney. Lawsuit after lawsuit was filed, and a federal appeals court in Atlanta finally ruled in 1984 that the Cougars owed him $220,000. In the meantime, he convinced Tom Meschery to get a real job, and made Larry Brown wonder why he'd ever wanted to be a coach in the first place.

TOM MESCHERY: I retired from Seattle after the 1970–71 season and I had signed up with the Peace Corps to coach basketball and teach in Venezuela. All during the summer of 1971, my wife and I waited for our orders from the Peace Corps at the summer home we'd always rented in Donner Lake, California. There were delays after delays and all kinds of governmental red tape. I was starting to get nervous about what I was going to do, because I wanted to be sure that I was doing something once basketball season started.

In August, I got a call from Carl Scheer about the Cougars job. I had known Carl from when he worked in the NBA office. As I listened to him, I got excited. They offered me $38,000 and a chance to find out if I belonged in coaching. It sounded like the Cougars were going to be a good team. They had Joe Caldwell and had just signed Jim McDaniels. I'd played against Joe in the NBA and had a lot of respect for him. McDaniels was considered a real promising rookie. And the following year, Billy Cunningham was coming over once his contract with Philadelphia was up. I went to training camp and met Gene Littles, who was truly inspirational. He was unselfish and just a damn good guard. We had other hardworking players, such as Ed Manning and Warren Davis. I remember that Davis wrote the Cougars for a tryout, his letter beginning, "I would just like to take a minute of your time to tell you how I can help your team." Tom Owens was another solid player, a 6-foot-10 center. The thing I remember about Tom was that he and his wife were from a tough neighborhood in New York and they used to sleep with a crowbar under their bed, even in Greensboro. Bob Warren was a steady player and person who had a degree in electrical engineering from Vanderbilt and was studying for his real estate license during the season. The reason I mention all these guys was because they probably will get lost in all the crazy stories about that year. I mean, how was I to know that Joe Caldwell, who was supposed to be my star, didn't want to play and had no interest in anything I had to say? How could I know that my great rookie, McDaniels, would jump leagues at midseason? My owner, Tedd Munchak, was a guy who took $6,000 and turned it into millions. He always told me that he didn't know much about basketball, but he also liked to tell his coach what to do.

McDaniels wasn't even close to being a big-time pro player when he signed. He was a face-the-basket, 7-foot jump shooter. He had some speed and some skills with the ball, but he was the worst defensive player I had ever seen as a big man who was supposed to be a high draft pick coming out of college. He couldn't guard anyone. With some patience and some hard work, he could have become a pretty good power forward in the NBA, but he was never going to be a franchise center in either league, yet he was supposed to be that for us.

GENE LITTLES: It didn't take long for McDaniels to become dissatisfied with his contract. He started trying to find a way out of the deal. He claimed that his contract said that his car was supposed to have a tilt steering wheel, but the car they gave him just had a standard steering wheel. He said the Cougars had reneged on his contract. The guy was just trying to get out of his deal. He didn't play hard most of the time. He was truly an awful defensive player. All he really wanted to do was take that turnaround jumper.

McDaniels's contract was supposed to be a six-year, $1.425 million deal. But it really was a classic ABA play-now-and-get-paid-later deal—there was a $50,000 signing bonus and the remaining $1,375,000 was to be paid over 25 years. It was announced as a $3 million deal.

TOM MESCHERY: McDaniels got hooked up with Al Ross, the agent who helped Spencer Haywood and John Brisker jump from the ABA to

Seattle of the NBA. Ross obviously wanted to do the same thing with McDaniels, but McDaniels had to get out of his contract. We played a game in Kentucky *(February 10, 1972)* and Jim didn't show up. Carl Scheer told me that McDaniels was upset because he found out that some of the tax shelters he thought he had weren't really tax shelters. Anyway, McDaniels was supposedly so upset that he was thinking about not playing that night. Here I am a first-year coach and my star rookie is trying to get out of his contract after four months—and it's a 25-year contract, mind you.

Ross made his demands. He wanted the $1.5 million spread over 15 years instead of 25. As he went on, the demands got more outrageous. As Munchak later told Ross, "You shouldn't be living in L.A.; you really belong in Disneyland." Ross made 16 demands in all. He wanted a $25,000 bonus if the Cougars made the playoffs, $25,000 for MVP, a $100,000 life insurance policy and the contract to be paid in one yearly lump sum. He also wanted Tedd Munchak to personally guarantee the contract and he wanted an immediate $50,000 bonus "for the aggravation of having to live in North Carolina."

A couple of weeks later, McDaniels was playing for Seattle.

TEDD MUNCHAK: After I sued Seattle over McDaniels, I got a call from Sam Schulman. He said, "These attorneys' fees are killing us; let's talk."

So we set up a meeting at the Denver airport. His plane came in one gate, mine came in another. We then went into the coffee shop, talked for 20 minutes and came to a settlement. I won't say for how much, but that was it. Good-bye, Mr. McDaniels. At least we still had Joe Caldwell.

The settlement was believed to be $400,000 and McDaniels signed a five-year, $1.5 million deal with Seattle.

CARL SCHEER: When I was hired by the Cougars in 1970, they were undercapitalized. Our highest-paid player was Doug Moe at $55,000, and then we traded him to Virginia. While Jim Gardner and his people had substantial wealth, they weren't interested in losing a couple of million a year. Then Tedd Munchak bought the team and Tedd was willing to spend money.

Joe Caldwell was Munchak's idea. Tedd was from Atlanta and he had a special feeling for Caldwell. Caldwell was an outstanding player with the Hawks. Tedd saw a chance for us to get him so we pursued it.

TEDD MUNCHAK: Carl Scheer wanted Joe Caldwell very badly. I wouldn't have known Joe Caldwell from a kick in the ass. My contact with Joe came when two black Atlanta businessmen came to me—Jessie Hill and Herman Russell. They said that they wanted to see Joe get a fair shake with his next contract and what could be done if Joe were to jump leagues and play for Carolina. I told Carl Scheer about the meeting, he was enthusiastic about getting Joe, so we started talking to Joe's agent, a guy who had shrunk Joe's head in a million ways.

CARL SCHEER: The agent's name was Marshall Boyer and he took me through the most bizarre negotiations I've ever experienced. Boyer's father was very wealthy and Joe's sister worked as a maid in Boyer's home in California. Marshall Boyer would give me speeches about racial oppression, about how pro basketball was just another version of the plantation system and how we were trying to keep people like Joe Caldwell down. I was listening to this and thinking, "Joe's sister is your maid, not mine."

Boyer was married to a Japanese photographer. He was very heavy into everything that was the 1960s, the Woodstock culture and all that. The only reason Joe signed with us was because Joe and his agent wanted to stick it to the Hawks. Boyer didn't care if the ABA was stable, if Carolina was a good franchise or anything. He just wanted to take Caldwell away from Atlanta, as if he were Abraham Lincoln freeing the slaves.

GENE LITTLES: When the Cougars were trying to sign Caldwell, they had him hiding out at the Americana Hotel under a phony name. The Hawks were looking for him to try and get him to sign. When Joe showed up, he wore a huge hat and long overcoat, sort of the Super Fly look. We didn't have anybody on the team who dressed like that. But right away, Joe was unhappy. He complained that we didn't stay in the top-of-the-line hotels like the Hyatts. I always thought the places we stayed were fine, and no one else but Joe complained. He didn't like the airplanes, the arena—he didn't like much of anything, because it wasn't the NBA.

TOM MESCHERY: Like a lot of NBA guys who came to the ABA, Joe thought he was going to be great. He figured that all he had to do was show up and he'd be the Emperor of the North. But Joe couldn't shoot well enough to be a superstar in either league. He was a great role player, yes, if he worked hard. A true star, no. Then you had Joe's personality— he had a chip on his shoulder and thought everyone was out to get him, that being black hurt him. I just couldn't get through to the guy.

TEDD MUNCHAK: Caldwell always wanted a new contract. He never understood the contract he did sign or how his deferred payments worked. He wanted the same benefits as NBA players, but he was in the ABA and he never would accept that. He was always telling me that the coach didn't know what to do, and he said that of all the coaches he played for in Carolina, not just Meschery. Joe would tell me, "We'll never win a game with this guy on the bench."

One day, he came in and said he wanted his own TV show. It was amazing, but we actually got him one. It didn't last long and when it was canceled, Joe sued me for that. Of course, he sued for everything. I had done very well in the carpet business and Joe asked me to help him. So I set him up in the business; he got a big job and mismeasured it. What else was I supposed to do for the guy?

Over the last 15 years, he has sued us for breach of contract several times. I've probably heard from maybe 15 different lawyers over that span claiming to represent Joe, and they tried to garnishee his deferred payments. There was a bankruptcy. Joe had a lot of problems, but he was paid every penny owed him, and that was established in court.

TOM MESCHERY: It got to be so bad with Joe that Atlanta started calling the Cougars about buying Joe back and we talked about selling him to the Hawks or some other NBA team. The cloak-and-dagger stuff that went on was astounding. Here Carolina had just signed the guy, got him to jump leagues, and then they were going to sell him back? That deal was never made, but it was amazing that it was even talked about.

I'll tell you, by the end of that 1971–72 season, with all the crap that went on with McDaniels and Caldwell and everything else, I kept seeing myself less and less as a coach. I had no real vision about how the game should be played. As a player, I had an individual view, but as a coach I had no overall philosophy. I was a bad disciplinarian. Another guy might have gotten more out of Caldwell, although I really don't know what I could have done with Joe. There were days when I thought I was pretty brilliant and other times when I knew I was pretty dumb.

There was pressure coming from all directions. McDaniels jumped the team, Caldwell wouldn't play and Tedd Munchak wasn't the easiest guy to work for.

Tedd was from New Jersey and he liked to play the tough guy. He was very domineering. He'd call me in the middle of the night and ask me why I wasn't playing this guy or that guy. He thought that players should have his 9-to-5, steel-hat work ethic. He'd tell me that I should play this player, "because he's a really tough kid."

Tedd would be right. The player was tough and he did work hard, but he did all that because he had no talent. No matter how hard he worked, it wasn't about to make up for the lack of talent, either. Tedd never understood that.

We ended the season at 35–49 and didn't make the playoffs. Everybody was very disappointed. I was going to just quit but *(GM)* Carl Scheer told me, "Don't do it. Go home and think about it."

I did, and the next day I went to see Carl and told him that I still wanted to coach. He said, "Good, we're 100 percent behind you."

I knew that Billy Cunningham was coming to the Cougars and that unlike Joe Caldwell, Billy was a superstar, a turnaround player. With Billy Cunningham on your team, you can become a good coach very fast. But in the end, I found that I liked and respected Carl Scheer. He is an honest, lovable guy. I couldn't say the same thing about Tedd Munchak or his management style. So I quit, or they fired me to hire Larry Brown. The semantics don't matter. I was out of coaching and glad about it. I changed my life completely. One year was enough to tell me all I needed to know about pro coaching.

o o o

This was the setting when Larry Brown was hired as the Cougars' head coach in the summer of 1972. Brown was 32 and hired good buddy Doug Moe as his assistant. Moe was 34 and had played until his knee would let him play no more. Brown was an All-Star during the first three years of the ABA; for his five-year career, Brown averaged 11.2 points and 8.3 assists and shot 42 percent. He was the ABA all-time leader in assists when he retired. Moe was an All-Star in his first four seasons. For his career, he averaged 16.3 points and 7.8 rebounds and shot 44 percent. The real value of Brown and Moe was their relationship with each other, their ability to communicate with the players and the fact that they had been in the ABA since Day One. In their first season, the Cougars improved 22 games and were 57–27, with Brown being voted the ABA Coach of the Year. Of course, Brown got a big boost when Billy Cunningham joined the team. The following season, the Cougars were 47–37. Then the team was sold to St. Louis, while Brown and Moe followed Carl Scheer to Denver.

TEDD MUNCHAK: After Meschery, I decided that I would take a more active role in hiring the next Cougars coach. I got tired of these geniuses telling me that Play 7 didn't work because Play 12 broke down and that was why we lost. Who the hell cared what play it was? That X and O crap is way overrated. I wanted a coach who could talk to the players and get them to play hard. I wanted a guy who knew what was going on in the ABA now and who didn't tell me how it used to be in the old days when he played.

My guy was Larry Brown.

LARRY BROWN: I had severely injured my hip and I was playing for Denver in 1972, knowing I couldn't play much longer. The hip was giving me too much trouble, and it's the same hip that I've since had replaced. At Carolina, Carl Scheer had been through several coaches, and I know that Carl called Dean Smith about me and Coach Smith recommended me for the job. Tedd Munchak flew me to Greensboro on his private jet and offered me the job. I was interested in coaching, but college coaching, not pro coaching. Still, the Cougars seemed like a great opportunity, so I took it.

CARL SCHEER: We hired Larry Brown for $30,000, which was probably the best $30,000 the Carolina franchise ever spent.

ALEX HANNUM: I was coaching in Denver and it was a last-place team. Larry Brown was one of the few guys I could count on. Then Carl Scheer came in and stole Larry from me. Larry could still play, but Carl talked him into coaching the Cougars. I don't hold that against Larry, but I do against Carl Scheer. I've never had any respect for Carl Scheer and I've never forgiven him for taking Larry Brown from me.

LARRY BROWN: Whether I liked it or not, I had to stop playing because of my hip, just as Doug Moe had to stop because of his knee problems. The first thing I did after getting the Carolina job was hire Doug as my assistant.

DOUG MOE: Larry came to see me in the hospital after I had had knee surgery. I knew that my knee was gone and I probably couldn't play anymore, which was going to about kill me. I was going to play until I was at least 50, you know? Larry was different. Larry always was going to be a coach. Larry knew what he wanted to do with the rest of his life. I had no idea. So when the doctor told me that my knee was shot and to forget about playing basketball, I was open for suggestions. Then Larry showed up and asked me to be his assistant and I said, "Why not? I don't want to get a real job."

CARL SCHEER: Doug Moe was exactly what Larry Brown needed. Larry was driven, intense. Doug had a calming effect on Larry, especially when he sensed that was what Larry needed. At other times, Larry and

Doug would argue as if they were about to kill each other. Doug understood how to be a second banana, yet he had enough respect from Larry that he could say, "Larry, just ease off a bit. You're going off the deep end," and Larry would listen to him.

TEDD MUNCHAK: Doug was the ideal foil for Larry. During a time-out, Larry would be all wound up and Doug would sort of push Larry aside and say, "Hey, guys, you know what to do. Just go out there and score some points, all right?"

LARRY BROWN: With Doug on the bench next to me, it was like we were co-coaches. He still is my friend. He has always been loyal and always wanted me to succeed. But he also would tell me when I was wrong. We just have a great friendship.

DOUG MOE: If I felt like saying something, I did. If not, I'd just sit there and say, "Way to go, Larry."

STEVE JONES: From the moment Larry and Doug came into the league, it was as if they were a package deal. They had such a strong bond, starting with growing up in Brooklyn, then playing together at North Carolina and then going to New Orleans at the start of the ABA. Then when Larry got his first coaching job, Doug was there to help him. I can't think of two guys in basketball who have shared so many experiences. Even today, with Doug coaching in Denver and Larry in San Antonio, Doug will say, "The hell with this, I think I'll just go back to being Larry's assistant."

DOUG MOE: Larry and I just always got along. I don't know why. I mean, why even ask the question? Either you get along with someone or you don't. We would have incredible fights, especially on the golf course. We'd call each other names and swear we'll never talk to each other again, but the next day it was over. The thing is that we never competed against each other. Not in basketball, golf, racquetball or anything. We always played on the same team, yet we'd still get into fights.

GENE LITTLES: When Larry Brown was hired, it was exactly what we needed. The guys knew and respected Larry and Doug because they'd played in the ABA, and they also knew what we could do. I liked how Larry played, his unselfishness and his ability to read his teammates. He has a real knack for knowing what players are thinking and what they worry about. He knew that players wanted to know what was expected of them. His practices were the same most days. His substitution patterns were the same in most games. His main rule was if you practiced hard and played hard, you would get your minutes. He was a coach who had no surprises, and the players appreciated that. He also knew that there were times when the guys were down and he'd say, "Here's my credit card. Go out and have dinner on me, just be ready to play hard tomorrow."

TEDD MUNCHAK: Larry didn't run a strict club, but I didn't care because we won. The guys played their ass off for him and Doug. So if on a trip from Denver to Texas they wanted to make a stop in Las Vegas for a good time, I wasn't going to say anything. I suppose Larry thought I didn't know about that, so I pretended I didn't know. What the hell, Larry won 57 and 47 games in his two years as coach, so what he did was all right with me.

BOB COSTAS: Before every game, it was fun just to see what Larry and Doug would wear. Most ABA coaches were into leisure suits with ridiculous shirts and those collars you could land an airplane on. Larry liked to wear Oshkosh B'Gosh farmer's overalls. Once in a while, he'd wear leather pants. And Doug, he looked like a flood victim. A complete disaster.

TERRY STEMBRIDGE: When Doug Moe first came into the league, he wore a white T-shirt, jeans and tennis shoes everywhere. When Doug became a coach, the only change was that sometimes he wore a different color T-shirt. With Larry wearing those overalls, it was hard to imagine someone dressing even worse, but Doug did.

STEVE JONES: Larry's real talent is his knack of walking into a disaster area, bringing order and stability and making players happy. I was traded by Dallas to Carolina, and it was a huge break for me to play with a really good team.

This was a learning season for Larry. No matter how well you think you're prepared to coach and how much basketball you know, there's nothing like getting that first coaching job and having to deal with all the egos and the insecurities. He developed a strong fraternal feeling on the team. Larry would go to bat for his players if they needed help with expenses, housing, that kind of thing. He made sure that management did right by you. In return, he expected an honest day's effort and a certain degree of loyalty.

His first big test was Joe Caldwell. And Caldwell and Doug Moe had no chemistry at all. None.

DOUG MOE: In our first day of practice, I threw Joe Caldwell out. He wasn't hustling or something and I yelled at him to shape up.

Joe yelled at me, "You don't tell me what to do."

I said, "You're outta here."

Caldwell just stared at me. He couldn't believe that an assistant coach had just thrown him out of practice.

I said, "Get your ass outta here. We only won 35 games last year with you here, we can win that many without you."

When Joe left the gym, the whole team went into shock.

STEVE JONES: The coaches were in a bind because the owners insisted that Caldwell play, and when it came to the games, Joe did give you all he had. But he just didn't see any sense to practice. He didn't like drills, he didn't like anything about it.

There was a time when Caldwell and Doug got into it so bad that Doug got mad and stayed away from the team for three days because of Joe. So one day, Larry came into a morning shootaround and told us, "Joe isn't going to be with the team anymore." Apparently Larry and Doug had gone to Carl Scheer and talked it over with him and Carl apparently said he would trade Caldwell.

That night, Caldwell showed up for the game. Nobody said a word to him, but all the players were looking at Joe and thinking, "Why are you here? You're supposed to be gone."

Then Larry told us, "We couldn't trade Joe. The owners said they were paying him too much money to trade him, so Joe stays."

I heard there was a deal for Caldwell set up, but Tedd Munchak had vetoed it. But that's something no one will ever know.

MACK CALVIN: Joe Caldwell was so moody. He wasn't on drugs or anything like that, he was just very unhappy. He would get upset about something and he'd walk home from the arena. And he lived seven miles away! He'd just follow the railroad tracks home to his condo.

GENE LITTLES: Joe had his problems and his moods, but everybody else on the team was focused and busting their butts, so Joe couldn't disrupt what we were doing. When guys like Billy Cunningham, Mack Calvin, Steve Jones, Ed Manning, Teddy McClain and the rest are hustling, Caldwell sort of just fell in line.

BILLY CUNNINGHAM: When Joe set his mind to it, he was a tremendous defensive player. Joe Caldwell took it as a personal challenge when he played Julius Erving and he guarded Julius as well as anyone in the ABA.

BOB RYAN: When the Cougars had Caldwell and Cunningham together at the forwards, they had a very dangerous front line. Cunningham would drive out of the right corner across the line and go up with his left-handed drive. Caldwell would come out of the left corner with the same move, only he was right-handed. They had two guys who could get to the basket.

The Celtics played their first exhibition game against the Cougars both years that Larry Brown was there. The Celtics hated it because Brown had his guys ready to go the first game; they were pressing and doing that jump-switch double-teaming defense of his. The Celtics were out there just trying to break a sweat and the Cougars were trying to win the damn game and run them off the court.

GENE LITTLES: No one else in the ABA trapped and used that jump-switch defense until Larry brought it in. We surprised a lot of teams, including the Celtics, because we double-teamed and got guys from the blind side. No one in the NBA did that, either. We had very quick guards and got a lot of steals. Also, our forwards could press, too, with Caldwell and Cunningham. At first Caldwell didn't like it, because it was a lot of work. But then he saw all the steals and the layups he was getting off those steals and he got with the defense and loved playing it.

LARRY BROWN: No one used the run-and-jump defense in the pros. When I told people that that was the defense I planned to play, they told me that I would get killed. But I was convinced that if you had a quick team, you could make up for your lack of size with this defense. And using that kind of pressure meant that you had to play a lot of guys, which was good for team morale, since more guys were involved. At the start of the season, Mike Lewis was supposed to be our center, but he got hurt and played only 15 games that season. So we alternated Ed Manning and Tom Owens in the middle. Both of those guys were really forwards, but we did what we had to do and with the run-and-jump defense, we got by with a smaller team.

CARL SCHEER: In terms of depth, the guards were the strongest part of our team. We had Gene Littles and Teddy McClain when Larry was hired. Then we picked up Mack Calvin in the dispersal draft after the Floridians folded, and we traded for Steve Jones. Mack and Steve had been All-Stars, 20-point scorers in the league. I thought Mack was the best of the ABA's little guards, and Steve was a great shooter, but not known for his defense. I wasn't sure how they'd fit into Larry's pressure defense, which was more suited for Littles and McClain.

One day Larry came to me and said, "I've got four good guards, but I don't think any of them can play 40 minutes."

I waited for what he would say next. I didn't know if he wanted to trade someone or what.

Then Larry said, "I'm going to play all four of them equal time."

I said, "You'll never get away with it."

Larry said, "Wait and see."

He started the game with Mack and Jones. That was his offensive unit. Mack was a great penetrator, a streaky shooter and an emotional leader. He pushed the ball up and down the court, he went to the basket, got fouled and made the foul shots. Jones had his spots outside; he went there and made the shots.

Then Larry would take them out for McClain and Littles, and those guys just pressed people off the floor. You couldn't dribble the ball up the court against Gene or Teddy. They would just take it away from you. You put all that backcourt talent together and we were a bitch. The great thing was how Larry was able to get these four talented guys to be happy with playing only half the game.

STEVE JONES: Larry used the passing-game offense, the same one Doug Moe now uses in Denver. The idea is simple: when you get the ball, you have two counts—1,001 and 1,002—to do something. If you haven't shot it or made a strong move to the basket by then, pass the ball and cut to the basket or go someplace. The idea was to keep the ball moving. He hated isolation basketball where a guy got the ball on one side of the court and everyone else stood on the other side and watched him go 1-on-1.

At the start of that season, Larry had four guys who were used to being the No. 1 scorers on their teams: Cunningham, Caldwell, Calvin and myself. Larry had all these offensive-minded players, yet he was spending most of his time on defense.

Sometimes, you'd get the feeling that if you passed the ball once, you'd never see it again. Mack Calvin would never take the ball inbounds because he worried that if he did, that would be the last time he touched it. If you threw the ball down Cunningham's side of the court, then Caldwell would say, "How about me?" Then you'd go to Joe and Billy would say, "Am I playing in this game?"

But by the end of the year, it was working. The ball was moving around, the egos were in check, the defense was great. Larry has done a lot of super coaching jobs in his life, but I still think this was his best.

THE KANGAROO KID JUMPS IN

When Billy Cunningham joined the Cougars, he was 29 and had been an NBA All-Star in four of his seven seasons with the Philadelphia 76ers. He was considered perhaps the best small forward in the NBA. In his first ABA season, the Cougars had the best record in the ABA. They beat the Nets 4–1 in the first round of the playoffs, then lost 4–3 to Kentucky in the second round. Carolina tied Utah for the scoring lead with 115.5 points. The Cougars also led the league in forcing turnovers, a tribute to their press. Cunningham led the league in steals, Caldwell was fifth, Ted McClain ninth and Gene Littles 10th. They also became the first team in ABA history to shoot 50 percent from the field. Billy Cunningham averaged 24.1 points and the rest of the scoring was balanced— Calvin 17.4, Caldwell 16.6, Jones 12.2, Tom Owens 11.8, Littles 9.8, McClain 9.6, and Ed Manning 9.5. Cunningham stayed with Carolina for its last two seasons before returning to Philadelphia when the Cougars were sold to St. Louis.

BILLY CUNNINGHAM: I was with Philadelphia when Jim Gardner approached me about jumping to the Cougars. I had gone to college at North Carolina and I liked the area. The season was 1969–70 and I was making $40,000 with the Sixers. That was after six years in the NBA. I was a first-team all-pro, third in the MVP voting, and given all that, I really wasn't making any money at all.

Gardner offered me a chance to increase five times *(to $200,000 a year)*. I kept thinking about all that money. I knew I wasn't going to play forever and it was time to make it while I could. So I took the Cougars' offer *($400,000 for two years)* even though I had a year left on my contract with Philadelphia. I played that last season with the Sixers—my option year—and then I went to Carolina for 1972–73.

But later I felt that Carolina had reneged on my contract. Certain monies were supposed to be delivered to me on certain dates before I even started playing, but those payments were never made.

(Cunningham received $40,000 upon signing, which was paid. He was due another $40,000 in April before he was to jump leagues, which Cunningham claimed wasn't paid. Cunningham then returned the first $40,000 and declared his contract void.)

I filed a suit claiming that my Carolina contract was void because of the missed payment and then I signed a long-term deal with Philadelphia. In the meantime, Tedd Munchak bought the Cougars. He filed a court suit and the judge ruled that my contract with Carolina was still in effect, so I reported to the Cougars.

TEDD MUNCHAK: In the summer of 1972, I called Cunningham and set up a meeting. I wanted to talk to him about the contract and make sure that he was happy.

I said, "Billy, you understand that the contract you have with the ABA is legal and binding."

He said he did.

Then I said, "Let's talk about that contract. I want you happy and I want you ready to contribute to our success. Before we talk about money, I want you to know that I won't be nickeled and dimed to death. I don't want to hear about plane tickets, cars, apartments. I just want to know, how much do you want?"

He said, "I want $300,000 a year."

I said, "Okay."

Billy was stunned, and so was his agent. There was a long silence. Then Billy asked, "Is that real dollars?"

I said it was.

Billy asked, "Nothing deferred?"

I said, "Nothing deferred. But that's it. No nickel and dime crap. Nothing but real dollars. Your agent can draw up the contract just like we talked about and I'll sign it, so long as there is no extra garbage in there."

That conversation with Billy took exactly five minutes and then we went out and played nine holes of golf.

BILLY CUNNINGHAM: In essence, that was what happened, although I remember the details a little differently. When Tedd called me in for a meeting, he said he wanted me happy and he wanted to talk about my contract. Then he made me an offer. I didn't like it. He asked me to leave the room for a minute. When I came back, he had two offers for me. I picked the one I liked and then Tedd said, "Let's go play golf." I'd say the whole thing took no more than 10 minutes.

CARL SCHEER: When Billy came over, especially in light of the lawsuit, we were concerned that he might have an "NBA attitude," acting as if he was too good for us and the league. But Billy quickly dispelled those fears. He was great from the first day of camp. He acted like a Cougar, had nothing but nice things to say about the ABA and didn't talk about his days in the NBA. Then he went out and had a great year. He got behind Larry Brown and the things Larry wanted done and the whole thing clicked. He played the total game—scoring, rebounding, passing and defense. It really was impressive to see a star of that magnitude play so hard.

GENE LITTLES: Billy never wore socks except when he played. He hated to dress up and loved to wear those baggy pants. With Billy, it was always loafers and no socks. When he got some money, he took the bills, wadded them up and shoved them in his pocket. When you walked into Billy's room, there would be all these bills wadded up on his dresser. One time, he threw one of those wads at me and said, "Looks like you're going out, why don't you get us something to eat from the store?" I unfolded the wad and it was a $50 bill.

LARRY BROWN: Billy had a career year. In fact, I've never had a player who has had as good an all-around season as Billy did with the Cougars. I loved everything about the guy.

STEVE JONES: Once Billy came to the league and saw the competitiveness, he realized these guys could play. He had a great year, but he didn't just walk out there and dominate the league. There were guys who scored more points, had more rebounds. There were nights when he could control the game and other nights when he had his hands full, just like he did in the NBA. He was the MVP *(in 1973)* and he earned it, because the guy had a knack for making the big plays, the plays that won games.

MACK CALVIN: At first, we had some problems with Billy and Joe Caldwell. Both guys were ex-NBA stars and both guys wanted the ball. If you threw it to one, the other complained.

Early in the season, Billy and I had an incident in Denver. Denver had this guard named Ralph Simpson who was 6-foot-5 and supposed to be the next Oscar Robertson. That never panned out, but Simpson had some excellent seasons. I was guarding one of their smaller players and Billy was on Simpson. But on a couple of plays, some picks were set and Ralph ended up scoring over me. Billy was getting pissed because Simpson scored, and decided to blame me because of how we switched on defense. Billy called a time-out and started screaming at me.

I stopped him and yelled, "You say one more damn word to me and I'm going to knock you right into the stands."

From that day on, I think I had Billy's respect. I spent the rest of the night looking to get him the ball, but I never congratulated him after he made a shot. I didn't want it to look like I was giving in to him or something.

When the game was over, Billy asked me to go out for a drink. He was that kind of guy; he never held grudges, no matter what was said on the court. We talked about what happened with Simpson and Billy said he just got frustrated. I said, "Billy, I love playing with you. You're a great player, but no one likes to be yelled at when he's busting his ass."

I think Billy saw that we were both the same kind of guys and wanted the same things, and we got along really well after that.

GENE LITTLES: For a guard, there was a balancing act between Caldwell and Cunningham. Not only did those guys want the ball, they called for it. But they also were the best forwards in all of basketball that year, and everybody played hard for Larry Brown. The more we won, the better everyone got along and got to know each other. People said that Larry would never be able to split playing time between four guards and make everybody happy, but he did. Then they said that he'd never be able to play Caldwell and Billy together because they'd both want to be the star, but that worked itself out, too. The key was Billy's having a good attitude. If he hadn't, he could have ripped the team apart.

BILLY CUNNINGHAM: I had the time of my life playing for the Cougars that year. I am very sincere when I say that this was the most fun I ever had playing pro basketball. I just felt bad that I was hurt in my second season.

Cunningham had two kidney operations and played only 32 games that season. The Cougars slipped to 47–37 in 1973–74 and were eliminated in the first round of the playoffs. Then the Cougars were sold to a group of New York businessmen and brothers by the name of Ozzie and Daniel Silna, along with a lawyer named Don Schupak, who moved the team to St. Louis and named it the Spirits of St. Louis. After selling the team, Munchak became commissioner of the ABA. Carl Scheer moved on to Denver, where he became general manager. He took Doug Moe, Larry Brown and Mack Calvin with him. Billy Cunningham returned to the NBA, and the only member of the Cougars playing in St. Louis by the end of the Spirits' first season was Steve Jones.

CARL SCHEER: I've always felt that if Tedd Munchak had lived in North Carolina instead of Atlanta, he would have stuck with the Cougars instead of selling the team to the Silna brothers. But he was becoming disenchanted and he was losing money, so when he saw a chance to sell the team, he did.

Actually, the Cougars were a pretty good franchise, but the regional idea was the problem. We were playing in Greensboro, Charlotte and Raleigh. In Greensboro, which was our headquarters, we drew great— about 12,000 a game. Charlotte was about 6,000 and Raleigh was terrible, as we were lucky to get 3,000. In the abstract, it made sense to try to involve the whole state in pro basketball, but in reality you just couldn't make it work. The feeling was that the team belonged to Greensboro and when we played in Charlotte or Raleigh, we were carpetbaggers. Our expenses were high, because we had to maintain three offices in the three different cities and that meant three different staffs. Even though we drew those big numbers in Greensboro, a lot of it was done with cut-rate tickets, so the actual cash wasn't as big as it seemed. Also, we had no network television revenue worth discussing, so you had to survive on what you made at the gate.

BILLY CUNNINGHAM: The regional franchise thing made travel a problem. We did a lot of busing to games in Raleigh and Charlotte, which made them feel like road games. Also, flying anywhere from North Carolina meant that we first had to go to Atlanta. To me, the Atlanta airport felt as much like home as anything did, because of all the time we spent there waiting for connections.

STEVE JONES: The regional concept did us in during the 1973 playoffs. We had a seventh game with Kentucky in the second round and instead of playing in Greensboro, which was really our home floor, we played in Charlotte and we lost (107–96). That year, we played two playoff games in Charlotte and lost them both. In Greensboro, we were 4–0. When that game was played in Charlotte, we didn't have the home-court advantage you'd expect in the playoffs and that had a negative psychological effect on the team.

TEDD MUNCHAK: I never thought that the franchise could survive in three different cities. Raleigh was a big mistake and I thought we should have been headquartered in Charlotte, but Carl Scheer liked Greensboro so we stayed there.

When I bought the Cougars, I needed a tax loss. By the time I sold them, I no longer needed that kind of loss. I made a commitment to the ABA to keep the team for three years and I kept it for three years and one day.

BILLY CUNNINGHAM: After my second season with the Cougars, I had my choice of staying in the ABA or going back to Philadelphia. I really respected Tedd Munchak, and he was selling the team. That worried me.

Here the Cougars were supposed to be one of the top four teams in terms of gate revenues, not just in the ABA but all of basketball, and Munchak was getting out. I didn't take that as a good sign. Also, I still had a home and my family liked Philadelphia, so I decided it was best to go back to the Sixers.

GENE LITTLES: It seemed like everybody knew that the franchise was being sold but me. In fact, they may as well have folded the team for all the good it did the players, because none of us got a chance in St. Louis. I'm sure that management told Billy Cunningham and Mack Calvin what was coming, but the other guys, the guys who weren't stars, we were caught by surprise. For me, it was a funny feeling for the team no longer to be in North Carolina. I was there for all five years. It seemed like every training camp there were a couple of young guards who were supposed to take my job, but they never did. I bet they went through 20 guards while I was with the Cougars.

Wendell Ladner: An ABA Original

Wendell Ladner was a 6-foot-4, 220-pound forward for five seasons, playing for four teams—Memphis, Kentucky, Carolina and New York. He averaged 11.6 points and 8.1 rebounds and shot 40 percent. He also was a member of the 1971 and 1972 All-Star teams. Ladner died in a plane crash on June 24, 1975, at the age of 26.

STEVE JONES: Wendell Ladner was a discovery and a disciple of Babe McCarthy. Babe had coached at Mississippi State and Wendell was from Necaise Crossing, Mississippi, and attended Southern Miss. Babe told me that he remembered Wendell from when Wendell was a kid and he went to one of Babe's basketball camps.

One day in our last season in New Orleans *(1969–70),* Babe told me, "Steve, you run practice for me today. I've got to go out scoutin'."

When Babe went "scoutin' " it could mean a lot of things. He wasn't necessarily scouting for basketball players, if you know what I mean. But this time, he did go look at a player, and it was Ladner.

"The first thing I noticed about Wendell was his size," Babe told me. "They said he was 6-foot-9, and he was about 6-foot-4. There were all these damn NBA scouts in the building and there was Wendell, this big old lard-ass just jiggling up and down the court. He wasn't in any kind of shape. He was just embarrassing."

After the game, Babe went up to Wendell and said, "Son, you're just a damn embarrassment to me. When I had you in my summer camps, you were big, but you were cat-quick. You were one of the quickest things I've ever seen in my life. And now look at you, you lard-ass. When are you gonna get in shape?"

Wendell said, "I'll get in shape when the pro season opens."

Babe said, "None of these damn NBA scouts will have your fat ass. But I'll tell you what—since I've known you about all your life, I'll take you and I'll give you a $500 bonus. You come down and try out for my team. If you make it, I'll play your ass."

Babe said Wendell was about 260 when he saw him. Come training camp in Memphis, Wendell was down to 220. He was the strongest 6-foot-4 guy I had ever seen in my life. No one hustled like Wendell. He'd throw a bad pass to himself. I mean, if he'd throw a bad pass, he would just chase it down, running over guys to get the ball. He loved to take 3-pointers and he missed most of them, but what he did well was crash the boards, get his own rebound and go back up with the shot. Physically, he could just brute you to death.

DAN ISSEL: I played with Wendell in Kentucky when he pulled the famous water cooler incident. Wendell was forever diving for loose balls and he chased one down in front of our bench. He went after it headfirst and came smack down into the water cooler, a glass water cooler, and he had to get 100-some stitches. The thing was that Wendell wanted to come back and play in the second half.

VAN VANCE: His favorite thing on the court was to crash into the stands after a loose ball. He ran into the scorer's table and knocked me off the air a couple of times going for loose balls.

As for the water cooler play, it was in Game 6 of the 1973 playoffs between our Kentucky team and Carolina. He barreled right into the cooler and took 48 stitches. Then he came back the next day and played in Game 7, helping us upset the Cougars and Billy Cunningham in Charlotte.

DAVE VANCE: I was publicity director for the Colonels during Wendell's dive into the water cooler. It was 48 stitches and there was blood all over the place—Wendell's blood. I distinctly recall a woman seeing that and then she fainted.

TERRY STEMBRIDGE: One day I was interviewing Babe McCarthy about Wendell and we talked about the water cooler incident. I said to Babe, "It seems Wendell doesn't know the meaning of the word 'fear.' "

Babe said, "That's right; of course, he doesn't know the meaning of many other words, either."

DAN ISSEL: Once we were flying into Washington, D.C., and from the window of the plane, Wendell looked out, saw the Washington Monument and said, "I bet that's the Washington Post."

STEVE JONES: Wendell would fight anyone. In his second pro game, we played Denver and Wendell got into it with Wayne Hightower, and right away Hightower backed off. He just didn't want any part of Wendell. The next day, we went to Pittsburgh back when the Condors had John Brisker, who was the meanest guy in the league. Before the game, Brisker said to me, "I hear you've got this tough white kid on your team."

That was how good the ABA grapevine was. Wendell was in the league for only two games and already the word was out on him.

I told Brisker, "Ladner can fight. I wouldn't mess with him."

Brisker said, "Well, we'll find out tonight."

Pittsburgh had a bad team and a very selfish team. Brisker was out there shooting the ball every time he got it, trying to get his 30. Once Brisker got his 30 points, he decided it was time to go after Wendell. John threw an elbow at Ladner, who didn't pay any attention to it and just ran down to the other end of the court. The next time down the court, Brisker threw another elbow, and Ladner went crazy. It became more like two bulls trying to gore each other than a basketball fight. These were just two big, strong, rough guys. In their next game, they got into a fight at the jump ball to start the game. But eventually, they learned that neither guy could beat the other.

RUDY MARTZKE: Wendell was crazy. He'd stick his head into Brisker's dressing room and yell, "Hey, John, we going to go at it now or after the game?" The three toughest guys in the league were Brisker, Ladner and Warren Jabali.

DAN ISSEL: When Wendell was traded by Kentucky to New York, he became Julius Erving's bodyguard. You'd better not lay a finger on Julius, or else Wendell would break your arm. One game, I got into a little altercation with Wendell. In Kentucky, our enforcer was Ron Thomas. I squared off with Wendell and I was waiting for Thomas to come to my rescue. He never did. Lucky for me, Wendell didn't want to hurt me, so not much happened.

After the game, I asked Thomas, "Where were you?"

He said that the ABA had sent out a memo saying if you left the bench to get into a fight, it was an automatic $100 fine.

I said, "Listen, if I ever get into anything with Wendell, you just come help me out. I'll pay the hundred bucks and I'll give you an extra hundred. It will be worth it to keep me out of the hospital."

Wendell just loved to fight. When we were teammates in Kentucky, he got into fights in practice. He would undercut guys and everything. I said, "Wendell, that stuff is fine in a game, but take it easy in practice."

Wendell would look at me and say, "What did I do?"

The thing was that Wendell really didn't know what he did. He just played the same way all the time—crazy.

ROGER BROWN: Wendell was built like a linebacker and when he guarded me, he tried to beat me to death. When no one was looking, he'd push me right into the stands. If there was a loose ball on the floor, he'd jump on it with his body like it was a fumble. We gave him a lot of room out there, if you know what I mean. With Wendell, you just never knew what he'd do on the court.

But the funny thing was that off the court, he was one of the most popular guys in the league. He was a white guy from Mississippi, but you'd never know it because he got along fine with everybody, black or white. He didn't have one of those attitudes you find in some players from the South.

BOB RYAN: I remember covering an exhibition game between the Celtics and the Nets. Wendell went right after John Havlicek, and tried to beat the hell out of him. The players on the Celtics looked at Wendell and said, "Who the hell is that lunatic out there?"

VAN VANCE: Two guys who always fought were Cincy Powell and Wendell Ladner. Those guys wouldn't be on the floor for five minutes and they would be swinging at each other. One official told me, "The best thing to do with Ladner and Powell is to let them fight it out early. Don't try to break it up, because they will just be at it a few minutes later. Once they fight and get it out of their systems, then they're fine for the rest of the night."

Wendell once swore to me that he fouled out of a high school game in 90 seconds. Hey, maybe he did.

BOB COSTAS: The league feared Wendell Ladner, yet he also entertained everyone, because he was a guy whose view of the world was just a little off.

In the second playoff game in 1975 between St. Louis and New York, the Spirits had a 30-point lead over the Nets at Nassau Coliseum. Ladner was running after someone and he ran right out of his shoe. Freddie Lewis was dribbling the ball away from Wendell, who was hobbling around in one shoe. Wendell was so frustrated that he threw his shoe right at Lewis, hitting Freddie in the back. Freddie was a little guy, but he was a fighter and his initial instinct was to take a swing at whoever had hit him with the shoe. But when he turned and saw it was Wendell, he just smiled. *(Some people have told this story as Ladner knocking the ball away from Lewis with the shoe, but the consensus is that the shoe hit Lewis.)*

TOM MESCHERY: I coached Wendell in Carolina and he was a big, overgrown kid. He had a two-track mind—basketball and sex. He used hair spray before games and at halftime so he'd look good for the ladies. He liked to shoot the ball from unbelievable distances and that would drive any coach nuts, but he played so hard you had to love him. Poor Wendell—he really was dumb as a post, but he had a great time while he was alive, and the women surely did love him.

DAN ISSEL: His vocabulary was pretty much limited to basketball and women, and he talked a lot more about women than he did about basketball.

VAN VANCE: Wendell was a handsome guy with a hairy chest like Burt Reynolds. For one promotion, the Colonels had him pose wearing only his basketball shorts and holding a basketball. Women just migrated to the guy.

DAVE VANCE: I was publicity director for the Colonels when we did the Wendell Ladner hairy-chest poster. We stole the idea from Burt Reynolds, who had posed for *Cosmopolitan.* Wendell's posters sold out in a day.

Wendell had a speech impediment that actually was quite endearing to some people. He had trouble with his *s*'s. He'd say, "I had four cup of coffees," or "Is my hair mess upped?"

VAN VANCE: Wendell and I made a commercial for tortilla chips. But Wendell couldn't say tort-te-ya. He'd say, tort-till-a. Nor could he read the script out loud that they had prepared for him. Finally, we just started talking off-the-cuff about how great these chips were for about an hour and somehow got a commercial out of that.

DAVE VANCE: This story is incredible, but I swear it is true. Wendell went to see a doctor and said he had a discomfort in his groin area. For the record, Wendell was single at the time. The doctor said, "It looks like you've been having sex too much."

Wendell said, "You think so?"

The doctor said, "Well, how many times a day do you have sex?"

Wendell said, "I don't know, three or four times."

The doctor said, "Wendell, that's too much."

Wendell said, "Well, it's never with the same girl."

The other story along these lines is that a woman appeared at Wendell's door saying she needed a cup of sugar.

Wendell said, "I don't have any sugar."

She said, "I drove all the way from Indianapolis for some sugar. Are you going to let me in or not?"

KEVIN LOUGHERY: After Julius, Wendell was the second most popular player on the Nets. It was the same way everywhere he played. When Kentucky traded him to us *(the Nets),* there was a big uproar from the fans in Louisville. When he was killed, there was a real and deep sadness all over the league.

DAVE VANCE: I was one of the pallbearers at Wendell's funeral in Necaise Crossing, Mississippi. There were about 600 people at the funeral and Julius Erving was the only black there. He delivered one of the eulogies for Wendell and he was a great comfort to Wendell's family. Julius and Wendell were two guys from completely different parts of the country, different racial backgrounds, different lifestyles. But you could sense the bond they had with each other, and that said a lot about Wendell.

Seventh-Year Notebook: 1973–74

The only franchise move in the ABA was Dallas traveling south to San Antonio, where they became the San Antonio Spurs. Tom Nissalke, the Dallas coach in 1971–72 and the 1972 ABA Coach of the Year, was hired to coach the Spurs . . . Julius Erving tried to jump from Virginia to Atlanta, where the Hawks had a signed contract from him. But New York Nets owner Roy Boe paid off both the Hawks and the Squires to bring Erving to New York. That became the ABA story that received the biggest nationwide media attention, because it happened in New York . . . Boe also signed Larry Kenon out of Memphis State. There was controversy over the signing because Kenon's ABA draft rights belonged to Memphis Tams owner Charlie Finley, who complained about Boe stealing his player. Little was done about it, because Finley did not have the money to sign Kenon and the ABA wanted Kenon in its league and away from the NBA . . . The Nets hired veteran NBA guard Kevin Loughery as coach and Rod Thorn as an assistant . . . Virginia sold Swen Nater and George Gervin to San Antonio . . . LaDell Andersen resigned as coach of Utah and returned to coaching at Utah State. The ABA Stars hired veteran Joe Mullaney as their coach. Mullaney and GM Mike Storen resigned in Kentucky in a dispute with owner John Y. Brown. Storen became commissioner of the ABA, replacing Bob Carlson. Brown hired Gene Rhodes as the Colonels' GM. Rhodes had been fired as coach by Storen in 1970. Brown also named Babe McCarthy to coach the Colonels . . . In the never-ending game of coaching musical chairs, Butch van Breda Kolff replaced McCarthy as coach of Memphis . . . Charlie Finley talked about selling the Memphis team to Providence, where the plan was to hire ex–Providence College coach Joe Mullaney to run the team, but that deal fell through . . . The ABA signed two more veteran NBA officials—Jack Madden and Ed Rush . . . Storen hired veteran ABA coach Bob Bass to be in charge of the league's officials . . . In the same week, van Breda Kolff was called for four technicals in a game, and Slick Leonard was whistled for three and was fined $1,000 and suspended for two games for throwing a ball rack at official Ed Rush. A week later, Loughery was whistled for three technicals when he threw a paper cup onto the floor in disgust, and the cup happened to be full of water . . . The December 20 game between Virginia and San Antonio at Hampton, Virginia, was called off when both teams had their equipment and luggage lost by airlines. A week earlier, the same two teams had a different problem in Hampton—their game was held up for 45 minutes because of travel problems and then a furnace failure at the gym made the temperature 58 degrees inside . . . George McGinnis had 33 rebounds against the Nets and Julius Erving . . . Backup center Garfield Smith asked San Diego for a guaranteed $100,000 contract. The Qs responded by putting him on waivers . . . When Adolph Rupp quit as president of the Memphis Tams in June, he called the ABA "bush-league" and said it "would never survive." Three months later, he took a spot on the board of directors of the Kentucky Colonels . . . Carolina's Ted McClain set a league record with 12 steals. The old mark was 10 by Joe Caldwell . . . Utah Stars owner Bill Daniels said he was going to sell the team and run for governor of Colorado . . . In terms of overall stats, no ABA player ever had a better game than when George McGinnis had 52 points and 37 rebounds as the Pacers beat Carolina 124–105 on January 12, 1974

... The East beat the West 128–112 in the All-Star Game, which drew 10,624 in Norfolk. Artis Gilmore had 18 points, 13 rebounds and four blocks to gain MVP honors, but the fans thought the award should have gone to Swen Nater, who had 29 points and 22 rebounds in only 28 minutes ... Denver released Warren Jabali, who was averaging 16 points and leading the league in assists. Any ABA team could have claimed Jabali for the $500 waiver price, but none did. He had a personality conflict with Denver coach Alex Hannum. Jabali's Muslim views upset the ABA establishment. He did not play for the last 35 games of the 1973–74 season. He resurfaced with San Diego in 1974–75, averaging 12 points and shooting 39 percent, and then his career came to an end ... Artis Gilmore set a league record with 40 rebounds against the Nets ... Asked if he was interested in buying an ABA team, UCLA booster and player representative Sam Gilbert said, "I'd rather have cancer" ... Louis Dampier set an ABA mark with 55 consecutive free throws. Right behind was Denver's Byron Beck with 54 ... The Denver Rockets and Coach-GM Alex Hannum were sued by the Colorado Civil Rights Commission because the Rockets gave out seat cushions, but only to women. This was considered a sexist act. The Rockets responded at their next game by giving away the 800 cushions they had left from the promotion, but they gave them only to men. The legal action then faded away ... The Nets led Indiana 60–40 at halftime, but the Pacers came back to hit 35-for-49 from the field in the second half and to outscore the Nets 80–39 en route to a 120–99 victory ... Petersburg (Virginia) High School star Moses Malone scored 31 points in the Dapper Dan Game, considered the top high school showcase in the country. Malone was being recruited by Maryland, Virginia, Clemson, and the Utah Stars. Talent scout Marty Blake said, "Malone is ready to turn pro right now. Colleges give you all that baloney about an education, but let's be realistic." After the Dapper Dan, Malone said, "College means a lot to me. I think I can get a lot out of it. People tell me how much money I can make, but I don't think much about the money" ... New York beat Utah in five games to win the 1974 title. Julius Erving was the league's scoring champ, plus the playoff and regular-season MVP. Utah's Joe Mullaney and Kentucky's Babe McCarthy tied for Coach of the Year honors, but McCarthy was fired shortly after his team was swept in the second round by New York. Six months later, McCarthy was dead of cancer ... Swen Nater was Rookie of the Year ... The all-ABA team was Erving, McGinnis, Gilmore, Utah's Jimmy Jones and Carolina's Mack Calvin ... New York led the league in attendance with an 8,923 average and San Diego was the worst at 1,864.

Coach Chamberlain

Only the ABA would make Wilt Chamberlain a coach, and only one thing could make Chamberlain coach the San Diego Conquistadors: money—$600,000 for one season. Chamberlain coached the Qs in 1973–74, although most people in the ABA would say that assistant Stan Albeck actually coached the team, since Chamberlain didn't make it to all of the games. Well, whoever coached the team had a 37–47 record and lost in the first round of the playoffs. The Qs did have a wide-open, run-and-gun team with Bo Lamar and Stew Johnson each averaging 20 points while Travis "Machine Gun" Grant scored 15. The Qs took 194 more 3-pointers than any other team in the league. Lamar hoisted 247 of them, which was more than three other teams. He only made 27 percent from long distance, so you have to wonder about that strategy. But San Diego owner Leonard Bloom didn't sign Chamberlain for the X's and O's. Chamberlain was supposed to play center, and did play in four exhibition games, averaging 18 points, but his old team, the L.A. Lakers, took Wilt to court in order to keep him on the bench. The courts ruled in the Lakers' favor, saying that Chamberlain couldn't play in the ABA because of his contractual obligations to the Lakers, but he could coach. Thus, Coach Chamberlain was born. Since the Qs played in a place called Golden Hall with only 3,200 seats, that led to a baffling advertising campaign of "The Tallest Coach in the Smallest Arena." Chamberlain was somewhat dedicated in the beginning as coach, usually showing up for practice. But as the season went on, Wilt wasn't exactly omnipresent. Center Gene Moore told Basketball Digest, *"Every day there seems to be a different star at practice. One day, Andy Williams was here, another time it was Archie Moore. Wilt works out with us, but a lot of times he has to stop and talk to some young lady on the telephone." Chamberlain would later call Moore "a fat pig" and cut him. Chamberlain didn't move to San Diego. He commuted by airplane or helicopter from his home in L.A. for practices and games. Chamberlain missed one game when he attended an autograph party for his book,* Wilt: Just Like Any Other Seven-Foot Black Millionaire Who Lives Next Door. *He was AWOL for two others when no one in the Qs' front office knew exactly where he was. The Qs won those games under Albeck. After one season, Coach Chamberlain was another footnote in ABA history.*

LEONARD BLOOM: I believe in giving people a chance to do things that they are supposed to do. Before I hired Wilt, I had K. C. Jones as my coach. K. C. was the first black coach in pro basketball history *(actually, the second)*. I had Alex Groza as my GM, and Alex wasn't supposed to be in pro basketball because he allegedly was tainted by the point-shaving scandals in the 1950s. In 1973, the merger was supposed to be near and the ABA was encouraging teams to go out, be aggressive and do something dramatic. I figured, why not get Wilt? He was with the World Champion Lakers, he may have been the greatest player in basketball history and he was a man who liked challenges. We said he could play and coach himself. He liked that idea. The other ABA owners laughed at me when I said I wanted Wilt, but after I signed him, the owners gave me a plaque because it was such a coup for the league.

Then the Lakers hit us with a lawsuit and it became a political thing. L.A. said they had an option clause in his contract, so if he was going to play for anyone, it had to be them. The NBA and the Lakers put a lot of pressure on the courts, and the courts bought their argument. But the option clause didn't cover coaching, so he could coach.

MIKE STOREN: When Bloom got the brainstorm to sign Wilt, he wanted the league to pay for it. We said, "No way, Lenny. That one is your baby." He signed Wilt to some kind of personal-services contract, and I understand that he is still paying Wilt to this day because of the deal.

LEONARD BLOOM: It's true that I still have a contract with Wilt, but other than that, I have no comment.

VAN VANCE: When San Diego signed Wilt the question was, would he play? But he never did. As for him coaching, well, let's just say it seemed like Stan Albeck had a lot of input, an awful lot. People around the league said it was really Stan's team.

ALEX HANNUM: The best thing Wilt had going for him was Stan Albeck, who is a student of the game and a good teacher. Wilt did show up occasionally and pretended to coach, but it was really Stan's team. It wasn't that Wilt couldn't do it or that he wasn't smart enough. Just the opposite. I've coached Wilt and I can tell you that he has a great feel for the game, he understands pro basketball. But the day-to-day things that are an important part of coaching just bored him. He didn't have the patience or desire to coach.

GENE LITTLES: Even as a coach, Wilt was a draw. When San Diego came into Greensboro to play the Cougars, we sold out. People just wanted to see the guy. But Wilt didn't show up for some reason. Stan Albeck coached the team and a lot of people were really upset because there was no Wilt.

CARL SCHEER: Wilt just wasn't very reliable. He showed up at halftime during a game at Charlotte. We tried to capitalize on his name, but Wilt didn't help because he didn't like to make appearances or deal with the media.

DAVE CRAIG: When Wilt was around, you knew it. Indiana had a fight with the Qs—Mel Daniels got into it with one of San Diego's guards. Mel was one of the biggest, strongest guys in the league, but Wilt went out on the floor and picked up Mel as if he were a toothpick. The Indiana bench started to come on the floor, but when the players saw Wilt grab Daniels, they decided it was best to go back to the bench. Nobody wanted to deal with Wilt.

DAVE VANCE: Wilt was very aware of his image. I was with him at the Executive Inn in Louisville and he dropped a quarter on the floor. I knew that Wilt saw he dropped the quarter, but he kept talking to me and wouldn't bend over to pick it up.

Finally, I said, "Wilt, you dropped a quarter."

Wilt said, "I know, but if I bend over to pick it up, people will talk about it."

Of course, Wilt was famous for this line: a girl asked him what sign he was born under and Wilt said, "The dollar sign, baby."

RON GRINKER: The joke around the league was that when Wilt traveled, he only took a change of underwear because he wore the same purple velour sweater everywhere he went. He also wore sandals.

MIKE STOREN: When I was commissioner, I had to talk to Wilt about his wardrobe. Some people complained that he was wearing sandals on airplanes, which wasn't supposed to be good for the image of the league. I'm not sure what that means, but people complained.

So I called Wilt in and said, "Wilt, whether you like it or not, you are going to have to wear shoes and socks on the road."

Wilt is so damn big and imposing. He is bigger than life and if you don't know him, he just scares the hell out of you. But Wilt is a very nice guy, thank God. I kept thinking, "Here I am telling this guy to wear shoes and he can just reach across the table and rip my head off with one hand."

But Wilt said, "No problem." And it wasn't a problem.

Of course, he didn't always show up for games. The team would be on a road trip and Wilt would decide that he wanted to go someplace else.

This could have been a great opportunity for him and it certainly would have been something for the league, but Wilt never took coaching seriously. He basically hung around Leonard Bloom all the time and then went to the bank.

In terms of his impact on the league, Wilt Chamberlain as coach didn't add up to a hill of beans.

Doctor J and the Rest

The Nets franchise lasted all nine years in the ABA. They were originally owned by Arthur Brown of the ABC Freight Forwarding Company. Brown wanted to call the team "the Freighters." Why not? Denver was named "the Rockets," weren't they? Eventually, Brown dropped the idea of "the Freighters" and decided to call the team "the Americans," since the ABA had a basketball with all-American colors. Brown also wanted to play in New York, but couldn't find an acceptable facility and ended up at the 4,800-seat Teaneck (New Jersey) Armory. The Americans had fewer than 50 season-ticket holders, and a crowd of over 500 was considered a mob. The Americans finished that first season with a 36–42 record, tying Kentucky for the last playoff spot. In a legendary ABA story, New Jersey was awarded the home court for the one-game playoff with Kentucky. The Teaneck Armory was booked, so Brown had to scramble for another facility, and found the Commack Arena on Long Island. When the two teams showed up for the playoff game, they found that the Commack floor was full of holes, loose nails and bolts. Commissioner George Mikan forfeited the game to the Colonels, and the Americans were out of the playoffs. The following season, Brown moved the Americans to—where else?—Commack, but this time they got a new floor. They changed their name to the Nets, to rhyme with the Mets, Jets and even the New York Sets of the old pro team tennis league. The Nets went 17–61 at Commack. Then, in 1969–70, Brown sold the team to Roy Boe, who hired Lou Carnesecca as coach. Carnesecca coached the Nets for three seasons (1970–73), compiling a 114–138 record. Boe did create some excitement when he bought Rick Barry from Virginia, but Barry lasted only two seasons before returning to Golden State of the NBA.

The Nets never became a major factor in the ABA until 1973–74, when Boe purchased Julius Erving from Virginia and hired Kevin Loughery as coach. The team moved from Commack Arena to the Island Garden, and finally into the brand-new Nassau Coliseum in 1973. Under Loughery and Erving, the Nets won ABA titles in 1974 and 1976.

JEFF DENBERG: In the early years, the Nets were just a local joke. I covered them occasionally for *Newsday* and they were owned by Sad-Faced Arthur Brown. When Brown moved the team to Long Island and changed the name to the Nets, he not only did it to rhyme with all the other New York teams, but because he was deeply offended that the New York tabloids had shortened the name of his team from the Americans to the Amerks. He thought that sounded sort of Communist, so in an act of patriotism he changed the nickname.

There are so many stories about guys freezing their butts off at Commack. Brown even installed several large heaters to blow hot air around, but that didn't have much impact. One game, Bob Verga was sitting on the bench wearing his overcoat.

Brown sent a note to the bench, "Tell Verga to take off his coat."

Verga refused.

Brown sent down another note, and Verga still wouldn't take his coat off.

Finally, Brown sent a note to coach Max Zaslofsky: "Put Verga in the game."

Verga went into the game and yes, he did take off his coat.

STEVE JONES: Guys would sit on the bench at Commack wearing coats and gloves trying to stay warm. Nobody wanted to play for the Nets and have that icebox as your home court.

DAN ISSEL: I never played at Commack, but when the Nets moved to the Island Garden, that wasn't any better. It still was cold. Guys on the bench still wore coats over their warm-ups. The dressing rooms were brutal. They should have called the place the Long Island Toilet.

RON GRINKER: The Island Garden was like an airline hangar. It gave you that kind of airy, vacant feeling.

BOB RYAN: Without a doubt, the Island Garden was the least professional, lowest-class facility in pro basketball. No one would dare dress in the locker room. Everyone dressed at the hotel first. On one side of the arena were about five rows of stands, reminiscent of a high school gym. The other side had about 15 rows. I couldn't believe how rinky-dink the place was.

ROY BOE: I bought the Nets in May of 1969 from Arthur Brown, who had no idea how much money he had lost in two years, but just knew it was a lot and he wanted no more of pro basketball. I paid about $200,000 for the team *(much of it in assuming debts)* and the highest-paid player made about $12,000. I had learned of the plans to build the Nassau Coliseum and I thought it would be a good business move to own a pro basketball team when that building was completed. Before I bought the Nets, I had seen one ABA game at Commack. The Nets were playing the Oakland Oaks with Rick Barry and there were about 150 people in the stands.

In other words, I knew what I was up against.

The first thing I did was move the team out of Commack and into the Island Garden. I really was just biding my time until the Nassau Coliseum was built. The Island Garden was terrible. We got all the complaints about the toilets not working and there being no hot water in the showers. If the circus had just left, the parking lot would be littered with elephant excrement.

In those early years, we drew about 2,000 to 3,000 a night, and half of them were kids we let in for free. Once, we had a Gerbil Night promotion where we were going to give away 50 gerbils. But our promotion managers stopped on the way from the pet shop to the arena at a McDonald's. Somehow, the cages got knocked over and the gerbils got out. He ended up chasing those animals on his hands and knees to get them back in the cages.

JIM O'BRIEN: I covered the Nets for the *New York Post,* so I got to know Roy Boe. He was from Yale, a guy who didn't think anything was important unless it appeared in *The New York Times,* where his Ivy League friends would see it. He got to be a very important guy just because he owned the Nets for so long. He also owned the New York Islanders of the NHL.

ROY BOE: I knew that we had to keep making dramatic moves until we started to win, or no one in New York would notice us. We purchased Rick Barry and we hired Lou Carnesecca from St. John's as coach, and that started us on the road to legitimacy.

RICK BARRY: I liked playing for Louie. He was new to the pro game and it was obvious that he missed college ball very much. None of us were surprised when he went back to St. John's.

BARNEY KREMENKO: I worked with Louie as the Nets' PR man. Louie was a college coach through and through. He couldn't believe how the pros would drink and chase women. He left St. John's because Roy Boe paid him well, but he found that when he was dealing with pros, he couldn't get on the phone and call a kid's mother when there was a problem, like he did at St. John's.

We got some attention with Louie, but not that much. To try and help our coverage, I would write game stories and send them to as many as six papers a night—the *Times,* the *Post,* all the big ones at some point—I'd just put a different lead on it. It was a way to help us get more publicity, and they would run the stories if they couldn't send a reporter to the game.

But what really made the Nets the focus of the ABA was when Roy Boe bought Julius from Virginia. That was something special.

In the summer of 1973, Roy Boe purchased Julius Erving and hired Kevin Loughery as coach. The Nets were 34–50 the season before, Lou Carnesecca's final year as a pro coach. The team had some talent with Billy Paultz, George Carter, Brian Taylor, Bill Melchionni and John Roche, but it clearly lacked personality. Loughery came from Philadelphia, where he had coached the Sixers during the last third of the season, going 5–26. Sound bad? That was an improvement, as the Sixers were 4–47 under Roy Rubin. Loughery was 33 when hired by Boe. He received a five-year contract worth $35,000 annually to coach the team. He hired Rod Thorn as his assistant. Thorn was Loughery's roommate when they played together with the Baltimore Bullets, and became a key man for Loughery because of his communication skills with the players and his ability to soothe egos after a Loughery outburst. Once, Loughery threatened to trade half the team by the next game. Loughery almost didn't last through his first season, as the Nets were 4–10 and had lost nine in a row when Loughery changed both his team's style of play and the lineup. The Nets then won 19 of their next 22 games. They rolled through the playoffs, winning 12 of 14 games and defeating Utah 4–1 in the finals. By the end of the season, only three players remained from the year before—Paultz, Melchionni and Taylor. In his first season with the Nets, Erving averaged 27.4 points, 10.7 rebounds and 5.1 assists and shot 52 percent. He was the league's MVP and averaged 41 minutes a night.

KEVIN LOUGHERY: I went to the Nets for the simple reason that it was a chance to go home to New York. I knew very little about the ABA, because I had spent my entire career in the NBA, but I liked Roy Boe because it was obvious that he would spend money to win. It just seemed like a great situation for a young coach, although I'll admit that I had a lot to learn.

ROD THORN: Kevin and I had both heard a lot about Julius Erving and frankly, we didn't believe 90 percent of it. How could some guy who was playing at UMass be that good? Well, in our first practice, we saw how good he could be. Kevin wanted to play pressure defense, a lot of full-court stuff. Julius just dominated the practice defensively. I mean, he made steal after steal, taking away guys' dribbles, picking off passes, and it seemed with those long arms and huge hands he came up with every loose ball. I had never seen a guy with such athleticism. Brian Taylor also was very good on the press, so we thought that was how we'd play.

We opened the season with John Roche and Melchionni in the back-court, Paultz at center, and Larry Kenon and Julius as the forwards. We broke out of the gate at 4–1 and everyone loved our pressing style.

Then the whole thing fell apart. We lost our next nine games. People started writing that Kevin was too young to coach, that he didn't know what to do with a talent like Julius. It got pretty ugly.

We were on a West Coast trip and we had a big meeting in San Diego. It was a real man-to-man thing where everybody spoke their minds.

We admitted that we made a coaching mistake by trying to press all the time. We were usually in front after three quarters, but then fatigue would catch us and we'd blow the lead down the stretch. We were wearing Julius out because he was working so hard on defense.

Then Kevin made some changes in the lineup, the biggest when he replaced Melchionni with John Williamson as the starting guard. Williamson was just a kid and he shot the ball too much, but he was a very physical player and he could score quite a bit. He gave us another weapon in the lineup, but that move was a difficult one, since Melchionni had been in the All-Star Game the last three seasons.

KEVIN LOUGHERY: Actually, we made two changes at guard. I put Brian Taylor and Williamson into the lineup. Not long after that, we traded John Roche to Kentucky for Mike Gale and Wendeli Ladner, and that became a great deal for us. Gale moved in as our third guard and Wendell gave us this hustling forward off the bench.

ROD THORN: We lost our first game at San Diego with the new lineup, but the next night, we played at San Antonio and won. Williamson drilled his first nine shots and had 20-some points for the game. You look back at it and you can see why we began to click. We were a young team that just jelled. Kenon and Williamson were rookies. Julius, Taylor and Gale were only in their third seasons. Our veterans were Paultz, Melchionni and Ladner. Also, all the guys were new to each other. The growth of Kenon and Williamson into big-time players as rookies *(both averaging 15 points)* really made our season. We also had a very colorful and aggressive team, because that was Kevin Loughery's personality.

A big factor was Julius's attitude. Kevin found that he could criticize Julius and Julius would not turn on him like most stars. In fact, I know that sometimes Kevin would scream at Doc just to let the other guys known that Doc was no different than they were.

And, of course, Kevin was all over the officials.

One night we were playing in Virginia and getting beat. He thought that there were a few illegal defenses called on us that were incorrect calls. Kevin then told our guys to play a real zone, to just stand there in a 2–3 with their arms up. So the refs started calling illegal defenses on every possession. It ended up being a farce.

Loughery received six technical fouls in that game, and was fined $1,000 for being ejected and another $750 for all the technicals. He also was suspended for two games.

KEVIN LOUGHERY: The irony about that game in Virginia was that we protested it because the officials had messed up some rule and we won the protest. The next time we were in Virginia, we had to replay the game from the moment of the protest, which was late in the first half. When that game was over, we had our regularly scheduled game to play. We ended up playing three halves of basketball, and we lost the game we protested anyway. We didn't get out of there until two in the morning and we had an afternoon game the next day in New York.

JOHN VANAK: Kevin loved to work the officials. He'd say to me, "John, that guy you're working with, what color underpants does he have on? He must be wearing red, because he's calling everything for the other guys. Check out that guy's pants, will ya, John?"

Or Kevin would say, "Gee, John, it's too bad that you have to work by yourself out there. That other guy you're with, he may as well have stayed home. I bet your back gets tired from carrying him around all game. I feel bad for you, John, because you deserve better than that."

Kevin could be a problem for some officials because he did get emotional, but I liked him and we got along great, and he did a terrific job with that team.

BOB COSTAS: My favorite Loughery story was during the 1974–75 season. Kevin and Rod Thorn were alike in their courtside demeanor. They pranced around, throwing their arms in the air, screaming at the officials and putting on the faces of men who had been unduly wronged. They both were superb when it came to seeing a call, throwing their hands over their heads, slumping down with great drama into their chairs, and then spreading their arms out to the heavens as if to plead for mercy.

Before I tell the story, you should know that during the regular season, the Nets beat St. Louis 11 straight times and they also beat us in the first game of the playoffs. But in Game 2, we were ahead by about 25 points and it was absolutely impossible for Kevin to fathom what had happened. This was the game when Wendell Ladner threw his shoe and hit Freddie Lewis in the back. They called a technical on Wendell for throwing the shoe. Kevin went nuts and put on a big show. Jack Madden ejected him.

As Kevin left the floor, he yelled at Thorn, "Rod, take a technical."

The action was still stopped, but now Thorn was screaming at Madden, "Hey, Jack, how long is this hosing going to continue? This is the most ridiculous thing I've ever seen."

On and on it went, but Madden paid Thorn no attention. Jack just stood at midcourt, blowing his nose.

Thorn, knowing that he was ordered to get a technical, finally screamed, "Hey Jack, don't blow it out of your nose, blow it out your ass."

With that, Thorn got his technical, which no doubt pleased Loughery.

JIM O'BRIEN: Kevin was a great coach for the Nets, because he had a New York background and was a down-to-earth guy. He would shoot around with the players, betting them that he could beat them in H-O-R-S-E and games like that. Kevin had a lot of parties at his house and you'd find a fascinating mix of people, from the players to the rich Ivy League types to the guys from Kevin's old neighborhood in Brooklyn who wore white socks. Kevin was as comfortable with one group of people as he was with any other. And at this point in his career, he was a very good coach, because he was young, enthusiastic, and wasn't worn down by the game.

ROD THORN: By the time we got to the *(1974)* playoffs, we were a monster. Kevin and I would sit there and say, "We're better than this team, or better than that team." We were just playing that great. We opened the playoffs against Al Bianchi and Virginia and we beat them

4–1. It wasn't much of a series. Next, we played Kentucky, and Babe McCarthy was coaching. Kentucky gave us more problems than anyone else in the regular season. They had a great team with Artis Gilmore, Dan Issel, Louie Dampier and those guys. We said, "We're just better than they are and we'll beat them, I know it."

We kicked Kentucky's ass in the first two games in New York. Game 3 was in Louisville and it was one of those 89–87 games where no one can make a shot. The score was tied with about 15 seconds to go and we set up a play to get Doc the ball in the middle of the court. That was exactly what happened. He had the ball and was dribbling, sort of yo-yoing up and down waiting for the clock to run down. With about four seconds left, he drove toward the foul line. The defense collapsed on him, so he veered a little right and then threw up a 15-footer fading right, shooting off his right foot, and it banked in. It was shot all wrong—a banker and he took it off the wrong foot—but Doc made it anyway and we won. We were all on the court, dancing around and hugging each other. I happened to look over at the bench and saw Babe McCarthy sitting there, holding his head and wondering, "What did I do wrong? How were we supposed to stop that shot?"

We beat the Colonels in the next game to sweep. Then we faced Utah in the finals and beat them 4–1. After Julius made that shot, there was no doubt in anyone's mind that we were destined to win the title.

DAVE VANCE: I was the GM of the Colonels when Julius made that shot, and Kevin tells a great story about what went on in the huddle.

When they called time-out with 15 seconds left, Kevin went down on his knee and started to draw up a play. He didn't get very far when this huge hand landed on his shoulder.

"Kevin," said Julius. "I'll take the last shot."

Kevin said he got chills when he heard Doc say that. It was almost like the voice of God.

So Kevin said, "Okay, guys, if Doc misses—"

The hand came back on Kevin's shoulder and Julius said, "Kevin, I won't miss."

That just stopped Kevin. Finally, he said, "Okay, let's get Doc the ball and let's go."

I can still see Julius floating to the right in the air, the shot leaving his hand, and he just ran right into the dressing room after he let it go. Julius knew it was in and he knew he had won the game.

The Rivalry

NBA owners and front-office types greeted the ABA as a sailor would scurvy. The NBA took every opportunity to assault the new league. It reached incredible proportions when Celtics GM Red Auerbach was quoted as saying in 1975, "Julius Erving is a nice kid, but he's not a great player." Indiana coach Slick Leonard countered by saying, "I played and coached in the NBA and things haven't changed from when I was in the league. He was the biggest mouth in the league then and he still is." Auerbach told Sports Illustrated, *"Leonard was a bad coach in the NBA and he will be a dog now, too." Obviously, the NBA had reason to gripe about the ABA. Some of the points were well taken and some weren't.*

WAYNE EMBRY: From the moment they first threw up that red, white and blue ball, we thought that the ABA was a maverick league, a gimmick league. The first time I saw them play with that basketball, I thought I was at a circus. It gave the league a bush atmosphere. I thought that the 3-point play would just encourage wild-ass basketball and that guys would just gun the ball up there the moment they touched it, instead of passing the ball around to get a good inside shot. To me, much of the beauty of basketball is passing, and I thought the 3-pointer would take some of that away.

From a business standpoint, we wondered how they were going to find enough cities to support pro basketball when a number of NBA teams were losing money. We also knew that the ABA was going to compete for some of the college players and try to lure some of our players to jump leagues, and that would raise salaries, which was great for the players, but we thought it could drive everybody out of business if we weren't careful.

My biggest complaint with the ABA was their business practices. A lot of the players they signed were lied to and didn't receive anything close to the money they were promised. There were a lot of under-the-table dealings, with agents getting money to deliver players to certain ABA teams. To me, it was almost like slave-trading. The agents were selling those kids down the river and the ABA was there with the money. The players were the ones who were hurt. They were, in my mind, bribing kids to leave school early to turn pro when a lot of the kids just weren't ready. They signed those incredible long-term contracts with payouts for over 25 years. The money they received sounded like a lot, but it was peanuts once you understood the payouts. You could bet your last dollar that some of those agents who were getting money under the table weren't being paid out over 25 years.

Some of the agents were double-dipping. They were getting paid to deliver their players to the ABA, and they also were taking a fee from the player for negotiating the contract. I lost a lot of respect for some agents and owners when I got a look at some of the ABA contracts.

RON GRINKER: There were some agents who were nothing but whores, who would sell their mothers for a deal. It was not uncommon for an agent to be paid more in the first year than the player would receive. He'd take his fee for the entire contract up front and whatever was left went to the player as a first-year salary. It was just robbery.

CARL SCHEER: I was working in the NBA office when the ABA was formed, and our approach was to pretend that the ABA didn't exist. We figured that in a year or two, they'd go broke and then go away and it would be business as usual. They started giving outrageous contracts— for that era—to people like Rick Barry. Two years later, I was on the other side of the fence as GM of the Carolina Cougars. That showed me how wrong we were at the NBA, because we had underestimated the resolve and the creativity of the guys running ABA teams.

BOB RYAN: My attitudes about the ABA were probably shaped by being around such people as Red Auerbach and other old-line NBA types. I wasn't parroting their view because I couldn't think for myself; rather, it was what I believed, too.

The common perception in the NBA was that the ABA was a second-rate, offensive-minded collection of people who didn't have the good sense to come into the NBA if they were good enough. It was a head-case league with thugs like Warren Jabali and John Brisker. A guy like Brisker—how could anyone let him on the court?

Then there were folks like Les Selvage who went 10-for-26 from 3-point range in one game! We said, "What the hell is going on over there?" And there was the famed story about how George McGinnis was going for the rebounding title and tapped the ball off the backboard to himself five or ten times to pad his total.

AL BIANCHI: The whole ABA was up in arms when Auerbach made his crack about Erving. The NBA went out of its way to insult all of us in the ABA. But it also brought us together. We were the underdogs, the have-nots, and that was fun. When we played them in exhibition games and beat them, which we did often, that was a whole lot of fun, especially listening to the excuses they made after the game.

BOB RYAN: The NBA felt that the ABA played no defense, certainly no team defense as it was known in the NBA. You could drive down the middle and do anything you wanted, because they had no real centers until Artis Gilmore. Really, we figured it was a glorified Eastern League—at least that was the opinion until we started playing exhibition games.

When the exhibition games began, the view in the NBA was, "Now we'll show those guys." But then you know what happened—the ABA teams won nearly as often as the NBA did. So the NBA took a different tack. They said, "Well, to us those games were exhibitions, while the ABA was playing them like the playoff finals. Besides, a lot of the games were in ABA arenas."

I distinctly recall a game at the Island Garden where the Nets beat the Celtics on Rick Barry's 3-pointer at the buzzer. Barry didn't surprise me, but Billy Paultz did. I considered Paultz just another nobody ABA center, but he showed no respect for Dave Cowens. He rebounded over Cowens, he scored on Cowens. I saw that and I said, "What's this?" I also started to wonder if I had dismissed the ABA too quickly.

LARRY BROWN: When the NBA refused to play us, they just said we didn't belong on the same court with them. When some exhibition games were arranged in the 1970s to make some money and we beat them, the NBA said they weren't up for the games. Come on. When I coached Carolina, we played the Knicks after they won a championship. I looked at their guys shooting around and I looked at my guys and I didn't want my players to take off their warm-ups because they looked so scrawny next to the Knicks—and we went out and beat New York. We also played the Celtics a couple of times and beat them. (Coach) Tommy Heinsohn would say that we were playing to win and they weren't, but I'd check the box score and see that Tommy played his regulars 35 to 40 minutes, so what does that tell you?

BOB RYAN: Those NBA-ABA games were intense. In one, Dave Cowens was ejected by Jack Madden for punting a basketball. Madden was one of the "renegade refs" who had jumped from the NBA to the ABA. In another game, Madden gave Tom Heinsohn seven technicals and ejected him. I went to ABA games, saw the Julius Ervings, the George Gervins and all the rest, and I respected their individual talent. But I never saw an ABA team play defense like the NBA did. Maybe I just didn't want to see it. So I refused to take the league seriously. When writers such as Jim O'Brien and Peter Vecsey wrote that the two leagues were very close, that some ABA teams were among the top five of all pro basketball teams, I thought they had no objectivity and that they were too close to the teams they were writing about to really understand pro basketball. Then came the merger, and Denver and San Antonio won division titles. What could I say? Guys like Jim O'Brien were right.

LARRY DONALD: The ABA had a far better grasp on public relations and marketing than the NBA. The typical NBA front office was a general manager, a coach, a public relations man, a business manager and a trainer. Their idea of promotion was to put a sign out in front of the arena that said, "Game Tonight."

Good ABA teams such as Denver, Indiana and Kentucky had all those people, plus marketing directors and sales directors. They gave away posters, basketballs, all the giveaways that are common today. The NBA just wrote that off as the ABA using gimmicks to attract fans and they weren't about to stoop to such a level.

At *Basketball Weekly,* we probably wrote more about the ABA than it deserved, because the people were so accessible. The Kentucky Colonels would call and say they had a free plane ticket if we wanted to come down and do a story. The magazine was in its infancy then and had a small travel budget, so we sometimes took them up on their offer. The NBA wouldn't think of doing something like that.

Of course, the ABA invented the All-Star weekend as we now know it. I recall going to an NBA All-Star Game in Chicago. It was held at night during the week, and even the players didn't want to be there. They went through the motions and the fans booed.

BOB BASS: When the leagues merged, the NBA owners and executives would look down their noses at the ABA people, if they bothered to look at us at all. They acted like we didn't deserve to be in the same room with them. Never would you find such arrogance in the ABA.

A Big Move Spurs a Texas Revival

Before they became the San Antonio Spurs in 1973–74, the franchise was in Dallas for five seasons. The Chaparrals had Cliff Hagan as their coach for the first 2½ seasons, then five coaches in the next 2½ seasons, making it six coaches in five years. They were never a factor in the playoffs, and things became very ugly after the 1972–73 season when several black players thought that management was trading blacks for white players. Donnie Freeman, a 24-point scorer, was sold to Indiana and Bob Netolicky came from the Pacers to Dallas in a separate deal, which brought the issue to a head. "Several other black players were traded and soon half of our roster was white," recalls Steve Jones. "The feeling among the black players was that management wanted to get as many white guys as it could to help attendance. Some public statements were made by the front office that they thought white players would give the team some fan appeal." The black players refused to attend training camp until the front office issued a retraction, which it did, but only after Jones went to the front office and demanded one.

After that early-season turmoil, the Chaparrals stumbled to a 28–56 record, last in the Western Conference, behind even the expansion San Diego Conquistadors. By December, talk was rampant about the club moving to New Jersey, but a prospective buyer fell through. Basketball Weekly's Dave Overpeck described the situation by saying, "Covering a Chaparrals game is a lot like going to a wake. In the ABA, it's not unusual to go into a town knowing that the club won't be there next year. But the Chaparrals are different. Never, not even in the floating craps game of the ABA, has it been announced so early that a team is leaving town before next season. . . . The crowds aren't down that much, primarily because they weren't that big in the first place." In six years in Dallas, the Chaparrals never drew more than 7,800; their average was about 2,500.

TERRY STEMBRIDGE: After the New Jersey deal fell through, we really were stuck. One day we were sitting around the office trying to figure out who we could get to buy the team. *(GM)* Bob Briner said, "You know, there's a guy down in San Antonio named Red McCombs who has been involved in minor league football. Maybe we should check him out." I said I'd call McCombs. I called down to San Antonio and found out that he was in North Carolina, visiting his daughter at Duke. I was real persistent and tracked him down at a Holiday Inn, told him about the Chaparrals needing an owner and asked if he was interested. Red came to Dallas and we ended up making one of the most unique deals in the history of professional sports: we leased the team to San Antonio. McCombs became very important in getting the team for San Antonio, and so was a guy named Angelo Drossos.

ANGELO DROSSOS: I knew nothing about the ABA when I heard from a friend in the advertising business that he had been contacted by some people in Dallas about buying the Chaparrals. I had never seen an ABA game, but the Houston Rockets of the NBA had played seven games in San Antonio and I had a season ticket—for all seven games. I went to Dallas to talk to Bob Folsom and Joe Geary and the Dallas people said, "We will loan you the team for two years, but you have to have $800,000 of working capital." They figured that it would take $400,000 a year to operate the team. Then after two years if we wanted to own the team, we'd pay them another $800,000.

TERRY STEMBRIDGE: Angelo Drossos is a unique guy. He's Greek and he spent some time in boxing, first as a fighter, then as a promoter. He came up the hard way and he even ran a Coney Island hot dog stand in San Antonio. He started working for Red McCombs as a car salesman at Red's Ford dealership. Then Angelo moved up to sales manager. He went to New York and worked his way up through stockbrokers' school. Angelo Drossos had to work and sweat and push for everything he ever had and he gained a reputation as a very tough negotiator, a guy who put together some great deals. He had been in some deals with Red McCombs and he was a stockbroker at Dean Witter when he got involved in basketball. At that time, Angelo didn't have any real big money.

ANGELO DROSSOS: After we made the deal with Dallas, we needed to raise the $800,000. We eventually did get $780,000, with 36 investors.

The $780,000 was supposed to last two years, but it was gone after three months. I spent $200,000 of it when I went to the city of San Antonio and said, "If you want basketball in this town, then we have to have the concession rights at the convention center." The concession rights were owned by Phil Sheridan, and the city told him that if he sold the concession rights to the basketball team, the city would give him the rights at the zoo, which was a very good deal for Sheridan. So he gave up the rights, and we had them for all events in the building, not just basketball games. You can make a lot of money off concessions and getting the rights for $200,000 was an incredible bargain, but spending that money before we even played a game set us back.

TERRY STEMBRIDGE: An example of the kind of deals Angelo made was when we had a contract with Coke to be our major radio sponsor. The reason Coke did that wasn't so much for the exposure on the radio, but to be the exclusive cola at the arena for the games. At this time, Pepsi was in an all-out war with Coke, and Pepsi wanted to get in on the action. I didn't see how Angelo could change anything because Coke had a year left on its contract with the team, but Angelo negotiated and negotiated and ended up with Coke and Pepsi becoming cosponsors, which was a first and probably a last-time occurrence. They both advertised on our radio broadcasts and both colas were available at the arena, and the Spurs made a lot more money than they would have with either one having an exclusive.

ANGELO DROSSOS: I had no training in basketball, informal or otherwise, when I took over the Spurs. Everything was on-the-job experience. If I made a mistake, I paid for it the hard way. The team I inherited from Dallas was a last-place team. It had only a few players worth keeping. It had no coach, no front office, nothing worth speaking of. The first employee I hired was Terry Stembridge; I didn't keep him as assistant general manager, which he was in Dallas, but I kept him as the radio voice of the team. He was a guy I could trust, a good person to have in the organization. The next person I hired was Bernie LaReau, who had been one of the trainers for the Chicago Bears. He came on as our trainer, business manager and traveling secretary. My biggest job was to find a coach.

TERRY STEMBRIDGE: Tom Nissalke had followed the Dallas situation closely, especially after he was fired in Seattle. *(Nissalke had coached Dallas to a 42–42 record in 1970–71 before leaving to take the Seattle job, where he was fired after 45 games with a 13–32 record.)* When the team moved to San Antonio, he called down here several times to see what the Spurs were doing. I advised Angelo against hiring Nissalke, because I just didn't like him when he was in Dallas, but Angelo interviewed Nissalke and was impressed with him. I don't know why Angelo went against my advice and the advice of some others and hired Nissalke, but he did.

ANGELO DROSSOS: I really didn't know that much about Nissalke. I interviewed him and he seemed all right. He had coaching experience and he was willing to coach for practically nothing because he was getting paid by Seattle.

The thing we needed more than anything our first year in San Antonio was a center. Nissalke was high on Swen Nater. I knew two things: first, Virginia had two centers and Nater was backing up Jim Eakins, so that made Swen expendable. Second, Earl Foreman needed money, which was always a given.

There are two kinds of owners of pro sports teams. The first is the guy who sits in the backseat and lets the GM run the franchise. The second is the guy who is a "hands on" owner. Earl Foreman and I fell into that second category, and that was part of the reason we got along so well. Dick Tinkham of Indiana was another owner just like us, and we three used to hang around a lot.

Anyway, there was a league meeting in New York *(in November of 1973)* and afterwards Foreman, Tinkham and I went to this place called Dionysus, a Greek nightclub. We were having a few drinks and Foreman got up and went to the bathroom. At the time, the two most important players in the ABA were Julius Erving and George McGinnis. Tinkham had McGinnis and he had run a strong operation in Indiana. I started talking about Nater. I don't know why, but the figure $300,000 stuck in my head and I said, "Dick, help me get Nater from Foreman. I'll pay $300,000."

Tinkham said, "You'll pay $300,000 for that stiff? I'll tell you what. You give me $300,000 and I'll give you McGinnis."

I said, "I don't want McGinnis. I need a center. I got Bob Netolicky playing center now and he's getting killed out there."

Actually, I don't know if Dick would have sold me McGinnis or not, but he did say he'd help me with Nater.

When Foreman came back to the table, I wrote out a check for $50,000 and put it right in front of him.

Foreman asked, "What's this for?"

I said, "That's a down payment on $300,000 for Swen Nater."

He said, "I can't sell Nater." He was very adamant about it. But I also knew that the ABA had Foreman up on charges because he hadn't met his league assessments. His franchise was frozen. Dick and I talked to him, saying how the money could really alleviate his problems.

I said, "Earl, you're in real trouble. Suppose I give you the $300,000 in 15 minutes. You then can write a check, get off charges and go back to running your franchise."

He said, "You're going to give me the money in 15 minutes? How are you going to do that?"

I said, "That's my problem. Just remember that I'll get you the money in 15 minutes, you can write a check and get off charges and all it will cost you is one player."

Earl said, "You got a deal if you can get it done in 15 minutes."

I called my bank in San Antonio and told them to deposit $300,000 in the Federal Reserve of New York in the account of Earl Foreman. The bank immediately approved a loan to me. I told them that I'd sign for the loan when I got back to San Antonio, and the deal was done in exactly nine minutes. We got Earl the $300,000 with six minutes to spare.

DICK TINKHAM: As usual, Earl Foreman had missed another $100,000 league assessment and the league was down on him.

Angelo said, "Earl, why don't you sell me some players."

Foreman said, "Ah, I don't know."

Angelo said, "How about Swen Nater?"

Foreman said, "He's not for sale."

Angelo said, "You mean if I offer you $300,000 for Nater right now, you won't sell Nater?"

Foreman said, "It's my team. I can't sell my team away."

Angelo then excused himself and went to the bathroom.

I said, "Earl, your assessment is due tomorrow. You can take the money, then replace Nater with eight other guys or something."

Earl agreed.

I got up and met Angelo coming out of the men's room. I said, "When you get back to the bar, make Earl the offer."

Angelo said, "Cake."

Then I watched them shake hands on the deal at the bar.

EARL FOREMAN: It was no secret that was I hurting for money when Dick Tinkham and Angelo Drossos took me to the Dionysus after the league meeting. Angelo was Greek and he loved the place. It was a great bar. Dick Tinkham and I would go out there and dance the Greek dances while Angelo watched and laughed his ass off. We were sitting at the bar, me on one side, Angelo on the other and Tinkham in the middle. We were going to make a deal for Swen Nater, right at the bar. It finally got done about two in the morning. Angelo left, then Dick and I went to P.J. Clarke's and stayed out till at least three in the morning. There was a league meeting set the next day at 8 A.M. and that was when we were going to finalize the deal. I was unshaven and a lot of us were half hung over. I remember Angelo seeing me in the morning saying, "Let me give you the check before you die."

So I got the check and I had Angelo's word that he wouldn't leak it to the press. I was worried about Al Bianchi hearing about it from someone other than me. I flew from New York back to Norfolk and met Al at the Norfolk airport, because the team was headed out somewhere. I had to call him over and say, "Coach, I want you to hear this from me: I sold Swen to San Antonio." Then I had to tell him about selling Nater in a bar at two in the morning.

Al didn't bat an eye. He just said, "If you had to do it, you had to do it."

TEDD MUNCHAK: Earl Foreman may have been the most creative mind in the ABA. He never had any money, but he always had a lot of ideas.

DICK TINKHAM: Whenever Earl called, you knew the conversation would probably turn to money. One night Virginia was scheduled to play us in Indiana and Earl called me to say, "Dick, we can't play tonight's game."

I said, "Why not?"

Foreman said, "Because the sheriff is going to pick up our uniforms."

I said, "The sheriff is what?"

Foreman said, "We owe two grand on our uniforms."

That was it. Foreman owed $2,000 for his uniforms and they were going to be repossessed. That night, the sheriff did show up and I had to do something. We had a full house. We couldn't cancel the game because Earl Foreman didn't pay on his uniforms.

So I said to the sheriff, "Look, if you take these uniforms, you really won't be hurting Foreman. I would just give Virginia our road uniforms to wear and the game will go on anyway. Besides, what good are a bunch of used uniforms anyway?"

We talked for a long time and the sheriff let Virginia keep the uniforms and play the game. And I heard that Earl even eventually paid that bill, although he probably had to sell a player to do it.

ANGELO DROSSOS: We had a lot of fun in that first year in San Antonio. We signed George Karl out of North Carolina in a unique way. He had been drafted by Memphis, but Memphis didn't follow up and lost his rights. I got a call from Karl's lawyer. He said that George was "the kind of player who can really help. He played for North Carolina, he's played some international ball against the Russians and he's a point guard. You can always use a good point guard."

We got to talking money. I really didn't know anything about Karl, although I knew that North Carolina was a good basketball school. I certainly had no idea what to pay him. I talked to his lawyer for several weeks and we still were about $40,000 apart. I'm an avid tennis player and I play practically every day. His lawyer wanted to set up an appointment to talk about George's contract, but I said I couldn't talk then because I had a tennis match. The lawyer seemed interested in tennis, so I said, "Why don't you come to San Antonio, we'll play some tennis and then talk about George's contract."

Then a light went on in my head. I said, "Tell you what. I'll play you for George's contract. If you win, you get what you want for George. If I win, you take my offer."

There was a long silence on the phone, and he said, "Angelo, I don't think you want to do that."

I asked why not.

He said, "I don't think you can beat me. It wouldn't be fair to you."

I was getting upset. I'm proud of my tennis and I'm an A player.

He said, "Angelo, I've played a lot of tennis. A lot of tennis at a very high level, so I suggest we work this out some other way."

It turned out that the lawyer was Donald Dell, who had played at Wimbledon and was on the Davis Cup team. We never did play for George's contract, but if Dell had insisted I stick to the bargain, I would have. George eventually signed and I was glad Dell did call, because George was a solid player for us.

But that was the kind of thing I'd do in the beginning—I'd challenge a guy to play tennis for a contract. I really had no idea what would happen that first season or how you were supposed to do business. I figured it out as I went along. The whole organization did.

JIM CHONES: That Drossos was something. I was with the Carolina Cougars and we played a game in San Antonio. Larry Brown and Angelo never got along and in one game, Angelo came right out of the stands and was yelling at Larry Brown, "Hey, you wanna have it out with me?"

Angelo wanted to fight Larry right in front of the scorer's table. Larry ignored him and said, "What's with that guy?"

You could say Angelo was a little intense.

TERRY STEMBRIDGE: San Antonio didn't know anything about pro basketball and the fans didn't seem to care about it any more than they did in Dallas. Most of our early crowds were in the 3,000 range. We lost our first four games and were 1–6 at one point. I began to wonder if we'd make the year. But three things saved us.

First, Angelo Drossos fell in love with running a basketball team. I mean head over heels in love. He truly did. He learned a lot very fast, he was tough and he was gutsy. It was his single-mindedness that carried the team through the first season.

Second, Angelo bought Swen Nater from Virginia.

Third, Angelo bought George Gervin from Virginia and fought in court to keep him.

Angelo made himself a force in the community and in the league. He came on strong and that bothered some people, but Angelo got things done and as the season went on, the team kept getting better and better.

GEORGE GERVIN: EARL FOREMAN'S LAST BIG SALE

AL BIANCHI: To this day, most people don't know that we had Julius Erving and George Gervin on the same team *(Virginia, 1972–73)*. That sounds like a foundation for a championship team, doesn't it? But Julius was only in his second pro season, Ice was a 19-year-old kid who should have been a college sophomore, and I was a young coach who probably didn't get the most out of those guys because I didn't know how to best use them. Really, everybody was so young. That made it fun. Just as we really didn't know what we had when we signed Julius, the same was true of Gervin, maybe even more so. He was less heralded than Julius because he barely played college basketball. I had heard about this kid playing semipro ball in Pontiac, Michigan. There was a mystery about why he had left Eastern Michigan—in fact, the whole thing was a mystery. All I knew was that we needed players and Johnny Kerr went to scout him.

JOHNNY KERR: The first I heard about George Gervin was when I was coaching the Bulls *(1967–68)*. I talked to George King, who was the athletic director at Purdue, and asked him if any college players caught his eye. King said, "There's this string bean of a kid at Eastern Michigan. He's only a freshman, but the kid was 16-of-19 from the floor against us in a freshman game. I think he's a real player." George King and I had played together in the NBA with Syracuse and I respected his opinion. I wrote down Gervin's name and it always stayed in the back of my mind. I tried to find out what happened to the kid, but it was as if he had just disappeared. It turned out that George had been suspended for getting into a fight on the floor and he quit school.

A few years later, I was watching some kind of all-star game in Michigan and there was this skinny kid making all these shots. I asked who the kid was and it turned out to be George Gervin. I felt as if I had just found out that Elvis Presley was alive. I told Al Bianchi that he had to sign Gervin right now. Then Al went to Earl Foreman, who got right on it.

EARL FOREMAN: I first heard about Gervin from Sonny Vaccaro *(who runs the Nike basketball camps)*. I mentioned Gervin's name to Al Bianchi, who said he'd check on it. He came back to me a few days later with his tongue hanging out saying, "Sign this kid." Al kept talking about making Gervin into a 6-foot-7 guard.

So I set up a meeting with Vaccaro in a restaurant. I said, "Okay, I want this kid. What is it going to take?"

I pulled out a pen, we took the napkin and I started writing down some numbers. I can't remember what the offer was, but it wasn't that high, nothing like $100,000 a year—much less. Vaccaro took the napkin with him and I guess he talked to George. The next day, I got a call and the deal was done. Then I started hearing that Gervin was a bad kid, that he had punched somebody in school and all that. I met George before he signed and he was so quiet and polite. All he did was look at his shoes. I figured he had to have been provoked really badly to hit anyone.

JOHNNY KERR: I did a lot of checking on Gervin and everybody said he was a good kid. The punch he had thrown at Eastern Michigan was just an isolated incident. If anything, he was almost too quiet, too reserved.

(Gervin punched an opponent who he thought was "pushing him around" during a game between Eastern Michigan and Roanoke College. Gervin was suspended from the team and later left school because of academic problems.)

Right after we signed Gervin, I took him to one of our games and he sat in the stands next to me. After it was over, we walked down to the court. George was wearing a T-shirt, jeans and tennis shoes. He said, "Why don't they use the 3-point shot more?"

I said, "Coach Bianchi doesn't think it's a good percentage shot unless we're behind at the end of the game."

George said, "Suppose you could make 15-of-20."

I said, "George, that's a really long shot."

He said, "But say you could make 15-of-20."

I said, "Then Al would probably change his mind."

The game had been over for a while and the lights were dimmed. It wasn't dark, but it wasn't easy to see the rim, either. George wanted a ball and someone threw him one. He went behind the 3-point line and started shooting. He took shot after shot and swish after swish.

Then he said, "That's 18 out of 20."

I said, "Hey, George, let's go make sure that the ink is dry on your contract."

MIKE STOREN: Right after he signed George Gervin, I got a call from Earl Foreman, who said, "I got a guy just like Julius Erving, only he shoots better."

I told Earl, "You gotta be kidding."

Then I went to see Gervin's first game. He came off the bench and lit it up pretty good. I said to Earl, "I can't believe it; you did it again. I mean, I never even heard of this guy."

AL BIANCHI: The problem I had with playing Gervin and Julius together is that I used them both at forward. Ice wasn't much of a rebounder and we were getting killed on the boards, but I didn't immediately want to switch Gervin to guard, because he came to me as a college forward and I figured getting used to pro ball was enough for a 19-year-old without having to learn a new position, too.

The 1972–73 Squires were 42–42 and eliminated by Kentucky in the first round of the playoffs. They did lead the league in scoring, averaging 115 points, but gave up 116 points. In the 30 games Gervin and Erving played together, the Squires were 15–15. Gervin averaged 14.1 points in those games. At the end of the season, Foreman sold Erving to the New York Nets.

ANGELO DROSSOS: A month after the Nater deal, I heard that Earl Foreman was in money trouble again, so I got on the phone. I said, "Earl, I need another player and I'm willing to buy another player from you."

Earl said, "Listen, I just can't sell you George Carter. He's my best player and it will devastate the franchise."

I said, "I don't want Carter, I want George Gervin."

Earl said, "Gervin? George is just a kid. He's not even 20 yet."

I said, "I'll give you $225,000 for him."

There was a long silence on the phone. I knew that money always got Earl's attention.

Earl said, "Angelo, I just can't do that. The All-Star Game is in Virginia in a couple of months. If I trade Gervin, I'll have no one at the game. Our fans won't like it. Gervin is our future. I lost Charlie Scott. I traded Swen Nater. I traded Julius Erving. I traded Rick Barry. I can't trade Gervin, too."

But I knew that he would trade Gervin for the same reason he traded all those other players—money.

I said, "Earl, suppose we do a delayed-delivery deal."

Earl said, "What do you mean?"

I said, "I'll pay you the $225,000 now. We'll wait until right after the

All-Star Game and then you deliver Gervin to me. Until then, you can keep him."

Earl said, "All right."

I don't believe I even told Tom Nissalke and I don't think Earl told Al Bianchi. Word never leaked out until the All-Star Game.

EARL FOREMAN: At the All-Star Game in Norfolk, the press got the Gervin rumor and the town was going crazy. Fans were ready to kill me. George was off to a good start *(averaging 25 points)* and I was already being hung in effigy. I'll never forget how good *(Commissioner)* Mike Storen was to me. He sat by me, said all the right things to try and take some of the heat off. He did everything but hold my hand.

During the game, I said to myself, "I don't care what has to be done, I'm going to reverse this deal." The problem was that the deal had been done two months before, and now I was feeling remorse. It really was too late, but I wanted to do something anyway.

After the game, I went into the dressing room, something I seldom did. I went up to George Gervin and said, "George, don't worry. No matter what happens, you're going to stay with the Squires."

George never said a word. He never looked up. Like always, he just looked at his shoes. The next morning, I tried to get in touch with George, but he and his agent had taken off for San Antonio.

ANGELO DROSSOS: When the All-Star Game was over, I said to Foreman, "Let's have a press conference and announce the deal."

Foreman said, "I can't give you Gervin. I just can't. I had to tell the commissioner about it because the deal was illegal."

I obviously didn't agree, but then we brought Storen into the room.

Storen said, "Angelo, I'm going to tell you what I'll do. You can have your choice of any player on the Virginia roster except Gervin. You can have your money back, plus 10 percent interest as a penalty on Earl. And you can even have George Carter if you want him."

I said, "No, we made a deal for Gervin. That's the player I want."

Storen said, "You can't have him. I'm not approving that."

I said, "I'm sorry, Mike, but a deal's a deal and that's the deal."

Storen said, "Then you don't have any deal."

I said, "We'll see. You take your best shot at me and I'll take my best shot at you."

Storen wouldn't give us Gervin because he had played for the Squires while he was our property, which was illegal, even though only three people in the world knew about it and Gervin wasn't one of them. I went back to San Antonio determined to get Gervin.

Right after the All-Star Game, Virginia was playing in Utah. I called Gervin and said, "If you step on the floor for the Squires tonight, I'm going to have federal marshals pull you right out of the gym, because we have your contract."

Gervin called his agent, Irwin Weiner. I didn't know Weiner from Adam, but he called me and said that Gervin was very nervous. Then he said, "Angelo, George says that you have his contract. Do you really have his contract?"

I said I did.

Weiner said, "Will you indemnify us if I bring him to San Antonio?"

That meant, would I protect Gervin from any sort of loss or legal action because of a breach of contract? I said I would. Then Weiner called George and they came to San Antonio, where I negotiated a new contract with them.

Then I got a telegram from Storen saying, "Every game that Gervin is in your town, you will forfeit it. If the player does not report back to Virginia by tomorrow night, you're going to be suspended from the league."

I sent a telegram back to him saying, "Fuck you. A stronger letter will follow."

Storen then sued us, but it was in a Federal Court in San Antonio. The judge was a family friend and a Spurs season-ticket holder. The judge listened politely to Storen's lawyer, then he said, "I find for Mr. Drossos."

That's how we got Gervin.

A few years later, I got a funny letter from Storen saying, "You may have Gervin now, but you'll never keep him as long as there's justice in the courts of Texas. Affectionately, Mike Storen."

MIKE STOREN: It was clear what was going on in the Gervin situation. Earl Foreman was selling all of his players to get cash, and he was trying to sell the team at the same time. As commissioner, what I wanted to do in the best interest of the league was to prevent Earl from selling all of his assets so he would have something left to attract a buyer. I mean, he had just sold Julius Erving and Swen Nater within a year, so it was obvious what his course of conduct was. I wanted Gervin to stay in Virginia so the league could go out and find a new buyer for this franchise. Then San Antonio created a legal situation and ended up having a federal judge hear the case in San Antonio. The deck was stacked. Why would a San Antonio judge rule any way but in favor of the Spurs?

We lost the case, and I remember coming out of the courthouse and a lady running up to me, yelling, "Are you Storen?"

I said I was.

She said, "You know what you are?"

I said, "What am I?"

She said, "You're nothing but a goat roper."

I turned to my local counsel and asked him what the hell a goat roper was. He said, "Well, that's an insult. It means it's somebody who's not even good enough to rope a horse."

ANGELO DROSSOS: After Storen lost in court, he tried to bring me up on charges at the league level. Charlie Finley owned the Memphis franchise and he stood up and said, "You crazy sons of bitches. Instead of bringing Angelo up on charges, you should be congratulating this man. In this weak-kneed league of ours, here's a guy willing to spend money to improve his team. I'm voting with Angelo."

The majority of the owners went with Finley and we ended up with the greatest player in the history of the Spurs.

MEANWHILE, BACK IN SAN ANTONIO . . .

TERRY STEMBRIDGE: George Gervin was great, especially when he played with James Silas. Silas was one of my all-time favorite players and one of the Spurs' first stars. Nobody heard about this guy. He went to Stephen F. Austin, an NAIA school in Nacogdoches, Texas *(where Silas averaged 30.7 points and his team went 29–1 in his senior year. Silas was a fourth-round pick by Houston in the NBA and wasn't even picked in the ABA draft).*

I first saw James when he was in training camp with Houston and Dallas played them in one of the ABA-NBA exhibition games. This one was in Tyler, Texas, and he played very little, less than a quarter. Then we played Houston in another exhibition game, this one in the Stephen F. Austin gym. Silas only played about a quarter, but he went wild. He was hitting everything. Then we played them in a third exhibition game, and Silas didn't play at all. The Rockets later cut him and I couldn't understand why, because they never gave him a real chance. We signed him quickly. Silas's first game with Dallas was against Kentucky in Freedom Hall. Babe McCarthy put James into the game in the third quarter, and he pushed the ball up the court, drove the baseline and stopped on a dime about 15 feet away and swished the jumper. It was one of those plays that only a really good guard can make. Right away, we just knew that James was a good player.

James was a tremendous clutch player. He had several 20-point *fourth quarters.* He won a lot of games with last-second shots. I started calling him "the late Mr. Silas" on the air because of his late-game heroics, but that sounded more like he had died. "The late Mr. Silas" evolved into Captain Late, which was the nickname that stuck with James for his career.

When Bob Bass became coach in 1975, he put Gervin in the backcourt with Silas, and that was the greatest guard combination the ABA ever had. They were a perfect pair. Gervin didn't like to handle the ball, he liked to shoot it. James could dribble and pass. He also was such a good offensive player that if the other team started to double-team Gervin, Silas would score and make them pay. He was one of those guards who controlled a game in a lot of different ways, with his scoring, passing and his clutch play.

Okay, George Gervin was the franchise, no one will deny that. But James Silas wasn't far behind. People don't know Silas because he went to a small college, because he was a very quiet guy who just did his job and didn't draw attention to himself off the court, and because he was overshadowed by Gervin. The tragic thing about Silas was that in the last year of the ABA, when we played New York in the playoffs, James messed up his knee. He came back and played, but he never had the same quickness, the same ability to just explode off the dribble. When the merger came, the NBA saw James Silas, but they never saw the real James Silas because of his knee problems.

In the final year of the ABA and Silas's last healthy season, he averaged 23.8 points and 5.5 assists and shot 52 percent, compared with 21.8 points, 2.2 assists and 51 percent for Gervin.

ANGELO DROSSOS: Probably the biggest thing that happened during that first season in San Antonio was that we bought 100 percent of the franchise. Early in the season, we weren't drawing well *(only a 1,600 average after the first month, up to about 3,000 by Christmas)* and I was buying players. In effect, we ran out of money. I told the Dallas people who had leased us the team, "I've got to give you back your franchise."

That shook them up, because the last thing they wanted was the team back and then to have to find another buyer.

I said, "We've run out of money and the only way we can make this thing go would be if we own 100 percent of the team."

They were listening.

The original deal was that we could buy the team in two payments of $800,000, or $1.6 million.

I said, "I'll give you the $800,000, but that's it. We get 100 percent of the team for that $800,000, not 50 percent."

They agreed to it. They didn't want the team back.

Once we got that squared away, the best thing I did was hire Bob Bass as coach, replacing Tom Nissalke.

TERRY STEMBRIDGE: Tom Nissalke and Angelo had some real differences about players. There also was a lot of maneuvering going on behind the scenes in terms of the owners and Angelo's standing among the owners. It was very political.

ANGELO DROSSOS: I was good friends with Charlie Finley and I remembered something he had told me about his coach in Memphis, Bob Bass. Charlie told me that you wouldn't find a more loyal, hardworking guy than Bob Bass. Charlie no longer owned Memphis when I fired Nissalke and needed a coach. Bass had moved into the Memphis front office as general manager. I understood that Bob loved coaching, so I called him and offered him the job and he took it right on the spot. And the irony was that we were playing in Memphis that night, so the team just met him there.

BOB BASS: Everyone in the ABA was aware that the Spurs were in some turmoil, especially between Nissalke and Angelo. Also, some of the players were unhappy with the style of play—Nissalke liked to play a very patterned offense. When I took over the team, the Spurs were the second-lowest-scoring team in the ABA, at 102 points a game. The team was 17–10, but 15 of those 27 games were at home. *(The Spurs were 13–2 at home, 4–8 on the road).* I got the job and 10 of our next 11 games were on the road. Talk about a tough spot.

The main thing I wanted to do was get the guys to feel loose and just play to their talents, because that was a talented team. When I took over, my backcourt was James Silas and Donnie Freeman—I hadn't moved Gervin to guard yet. My center was Swen Nater and the forwards were Rich Jones and Gervin. These guys could play and they could score. I let them loose, and by the end of the season we were averaging 116 points, second-best in the ABA. So we went from second-worst to second-best, which tells you something about our firepower.

TERRY STEMBRIDGE: I've always said that Tom Nissalke's teams played the most boring basketball known to mankind. Even when they won, they were still boring to watch. That's a personal opinion, but I was announcing the games and I could really see the change when Bob came in.

BOB BASS: There was a lot of pressure right after I got the job. We went on one of those trips that only the ABA had and we got our butts whipped pretty good.

Bass is referring to a nine-game, fourteen-day trip where the Spurs played every ABA team on the road but Memphis. They went 2–7. After that trip, the Spurs finished 30–15 under Bass, then lost to Indiana in the first round of the playoffs.

TERRY STEMBRIDGE: The fans responded to the team. *(The Spurs averaged 7,853 fans).* They liked Bob's feisty style on the sidelines and they liked how the team raced up and down the court. Our crowds were lively and the loudest in the ABA. We had the Baseline Bums, a group of blue-collar guys who were a creation of *(business manager)* John Begzos. John wanted a group of loyal, hard-core fans and he had something like the Bums when he was a minor league baseball general manager. So these guys had T-shirts and they got discounted tickets. In a sense, they became a big part of the franchise. Now, you'd call it a great marketing idea. Back then, it was just getting a bunch of guys together to make noise and have fun.

WAYNE WITT: When Begzos was hired, he called a couple of his buddies and said why don't they start a Bleacher Bums kind of group at the Spurs games? We gave them a 120-seat section *(in the corner above the tunnel that led to the visitors' dressing room).* They really didn't know much about basketball, but they adopted the team, drank a lot of beer and screamed their lungs out.

JOHN LOPEZ: I grew up in San Antonio and I covered the Spurs for the *San Antonio Light* from 1986 to '89. There's a misconception that the fans loved the Spurs from the first day they came to town. That's really not the case. I loved that team because I loved basketball and I was aware of what the ABA was, but when the Dallas Chaparrals moved here, it just wasn't a big deal. What's more, Dallas wasn't even a good ABA team, so there seemed to be little reason to get excited.

In the first year, I was 13 and the Spurs had something called the Go Spurs Go club for kids. Every kid could buy tickets for five games a year at something like a buck each. I had four friends and the five of us would pile into my father's station wagon and he'd drop us off at the games. We found that there was a back door you could open from inside. Security? The ABA didn't know the meaning of the word. So we'd all chip in so one of us could buy a ticket and then he'd open the back door and let the other four of us in.

After we got in the arena, we could pretty much sit where we wanted. Again, this was in the early days before the crowds started to come. I remember distinctly sitting about six rows up from the floor right at halfcourt and seeing Wilt Chamberlain spread out on the bench coaching the Qs. The Spurs lost that game in the last few seconds when Caldwell Jones hit some free throws. In another game, we sneaked down by the Spurs bench and sat right behind the team when George Gervin went for 51 points against Memphis. It was that kind of feeling—adventure, watching something brand-new, sitting in different spots in the arena and trying to get close to the players. I went to 25 to 30 games a year.

The ABA caught on in San Antonio for two reasons: first, the team became good right away when the Spurs got players such as Gervin and Swen Nater. But second, the real turning point came after Bob Bass was named the coach and he opened up the style of play.

The ABA games were always fun to watch, but the Spurs, playing that run-and-gun offense, were like a circus, and I mean that in the best, most entertaining sense of the word. Here were these graceful athletes dashing up and down the floor as no athletes ever had done in San Antonio, and they were playing with the red, white and blue ball, which in itself was a lot of fun to watch. By the 1975 playoffs, the team had taken hold in the town. The arena sat 9,900, but there were over 11,000 people at those games, wall-to-wall people, and that was before the fire marshal made them control the crowd.

The Baseline Bums were their own show. Mostly they were Mexican guys who would go straight from work to the Lone Star Pavilion, where they sold pitchers of beer for a buck. So these guys would load up on Lone Star beer for a couple of hours before they even got to the game. They were just wasted and they'd yell and give the other team hell. The leader was Dancing Harry, this fat Mexican guy with a big mustache who'd dance during time-outs. That also was back when they sold beer in the can during the games and they let the fans keep the can. So when the officials blew a call or when a player did something to the Spurs, the Bums would pelt the court with cans. Finally, they stopped selling the cans before someone got really hurt.

WAYNE WITT: The whole thing mushroomed between the fans and team. The town really embraced the Spurs. There was a game with Denver when Larry Brown was coaching the Nuggets. Every time Gervin would go by the Denver bench, somebody was yelling at him. We didn't know who was doing the yelling, if it was a player or a coach, but Bob Bass was hot about it. In the ABA, coaches could walk all the way down to the halfcourt line. Bass did and he yelled to Larry Brown to come over. Brown met Bass at halfcourt and Bob said, "Larry, if you don't stop yelling at Gervin, I'm gonna whip your ass right here in front of everybody." They had some more words, and after the game Larry told reporters, "All Bob Bass wears is polyester and the only good thing about San Antonio is the guacamole salad."

Well, this became a big duel in the papers and we really hyped it, because we knew it would help the crowd. The Baseline Bums got in the act and before the next Denver game in San Antonio, the Bums gave Larry Brown a crate with all the ingredients for guacamole salad. They presented it to Larry in a little pregame ceremony at halfcourt. Everybody got some laughs out of it, and we sold some more tickets.

JOHN LOPEZ: Obviously the Baseline Bums lived for something like what Larry Brown said. I was at the game, and when it was over Brown was heading down the tunnel right under the Bums and they dumped guacamole and all kinds of stuff on him. That made it a bigger deal, and thirteen years later when Larry Brown was hired to coach the Spurs, they had a Meet the Coach Day at a local shopping mall and some fans showed up with guacamole salad for Larry. That incident is forever a part of the Spurs lore.

WAYNE WITT: We had a lot of different promotions. One time we had Dime Beer Night. Think about that. For a buck, you could have 10 beers . . . it's amazing there wasn't a total riot. We cut back on that but stuck with 2-for-1 beer nights.

One of the more bizarre things we did was to have a Merchants Night. We had a "boiler room" operation, where we set up shop in one of the local businesses and had a dozen people on the telephones, calling businesses and selling them 10 tickets for 10 bucks. It got out of hand. By 6:30 that night, the arena was packed with people with those dollar tickets and there were lines outside. We had to shut the doors, and there were fans outside actually trying to beat down the doors to get into an ABA game. Of course, the reason was the dollar tickets. We had to have another Merchants Night for the people who still had tickets. The guy running our "boiler room" operation was getting paid by commission; all he wanted to do was sell tickets, he didn't care how many, and he just lost track. I figure he must have sold 20,000 tickets because we had two sellouts.

JOHN LOPEZ: An important part of the fans' feeling like they knew the team was Terry Stembridge. He was the team's first announcer and he was the guy who really introduced basketball to the city. Terry had a flair. He called the game as if he were a volcano on the verge of eruption, yet he'd never explode. He was on the verge a lot, but he didn't lose track of the game. Instead, he made you feel like you were in the game and a part of the team. When Terry called a game, he made it sound like something important and exciting was happening. On certain plays, he'd go bananas. He made you care about the Spurs.

WAYNE WITT: We wanted everything about the Spurs to be a show, to cause your heart to beat just a little faster, and that was especially true of the 1975 All-Star Game. I was hired by the Spurs as their PR man in May of 1974, and a month later our GM, Jack Ankerson, left to work for the Squires. Angelo ran the team and we had a four-man front office—Terry Stembridge, *(business manager)* John Begzos, *(trainer)* Bernie LaReau and myself. Every Monday morning, the four of us and Angelo would meet at LaReau's condo for our weekly staff meeting. We sat around Bernie's kitchen table and talked. One morning, Angelo said we were having the All-Star Game in San Antonio. Then he looked at me and said, "Wayne, you're our All-Star Game general chairman."

I said, "Jeez, Angelo, I've never even been to an All-Star Game, how can I be the chairman of one?"

He said, "You'll figure it out."

So we started calling all the people who had had All-Star Games before, in Utah, Kentucky, places like that. We wanted to make the game in San Antonio a real Texas show. Terry Stembridge did a heckuva job in contacting local businesses and getting them to donate gifts for all the ABA people coming to town. We had glasses, ABA mugs, boxes of cigars, fruit baskets, cases of beer . . . on and on. People were saying, "How are we going to take all this stuff home with us?" That was exactly the response we wanted.

Our big thing was that we got Willie Nelson to perform at our dinner, which was a Mexican fiesta. We in Texas knew who Willie Nelson was, but this was before he was a national name, and I think a lot of people had no idea what they were watching. In fact, the deal we cut with Willie shows how much he wanted the national exposure—he agreed to entertain at the dinner provided he could sing the National Anthem at the All-Star Game the next day, because the game was going to be on national television.

We were a little concerned about Willie getting to the game on time for the anthem. Willie has always been a fine fellow, but he never looked that good and he probably looked even worse back then. We even assigned a guy to make sure that Willie showed up, but 15 minutes before the game, there was no Willie. People started going berserk and there were nine guys running around asking each other, "Have you seen Willie?" Now it's pretty humorous, but we were close to panic back then.

Five minutes before the game, Willie strolled in wearing his jeans jacket, his jeans shirt, his jeans, his boots, and a bandanna on his head. We all held our breath as he walked out on the court. You never know exactly what Willie will do, but he did a great job.

The kicker was that there was a snafu in the time and the anthem never was shown on national television.

ANGELO DROSSOS: The ABA believed in grand gestures and gala All-Star Games and we threw the biggest party of all. We spent thousands of dollars to give the players TVs, rings, furniture, radios. The players all took it for granted, except for one. I got a real nice "Thank You" note from George McGinnis.

JOHN LOPEZ: What I remember about that All-Star Game was the warm-ups. This was before the first Slam Dunk Contest, but it was like the players were having their own contest. There was Doctor J, Ice, Marvin Barnes trying to outdunk each other. It was BAM-BAM-BAM, dunk after dunk. Doctor J did a version of the taking-off-from-the-foul-line dunk that he did the following year at the contest in Denver. Now when I see the NBA Slam Dunk Contest, I'm just not that impressed, because guys were doing that in the ABA back then and it had more spontaneity because it all happened in warm-ups.

WAYNE WITT: We wanted to give our All-Star MVP something special, something very Texan. We decided on a horse. We were going to give the player a saddle and everything along with a big Western hat and a quarter horse. The horse was donated to us and its name was Turf Julie. We hired a guy to take care of the horse for a month before the game. A few weeks before the All-Star Game, we started bringing the horse to our regular-season games, parading it around the arena and telling the fans that the horse was going to be there for the All-Star Game. Seeing the horse always got the crowd revved up.

Freddie Lewis ended up being the MVP *(26 points, 10 assists as his East team beat the West 151–124 before a sellout crowd of 10,449).* Freddie didn't know a horse from a cow and he had no idea what to do with it, so we struck a deal. We'd auction off the horse and give Freddie the money, which ended up being something like two thousand dollars. One of our investors, Dr. Linton Weems, bought the horse and the poor thing died two weeks later because of malnutrition. The guy taking care of the horse apparently was taking the feed money and buying himself Pearl beer. He disappeared on us and the horse died. That was a really sad ending to what should have been a great promotion.

JOHN LOPEZ: I loved that All-Star Game, probably because it was my first. In my office, I still have an ABA All-Star banner hanging on the wall, and it's signed by Freddie Lewis and Dave DeBusschere, whose autographs I got that day.

NATER GOES, ICE BREAKS THROUGH

ANGELO DROSSOS: Even though we had a good year at the gate and were 51–33 in our second year, we did lose in the first round of the playoffs to Indiana. I also had gotten a little disenchanted with Swen Nater. I was beginning to wonder just how far we could go with the guy.

Anyway, it was one night after the season and I was in bed with my wife. She was reading a book and I reached for the phone and called Roy Boe in New York and said, "Roy, we got knocked out of the first round of the playoffs by Indiana and you lost to St. Louis. We should do something. We should make a trade just to make one, even if it isn't any good."

Boe said, "You only have one player I want."

I didn't say anything. I was afraid he was going to ask for George Gervin.

But Boe said, "I'm interested in Nater."

I decided to pull an Earl Foreman and I said, "Roy, I don't know. Swen is a very important player to us; I don't think we can give him up. But just in case we could, who would you trade for him?"

Boe asked, "What do you want?"

I said, "It will take more than one player, and I've got to have a center."

Boe said, "Okay, I'll give you Billy Paultz."

I said that was a good start and we kept talking. When it was over, he gave me Larry Kenon, Mike Gale and Paultz. Then I asked for some cash and he gave me $300,000. In addition to Nater, we gave up four other guys I didn't want—Rich Jones, Kim Hughes, Chuck Terry and Bobby Warren.

I knew that I would catch some flak from the fans and I did. Nater was the first Spur to have a fan club, "Nater's Raiders." Those people really chewed me out. But I didn't care. I wanted to get rid of Nater and I would have traded him straight-up for Paultz.

As it was, we got two starters in Paultz and Kenon and a damn good guard in Mike Gale, who started for us when James Silas hurt his knee. None of the five guys we traded were going to play a significant role for us. I loved that trade.

BOB BASS: The Nater deal with New York is a trade that this franchise lived off of for years. After the Gervin deal, it's the most important trade this franchise ever made. I really think we became a winning team for the next eight years because of that deal.

JOHN LOPEZ: When Bob Bass talks about the Nater deal being crucial to the franchise, he's right. To this day, Larry Kenon is the best I've ever seen as a forward on the wing during a fast break. He could outrun anyone and finish the play. The rest of his game was maddening—he was the epitome of streaky. But he was thin, 6-foot-9, and had a huge Afro. Watching him seemingly glide up the court and then finish the break with a slam, it really was a sight. Most people only remember Kenon as the guy from Memphis State who had a good game against Bill Walton and UCLA in the NCAA finals, but he was a good player.

As important as that trade was to the Spurs, Bass's decision to move Gervin to guard really made Ice a superstar. Once Ice got used to the position, he went from scoring in the low 20s to the high 20s, and that increase happened *after* the Spurs went into the NBA.

BOB BASS: I'd like to say that making Ice a guard was a stroke of genius, but it was done more out of necessity. We had lost the first three games to Indiana in the 1975 playoffs. Don Buse was a 6-foot-4 guard, and he was covering James Silas. Buse was a helluva defensive player and he just shut down Silas. The Pacers' other guard was Billy Keller, and he was on Donnie Freeman. Donnie was a great scorer earlier in his career, but by 1975 he had started to show some age. So I shifted the lineup around, putting Ice in the backcourt with Silas. That meant Buse had to try and guard Ice, and I use the word "try" intentionally because no one could really guard Ice. That meant Keller switched over to Silas, and he couldn't guard James. With the new lineup, we won the fourth game *(110–109 at Indianapolis)*. Ice got his usual 29 and Silas went for 39. The idea was to create as many isolations for Gervin as I could because when there is only one man between him and the basket, Ice will score. That's also why I picked up the tempo when I became coach. Ice was a great open-court player because it gave him room to operate, so why saddle him with a halfcourt offense?

In that six-game playoff loss to Indiana, Gervin averaged 34 points and an amazing 14 rebounds. Why amazing? Because Gervin was 6-foot-7 and 170 pounds at this stage in his career, and he got just as many of those rebounds when he was at guard as when he played forward.

JOHN LOPEZ: What Bob Bass did that was brilliant was that he played Ice at guard, but only technically. He actually used a 1-4 offense. The ball was in James Silas's hands. He not only was the point guard, he was really the only guard. Ice still played in the same area of the floor that he did when he was a forward, only now he was being guarded by a smaller player, by the opposing team's guard. So Bass didn't ask Ice to do anything differently, yet he created a better defensive matchup because at 6-7, Ice was taller than virtually every guard in the ABA.

BOB MACKINNON: I coached in the NBA with Buffalo and in the ABA with St. Louis. When the Spurs got Gervin and Silas playing together, I thought they were better than any backcourt in basketball, and that included Earl Monroe and Walt Frazier with the New York Knicks.

BILLY KNIGHT: When I came to Indiana, George Gervin and I were two of the highest-scoring players in the league and sometimes we were matched up. The unbelievable thing was how easy he made it seem, how many different shots he had. Ice was the perfect nickname for him.

The Iceman nickname came from one of Gervin's teammates in Virginia, Fatty Taylor, who said Gervin was "just so cool."

DOUG MOE: I'm not saying that George Gervin was a better overall basketball player in the ABA than Julius Erving. Understand, that's not what I'm saying. But what I am saying is that Ice had more polish, a better variety of shots, and more ways to score than Julius. In terms of pure offense, Ice was probably better than Julius at that stage of their careers.

TERRY STEMBRIDGE: After Gervin came to San Antonio, the comparisons started with Erving. Ice was a better scorer than Julius, but Julius was more of a force. Julius won more games for you, he carried his teams to ABA titles. George was not that type of talent. He was singular, cometlike. While he won a lot of games for us, he won them early. By that I mean Ice would have 20-point first quarters, 30-point first halves. He could be shut down for a while down the stretch because he was vulnerable to the good double-team. Ballhandling and passing were never his strengths, and that was why the double-teaming defense would sometimes work against him.

George was great for the franchise, because he was friendly, always smiling and good with the fans. He wasn't the most dependable guy in terms of showing up for public appearances on time, but when he did get there he was usually so nice that everyone just forgot he was late. He had a very warm smile that counted for a lot.

ANGELO DROSSOS: George Gervin was to San Antonio what Babe Ruth was to New York. Babe Ruth was baseball in New York City, he was the New York Yankees. Well, Gervin was the San Antonio Spurs and he was the symbol of basketball in this town. He was rather immature, but a nice kid and he didn't have a prima donna attitude, which made him even more popular.

JOHN LOPEZ: I remember when George Gervin appeared on the cover of *Sports Illustrated* in his San Antonio Spurs uniform. It was a great moment for the entire town. San Antonio was considered nothing more than a high school football town. In terms of national sports, there was nothing to talk about until Ice came along. But the Spurs team, especially Ice, gave the city an identity and all the players became heroes in their own way. Hey, they were—still are, for that matter—the only pro athletes in town. So it doesn't matter how many times George Gervin has screwed up—and he has screwed up a lot the last few years—he's still George Gervin and he could do no wrong in San Antonio.

TERRY STEMBRIDGE: You can't underestimate the fact that the team was a winner from the first moment it stepped on the court in San Antonio, and Angelo Drossos just kept making it better and better. The Spurs became his life. He was on every ABA committee and had a hand in every major move the ABA made in its last few years, and that way he protected the team's interests. In the last year of the ABA, we were 50–34, and that was our second straight 50-win season.

San Antonio's three-year ABA record was 146–106, although the Spurs could never get past the first round of the playoffs.

HUBIE BROWN: By the end of the ABA, San Antonio was the deepest, most talented team in the league in terms of players one through ten. They were the biggest team in the league when they started Silas, Gervin, Paultz, Kenon and Coby Dietrick. Silas was the only guy under 6-foot-7; their front line was 6-foot-11, 6-foot-9 and 6-foot-11. They also had athletes who could run. It was a nightmare to coach against them.

TERRY STEMBRIDGE: The playoffs were always this huge obstacle for us in the ABA. That last season, Denver clearly had the best talent in the league, but we thought we would get a crack at the Nuggets in the finals. We played Julius and New York in the first round in a seven-game series and we were up 2–1. In the opening game, we lost Silas *(knee injury)*. Gervin had a broken bone in his wrist, but he still played. The key was Game 4 in San Antonio. Mike Gale filled in for Silas at guard and was doing a great job, so we still liked our chances. It was Easter Sunday and the game was being carried on CBS at noon. George Karl came off the bench and in the middle of the second quarter, he and the Nets' Brian Taylor got into a fight that turned into one of the biggest brawls I've ever seen on the court. Rich Jones was with the Nets then, and he teamed up with John Williamson to go around slapping and punching everybody. Even Julius Erving got into it, and I believe this was his first and last real fight. He took a swing at Tom Owens, our backup center. Owens just looked at Julius and said, "Doc, don't you know I can end your career the next time you go flying down the lane?" Julius then apologized.

Finally, things settled down . . . sort of. Guys stopped throwing punches, but it was a brutal game after that. Williamson had a great game for them, scoring a ton of points off the bench.

With 17 seconds left, we were ahead by one point, 108–107. There was a time-out and Bob Bass told the team not to let Julius get the ball and to force Rich Jones to take a shot if possible. That was exactly what happened. Jones forced up a long shot that banged against the rim and Gervin grabbed the rebound on the baseline.

That should have been the ballgame.

But instead of covering up the ball with both hands, almost cradling it as players do, George sort of raised the ball over his head.

He was right on the baseline, just inbounds. I can still see this play and I can still see the Nets' Brian Taylor standing out-of-bounds. Taylor saw Gervin hold the ball out. He gave Gervin a push with his left hand and then whacked the ball away from Ice with his right hand. The ball deflected right to Julius, who grabbed it and slammed. Coby Dietrick then fouled Julius and our one-point lead became a 110–108 loss.

There was no question that Taylor was out-of-bounds, so he should not have been permitted to take the ball away from Gervin. Norm Drucker was the official and he was standing right there! I mean, the play was right in front of him and he didn't call a thing. I couldn't believe it. Bob Bass and I have probably watched that film a hundred times and it never changes. Taylor was out-of-bounds.

So New York won that game in San Antonio, making the series 2–2, and the Nets ended up beating us in seven games. But to this day, that is another famous incident in Spurs history—the day Norm Drucker didn't make the call.

COTTON FITZSIMMONS: The ABA has been dead for a long time now, but they still love to talk about it in San Antonio. When I coached the

Spurs *(1984–86)*, all I ever heard about was the ABA, the great teams and the great players. Given the choice, those people would probably rather go back and play in the ABA than play in the NBA. Of course, I was the guy who coached George Gervin at the end of his career and I had to trade George in order to clear the decks for Alvin Robertson to play. But trading Ice—it's lucky I wasn't lynched. Ice hung a lot of those championship banners up there and I heard a lot about Spurs tradition.

JOHN LOPEZ: When the Spurs went into the NBA after the merger, it was a tremendous moment for the town. It was like San Antonio was recognized as a major league city and that caused the fans to embrace the team all the more. Making the situation better was that the team was very successful in the NBA. *(The Spurs won five division titles in six years from 1977 to 1983.)* But the attachment to the ABA, to those players and stories, is still very strong, because that was really where it began and Texans love their own history. You can get some Spurs fans together and just mention some old names from the team—Bird Averitt, Goo Kennedy, Collis Temple—and people start to smile and tell stories. My first favorite Spur was Skeeter Swift. Not because he was any good; he probably would have a tough time making a decent European team today. But I just liked the name—Skeeter Swift. San Antonio was quick to make heroes out of these players, and not just George Gervin or James Silas, but guys who were average players such as George Karl and Coby Dietrick. In the basketball world, they may not have been special, but the mere fact that they played for the Spurs and played hard made them special in San Antonio.

Part III

ENDGAME

The Legend of Doctor J

Julius Erving played in the ABA for five seasons, averaging 28.7 points and 12.1 rebounds while shooting 50 percent. Erving raised those numbers to 31.1 points, 14.6 rebounds and 52 percent in 48 playoff games. He won the league's MVP award in each of the last three seasons, sharing it in 1975 with George McGinnis. He also won three scoring titles and was a first-team ABA player in the league's last four seasons. His high game was 63 points against the San Diego Conquistadors on February 14, 1975, when he was 26-for-46 from the field, doing most of the damage against Travis "Machine Gun" Grant. In four of his five seasons, he never missed a regular-season or playoff game. But Erving meant far more than numbers to the ABA.

KEVIN LOUGHERY: When Julius came to the Nets from Virginia, the word was that he could do things that had never been done before on the court. I was in the NBA, so I hadn't seen him with Virginia. You hear things about a guy and you say, "Yeah, right." Hey, I had been watching the world's greatest players in the NBA, so I had some real doubts that Julius was going to show me something I had never seen before.

In the first game that I coached Doc with the Nets, he had the ball right at the end of the first half. We were playing Indiana and the clock was running down. Doc drove the baseline and found himself under the basket with both George McGinnis and Darnell Hillman—two big guys—going for the block. Somehow, Doc floated between McGinnis and Hillman and then almost tore down the rim with a slam. To that point in my life, that was the greatest dunk I had ever seen, and Doc did it in the first half of my first game with him. After that, there were a lot of "greatest dunks" when you watched him every day.

What impressed me even more was that here was a player who really was *the league*. He could have done almost anything he wanted, but Doc never missed a game and never even missed a practice in his three years with me. We used to play three games in a row all the time, Friday, Saturday and Sunday. Come Monday afternoon's practice, everybody

317

was dead. Doc could have said to me, "Kevin, I'm tired." But he never did. I would ask him, "Doc, want to rest your legs?" He was playing 40 minutes a night. But he'd always play. He loved the game and he'd play so hard in practice that he'd lift the rest of the team. He was usually the last guy to leave practice, because he was always asking somebody to play him 1-on-1.

JOHN STERLING: I did the Nets games on television and I did a talk show in New York. I can say without a doubt that what finally convinced the NBA to merge was a chance to get Julius in the league. There were a lot of other reasons, having to do with money and all that. But Julius was about money, too. The NBA knew this guy could be a great drawing card.

Julius had class and dignity and the fans sensed that and were attracted to him. But it was truly a case of word getting out on Julius, because so few people could see him. As his legend grew, he was *underexposed* instead of overexposed, because the league had no significant national television contract, nor was there cable television. Fans outside of ABA markets may have heard about him and read about him, but they didn't see him. And when they finally did get a look at him, it was an event. Of course, if Julius didn't have such overwhelming talent and if he wasn't so great, then it wouldn't have worked. But despite most people's expectations, when people finally got a look at him, Julius was even better than they thought.

BOB COSTAS: I wouldn't underestimate Julius's looks in his popularity. He is a handsome guy, almost regal in his bearing. He was one guy who was helped when he cut his Afro, because he may have had the biggest one in pro basketball when he was a kid. There was electricity in his game and kindness in his personality that added up to a lot of charisma.

ZELMO BEATY: I spent most of my career in the NBA. I saw Elgin Baylor in his prime and I saw Connie Hawkins. Both of those guys could do some of the things that Julius later did, but he carried it a step beyond. No one could run and dunk and swoop down on the basket with the style of a young Julius Erving.

STEVE JONES: Julius was hardly a finished product when he came into the ABA. He was strictly an over-the-rim player, a pure athlete, and his greatest attribute was offensive rebounding. But he worked on his game, developed a jumper and some drives, to the point where he could make a shot from any angle. Even when you thought you had forced him out-of-bounds, he would just rise up and fly around you. When a player as gifted as Julius takes the court, he believes that he has no limitations. He can try any move because he can make any shot. I guarded Julius when he was in that stage of his career; it wasn't much fun. If you put him in historical perspective, the only other player in the same class is Michael Jordan. Michael has a much better jumper than Julius, but believe it or not, Julius played much higher above the rim and he was a far better rebounder than Michael. It would be fun to see a young Erving play a young Jordan just to see how it came out, because those two guys are players who have no limits.

DAN ISSEL: Julius would begin to work on you during warm-ups. You'd be at one end of the court, shooting around, and then you'd hear the crowd cheering. You'd look and see Julius doing windmill dunks and stuff like that. When the game began, he'd look for a chance to make a great play. I never saw anyone dunk on Artis Gilmore like Julius did. He'd go right up to Artis, sort of chest-to-chest, then dunk the ball right over Artis's shoulder. People would go crazy, even your own fans, and all you could do was put your head down and run to the other end of the court.

HUBIE BROWN: Nobody in the league could turn your own sellout crowd against you like Doctor J. At Kentucky, we had a rule: if Doctor J was coming down on the fast break, foul him. I didn't care if he was 20 feet from the basket. Just foul him before he took off. If you didn't foul him and Julius dunked, it was a $50 fine. I learned that the hard way. In my first year in the ABA, we had six crowds of over 16,000 for our games with the Nets in Louisville; Julius would do something spectacular and the next thing I knew, the fans were cheering for him instead of us. He had a move from the right side where he'd drive, raise up and take the ball in both hands, touch it against the top of the square over the rim, then slam it home. Do you realize how high you have to jump and how long you have to stay up to do something like that?

I was in awe of what the guy could do. He was great in the NBA, but by then his knees had started to hurt and he had been physically knocked around. But in the ABA, he was fearless. He played with reckless abandon. He made plays no one has seen before or since, plays that not even Michael Jordan can do.

ROD THORN: Two plays stand out in my mind.

One of them was almost routine for him: Doc was the first player I had ever seen run the court on the fast break, catch a lob with one hand

and then slam it without bringing the ball to his body or using another hand. It was like someone threw him a softball, not a basketball, because of how he could control the ball in one hand.

The other was a specific play against Kentucky. Julius brought the ball down the court on the fast break and Teddy McClain was between Doc and the basket. Teddy crouched a bit in the standard defensive stance. Doc just took off, high-jumped over Teddy and then dunked. I can still see McClain looking up and watching Julius fly over him.

JOHN STERLING: In the last year of the ABA, Julius was having a great game, even by his incredible standards. He was making one mind-boggling play after another and there was hardly any noise because it was a very small crowd. After one dunk over three guys, Kevin Loughery called a time-out. When the players came to the bench, Kevin went up to Julius and said, "I called that time-out because I wanted to tell you that you've just played the greatest three-minute stretch of basketball I have ever seen."

TEDD MUNCHAK: I once had a friend who told me that Julius walked when he drove to the basket. I told the guy, "Yeah, he takes four steps while he's in the air."

ALEX HANNUM: Julius was one of the few guys in basketball history who really could be a one-man team, at least in the ABA when he had those young legs and could leap over everybody. When I coached against him, I would run three men at him in the last five minutes of a close game. I recall once setting up a defense where I sent four guys at him to stop him. Even then, you couldn't shut him down because at the very least, he'd draw a foul.

BILLY CUNNINGHAM: Julius was the best player I've ever seen in the open court, and that includes Jordan. In the ABA, where the style of game was faster and wide open, Julius had more opportunities to do amazing things than he did in the NBA, where the offenses were more conservative. After I came back from the ABA to the NBA, I would start telling Julius Erving stories and guys would say to me, "Yeah, he was great in that league, but wait until he has to play against us."

I'd say, "Who are you kidding? There has never been a player like this guy."

ROD THORN: Of all the players I've been around, no one has had a more dramatic effect on his teammates, his league and even how the game is played than Julius. Jordan is a better overall player, because he can do some of the things that Doc couldn't, and certainly Jordan has had a profound impact on pro basketball. But Julius was such a leader and he understood his position on the team and in the league as a spokesman. He knew that how he acted and what he did was very important.

He would do little things for the other guys on the team. In Larry Kenon's rookie season, he was having a tough time and was depressed. After our pregame meeting one night, Julius told me, "Don't worry about Kenon. I'll take care of him."

Early in the game, Doc had a clear lane for a dunk, but he spotted Kenon open and passed off so Kenon could dunk. By the end of the first quarter, Kenon had 12 points, most of them on passes from Julius. Kenon ended up with a 30-point night and was all smiles. After the game, Julius told the reporters about how great Kenon had played and how Kenon was very important to the team.

Julius was aware that his teammates needed attention and a pat on the back. He also knew that reporters would come to him for quotes because he was so patient with everybody. So Julius would talk about different guys on the team and he did it sincerely, so it didn't sound like he was just some star blowing smoke.

Another player Julius helped was Brian Taylor, a guard from Princeton who was a very sensitive kid. Brian sometimes felt as though he had gotten lost in Julius's shadow. Julius would occasionally take him to dinner, talk to him and talk about Brian to the reporters. Julius just had a sense of what it meant to be a teammate.

I think it's because he came from such a strong family background. He was taught to respect people, to be polite and to appreciate what he had. Stardom came late in his basketball life. He wasn't like some of these kids who have been recruited since they were in junior high. At UMass he was a helluva player, but the nation didn't know him. Since he hadn't been catered to all of his life, he knew that he wasn't the center of the universe.

I think that other teams knew what Julius meant to the league. No one ever tried to deck him. A lot of players would rough up Julius, but no one wanted to hurt him. You weren't going to take a punch at Julius Erving. That would have been like fighting in church.

MACK CALVIN: The players were in awe of Julius. His talent was overwhelming, but the credibility he had on and off the court kept the league going the last two years. I was involved with Julius in the ABA Players Association and he had a clear sense of what was best for the league. He also had a stake in the league after he was traded to New York. He could have tried to jump again, as he did in Virginia, and it probably would have worked. But he committed himself to keeping the ABA alive. I remember in 1974 when some of the players were threatening to strike at the All-Star Game, Julius talked to the guys and convinced them to play.

JULIUS ERVING: Some of the guys were complaining that the gifts they got weren't the best, or that they wanted some little things changed. I said, "Wait a minute. This game isn't for us personally, it's the showcase for the entire league. We're here to represent our teams and all the guys in the league. It is an honor to be here, and I think we should just go out and play." Most of the other guys felt the same way, so it really wasn't that big a deal. The ABA had a tremendous support group of players looking out for each other and the league, even if we sometimes tried to take off each other's heads on the court. We really did know what was best and we weren't afraid to remind each other of what we should do.

ANGELO DROSSOS: During the last season when the league was in serious trouble, Julius came to my office. The Nets were playing in San Antonio and Julius was aware that I was very active in the league and on things such as the merger committee. He came to my office and said, "Mr. Drossos, what can I do to help the league survive?"

I didn't invite Julius, and really, it didn't matter to him personally if the league made it. There was a job waiting for him in the NBA. But he was concerned about the other players and since he had grown up as a pro in the ABA, he had a stake in the league. No other player ever came to me and said that.

Unfortunately, there was nothing more Julius could do. He already was giving the league a great image and the other issues such as the merger were going to be decided by the NBA owners.

CARL SCHEER: The spirit of the ABA was the spirit of Julius Erving. On the court, he expressed it in his style of play. Off the court, he became the league's ambassador. One night, I came into the old Charlotte Arena. The game had been over for at least an hour and I saw about 50 kids in the balcony and Julius sitting in the middle of them, signing autographs and talking. There was no press around or anything like that. He took the time because he wanted to do it. That was the thing about Julius. He'd make time for everybody.

Moses Malone: The Ultimate Underclassman

The first high school basketball player to sign a pro contract was Moses Malone, who went directly from Petersburg (Virginia) High to the Utah Stars in 1974. The drafting of Malone was announced by Utah assistant coach Larry Creger on April 17, 1974, when Malone was selected in the third round. While Stars GM Bucky Buckwalter signed Malone, the groundwork and initial wooing of the 6-foot-11, 210-pound 18-year-old was done by Creger. Moses is the only child of Mary Malone. His father left home when he was about 18 months old. Mary Malone first worked as a practical nurse, then was a $100-a-week meat packer when the wooing of Malone began. The Malones lived in a poor section of Petersburg, in a duplex on St. Matthews Street. In his first high school varsity game, Malone scored 32 points; he was a ninth-grader at the time. His high school team won 50 consecutive games and two state championships. After his junior year in high school, Malone went to Howard Garfinkel's Five-Star camp and was given a full five-star rating—"which is infinity," according to Garfinkel. By his senior year, Malone was being recruited by over 200 colleges. According to a Larry Donald column in Basketball Weekly, *ACC Commissioner Bob James called the Malone case "the worst recruiting mess I've ever seen." Donald said that Malone's uncle allegedly received envelopes containing $1,000. Another recruiter allegedly deposited a Chrysler Imperial at Malone's doorstep. Donald also reported, "An indifferent high school student through most of his days, Moses Malone became an A student in his last semester, which made him eligible, barely, to accept an NCAA scholarship. Malone's standard request as a junior was $200 to make a visit to some campus, any campus." According to a* Basketball Digest *story, Utah's Buckwalter had to sneak through a field to see Malone, and Buckwalter ended up being bitten by a dog that the Malone family had bought to guard their house. In Malone's home, Mary Malone had pictures of Martin Luther King Jr., John and Jackie Kennedy, Jesus Christ, and her son. Malone's final three schools were Clemson, Maryland and New Mexico. According to Tates Locke's book* Caught in the Net, *New Mexico assistant coach John Whisenant lived at the Howard Johnson's in Petersburg for over two months to recruit Malone. Maryland ran up* *over $20,000 in expenses at the Petersburg Holiday Inn. At first, Malone verbally committed to Clemson. Then he said he was signing with Maryland, which pleased his mother, who liked Terps coach Lefty Driesell. In the end, Malone turned down all the colleges and went with the ABA and Utah. In his two ABA seasons, Malone averaged 17.2 points and 13 rebounds and shot 55 percent. When he went into the NBA after the merger, he was 21 years old.*

LARRY CREGER: We were looking to get talent anywhere and wanted to beat the NBA to that talent. What the heck, we were free to sign anybody. We certainly didn't have to follow NBA rules. The courts said that the NCAA had no right to deny a kid a chance to leave college early and earn a living playing pro basketball. So why not sign a high school kid if he was good enough to play? Baseball had been signing kids out of high school for years. From a psychological standpoint, I was against it, because I felt kids needed some college, even if they were physically mature enough to play pro ball. Players need some time to grow up, even just a year or two on campus. But I had been hearing about Moses for some time, that he was good enough to be a pro while he was a senior in high school and that he wasn't exactly academically college material. So I went to Petersburg to check out the situation and I spent a month there at the Howard Johnson motel, along with all the other college coaches trying to get him.

The first time I saw him was in a charity game between the school's varsity team and an alumni team. Late in the first half, Moses's team was ahead by over 50 points. So they said, "Let's put Moses on the alumni team for the second half."

The alumni team was awful. It looked to me like they had one guy who had played some high school ball and that was it. Moses was at least six inches taller than everyone else on the court. He'd get a rebound, dribble it the length of the floor and score. Sometimes he'd throw the ball to his one decent teammate, then post up, catch a return pass and score. In the end, the alumni team lost by two points. Moses must have had 100 points in that game, if you added together what he scored for both teams.

So physically, I had no doubt that Moses was a pro talent—now.

Then I got to know his mother, Mary, and she had some serious health problems and wasn't supposed to work anymore. She had ulcers that were bleeding internally and if she wasn't careful, she could go.

It was obvious that they were broke. The house had no paint. There wasn't any grass where the lawn was supposed to be. The whole neighborhood was like that, extremely poor.

The inside of the house was decent. I had a feeling that some of the colleges had sent them some furniture. They had a nice color television set, new carpeting and a new sofa. They also seemed to have the only home in that area with an air conditioner in the window. Maybe Mary Malone earned the money for that stuff, but I found it very hard to believe.

So I knew that Moses needed money. I also heard that whatever college got Moses would end up on probation because there were NCAA investigators all over the place and everybody was supposedly breaking all kinds of rules to get him.

If anybody had Moses, it was Maryland. I know they had pulled some illegal stuff, not as bad as what the other schools were doing, but still against NCAA rules. Maryland had sent John Lucas and a couple of their other players over to see Moses a few times, and that was an NCAA violation. They'd pick Moses up, take him to dinner and then to a game. You can't do that, either. Lefty Driesell had 17,000 people talking to Moses and writing Moses.

I remember running into Houston's Guy Lewis down there. He told me, "There's no way I'll get this kid. Lefty has him wrapped up. But if I don't show up here for a few days and give it a try, my alumni will kill me. I at least have to pretend that I'm trying."

What a joke it was for some of these coaches to be talking to Moses about the value and sanctity of a college degree. At that stage of his life, Moses couldn't even put a sentence together.

You asked him, "Moses, what do you think of this or that?"

He'd just say "yes" or "no," or he'd grunt or give no answer at all. From that school system, I could understand why he was so far behind. I've been a high school instructor and I know when a school is a good one or not. I was around that school almost every day for a month. They had problems. It was ludicrous for Lefty Driesell and all these guys to talk to Moses about how a college education was what he needed.

I talked to Moses and his mother a lot. Moses's uncle, his mother's brother, sort of acted like the agent. He was a neophyte and he admitted that all this was new to him. He was a nice guy, he had a job and wanted to figure out what was best for Moses. He didn't know much, but talking to him was better than talking to Mary, because she didn't know the first thing about athletics.

To me, the key point was that no one ever said, "Moses has to go to college."

They agreed that they needed money and they agreed that Moses wanted to play basketball. When I heard that, I knew we had a great shot at getting it done.

When we drafted Moses, all these people were trying to lay a guilt trip on us, as if we were robbing the cradle. I said that I believed in college for 99 percent of the players in the country, but not for Moses. Think about it. What was Moses Malone better prepared to do, sit in a classroom or play basketball? Also, what did his family need more, Moses at school or some immediate financial help?

MIKE GOLDBERG: The press conference where we announced the signing of Malone was held at the Americana Hotel in New York. It was my first look at Moses, and I couldn't believe how he looked. He was pencil-thin. He was 6-foot-11, but he had the body of a high school kid. Never in a million years would you believe that the skinny kid who stood before the press that day would become one of the greatest workhorses in pro basketball.

LARRY CREGER: Moses wasn't the only player I tried to sign with the ABA. I talked to Marvin Webster about leaving Morgan State early, but he ended up staying four years because he felt loyal to his coach.

I really spent a lot of time with Robert Parish. I first saw Robert in a high school all-star game and I thought he had pro potential at 18. He went to Centenary College, and I first approached him about turning pro between his freshman and sophomore years. Then I went to see him the following two summers, so for three years I tried to get Robert to turn pro. I'd say things like, "Robert, you can start earning six-figure salaries right now. Over the next four years you'll spend in college, that would add up to a lot of money."

I got to know Robert and his family very well. His father worked as a riveter on railroad cars. His mother worked at the local school on the school lunch program. A few times, I drove her to and from school. They had a lot of relatives living with them. I'd want to take the whole family out somewhere nice to eat, but they'd say, "Oh, don't spend that kind of money." I'd want to buy them some food and we'd end up going to a fast food joint, buying 20 burgers and a bunch of fries, and taking that stuff to eat at their house. They were great people.

But his mother always said the same thing: she wanted Robert to become the first member of that family to graduate from college. She didn't care about the money and in that house her word was law.

While Moses was one of my success stories, there were several players like Parish and Webster who decided to stay in school.

BOB RYAN: Moses was a legend before his first pro game. I went to the Salt Palace to see the Stars in an exhibition game during Moses's rookie year. Larry Brown came up to me and said, "Moses Malone is the greatest offensive rebounder I have ever seen in my life."

I said, "Larry, he's just a kid out of high school. You mean to tell me that he's better than Paul Silas?"

He said, "Just watch and wait a few years and you tell me who is a better offensive rebounder than Moses Malone."

With the Stars, Moses had hooked up with Gerald Govan, who had been in the ABA since Day One and was sort of Moses's patron and protector. Govan started telling me what kind of rebounder this kid was. So the early line on Moses was that no one knew what else he could do, but he could rebound.

JIM O'BRIEN: Moses's first regular-season game was a loss at New York *(105–89)*, and Kevin Loughery's plan was to beat up on him because Moses was just a high school kid. That was pretty much what the Nets did—they went right at him inside. That's hard to imagine when you see Moses today. Now you see a guy whose body is like the shores of Long Island and whose shoulders are rounded from all the poundings he's taken over the years. Back then he had a big Afro, his shoulders were straight and his skin had the glint to it that you find in a teenager.

TOM NISSALKE: The young Moses Malone had virtually no offensive moves other than a devastating ability to get the ball off the glass. He was so lightning-quick and just seemed to know where a rebound was going. I saw a playoff game in his rookie season where he had 38 rebounds, 23 of them off the offensive glass.

DEL HARRIS: I coached Moses with Tom Nissalke in Utah and Moses just lived off his offensive rebounding. He was so young; 6-foot-11 and 217 pounds in his second pro season. He could run faster than anyone on the team, even our guards. We had a player who said that he could run up, jump and touch his head on the rim. The guy did it, but Moses wasn't impressed. He just grunted, walked under the basket and, standing still, jumped up and touched his head on the rim, which is pretty amazing when you think about it.

In his second year, Moses broke his foot in an exhibition game. The trainer looked at it and said he couldn't find anything wrong.

"Foot broken," Moses said, and he refused to play.

Later, we found out that his foot *was* broken. We lasted only 19 games that season and Moses didn't play for us because he had his foot in a cast. My last ABA memory of him was when we folded, and guys were grabbing anything they could find. Moses had loaded up one of the dumpsters on wheels with tennis shoes and uniforms. Dragging his broken foot behind him, Moses pushed that cart filled with equipment out of the arena.

MOSES MALONE'S CONTRACT WITH UTAH

1. The contract calls for $565,000, to be paid out over four years:

   1974–75: $125,000
   1975–76: $130,000
   1976–77: $150,000
   1977–78: $160,000

2. During the length of the agreement, the club agrees to pay the mother of the player $500 a month.
3. The club shall provide a housing allowance for the mother of the player up to a total of $25,000, to be paid out at $335.00 a month during the length of the agreement; if the contract expires before the full $25,000 is paid, the club may either continue making monthly payments or settle the difference in a lump sum.
4. The player will receive a $40,000 signing bonus.
5. The mother of the player will receive $10,000 upon the signing of the contract.
6. The player will receive $10,000 for each academic quarter completed by the player at an accredited institution of higher education, up to 12 quarters.
7. The player will receive $10,000 if he has the most playing time of anyone on the club, $5,000 if he has the second-most playing time.
8. The player will receive $10,000 if he leads the club in rebounding, $5,000 if he is second in rebounding.
9. The player will receive $10,000 if he leads the club in scoring, $5,000 if he is second in scoring.
10. The player will receive $10,000 if he is selected to the first-team ABA All-Pro Team.
11. It is understood that this is a guaranteed, "no-cut" contract.

(After the 1976 merger, Malone signed a new deal with the Buffalo Braves that paid $300,000 a year for three seasons and a $25,000 signing bonus, for a total of $925,000 for three years. He also would receive $50,000 if he were traded.)

The Kentucky Colonels: The ABA's Frontline Team

In a league where big men were as common as balanced budgets, the Kentucky Colonels had not one but two big-time big men in Dan Issel and Artis Gilmore. They played together for four seasons, then went on to become stars in the NBA after the merger. Yet the Colonels won only one championship. They were a team that broke your heart. They went 68–16 in 1971–72 and were knocked out of the playoffs in the first round. Twice they made it to the ABA finals, in 1971 and 1973, and lost. It was a team of "almost," yet a fun team to watch. In addition to Issel and Gilmore under the basket, the Colonels had Louis Dampier, the king of the 3-pointers. In their early years, they also had Darel Carrier, who played in the same backcourt as Dampier and shot nearly as well. In their first three seasons, they were owned by Joe and Mamie Gregory, whose dog Ziggy appeared in team pictures and in the team logo. The joke was that the Colonels didn't have a team doctor, they had a pediatrician who also was a dog-lover. Only it wasn't a joke, it was a fact. So was the fact that in those first three years, the Colonels weren't very good and averaged about 4,000 fans a game, usually operating with a front office of only five full-time people. The Colonels had two guys named Vance—no relation. Van Vance was their radio broadcaster and Dave Vance began as their PR man and was eventually general manager under John Y. Brown. And later, they had Hubie Brown in his first head coaching job. Put it all together and, for the last six years of the ABA, Kentucky was, in the words of Brown, "always a huge factor."

DAVE VANCE: In the early years of the franchise, they did things like signing Peggy Ann Early to a contract. Peggy was a female jockey and she was doing pretty well at the track. The Colonels decided it would be a good gimmick to make her the first female pro basketball player. They signed her and had her sit on the bench for a couple of games, which didn't thrill Coach Gene Rhodes at all. One day, she even played a little, and that stunt got them some publicity. I was a local newspaperman and I remember writing a story about it.

(Early was put into one game. She threw an inbounds pass, and Kentucky immediately called time-out and took her out of the game, never

to return. She is listed in The Sports Encyclopedia: Pro Basketball—*one game, one minute—but not in* The Official NBA Basketball Encyclopedia.*)*

The turning point for the Colonels came in 1970 when Wendell Cherry put together a group that included John Y. Brown to buy the team from the Gregorys. They hired Mike Storen from Indiana, where he was really the best GM in the ABA. Mike came in and traded away eight of the eleven veterans. They signed Dan Issel from the University of Kentucky, and for the first time people started to take them seriously.

MIKE STOREN: One of the last things I did before I left the Pacers was to write a letter to Kentucky, proposing that "we play four exhibition games in 1970." Then when I got to Kentucky, I wrote a letter back saying "we would love to play those games." So I made a deal for both teams myself, and the exhibition games made money because of the natural basketball rivalry that exists between Indiana and Kentucky on any level.

The other thing I did right in the middle of my move was to get together with my old boss from Indiana, Dick Tinkham, and agree to push the league to move Indiana out of the Eastern Division to the West. I figured that Kentucky and Indiana would have the best two teams in the league, so why put them in the same division? This way, we could meet in the finals and travel by bus, which would save both teams a lot of money. The league approved that plan, and we did play in the 1973 finals.

I'll take credit for doing a lot of things to get Kentucky on its feet, but the most important move was signing Dan Issel, and I had very little to do with that. The Colonels' owners were all Kentucky alumni and had strong connections to the college. They did about 90 percent of the groundwork by the time I got there. I just finished it and a lot of people said I signed Issel, which was technically correct, but the owners were the ones who really cut the deal with Issel and Mike Pratt.

DAN ISSEL: I signed with the Colonels even before the NBA draft. My attorney and I did talk to some NBA teams, Atlanta and someone else. The money they mentioned was in line with what the Colonels were offering. But I had loved playing at the University of Kentucky. My wife is from Kentucky and I looked at the Colonels as an extension of my college career. Originally, Dallas had my draft rights, but those rights were sold to Kentucky *(for $25,000).* If Dallas had tried to sign me, I probably would have gone to the NBA. It was announced that I had signed for $1.4 million for five years, which wasn't even close. The only way that number meant anything was if you counted the Dolgoff Plan, which didn't pay off for 20 years. My first-year salary was $52,000.

My first training camp was unbelievable. All we did was play exhibition games. I think we played at least 10, and it seemed like we were always playing Indiana. We had no players' union to speak of, so management could play as many exhibition games as it wanted. Then the coach (*Gene Rhodes*) was fired after about a month, and that was certainly new to me.

MIKE STOREN: We were in first place with a 10–5 record and I fired Gene Rhodes, who basically was the only coach the franchise ever had. They had one other coach (*John Givens, who was there for only 17 games*), but Rhodes was established with the team.

I announced that "I am not retaining Gene Rhodes because it is not in the best long-term interest of the team." That is all I ever said about it. Rhodes's old college roommate was the sports editor of the Louisville paper. They put the story on page A-1 and they fried me.

DAN ISSEL: To the players, it was pretty clear what happened. Rhodes was a holdover from the old regime and Storen came in with his people and his ideas. He also wanted his own coach. I like Mike Storen a lot and think he did a great job, but he is a guy who will run his own show his own way.

MIKE STOREN: I knew that I had to come up with a highly credible person to replace Rhodes and take the heat off the situation. I didn't have anyone in the wings. When I decided to fire Rhodes, I brainstormed with some people, and then Frank Ramsey's name was mentioned. Ramsey had been a great player at the University of Kentucky and with the Boston Celtics. He was living in Madisonville, Kentucky, where he owned a bank, a nursing home, a grocery store—just about the whole town. I really had to talk him into it because he didn't want to leave Madisonville, and he only agreed to take the job for the rest of the year. But Frank came in and coached us to the ABA finals.

DAVE VANCE: Hiring Ramsey was a stroke of public relations genius by Mike. The guy was a Kentucky folk hero and no one would dare say a bad word about him. Mike knew he had to do something dramatic to get out from under the Rhodes firing.

DAN ISSEL: Madisonville is about three hours from Louisville and Ramsey would commute back and forth. He had cut a deal with Storen whereby he didn't have to live in Louisville. There were times when he didn't make it to practice and the trainer ran things, because we also had no assistant coach. But the players liked and respected Frank. He knew what he was talking about and obviously was a great player, so the setup worked.

MIKE STOREN: Frank was almost a god in Madisonville. While he was with the team, people from that town would call him and ask him what they should do for a hangover, or a cold, or anything. He wasn't a medical doctor, but he had all these down-home cures and I'd hear him telling people to do things like "take three aspirin and put a cold wash-cloth over your forehead for a half hour." It was almost mystical.

He had theories on everything. One of the things he'd say was that in every gym, a player should go to the free throw line during warm-ups and find a little indent of paint. That will tell you exactly where you'll find the middle of the free throw line, directly in front of the basket. That indent came from where they pounded a nail in the floor to tie a string from under the rim to where the free throw line was supposed to be. Frank felt that people missed free throws because they didn't line up dead center in front of the basket. He had a thousand things like that.

VAN VANCE: Frank really didn't want to coach. But he felt that Kentucky's only pro team was in trouble and he was needed to help out. But he took the job on his own terms. He had a private plane and would fly back and forth between Madisonville and Louisville. He was a precise, detail guy. He even taped the players' ankles himself, because he felt they should be taped a special way and only he could do it. Frank also used to bring along vials of ammonia when we played in Denver because he thought that sniffing ammonia would help players deal with the thin air. He believed in taking the first flight out in the morning, which was a change from the previous regime and severely cut into the late-night entertainment factor.

DAN ISSEL: After Frank came in, we struggled for a while and lost more games in a month than I did in my entire college career. *(Ramsey's regular-season record was only 32–35.)* I was a rookie and the toughest thing for me wasn't the games themselves, but the number of games. We did things like playing ten games in twelve days in nine different cities. We didn't fly first class, and most of the flights were two- or three-stoppers because the ABA cities weren't on the main airline routes.

VAN VANCE: I know Dan was stunned by the ABA lifestyle on his very first pro trip. We had played a night game at home, then went to the airport and caught a two-stop red-eye to Raleigh, where we had a game with the Carolina Cougars the next afternoon. We got to the hotel, I think it was a Holiday Inn, in the early hours of the morning and there were no rooms. The hotel had been taken over by the cast from "Hee Haw," which was performing at the North Carolina State Fair that day. So we sat around the lobby for a couple of hours until some people checked out. Then when we finally got to the rooms they weren't made up, and we slept for a couple of hours on the dirty beds. We staggered onto the bus and went to the arena. The game was being played at a facility on the grounds of the State Fair to hopefully get a bigger crowd. We went inside and there was still dust in the air, because they had just finished a cattle show. They were putting down the floor over the dirt. That also was the first time I saw Carolina GM Carl Scheer. He had a rag and he was dusting off the folding chairs before the fans came in. After all that, Dan went out and scored 30-some points. It was right then that I knew he was going to be a great pro.

MIKE STOREN: All of the things Frank Ramsey had been teaching the team just came together in the playoffs. We drew Miami in the first round and beat them, which wasn't a surprise, because we were better. But in the second round, we played Virginia, which was 55–29. Al Bianchi had Charlie Scott, George Carter and Doug Moe. They were a damn good team and obviously the favorite, but we knocked them off in six games. Coaching is more of a factor in the playoffs than the regular season, because you have more time to prepare and you keep playing the same team. Frank was just super. He had a tremendous basketball mind and it showed.

DAVE VANCE: We went against Utah in the finals, and that was a great team. They had Zelmo Beaty, Willie Wise, Merv Jackson, Ron Boone, Red Robbins and Glenn Combs, all terrific players. They had the best record in the league at 58–26, and I don't think anyone gave us much of a chance.

Frank knew that his players were concerned about the high altitude in Salt Lake, so he put an oxygen tank next to the bench. During time-outs, the players would come in and breathe into the mask. They all said it made them feel better. After the playoffs, Frank told me that there was nothing in the tank. It was all psychological.

DAN ISSEL: The series went seven games. Right before the seventh game, Goose Ligon did something to his back. I remember watching as

Goose was in the trainer's room and a doctor pulled out a six-inch needle. It was the longest needle I had ever seen.

MIKE STOREN: Frank Ramsey and I were in the trainer's room when the doctor was working on Ligon. Frank whispered to me, "If Goose sees that needle, he'll never be able to take the shot." The doctor had Goose lean against the wall, sort of spread-eagled. Frank was right there with Goose. He put a towel over Goose's head, an arm around his shoulders, and he was whispering something to Goose as Goose took the shot. Frank really had a calming effect with players and this was just another example.

DAN ISSEL: Goose tried to play that day, but lasted only a quarter. We lost by 10 points *(131–121)*. It was one of those things. I don't know if we would have beaten them with Goose, but we didn't have much chance without him because he was so important to us defensively.

DAN ISSEL: After the season, I was physically exhausted. I had played about 110 games, counting the endless exhibition season. For the first time in my life, I took the entire summer off. I didn't touch a basketball. I think that year took a lot out of Frank Ramsey. He never looked at the job as long-term. Coach *(Adolph)* Rupp told me right after Frank became coach that even if we won a championship, Frank would coach for only one year. We lost in the finals to Utah, then Mike Storen signed Artis Gilmore, the best center in college basketball that year, but Frank resigned. One year was enough for him.

ARTIS GILMORE: MIKE STOREN'S BIGGEST CATCH

Artis Gilmore was a 7-foot-2, 240-pound center for Jacksonville University with a 32-inch waist and 27-inch thighs. He averaged 22 points, 23 rebounds and 8.2 blocked shots per game. He signed with Kentucky before the March 29, 1971, NBA draft. Gilmore's agent, Herb Rudoy, told Basketball Weekly, "The NBA made us a big offer. An owner was authorized by the league to make an offer, but it didn't come from the team (Cleveland) that won the coin flip for the first pick in the draft." Gilmore's contract was announced at $2.7 million, but as was the case with Dan Issel, those figures weren't even close. Gilmore signed a 10-year, $1.5 million deal—he received $150,000 a year for 10 years plus a $50,000 bonus. He also had a Dolgoff Plan that paid him $40,000 a year for 20 years starting in 1981.

MIKE STOREN: In the middle of the 1970–71 season, we had a league meeting to determine who would get the draft rights to Jim McDaniels and Artis Gilmore, who were the two top college seniors. People in Kentucky wanted us to sign McDaniels because he played at Western Kentucky and was running up big scoring numbers, but we felt that we had a player like McDaniels in Dan Issel, only Issel was better. What we needed was a legitimate center, and that was Gilmore. So we wanted Artis. I recall someone telling me, "All Gilmore can do is play defense."

I said, "Wait a minute. The guy is at least 7-foot-2 and if all he does is play defense, that's an awful lot, since all defense does is win games." So we knew we wanted Gilmore; now we had to get the rights to him.

The league set up a system whereby each team would submit a sealed envelope containing a bid of how much they were willing to pay to sign Gilmore. The team willing to put out the most money would get his rights, and we outbid the rest of the league for Artis.

DICK TINKHAM: This whole sealed-bid business was just Mike Storen pulling a fast one on the league to get Gilmore's rights. The Floridians wanted Artis because he played at Jacksonville and they were talking about territorial rights. Of course, they also were on the verge of going belly-up, so why listen to them? We all put our bids in the envelope. We at Indiana didn't have a chance of signing Gilmore, so we didn't care. I remember that Storen said he'd pay $3 million for Gilmore and that blew the rest of the league away. Then he signed Artis for half that amount.

MIKE STOREN: Herb Rudoy was Artis's agent and he was the key guy. Artis was 22 years old from Chipley, Florida, and at this point in his life Artis was going to do what his agent told him to do. Our theory was to put enough money in front of Rudoy so that he would have no reason to think about the NBA. We wanted to get him signed before the NBA draft. We started talking money and kept talking money until we got a deal done. Artis said he wanted security, so we gave him a 10-year deal worth over $1 million with a lot of other money in deferred payments. For the time, it was a very fair contract.

DAVE VANCE: We wanted to make a big deal about the signing by introducing him during a game. We smuggled Artis into Louisville and put him up at the Executive Inn. Alex Groza worked for us and he picked up Artis at the airport and took him to a tall man's store and bought Artis some clothes. Artis said that this was the first tie he ever had in his life. Word had leaked out that Artis was in town—it was very hard to hide somebody 7-foot-2—and there were about 12,000 people at the game that night. At halftime, we turned out all the lights, then introduced Artis, who walked the length of the court with just a spotlight on him as the crowd stood and cheered. He is a very shy person and had little to say, but it made for a very dramatic moment to see someone that big walking under a spotlight in a dark arena.

Later, we had a press conference for Artis at the "21" Club in New York, because signing Artis was a national story, a real coup for us. Artis was wearing platform shoes and he had a huge Afro. The writers took him outside and measured him—he was 7-foot-8 at the top of his Afro. They wanted him to pose all these different ways for pictures and Artis said, "Get me out of here; I'm not a monkey." He got all these questions about his height and he said, "Nobody goes up to a fat person and says, 'Hey, how much do you weigh?' But they'll ask a tall person about his height." One time, the Colonels were getting off a plane and Artis had a tennis racket in his hand. A guy said, "Who's that?"

Dan Issel said, "That's Arthur Ashe."

The guy just nodded. Artis smiled. He liked that. Artis was a very good person, very cooperative in the ABA and with the writers in Kentucky, but I think that press conference in New York just scared him.

JOE GUSHUE: After he signed with Kentucky, Artis and Mike Storen did a commercial where they each were smoking cigars and Artis smiled and said, "I'm gonna make a whole lotta money." Then they blew smoke rings.

MIKE STOREN: After signing Gilmore, I wanted a coach who could win instantly at the pro level, a guy who had a track record. This was not a time to break in some kid. I noticed that the Lakers had just fired Joe Mullaney. I called him immediately and when I met with him, I liked him right away. We developed more than a professional relationship— we became close friends. He later coached for me in Memphis *(1974–75)* and with Pensacola of the CBA *(in 1988–89)*.

JOE MULLANEY: At this stage of their careers, Issel and Gilmore were intriguing cases.

When Issel was in college, a lot of people looked at his body—which was never very muscle-toned—and they were convinced he would get fat in a few years, that his career would be short. Of course, the opposite was true. He played forever and as he got older, he got thinner. That's because the guy has the heart of a tiger. All he did was work on his game and on conditioning, but his body was one of those that was never going to look muscular no matter what he did. I know that it was hard for him to keep the weight off, but he did it because of that desire. Issel spent his career making people eat their words. He was a polished player whose outside shot was as good as any big man's who ever played. He had some defensive deficiencies, but he made up for them well and we also were able to hide them because of Artis.

As a rookie, Artis was a tremendous prospect. His offense was very weak because he had no real low-post moves at that time. But he loved to block shots and rebound, and we set up a defense where we'd make it appear there was an open lane to the basket, but what we were doing was funneling people right into Artis. We did it along the baseline. A guy would get the ball in the corner and see a lane along the baseline to the basket and he couldn't resist, he'd take off. Artis would then sort of meet him at the pass, cutting down the shooting angle and almost smothering the guy. No one in the ABA was using a defense like that. We became a monster that season because of our defense. Even Rick Barry was being sucked in, driving the baseline and getting his shots blocked. He said that Artis was the greatest shot-blocker he had ever seen.

VAN VANCE: Joe Mullaney was a basketball genius. I once sat on an airplane and he drew up the whole offense Babe McCarthy was using at Memphis, then diagrammed how his defense could stop them. He did it all from his head, no notes or anything.

DAN ISSEL: While Frank Ramsey was a brilliant coach, the fact that he was commuting from Madisonville and that he knew he was only doing it for one year meant that he took a very laid-back approach to discipline. Mullaney was strict with us, and that was good. That was why we were so great in the regular season. We went 68–16 and people just assumed we'd win the ABA title. Of course, the players felt the same way. No one had stopped us in the regular season; why would they do it in the playoffs?

JOE MULLANEY: In our division, four teams made the playoffs. Since we were No. 1, we should have played No. 4, which was Miami. Instead, they made it No. 1 plays No. 3 and No. 2 plays No. 4. So we would have been better off finishing second than first in terms of drawing a weaker playoff opponent. Instead of playing Miami, we drew New York with Rick Barry.

Kentucky was 10 – 0 in the regular season vs. Miami and 7 – 4 vs. New York, but the Nets had won three of the last four regular-season games.

DAN ISSEL: New York had a great game plan against us in the playoffs. They guarded Louie Dampier, Artis and myself. Darel Carrier was hurt and couldn't play and we missed his outside shooting. So they wanted to shut down the three of us and see if anyone else could beat them, and no one could. I was double-teamed every time I got the ball.

Issel averaged 22 points, but shot only 42 percent in the playoffs. Dampier also struggled, scoring 13 points and shooting 39 percent. Gilmore averaged his usual 21 points and 18 rebounds. The Colonels lost in six games, and four times they failed to score 100 points.

JOE MULLANEY: The Nets were the first to realize what we were doing on defense, and they adjusted. Barry would start to drive the baseline, then stop and take the jumper. The other players did the same. Suddenly, we stopped blocking shots, our defense wasn't as effective and our confidence was shaken.

The next year, we had a great team again. We went 56–28 in the regular season and got to the finals, losing to Indiana in seven games. But by then, people were getting frustrated because they thought we had the best team in the league, yet we didn't win a title.

LARRY DONALD: Artis became to the ABA what Wilt Chamberlain was to the NBA—the most physically dominating big man in the league, yet he couldn't take his team to a championship. With Issel and Gilmore, Kentucky became an NBA-style, grind-it-out team with two low-post players, while just about everyone else in the ABA was playing a wide-open, fast-break style. They were coached by Joe Mullaney for two years, then by Babe McCarthy, and those guys were very good coaches. But there was no title and people hung the "bridesmaid" name on the Colonels, saying they couldn't win the big game.

JOHN Y. BROWN TAKES OVER

After the 1972–73 season, Wendell Cherry sold controlling interest in the Colonels to a group from Cincinnati, but that group then sold it to John Y. Brown, who had been one of the minority owners under Cherry. Brown made his fortune as the owner of Kentucky Fried Chicken.

DAVE VANCE: Here's why John Y. bought the Colonels so they wouldn't move to Cincinnati: the Browns were having dinner and young John, who was about 10 at the time, said, "Dad, I don't want the

Colonels to leave." So John Y. decided to buy the team and put his wife and a 10-woman board of directors in charge of the team. John thought it would be a good marketing tool, showing that women could like basketball if they just gave it a chance.

MIKE STOREN: When the team moved from Cherry to the Cincinnati group, then to John Y., I didn't think there would be a problem. John Y. worked out a contract with me quickly and I figured we'd keep doing what we had been doing, which was putting together a damn good team. Then he announced that his wife Ellie and the all-women board of directors were going to run the team.

I told John Y., "What's all this about? It's okay if the ladies want to sell season tickets or whatever, but I refuse to sit down with a group from the Junior League to talk about running a basketball team."

John Y. said, "I'm giving them control of the team."

As usual, John Y. was thinking about his political career, and saving the Colonels for Louisville—which he did—was very good public relations. He got to wear the white hat in the state. His position was that women were a great untapped resource in sports marketing, and he talked a lot about "woman power."

I said, "You can't be serious about letting Ellie and her friends run the team."

John Y. said he was.

I said, "Adios, John Y. Get yourself a new GM."

VAN VANCE: After John Y. took over, he had a meeting with Joe Mullaney. Brown loved to talk in hypothetical terms. He asked Mullaney, "If you were going to build a team, would you rather start with Julius Erving or Artis Gilmore?"

Mullaney picked Doctor J, and that wasn't the answer John Y. wanted to hear, because he already had Artis and he loved Artis. Mullaney told me that the more he and John Y. talked, the more it became evident that John Y. was going to take a very active role in the team, and Mullaney didn't like that. So he left the Colonels to coach Utah.

JOE MULLANEY: Mike Storen made it clear that he wouldn't work for John Y. Since Mike had hired me and we were together for two years, I felt very close to him.

Mike told me, "I can't work for this guy. He wants to meddle. He says things that make no sense such as, 'I can't understand why Artis doesn't average 35 points a game.' I'm getting out of here."

I went home and told my family that I didn't like how things were going in Kentucky. At that time, Utah's *(GM)* Vince Boryla was looking for a coach.

Van Vance asked me why I was leaving Kentucky and I told him, "Vince Boryla is a basketball guy. I don't want to work for a guy who made his money in fried chicken and thinks he knows basketball. If we don't win like he thinks we should, I'd be in real trouble. It's best that I get out now before the inevitable happens."

VAN VANCE: Babe McCarthy became the coach after Mullaney left. Babe would tell stories about John Y. calling him. We left for the West Coast and changed planes in Atlanta. John Y. had Babe paged at the Atlanta airport. John Y. talked to Babe for a while, then he said that he was going to Fort Lauderdale. We flew to California and John Y. went to Florida. When Babe walked into his hotel room in San Diego, the phone was ringing and it was John Y., who said he was calling from Florida and he wanted to continue the conversation they were having when Babe was at the Atlanta airport.

JOE MULLANEY: When Babe McCarthy took over, he and I were at a social event. Babe yelled to me, "Joe, you know what kind of team I have in Kentucky. Tell these boys that I have the best team in basketball."

I heard that and thought, "Babe, you're not as good as you think you are, and Lord help you if you don't win it all."

That season *(1973–74),* Babe lost in the second round of the playoffs and was immediately fired.

RON GRINKER: When the Browns took over Kentucky, someone asked Ellie if the basketball team was just a toy given to her by her rich husband. She said, "You're absolutely right in saying that I know nothing about basketball, but my husband knows nothing about making chicken and he's done all right."

VAN VANCE: The female board got the team a lot of publicity. The women would go to New York, lunch at "21" and meet Howard Cosell. But they also sold a lot of tickets. These women were well-connected to the business community and people bought tickets who otherwise would not have given the Colonels a second thought.

GENE LITTLES: Occasionally, Ellie and her ladies would come to practice, and that was a big deal for them, to watch us work out and then meet with us afterwards.

DAVE VANCE: John Y. was very discouraged after we got swept by New York in the second round of the playoffs when Babe McCarthy was our coach. John Y. wanted another coach, a younger guy, to get us over the top. We talked to Lake Kelly, who was Fly Williams's coach at Austin Peay. We talked to Al Bianchi and we talked to Bill Musselman, who was at the University of Minnesota. We also talked to Bobby Knight about Musselman, and Knight had a very high opinion of Musselman. But the name we kept hearing the most was Hubie Brown, who had earned quite a reputation as an assistant under Larry Costello in Milwaukee. He came in to interview and struck me as one of the most organized people I had ever seen. He knew what questions we would ask and how he wanted to answer them. But you also knew that Hubie was interviewing us, sizing us up to see if he wanted to work for us. He was a very impressive guy. He was very realistic, too. He knew that John Y. expected his new coach to win a championship. The Colonels had been the ABA's bridesmaids for too long; a championship was the next logical step.

THAT CHAMPIONSHIP SEASON

The Colonels finally won it all in 1975 with Hubie Brown as coach, Stan Albeck as his assistant and five new players—Ted McClain, Gene Littles, Bird Averitt, Wil Jones and Marv Roberts. Under Brown, the Colonels led the league in defense, allowing 101.6 points per game. They finished 58–26, winning 22 of their last 25 and a one-game playoff against New York for the regular-season Eastern Division title. In the playoffs, the Colonels were a machine, beating Memphis, St. Louis and Indiana, all 4–1. They lost only three home games all year, going 49–3 at home counting the playoffs. They gave notice early that this would be a special season when they beat New York after trailing by seven points with only 30 seconds left on November 13.

HUBIE BROWN: When I got the job, I knew the pressure was tremendous to win it all. The town, management and the players were accustomed to winning and expected to win. What we needed to do was find that right chemistry, that spark which takes a team from being good in the regular season and carries them through the tense playoff situations. The first thing I did was to hire Stan Albeck as my assistant. I had never spoken to Stan until he called me asking if he could be my assistant. He had been an assistant in Denver, and was Wilt Chamberlain's assistant with San Diego. We met at a hotel near O'Hare Airport in Chicago, sat by the pool and talked for hours. I had other people in mind, but after listening to Stan I knew that I needed someone who knew the ABA. Stan was a great scout and he believed in my system, which included a lot of charting and statistics. He was laid-back, while I was intense. We were a good combination.

I felt that the key to coaching in pro ball was to keep 10 guys happy instead of eight. For a player to be happy, he needs minutes. Most teams only used eight players a game, but if you use 10 guys, then you only have two guys on the end of the bench, and those two guys are usually marginal players who are just happy to be there. But the key is winning with 10 guys. If you're going to play 10, then you have to use pressure defense. Pressure defense hides a player's weaknesses. If you're playing a straight man-to-man defense, the opposition can pick out a player to exploit. In a press, where people are scrambling and double-teaming, it's hard to find the weak player, so I told the guys that we were going to use 10 players, and that meant 10 guys would be contributing to a championship.

I looked at the Colonels and I knew they could score. Dan Issel, Louie Dampier, Artis Gilmore—these guys could put the ball in the basket.

To me, a crucial statistic is point differential. If you average 100 points and give up 100 points, then you'll win half of your games. If your point differential is three—you score 103 and give up 100—you have a very good chance of winning 50 games. You want to win 55 games? Then score 105 and give up 100. I'm telling you right now, a team that has a point differential of five will win at least 50 games. You can write that in cement. By the end of the season, our point differential was seven— 109 to 102. That's astronomical. That's the stuff of champions. And in the last 25 games where we won 22, we averaged 108 points and allowed 92, which is off the charts.

I didn't talk about point differential when we started camp with the Colonels. The guys had enough to worry about with the defense we were asking them to play. I also was trying to develop two full units so that I could play 10 guys. I liked my first group to play 32 minutes a game, my second group to play 16. I made an exception with Artis Gilmore, who played 39 minutes. We needed Artis on the floor.

I thought the ball wasn't being distributed correctly before I came to Kentucky. Artis was taking only seven to nine shots a game *(actually 14, averaging 18.7 points)* and we raised that *(to 16 per game and 23.6 points)*. Artis just had to see the ball more. I thought he had an unfair rap when people said he had bad hands. But you had to figure out what he could do. Put him on the low block, the right-hand side. Get him the ball and watch him shoot that little left-handed hook. Aside from Wilt

Chamberlain, Artis Gilmore is the strongest man ever to play this game.

One of the guys who suffered with Artis getting the ball more was Dan Issel. I asked him to take fewer shots, and I know that was a burr under his saddle, and he had the worst shooting year *(47 percent, 17.7 points)* of his ABA career to that point. But in the playoffs, he was ready. He scored his 20 points and he was a huge contributor. I believe that you go through your power people, and in this case it was Artis. I also had Louie Dampier at guard, and he was the guy who got the ball when the game was on the line.

GENE LITTLES: You could feel the discipline Hubie wanted from the moment you walked into the dressing room for practice. He wanted you to "think practice." There was no grab-ass, no screwing around or laughing. When you stepped on the practice floor, you didn't just shoot around. We had prepractice drills, and you better be doing the drills when Hubie came onto the practice floor. If not, no one knew what he would do. He was so intense about it that no one wanted to find out. Basically, you knew that if you didn't do it Hubie's way, you were going to be on the end of the bench for a long, long time. As the season went on, he talked more and more X's and O's, and more and more about things like number of possessions, fast-break conversions, defensive stops and point differential. None of us had ever run into a coach like Hubie before. He knew all these numbers off the top of his head. Most of us thought he was a basketball genius.

VAN VANCE: All Hubie and Stan Albeck did was talk basketball, and their enthusiasm was contagious. Hubie has a way of looking right at you and saying, "How are you?" that makes you feel like he really wants to know, that he's listening. Sort of like, "Cut through the crap, let's talk about what's really going on here." He was so new and fresh and brought so many insights to the team.

Hubie also could really cuss. We had a game in Virginia where there was no one in the stands. I was broadcasting it, and it was so quiet that you could hear the shoes squeaking, the ball hitting the floor on a dribble and banging against the rim. You also could hear Hubie and his imaginative cussing. I was trying to talk as much and as loudly as I could, but Hubie was still going over the air. At halftime, Hubie's wife called and said, "For God's sake, you can hear Hubie swearing on the radio. Can't you do something?"

I said I'd try to talk a little louder.

I am convinced that Hubie pushed the team to the top. You know, he was already a legend, a guru to young coaches. On the road, they just flocked to him. The idea of hiring Hubie was that Milwaukee had won with a big-man offense with Kareem Abdul-Jabbar. The hope was that Hubie would do the same with Artis. Hubie came in with the plays Costello had for Kareem and he developed some more and for the first time in his career, Artis became a force on offense.

HUBIE BROWN: I like Artis immensely. He was never late, always coachable, and got along with the other guys. He was terrific, period. And look at the progress he made. The guy had huge games in the clutch. He had 33 rebounds when we beat New York in the one-game playoff for the division title. In the five-game series against Indiana in the finals, he never had fewer than 13 rebounds and he had games of 28 and 31 rebounds. Those numbers have to blow your mind.

DAVE VANCE: A guy who was a key for us was Wil Jones. This was John Y.'s idea. John Y. went around asking everyone who guarded Julius Erving best in the ABA, and he found out that Doctor J said that Jones gave him the most trouble. So he went out and got Wil Jones as a free agent after Wil played out his option with Memphis. We had to beat New York three times in the last 10 games of the regular season to force that playoff, and we did. Wil was instrumental in that because of how he played Julius. He certainly didn't shut Julius down, but he made it tough for the Doctor.

HUBIE BROWN: We had Wil Jones and Marvin Roberts who split time at small forward and they both were great. Wil played the first and third quarters, Roberts the second and fourth. In the championship series, Roberts played so well that he finished second to Artis in the MVP voting, losing by one vote. They combined to give us a helluva small forward.

DAN ISSEL: Winning the championship was both a thrill and a relief. We got tired of hearing that we were bridesmaids, that we choked and all that. We also knew that we had a great team and we had reached our goal. That was special.

GENE LITTLES: When we won the championship, we threw Ellie Brown in the shower. After all, she was the owner, and owners get thrown in the shower.

DAVE VANCE: At the celebration after the championship game, John Y. said, "Suppose we challenge (NBA champs) Golden State to a game. Think we can beat them? Think they'll play us?"

I said, "John Y., just let it rest for a while. Why not just savor this moment? It isn't every day we win a championship."

HUBIE BROWN: The 1975 Kentucky Colonels were the best team I have ever coached. No other team has even come close. They were just a great, great team because they had perimeter scoring in Dampier and Issel, they had Gilmore at the low box. Teddy McClain could guard anybody in either league. Gene Littles was a helluva defensive player. Wil Jones and Marv Roberts combined for over 20 points a game and we never ran any plays for them. They were 6-foot-9 small forwards before anyone had a 6-foot-9 small forward. Louie Dampier was a tremendous clutch player and the team had a lot of great guys. We went 22–3 in the last 25 games of the season and 12–3 in the playoffs. That was why I had the word "pressure" engraved on our championship rings. This Kentucky Colonel team knew how to play under pressure.

THE COLONELS' LAST STAND

DAVE VANCE: Even though we won the championship in 1975, we still lost money. To make sure we didn't lose money again, John Y. determined that we had to get $500,000, and the easiest way to do that was to make a deal. John Y. felt that he had to trade either Artis or Dan Issel. Those were the two players who would bring the maximum dollars. Artis was more valuable to the Colonels because he was a 7-foot-2 center, the best center in the ABA. It would have been impossible to replace Artis, because the league never had a big man like him before. So he put Issel on the market and sold him to the Baltimore Claws, who were the old Memphis franchise. There was a huge outcry from the public and Issel wasn't very happy. John Y. took a lot of heat and he honestly couldn't understand why. He believed that selling Issel was preserving the franchise.

VAN VANCE: John Y. said he bought the team when it was ready to move to Cincinnati, and he spent the money to finally bring the city of Louisville a championship team. He wondered how people could forget all that when he sold Issel. But no matter how he explained it, the Issel deal was the beginning of the end of the love affair between the Colonels fans and John Y. Brown. Issel and Louie Dampier *were* the Colonels in the eyes of the fans. To see Issel sold right after winning the championship just took the luster off everything. Even though John Y. made a good deal after that to get Maurice Lucas, interest in the team really started to wane.

HUBIE BROWN: There was a lot of turmoil that year. We sold Issel for $500,000, then we sold Teddy McClain to New York for $150,000. McClain was the heart of our defense, and we missed both of those guys. You know, those deals netted $650,000, which was a lot of money in 1976. It was a transition year, with a lot of new players coming and going. We lost in the playoffs in the second round to Denver in seven games. As for my relationship with John Y., I won't get into that.

DAVE VANCE: John Y. and Hubie just clashed. It was little things. If you asked Hubie a question, he had a way of staring at you, a little sideways glance. He would stare at you for maybe a minute. The silence would drive John Y. crazy. He'd say, "Come on, Hubie, say something already." Of course, the silence was calculated on Hubie's part. Both of these guys had strong wills and egos, and I think their parting was inevitable. After the Issel deal, everyone was under a lot of strain and Hubie put incredible pressure on himself to try to win a second championship. There was a game against Denver when Hubie was all over Artis. He was screaming right in Artis's face and Artis wasn't saying anything. He just took it. Suddenly, Maurice Lucas came up to Hubie and screamed, "Get the hell out of Artis's face." Hubie went off on Lucas and benched him for the rest of the game. We lost, and afterwards Hubie was visibly shaken. He pulled me aside and said, "You know, Lucas left me no choice. He tried to get me to back down in front of the whole team in the most critical part of the game. I didn't want to do it, but I had to." That last season just wasn't much fun for anyone.

When the merger came, Kentucky wasn't one of the four teams going into the NBA. Instead, John Y. took a financial settlement of $3 million. A lot of the fans were down on John Y., but he made what he thought was the best business decision.

VAN VANCE: To John Y., the merger was a big holdup. Why should an ABA team pay over $3 million to get into the NBA? So he took a settlement and got out. Then he bought the Buffalo Braves of the NBA *(for about $1.5 million)* and later traded franchises so that he ended up with the Boston Celtics. It was a great deal for John Y., but the fans of Kentucky were left out in the cold with no NBA team, after the Colonels had the sixth-best attendance in all of pro basketball in 1975–76.

LARRY DONALD: The prevailing attitude was that John Y. sold the ABA down the river. He wanted to be a hero. He kept meeting with the NBA, working on a merger. Then he folded his franchise for big bucks, and sold Artis Gilmore to Chicago *(for $1.1 million)*.

I did a big story where John Y. said he was disillusioned by basketball and had had enough. He told me, "Ellie and I decided that basketball isn't the kind of business we want to be involved in." Then he went out and bought the Buffalo Braves, putting together a deal where he ended up with the Celtics. What does that tell you about the man?

RON GRINKER: When John Y. owned the Celtics, Red Auerbach just hated working for him. One day, Auerbach walked into the office of another of the Celtic owners and said, "You either get rid of John Y. or I'll sign this." Red then put a contract on the desk that would have made him the president of the New York Knicks.

Red told me, "I never met a guy in business who constantly looks for the edge like John Y."

I said, "What do you mean?"

Red said, "You know how most people want to have an edge in the deal? They say they want to be equal partners, but then they give you a proposal where they get 51 percent and you get 49 percent. Well, John Y. would take a 50-50 deal. But then he'd tell you, 'Okay, we'll go 50-50, but I'll make you so miserable that either you will sell your 50 percent to me or you'll end up overpaying me to get my 50 percent. Either way, I win.'"

DAVE VANCE: Like him or not, John Y. came out of the merger better than the teams that went into the NBA. He did what he thought was best from his business viewpoint. You may not like it, but that was how John Y. operated.

Eighth-Year Notebook: 1974-75

As usual, teams were sold and teams moved and there was another new commissioner. Tedd Munchak sold the Carolina Cougars to a group of New York businessmen, who then moved the Cougars to St. Louis and named them the Spirits. Munchak then was hired as commissioner, "for one dollar a year," he said, replacing Mike Storen. In what would become the only dark spot on his ABA record, Storen tried to put together a group of investors to buy the Memphis Tams, who had been taken over by the league after Charlie Finley lost interest and got tired of losing money . . . GM Carl Scheer, Coach Larry Brown and assistant Doug Moe all left Carolina and went to Denver. Scheer changed the name of the team from the Rockets to the Denver Nuggets. Alex Hannum was relieved as coach of Denver . . . Scheer signed Bobby Jones out of North Carolina to play for the Nuggets . . . Moses Malone became the first player to go directly from high school to the pros when he signed with the Utah Stars . . . Indiana signed college stars Len Elmore and Billy Knight. It appeared that George McGinnis was going to jump from the Pacers to the New York Knicks, but he decided to stay in Indiana for another season . . . Joe Mullaney left Utah to coach under Mike Storen in Memphis. Bucky Buckwalter was named the new coach of Utah . . . Billy Cunningham returned to Philadelphia of the NBA . . . Wilt Chamberlain quit as coach of San Diego . . . St. Louis signed two college stars in Maurice Lucas and Marvin Barnes . . . Earl Foreman sold the Virginia Squires to a group of local businessmen . . . By midseason, Mike Storen's Memphis investors ran into money problems and Storen ran out of money for his team, newly named the Sounds. The ABA took over the Memphis franchise for the second straight season . . . The league also took over the ever-troubled San Diego team . . . Indiana nearly went broke when the Pacers' owners also became involved in the new World Hockey League. The Pacers were sold at midseason, or else they would have folded . . . One of the people involved in the new World Hockey League was Dennis Murphy, one of the ABA's founding fathers . . . The East beat the West 151–124 in the All-Star Game, which drew a sellout of 10,449 in San Antonio. Freddie Lewis was the MVP with 26 points and 10 assists. George Gervin led the losing West team with 23 points . . . Hubie Brown was hired by Kentucky with the sole goal of making the Colonels the ABA champs, and he did just that, Kentucky defeating Indiana in five games in the finals. The biggest playoff upset was St. Louis dumping defending champion New York in the first round . . . In the regular season, Denver was the biggest success with a 65–19 record, second best in ABA history. Larry Brown's Nuggets were led by Mack Calvin, who averaged 19.5 points and a league-best 7.7 assists. George McGinnis and Julius Erving shared the MVP honors. McGinnis edged Erving for the scoring title and Swen Nater was the top rebounder . . . Larry Brown was the Coach of the Year and Marvin Barnes was Rookie of the Year . . . The all-ABA team was Erving, McGinnis, Gilmore, Calvin and Ron Boone . . . Veteran ABA forward Wendell Ladner was killed in a plane crash . . . Tedd Munchak resigned as commissioner and was replaced by Dave DeBusschere.

The Wildest Team of Them All

When the ABA folded, the Spirits of St. Louis had a starting front line of Marvin Barnes, Caldwell Jones and Moses Malone, with Don Chaney and Freddie Lewis in the backcourt. On the bench were M. L. Carr and Ron Boone. The Spirits also had Lonnie Shelton under contract for the following season. Yet that team didn't even make the playoffs and had a 35–49 record, which tells you a lot about the Spirits of St. Louis. It was a team of names and legends. Fly Williams and Maurice Lucas also wore their colors. They had a guy named Bob (then Bobby) Costas fresh out of Syracuse University at the broadcast table. They had Rudy Martzke, now the sports television critic for USA Today, as assistant general manager. The team president was Harry Weltman, the GM of the New Jersey Nets from 1987 to 1990. The coaches were all respected basketball men—Rod Thorn, Bob Mac-Kinnon and Joe Mullaney. Yet in their two seasons, the Spirits won few games (a 67–101 record) and made few fans. Their one moment of glory came in the 1975 playoffs, when they upset defending champion New York in the first round, but then the Spirits were dumped 4–1 by eventual champion Kentucky in the second round. And their best move was made by the team's owners, who made a financial killing by not going into the NBA after the merger.

HARRY WELTMAN: I knew a group of guys from New York—Ozzie and Daniel Silna and their lawyer, Donald Schupak—who were interested in getting into the basketball business, primarily the NBA. I had known *(NBA Commissioner)* Walter Kennedy for some time and Walter told me that the Pistons were available. This was in 1973. I begged these guys to buy the Pistons, because I thought it would be a great investment. The Pistons wanted $5.1 million, the Silnas offered $4.75. Now it sounds like a deal could be made because the two sides weren't that far apart, but the Pistons' owners were not about to budge from that $5.1 figure. I advised my people that $5.1 was the price, it was not negotiable, and we should pay it. But they stayed at $4.75 and were summarily dismissed. The Pistons made the playoffs that season, and six months later I was advised that the Pistons were still for sale, only the bidding would start at $8.5 million. So if my people had moved on the $5.1 price tag, they could have made over $3 million in six months.

At this point, the group still wanted a basketball team, but the NBA was getting very expensive. So we looked into the ABA and targeted what was left of the Carolina Cougars. Tedd Munchak still owned the team, but he was in the process of dismantling it. He had lost Billy Cunningham back to Philadelphia. He had sold Mack Calvin and Steve Jones to Denver and Ted McClain to Kentucky. So we bought what was left for $1.5 million—$500,000 down and the $1 million to be paid out over a number of years.

We decided to put the team in St. Louis because it was the largest city at the time without a pro basketball franchise. You were talking about the 12th-largest market in the country and an arena that sat 18,000. It was a big league situation all the way and we felt it would give us more credibility with the NBA whenever there was a merger. Certainly there was no reason to keep it in Carolina, which had proved conclusively that the regional franchise idea just wouldn't work.

BOB COSTAS: I've always said that Harry Weltman has spent his time in basketball purgatory. First, he ran the Spirits of St. Louis, which gave the world Marvin Barnes and Fly Williams. Then he went to the Cleveland Cavaliers before they were good. Next were the New Jersey Nets, who haven't been any good since the merger. Harry is a great, warmhearted guy, a man of tremendous compassion. He cares about the people who work for him, guarding and nurturing them. Losses eat away at Harry, and he's had to endure a lot of losses. He would take long walks. As the frustration mounted he'd mumble to himself. He put together an excellent group of players at St. Louis, but at that stage of the ABA there were too many factors working against him.

When Harry Weltman became involved in the Spirits, he had no formal basketball background. He had been a very successful executive for NFL Films and he had worked in the advertising business. He was a very good college basketball player *(at Baldwin-Wallace College in Cleveland)*. He knew a lot about sports marketing, but had never run a pro basketball team. He lived in New York and was a Knicks season-ticket holder. Harry loved basketball and wanted to run his own team. He convinced the Silna brothers to invest in the ABA.

The Silnas were textile magnates, one of the first to manufacture polyester for clothing. Now we laugh when we think of the kind of double-knit clothes you could wear through a hurricane and afterwards look no better or worse, but a lot of people still have the Silnas' polyester buried deep in their closets. They were making a lot of money on double-knits and their business was in New York, so they weren't about to move to St. Louis and run the Spirits. That's where Harry Weltman came in and said, "Don't worry, guys, I'll watch the store."

HARRY WELTMAN: I got a chance to run the Spirits because some people were impressed by my media contacts, my business and marketing experience and my overall understanding of the game. I admit that the area of my least experience was talent, but I always thought I could recognize a good basketball player when I saw one.

We had to operate first class and have the best team we could as fast as we could so that we would be attractive to the NBA when the merger came, and we thought it was coming within a year or two.

We were fishing for a nickname, and we must have gone through a thousand names. We wanted something that would be indigenous to the St. Louis community, something that would be memorable on a logo and sell the team with a certain image. We talked about the St. Louis Arch, but I could just see us losing a few games and being called the Fallen Arches—too many bad jokes. I didn't want to be the basketball Cardinals; there already were the baseball and football Cardinals, which was probably one Cardinals too many. One day we were negotiating with Sidney Solomon, who owned the St. Louis Blues hockey team and the arena. We were talking about playing dates or something and Solomon said something about "Spirits."

We said, "That's not bad. But we don't want to be the St. Louis Spirits." Then we talked some more and got on the subject of Charles Lindbergh's plane—*The Spirit of St. Louis.* I got very excited when I heard that. It was something that could really tie into the image we wanted. It was pure St. Louis, would easily lend itself to a logo with an airplane.

BOB COSTAS: I always thought the Spirits had the best logo and uniforms in the league. The uniforms were burnt orange and silver with a jet stream from Lindbergh's plane spelling out "The Spirits of St. Louis." Maybe not all of the players in the uniforms had class, but the clothes they wore on the court sure did.

BOBBY COSTAS BLOWS IN

BOB COSTAS: In September of 1974, I got a call from Roger Holstein, who was the Spirits' new promotions director. He went to Syracuse with me, but later transferred to Swarthmore. Roger remembered that I had done some sports on the campus radio station, WAER. Roger told me about the Carolina Cougars moving to St. Louis and that they were starting an organization from scratch and they needed a radio broadcaster because the games were going to be done on KMOX.

The only basketball tape I had was from my sophomore year, a Syracuse-Rutgers game. I listened to that tape, and there just weren't very many good moments on it. I knew I had to splice something together; I couldn't just pick out 10 minutes during the game. So I had plays from the first half followed by plays from the second half and then a few more plays from the first half. In terms of content, it made absolutely no sense. Then I listened to the game again and I realized that I didn't sound old enough. I sounded like some college kid, which was exactly what I was. I wanted my voice to sound lower. I had grown up listening to Marv Albert do the Knicks, and I was doing a poor man's Marv Albert. So I took my spliced tape and recorded it onto a second tape, turning down the treble and turning up the bass to make my voice deeper. I sent the tape to Harry Weltman, the Spirits, and to KMOX. All the tapes were going to Rudy Martzke, who had a box with about 200 of them on his desk.

That was when my guardian angel stepped in again for me, as Roger Holstein dug deep into that box and found my tape. Then he waited until Harry Weltman went to lunch and he laid the tape on Harry's desk. It was one of those old reel-to-reel tapes. Roger cued it up for Harry while Harry was eating.

When Harry got back into the office, about the last thing on his mind was the new broadcaster. He had no players, no coaches, and the season was only two months away. Anyway, Harry sat down behind his desk and Roger said, "Harry, listen to this."

Roger pushed the button. Harry listened and said, "That kid is pretty good; who is he?"

It's not fair to say that I got the job right there, but it did put me among their 10 finalists and it got me out of the bottom of the box. I don't care what anyone says, these things never are done very scientifically, and when you end up in the bottom of the box, you can easily just stay there because no one has time to listen to all those tapes.

HARRY WELTMAN: Bob was recommended to me by Roger Holstein and I was intrigued by what Roger had to say about him, but I withheld judgment until I heard his tape. I was impressed by his voice, so we brought him in for an interview.

BOB COSTAS: When I came to St. Louis for my interview, it was September and I wore a suit—my only suit—a glen plaid that I thought was pretty snappy. It was a wool suit and I thought that since it was September, it might be a little chilly in St. Louis. What did I know? I had never been to St. Louis. When I got off the plane, it was 106 degrees and the humidity was about the same. By the time I walked through the doors of KMOX, I was wilted.

When I thought of KMOX, I thought of Harry Caray, Jack Buck, Dan Kelly—legendary sportscasters. When I was a kid, I'd sit in my father's car in our driveway and listen to games on KMOX, with its 50,000-watt signal.

KMOX was interested in me for a couple of reasons. First, the Spirits were not that important to the station. Whenever there was a conflict with the Blues, the hockey games went on the air and the Spirits were bumped. Second, if the team folded, which was a distinct possibility with any ABA team, if the station hired a young guy they could dump him without his having moved his family to St. Louis and settled in. Third, if the kid ended up being good, they'd have him available for something else. It was almost like a baseball team trying out a prospect in the minors.

The final factor also counted for a lot: I was absolutely delighted by the idea of working for $11,000.

One of the things they did during my interview was to take me over to meet Jack Buck. He was getting a haircut at the time. When I walked in, he was in the chair, his white mane being trimmed, and I was standing behind him. He was looking at me in the mirror and I was talking to the back of his head.

He said, "Kid, how old are you?"

I said I was 22.

He said, "I have ties older than you, kid."

That was the end of that encouraging exchange, in which I learned that the guy I had listened to from my father's driveway in Long Island had some very old ties.

HARRY WELTMAN: Bob was not the most mature kid when we hired him and he certainly had some moments when he didn't cover himself in glory, but he was a lot of fun.

BOB COSTAS: The Spirits' regular-season opener was at home against Memphis. With 1:10 to play, St. Louis had a five-point lead and Gus Gerard got a rebound. Remember that the ABA had a 30-second clock. Anyway, Gus took the ball deep in the corner and let loose with what was nearly a 3-pointer, and he had used up only five seconds on the shot clock. A couple more plays like that followed and the Spirits blew the game and lost 97–92.

Two nights later, the Spirits' second game was against Utah and Moses Malone. Joe Caldwell guarded Moses that night and held him to four points. I'm feeling great. I'm 22, I'm on KMOX, and I figure the entire nation is sitting in their driveways, listening to me do the Spirits games.

When the Spirits played at home, I did the games with Bill Wilkerson, who served as our color man. On the road, I did them myself because no one wanted to pay for a second guy to travel.

Anyway, the Spirits had a seven-point lead with about a minute to go and I turned to Wilkerson and said right on the air, "Bill, it would seem that the Spirits have this one well in hand. But you can bet that the last thing Coach Bob MacKinnon wants to see is a repeat of Friday night's blow job."

Naturally, what I wanted to say was that MacKinnon didn't want to blow the game, but that wasn't what I said, and it wasn't what I figured half the country heard me say on KMOX.

Bill Wilkerson was just looking at me. He's a big guy; at that time he probably weighed 300 pounds and had been a former lineman at Southern Illinois University. His eyes were as wide as saucers and he pushed away from the microphone and whispered to me, "Are you kidding?"

At that moment, I figured I was fired. But the engineer kept signaling to me to keep talking, so I just did the rest of the game and the Spirits won.

But nothing happened. I guess the station was more amused than anything, and now I still run into guys in St. Louis who say to me, "Remember when you first came to town?" and then boom, they're telling me the story and saying they drove into a ditch when they heard it.

WARNER FUSSELLE: I was broadcasting the Virginia games and the Squires' Cincy Powell came up to me and said, "Who's this Costas and how come he called me a 'hatchet man'?"

Bob had one of those ABA guides that gave you a capsule comment on each player and he simply read it on the air, and it said that Powell was a hatchet man. Bob didn't mean any harm and he certainly didn't know any better.

Well, Cincy did confront Bob about it by saying, "I heard you called me a hatchet man."

Bob didn't deny it. He just tried to tell Cincy that he was sure Cincy was a good player, a hard worker and all that.

Cincy worked Costas over pretty good, chewing him out and glaring at him. We all got a kick out of watching the rookie announcer sweat and squirm.

BOB COSTAS: I almost ended up being a rookie announcer who didn't see the end of my first year.

Late in November the Spirits had a game in Memphis. As usual, I had no money and our checks weren't going to be available until noon.

Consequently, I didn't take the morning flight with the team. I waited until noon, picked up my check and took it to the bank. I had a 3 P.M. flight to Memphis, which should have gotten there in plenty of time because it took about an hour. But when I got to the airport, there was fog in Memphis, flights were canceled and delayed. The flight didn't leave until about 6 P.M. and when it landed, I did my best O. J. Simpson imitation running through the airport. I got into the cab at game time. I had the driver put the game on the radio—the Memphis broadcast— and you have no idea how sickening it feels to listen to a game you're supposed to be announcing.

KMOX didn't know I wasn't there, and they went to me and all they were getting on the air was "Basket by Jones." It was the public-address announcer. After a minute or so of that, they went back to the station. I got to the game and back on the air with the score something like 17–14, about five minutes into the first quarter. At that point, I was sure I was going to be fired and that this would be my last broadcast, so I decided that I'd make it the best basketball broadcast the world has ever known. I pulled out all the stops, and then the game was over and I felt awful. I was washed up at 22.

Back at the hotel, I was sitting with several of the players, telling them what had happened and how I was in big trouble.

Gus Gerard said, "So what can they do to you? They'll just fine you, you'll pay it and then it's over."

I told the guys that they don't fine people in radio, they fire them for missing games. The guys were listening to me, offering their sympathy. Then Marvin Barnes said, "Hey, bro, don't worry about it. I've been looking for a little white dude to drive me around in my Rolls-Royce."

It was nice to know that I had something to fall back on.

When I returned to the station, they chewed me out but didn't fire me. Later, I saw Jack Buck and he said, "Kid, I've been in this business for 32 years and I've never been late for anything."

Then he walked away.

In the second year with the Spirits, the brainstorm was to have Harry Weltman's wife, Arlene, do the color on the television broadcasts. Arlene had been interviewed at halftime of a game during the first season and she came off as witty, charming and nice. She also did know something about basketball. There was an advertising agency guy who saw the tape and said, "Arlene was great; why don't we let her do the color on the TV games? Maybe we can get women to watch the team and we'll tap into this new source of fans."

Arlene did all right, but she had no chance. The idea was doomed from the start. I'm still not sure that the public is ready to accept a woman doing the color, but I know that it certainly wasn't in 1975. Add in the fact that she was Harry Weltman's wife . . . well, it was almost comical. And the thing was, I had virtually nothing to compare this to. The Spirits were my first pro sports experience. I thought every team had players like Marvin Barnes and Fly Williams and every team did things like we did.

BUILDING THE SPIRITS

RUDY MARTZKE: Before coming to the Spirits, I had been a PR man with the Buffalo Braves and I knew Bob MacKinnon very well. Bob was an assistant at Buffalo and I thought he was the kind of patient, older guy we'd need with a young team. So I said to Harry Weltman, "How about Bob MacKinnon?"

HARRY WELTMAN: Rudy Martzke recommended MacKinnon to me. We had interviewed several other people, then brought in Bob. He had experience and an understanding of the kind of team we wanted to build, so we hired him.

BOB MACKINNON: Harry had definite ideas about what he wanted to do. He wanted a young team, yet a team that would make the playoffs. The next step was to challenge for the ABA title. Finally, he wanted a team that could eventually compete for an NBA championship after the merger. Harry had grand plans and he went about it in a grand way, starting with the signing of Marvin Barnes.

HARRY WELTMAN: Philadelphia had drafted Barnes in the first round and we went after him because he was 6-foot-9 and had tremendous basketball skills. Denver had his ABA rights, but we cut a deal with Denver to get the right to go after Barnes. I wanted him badly. He would make an immediate impact for us, give us a big man who could help us be competitive right from the start. I don't think that Philadelphia considered us a threat to sign Marvin, so they didn't move very quickly. But we were able to cut a deal because we offered some serious money. It was reported as $2.1 million over seven years. Actually, the payout was over 14 years, so we were basically talking about $150,000 a year for a guy who was the second pick in the NBA draft.

RUDY MARTZKE: Marvin was our first real player. From the Cougars, we inherited four guys—Joe Caldwell, Ed Manning, Tom Owens and

Gene Littles. Only Caldwell was considered a starter, and he had his problems off the court.

GENE LITTLES: Those of us who did go to St. Louis knew that the Spirits owners were mad because they didn't get the good players from Carolina. But they did get a few of us, and then they started releasing us one by one.

HARRY WELTMAN: Our other key signing was Maurice Lucas from Marquette. Chicago had Lucas's NBA rights. I thought Lucas had a chance to be good, but it was Barnes whom I thought would be great. Lucas exceeded my expectations. Of course, we thought more of Maurice than Chicago did. We signed Maurice to a six-year deal starting at $120,000 and ending at $150,000. *(Chicago offered him a multiyear deal worth about $40,000 annually.)* When I signed Lucas to that contract, I was widely criticized for giving away the store. But when the merger came, one of the things that made Lucas extremely attractive to the NBA was his contract, because he was signed for a long time at very affordable dollars for a player of his ability.

BOB MACKINNON: With the exception of Marvin and then Lucas, I had no idea what I would do for players. We had nearly 50 guys in training camp. We broke them down into two groups of 25. Then we had double-sessions for each group. Group 1 started at 9 A.M., then Group 2 came on at 11 A.M., Group 1 was back at 1 P.M. and then Group 2 at 3 P.M. Anyone who wrote a good letter or sounded decent on the phone got a tryout and we just kept weeding people out.

HARRY WELTMAN: I watched training camp and I thought to myself, "With these guys, we'd have a hard time trying to be a good Rucker League team. We couldn't even win the Harlem summer league." Then I watched these guys shoot and I thought, "I was born too soon."

RUDY MARTZKE: I started getting calls from guys who said they represented Fly Williams from Austin Peay. Notice, I said "guys." At least three different guys claimed to be his agent and we sort of guessed which one sounded the best and we dealt with him.

HARRY WELTMAN: Fly Williams was just a gamble and nothing more. An inexpensive gamble, may I add, because we signed him for only $35,000. He was a colorful player, a playground legend from New York, a gunner who we thought might sell a few tickets and get us some publicity. More important to us than Fly Williams was signing Gus Gerard out of the University of Virginia, a 6-foot-8 athlete who was very talented and averaged 16 points for us as a rookie.

RUDY MARTZKE: Another guy who helped us a lot more than Fly Williams was Mike Barr, a guard from Duquesne who had played with Virginia. I was talking to a basketball person I knew and he said I should check into Barr, who was a free agent after two years with the Virginia Squires. The only other team after him was Memphis. I said to Mike, "Look, Memphis is not a real good team, but we're even worse. We don't have anybody who can play. Come here and you'll get a lot of minutes."

Some selling pitch, huh? But it worked. Barr was our starting point guard until we got Freddie Lewis from Memphis, and Mike then did a nice job for us coming off the bench *(averaging 5.6 points and shooting 51 percent).*

BOB COSTAS: They even brought in Walter Bellamy for a tryout. Walter always had a prominent rear end, but the "Bellamy Caboose," as it was known in the annals of sport, had spread to where you could have set a table for eight on his ass. As you can guess, Bells didn't stay around.

RUDY MARTZKE: It seemed like the word around basketball was that before you drop a player off at the city dump, call St. Louis, maybe they'll take him. One day the phone rang, and it was Carl Scheer from Denver.

He said, "Would you like Steve Jones?"

I said, "Sure." I liked anybody who had at least played in the league.

We had just played our first exhibition game, against San Antonio at Pan American University. Allie McGuire was the point guard and we were still looking for guys who could play. But Marvin Barnes was there. I didn't go to the game, but Bob MacKinnon was supposed to call me after it was over and tell me what happened, so I could call the owners.

So MacKinnon called and I asked him what happened.

He said, "I don't know. We played a lot of different people, probably lost by 20 or 25 points."

I said, "How did Marvin do?"

He said, "Marvin had six points."

I said, "Six points!!! We're paying this guy $2 million and he got six points? How can I tell the owners Marvin got only six points?"

He said, "Well, Marvin had a great warm-up."

I said, "A great warm-up?"

MacKinnon explained that after the warm-up, there was a phone call in the dressing room for Marvin. It was from his girlfriend and she had just totaled his new Cadillac. Marvin was bummed out by the whole thing and he scored six points. A footnote to this story was that when Marvin came home, he replaced the Caddy with a Rolls-Royce.

That was what was going on when Denver called me about Steve Jones, so you better believe we were interested in Steve Jones.

STEVE JONES: Denver told me, "We like you, but we don't think you can play like you used to. You're going to be 32 . . ." I had made $75,000 in 1973–74. They offered $50,000. I said I couldn't take that much of a pay cut. Then they moved me to St. Louis.

The first guy I dealt with there was Rudy Martzke. I think Rudy said that the Spirits were looking for some veteran leadership or something. I don't think they had any idea what they were looking for. They did pay me the $75,000 I wanted and I ended up on the most incredible, bizarre basketball team that the world has ever seen.

BOB COSTAS: When the season opened, the Spirits' first starting lineup was Marvin Barnes at center, Joe Caldwell and Gus Gerard at the forwards, Bernie Fryer and Milt Williams as the guards. By the end of the season, the only starters still on the roster were Barnes and Gerard. Players of note on the bench were Maurice Lucas, Steve Jones, Mike Barr and Fly Williams. We lost and kept losing. Fryer got hurt after nine games, retired and became an NBA official. Caldwell was later suspended. Milt Williams was cut. We had lost four in a row and our record was 3–7 when Harry Weltman made a trade that turned the team around, sending Tom Owens to Memphis for Freddie Lewis.

HUBIE BROWN: Freddie Lewis was one of the all-time great guards in the ABA. Like Louis Dampier, he is one of those stars who never had a chance to show what he could do in the NBA, but Freddie was definitely an NBA-caliber point guard. He really took over that St. Louis team and shaped up some of those wild kids they had.

A SIDE TRIP TO FLYLAND

Fly Williams was never better than in his freshman year at Austin Peay (pronounced pee) when he led "The Peay," as he called it, to the NCAA tournament. He averaged 30.6 points and 8.7 rebounds. He also averaged 30 shots in a 40-minute game in a gym called "The Little Red Barn" that sat 2,305. Fans were lining up for six hours before games to get tickets to see this freshman from Brooklyn, New York. For James "Fly" Wil-

liams, Clarksville, Tennessee, was a long way from home, and he spent a lot of time talking about pigs and farms and saying, "If I had to spend my life here, I'd go crazy." He named himself Fly after Curtis "Super Fly" Mayfield, the soul singer. Williams was suspended several times by Coach Lake Kelly. Once, he didn't like the coach's strategy, so he walked off the court and sat two rows behind the bench in full uniform to watch the game. But another time he met some people from a poor section of Claxton, Georgia, where Austin Peay was in the "Fruitcake Classic." Each player was given a fruitcake, and Williams collected them all and took the fruitcakes to the poor of the town. By his junior year, his problems with his coach had greatly increased, and his value to the pros had dropped to the extent that only St. Louis would sign him. He lasted one year in the ABA, averaging 9.4 points and shooting 47 percent as a sub for the Spirits. A number of years later, he was shot in an incident in a New York bar. Life has been a struggle for him.

BOB COSTAS: Fly was a legend long before he got to St. Louis. The story that went around with the Fly, and I always thought it had to be apocryphal but it still makes the point, was that when Fly was recruited by Austin Peay, he got on a plane in New York and flew to Austin, Texas. That was where he figured Austin Peay had to be. When he got off the plane, he said to the first guy he saw, "Hey, where's The Peay, man?" Heaven only knows what the man thought Fly was asking. Anyway, Fly then called his coach and said he was in Austin, Texas, and "There's no Peay here, man." The coach was telling him that Austin Peay was in Clarksville, Tennessee, and he started routing him from Austin to Clarksville. Fly became confused and said, "No, man, I'm going home." Then he flew to New York and called the coach from LaGuardia Airport, and from there he flew to Clarksville.

Fly did things in college such as dribbling the ball off the court during a game to get a drink from a fountain in that old gym of theirs.

Fly loved Don Rickles. If Rickles was on television, Fly would watch him, and the next morning on the bus he'd do Rickles's entire routine. He'd go up to Gus Gerard and say, "Hey, you hockey puck." He'd do these lame Rickles imitations, then throw his head back and say, "Man, that dude was hot."

STEVE JONES: In our first game, Fly Williams had a wide-open layup. He was going 100 miles per hour on a breakaway. All he had to do was just lay the ball over the rim or dunk it. Instead, he went for a 360-degree layup. He turned himself completely around and nearly spun himself into the floor and threw the ball right over the rim and the backboard.

It was a total nightmare, but it also was an example of what this team was about—the total free spirit, no discipline; talent, but talent that was completely out of control.

BOB MACKINNON: The first time I saw Fly was in the NCAA tournament when he was playing for Austin Peay. He took a shot from the corner, missed it and screamed he was fouled. When there was no call, he just lay right down on the court in the middle of the game.

I was scouting for Buffalo and I told the people I was sitting with, "I don't know who we will draft, but it won't be that guy."

Then I got to St. Louis and there he was.

BOB COSTAS: The Spirits always lost in Denver and one night they were down by about 25 points in the third quarter. Bob MacKinnon had called a time-out and chastised them for their lack of team play. He told the team that they had to pull together and pass the ball. Then there was a long silence and MacKinnon said, "Anybody else have something to say?"

Fly said, "Yeah, man, just give me the damn rock and I'll take care of it."

So much for team play.

HUBIE BROWN: One night we were playing the Spirits in the Checkerdome and there must have been about 500 people in that 18,000-seat building. All of a sudden, Fly got into a fight with one of his own teammates during the pregame layup drill. I can't remember who it was, but I had never seen a fight during warm-ups before.

BOB COSTAS: The fans liked Fly. He was a very flamboyant character and he smiled a lot, like a big kid. A couple of times a month, he'd have some games where he'd come off the bench and go for 25 points, and people would go crazy.

RUDY MARTZKE: I recall a game where we were losing to Kentucky by 12 points going into the fourth quarter. John Y. and Ellie Brown were there watching the game and this was their Colonels team that went on to win the ABA title. Fly came off the bench, scored about 20 points and single-handedly beat the Colonels. So, yes, Fly had his moments.

ROD THORN: When I was hired by the Spirits, the famous Fly Williams story was that Fly had no teeth and Harry Weltman wanted to send Fly to the dentist. The team would pay for everything. The dentist told Fly what he needed to do and pulled out a big needle for a Novocain shot. Fly took one look at that needle and he was out of the chair and ran out of the dentist's office.

The dentist called Harry and told him what happened. Then Harry called Fly and said, "What's going on? You've got to have some teeth."

Fly was always so skinny, and part of the reason was that he didn't eat right as a kid, and when he got older he couldn't eat right because of his missing teeth.

But all Fly would say was, "Man, I wouldn't be the Fly if I had teeth."

HARRY WELTMAN: Fly was not the kid whose reputation preceded him. First, he was not a bad person. He was my daughter's favorite player and he was always nice to the fans. When we cut Fly, my daughter cried. But he also wasn't as good a basketball player as he was supposed to be, either.

ROD THORN: I was hired to coach the Spirits for their second year. Early in training camp, I told Fly, "I've heard some things about you, but as far as I'm concerned, you're starting with a clean slate. All you have to do is play hard and stay straight and you'll be fine."

Then we started seriously practicing and the first thing I saw was that the guy just wasn't that good. He was a 6-foot-5 small forward with no upper-body strength. He didn't have the ballhandling skills to play guard and he seemed to be just going through the motions. Everybody talks about this guy as if he were a great player, but he just wasn't that good.

The day I cut him, he was sitting up against the wall in one of his moods. I went up to him, told him that we had to let him go, and he showed the first real emotion in a month. He was really upset. He couldn't believe that anyone would cut him.

MARVIN GETS READY TO MAKE A MOVE

JOE MULLANEY: People ask me what kind of guy Marvin Barnes was and I tell them about this play: I was coaching the Spirits and it was right at the end of the first half. Marvin got the ball about 20 feet from the basket on a breakaway and there were about four seconds on the clock. He could have walked in and dunked it or just dropped the ball into the rim. Instead, he took three steps *backwards* and heaved up a 3-pointer. It was the most undisciplined, outrageous play I had ever seen at any level of basketball, and yet the Spirits didn't seem to think that was a big deal. It was just "Marvin being Marvin." It certainly was, because Marvin only cared about Marvin.

GENE LITTLES: The Spirits were a bunch of young guys let loose in the city who had money for the first time in their lives. They didn't think about anything but what made them happy right now. It was all big cars, fancy clothes and fast women. One time Marvin was late for a practice in training camp. Bob MacKinnon asked him why he was late and Marvin said, "I lost my car in a lot downtown."

McKinnon said, "What kind of car is it?"

Marvin said, "A Bentley."

There couldn't have been three Bentleys in all of St. Louis. A blind man could pick out a Bentley in a parking lot.

Just looking at MacKinnon, you could see that Fly and Marvin aged him at least 10 years that season.

VAN VANCE: When Kentucky played in St. Louis, we stayed at a Quality Inn near Stan Musial's restaurant. Several of us went there for lunch and we saw Bob MacKinnon there. Bob was telling us about all these wild kids he had on his team. We could see the parking lot.

A huge silver Mercedes pulled up and Maurice Lucas got out.

Then Joe Caldwell came and got out of his Porsche.

Then Fly Williams came and got out of his Caddy.

Finally, Marvin Barnes pulled up in his Rolls-Royce.

It was like "Can You Top This?" The players came into the restaurant and they were all talking about their cars, saying things like, "If you like that one, you should see what I have at home."

BOB COSTAS: In my mind, the symbol of the Spirits will always be Marvin Barnes tooling down the street in his Rolls. He'd spot some kids on the corner, stop and pick them up and drive them in that big car to an ice cream stand, where he'd treat them, then drive them home. He felt like the Pied Piper, and he was nothing more than a big kid himself. But this was the same Marvin Barnes who must have missed 100 personal appearances in his two years—everything from lunches to charity events to boys clubs. He was constantly giving away tennis shoes and shirts to kids on the street, yet he couldn't make it to practice or catch a team flight. He had great talent, yet that talent was lost in all the excess, and after just a couple of years, he was finished when he should have been just entering his prime.

STEVE JONES: Early in the season, it was incredible. Nobody passed the ball, no one helped out on defense, everyone just wanted the rock and went 1-on-1. In the huddle they'd say, "Don't sweat it, we'll stop this guy or stop that guy." They never stopped anyone, because they had no idea of what it meant to play pro basketball.

This ended up being my most difficult season as a pro. I was at the point in my life where I really understood the pro game and what it took to win, but I also was losing my physical edge. Yet I was playing with all these young bucks who seemed to be all talent and no brains. I guess I envied them for their youth, but their lack of discipline drove me crazy.

RUDY MARTZKE: Before the first game in which Marvin played Caldwell Jones, someone told Marvin that Caldwell was a great defensive player. Apparently Marvin wanted to show that no one could stop him, because he went out and took Jones apart for something like 51 points and 30 rebounds. He looked liked the best player ever to wear a uniform that night.

STEVE JONES: The morning after a game, we'd be on the bus ready to go to the airport and Marvin would come out with a woman on each arm. He would kiss them both a couple of times before he got on the bus.

Marvin had a number of good things going for him on the court. He just attacked the ball off the glass. If he was on the right side of the rim and the ball went off to the left, he didn't just stand there like most guys and figure he had no shot at it, he went across the lane and got the ball. When he was in the mood, he could get a rebound, throw an outlet pass to a guard, then race down the court and catch a return pass for a dunk as well as any big man in basketball. He had 18-foot range on his jumper and a good power game inside. He had every physical ingredient you'd want in a big man and he had the killer spirit to go with it. He didn't just want to beat you, he wanted to embarrass you.

But so much of what Marvin did was counterproductive to his career. He disdained practice. He stayed up all night. He didn't listen to anyone about anything, but then he'd come out and play a great game. You'd see that and know that the gods had touched this man and made him a great player, only he had no idea what he had. And he kept pushing things and pushing things, like a little kid trying to see what he could get away with. He was the star and he knew it. Also, management gave him carte blanche to do what he wanted, and what he wanted to do was run amok. The whole thing reached a boiling point when Marvin jumped the team.

MARVIN MAKES HIS MOVE

Marvin Barnes disappeared from the Spirits on November 20, 1974. His pro career was exactly 17 games old and the Spirits were 7–10 and preparing to play the Nets in New York. Barnes had grown close to Joe Caldwell. Barnes told Rod Sieb of Basketball Weekly, "I grew up respecting Joe Caldwell. He showed me certain things in his contract and he said I should have them, too. Then he said I ought to see his agent, Marshall Boyer. I thought that was the right thing to do." According to Sieb's account, Barnes checked out of the team's hotel in New York and was driven to the airport by Caldwell. He flew to a meeting with Boyer in Dayton, Ohio. Barnes told Sieb, "Boyer wanted me to sue the ABA, to sue the owners of the Spirits, to sue (his agent) Bob Woolf, sue everybody. He told me to leave St. Louis, to jump leagues." Barnes returned to the Spirits two weeks later. Then Caldwell was suspended, "for activities detrimental to the best interests of professional basketball," according to the Spirits' press release. Caldwell, 33, never played another game of professional basketball, and many lawsuits followed as Caldwell claimed he was blackballed. Caldwell also said in court that he told Barnes not to leave the team.

STEVE JONES: Management knew that Caldwell was close to Marvin and they came to Joe and said, "We've got to do something about Marvin."

Joe told them something to the extent of, "You've got to fine him and fine him big."

Then Marvin went to Joe and said, "Man, they're taking all of my money."

Joe said, "Well, you need to talk to my agent."

So Joe put Marvin in touch with his agent. Back then, agents didn't worry about contracts. Agents would tell you that they'd get you a new contract or they'd help you jump leagues. They'd try anything.

Marvin was gone and no one could find him, because he was with Joe's agent.

HARRY WELTMAN: Joe Caldwell was behind Marvin leaving the team. Joe would do things such as go to Bob MacKinnon and tell him that he ought to fine Marvin for being late, then Joe would tell Marvin that management was treating him unfairly. When Marvin bolted the team, we suspended him without pay. He did have a problem with his contract in that he was being paid through his own corporation, which meant they didn't take out the withholding taxes. So he got hit with a big tax bill. Marvin also was very generous and was having some financial difficulty. The only thing he had of significant value was his Rolls-Royce. So we helped him restructure his contract to deal with the tax problems.

We would have been glad to do that. He didn't have to jump the team and he would have saved me a lot of grief from talking to Marshall Boyer. I had a lot of conversations with the guy and none of them made any sense. He would close his conversations by saying, "Men move at night."

What the hell did that mean?

I remember a George Raft movie where someone said, "Men drive by night." I guess Boyer just wanted to sound mysterious and all that crap, but I needed to hear "Men move at night" as much as I needed a hole in the head. What I really needed at night was a good night's sleep, because we were losing and my star player turned up in a pool hall in Dayton with Boyer and Boyer's wife, who was supposed to be playing in the tournament.

STEVE JONES: All the different things in Marvin's disappearance started coming out, and the finger pointed right at Joe Caldwell. One day in early December we were ready to leave on a trip and they told us that Caldwell was going with us. Then they suspended Joe, and that thing has been in the court system ever since. The Spirits had a lot of inexperienced people in the front office and they had no idea how to deal with this situation. They would talk about rules to Marvin, but I swear Marvin learned all the rules just so he could break them. He did things like send the ballboy out right before a game to polish his Rolls, and that was when the ballboy was supposed to be around to help the other players and the trainer.

Marvin just figured that everybody would take care of him. "Everybody loves News," which was what he called himself. Time meant nothing to him. Rules meant nothing. Money meant nothing. For being late, they started fining him $1 a minute, then $5, then $10. I think it got up to $50 a minute, but he didn't care. They'd take the money out of his paycheck, but he knew that he'd usually get it back. He knew the front office wanted to keep him happy, so they wouldn't stick to their fines and they wouldn't bench him. They closed their eyes to a lot.

And I do mean a *lot*. Marvin would walk into a game 20 minutes before it was time to start. People would be taped and ready to go out for warm-ups, and Marvin would stroll into the dressing room with all this food—steak and gravy, black-eyed peas, greens, mashed potatoes. He would be eating it while someone taped his ankles, then he'd tell the ballboy, "I got some women coming in tonight. I need five tickets—and get me some body lotion, too." He loved to stand in front of a mirror and put lotion on himself. I think he saw himself as this great ladies' man, a guy with his own harem. Once, he spent the entire pregame layup drill in full uniform, sitting in the stands and talking to this girl. MacKinnon ripped into Marvin for that and didn't start him. Then he brought

Marvin off the bench and Marvin went for 40 points and 20-some rebounds. That was the kind of talent he was. He thought he was Superman, and for a while, he was.

BOB COSTAS: Looking back, the whole thing is pretty funny. The Spirits claimed that Joe Caldwell had led Marvin Barnes "astray." Believe me, Marvin spent much of his life "astray." He didn't need a map or someone else to take him there. He was found in a pool hall in Dayton, Ohio, of all places. Then Marvin came back, Caldwell was suspended, and then Joe showed up at a Spirits game. They wouldn't let him in, so he had to buy a ticket and he sat by himself upstairs. Really, the whole thing was crazy.

Very early in Marvin's rookie year, a story came out about him having 13 telephones in his six-room condo. It wasn't true, as it turned out, but suddenly, "13 telephones" became the watchword for Marvin.

WARNER FUSSELLE: I once had Marvin on a postgame show and I asked him about the 13 phones. He said, "No man, I ain't got no 13 phones. Let's see, I got one in the living room, one in the kitchen, one in the bathroom, two in the bedroom . . ." He named about seven different places that had phones. By then, we both were laughing so hard that we had to stop.

BOB COSTAS: A lot of people in St. Louis resented Marvin. He had the Super Fly image—the wide-brimmed hats, the long, floor-length mink coats, the platform shoes, the big cars and, of course, the 13 telephones. He became the trademark of the team, and the town did not relate very well to "that sort of Negro," to use Marvin's phrase.

HARRY WELTMAN: Look at what Marvin did for us as a rookie. He averaged 24 points and 15.6 rebounds and shot 50 percent, and he did it with the worst shot selection I had ever seen on a pro player. He would get the ball, turn around and shoot it. He didn't care where he was on the court.

He had reflexes like a snake's tongue. He would just go out and get the ball, and it was so quick you almost heard the hiss. For all his excesses—and no player ever had as many excesses as Marvin—he was a tremendous competitor. Bob MacKinnon had great patience with Marvin, and by the end of the year it paid off. Marvin was a helluva player and we were a damn good team.

THE SPIRITS MAKE THEIR MOVE

Once Marvin Barnes came back and Joe Caldwell left, all still wasn't well with the Spirits. Harry Weltman's hopes of having a young team that also made the playoffs appeared grim. The Spirits went through late January, all of February and early March on a streak in which they lost 18 of 22, including 9 of the last 10. On March 8, their record was 24 – 48 (.333) with 12 games left. Then the team won 8 of those last 12 games to finish at 32–52 and beat out hapless Memphis (27–57) for third place in the Eastern Division. In addition to Barnes's 24 points and 15 rebounds, the Spirits received nice seasons from Maurice Lucas (13 points, 10 rebounds), Freddie Lewis (22 points, 5.5 assists) and Gus Gerard (15.6 points, 8.1 rebounds). Steve Jones had the lowest-scoring season (10.9 points) in his eight-year ABA career, but he also had a career high with 197 assists.

BOB COSTAS: In the end, it was the veterans who pulled the team together. Freddie Lewis was sensational all season at the point guard. Steve Jones or Mike Barr started at the other guard. Jones really sacrificed a lot of his scoring to get the ball to the guys inside, and Barr was a very unselfish player. Then the Spirits picked up two other veterans who were a big help—Don Adams and Goo Kennedy.

RUDY MARTZKE: With about a month to go in the season, the Detroit Pistons cut Don Adams. He was a balding, heavyset guy from Northwestern, 6-foot-7, maybe 220, and he had played in the NBA for six years. He didn't score much, but this was the kind of hardworking rebounder any team needed. I got a call from Adams's agent, who told me that Adams had a guaranteed $90,000 deal from Detroit and he was willing to play for us for the minimum. All he wanted to do was play somewhere to keep his name in circulation so that he could get back into the NBA next year. I called the ABA office and found out that the minimum was $200 a game. So for that kind of money, we signed him.

When Adams showed up, he was out of shape. I can remember Marvin, Lucas and Fly Williams all laughing at him, calling him the old man.

One of his first games was against San Antonio. Swen Nater was the Spurs' center, a huge guy at 6-foot-11, 250 pounds, all muscle. Marvin got into a tussle with Nater under the basket and Nater just flung Marvin down to the end of the court as if he were a rag doll. Marvin flopped to the floor. He couldn't believe that Nater would just throw him like that.

Marvin got up and was waving his dukes, like he was going to take Nater on. But you could see that Marvin was worried and really didn't want to fight Nater, who was just staring at him. Then Adams came from Nater's blind side and decked him with one punch. Swen never saw it coming, but the guys on our bench were looking at Old Man Adams in complete awe.

BOB COSTAS: Adams just knocked Swen out cold. Nater was on the floor, bleeding. Marvin saw that and then he was standing over Nater yelling, "Get up." Guys were holding Marvin back and he's yelling, "Let me at him." When Swen finally got up, I heard Marvin yell, "Boy, are you lucky that I didn't get to you first."

This was one of the things Marvin did best—pointing a threatening finger at a guy and insulting him when there was a mob of people between him and a guy like Nater. If everyone had gotten out of the way and let Nater at Marvin, Marvin would have died of a heart attack. That was the last thing he wanted. He was a talker, not a fighter.

What Adams did changed the whole team's attitude toward him. This man was built like Mickey Lolich, but he was a man to be reckoned with. He was a smart player and he fell right in there with Steve Jones and Freddie Lewis, giving us more maturity on the court. The team just shaped up after we got him, even though he only played 20 minutes a night and averaged six points. The guys started playing together. When Lewis, Jones, Barr or Adams was on the court, the ball moved around, guys played defense. They started to look like a basketball team.

RUDY MARTZKE: Don Adams's punch turned the team around. When we played New York in the playoffs, he worked Doctor J over so badly that there were a few instances when they had to take Julius out of the game to let him cool down. On a team that needed all the maturity it could get, Adams was perfect. And we paid him only $200 a game. That was the best money we spent all season.

BOB COSTAS: When we made the playoffs, we drew New York in the first round. The Nets were the defending ABA champions. They had a regular-season record of 58–26. And the Spirits had played New York 11 times during the regular season and lost all 11 games, and hardly any of the games were close.

Nine of the eleven losses were by at least 17 points. The average defeat was by 19 points. Before the playoffs, the last time the two teams met was March 12, and the Nets won, 124–96, their widest margin of victory during the season. Barnes especially had a rough time against the Nets during the regular season, as he was often held to single-digit scoring.

STEVE JONES: This had to be one of the most remarkable turnarounds in basketball history. It wasn't just that we lost to the Nets all 11 times, but we were drilled. It felt like we lost to them 200 times, and we never wanted to see them again. Then came the playoffs and we just ambushed New York. Marvin was sensational and Freddie Lewis showed why he was on those championship teams in Indiana.

BOB COSTAS: We opened the best-of-seven series in New York and lost 111–105. Marvin was great. He had 41 points and we played the Nets better than we had during the regular season, but that made it 12 in a row. But in Game 2, we just killed them, 115–97, and it happened on the road. With 10 minutes to go in the game, Julius had only six points; Don Adams had done a great job on him. Marvin had 37 points and 18 rebounds. That was the game where Wendell Ladner threw his tennis shoe at Freddie Lewis, which was a technical foul and a lot of comic relief.

The series moved to St. Louis, and there were actually some people in the stands. Most of the year, we were lucky to get 3,000. *(The Spirits drew 6,199 and 7,719 for their two home games against the Nets.)* Anyway, we won both of those games at home, and suddenly we were up 3–1 with the series switching back to Nassau Coliseum.

Early in the fourth quarter, the Nets were up by 14, but the Spirits hung in there and were down by a point with 15 seconds to go. New York had the ball out-of-bounds and the Nets could dribble out the clock, or at least force the Spirits to foul. But Julius Erving, of all people, made a turnover. The Spirits got the ball. Freddie Lewis caught a pass at the top of the key, sort of elbowed Brian Taylor out of the way, and swished a 20-footer at the buzzer to give the Spirits a 108–107 victory.

It remains one of the most dramatic things I have ever seen in my life. Of course, me being 22 years old, the Spirits were my life. But also, given the fact that they were such underdogs and winning on the road with Julius Erving making the final turnover and Freddie Lewis hitting the 20-footer at the buzzer—it was great theatre. Freddie scored the last 10 points of that game. It was truly a clutch performance.

In the St. Louis dressing room, guys who had hated each other all year were embracing. The owners were thrown into the shower and lathered up with shampoo by the players. Everyone was exhilarated, not just by the moment, but because we thought this was just the start. Wait until next year. We have all these young players. It was like, "Look out world, here we come." That kind of feeling.

ROD THORN: Marvin showed up for those playoffs. He showed what a great talent he was. But even then, I heard a story that before one of the playoff games, Marvin ate a huge helping of nacho chips in the dressing room while he was changing into his uniform. Most guys would throw up doing that, but he went out and played like King Kong against us.

HUBIE BROWN: Since we were going to play the winner of the St. Louis–New York series, I watched it very closely. Marvin was just incredible. In three of those games, he went for at least 40 points. You'd see that and think that this guy was heading to the Hall of Fame. For that one year, Marvin was something to behold.

BOB COSTAS: Kentucky had a great team that year, with Dan Issel, Louis Dampier, Artis Gilmore and all those guys. They had won 58 games, just like New York, and then the Colonels chewed up Memphis in the first round. But the Spirits thought they could beat them. They figured they could beat anybody after what happened to New York.

The series opened in Kentucky and the Spirits nearly won, but Louis Dampier made a steal with 10 seconds left to save the game for the Colonels (112–109). The second game also was close (108–103), but Kentucky won again at Louisville.

The Spirits came home. There was a big crowd (10,142) and they beat Kentucky, making the series 2–1. In Game 4, the Spirits were up by 10 points in the second quarter and then Freddie Lewis sprained an ankle. He was finished for the series, and so were the Spirits. Until Freddie got hurt, the Spirits were confident. But when he went down, the players knew it was over.

HARRY WELTMAN: After that season was over, it really was a case of not being able to wait until next year. Bob MacKinnon had done a super job coaching. His patience paid off. We lost some games early that we should have won because he went with the younger players and stayed with them in crucial situations. We played well down the stretch, and then beat New York in the playoffs. I was convinced we would have come back to beat Kentucky if Freddie Lewis hadn't gotten hurt. After we lost Lewis, Hubie Brown had the Kentucky guards press Mike Barr and make him give up the ball. We had no other ballhandlers, so we were in trouble. But we had to be excited about next year.

MacKinnon Goes

Just as the Spirits never should have beaten New York in the first round of the playoffs, they never should have had such a disappointing second season. Coach Bob MacKinnon left, as did assistant general manager Rudy Martzke and Steve Jones. Martzke said of his departure, "Harry Weltman just wanted to run things himself." Rod Thorn was hired to replace MacKinnon. Thorn had turned down the job the year before; "That was a mistake," he said at the press conference where he was introduced as coach. "This is one of the finest jobs in professional basketball." But by midseason, Maurice Lucas had been traded, Marvin Barnes had pulled another disappearing act, and Thorn was already the former coach of the Spirits of St. Louis. When it was over, the Spirits had failed to make the playoffs, and there would be no next year.

HARRY WELTMAN: It hurt us when Bob MacKinnon quit to go back to the Buffalo Braves as their player personnel director. He is a very security-conscious guy and the reports about the league having financial problems worried him. He was an excellent, patient coach; even though we had upset New York in the playoffs, we still were a young team and we needed Bob.

STEVE JONES: Maybe Bob MacKinnon liked the security of the NBA, but I also think the Spirits just wore him out. He was 47 years old, had five kids and had to listen to Fly Williams saying, "Coach, Coach, put me in the game. I'll turn this game out. What are we losin' by, 15 points? Hey, I get 15 points in a quarter, easy. You just put me in the game and give me the rock. I'll win this game for you. You don't put me in and I don't know if you really want to win."

Then he had to worry about Marvin—would he get to the game on time? Would Marvin and Maurice Lucas get along? If Bob fined Marvin, management gave the money back. If he wanted to suspend somebody, he wasn't allowed to. I think he felt that so much was out of his hands that he couldn't coach the team as he would have liked and he just didn't want to go through it again. Yet, Bob was the perfect coach for that team, because he could just sit there and listen to all that garbage. He let a lot of things just defuse themselves. In retrospect, losing him was a major setback for the Spirits, which is no reflection on Rod Thorn or anyone else who later coached the team. It was just that Bob was one of the few men on the face of the earth who had the temperament to deal with the likes of Marvin Barnes.

BOB MACKINNON: Buffalo was home for my family and there were a lot of questions about the ABA's future, so I decided to go back to Buffalo and a sure thing. It was no reflection on the Spirits. I loved Harry Weltman, the owners and everybody. This was just a decision I made for my family.

ROD THORN: I had seen a lot of the Spirits because I was an assistant with the Nets. When I interviewed with Harry Weltman, it was obvious that Harry was very proud of the talent he had and the front office believed that it would be good enough to compete in any league. I was 34 years old and I wanted the chance to be a head coach. The team had potential, at least on paper. Of course, this was a prime example of how paper doesn't win games. Harry had gone out and signed Don Chaney away from the Boston Celtics. He picked up M. L. Carr and thought he had Lonnie Shelton. Chaney was a guard and the backcourt was St. Louis's weakness, especially when Steve Jones played out his option and went to Portland of the NBA. So you take a backcourt of Chaney and Freddie Lewis with a front line of Barnes, Lucas and Gus Gerard—the team did have some talent.

STEVE JONES GOES

The 6-foot-5 Jones played in the ABA in the first eight years of the league. He missed only seven games in the first seven years, then sat out 15 in his final season with the Spirits. Jones played for six different teams—Oakland, New Orleans, Memphis, Dallas, Carolina, Denver and St. Louis. He was a three-time All-Star, and left the ABA averaging 16 points and shooting 45 percent from the field, 34 percent from 3-point range and 82 percent at the foul line. He also did a stint as president of the ABA Players Association. After a year as a backup guard with Portland, Jones retired and went into broadcasting, working his way up from doing the Portland games to becoming one of the voices of the NBA on Turner Network Television.

STEVE JONES: The league was at the point where it was starting to lose teams, and when Denver and the Nets applied to join the NBA on their own, there was real concern about where the league was heading. From being on the Players Association Merger Committee, I knew that a merger wasn't far off, and I felt that if the two leagues were going to get together I should make a move to a team I knew would be secure. I really wasn't sure if I wanted to go through another season with the Spirits. Living through that was amazing once, but I'm not sure that anyone should go through it again. Also, I grew up in Portland, so this was a chance to go home, and I took it.

CHARLIE WILLIAMS: In a sense, Steve was the diplomat among the players. He was very active in the Players Association, pushing for a stronger union and more benefits, yet his personality was such that he got along with everybody. He was one of those players who was good for the league—a guy with ability, a smart player and a gentleman. He really took the ABA to heart.

BOB COSTAS: Steve was a source of sanity on the Spirits. Most young players in the league looked up to him because he carried himself with such dignity and because he had time to talk to everyone. The Spirits really missed his leadership that second year. He was the kind of guy you could sit down and talk with. When you mention the ABA to those in the league, Steve Jones is one of the people who comes to mind.

DON CHANEY COMES

HARRY WELTMAN: I knew I had to do something about our backcourt and I wanted a veteran. Don Chaney was one of those guys we had targeted. His contract was up, he had played for great teams with the Celtics. He was mature, a strong defensive player and unselfish.

People would ask me, "What kind of team do you want?"

I'd say, "We'd like to play like the Boston Celtics."

Then someone would ask how we planned to do that.

I'd say, "We've got some great kids on the front line; now what we need to do is to sign a Boston Celtic guard."

BOB RYAN: There was no question that Harry Weltman wanted a Celtic. You could almost say that Harry wanted any Celtic. He just felt he had to have one.

At the end of the 1974–75 season, both of the Celtics guards—Don Chaney and Paul Westphal—had contracts that had expired. Chaney was being represented by Larry Fleisher, Westphal by Howard Slusher. Suddenly, what we had was a case of contractual intrigue.

It was the opinion of the Celtics that Chaney and Westphal—or, to be more exact, their agents—had joined forces to market these guys collectively. The Celtics acted as if this were another Hitler-Stalin pact.

But still, Red Auerbach didn't comprehend the seriousness of the situation. The moment Chaney declared that he had hired Larry Fleisher to represent him, Red should have taken that as a warning to negotiate seriously, that Chaney meant business. But Red thought that Chaney was a little boy and that "Duck" *(Chaney)* wouldn't dare leave the Celtics.

DON CHANEY: St. Louis moved in on me early and started talking big contract numbers right away. I loved the Celtics, but I had to listen. Harry Weltman gave me what I considered a great offer *($600,000 for three seasons)*. Red just let things ride, so I signed with the Spirits. I thought that St. Louis would be a good team. I felt a merger was coming and St. Louis would be one of the teams admitted to the NBA. I got a super three-year deal. I just didn't see how I could turn it down when I couldn't even get a serious counteroffer from the Celtics.

BOB RYAN: I don't know if Harry Weltman realizes it to this day, but he signed the wrong guard. He should have signed Westphal. Westphal was a scorer, he was flashy, his athleticism made him much better suited for the ABA's game than how Chaney played. Duck was a defensive specialist, not a marquee player. He fit in a system, he didn't create things. Westphal would have given the Spirits what they needed, a big-time guard. I remember when Chaney signed with St. Louis. It was in November of 1975 and I was sitting in a coffee shop in Asheville, North Carolina, with *(Boston coach)* Tom Heinsohn. He was moaning and groaning, saying, "Duck is going to regret this."

And Duck did regret it.

DON CHANEY: My year in St. Louis was a lost season for me. I tore up my knee early in the season and couldn't play. I wasn't very happy. I was hurt and the team was in disarray. It was not something I enjoyed.

BOB COSTAS: I'd see Duck in the whirlpool getting treatment on his knee. He felt like he had walked into a zoo. He had never seen anything like Marvin Barnes and the Spirits. Compared to the Celtics, it was like being on another planet. He would be in the whirlpool, we'd make eye contact and then Duck would shake his head. He never said a word and he didn't have to. I knew exactly what he was thinking.

LONNIE SHELTON ALMOST COMES

RON GRINKER: One day I got a call from two brothers named Ron and Ken Delpit. They said they were working with Lonnie Shelton, and

Lonnie wanted to leave Oregon State after his junior year and turn pro. They said that they had represented football and baseball players before, but they had never done anything in basketball. I said that I was reluctant to get involved with an underclassman because too many agents had been talking kids into leaving school early, kids who had no business turning pro. But they said regardless of what I decided, Lonnie was leaving school. He and his family needed the money. Since I knew Lonnie Shelton as a player and I knew that he was a tremendous physical specimen—about 6-foot-7, 260 pounds and very agile at that time—and would make a terrific pro, I agreed to represent him.

Something I didn't know about and something that became a problem later on was that Ralph Miller had just become Lonnie's coach at Oregon State. When Ralph was at Iowa, he was very close to an agent named Arthur Morse, and nearly all of Ralph's players eventually were represented by Morse. But I didn't know about this when I got involved with Lonnie.

St. Louis had the ABA rights to Lonnie. I brought Lonnie to my office in Cincinnati and set up a workout at the Jewish Community Center, where Rod Thorn could come down and take a look at him. Rod did and he loved what he saw, so we set up a meeting in St. Louis to talk about a contract.

HARRY WELTMAN: Lonnie was very close to his high school coach and the coach came to St. Louis for a meeting. We told the coach, "Look, we're not here to take advantage of the kid. If he wants to play professionally, we have his rights and we'll make him a fair deal. If he wants to play, we'd like him to play for us. But the big question is, what does Lonnie want to do?"

Lonnie said he wanted to play. The coach said he wanted to play, so we sat down to do the contract.

RON GRINKER: When we went to St. Louis for a meeting, a couple of strange things happened. Lonnie's mother was supposed to come, but she couldn't make it through airline security because they found a butcher knife in her handbag.

Then in St. Louis, Lonnie didn't want to sit through all the preliminary talks so he decided that he'd like to go out. Marvin Barnes was around and always interested in going out, so Marvin pulled up in his Rolls-Royce and picked up Lonnie.

HARRY WELTMAN: That's where the stories that we got Lonnie drunk or drugged or whatever came from—because he went out with Marvin.

We never took advantage of Lonnie. He went out with Marvin Barnes. Maybe they had a drink and maybe they didn't. They were only gone two or three hours and I don't know where they went or what they did. Maybe they sat around looking at Marvin's scrapbook. Who knows?

RON GRINKER: At one point during the negotiations, Harry called Marvin in his Rolls to talk to Lonnie. We asked Lonnie something and Lonnie said, "I don't know who I can trust, but I do know that I can trust Marvin."

We all rolled our eyes. Now Marvin Barnes was Lonnie's trusted advisor, and he'd just met Marvin about three hours ago. Lonnie was told to come back and bring Marvin into the contract talks if that was what he wanted to do, because we had a preliminary deal for him to look at.

HARRY WELTMAN: We thought we had a deal about three-thirty in the morning. In essence, we offered Lonnie a five-year deal that started at about $150,000. It was big money. Ron Grinker has always had an excellent reputation as an agent and is totally honest. We told Lonnie what was being offered and said, "It's up to you. If you want to tear up the contract and go back to school, no hard feelings. Whatever you want to do."

RON GRINKER: Lonnie showed the contract to Marvin. Marvin said, "Man, you're getting $150,000 a year, a house for your mother, a car. Boy, you better sign that damn contract. It's not as much as I'm making, but you're not as good as me."

So Lonnie signed the contract.

ROD THORN: When Lonnie went back to Oregon State, people were very upset about him leaving school early and they tried to say that he had been coerced into signing. The opposite was true. The kid wanted to sign, he had excellent representation and he was going to get what, for that time, was huge money. Lawsuits were filed, and if our owners had decided to pursue it, Lonnie would have had to play, because we had a deal. But they let it drop.

RON GRINKER: After Lonnie signed, Arthur Morse was very upset. Lawsuits were filed against the Spirits, the ABA, the Delpit brothers and myself saying that Lonnie was drunk or whatever and forced to sign the contract. Those suits were settled out of court. But the remarkable thing was that Lonnie went back to Oregon State and played his senior year. I was amazed that the NCAA let him play, but they did.

MORE MARVIN

When the Spirits' second season started, the hope was that Marvin Barnes would mature. Even Barnes laughed at that. This was a guy who said just out of college, "If I don't get paid a million dollars, I'll go to work in a factory." Later, he would say, "I'm a basketball player, not a monk. I play the women, I play the clothes, I play the cars, I play everything I can play. There's players and there's playees. The playees are the ones who get played on by the players. I'm a player." Barnes also said, "I'm 22 and a 22-year-old kid ain't no genius." And he said, "I don't want to act like an old man of 30 when I'm 22. But they keep telling me, 'You can't make any more mistakes, Marvin. Don't miss any more planes. Be on time, Marvin. Drink your milk, Marvin. Eat your vegetables, Marvin.' I'm tired of being 'the franchise,' and all those responsibilities." In his second season with the Spirits, Barnes was hit with a $1.5 million lawsuit by Larry Ketviritis, a teammate of Barnes's at Providence College. Ketviritis claimed that Barnes hit him with a tire iron. A trial was held and Barnes denied using a tire iron. The trial caused Barnes to miss plenty of practice time and some games under new coach Rod Thorn. Barnes was ordered to pay $10,000 in damages to Ketviritis.

BOB COSTAS: With Marvin Barnes, it never ended. Even when it seemed that he wasn't doing something, he was saying something that caught everybody's attention. We'd get back to the hotel lobby after losing a road game and you'd hear Marvin's voice: "Party hardy, gentlemen. Party hardy." Then he'd start dancing around the lobby, and, as you can imagine, this didn't sit especially well with the coaches.

In October of 1974, we were playing San Diego, and it was the same night that Ali beat Foreman in the great heavyweight fight in Zaire. With three minutes to go in the game, my old friend Roger Holstein was on the public-address system and he announced that Ali had won. The players on the court started dancing, and slapping five with each other. We were ahead when that announcement was made and whether it was coincidental or not—Bob MacKinnon thought not—we blew that game to San Diego, which was a very weak team.

Marvin had a great night, 48 points. After the game, I saw him in the dressing room and he started giving me his State of the Spirits speech.

He told me, "Bro, you know what's wrong with this team? We don't have any team play. We don't care about each other."

I thought, "Maybe Marvin is starting to see what the problem is—this team has no unity."

Then Marvin continued, "Let me give you an example. Tonight, I had 48 points with two minutes to go. Did anybody pass me the ball so I could get 50? Huh? No, they just kept the ball to themselves and I got stuck at 48. Stuff like that; that's what's wrong with these guys."

The mental world of Marvin Barnes was a bizarre place.

He used to like to talk to me if he saw me going through the dressing room. One day before a game he spotted me in the mirror. He loved to stand in front of a mirror naked, rubbing himself down with oil. I don't know if it was supposed to prevent dry skin or just make him sort of glisten under the arena lights. He was going on and on about something, I don't remember what. But after he was done with the oil, then he was trying to part his hair. Even in those days of Afros, Marvin never really had one. The players called him "BB," because his head was supposedly as small as a BB. Guys all over the league had nicknames because of their hair. Indiana's Billy Knight was TWA—Teeny-Weeny Afro—because he couldn't grow one.

So Marvin had finished applying his lotion, finished his hair, and now he was supposed to be ready to play. Instead, he stared in the mirror and said, "I've always had the bitches, man."

DON CHANEY: One day, Marvin came into the dressing room with a 9-millimeter gun. He started pointing it at people and guys were hitting the floor. We figured he had finally freaked out, but he was just messing around. He didn't have a magazine in the gun.

I don't know how many times I saw him stay out all night, get about an hour's sleep and then score 35 points. His pregame meal usually was hamburgers, hot dogs and Twinkies.

BOB COSTAS: Making airplanes just about killed Marvin. I'm trying to remember a morning flight where Marvin was on the plane. There were few—very, very few. In the Spirits' two years, they would take an 8 A.M. flight the morning of the game to Kentucky. There must have been about 15 of those flights in two years, and I know for a fact that Marvin never made one. Not a single one. It also was just a given that he'd miss the 11 A.M. shootaround in Kentucky. Once, he got the itinerary for that trip and noticed that the flight was exactly one hour. Because of the change of time zones, our return flight would leave Louisville at 8 A.M. and arrive in St. Louis at 7:59.

Marvin looked at that and announced, "I ain't goin' on no time machine. I ain't takin' no flight that takes me back in time."

STEVE JONES: The classic Marvin Barnes story came when we played a game in New York and the next day we had a game at Norfolk. We had an early-morning flight out of LaGuardia and, naturally, Marvin wasn't there. One of the Spirits owners, Donald Schupak, asked Freddie Lewis about Marvin and Freddie said, "Marvin said he was going to catch a later flight."

Schupak called Marvin and said, "Marvin, you get here now."

Marvin just mumbled something and hung up the phone and went back to sleep.

BOB MACKINNON: Next, I called Marvin and said, "Marvin, if you don't get to the game, I'm gonna have to suspend you. I'm not kidding this time." Marvin said, "Don't worry, man." Then he hung up.

RUDY MARTZKE: About three in the afternoon, I got a call from Mac-Kinnon. He said that Marvin had missed the 9 A.M., the 11 A.M. and the 1 P.M. flights to Norfolk. He hadn't heard from Marvin and figured there was no way Marvin would make the game.

BOB COSTAS: When Marvin finally got to LaGuardia, he found that all the flights to Norfolk were gone, and he was in real trouble. He started explaining his plight to some people and was told that the only way he could get to Norfolk was to charter a plane. So he cut a deal and got a private plane to take him to Norfolk. The plane landed and Marvin got a cab to rush him to the arena. About 10 minutes before the game, Bob MacKinnon was at the blackboard talking strategy, especially what they would do without Marvin that night. There were some double doors at the back of the dressing room and Marvin burst through the doors wearing a huge grin and proclaimed, "Boys, game time is on time."

STEVE JONES: Marvin was wearing a big, wide-brimmed hat and his floor-length, $10,000 mink coat. He had a bag of McDonald's hamburgers and fries with him. Then he proclaimed, "Have no fear, BB is here." He opened the coat, and underneath he was wearing his Spirits uniform.

BOB COSTAS: MacKinnon didn't start Marvin that night, but he put him in late in the first quarter and Marvin ended up with 43 points and 19 rebounds. The funny thing was that late in the first half, the pilot of the charter flight appeared by the Spirits' huddle. He wanted to be paid right now and he wasn't about to trust Marvin to send him a check through the mail. So Marvin sent the trainer into the dressing room to get his checkbook. During the next time-out, while everyone else was huddled around MacKinnon, Marvin was standing up with sweat pouring off his face and saying, "Hey, man, who should I make this check out to?" He wrote the pilot a check *(reportedly for anywhere from $520 to $800 to $1,200)* right in the middle of the game.

VAN VANCE: There are so many stories about Marvin Barnes that after a while, you don't know what to believe. One guy swore to me that Marvin had just bought his girlfriend a new Buick and he drove that car to the airport. As usual, he was late for a plane. He pulled right up to the airport, tossed the keys to a skycap and told him to park the car, he had a plane to catch. Supposedly the skycap took off with the keys and Marvin never saw him or the Buick again.

ROD THORN: When training camp *(in 1975)* began, Marvin was gone most of the time at his trial for allegedly hitting that kid with the tire iron. He'd show up for a few days, then be gone for a week. Practices went great; everyone was enthused about the team. Maurice Lucas looked especially good. Don Chaney and Freddie Lewis gave us a good backcourt. Gus Gerard was a talented kid. We played five exhibition games—four against NBA teams and one against an ABA team—and we won them all. Marvin came back toward the end of camp and even though he hadn't worked out much, he was playing great. But when the season began, we couldn't sustain anything. We'd win one game, lose two. That kind of thing.

Marvin was a problem. A big problem.

On the court, he could do everything but pass. I never saw any passing skills from him. I don't know if he couldn't pass or just wasn't interested in passing. But he didn't pass.

Otherwise, he could guard any power forward, most small forwards and most guys who were then playing center in the ABA. He could score inside, outside—the whole package.

But off the court, I have never seen a player who was so totally disruptive. Anything a player could do that was disruptive and negative to his teammates or in terms of his responsibility to the team, Marvin would do it. I told our trainer that if Marvin had one of those rare days where every light was green and everything happened just right and in spite of himself he got to the gym on time for practice, he'd wait outside for a few minutes just to make sure he was late.

His whole mind-set was, "I'm too good for practice. Only the other guys need practice. It's just a waste of my time."

I started to think that the only times I talked to Marvin were after he messed up. So I figured I'd talk to him after he did something right. We were playing in Utah and won a very close game. Marvin was magnificent. I asked him to stop by my hotel room after the game and he did, which was a good sign since that meant he remembered. We had what I thought was a great conversation. It went on for two and a half hours. We talked about the team, about how Marvin was perceived by his teammates, by the press and by the fans. We talked about the future and his responsibilities. Marvin promised me that he would change.

The next morning he missed the team flight. And he also disappeared for a day. We were going from Utah to Denver and had a travel day in between and he just disappeared for that day. When he came back, I screamed at him, I fined him, then I played him. I didn't know what else to do with the guy.

It all came to a head right after we had beaten Denver and Kentucky back-to-back, two very strong teams. Those were our best two games of the season and I started to think, "We're gonna finally turn this around."

We had from Monday until Thursday before we played another game. I gave the players Monday off. Tuesday we had practice and there was no Marvin. Wednesday, practice again, no Marvin. We didn't hear a word from him. People were calling his place; no one could find the guy. I decided that when he came back, I just wasn't going to play him. Marvin had already been fined over $12,000 and that certainly didn't change his behavior.

Thursday was the day of the game. About 4 P.M., I got a call and it was Marvin.

He said, "Coach, how's it going?"

I said, "Not very good."

He said, "Don't worry, I'll be at the game tonight. I'll take care of things."

I said, "Don't even bother because you're not going to play."

We were playing Kentucky that night and there was some kind of promotion. Instead of our usual 2,500 fans, we had over 10,000, our biggest crowd of the season up to that point. I was in the dressing room, giving my pregame talk, and Marvin wandered in, late as usual. I just pretended he wasn't there. I had prepared the team for the game without Marvin and I wasn't going to use him.

It was just my luck that this was a game where we got down by 15 points early and we just weren't playing well.

I was sticking to my guns, keeping Barnes on the bench. The fans were chanting, "We want Marvin, we want Marvin." I didn't play him and we got beat.

After the game, Harry Weltman was furious, and in retrospect I can understand why. We finally had a big crowd; if we could have won then maybe some of the people would have come back. Instead, we lost and it turned into a sideshow because Marvin didn't play. Harry saw it as an important night for the franchise. For me, it was a matter of principle. I had made my stand on the wrong night. But I'll tell you, I slept better that night than I did about any time that season.

LUCAS GOES, MARVIN STAYS

ROD THORN: That same night, Maurice Lucas and I talked for a long time after the game. Lucas was saying how he was sick of Marvin, that this garbage had been going on for two years and the guy was completely out of control. Maurice was a very professional, hardworking player and he was totally fed up with Marvin. He just couldn't stand the guy anymore.

Maurice Lucas was on time. He didn't complain. He was unselfish and he passed the ball. I loved the guy.

In his rookie season, Lucas was second on the Spirits in assists, only behind point guard Freddie Lewis. That is rare for a 6-foot-9 power forward.

GENE LITTLES: Maurice Lucas was the first player I had ever seen who was into serious stretching. Guys would be shooting around during warm-ups and he would be on the floor, turning his body into a pretzel. Now most guys do that. Back then, no one did and it was strange. He also was into a health-food diet—no red meat, just chicken and fish, when everyone else was eating steaks and hamburgers. Maurice was doing anything he could to get an edge.

BOB COSTAS: It was interesting to watch Lucas develop. Early in his rookie year, he was coming off the bench. One night the Spirits were playing Kentucky in Freedom Hall and Lucas was trading elbows with Artis Gilmore. At 7-foot-2 and 240 pounds, Gilmore just towered over Maurice. Lucas's only chance was to beat Gilmore to a spot on the floor and then try to hold off Artis. Despite his enormous size and strength, Gilmore was never known as a ferocious player and he seldom was in a fight. But all of a sudden, Artis just got sick of Lucas's bodying him and you could see that the big guy was really hot. Gilmore took a swipe at Lucas and missed. Lucas put up his fists, but he was backpedaling like any sane man would when confronted by Gilmore. It started at the foul line, and Lucas was backing up toward the corner. It was almost slow motion—Gilmore would take a step, then Lucas would take a step back. It was obvious that Lucas didn't want to fight and was trying to figure out where he could go. Finally, he was trapped in the corner; he had run out of court. He didn't know what else to do, so he planted his feet and threw this tremendous punch at Gilmore, and it caught Artis square on the jaw. It was a frightening sight. Artis hit the deck. Lucas was going crazy. Now he really did want a piece of Artis. Guys were holding Lucas back and Artis was still down. For whatever reason, from that point on Lucas developed into a helluva player.

BOB MACKINNON: After punching Gilmore, Lucas was ready to take on everyone else in the league and no one wanted any part of Maurice Lucas.

HARRY WELTMAN: When Lucas first came into the league, he didn't say anything about Marvin, because he wasn't even starting at first and had to work his way into the lineup. By the second season, some of the things Marvin did were rubbing Lucas the wrong way—rubbing him raw, in fact. As he proved his worth, Lucas earned a platform to speak out, and he did about Marvin. It was one of those things where it came down to a choice between Lucas or Marvin; one of them had to go. It was a tough decision, but Marvin was one of the most valuable talents in all of pro basketball. We thought a merger was coming and having Marvin might make us more attractive to the NBA, so we traded Lucas to Kentucky for Caldwell Jones, who was a legitimate, shot-blocking center. Jones was a good player and he enabled us to use Marvin exclusively at power forward, which was his natural position.

THORN GOES, MARVIN STAYS

BOB COSTAS: Rod Thorn was a young, intense guy who wanted desperately to be a great coach when he got the St. Louis job. He was a screamer on the bench. He almost was like some big bird prancing on the sidelines, his long arms flailing as he was jumping up and down to protest some call or admonish one of his own players. He kicked over chairs. He took off his sports coat and threw it down. His face would be crimson.

By the end, I think Rod was totally drained emotionally, and all the stuff with Marvin and the losing got to him. Harry Weltman was very disappointed that the team was well below .500 and I think he wanted an older, more experienced coach—a Bob MacKinnon type. So he fired Rod Thorn and replaced him with Joe Mullaney.

HARRY WELTMAN: Rod was thrown into a situation that was very difficult and very pressurized. We had a feeling that the merger was coming soon and we felt we had to win now to prove our legitimacy to get a better shot at getting into the NBA. Rod worked hard, but the team just wasn't winning and we had to make a change. Joe Mullaney was an experienced coach and I thought he might be more effective with the team. It was nothing personal about Rod, it was just a judgment I made at that time.

BOB COSTAS: Joe Mullaney came to town as a venerable, respected figure with wavy silver hair. He had been a successful college coach at Providence with the great Lenny Wilkens as his point guard. He had coached the Lakers in the NBA and had been with Kentucky, Utah and Memphis in the ABA. *(His pro winning percentage was .601.)* He seemed like a good choice to coach the team. If anyone could deal with the Spirits, a man of his experience should. As for Rod Thorn, the losing, Marvin and everything was just eating him up. He dreamed all his life of being a head coach and then he ended up with the Spirits and Marvin. That could be very disillusioning.

JOE MULLANEY: If I knew then what I know now, I never would have taken the Spirits job. I had five kids, I was out of work, and I heard from Harry Weltman. I needed a job, so I took it. I knew there was a problem with Barnes and I knew they wanted him to play no matter what. So against my better judgment, I played the guy.

Right after I was hired, we had a road game in Kentucky and I was at the airport. The whole team was there except for Marvin.

The trainer came up to me and said, "I just got a call from Marvin. He said he had a flat tire on the way to the airport and he can't make the flight."

I nodded.

The trainer said, "You know, Marvin must like you. He never called any of the other coaches to tell them he was going to be late."

I thought, "Well, that's just great. He's still not here."

As time went on, Marvin pulled the same things on me that he had done to the other coaches—being late, disappearing, not listening. There was nothing in all my years of coaching that would have prepared me for this guy.

I went to the front office and said that something had to be done about Marvin.

I said, "Let's really fine the guy."

They said, "We fine the guy all the time. He owes us $11,000 this year and $13,000 from last year."

I said, "So suspend him without pay."

They said, "We can't do that. He's liable to just pick up and leave town. Last year, he disappeared for a week and we couldn't find him until he showed up in a pool hall in Dayton."

They had one guy in the Spirits office keeping track of all the money they took from Marvin in fines, and they had another guy in a different room trying to straighten out Marvin's messed-up finances and figuring out his taxes. Marvin led the league in fines and accountants.

I said, "So how am I supposed to coach the guy? What kind of hammer can I hold over his head? You tell me how to motivate this guy. He's missing practices, flights, he gets to the gym late. He's disrupting the whole team."

They told me just to do the best I could, and the implication was no matter what, play Marvin Barnes. They thought that the future of the franchise rested on the shoulders of Marvin Barnes. To me, that was a frightening thought. They believed that Marvin made them more attractive to the NBA. I don't think they had a realistic view of the situation.

And I'll tell you something else—Marvin was good, but he was not the greatest player who ever lived, as some people made him out to be.

BOB COSTAS: Marvin and those guys just drove Joe Mullaney nuts. There was one game—and this is almost impossible to believe, because he has become one of the great centers in NBA history—where Moses Malone was playing center and doing things like throwing the ball behind his back and dribbling through his legs. Moses made 13 turnovers that night. It was insane.

Mullaney sat on the bench, and he reminded me of Brian Keith on the old "Family Affair" television show. When one of his kids would do something stupid, Keith would run his hand across his face and sort of shove his nose up into his forehead because he didn't know what else to do. Mullaney would do that. He'd bury his face in his hand. The players all sat a couple of chairs away from him—it was almost like he had to endure this alone. One night, I was sitting near the bench and Marvin was doing something crazy and Mullaney was saying, "He's killing me, he's killing me," over and over.

THE FINAL DAYS

Right before the Utah Stars folded, there was talk of combining the Utah and St. Louis franchises, making one super team out of two that had pretty decent talent. Then the super team would move to Salt Lake City. That never happened, but the Stars sold their best players—Ron Boone,

*Randy Denton, Steve Green and Moses Malone—to the Spirits in early
December. Among the players waived by the Spirits to make room on
the roster for the new acquisitions was Don Adams, who averaged 13
points and 5.8 rebounds in 20 games. A few days after the fire sale with
Utah was conducted, the Spirits made the Maurice Lucas–Caldwell
Jones deal with Kentucky. That was supposed to give St. Louis a starting front line of Marvin Barnes and Moses Malone at the forwards
with Jones at center. But Malone was recovering from a broken foot
and Gus Gerard started more games than Malone did at forward. With
the Spirits, Malone averaged 15.2 points and 9.5 rebounds in 27 minutes a night. Boone averaged 21 points as he teamed with Freddie
Lewis in the backcourt. Nothing mattered in the standings. The Spirits
were 10–10 before the acquisitions and 25–39 after. They were 20–27
under Rod Thorn and 15–22 under Joe Mullaney—seven games under
.500 for each coach.*

BOB COSTAS: It became pretty sad towards the end of the second year.
There was this dream of building a great franchise with all this young
talent, and what happened was that the team was losing, Marvin was
running wild, and nobody was coming to the games. There was a game
against San Antonio where we had an announced crowd of 808 in an
18,000-seat arena. Terry Stembridge and I started counting the crowd.
We came up with a little over 500.

I said to one of the Spirits' PR men, "It's bad enough that we announced 808 fans, but I don't think there's even 500."

He said, "Listen, little wise-ass, why don't you mind your own business? Did it ever occur to you that some of the people could be out buying
a hot dog or in the rest rooms?"

I said, "Let's consider the premise of what you're saying. There's 500
in the stands and 300 fans missing. That would be the same as saying
that with 8,000 in the stands, there are 3,000 in the rest rooms or at the
concessions stands at any given moment. It's the same percentage."

He said, "You're just trying to be a wise-ass." Then he stormed away.

In another game against the Spurs, the final score was 102–100 and
George Gervin had 43 points in front of 1,800. We averaged about 3,000
fans.

It was against this bleak backdrop that there were some crazy promotions.

We had Toys for Tots Night, which was sponsored by Burger Chef.
They had two mascots—Burger Chef and Jeff. Burger Chef was this guy
in a hamburger costume and Jeff was his friend, a little kid.

During halftime, they had a mini-trampoline and were jumping around. It really wasn't very entertaining. Then Burger Chef put Jeff on his shoulder. Jeff was really this little man, not a kid. They went up to the rim and Jeff started doing chin-ups on the rim. Then the hamburger head put Jeff down, got on the trampoline, and he was doing chin-ups on the rim. Burger Chef bent the rim and Harry Weltman came running out of his seat to try and get this walking piece of meat to stop destroying the rim. The game was held up for 20 minutes while they fixed up the damage done by the hamburger head.

As the year went on, it just got worse.

During the last few weeks of the season, people in the office were answering the phones by saying, "Spirits of Utah," because it seemed that the team would move there for the next season.

Every night, we had a "Lucky Number Shootout," where some fan got a chance to take a shot from halfcourt when his program number was drawn out of a hat. The prize was a trip around the world, and in two years no one had even come close. It was sponsored by the travel agency that booked the Spirits' flights.

Since it was the second-to-last home game of the year, the contest was rigged. The public-address announcer was Ken Bland and he had a friend named David Elkin. The Spirits were playing Virginia, a truly horrible team, and there was no one at the game. Bland fixed the contest so that his friend could have his moment on the court, take a shot and miss by 20 feet. Bland announced that "Mr. David Elkin" would take the shot. It was a very elaborate introduction and Bland was looking at me, giving me the high sign, and we were both laughing. Elkin went to midcourt and bowed in two different directions. He took the ball, dribbled it once and heaved it up there with one hand—swish.

So here was a team that was getting ready to board up its windows, and now they had to make sure that they and their travel agency paid for David Elkin's trip, knowing that after two days the franchise probably would never play another game in St. Louis.

HARRY WELTMAN: I thought we did very well in the face of overwhelming odds. We got no help from the team from Carolina. We were like an expansion team and we pulled together a lot of talent very quickly. You take the guys who played for us in the two years and you'll find that about 11 guys were playing in the NBA in 1976–77. Nine were starting if you count Lonnie Shelton, who was under contract. We had the makings of a great team, especially when you have frontcourt players such as Barnes, Jones, Malone, Gus Gerard and M. L. Carr.

Those Spirits who played in the NBA in 1976–77 were Maurice Lucas (Portland), Ron Boone (Kansas City), Marvin Barnes (Detroit), Cald-

well Jones (Philadelphia), Lonnie Shelton (New York), Steve Green (Indiana), Gus Gerard (Denver), Don Adams (Buffalo), Don Chaney (L.A. Lakers), M. L. Carr (Detroit) and Freddie Lewis (Indiana).

ROD THORN: You look at the character of the people and that told the story of the Spirits after the merger. Malone, Lucas, Chaney, M. L. Carr—these were good people and hard workers and they went on to good careers. Then you take Barnes. I have never seen a player lose so much talent so fast. He had two good years in the ABA, then he was finished. In the NBA, he was just a shell of himself, and he hadn't turned 25. All the late nights, all the missed flights, all the lack of discipline caught up to him all at once and he just couldn't play anymore. It was sad to see him just waste that talent.

After averaging 24 points and 13 rebounds in his two ABA seasons, Barnes went to Detroit for $500,000 in the dispersal draft after the merger. He played for five different NBA teams in four seasons, averaging 9.2 points and shooting 44 percent. He was out of the NBA by his 29th birthday.

BOB COSTAS: In 1979, the Kansas City Kings played three games in St. Louis, and one of them was against Boston, which was Marvin's latest stop. I was waiting at the Chase Park Hotel in the lobby with my tape recorder to get some interviews. Marvin came in, saw me and said, "Bro, Bro, Bro . . . how are you?"

I said I was fine and asked him for an interview.

He said, "Give me 15 minutes to go up to my room and then we'll do it."

Fifteen minutes went by; no Marvin. I called his room and he said he would be right down. Another 20 minutes passed; still no Marvin. I called him again and he said he would be right down. That went on a few more times, then Marvin said, "Bro, you got a car?"

I said, "Of course I have a car, I live here."

Marvin said, "I want to see some dudes on Kings Highway, can you take me there?"

I said I would if I could put the tape recorder on the front seat and do an interview. He said he would be right down.

Another 15 minutes went by; still no Marvin. I'd been messing around for about 90 minutes trying to get him. I called Marvin again and he said, "Listen, Bro, why don't you go see those dudes without me?"

I said, "Marvin, I don't want to go see those guys, whoever they are. I don't even know those guys."

Marvin said, "Oh . . . yeah."

Then I said, "Listen, why don't I go to the station and I'll just call you and we'll do the interview on the phone."

Marvin said that was fine with him.

I called Marvin. He answered and seemed totally out of it. He said a few words, then dropped the phone and just tailed off. Amazingly, three hours later he played in the game, was red-hot, and scored 29 points.

Ten years later, I spoke to him as he was finishing off a prison term in San Diego. He said he was going to turn his life around, and sounded sincere. I hope he can; strange as it sounds, in spite of everything, he was really a very likeable guy.

Escape Claws

The Memphis Sounds took up residence in Baltimore for the start of the 1975–76 season. The ABA was relieved to find anyone willing to take over the nearly comatose franchise. The Baltimore group claimed it was worth $2.25 million; there would be $1.25 million for operating funds and the remaining $1 million would be paid to the league as a purchase price for the team. But Baltimore never played a regular-season game, folding on October 20, five days before the scheduled opener, after selling only 300 season tickets and going deeply in debt.

MIKE GOLDBERG: Baltimore was trouble right from the start. The first nickname they picked was ridiculous—the Hustlers. We in the league office liked being in the forefront of things, but the connotations of "Hustler" were a bit much, and we encouraged them to find another name. They came up with the Claws, which was fine with us. But when they didn't have money to pay the bills, that was a much bigger problem than a nickname. They were in business for 40 days, at the end of which they forfeited their letter of credit and were never heard from again.

JOE MULLANEY: When the Memphis team was sold to Baltimore, I was told that I was sold with the team. I met the new owners and told them exactly what they had bought. I said, "This isn't a good team, nor does it have any real chance of becoming good. It isn't a young team that will improve with experience. It isn't an old team that can rely on a winning tradition. It isn't anything at all. Mel Daniels is your biggest-name player, and I don't know if he has anything left at his age. No matter how you look at it, this is a bad situation."

The owners asked me to leave the room. Ten minutes later, they brought me back in and said, "We want you to coach the team." That wasn't exactly bighearted on their part, since I had a year left on my contract and they were going to have to pay me regardless of what I did.

Then the owners started telling me the kind of team they wanted. They said, "We want a team that hustles, that dives for loose balls. That's why we called the team the Hustlers. We want to get players like the kind Washington has, that Mike Riordan kid."

I said, "I coached Riordan at Providence College. He was great and he really hustled, just like you said. But the guys you have, they don't play like that. Guys like Stew Johnson, they never have played defense in their lives and they're not about to start now."

I didn't think they had any idea what I was talking about, and they certainly had no idea what they were doing. About a week before training camp, I found out that none of the players had received contracts. I told the owners, "Listen, according to league rules, these guys have to be under contract so they can practice."

The owners said, "Don't worry about it, Coach, we'll take care of it."

When the players showed up, a lot of them didn't have signed contracts. Mel Daniels sort of emerged as the team spokesman and he told me, "Coach, what should we do? The agents are telling the guys not to practice unless they have contracts."

I said, "Mel, I have no control over that. Do what you think is right."

Before every practice, the players would get together and vote if they should work out that day. Usually, they practiced. Mel told me, "Coach, we figured if we don't practice, we may not have any kind of team at all."

Meanwhile, I was begging the owners to sign the players, but they wouldn't do it. Then the players began telling me that they were going to get thrown out of their hotel rooms because the team wasn't paying the bills. The players also weren't getting their meal money every day.

DAN ISSEL: To this day, people don't know I was a member of the Baltimore Claws—for about five minutes. After Kentucky won the 1975 championship, I got a call from my attorney, who said he had talked to John Y. Brown, and John Y. had said that even though the team won the title, it lost money. I went to see John Y. and he said that he either was going to sell Artis or myself and it would probably be me because he thought that Artis would have a longer career than I would. Then the next day I talked to John Y. and he said not to worry, I wasn't going anywhere.

It went back and forth like that for a while until one day I was at Louisville Downs, the harness track, and I was paged. Ellie Brown was on the phone and she said that I had been sold to Baltimore.

I talked to the Baltimore owners and they kept telling me, "You'll love it. You're going to be the next Johnny Unitas in this town."

I really didn't care about being the next Johnny Unitas, but they thought this was a great selling point. The coach was Joe Mullaney and I had played for him in Kentucky and liked him a lot. Look, I wanted to play, so I went to Baltimore and hoped for the best.

This was the only team where, instead of having double practice sessions in training camp, we had a morning workout and then went to Bowie racetrack in the afternoon. Mullaney loved the horses and so did some of the guys on the team, so we spent a lot of time at the track. Hey, we all knew that the owners didn't have a clue and that the team wouldn't last. Guys weren't getting paid. You don't have to be a genius to know that there's trouble when your first paycheck doesn't show up.

JOE MULLANEY: Word was that John Y. had determined that if he could get an extra $500,000, then the Colonels would make a profit for the season. So he put Issel on the market for $500,000. I may not agree with that thinking, but I could see his point of view. But why he picked Baltimore as the place to sell Issel . . . I mean, these owners couldn't even pay the hotel bill, and he thought he would get $500,000 out of them?

A few days after the trade, I got a call from John Y. wanting to know what was going on in Baltimore. The way John Y. was talking, it was obvious that he hadn't gotten his money yet. So I told him what a mess it was and a few days later they worked out another deal where Issel went to Denver and we got Dave Robisch.

DAN ISSEL: I was in Baltimore about 10 days and John Y. was taking a lot of heat in the Kentucky newspapers for trading me. One day he showed up at my hotel and said, "I'm gonna get you outta here. You're going to Denver, a good team with a lot of money. But in exchange for that, you have to say something nice about me to the Louisville newspapers."

I was willing to do about anything to get out of Baltimore, so I agreed. I told the papers that basketball was a business and what John Y. did was purely a business decision, nothing personal. I said anything I could think of, just so I could get away from Baltimore.

The guy I felt sorry for was Dave Robisch. The record book says I was traded for Dave Robisch and cash, which is just a smoke screen. The money went from Denver to Kentucky and they shipped poor Robisch to Baltimore just to make the trade look good.

DAVE ROBISCH: I loved Denver, and in 1974–75 we were 65–19, the best record in the ABA. But we lost to Indiana in the semifinals of the playoffs. We were in training camp and had signed Marvin Webster and David Thompson. The team looked great and I was excited, but 10 days before the regular season I was traded to Baltimore, of all places. Denver wanted Issel and I understood that, but I didn't know why I had to be the guy they gave up for Dan. Baltimore was going under. All Denver had to do was sit tight and then they could have gotten Issel without giving up a player.

I was very unhappy about the trade and I refused to report until my contract was renegotiated. I sat out until Baltimore reworked my contract and I tried to sit out as long as I could, because I heard that Baltimore was a disaster and they'd never make the season. Finally, I signed. I was there for about 10 days, then the team folded.

JOE MULLANEY: One of the owners' brainstorms was to sign Skip Wise out of Clemson after his sophomore year. He was the ACC Rookie of the Year and I thought that signing a kid that young would create quite a stir, but not as much as I imagined. I guess the Clemson people knew that Wise was on drugs already.

(Wise reportedly signed a five-year, $1 million deal. Two of the years were guaranteed, but much of the money was deferred.)

Wise was supposed to be a great talent, but in camp he couldn't do anything—he was that deep into the stuff.

The owners would ask me, "What do you think of Wise?"

I'd say, "He doesn't look very good. I know he can't start for us and I'm not sure he can play at all."

Dave Robisch came up to me and said, "Are the owners going to make you play Wise? They can't do that. This kid is killing us."

Wise was in such bad shape that one day I saw him sitting off to the side of the practice court. He was shivering. I asked him if he was all right and he said, "No, man, I'm cold. I just feel so cold."

Finally, I just couldn't take it anymore. The guys weren't getting paid. Dan Issel was there and gone. My star rookie was on drugs. I just called the league office and told them exactly what was going on. Then *(Commissioner)* Dave DeBusschere came in, checked out the situation and folded it.

I never was paid for the last year of my contract because my coaching contract was with the team, not the league, and the league didn't honor it. I had moved to Baltimore, then I had to pack up and leave. One day I got a bill from United Van Lines for $4,200 for my move from Memphis to Baltimore. The owners had given me a check to cover that bill, but the movers said that the check bounced and since the team was no longer in business I was liable for that bill.

So Baltimore was a place where I didn't get to coach, I didn't get paid, and I got stuck for a $4,200 moving bill.

MEL DANIELS: When the team folded, the players showed up at the Claws office. We were angry. They owed us money and we weren't going to get it. There was a guy in the office and he said, "Look, we can't pay you but you can take anything you want out of here." Players went in there and were walking out with typewriters, telephones, anything they could get their hands on. And that was how my ABA career ended. I had been with the ABA from Day One and had great memories, but this was an awful way to go out.

DAVE ROBISCH: When Baltimore folded, a dispersal draft was held for the players and I was taken by San Diego, where Bill Musselman had just been named coach. I went to San Diego and played 11 games. We weren't drawing well, but I figured the team would make the season. I guess I just didn't think I could be with two teams that folded in one year.

I picked out a condominium and moved my family out there. This is the honest truth: the day the moving van arrived with our stuff, the Sails announced that they had folded. I told the guys just to keep the stuff on the truck and I'd tell them where to take it in a few days. There was another dispersal draft, and this time I went to Indiana. I called the movers and sent them to Indianapolis.

DAN ISSEL: My attorney makes collages of things—pictures, matchbooks, things like that. He was doing one on my career and he wanted something from the Baltimore Claws. He had no luck as he searched, so he wrote someone from the *Baltimore Sun*. The guy wrote back saying, "As far as we can find out, there were no pictures of Dan in a Baltimore uniform. All they wore were Baltimore Claws T-shirts. I wish you the best of luck, but I don't know what to tell you, because trying to find someone associated with the Baltimore Claws is like trying to find last night's thunderstorm."

Denver: A Rock in the ABA

Denver and Indiana were the only two ABA teams to play virtually all their home games in the same city during the nine years of the ABA. Byron Beck played all nine ABA seasons with Denver. When GM Carl Scheer and Coach Larry Brown left Carolina and moved to Denver in 1974, the name of the team was changed from the Rockets to the Nuggets, which had been the name of a Denver team in the NBA in 1949–50. Those Denver Nuggets were 11–51. Scheer liked the Nuggets nickname, mostly because it was different from the Denver Rockets; the modern NBA had the Houston Rockets and Scheer was determined to get the Denver franchise into the NBA, so the last thing he wanted was for something as trivial as a nickname to become a problem. In its first seven seasons, Denver had four winning records but could never get past the first round of the playoffs. Under Scheer and Brown in 1974–75, the Nuggets went 65–19 and were led by guard Mack Calvin, who made first-team all-ABA as he topped the league in assists (7.7 per game) and averaged 19.5 points. The Nuggets lost in the Western Conference finals. Before the 1975–76 season, Scheer purchased Dan Issel, traded Calvin to Virginia for the draft rights to David Thompson, and then outbid the NBA's Atlanta Hawks for Thompson. Scheer also signed Marvin Webster, another NBA first-round draft pick. The Nuggets went 60–24 and lost to New York in the ABA finals. In their first NBA season, the Nuggets went 50–32 and won the Midwest Division.

DAVE ROBISCH: Denver has always been a good basketball town. In the early years they had Spencer Haywood, and they won the division title in 1970. They were selling out and everything was great, but Spencer jumped to the NBA and the franchise went down. I signed with Denver out of the University of Kansas in 1971.

Alex Hannum was coaching and trying to pick up the pieces of what was once a pretty good franchise. They were disorganized and Alex brought some stability in his three years there, but the best we could do was 47–37 in 1972–73. Alex is a very hard-line guy. By the time he was through coaching in Denver *(in 1973–74),* I think he knew that it was time for him to get out. He wasn't dealing with the same kind of players he had in the past, and Alex isn't the kind of guy to let things pass, to roll with the punches. He was an old-school coach and that era was gone.

ALEX HANNUM: Toward the end in Denver, I had trouble communicating with some guys. Also, that was when drugs were starting to become a factor. I remember hearing guys say that cocaine was the greatest thing, if you could just afford it. It was a very discouraging situation and I was glad to get out in 1974.

STEVE JONES: Alex Hannum's last season in Denver was dismal. Alex and his wife had run the entire front office, but the owners weren't happy with that situation. Alex said he had to have complete control or he was out. Well, they told him that he was out. The owners *(Bud Fischer and Frank Goldberg)* called me in and asked who I thought would be a good coach. Since I had been in the ABA from the beginning, they knew that I had played for a lot of different people and knew just about everyone in the league. I had just been traded from Carolina to Denver and I told them that the guy who could turn their team around was Larry Brown.

The owners started talking to Carl Scheer, who was GM in Carolina. It became apparent that Carl and Larry Brown were going somewhere as a package deal, much like Doug Moe was going to be an assistant coach wherever Larry landed. Since the owners didn't want another Hannum situation where the coach was the GM, they were glad to talk to Scheer about the job. I think they were more interested in Larry than Scheer, but they were willing to take Carl in order to get Larry.

CARL SCHEER: We inherited some decent players in Dave Robisch, Byron Beck, Mike Green and Ralph Simpson. But the guy who made us go was Mack Calvin, who had played for us in Carolina. We brought him in and he set the tone for Larry's running-and-pressing style. We also signed Bobby Jones out of the University of North Carolina. Houston also drafted Jones, but they didn't pursue Bobby nearly as hard as we did.

DAVE ROBISCH: Bringing in Carl Scheer and Larry Brown probably saved the Denver franchise and was the reason it was strong enough to get into the NBA two years later. When they came to town, the Broncos owned the city and there was serious apathy about the basketball team. There were absolutely no expectations about the team, because most people paid no attention to it. We lost our first game *(117–99 at Kentucky)* and those who did notice us just figured it was the same old thing. But then we won our next nine in a row, people started packing the arena and we became the hottest ticket in town. It was one of the fastest turnarounds in pro basketball history, from 37–47 to 65–19 in one year.

CARL SCHEER: I wanted to change the image of the team, so we held a contest for a new nickname. It made no sense for the team to still be named after Bill Ringsby's trucking company, because Ringsby was long gone. We picked "Nuggets" as the winner and said we are now the Denver Nuggets. It just sounded good. We played in an old downtown arena with 6,900 seats. It was a depressing building that was more of an auditorium than anything else. They had broken ground on McNichols Arena, but we had to play in the Denver Auditorium for a year.

I wanted to create all the excitement I could. We had promotions for everything; we gave away cars, fur coats, basketballs, T-shirts. But the big thing that happened was that Larry made us a great team immediately. You win nine games in a row and you get people's attention; soon we had a string of 25 consecutive sellouts going.

LARRY BROWN: Doug and I did the same things we had done in Carolina. We got the players believing in themselves and got them playing the kind of up-tempo basketball that's a lot of fun. It all just snowballed and we started getting over 7,000 fans in that small building every night, and they were so loud. We became more than a basketball team; we were a happening.

DAVE ROBISCH: Larry and Doug Moe worked together so well. In practice, Larry was the teacher. Doug would slap you on the back or maybe kick you in the butt to get you to play harder. They came at you from different directions, Doug more emotional, Larry more cerebral. In the huddle, Larry did the talking to the entire team. Doug might say something to one guy as the time-out ended and you were about to step onto the floor.

Our guards were so strong. Mack Calvin was the classic small guard who pushed the ball up the floor. He had a good outside shot and a great first step on his drive to the basket. He led the league in foul shooting and played so hard. Fatty Taylor was one of the best defensive guards in the league. Ralph Simpson was a scorer. That was as good a guard combination as you could find in the NBA.

On the front line was Byron Beck, who was a legend because he went to the University of Denver and then spent his entire career with the Nuggets, going back to their first game in the ABA. He was 6-foot-9, 240 pounds, a blue-collar guy under the boards with a great hook shot. He just played so hard, fought for every rebound; that was what impressed me. Byron's attitude carried over to the whole team. We were a bunch of good guys and hard workers and Larry Brown got the most out of us.

CARL SCHEER: Beck was one of those guys who was good for 12 points and 10 rebounds every night. He was so hard-nosed on the court, but off the court his wife ran the show. I mean, she negotiated his contracts. She was a tough lady. I told Byron that I would have rather dealt with some agents than his wife.

With our strong backcourt and with such solid guys as Beck, Robisch, Mike Green and Bobby Jones up front, we had a great first season. We were 65–19, but lost to Indiana in the Western Conference finals.

After that season, I wanted to do something dramatic to make us viable for the NBA. When I first came to Denver, the football team owned the city. The few people who still paid attention to the ABA were bitter because Spencer Haywood had jumped leagues. Denver is a new city with people from all over the country, many of whom came from NBA towns. They thought the ABA was minor league.

We were determined to sign David Thompson.

○   ○   ○

David Thompson spent only one season in the ABA, and it may have been his best and most enjoyable season as a pro. It was before his knee problems and his drug problems led to many other problems. He was still "The Skywalker," a 6-foot-4 guard out of North Carolina State with a 42-inch vertical leap. He had passed up multimillion-dollar offers to turn pro after his sophomore and junior years because his mother wanted him to graduate from N.C. State. He would make unannounced appearances at rest homes and orphanages. He was one of 11 children of a Shelby, North Carolina, truck driver, who spent much of his youth helping out in the Baptist church where his father was a deacon. After he signed with Denver, the Nuggets' season ticket base jumped from 2,200 to 6,000. With a team led by Thompson and including such stars as Dan Issel, Bobby Jones, Marvin Webster and the omnipresent Byron Beck, the Nuggets were 60–24. They moved into 17,000-seat McNichols Arena and averaged 13,000 fans, fourth best in all of pro basketball and far more than anyone else in the ABA. Thompson brought the team national attention, all of it positive. As Larry Brown said not long after Thompson signed with the Nuggets, "He is as great a person as he is a player." As a rookie with the Nuggets, he averaged 26 points and led Denver to the ABA finals against New York. But Thompson was using cocaine daily by 1978. In 1983, he got into a scuffle at Studio 54, fell down a flight of stairs and ripped up the ligaments in his left knee. By then, he was 29 and pretty much finished as a pro. Thompson later did stints in drug rehabilitation centers. He spent time in a Seattle jail in 1987 after being charged with simple assault.

CARL SCHEER: David had led N.C. State to a national title and seemed like the second coming of Julius Erving—he was that good and that exciting. The team that signed David Thompson was going to be part of the merger, or at least that was my feeling.

Virginia had the draft rights to Thompson, but our drafts were hilarious. We said we could sign Thompson, so Virginia said, "Great, go ahead and do it."

Since Larry Brown and I had worked for the Cougars and we both had gone to college in North Carolina, we had a lot of contacts in the state. We had watched David grow up as a basketball player. We knew his high school and college coaches. We knew David's father quite well. We spent a lot of time in his hometown of Shelby, trying to figure out what made David tick, what he wanted. We recruited him like a college would a high school kid. We knew that 5-foot-7 guard Monte Towe was his best friend on the N.C. State team, so we signed Towe in Denver. Monte was a nice little player, sort of a poor man's Muggsy Bogues. Monte was a nice kid, worked hard in practice and all that. But the real point of his being there was to get David.

We brought David to one of our playoff games in Denver, had a big party for him. In the arena was a huge sign that read, "Welcome David Thompson." David was introduced to the crowd and received a standing ovation from our packed house. Atlanta had his draft rights in the NBA. David went to see the Hawks play and there were about 3,000 people at the Omni. We came off as far more major league than the Hawks did, so we knew we had a real shot at David.

DAVID THOMPSON: I really could have played for any ABA team that I wanted. That league would just ask you, "Where do you want to play?" Denver had a great franchise. I knew Carl Scheer and Larry Brown, so they were a natural for me. Atlanta wasn't in good shape back then. Really, it was an easy choice. It didn't matter that Denver was in the ABA, because the Nuggets were very big league.

CARL SCHEER: We cut a deal to pay David $450,000 a year for three years, which made him the highest-paid player in the ABA. The league chipped in and helped us pay some of the salary, although I don't recall how much. It wasn't as much as 50 percent or anything like that.

Once we signed Thompson, then we made a deal with Virginia for his rights. It was almost after the fact. They wanted something, so we gave them Mack Calvin, Mike Green and Jan van Breda Kolff for the rights to Thompson and George Irvine.

GEORGE IRVINE: Going from Virginia to Denver was going from the outhouse to the White House of the ABA. While just about every other ABA team was in turmoil, Denver was an oasis. The fans were great, the team was great, we had great coaching, great ownership. Teams in Baltimore, Utah and San Diego would fold, but none of that mattered to us because we knew that we were so good that the NBA would have to take us when the time for a merger came.

At that time, David Thompson was an unbelievable player. His leaping ability was well known, but the guy also was a great jump shooter and he could defend extremely well. Before David ran into his problems, he was the closest thing to Michael Jordan basketball had ever seen. When you have an exciting talent like that on your team, you know that your franchise is in great shape.

CARL SCHEER: It's hard to believe now, but the big debate was, who would become a better player down the line, Julius Erving or David Thompson? Al Bianchi, who had coached Julius when he came into the league, said that Thompson was the same kind of talent. I thought David had a chance to be better than Julius because he had the same athleticism and leaping ability, but he was a better shooter.

DAN ISSEL: Before he ran into his problems, David Thompson was as good as anyone I ever played with. He wasn't 7-foot-2 like Gilmore and he didn't have the huge hands to make a basketball look like a softball as Julius did, but he was a pure basketball player and could outleap anyone—including Julius Erving.

LENNY WILKENS: I coached David when he was in Seattle (in 1982–83) and by then he was having his drug problems and he had hurt his knee. But I saw him play a lot for Denver. I'll tell you, a young David Thompson wouldn't have to take a backseat to anyone. He could have been a Michael Jordan before Michael. He was that great, that exciting. But David's inherent problem was that he always was a follower.

GEORGE IRVINE: There weren't any early signs that David would have drug problems. He was friendly with everyone. He liked to drink a lot of beer, but a lot of guys drink beer and you don't think they'll use cocaine. At that time, you have to remember that cocaine was just coming out. It wasn't like today where there are all these warnings about what cocaine can do to you. It was something new, supposedly something special. David had no idea what he was getting into.

CARL SCHEER: For all of David's talent on the court, he had very little sense of self-worth away from basketball. He would surround himself with these low-life people who easily influenced him. Denver was emerging as a real yuppie, fast-lane city. There were parties, and the drug culture was very strong. I know that now. Back then, I was ignorant about drugs. I didn't even know the signs of what to look for when a guy has a problem. People came to me and told me that David had a problem. For a while, I didn't want to believe it. I guess I was naive. David was producing on the court, he was gracious to the fans and very personable when I was around him. It wasn't until three or four years after the ABA folded that his behavior became erratic. By then, people tried to help him, but I guess he was in it too deep. In a sense, David is one of those tragic "what could have been" stories. He made our franchise. He helped get us into the NBA and gave us a team that was an immediate factor in the NBA, yet he destroyed himself.

DAVID THOMPSON: I had a chance to be the greatest basketball player ever and I blew it because of drugs. It's that simple. It started at the end of my rookie season. After the exhibition games, the regular season and the playoffs, we had played almost 100 games. One day I was very tired and I started telling a teammate about that. He said, "Hey, I've got something that will help you." Then he started putting some lines of cocaine on the table. It gave me a lift, but it later ruined my life. In 1978, I signed a five-year, $4 million contract that made me the highest-paid player in basketball history, and I could have made a lot more money, but I messed up everything because of drugs. It's no one's fault. I did it to myself, because I never thought I'd get hooked. I thought I was a special basketball player, so drugs couldn't touch me.

CARL SCHEER: After I became GM of the Charlotte Hornets, I hired David to speak at basketball clinics and to kids' groups about drugs. We wanted to give him a last chance to put his life together. For all the trouble and all the grief he caused me, I always liked David as a person. With the Hornets, he is a very effective speaker and very good with kids. But he also is a recovering cocaine addict, and we know that. We know there are risks. Every day is a struggle for him. It really is one of those situations where he has to take his life one day at a time.

Ninth-Year Notebook: 1975–76

The final ABA season began with the stunning news that the New York
Nets and Denver Nuggets had applied for membership to the NBA on
their own, which upset the rest of the league. Losing Denver and New
York would have meant the end of the league, as those were two of the
ABA's most successful franchises. But the NBA turned down the appli-
cation, so the ABA was set to start the year with 10 teams. However,
the Baltimore Claws never made it out of training camp, making the
ABA a nine-team league. Eleven games into the season, the San Diego
Sails and new coach Bill Musselman were history. Sixteen games into the
season, Utah went under and four of the Stars' best players were sold to
St. Louis—Moses Malone, Ron Boone, Steve Green and Randy Denton.
That left the ABA with seven teams, one of which was Virginia. The
Squires were destined to stagger through the season on the verge of
bankruptcy. They had six coaches—Al Bianchi, Mack Calvin, Willie
Wise, Jack Ankerson, Zelmo Beaty and Bill Musselman—but only 15
victories compared to 68 losses . . . Good news was that Denver signed
two college stars in David Thompson and Marvin Webster. Denver also
obtained Dan Issel from Kentucky by way of the defunct Baltimore
Claws . . . Webster missed most of the season because of a liver ailment
. . . The financially struggling Indiana Pacers lost George McGinnis to
Philadelphia of the NBA . . . For the first eight years of the league, the
ABA used the 30-second shot clock. For the ninth season, in preparation
for a possible merger, the ABA went to the 24-second clock, which is
what the NBA uses . . . John Y. Brown said that Kentucky had lost $3
million over the last five seasons . . . The biggest trade of the year came
when St. Louis shipped Maurice Lucas to Kentucky for Caldwell Jones.
Lucas was traded because he had a personality conflict with Spirits star
Marvin Barnes, who missed games and racked up fines at a rate that
would have been a record in any league. (Before leaving for the NBA,
McGinnis had declared that the Spirits "lead the world in crazies.")
. . . Spirits coach Rod Thorn was fired at midseason and replaced with
Joe Mullaney, whose last stop had been the Baltimore Claws. Thorn
returned to New York and to his old job as an assistant under Nets coach
Kevin Loughery . . . Part of the reason the San Antonio Spurs made a
profit was that they paid only $500-a-night rent on their arena, the lowest
in either league . . . Another big trade had San Antonio sending Swen
Nater to New York for Billy Paultz, Larry Kenon and Mike Gale

... The ABA had its All-Star Game in Denver, where the Nuggets faced All-Stars from the remaining six teams. The game was highlighted by the world's first Slam Dunk Contest, won by Julius Erving. Denver beat the All-Stars 144–138 before 17,798 fans. Thompson was the MVP with 29 points, 12 in the fourth period. Erving had 23 points. Billy Knight had 20 points and a game-high 10 rebounds ... With only seven teams, the ABA junked its two-division setup and went to one league with seven teams. Five teams made the playoffs. Indiana and Kentucky played in the first round and the Colonels prevailed. In the semifinals, New York beat San Antonio and Denver beat Kentucky. That set up a New York–Denver finals, which opened in Denver before 19,034 fans. Erving had 45 points, including a jumper at the buzzer to give the Nets a 120–118 victory. In Game 2, Erving scored 48, but Denver won, 127–121, before 19,017 fans. The series continued back and forth before the Nets won the seventh game, 112–106, outscoring Denver 34–14 in the fourth quarter. Erving, the playoff MVP, had 31 points and 19 rebounds in the final game. David Thompson had 42 points for the losers ... Erving was the ABA's MVP and scoring champ ... Larry Brown was the ABA Coach of the Year for the third time in the last four seasons ... David Thompson was Rookie of the Year ... The final all-ABA team was Billy Knight, James Silas, Ralph Simpson, Gilmore and Erving ... Only three of the original ABA players were around nine years later—Louis Dampier, Byron Beck and Freddie Lewis. Denver's Beck and Kentucky's Dampier went the distance with their original teams ... When the merger with the NBA finally came, New York, Denver, Indiana and San Antonio were admitted to the NBA. St. Louis, Kentucky and Virginia were left out, as was the red, white and blue ball.

Down the Tubes with Virginia

In a league that spent nine years teetering on the edge of disaster, no franchise went through more instability than the 1975–76 Squires. It was ready to fold at least six times, went through six coaches and achieved only 15 victories. Here is how it was, in the words of those who lived it—their memories, old news clippings, and a diary kept by Warner Fusselle, their radio broadcaster.

June 20, 1975
NEWS ITEM: Denver had the first selection in the ABA draft and the Nuggets chose Marvin Webster from Morgan State. Virginia came next

and the Squires took North Carolina State's David Thompson, knowing two very important facts: 1. They didn't have the money to sign Thompson; 2. Denver GM Carl Scheer had been close to Thompson from Scheer's days with the now-defunct Carolina Cougars and was convinced he could sign Thompson to play in Denver and would probably try to do just that, even if his rights belonged to Virginia.

July 25, 1975
NEWS ITEM: Denver signed Thompson and everyone in the ABA was happy about it. At least Thompson wouldn't be in the NBA. He was billed as a 6-foot-4 Julius Erving. Of course, a 6-foot-4 Julius Erving was exactly what the depressed Squires needed, but they weren't going to get him.

AL BIANCHI: We did the best we could—we cut a deal with Denver. We got three players *(Mack Calvin, Mike Green and Jan van Breda Kolff)* and cash *($250,000)* for Thompson and George Irvine. I would have loved to have had David, but I had been in Virginia long enough to know that you make do with what you can.

WARNER FUSSELLE: It seemed like a decent deal since Thompson was not coming to Virginia under any circumstances. Calvin had been an All-Star guard, Green was Denver's starting center *(averaging 17.4 points and 9.3 rebounds)* and the Squires really needed a center, while van Breda Kolff was a decent forward off the bench. Al also signed Ticky Burden, a guard from Utah who could really score, and Mel Bennett, a forward from Pittsburgh. It's hard to imagine now, but there was reason for optimism before that last season.

MACK CALVIN: You didn't have brain surgeons running some of those franchises back then, and that was especially true the last few years in Virginia. I had heard rumors about being traded to Virginia, but Carl Scheer assured me that it wouldn't happen. Of course, it did happen, and I was very, very bitter. Larry Brown didn't even bother to call me. He just wrote me a letter. He later said that he was too ashamed to call, which was typical Larry. I ended up telling the press that Larry Brown was a Dr. Jekyll–Mr. Hyde; he preached a family atmosphere and didn't hold to it. That was just my frustration coming out. The thing was that on paper, Virginia didn't look bad. They had Willie Wise, Dave Twardzik, Mike Green, myself. But they also had no money, and that worried me. In retrospect, I can see where the Denver management was coming from. They had to get Thompson, and if I were in their shoes I probably would have done the same thing. But being traded to Virginia really hurt.

July 27, 1975
NEWS ITEM: Virginia Squires center David Vaughn was shot by a Chesapeake policewoman after a high-speed chase. It began when Vaughn filled up his rented Mark IV at a Shell station in Great Bridge, Virginia, then pulled away without paying for $14 worth of gasoline. Three police cars ended up chasing Vaughn, who refused to pull over. Police said that the upper part of Vaughn's body could be seen through the sunroof during much of the chase. During the chase, Vaughn rammed into three police cars and the automobile of a woman. When police finally blocked Vaughn's car, there was a struggle to get him out, and in the process Vaughn was shot by a policewoman who had been on the force for only a month. Vaughn was charged with four counts of "attempted murder with an automobile," one charge of felonious hit-and-run and reckless driving. The day before this incident, he was arrested for indecent exposure in Virginia Beach while walking outside his home wearing only a T-shirt. Vaughn told arresting officers, "God is naked, too."

DAVE TWARDZIK: When Virginia signed Vaughn *(in 1974),* he was supposed to be our foundation, the 6-foot-11 guy we needed in the middle. We got rid of Jim Eakins *(traded to Utah for Johnny Neumann in August of 1974),* who had been a very good center for us. Not great, but solid; he'd get 12 points, 10 rebounds a night. I mean, you could take one look at Eakins and one at Vaughn and know you'd win more games with Eakins than Vaughn. Poor Vaughn was just screwed up back then. He had a finesse game, not much off the boards. He was basically a 6-foot-11 jump shooter and really out of touch with reality.

September 23, 1975
NEWS ITEM: Vaughn joined the Squires for training camp while awaiting trial. Friends blamed Vaughn's problems on the breakup of his marriage.

September 25, 1975
NEWS ITEM: The New York Nets and Denver Nuggets announced their intention to leave the ABA and join the NBA as expansion teams. Denver and New York were considered two of the strongest ABA franchises.

WARNER FUSSELLE: If Denver and New York had left the ABA, it could have meant the end of the league, and certainly the end of the Squires. Those teams were two of our strongest links, while we were among the weakest. Everybody else in the ABA was upset with New

York and Denver. We felt it was a move that was like being a traitor to the league. They were giving up the fight and trying to leave everyone else behind. I know Al Bianchi was really mad *(Bianchi said, "If those teams want to leave, then kick 'em out"),* but I think everybody was relieved when it became apparent that Denver and New York were not going to get into the NBA.

October 10, 1975
NEWS ITEM: The Baltimore Claws fold before playing their first game.

WARNER FUSSELLE: Everyone asked if Virginia would be next. Some way to start a season. The team was not shaping up that well. Mack Calvin was out with knee problems; Mike Green was also hurt. The David Vaughn situation was up in the air. I really felt bad for Al Bianchi, because I knew the team was in trouble.

November 1, 1975
FUSSELLE DIARY: Opened the season with five straight losses, then finally won at San Diego. Had a game the next night in St. Louis. Had a 5 A.M. wakeup call and didn't get to St. Louis until 5 P.M. One of our planes was fogged in. Another plane refused to wait for us. Then lost to St. Louis. Coming home from St. Louis, we got stuck in the Chicago airport for a five-hour delay while waiting to get our flight to Norfolk. Record is 1–6, team is depressed and exhausted.

November 3, 1975
NEWS ITEM: The Squires fired Al Bianchi after a 1–6 start. Four of the seven games were on the road; Calvin and Green hadn't played because of injuries. A banged-up Twardzik played in only four games and Vaughn had played exactly four minutes while still awaiting trial. After three home games, the team was averaging 4,300 fans. Bianchi had been the only coach the Squires ever had, coming with the team from Washington. His final ABA record was 230–281. The media ripped the firing; the prevailing opinion was best expressed by Mike Littwin of the *Virginia Pilot,* who said the Squires didn't need a new coach, they needed a new center. The void in the middle forced Bianchi to play 34-year-old Gerald Govan, who was really a forward, there.

AL BIANCHI: After Earl Foreman sold the team, it was really a crazy situation. Van Cunningham was the front man for about 100 investors. *(Cunningham owned a company that sold premade sandwiches to convenience stores. He even had the Squires put a small sandwich logo on their* *uniforms to advertise his business. After he was fired, Bianchi said, "I hope they sell a lot of tickets . . . and a lot of sandwiches.")*

Actually, Cunningham didn't fire me. This guy from the bank fired me. I'll just say that the guy's name was John. Anyway, he brought me into his office and he was stuttering around and not looking me in the eye and all that. Finally, I said, "John, are you trying to tell me that I'm fired?" I had a big grin on my face.

He said, "Well, you know . . . blah, blah."

I said, "Hey, John, just tell me."

He sort of nodded or something.

Then I said, "Remember, you still have to pay off my contract *($60,000)* for this year."

November 5, 1975

FUSSELLE DIARY: It just gets worse. They fired Al and had no idea who to hire, so finally they asked Mack Calvin to coach because he's hurt and not doing anything else. Played San Diego and got killed at home. I did a pregame editorial about Bianchi that didn't make the owners very happy. At the half, I interviewed some fans about the firing and they didn't like it any better than I did.

MACK CALVIN: This was one of the more amazing things I've ever seen in basketball. After firing Al, the front office came to me and said, "We know you're out for a couple of months with a knee injury, so we figured you might have time to coach the team for a while." I said I did one day want to coach, but I'm 27 and I'm still a player. I also was worried about coaching a group of guys when the day before I was one of their peers—a player. Anyway, I agreed to do it because somebody had to coach the team, so they hired me on an "interim basis," but no timetable was given for when they would find a regular coach. I lasted exactly six games, then I told them I wouldn't coach anymore. The reason I quit was simple— my checks were bouncing. My attorney would send them a letter saying that they had to make good on a check in a 10-day period or face legal action, and they'd make good on the check. Then my next check would come in, it would bounce and my attorney would have to send another letter. The least you can do is make sure the coach's checks don't bounce.

November 7, 1975

FUSSELLE DIARY: We lost to Indiana 104–100 before 3,293 in Hampton. Billy Knight played only two minutes for the Pacers, but we got beat anyway and Knight is the second-leading scorer in the league. Squires offered the coaching job to Doug Moe, who turned it down. Said he didn't want to leave Denver and liked working for Larry Brown. Morale down. Record 1–8.

November 11, 1975
FUSSELLE DIARY: Lost to Kentucky in Cincinnati. San Diego folded; rumors that the Squires will be next. Also rumors that since Bill Musselman is out as San Diego's coach, he'll be the next Squires coach.

November 13, 1975
NEWS ITEM: The ABA held a "dispersal auction" for the San Diego players. The Squires really wanted Caldwell Jones to fill their gap at center, but he went to Kentucky. Colonels "owner" Ellie Brown said, "I don't think there's a woman in the world who could pass up this kind of bargain. It would stun you to know what Caldwell makes." Jones earned $50,000. There were rumors that the ABA would soon be down to six teams.
FUSSELLE DIARY: Airlines lost my radio equipment on the way back from San Antonio. Team depressed about not getting Jones.

November 14, 1975
FUSSELLE DIARY: Squires lost 106–102 in overtime to St. Louis. Mack Calvin didn't show, so Willie Wise coached the team and did a great job. He also played 30 minutes and had 12 points. Rumors that the team won't be able to make payroll in three days, rumors of the team folding. Big investors meeting set.

November 18, 1975
FUSSELLE DIARY: Team is saved, for the day anyway. Kirk Saunders led a group of black investors who pledged $200,000 to the team. Another group of investors put in money to make the payroll.
NEWS ITEM: The players were paid two days late. They didn't practice for those two days because they had neither a coach nor paychecks. The Chicago Bulls filed suit for $13,000 that they claimed the Squires owed them as gate receipts from an exhibition game.

November 19, 1975
NEWS ITEM: Bill Musselman was hired as coach of the Squires and Virginia beat New York 110–100 before 7,100 fans in Norfolk. A promotion of 1,000 regulation ABA basketballs given to children helped the gate. Musselman played Fatty Taylor, Willie Wise and Ticky Burden all 48 minutes and Gerald Govan and Jan van Breda Kolff 44. GM Jack Ankerson said, "Musselman is a disciplinarian, a taskmaster and a win-

ner. We need someone with Bill's ingredients." Musselman had previously coached at Ashland *(Ohio)* College, the University of Minnesota, and then 11 games with San Diego, going 3–8. At Minnesota, Musselman was the key figure in an NCAA investigation that landed the program on probation. He also was accused by some members of the media of instigating the basketball riot in which several Minnesota players beat up Ohio State's Luke Witte. Musselman told reporters in Virginia, "It's funny, I was rapped for motivating my Minnesota team too much. And almost every day you read about a coach losing his job because he couldn't motivate." Musselman also told the Virginia writers, "Indiana University could compete in the ABA right now." And he said his new Virginia team had "too many guards. The game isn't won with guards." And he said that "one of my strengths always has been my rapport with the players. I don't anticipate any problems here."

November 21, 1975
NEWS ITEM: The Squires won their second game in a row with Musselman coaching, 106–98, over Utah in Norfolk. Once again, three players were on the floor for all 48 minutes—Govan, Burden and Wise. Van Breda Kolff played 46 minutes. Burden had 34 points, Wise had 28. Squires' record moved to 3–12.

December 2, 1975
FUSSELLE DIARY: The Utah Stars folded, leaving seven teams in the ABA. Utah sold Moses Malone, Ron Boone, Mike Green and Randy Denton to St. Louis. After winning their first two games under Musselman, Squires lost the next four. Strong rumors that the team will fold. The group of black investors didn't come through. Paychecks still late. Players not happy with Musselman.

December 12, 1975
FUSSELLE DIARY: There are rumors of a rebellion by the players against Musselman. Squires lost 110–107 to Denver before 5,564 at Hampton. Musselman was ejected. *(Musselman said he didn't swear at official Jess Kersey. Musselman explained, "I told him that he needed a haircut. I told him he looked like a broad.")* After Musselman was ejected, he asked Mack Calvin to coach the team in his place. Mack refused. *(Calvin said, "How about Willie?")* Willie Wise took over as coach. Fatty Taylor and Jan van Breda Kolff—are they hurt or not? They're not playing. Rumors that Ticky Burden was upset and wouldn't show up for the game, but he did and scored 23—21 in the second half. Mel Bennett dunked and bent the rim, holding up the game for 28 minutes. Fans got

mad at the officials and pelted the floor with ice. The game also was held up because the 24-second clock continually malfunctioned. Dave Twardzik was solid—22 points, 10 assists. Squires now 4–20.

DAVE TWARDZIK: Musselman wanted to rule the team with a very authoritarian hand. In one of his first practices, he showed us this defensive drill. His assistant was Gerald Oliver, who took everybody on the floor for a drill where Musselman would blow the whistle once and point to the right and in your defensive stance you'd move to the right. He'd blow the whistle again and point left and you'd go left. But the killer was that he said when he blew the whistle twice, he expected everybody to dive on the floor then bounce back up into a defensive stance. He blew the whistle and pointed right and everyone sort of shuffled right. Blew the whistle again and pointed left, people shuffled left. Not a lot of enthusiasm. Then he blew the whistle twice, guys went down to the floor real slowly, first on one knee, then the other.

Musselman screamed, "What the hell are you guys doing? You're supposed to go down quick and get back up. Now try it again."

So Musselman went back to blowing the whistle and guys went back to taking their time. Musselman was getting really hot. He said, "Coach Oliver, these guys don't know what we want. You blow the whistle and I'll show these guys how to do it."

Oliver then blew the whistle and Musselman was sliding right, then left, then hitting the floor and jumping back up. The players looked at Musselman then looked at each other as if to say, "What the hell is this guy doing?"

Then Musselman went back to blowing the whistle. But the guys didn't change. Finally, Musselman just said, "The hell with it," and that was the end of the drill.

MACK CALVIN: I don't think Bill knew what he was up against in Virginia. He was a drill-sergeant type, very aggressive with the players. But the attitude of the team was so bad with all the losing and the checks bouncing. Musselman's style just wasn't going to work.

He had a drill where he rolled the ball on the court and wanted guys to dive after it. He had these vicious rebounding drills. It got pretty ugly. Guys were killing each other, taking out their frustrations on their own teammates in practice. There were fights in nearly every practice. Joby Wright, now an assistant coach at Indiana University, was on the team and he seemed to get into a fight in every practice. Musselman loved it and he played Joby. Mel Bennett did the same thing and he got to play. Frankly, I was never on a team before or since that fought as much in practice.

DAVE TWARDZIK: Bill lost credibility with the players pretty fast. Whether it was just the lousy situation he was thrown into or his personality and what he said to the players, I don't know. I just know that he lost control of the situation.

After one game in Richmond, I was one of the last guys in the dressing room. I was icing my knee and Musselman said to me, "Man, I am so pissed off."

As usual, we had lost.

Musselman said, "There are two guys who will never play again for me. I mean not one minute."

I said, "Look, Coach . . ." I really didn't want to get into this conversation, but I was stuck. I wasn't dressed. I was the last one in the dressing room and I had ice on my knees.

Musselman said, "I'm not ashamed to tell you who they are."

I said, "You're the boss. That's your decision."

He told me that the two guys were Fatty Taylor and Jan van Breda Kolff. I thought to myself, "Well, Fatty is a point guard like me, so maybe I'll get some more minutes."

Well, the next game came and Fatty Taylor played 35 minutes, so there you are. I still didn't play much. There was a game when I swear he played five guys 48 minutes. I guess he just didn't like me or didn't think I could play. I thought I was okay *(Twardzik had been an All-Star point guard in 1975)*. One time, Musselman put me in a game to guard David Thompson. Not a good idea. I'm 6-foot and not exactly a leaper. Thompson was 6-foot-4 and could jump over the moon. I don't know what Bill was thinking, but all I could do was foul Thompson. I got about five fouls in 10 minutes; it was ridiculous. This situation was pretty hard for me to take. Why didn't I play when the team was so bad? I grew up with the Squires. I went to Old Dominion in Norfolk and in their first year, the Squires even played some games in our college gym. I worked for the team as a stat runner. I'd go into the dressing room with the box scores and I'd be in awe of the guys. I used to joke to people that I guess I wasn't good enough for Earl Foreman to sell me, but that was fine because I was very content in Virginia until all this stuff with Musselman started. Bill was a screamer and that just didn't fly with the players. I think even Bill would tell you now that he has learned a lot from that experience and that he probably didn't handle things like he should have. *(Twardzik averaged 10 points in the ABA and was known as a solid ballhandler and a fierce defender. He later played on Portland's NBA championship team.)*

December 17, 1975

FUSSELLE DIARY: Jack Ankerson called a big staff meeting and discussed the front office taking pay cuts. Talk about bad signs. The commissioner *(Dave DeBusschere)* came to town to talk to investors. The record is 4–22.

MIKE GOLDBERG: I was the ABA's general counsel and it seemed like we were always putting out fires, especially in Virginia. They had their 100 investors at the meeting and I remember Dave telling them, "There's no guarantee that you'll eventually get into the NBA and it's hard to know what will happen with a merger, but I'd stick it out if I were you." Then one of the owners stood up and yelled, "There you are. The man just said we're going into the NBA." These guys heard what they wanted to hear and they wanted the league to make it so bad that they really weren't listening. I think that was why Virginia managed to stagger through the season. The amazing thing was that they didn't fold, because you never knew from week to week if they'd be around.

December 27, 1975

FUSSELLE DIARY: Lost to Indiana at the Scope. Only funny thing that happened was that a fan hit official Ed Rush with a rubber chicken.

December 28, 1975

FUSSELLE DIARY: Lost 102–97 at St. Louis. Lamar Green missed the team flight. Ticky Burden forgot his uniform and had to wear a road Spirits jersey, inside out to hide the St. Louis name. Squires' record for the 1975 calendar year—11–75.

January 9, 1976

FUSSELLE DIARY: Squires scored 53 points in the fourth quarter to tie an ABA record, but still lost 155–128 at Denver.

January 15, 1976

NEWS ITEM: Mack Calvin played his first game for Virginia and the Squires lost to San Antonio 129–93. Calvin looked like a guy who had been hurt. He had 24 points, but was 7-for-26 from the field, with 13 turnovers; the Squires had 31 turnovers and shot 31 percent from the field. The game was played in Richmond before an announced crowd of 1,296. Writers estimated it was half that total. Telephones were removed along press row and neither radio broadcast made the airwaves.

January 16, 1976

NEWS ITEM: David Vaughn was convicted on two charges of assault. Two of the attempted-murder charges were dismissed by the court, two others reduced to assault. He was sentenced to 60 days in jail and fined

$850. Vaughn appeared in 10 games for the Squires, averaged 2.9 points and shot 36 percent.

January 20, 1976

NEWS ITEM: Bill Musselman "resigned." Musselman's record was 4–22 with the Squires, and the team had lost 18 of the last 20 games. Ticky Burden had not played or practiced during Musselman's last week, and he said he would return now that Musselman was gone. GM Jack Ankerson took over as coach. Ankerson said that Musselman resigned "by mutual consent."

January 21, 1976

FUSSELLE DIARY: Jack Ankerson and Willie Wise were co-coaches. It's Willie's second time filling in. Lost 119–106 at Indiana. Mack Calvin didn't travel with the team—contract problems. Ankerson said he does not want to coach and is looking for someone.

January 22, 1976

FUSSELLE DIARY: Broke a 13-game losing streak by beating St. Louis at the Scope in Norfolk before 4,130 fans. Spirits started a front line of Marvin Barnes, Moses Malone and Caldwell Jones and the Squires outrebounded them 40–17 in the first half. Squires had 23 offensive rebounds by the half, which was why the Squires led by 22 points despite shooting only 38 percent. Mack Calvin was back and had 24 points off the bench. Ankerson and Willie Wise coached the team, but Zelmo Beaty is in town to interview for the job.

January 23, 1976

NEWS ITEM: Zelmo Beaty was hired as coach of the Squires. He is their sixth coach of the year, following Al Bianchi, Mack Calvin, Willie Wise, Bill Musselman and Jack Ankerson. The Squires are 6–35.

ZELMO BEATY: I had retired after the 1974–75 season and I was sitting at home still trying to adjust to not being a basketball player and trying to find out what I wanted to do. I had been very close with Willie Wise from our days together in Utah. Willie called me and told me that Musselman had just been fired and did I want the job? I thought, "Why not?" I had been interested in coaching. Twice I had turned down a chance to be a player-coach in Utah because I wasn't sure that being a player-coach was a good idea—too much responsibility. But I did want to coach eventually. Willie mentioned my name to the front office, they brought me in for an interview and hired me. The situation was a mess, but I thought I could help. At least I wanted to try.

DAVE TWARDZIK: The best thing the Squires did all that year was hire Zelmo. He brought some order to the mass confusion. For a while there, it seemed we had a new coach every game. Zelmo was a former player, a guy you could respect. I can't say enough good things about him.

MACK CALVIN: I always thought Zelmo could have been a good coach, but he never had the horses. Willie Wise's knee was bothering him. I had a knee problem. But the thing about Zelmo was that he was always positive and very determined. He got as much out of that team as anyone could, and it was a relief when he was hired.

WARNER FUSSELLE: Zelmo saved the year for us. He was the epitome of class and he really knew what he was doing. Unfortunately, he didn't have any talent to work with and there was no money in the front office. He deserved better than the Squires.

January 25, 1976
NEWS ITEM: The Squires' latest plan to raise money is to sell 100 banners, at $5,000 each, that would hang from the ceiling of the arena.

February 2, 1976
FUSSELLE DIARY: Willie Wise came into a restaurant in our hotel in Denver and told us that he heard that unless 50 banners were sold by tomorrow, the team would fold.

February 3, 1976
FUSSELLE DIARY: They didn't sell 50 banners, but they're working on it. The team has set a meeting for tomorrow to vote if they will play tomorrow's game. The payroll is two days late. Rumors that the team will fold are everywhere.

February 4, 1976
FUSSELLE DIARY: The team voted to play the game. Squires lost 135–131 in Denver in overtime after leading with 30 seconds left. Heard they've sold 46 banners. The players have said that they won't play two days from now in Indiana if their checks don't show up. We were locked out of the hotel in Denver because the Squires didn't pay the bills the last time we were in town. Carl Scheer came down and said the Nuggets would pay the hotel bill and the Pacers said the same thing for when we arrived in Indiana.

ZELMO BEATY: The incident in Denver was something I had never faced in 12 years of pro basketball. I had to go in front of the team and see if there was a way these guys would play without being paid. I found myself saying things like, "Listen, guys, no matter what you do, I won't blame you. I know that the checks are late again. I know how that feels. Personally, I'd like to see us play, but if you don't, I'll understand that." There were several times when I'd walk into the dressing room and I'd say, "Are we going to play tonight? I hope we can." Then I'd leave and let the players take a vote. There were days when I didn't know if we'd play that night until four in the afternoon. In the end, it was so bad that our trainer didn't have enough money to buy tape for the guys' ankles. I think he was getting supplies from the other team.

February 6, 1976
FUSSELLE DIARY: Arrived in Indiana and the players received their checks—certified checks so they wouldn't bounce. Heard that Squires got a $250,000 bank loan to save the team. Lost to the Pacers by five points.

February 8, 1976
FUSSELLE DIARY: Lost 112–105 in San Antonio. The Spurs scored the last 12 points of the game as Squires couldn't score in the final 3:07.

February 9, 1976
FUSSELLE DIARY: Lost 112–105 to St. Louis. Second game in a row that the opponent scored the last 12 points of the game against the Squires. This time, no points in the last 5:07.

February 19, 1976
FUSSELLE DIARY: Beat Kentucky 102–82 at the Scope. Zelmo suspended Ticky Burden.

ZELMO BEATY: About the only player I had trouble with was Ticky Burden. He was very immature and was mad because I was playing Mack Calvin in front of him. Mack had just gotten healthy and was playing well. Ticky didn't want to practice. He was a problem and he really stood out, because the rest of the guys were working so hard under the most trying circumstances I've ever seen in pro basketball. I really grew to admire Dave Twardzik. He played with a very painful hamstring muscle. Dave could have said, "Hey, we're losing, we're not getting paid, my leg hurts. I think I'll rest a few games." But he played and always played hard. Mel Bennett is a kid who came out of Pittsburgh as a Hardship Case. He put his heart on the floor every night. When we lost a tough game, he'd cry. I'm not kidding—he'd actually cry. I've never seen a player do that. Really, about all the guys but Ticky were good. Now when I think about it, I always feel good about how hard those guys played for me. They showed a lot of character.

DAVE TWARDZIK: I was just so happy that Zelmo came along, because he gave us direction. We had so many different kinds of guys come and go that year. We had Lionel Billingy. One day we were writing checks for a charity—$12. Billingy yells out, "How do you spell 'twelve'?" Somebody yelled back, "Write two checks—one for $10, the other for $2." Maybe he couldn't spell "twelve" or maybe he just had a bad day at practice, I don't know. The whole year was just bizarre.

March 1, 1976
FUSSELLE DIARY: Lost to Denver at home. Van Cunningham criticized me for saying on the air that the fans were leaving early. But they were. Ticky Burden is back.

March 21, 1976
FUSSELLE DIARY: Lost in double overtime 138–129 at Kentucky, 13th loss in a row, 28 in a row on the road. Only seven players were healthy. Burden and Mack Calvin each played 58 minutes, Mike Green played 56. Mel Bennett cried on the way home.

April 7, 1976
FUSSELLE DIARY: It's finally over. New York wins 127–123 at the Scope before 7,000. Julius Erving had 38 points and 15 rebounds in 35 minutes. Mel Bennett dunked and tilted the backboard—another 28-minute delay. The Squirette dancers walked out of the game at the half. That's it; final record: 15–68.

May 11, 1976
NEWS ITEM: The Squires fold. The team didn't have enough money to meet its league assessment. The ABA ends with six teams—Denver, New York, Indiana, San Antonio, Kentucky and St. Louis.

June 17, 1976
NEWS ITEM: The NBA agreed to a merger, accepting Denver, New York, Indiana and San Antonio into the league. Kentucky and St. Louis agreed to a financial settlement not to go into the NBA. Because it had folded a month earlier, Virginia was not a part of the merger.

ZELMO BEATY: Jack Ankerson called me one day to say the team had folded. I was so disappointed. I liked coaching. I did get an interview with Angelo Drossos in San Antonio, but Angelo told me that he wasn't interested; I asked why not, and he said because I had a negative attitude about the ABA. I couldn't believe it. I jumped to the ABA and I played on bad knees. I came back and coached Virginia when most guys would have said forget that situation. Now you look at my coaching record (9–33) and people figure I can't coach. But that Virginia team was the only chance I ever had.

The Last Championship

The Nets defeated Denver in six games to win the last ABA title. The Nuggets had the ABA's best record at 60–24, New York finishing in second place at 55–29. Denver had a 15–7 record over New York in the last two regular seasons. In the finals, Erving faced Bobby Jones, considered the ABA's best defensive forward. Erving's six-game scoring totals were 45, 48, 31, 34, 37 and 31. He averaged 37.6 points and 14.2 rebounds and shot 60 percent from the field. Erving won the opening game with an 18-footer from the corner that went in at the buzzer, giving New York a 120–118 victory. In the final game, New York trailed by 22 points with 17 minutes left, but came back to win at the Nassau Coliseum. Erving had 31 points and 19 rebounds in the final game, but he was far from the only hero. John Williamson scored 16 of his 28 points in the fourth quarter, Brian Taylor had 24 points, and journeyman center Jim Eakins had 15 points and 13 rebounds as the Nets outscored Denver 34–14 in the final period. The Nuggets were 4-for-20 from the field. They did get 42 points from David Thompson, while Dan Issel had 30 points and 20 rebounds. A player who had a game to forget for Denver was Ralph Simpson, who shot 1-for-9 for four points and had nine turnovers in 35 very long minutes.

JIM O'BRIEN: The Nets were one of those great teams that no one knew. Even when the Nets won the 1974 title and even though they had Doctor J, they couldn't begin to put a dent in the Knicks' hold on New York. People on Long Island who could make it to a Nets game in 15 minutes would rather fight the traffic and go to Manhattan for a Knicks game. After the first championship, you might have thought that Madison Avenue would have tried to do something with Erving, but that never happened.

I worked at the *New York Post,* and the *Post* has a strong basketball tradition. We were the first paper ever to go on the road with an NBA team. Despite all that, the people at the paper just weren't open to the ABA. I would write stories about Julius, George Gervin, Moses Malone and those guys and I was held up to suspicion in the newsroom. How could any of those guys be any good? They're in the ABA. The attitude was that the Nets could never be anyone because they weren't in the same league as the Knicks.

KEVIN LOUGHERY: I'm from New York and I know how the Knicks own the town. But I still was surprised that our team had absolutely no impact on the city's sports scene, despite winning the title. We had the most exciting player in basketball in Julius, a guy who was a hometown kid from Long Island, and we still didn't draw that well. It was really frustrating to us. But in the end, we realized that we were playing for ourselves and we stopped worrying about the Knicks or anything like that. In the last season, we wanted to win a championship for our own satisfaction and we wanted to win one for Julius, because if that was going to be the last year of the ABA, Julius deserved to be on the last championship team.

BOB COSTAS: The Nets were a very attractive team, a team with a lot of personality. It began with Doctor J, but they were more than that. Loughery was a colorful, fun coach to watch on the sidelines. He had some rough characters on the team, a strong element of intimidation. It was almost like hockey, where they have a couple of bodyguards to protect the star. They had John Williamson and Rich Jones, and those were two guys who could scare the hell out of anybody. They just stared at you with an expression that made you think that these guys would rather fight than play. And Williamson was an ass-kicker as a guard, which is something you seldom see. His game was to be physical, to pound you.

JOHN STERLING: You couldn't take the ball away from Williamson. He would dribble the ball with one hand and have the other arm out to protect, literally stiff-arming anybody who tried to take it from him. He would just throw that arm out and—whack!—nail the guy guarding him. And the officials let it go because John had established that that was how he played. Soon word got around and everybody in the league just gave John a lot of room.

STEVE ALBERT: John Williamson's nickname was Super John and he led the team in personality. He was free-spirited, always upbeat and just a fun guy to be around, because he liked to play so much. That was before he got fat. He was about 6-foot-2 and 200 pounds of muscle. He was more of a warrior than a player, a guy who went out there and physically punished you. He also had the kind of ego where he had a knack for making clutch shots. In the final game he had 16 points in the last quarter against Denver. He delivered.

BOB COSTAS: Another good player the Nets had was Brian Taylor, a poor man's Walt Frazier. He wasn't quite as good as Frazier, but the things Frazier did well were also Taylor's strengths. Brian had lightning-quick hands and a knack for stealing the ball. He also could back into a guy like Frazier and then hit the jumper over a defender. He was a cerebral player, an excellent passer and a perfect complement to Williamson in the backcourt.

ROD THORN: With only seven teams left at the end of the ABA, rivalries became very heated and bitter because you played the same teams so often. If you had a fight with a guy, you probably would see him again next week. There was no time to cool off. In the first round of the playoffs, that was really evident when we faced San Antonio. The Spurs and Nets had a lot of common history, because Roy Boe and Angelo Drossos liked to make trades. They had Billy Paultz, Larry Kenon and Mike Gale, who had once played for us. We had Rich Jones, who had spent much of his career in San Antonio.

JOHN STERLING: Rich Jones's nickname was "House," and he had had some financial problems when he played for the Spurs. When he came back to San Antonio for the playoffs, someone had leaked word of House's troubles to the local press and it ended up in the newspapers. House saw the stories and was so distraught that he wouldn't even leave his hotel room.

STEVE ALBERT: Supposedly, Jones might have gotten in some sort of hot water had he played in San Antonio, so he didn't go to the game. Kevin Loughery hid Rich out in a hotel room down there.

JOHN STERLING: Jones not playing in San Antonio became a big deal, and when we came back to Nassau Coliseum for the next game, House was in the lineup. When he was introduced, he went out on the court and some fans held up a sign saying, "This is Rich Jones's Home." It was the first time House had smiled in a week. Then when the Nets beat San Antonio to get into the finals, House was the happiest guy in the dressing room.

JULIUS ERVING: When we got to the finals against Denver, most people figured we didn't have a chance. We hadn't won a game in Denver all season and they had the home-court advantage. They were a power-house—Dan Issel, David Thompson and Bobby Jones were great players. Guys like Byron Beck, Gus Gerard, Ralph Simpson and Chuckie Williams were very good. They clearly had more depth and more talent. Also, the year before we had been knocked out of the playoffs in the first round by St. Louis. We were a good team, but they were a great one.

ROD THORN: If there ever was a case where one man won a title, it was this. We had some good players—Brian Taylor, Williamson, Jim Eakins and Rich Jones—but we couldn't come close to Denver except in one area. We had Julius and they didn't, and Julius had a gut feeling that this was the last year for the ABA and he was determined to go out a champion.

KEVIN LOUGHERY: That last championship is a tribute to Doc. He was just ungodly. They had Bobby Jones on him, one of the greatest defensive forwards ever to play the game, as he proved after the merger when he played for Philadelphia. But Bobby couldn't do a thing with him. If we needed Julius to get 40 points, he got 40. He wouldn't let us lose. The team became so single-minded. In the huddle, guys would say, "We are going to win this game. We're gonna make our move now." They were saying that in the final game when we were down by 20 points in the third quarter. That championship game, coming from 22 points down, probably was the greatest game I was ever associated with.

STEVE ALBERT: In that championship game, there still were a few empty seats way up top. But that also was the loudest crowd I've ever heard. They sensed that even when the Nets were down by 20, they could come back and win. They screamed and screamed and the whole thing snowballed. It was a strange situation for me because I was announcing the Nets games and my brother Al was doing Denver's games. Ironically, Al had been the Nets broadcaster the year before, and when he left to go to Denver, he helped me get the Nets job.

When the Nets came back to win that game, Al was broadcasting the game back to Denver from his old stomping grounds and he almost got stomped. The fans poured out of the stands, overran his broadcasting station and ripped him right off the air. Tape recorders, mikes, all kinds of equipment were just carried off by the fans. I looked across the floor and saw Al. It was a helpless situation, because he couldn't even wrap up the championship game. For whatever reason, they let us go, but poor Al was nearly run over.

JIM BUKATA: The Nets had a chance to wrap up the championship in Game 5 in Denver. I was in charge of the championship trophy and I took it with me from the ABA office in New York to Denver for the game. I left the trophy in a rental car overnight and someone stole it. That meant if New York had won Game 5 in Denver, we were in real trouble because we had no trophy to give the Nets. I prayed Denver would win, and they did. When we got back to New York and the Nets took Game 6, we gave them the same trophy they had won in 1974. About two months later a package showed up at the league office. It was the trophy. No return address or anything, but it was mailed from Denver.

Surrender

When Dennis Murphy pulled together his group of 12 investors with the idea of hiring George Mikan and having their own pro basketball league, the plan was simple: "We figured that within three years, we would be part of the NBA," Murphy recalls. "Certainly by five years we would have either merged with the NBA or been out of business." Merger talks, merger deals and merger rumors were the lifeblood of the ABA, always close enough to lure new money, always far enough away to create the need for new money.

The closest the ABA and NBA came to merging during the ABA's life was in 1971. An agreement was reached between the two leagues on May 4, 1970, and was ratified by the NBA in May of 1971. The NBA was to accept 10 ABA teams, all but the Virginia Squires, who were too close to the territory of the Baltimore Bullets and would have to either move or be folded. The ABA would drop its antitrust suits and other legal actions against the NBA, each ABA team would pay the NBA $1.25 million over a period of 10 years, no ABA team would share in television money for two seasons, and the leagues would hold a common draft for college players. The agreement was derailed, however, by a lawsuit brought by the NBA Players Association, headed by Oscar Robertson, claiming such a merger would create an illegal monopoly in the basketball business.

The so-called Oscar Robertson suit was a major roadblock facing any merger efforts. So was the combative attitude of owners on both sides. But in the end, the cost of waging war was too great to keep peace from breaking out—somehow.

MIKE STOREN: There are about 38 different guys who would like to take credit for the merger. I wish I had a buck for every guy I met who said, "I want to be the architect of the merger." If you talk to Tedd Munchak, he'll tell you that he did it. Carl Scheer will say he did it. So will Angelo Drossos, John Y. Brown and Dave DeBusschere. Dick Tinkham and I weren't around at the end for the final merger, but we will tell you that we laid the groundwork. But in the end, the guy who put the merger together was Larry O'Brien. He was the commissioner of the NBA and he got the support of his owners for a merger plan. No O'Brien, no merger, because with no O'Brien, there was no NBA, and the problem all along was that we wanted a merger and the NBA didn't and there would be no merger until the NBA was ready.

MIKE GOLDBERG: Every time the ABA hired a commissioner, the owners figured that this guy would get them on national television and get them a merger. The first commissioner was George Mikan. He was there for his name and also because he knew everybody in basketball. Then there was Jack Dolph, a former head of CBS Sports who was supposed to use his connections to get a national television contract. Mike Storen had the job for his basketball experience. Tedd Munchak had it for his business acumen. The last commissioner was Dave DeBusschere. Like Mikan, he was a marquee name, a former great NBA player who had a lot of connections in the NBA, so DeBusschere had credibility. There were other commissioners, but why go on talking about it? All of these men brought something positive to the job, but none of them could get the national television contract or the type of merger agreement that the ABA owners dreamed of. Looking back at it, I don't think any man could have done that.

MIKE STOREN: Anyone who was ever commissioner had to deal with an incredible amount of legal fees. We were suing the NBA for being a monopoly, breaking antitrust laws and anything else we could think of. When I took over in 1973, we had so many lawsuits going that our legal fees were over $1 million annually. That alone was reason to want to merge.

TEDD MUNCHAK: We were suing the NBA, the NBA was suing us. We were suing players, players were suing us. It would never end. Nothing ever came of 99 percent of those lawsuits, other than a lot of lawyers got rich.

ROY BOE: I suppose we all thought if we could find our own Pete Rozelle, a guy with a lot of influence, then we'd get a merger and everything would be great. Television was the key. Back then, there was no cable, so you had to deal with the three networks, and ABC already had the NBA, so that meant CBS or NBC. But the NBA didn't have good ratings, so why would another network put on a second pro basketball league? That was the question we couldn't answer.

DICK TINKHAM: We were able to get the NBA to the bargaining table in 1970 because of all our legal action against them. We had a very strong antitrust suit against them dating back to the 1968 draft when the NBA pooled its resources to sign players such as Elvin Hayes, Wes Unseld, Tom Boerwinkle and Don Chaney.

We had gotten ahold of a document that was the NBA's battle plan to sign these guys. It was leaked to us by a disgruntled NBA employee who had been fired. The document contained:

1. The order of the draft.
2. The names of the teams and the college players they'd receive.
3. What each player would be paid.
4. How much each NBA team was to contribute to make sure that the college stars signed with them and stayed out of the ABA.

This approach was illegal and the document was the basis of our suit against the NBA. Of course, we were doing the same thing, but nothing was on paper, so how do you prove it? When the NBA saw that we had the document, they knew they were in trouble and so they started merger talks to avoid a court fight.

Both leagues were nearly bankrupting each other, between the lawsuits and the outrageous contracts being given to players. The NBA was livid at us for signing underclassmen, but we did that to hurt the NBA, to force them to merge and have a common draft.

Seattle's Sam Schulman ran the show for the NBA. He would call Walter Kennedy and say, "Walter, here is what we agreed upon."

One day, Schulman said the NBA wanted us to cease signing underclassmen while we were negotiating a merger. I agreed to that, but a week later I told Schulman, "Sam, we have one more underclassman signing."

Schulman said, "What crazy son of a bitch did that?"

I said, "I did."

Schulman said, "Well . . . who did you sign?"

I said, "George McGinnis."

Schulman said, "Oh boy, they're *(the NBA)* not going to like this."

But McGinnis wasn't the reason this merger deal fell apart. It was because of the Oscar Robertson suit, a legal action taken by the players to prevent a merger. The advent of the ABA and the bidding for talent was the greatest thing that ever happened to the players in either league. They never dreamed of making those kinds of dollars.

One of the major issues was the reserve clause, which bound a player for life to a team. Everyone knew that the reserve clause was illegal. How could you say that a player belonged to a team after his contract had expired? In one of the merger meetings, we were going to drop the reserve clause, because we knew that eventually it would be struck down in the courts. But the Knicks and Ned Irish said, "We'll never give up the reserve clause." Then Irish stormed out of the meeting.

I told Sam Schulman to go get Irish, but Schulman said, "He won't change his mind. Besides, whatever the Knicks want, the NBA will do."

So that was the end of our putting an end to the reserve clause in our 1971 merger agreement. The reserve clause stayed and that gave players such as Oscar Robertson, Bill Bradley and other heavy hitters in the Players Association grounds for their lawsuit saying that we were restricting trade and were trying to form a monopoly by combining leagues.

On September 8, 1972, the U.S. Senate Antitrust Subcommittee approved the merger of the ABA and NBA and said it was not a violation of antitrust laws. But the committee said that the reserve clause was illegal and could not be a part of the merger agreement. Oscar Robertson and John Havlicek testified before the committee, saying that the merger would not be in the best interests of the players. Robertson said, "If my NBA team were to fire me, I could get a job in the other league. With a merger, there would be no place for me to go." The Senate subcommittee prepared a bill that would outlaw the reserve clause and replace it with an option clause, meaning a player could switch to another team a year after the end of his contract without his original team retaining his rights. The subcommittee also said that the ABA teams did not have to pay $1.25 million to get into the NBA. The subcommittee said that players should all be signed to one-year contracts with an option for a second season, then become free agents. NBA Commissioner Walter Kennedy didn't like the Senate's amendments to the bill; "They put things into the merger that I don't think owners in either league can live with," said Kennedy.

DICK TINKHAM: The merger got bogged down in the Senate for over a year. Also, the subcommittee changed the merger agreement, and the NBA didn't like the changes. So it was back to square one. We went back to suing each other and trying to bankrupt each other to sign players, and no one was making any money. Now and then, we'd have more merger meetings, then we'd break up and declare war on each other, and it stayed like that until the last season, when the ABA was down to seven teams and had no choice but to merge on any terms it could get.

o   o   o

THE LAST YEAR: DENVER AND NEW YORK'S END RUN

Before the 1975–76 season, the Denver Nuggets and the New York Nets made independent applications to the NBA, basically saying, "Take us. We are the two strongest franchises and forget the rest of the league." Kentucky reportedly was approached to join Denver and New York in jumping to the NBA, but Colonels owner John Y. Brown refused, saying he was staying loyal to the ABA. Denver and New York did not get into the NBA, although they might have been accepted if they had been willing to pay the $6.15 million the NBA had been charging for expansion teams. NBA Players Association president Larry Fleisher said that the two teams couldn't join the NBA, because that would constitute a merger, which would have to be approved by the courts to see if there was a violation of antitrust laws. Fleisher also said that the Players Association would fight this type of merger in court because without Denver and New York, the ABA was likely to fold and there would be only one pro basketball league.

JULIUS ERVING: That last season started on a terrible note. Nearly all of the ABA players were shocked and bitterly disappointed when Denver and New York tried to abandon the ABA. It was like those teams were saying, "Screw everybody else, we're out to get what we can for ourselves." The thing that kept the ABA alive for nine years was the togetherness of the league, the sense that we were all pulling together so that we could survive. The players never viewed the ABA as a stepping-stone to the NBA or a league designed for a merger. Surely that was the owners' intent, but the reason we filed lawsuits and did the things we did to keep two leagues was that we wanted the league to grow independently, much like the American and National Leagues in baseball, and then have a World Series of basketball. In the ABA, the theme was unity, and Denver and New York nearly destroyed that spirit.

CARL SCHEER: I don't see why such a big deal was made of us in Denver and New York applying to the NBA. Over the years, several other teams had quietly done the same thing, but it was just never made public.

ROY BOE: Every ABA owner of significance approached the NBA at one time or another about getting in. We in New York had done it long before 1975. Really, Carl Scheer and I didn't think we had much of a chance of getting into the NBA, but we thought that our applications might get the merger talks going again. Someone had to do something dramatic, because the merger issue had gotten bogged down. And if there was no merger, we all were in deep trouble.

TERRY STEMBRIDGE: In the last two seasons, the ABA lost that community spirit. With guys like Roy Boe, John Y. Brown and Carl Scheer running the league, the attitude became very narrow and selfish. The waters were shark-infested and it was every franchise for itself. There was no way the league could go on another year, because the attitude that had kept it alive was gone.

TEDD MUNCHAK: In my year as commissioner *(1974–75)*, we talked to the NBA about a merger, and what they were really interested in was our players. They were talking about how to get Julius Erving to the Lakers or the Knicks without getting sued by the NBA Players Association. They wanted to take our best players and distribute them among the NBA teams, then hold a draft of the remaining ABA players and the NBA players no one wanted. They wanted to break up our best franchises and treat us like expansion teams, and there was no way we would go for that.

We knew that we had to do something to get a deal, so I spent at least nine months talking to Dave DeBusschere about becoming commissioner. He was an NBA guy, he had a high profile in New York and maybe he could get a deal. We said, "Hey, Dave, this can be a great thing for you. A merger of some type is coming and you can take credit for it. After it's done, you'll be an important guy in basketball." We also offered him a raise from the $75,000 he made as GM with the Nets to $100,000 as a commissioner.

JIM BUKATA: One of our biggest problems was getting the owners to pay their league assessments. A number of teams just didn't want to do it. They were owned by guys who ran them on a shoestring, thinking that a merger was around the corner and all they had to do was hang in there and they'd get rich once their franchise was in the NBA. Every day was an adventure: What teams were folding? What teams needed help to make the next payroll? What teams owed the league money?

DEL HARRIS: I went to Norfolk to scout an exhibition game between the Virginia Squires and Phoenix Suns and the game was held up because the Suns refused to take the court until they got the money they were promised for playing the game.

KEVIN LOUGHERY: When San Diego and Utah folded so fast, the league was in chaos because we didn't know who we were supposed to play. Our next game was against a team that no longer was in business. We were on a West Coast trip when Utah and San Diego went under. We sat around hotels for days waiting for the league to tell us where to go next. It was a strange feeling, like being in limbo.

JIM BUKATA: Not only was I the league's PR director, but I was in charge of drawing up the schedule. I would get a call from a team saying, "We're at the Salt Lake airport. Utah is getting ready to go down; should we stay here or fly somewhere else?" I tried to keep reworking the schedule to stay a few days ahead of everyone, but sometimes I was lucky to be a few hours ahead. It was funny. We never worried about the league folding at midseason. DeBusschere was convinced that we had six solid franchises. But the other teams . . . well, we worried a lot about them.

BOB COSTAS: By the end of the ABA, there were only five viable franchises—Denver, New York, Indiana, Kentucky and San Antonio. The St. Louis owners had money, but were lucky to draw 2,000 a game. Virginia was in shambles. The league was finished and everyone knew it.

A SETTLEMENT, AND THEN THE END

The Oscar Robertson suit was alive in the court system for six years before it was finally settled on February 3, 1976. Before the settlement, both the NBA and ABA believed that even if they had struck a merger deal, the players would have prevented the merger through legal action. According to the original suit filed on April 16, 1970, there could be no merger until issues such as free agency and "freedom of movement" were settled. The key points of the settlement were these:

1. The option clause, which bound a player to his original team a year after his contract expired, would no longer exist. The option clause was the reason that players such as Rick Barry and Zelmo Beaty had to sit out a season before jumping from the NBA to the ABA, even though their NBA contracts had expired.

2. When a player is selected in the college draft, his rights would belong to the pro team for one year. If he hasn't signed by the next draft, then he is eligible to be drafted again. It used to be that his rights belonged to the team that drafted him for two years.

3. Players whose high school class had graduated were eligible to apply for the pro draft, assuming they had renounced their college eligibility. In other words, underclassmen could be selected in the draft if they wanted to turn pro.

4. The "First Refusal" rule was put in place. Suppose a player with Boston plays out his contract, becomes a free agent and signs with Philadelphia. Boston has the right to match the offer the player received from Philadelphia, thereby keeping that player with the Celtics.

5. The NBA teams had to pay a total of $4.3 million to the players as a settlement. There were 479 players who received money, based upon how long they had played pro basketball prior to the agreement. The most any player received was about $32,000.

With the Robertson suit out of the picture, after nine years and 28 different teams and about $50 million in losses, the ABA came to an end in the summer of 1976 when four teams were admitted to the NBA— Indiana, New York, San Antonio and Denver.

MIKE GOLDBERG: First of all, the NBA never called this a merger. The four ABA teams in essence bought their way into the NBA and the NBA considered it an expansion.

Why did it happen?

In the end, it was the fatigue factor. The ABA owners were tired and on the road to bankruptcy. For nine years, millions upon millions of dollars were spent. It took so much energy, so much creativity just to stay in business, the ABA simply ran out of gas. They wanted to fight the good fight, but for how long? Everything has its limits, and the ABA had reached its limit. It ended the season with seven teams and had only six in operation when these last rounds of merger talks began. To most ABA people, it was impossible to imagine playing another season.

On the NBA side, fatigue also was a factor. The ABA had turned their world upside down. Guys were jumping leagues, guys were leaving college early, guys were getting paid astronomical salaries.

Both sides just said, "Enough already. Let's end the madness."

JIM BUKATA: There was an ABA merger committee composed of Roy Boe, Carl Scheer and Angelo Drossos. And there was an NBA committee that included Jim Fitzgerald and a number of others.

But the names aren't important, because the committees didn't do that much. The deals were cut in meetings between Dave DeBusschere and Larry O'Brien. They met in out-of-the-way restaurants on the East Side of New York. O'Brien believed that the time had come for a merger. A number of NBA teams, such as Atlanta, weren't exactly rolling in dough. In fact, the Hawks' losing David Thompson and Marvin Webster to Denver of the ABA was one of the forces behind the merger. Economics was the sole reason for the merger.

Our original proposal to the NBA was for six teams to get in, everyone but Virginia *(for an entry fee of $4.5 million, paid over six years)*. But the NBA didn't want Kentucky or St. Louis. Kentucky talked about moving from Louisville to Cincinnati, but that still didn't interest the NBA. St. Louis said it would move to Hartford, but the Celtics went crazy, saying that violated their territorial rights.

Everybody had their special interest.

Chicago's Bill Wirtz didn't want Kentucky in the league because he desperately wanted Artis Gilmore. He figured the only way he could get Gilmore would be if Kentucky folded.

The NBA said that they would accept only four teams—take it or leave it.

ROY BOE: Only taking four teams was a problem. We wanted to get all six franchises in the league, but we had no real grounds to negotiate. We were dead on our feet and the NBA knew it. We couldn't play another season.

ANGELO DROSSOS: The difference between a good negotiator and a bad negotiator is that the good one knows when someone has him by the proverbial balls. Well, at our final merger talks in Hyannis *(Massachusetts)*, that was how the NBA had us, and we knew it.

Okay, so it had to be four teams. We offered to pay them $5 million per team; that was $20 million. That money would be paid out over several years. We also had to settle with St. Louis and Kentucky, because they weren't getting into the league. It just seemed like it would never get done.

After one meeting, it was after four in the morning and I had been working on a deal all night with Larry O'Brien.

Finally, I said, "Larry? Uncle."

He said, "What do you mean, 'Uncle'?"

I said, "That means I'm giving up. I'm not making any deal. It's like building a house. You start out thinking you'll spend $30,000. Then you decide to add a bedroom, then there are cost overruns and the next thing you know it's $60,000. It cost you double what you expected. That's what has happened here. The NBA should just go on doing what it does and the ABA will do whatever it will do next."

I called John Y. Brown and said, "John, there's no merger."

He said, "Good, we'll just go on our merry way."

I said, "But there's only six teams left and I don't know how many of those will stay around. Maybe we can fight *(the NBA)* in court."

When I left the meeting, Carl Scheer, Roy Boe, and Bill Eason from Indiana were still talking to O'Brien. About nine in the morning, or four hours later, I went back into the room and those three guys were still talking with O'Brien.

O'Brien said to me, "I understand that you're ready to make a deal."

I said, "Larry, I must have been in a coma, because I don't remember anything. I've been in my room packing to go home."

O'Brien said, "While you were gone, we've been discussing this thing, and what are we playing games for?"

I said, "I'm not playing games. If my partners and I can meet and if you let me make an offer on their behalf, then I'll give you my last best offer."

Roy Boe, Carl Scheer and Eason all agreed that I could speak for them.

Then I made what became the final merger deal. The NBA said they wouldn't take it. I went back to my room to finish packing. Carl Scheer and Roy Boe were there and we all were saying that it was great that we stayed together and we'd try to put the league back together for another year.

Then there was a knock at my door. A messenger said that we were wanted by the NBA in a conference room. When I walked into the room, Mike Burke from the Knicks came up and hugged me. He said, "Welcome to the NBA."

That was how we got into the league.

CARL SCHEER: The pressure was enormous. We were fighting for our very lives. It reminded me of what it must have been like to be Japan at the negotiating table at the end of World War II. What did we really have to offer? I was convinced that there would be no deal. We were making ridiculous promises about playing again and more hollow threats about taking those NBA sons of bitches to court. We were packing to leave when word filtered down that there was a deal.

DICK TINKHAM: While I wasn't at the Hyannis meeting, I felt that Sam Schulman and I had something to do with the merger, because we had laid the groundwork years earlier.

MIKE GOLDBERG: While Larry O'Brien was important to the merger, so was a young lawyer named David Stern. You may know him today as NBA Commissioner David Stern. O'Brien was given a lot of latitude by the NBA owners to get the deal done, and O'Brien relied a lot on Stern for legal advice and all that. On the ABA end, DeBusschere laid the groundwork before Hyannis, then Scheer, Boe and Drossos finished the deal. As for the Indiana people, they sort of went along for the ride and ended up in the NBA.

MIKE STOREN: Dick Tinkham should get some credit for the merger, if for no other reason than he brought in Fred Fruth, who was a brilliant antitrust lawyer. He handled our case against the NBA and he scared the hell out of them. I don't think the NBA wanted a fight to the death in court with Fruth.

MIKE GOLDBERG: Fruth definitely was a high-powered guy in the world of antitrust litigation. Fruth liked money and made a lot of it. He also lived high on the hog. He had a suite at the New York Regency with his own personal servants. He went around town in a limo . . . you get the picture.

After a while, the ABA owed Fred quite a bit of money. One day we went to see him in his hotel suite. He was sitting there having a manicure.

He said, "Mike, there is something I want to talk about."

I said, "If it's your fee, we'll take care of that."

Fred said, "I know you will, because if you don't have $25,000 on my desk by Friday, Julius Erving will be working in my garden."

MIKE STOREN: Another guy who could have killed the merger was Larry Fleisher. If he and the Players Association had wanted to start some new legal action, it could have thrown the whole thing into jeopardy. In a sense, he was like O'Brien. Fleisher had the power to kill it.

MIKE GOLDBERG: For the merger to work, everybody had to see that they would get something they wanted. The Bulls wanted Artis Gilmore, so they were for it. The Knicks wanted a merger because the Nets would have to pay them millions for violating their territorial rights. St. Louis wanted in the league, but the other ABA owners had to cut a deal with them to keep them out. John Y. Brown had had enough of the ABA and he was willing to fold Kentucky, but he wanted his price. So the ABA owners had to negotiate with the NBA, and also among themselves to get St. Louis and Kentucky out of the picture.

JIM BUKATA: St. Louis went right into the eve of the merger demanding to become a part of the NBA. Donald Schupak was one of the Spirits owners and he was a sharp attorney. He knew that the Spirits would never get into the NBA, but he also knew that there would be no merger until he was satisfied.

MIKE GOLDBERG: Of all the deals cut in Hyannis, St. Louis made the best one. Schupak just wore everyone out with his demands. He is a hard-driving New York lawyer, and the other ABA owners were these nice men from the hinterlands. He just kept talking and talking, pushing and pushing, and exhausted everyone who was listening to him. In the end, they gave him what he wanted.

THE MERGER SETTLEMENT

1. Four ABA teams would be admitted to the NBA—Denver, San Antonio, Indiana and New York—giving the NBA 22 teams.

2. Each ABA team would pay the NBA $3.2 million by September 15, 1976.

3. The ABA teams would receive no money from the national television contracts for the first three seasons—1976–77 through 1978–79.

4. The ABA teams would take no part in the 1976 college draft. Thereafter, there would be a common draft for all the teams in the NBA.

5. The ABA teams would be referred to as expansion teams.

6. The ABA teams would have no votes pertaining to the distribution of gate receipts or the alignment of divisions for two years.

7. The New York Nets had to pay the New York Knicks $4.8 million for indemnification, for playing in the Knicks' territory.

8. The four ABA teams got to keep their players. The remaining ABA players would be distributed among NBA teams in a draft.

9. Chicago was given the first pick in the ABA dispersal draft so the Bulls could take Artis Gilmore.

THE ABA'S SETTLEMENT

1. Kentucky owner John Y. Brown received $3 million for not going into the NBA and folding his franchise.

2. St. Louis owners Ozzie and Danny Silna and Don Schupak received $2.2 million in cash and 1/7th of a share of the television money from each of the four ABA teams—in other words, the Spirits got 4/7ths of an annual television share. The television money would be paid in perpetuity.

3. All ABA contracts were guaranteed in order to appease the Players Association.

4. All ABA players who were in the league after 1971 had their pensions upgraded.

The deal cut by the St. Louis Spirits with the four ABA teams that went into the league may indeed be the greatest in all of sports. The latest NBA television contract, signed in 1990, pays over $200 million a year in cable and network revenue over the next four years. The Spirits owners will receive about $4.4 million annually as their ⁴/₁₇th of a television share, and that money is destined to go up, seemingly forever, as long as the NBA remains popular. During the 1980s, the Spirits owners received about $8 million in television revenue as part of the merger, and they did nothing for it other than be at the right place at the right time with the right demands.

Aftermath

ANGELO DROSSOS: When I got back from the merger meetings, the town was naturally excited about going into the NBA. I was met by a big crowd at the airport and things like that. But I told people, "This is no time to break out the champagne, because this isn't a good deal. We paid dearly to get in."

Between what we had to pay the NBA and what we had to pay Kentucky and St. Louis for a settlement, we had to go to a consortium of banks to borrow $5 million. The banks didn't think the loan was a good risk, but they did it anyway, because they wanted San Antonio to have NBA basketball. It wasn't like today when people know that pro basketball is a great investment. There still was uncertainty about the NBA, because attendance and television ratings were down.

ROY BOE: The merger agreement killed the Nets as an NBA franchise. I also owned the New York Islanders hockey team, so I had a lot of financial responsibilities. But to be hit with $3.2 million to get into the NBA—actually it was over $4 million because there were some extra charges and we had to settle with the teams who didn't get in. I owed the Knicks $480,000 a year for 10 years in indemnity charges. I needed to get some cash, about $5 million, by September 15. And Julius Erving said he wanted a new contract. He was making $350,000 with several years to run. Julius said that we made him a promise that we'd renegotiate his contract if we got into the NBA. Well, he had a 60-some-page contract and there wasn't a word in there about that.

I offered Julius to the Knicks for a cash settlement and in exchange for dropping that $480,000-a-year indemnity charge. They turned it down. I didn't have the $3.2 million in liquid cash to get into the NBA and it was due on September 15. I was offered $3 million for Julius from Philadelphia and I took it, because I had no choice. The merger agreement got us into the NBA, but it forced me to destroy the team by selling Erving to pay the bill.

JULIUS ERVING: In general, the ABA players felt as if we were sold down the river by the merger. At the very best, we got a second-rate deal from the NBA and not nearly the respect that we deserved. Guys lost jobs because three teams didn't get in. Other guys lost benefits or had their contracts broken. For years, we stood together against the NBA. To have the whole thing come apart like that—it really hurt.

Ask yourself this: Who made out?

The ABA owners got a good deal because by getting into the NBA, their franchises increased in value. In the long run, they got more than just their money back from the fee they paid to get into the NBA.

The ABA owners who didn't get in received incredible financial settlements.

The NBA owners got a great deal. They got all the money from the ABA teams, who wanted to get into the NBA. But they also got all the best ABA players, which made the NBA a more exciting and popular league.

But what happened to the average ABA players? Most didn't get jobs or played maybe a year or two in the NBA. They basically were left out in the cold.

ROY BOE: To me, the guys who got the best deal were John Y. Brown and St. Louis. Brown got $3 million, then bought the Buffalo Braves for half that amount. So he got into the NBA for $1.5 million. The guys from St. Louis will be rich forever with all that TV money coming in.

MIKE GOLDBERG: It's ironic how time changes everything. In 1976, guys were complaining about paying $3.2 million to get into the league. Now those same franchises are worth $50 million, $75 million, maybe more. While some people thought the ABA was fleeced by the merger, it turned out to be one of the great business bargains of all time.

THE DISPERSAL DRAFT

The NBA held a dispersal draft for the ABA players whose teams weren't a part of the merger. Price tags were assigned to each player by the league, according to what each player was worth. The draft was held according to usual NBA rules—the teams with the worst records draft the highest.

Here is how the draft went:

1. *Chicago—Artis Gilmore, $1.1 million.*
2. *Portland (from Atlanta)—Maurice Lucas, $300,000.*
3. *Kansas City—Ron Boone, $250,000.*
4. *Detroit—Marvin Barnes, $500,000.*
5. *Portland—Moses Malone, $350,000.*
6. *N.Y. Knicks—Randy Denton, $50,000.*
7. *Buffalo—Bird Averitt, $125,000.*
8. *Indiana—Wil Jones, $50,000.*
9. *Houston—Ron Thomas, $15,000.*
10. *San Antonio—Louis Dampier, $20,000.*
11. *N.Y. Nets—Jan van Breda Kolff, $60,000.*
12. *Kansas City—Mike Barr, $15,000.*

Players eligible but not drafted: Johnny Neumann, Al Murphy, Steve Green, Freddie Lewis, Mike D'Antoni, Jimmie Dan Connor, Jim Baker.

Teams that passed in the draft: L.A. Lakers, Phoenix, Seattle, Philadelphia, Washington, Golden State.

Deals: Portland traded Geoff Petrie and Steve Hawes to Atlanta for the second pick in the draft, which became Maurice Lucas.

Of the 84 players in the ABA at the time of the merger, 63 were in the NBA in 1976–77. Here are some other facts about the first season after the merger:

- *Of the league's 10 top scorers, four were former ABA players—Indiana's Billy Knight, Denver's David Thompson and Dan Issel, and San Antonio's George Gervin.*
- *Indiana's Don Buse led the league in steals and assists.*
- *Former Spirit Moses Malone was third in rebounding, former Colonel Artis Gilmore was fourth. Gilmore and former Colonel Caldwell Jones were among the top five in blocked shots.*

- *Five of the ten starters in the NBA finals between Portland and Philadelphia were former ABA players: Portland's Dave Twardzik and Maurice Lucas, and Philadelphia's Julius Erving, Caldwell Jones and George McGinnis.*
- *Denver won the Midwest Division with a 50–32 record, second best in the NBA. San Antonio was 44–38, Indiana 36–46, and the Erving-less Nets 22–60.*
- *Houston, the Midwest Division champ, was coached by ex-ABA coach Tom Nissalke, who was the NBA Coach of the Year. Other ex-ABA coaches were Hubie Brown in Atlanta and Doug Moe in San Antonio, along with Indiana's Slick Leonard, Denver's Larry Brown and the Nets' Kevin Loughery.*
- *Ten of the twenty-four All-Stars were former ABA players: Julius Erving and George McGinnis of Philadelphia, Bobby Jones, Dan Issel and David Thompson of Denver, Don Buse and Billy Knight of Indiana, George Gervin of San Antonio, Maurice Lucas of Portland and Rick Barry of Golden State. Of these players, only Barry didn't begin his career in the ABA.*

THE LAST WORD

DAVE ROBISCH: It took a while for people to realize how good we were in the ABA. Until the merger, the NBA didn't respect our teams or our players. But we in the ABA knew how good we were. George Gervin, Dan Issel, Julius Erving, Artis Gilmore and the others were great players, period, and it didn't take long for the NBA to find out.

DAN ISSEL: Most of the players were excited about the merger, because finally we were getting a chance to play the NBA teams. We had played them in exhibition games, but the regular season is different. At first, the NBA players were very skeptical about us. We had to prove that we belonged, but we did that. The only thing I wished was that there were more survivors from the ABA instead of just four teams getting in.

JULIUS ERVING: No matter what league I played in, I never had any doubts about my ability. Growing up on Long Island, I had played against great players on the playgrounds of New York. I came up the hard way, because I wasn't a star in high school or college. There weren't a lot of pro scouts at my door. But I also had the advantage of being a late bloomer; I didn't start to hit my stride as a player until I turned pro, while a lot of kids peak at a young age. So when the merger came, I was

26 and I knew I was still improving. I just figured that I'd do well in the NBA whenever I got the chance, and most of the guys in the ABA thought the same thing.

BOB COSTAS: The ABA had a strange split personality. On the one hand, the ABA people knew what a great thing they had, how talented their players were and how entertaining. It was almost like we didn't want to share our little secret with the world. Yet there was such pride in a league that had to endure so much simply to survive, and we wanted the world to know how great our players were. It was an obvious contradiction, but both feelings were understandable. I'll tell you this: we saw so many of our players do well after the merger, it was an incredible feeling for those of us who had been in the ABA. We could say to the world, "See, we told you so."

Index

A server passed by and offered me a warm Parmesan crostini from his tray. I forced myself to smile and take one, but I folded it into a napkin.

I paused for a moment, until the same server reached the group that contained Emma, then I approached.

"You have to try these," I gushed. I forced a laugh. "You've got to keep up your strength if you're working for Richard."

Emma briefly frowned, then her face cleared. "He does work long hours. But I don't mind."

She took a crostini and bit into it. I could see Richard begin to approach us from across the room, but George intercepted him.

"Oh, it's not just the hours," I said. "He's very particular, isn't he?"

She nodded and quickly popped the rest of her appetizer into her mouth.

"Well, I'm glad everyone finally has something to eat. You'd think the caterers would at least show up on time with what they charge." I spoke loudly enough so that the middle-aged man holding the platter of food could hear, and more important, so Emma would think I'd lobbed the harsh comment at him. I could feel my cheeks burn, but I hoped Emma assumed it was from too much wine. When I met her eyes, I saw disdain in them for my rudeness.

Richard extracted himself from George, walking directly toward us. Right before he arrived, I pivoted and headed in the opposite direction.

Give them one more reason. I knew I had to do it now or I'd lose my nerve.

Every step was a struggle as I slowly crossed the room. My pulse throbbed in my ears. I could feel a thin film of cold sweat gathering on my top lip.

All of my instincts were screaming at me to stop, to turn around. I forced myself forward, weaving through the clusters of smiling people. Someone touched my arm, but I pulled away without a glance.

Only the thought of Emma and Richard watching propelled me forward.

I knew I wouldn't have another chance to be near her anytime soon.

I reached the iPod that was attached to our speakers. Richard had carefully arranged a playlist, alternating jazz with some of his favorite classical compositions. The elegant music soared through the room.

I clicked to the Spotify app and selected seventies disco music, as I'd practiced doing. Then I cranked up the volume.

"Let's get this party started!" I shouted, raising my arms into the air. My voice cracked, but I continued, "Who wants to dance?"

The murmured conversations halted. Faces turned toward me in unison, as if they'd been choreographed.

"Come on, Richard!" I called.

Even the caterers were staring at me now. I caught a glimpse of Hillary averting her eyes, then of Emma gaping at me before quickly turning to look at Richard. He strode toward me quickly and my insides clenched.

"You forgot our house rule, honey," he called, his voice filled with a forced merriment. He turned down the volume. "No Bee Gees until after eleven!"

Relieved laughter cut through the room as Richard flipped the music back to Bach and reached for my arm and led me into the hallway. "What is wrong with you? How much have you had to drink?" His eyes narrowed and I didn't have to conjure the panicked note of apology in my voice.

"I can't—just a couple glasses, but—I'm sorry. I'll switch to water right now."

He reached for my half-full goblet of Chardonnay and I quickly relinquished it.

For the rest of the night, I felt my husband's glare. I saw his fingers clenching his glass of Scotch. I tried to remember the sympathy mixed with admiration on Emma's face when he'd smoothed over the scene I'd created; that was what got me through the rest of the party.

I'd accomplished everything I'd set out to do.

It was worth it, even though my bruises didn't heal for two weeks.

Richard never sent me a new piece of jewelry to make amends for that misunderstanding. This was confirmation he was no longer as invested in us; his focus was shifting.

"I'm in love with Richard," I say a final time as I peer into the empty hallway. "I am supposed to be here."

It wasn't difficult to get into Richard's office building. Just a few floors below his firm was an accounting company that handled high-net-worth individuals. I made an appointment, explaining that I was a single woman who had recently come into an inheritance. It wasn't far from the truth. After all, I still had the receipt from Richard's check in my wallet. I booked the last appointment of the day, six o'clock, and sailed past the guard's desk with my visitor sticker attached to my new dress.

After my appointment, I took the elevator to Richard's floor and walked quickly to the ladies' room. The code hadn't changed, and I slipped into the end stall. I already looked as much like Emma as possible on the outside; my new red lipstick and fitted dress and curled hair completed my physical transformation. I tore my visitor's pass into a dozen pieces and buried it in the trash can. I spent the next couple of hours practicing her voice, her posture, her mannerisms. A few women came in to use the bathroom, but no one lingered.

Now it is eight-thirty. I finally see the three-person cleaning crew emerge from the elevator, pushing a cart filled with supplies. I force myself to wait until they reach the door of Richard's firm.

I am confident.

"Hello!" I call as I stride briskly toward them.

I am poised.

"Nice to see you again."

I belong here.

Surely this crew must have encountered Emma on nights she worked late with Richard. The man who has just unlocked the double glass doors gives me a hesitant smile.

"My boss needs me to check something on his desk."

I gesture to the corner office I know so well. "I'll just be a minute."

I hurry past them, taking longer steps than I would normally. One of the cleaning women picks up a duster and follows me, which I expected. I pass Emma's old cubicle, which now holds a potted African violet and a flowered tea mug. Then I open the door to Richard's office.

"It should be right here." I walk behind the desk and open one of the two heavy lower drawers. But it is empty save for a squeezable stress reliever, a few Power-Bars, and an unopened box of Callaway golf balls.

"Oh, he must've moved it," I say to the cleaner. I can feel her energy heighten; she's clearly a little nervous now. She moves closer to me. I can read her mental process. She is telling herself I must belong here or I could never have gotten through the guard. And she doesn't want to offend an office employee. But if she's wrong, she could be jeopardizing her job.

My salvation is staring at me: a silver-framed photograph of Emma on the corner of Richard's desk. I pick it up and show it to the cleaning woman, making sure to hold it a couple of feet away from her. "See? It's me." She breaks into a relieved smile, and I'm glad she doesn't think to ask why my boss keeps a photo of his assistant on his desk.

I pull open the second drawer and see Richard's files. Each has a typewritten label.

I find the one marked AmEx and leaf through his statements until I find the itemized one for February.

What I'm searching for is right at the top: Sotheby's Wine, $3,150 refund.

The cleaning woman has turned toward the windows to dust the blinds, but I can't allow myself even the briefest of celebrations. I slip the piece of paper into my purse.

"All done! Thank you!"

She nods and I start to exit the office. As I round the edge of the desk, I reach out and touch Emma's photo again. I can't resist. I twist it so she faces the wall.

CHAPTER
THIRTY-THREE

THE NEXT MORNING, I awaken feeling more refreshed than I have in years. I've slept straight through for nine hours without the aid of alcohol or a pill. Another small victory.

I can hear Aunt Charlotte puttering in the kitchen as I approach. I walk up behind her and envelop her in a hug. Linseed and lavender; her scent is as comforting to me as Richard's aroma is unsettling.

"I love you."

Her hands cover mine. "I love you, too, honey." Surprise threads through her voice; it's as if she can sense the shift within me.

We have hugged dozens of times since I moved in. Aunt Charlotte embraced me as I sobbed after a cab left me on her building's doorstep. When I was unable to sleep as the memories of the worst times in my marriage tormented me, I felt her slip onto the bed and wrap me up in her arms. It was as if she wanted to absorb my pain. For every page in my notebook that

I filled with descriptions of Richard's deceit, I could write an equal number recounting times throughout my life when Aunt Charlotte has buoyed me with her steady, undemanding love.

But today I'm the one reaching out to her. Sharing my strength.

When I let go, Aunt Charlotte picks up the pot of coffee she has just brewed, and I pull the cream out of the refrigerator and hand it to her. I crave calories—nourishing food to fuel my newfound fortitude. I crack eggs into a pan, scramble in cherry tomatoes and shredded cheddar cheese, and slide two pieces of whole-grain bread into the toaster.

"I've been doing some research." She looks up at me and I can tell she knows exactly what I'm talking about. "You are never going to be alone in this. I'm here for you. And I'm not going anywhere."

She stirs the cream into her coffee. "Absolutely not. You're young. And you are not spending your life taking care of an old woman."

"Too bad," I say lightly. "Like it or not, you're stuck with me. I found the best macular degeneration specialist in New York. He's one of the top guys in the country. We're seeing him in two weeks." The office manager has already emailed me the forms that I'll help Aunt Charlotte fill out.

Her wrist moves in more rapid circles, and the coffee is in danger of sloshing over the edge of her mug. I can tell she's uncomfortable. I'm sure that as a self-employed artist, she doesn't have a great health-care plan.

"When Richard came by, he gave me a check. I have plenty of money." And I deserve every cent of it. Before she can protest, I reach for a mug of my own. "I can't argue about this before I have coffee." She laughs, and I change the subject. "So, what are you doing today?"

"I thought I'd go to the cemetery. I want to visit Beau."

Usually my aunt makes this trip only on their wedding anniversary, which is in the fall. But I understand she is seeing everything anew now, fixing familiar images into her memory bank to revisit them when her eyesight is gone.

"If you're up for company, I would love to join you." I give the eggs a final stir and add salt and pepper.

"You don't have to work?"

"Not today." I butter the toast and slide the eggs out of the pan, dividing them between two plates. I serve Aunt Charlotte, then take a sip of coffee to buy some time. I don't want to worry her, so I come up with a story about storewide layoffs. "I'll explain it to you over breakfast."

At the cemetery, we plant geraniums by his headstone—yellow, red, and white—as we trade some of our favorite Beau stories. Aunt Charlotte recounts how the first time they met, he pretended to be the blind date she was meeting at a coffee shop. He didn't reveal the truth until a week later, on their third date. I've heard this story many times, but it always makes me laugh when she tells the part about how relieved he was to no longer have to answer to the name David. I share how I loved the little journalist's notebook he kept in his back pocket with a pencil threaded through the spirals. Whenever I came to New York with my mother to visit, Uncle Beau gave me a duplicate one. We'd pretend to report on a story together. He'd take me to the local pizza parlor, and while we waited for our pie, he'd tell me to record everything I saw—the sights, the smells, what I overheard—just like a real reporter. He didn't treat me like a little kid. He respected my observations and told me I had a sharp eye for detail.

The midday sun is high in the sky, but the trees shade us from the heat. Neither of us is in any rush; it feels so good to be sitting in the soft grass, chatting comfortably with Aunt Charlotte. In the distance I see a family approach—a mother, father, and two kids. One of the little girls is riding on her father's shoulders, and the other is holding a bouquet of flowers.

"You were both wonderful with children. Did you ever want to have any?" I'd posed the same question to my aunt once before, when I was younger. But now I'm asking as a woman—as an equal.

"To be honest, no. My life was quite full, with my art and Beau traveling on assignment all the time and me joining him. . . . Plus, I was lucky enough to get to share you."

"I'm the lucky one." I lean over to briefly rest my head on her shoulder.

"I know how much you wanted children. I'm sorry it didn't happen for you."

"We tried for a long time." I think of those slashing blue lines, the Clomid and resulting nausea and exhaustion, the blood tests, the doctor's visits. . . . Every single month, I felt like a failure. "But after a while, I wasn't sure if we were meant to have kids together."

"Really? It was that simple?"

I think, *No, of course not, it wasn't simple at all.*

It was Dr. Hoffman who finally suggested to me that Richard should have a second semen analysis. "Didn't anyone tell him that?" she'd asked as I sat in her immaculate office during one of my annual physicals. "There can be errors in any medical test. It's standard to repeat the sperm analysis after six months or a year. And it's just so unusual for a healthy young woman like yourself to be having this much trouble."

This was after my mother had died; after Richard had promised things would never get bad again. He'd made an effort to come home by seven o'clock several nights a week; we'd taken a long weekend trip to Bermuda and another to Palm Beach, where we golfed and sunbathed by a pool. I'd recommitted to our marriage, and after about six months, we'd agreed to start trying anew for a baby. The job Paul had suggested never came through, but I continued my volunteer work with the Head Start program. I'd told myself I'd been partly to blame for Richard's violence. What husband would be happy to learn his wife was sneaking into the city and lying about it? Richard had told me that he'd thought I had a lover; I reasoned he would never have hurt me otherwise. As time passed and my sweet, attentive husband brought me flowers just because and left love notes on my pillow, it became easy to rationalize that all marriages had low points. That he would never do it again.

Just as my bruises faded, so, too, did the small, insistent voice inside me that cried out for me to leave him.

"My marriage was kind of . . . uneven," I tell my aunt now. "I began to worry about bringing a child into such an unstable environment."

"You seemed happy with him at first," Aunt Charlotte says carefully. "And he clearly adored you."

Both statements are true, so I nod. "Sometimes those things aren't enough."

When I told Richard what Dr. Hoffman had said, he immediately agreed to get retested. "I'll make the appointment for Thursday at lunch. Think you can keep your hands off me for that long?" We'd learned the first time that he had to wait two days to build up a good number of mobile sperm.

At the last minute, I decided to join Richard for this test. I thought back to how he was always beside me at my fertility appointments. Besides, I didn't have much else to do that day and figured it might be nice to spend the afternoon in the city, then meet him after work for dinner. At least those were the reasons I told myself.

When I couldn't immediately reach my husband on his cell phone, I called the clinic. I remembered the name from the first time Richard had gone years earlier—the Waxler Clinic—because Richard had joked that it should really be called the Whack-Off Clinic.

"He just phoned to cancel a little while ago," the receptionist said.

"Oh, something must have come up at work." I was grateful I hadn't begun the journey into the city.

I'd assumed he'd go the following day, and I planned to suggest at dinner that I accompany him.

That night, when I greeted him at the door, he folded me into a hug. "My Michael Phelps boys are still going strong."

I remember time seemed to shudder to a stop. I was so stunned I couldn't speak.

I pulled back, but he just hugged me tighter. "Don't worry, sweetheart. We're not going to give up. We'll get to the bottom of this. We'll figure it out together."

It took everything I had to look him in the eye when he released me. "Thank you."

He smiled down at me, his expression gentle.

You're right, Richard. I will get to the bottom of this. I will figure this out.

The next day, I bought my black Moleskine notebook.

My aunt has been my confidante for much of my life, but I will not burden her with this. I reach into my purse for the bottles of water I brought along and give one to her, then I take a long sip from mine. After a little while, we stand up. Before we leave, Aunt Charlotte slowly runs her fingertips across the engraved letters of her husband's name.

"Does it ever get easier?"

"Yes and no. I wish we'd had more time. But I'm so grateful I had eighteen wonderful years with him."

I link my arm through hers as we walk home, taking a long route.

I think of what else I can do for her with Richard's money. My aunt's favorite city in the world is Venice. I decide that when this is all over—when I've saved Emma—I will take my aunt to Italy.

After we arrive home and Aunt Charlotte goes into her studio to work, I am ready to execute my plan to get the AmEx statement to Emma. I know how I'm going to do it, because Emma never changed the cell phone number she used as Richard's assistant. I will photograph the document and text it to her. But I need to transmit it when Richard won't be near, so she can absorb the full implications of what she is seeing.

It was too early when Aunt Charlotte and I left this morning; they might have still been together. But by now he should be at work.

I take the statement out of my purse and smooth it open. The AmEx is Richard's business card, the one he keeps for his sole use. Most of the charges on this statement are for lunches, taxis, and costs associated with a trip to Chicago. I also see the fee for the caterers for our party; I signed the contract and specified the details, but since it was primarily a business function at our home, Richard had said to use the AmEx card they had for us on file. The four-hundred-dollar charge from Petals in Westchester covered the cost of our flower arrangements.

The Sotheby's wine refund is at the top of the statement, a few lines above the charge for the caterers.

I use my phone to take a photograph of the entire page, making sure the date, the name of the wine store, and the amount stand out clearly. Then I text it to Emma with a one-line message:

You placed the order, but who canceled it?

When I see that it has been delivered, I put down my cell. I didn't use my burner phone; there's no longer any need to conceal what I'm doing. I wonder what Emma's memory will reveal when she looks back at that night. She thinks I was drunk. She believes Richard covered for me. She is under the impression that I polished off a case of wine in a week.

If she realizes one of those things is not true, will she question the others?

I stare at my phone, hoping this will be the thread she begins to worry between her fingertips.

CHAPTER
THIRTY-FOUR

EMMA'S RESPONSE ARRIVES the next morning, also in the form of a single-line text message:

Meet me at my apartment at 6 tonight.

I stare at the words for a full minute. I cannot believe it; I've been trying to reach her for such a long time, and now she is finally welcoming me in. I've created the necessary doubts in her mind. I wonder what she already knows, and what she will ask me.

Exhilaration floods my body. I don't know how long of an audience she will grant me, so I write down the points I must make: I can bring up Duke, but what proof do I have? Instead I write *fertility questions.* I want her to ask Richard why we weren't able to become pregnant. He'll surely lie, but the pressure will build in him. Maybe she'll see what he fights to keep hidden. *His surprise visits,* I write. Has Richard ever shown up unexpectedly, even when she hasn't told him her schedule for the day? But that won't be enough; it certainly wasn't for me. I will need to tell her about the times Richard physically hurt me.

I have never shared with anyone what I am about to reveal to Emma. I need to harness my emotions so they don't overwhelm me and reinforce any lingering suspicions she might have that I'm unbalanced.

If she listens to me with an open mind—if she seems receptive to what I am saying—I must explain to her how I meticulously crafted a plan to free myself. That I set her up, but that I had no idea it would go this far.

I will beg for her forgiveness. But more important than my absolution is her own. I will tell her she has to leave Richard, immediately, tonight even, before he ensnares her.

When I last saw Emma, I tried to craft the image I wanted her to see: that we were interchangeable versions of each other. Now I strive for plain honesty. I shower and put on jeans and a cotton T-shirt. I don't fuss with my makeup or hairstyle. To burn off nervous energy, I plan to walk to her apartment. I decide to leave at five o'clock. I cannot be late.

Be calm, be rational, be convincing, I repeat to myself. Emma has seen the act I've put on; she has heard Richard's rendering of my character; she knows of my reputation. I need to reverse everything she believes about me.

I am still practicing what I will say when my cell phone rings with a number I don't recognize. But I know the area code well: it's in Florida.

My body tenses. I sink onto my bed and stare at the

screen as the phone rings a second time. I must answer this.

"Vanessa Thompson?" a man asks.

"Yes." My throat is so dry I cannot swallow.

"This is Andy Woodward from Furry Paws." His voice sounds hearty and affable. I've never spoken to Andy before, but I began to anonymously donate to the shelter in Maggie's honor following her death, since she'd volunteered there in high school. After Richard and I married, he suggested that we increase my monthly contribution substantially and fund the shelter's renovation. As a result, Maggie's name is on a plaque by the door. Richard has always served as the contact to the shelter; he suggested it, saying it would be less stressful for me.

"I got a call from your ex-husband. He told me the two of you have decided that in light of everything, you can no longer afford your charitable gifts."

Here is my punishment, I realize. I took Richard's money, so this is how he'll exact revenge. There's a symbolic flourish to it, a balancing of the scales, that I know Richard is relishing.

"Yes," I say when I realize the silence has stretched on too long. *This was for Maggie, not for me,* I think furiously. "I'm really sorry. If it's okay, I can still contribute a small amount each month. It won't be the same, but it's something."

"That's very generous of you. Your ex-husband explained how terribly he feels about this. He said he would personally call Maggie's family to let them know what happened. He asked me to relay that to you so you didn't have to worry about any loose ends."

Which of my actions is Richard retaliating for? Am I being punished for the photograph of Duke, my letter to Emma, or cashing the check?

Or does he also know I've texted the AmEx statement to Emma?

Andy doesn't understand; no one does. Richard would have been charming when they chatted. He'll be the same way when he calls Maggie's family. He will make sure he speaks to them all individually, including Jason. Richard will mention my maiden name—it will seamlessly slip into the conversation—and perhaps he'll say something about how I've moved to New York City.

What will Jason do?

I wait for the familiar panic to set in.

It doesn't.

Instead, I am struck by the realization that since Richard left me, I haven't thought of Jason at all.

"The family will be delighted to have a chance to thank you both personally," Andy says. "Of course, they write notes every year that I forward to your husband."

My head jerks up. *Think like Richard. Stay in control.* "I don't—you know, my husband didn't share those notes with me." Somehow my tone is casual and my voice remains steady. "I was really affected by Maggie's death, and he probably thought it would be too painful for me to read them. But I'd like to know what they said now."

"Oh, sure. They mostly sent emails for me to forward. I remember the content, if not the exact words. They always expressed how grateful they are to you, and how they hoped to meet you one day. They visit the shelter occasionally. What you've done has meant so much to them."

"The parents come to the shelter? And Maggie's brother, Jason?"

"Yes. They all do. And Jason's wife and his two children. They're a lovely family. The kids cut the ribbon on opening day after the renovation."

I take a half step backward and nearly drop the phone.

Richard must have known this for years; he intercepted the correspondence. He *wanted* me to be afraid, to be his nervous Nellie. He needed to pretend to be my protector because of some depravity within him. He cultivated my dependence upon him; he preyed upon my fear.

Of all of Richard's cruelties, this is perhaps the worst.

I sink down onto my bed at the realization. Then I wonder what else he did to pique my anxiety when we were together.

"I would like to call Maggie's parents and brother, too," I say after a moment. "May I have their contact information?"

Richard must be on edge; he should have realized Andy might mention the emails and letters to me. My ex-husband is the one who isn't thinking clearly now.

I've never pushed him this far before, not even close.

He is probably desperate to hurt me, to make me stop. To erase me from his tidy life.

I say good-bye to Andy and realize I need to get to Emma. It is almost five o'clock, the time I'd planned to leave. But I'm suddenly overwhelmed by the worry that Richard is waiting outside. I can't walk there, after all. I will take a cab, but I still need to get to one safely.

A second exit in the back of the building leads to a narrow alley where trash cans and recycling bins are kept. Which door will Richard expect me to use?

He knows I suffer from mild claustrophobia, that I loathe being trapped. The alley is narrow and usually empty, penned in on both sides by high buildings. So that's the route I choose.

I change into sneakers, then I wait until five-thirty. I take the elevator downstairs and fumble with the latch on the fire door. I ease it open and look out. The alley appears vacant, but I can't see behind the tall plastic waste containers. I take a deep breath and push away from the door, sprinting down the passageway.

My heart is exploding. I expect his arms to shoot out and grab me at any moment. I push myself toward the sliver of sidewalk I see ahead. When I finally reach it, I whip around in a full circle, gasping, as I scan my surroundings.

He isn't here; I am certain I would be able to feel his predatory gaze upon me.

I lift my arm to signal passing cabs as I hurry down the street. It doesn't take long for one to pull over, and the driver expertly weaves through rush-hour traffic toward Emma's place.

When we arrive at her corner, I see it's four minutes before six. I ask the driver to keep the meter running while I mentally rehearse a final time what I need to say. Then I exit the cab and walk to the door of Emma's building. I press the buzzer for 5C and hear Emma's voice through the intercom: "Vanessa?"

"Yes." I can't help it; I glance behind me a final time. But no one is there.

I take the elevator to her floor.

She opens the door as I approach. She is as lovely as ever, but she looks worried; her brow is creased. "Come in."

I step over the threshold and she shuts the heavy door behind me. At last, I am alone with her. I feel a rush of relief so intense I am practically giddy.

Her apartment is a small, neat one-bedroom. A few framed photographs are on the wall, and a vase of white roses is on a side table. She gestures toward the low-backed couch and I perch on the edge. But she remains standing.

"Thank you for seeing me."

She doesn't respond.

"I have wanted to talk to you for so long."

Something seems off. She isn't looking at me. Instead she is glancing over her shoulder. Toward her bedroom door.

Out of the corner of my eye, I see that door begin to open.

I recoil into the couch, my hands instinctively flying up to protect myself. *No,* I think desperately. I want to run, but I cannot move, just like in my nightmares. I can only watch as he approaches.

"Hello, Vanessa."

My eyes shift to Emma. Her expression is inscrutable.

"Richard," I whisper. "What are—why are you here?"

"My fiancée told me you texted her some nonsense about a wine refund." He continues moving toward me, his gait fluid and unhurried. He stops next to Emma.

Some of the terror eases out of my body. He isn't here to hurt me. Not physically, anyway; he would never do that in front of anyone. He is here to put an end to this by defeating me in front of Emma.

I rise to my feet and open my mouth, but he wrests away control of the situation. The element of surprise is on his side.

"When Emma called me, I explained to her exactly what happened." Richard longs to close the distance between us. His narrowed eyes tell me so. "As you well know, I realized that wine wasn't technically a business expense since I wasn't sure we'd drink any of it at the party. The ethical thing to do was to cancel the AmEx payment and put it on my personal Visa. I remember telling you this when Sotheby's delivered the Raveneau to the house and I stored it in the cellar."

"That's a lie." I turn to Emma. "He never ordered the wine at all. He's so good at this—he can come up with explanations for anything!"

"Vanessa, he told me instantly what happened. He

didn't have time to concoct a story. I don't know what you're after."

"I'm not after anything. I'm trying to help you!"

Richard sighs. "This is exhausting—"

I cut him off. I am learning how to anticipate his line of attack. "Call the credit-card company!" I blurt. "Call Visa and confirm that charge while Emma listens in. It'll take thirty seconds and we can settle this now."

"No, I'll tell you how we're going to settle this. You've been stalking my fiancée for months. I warned you last time what would happen if this continued. I'm sorry about all your issues, but Emma and I are filing restraining orders against you. You've left us no choice."

"Listen to me," I say to Emma. I know I only have this final chance to convince her. "He made me think I was crazy. And he got rid of my dog—he left the gate open or something."

"Jesus," Richard says. But his lips are tightening.

"He tried to convince me it was my fault we couldn't have kids!" I blurt.

I see Richard's hands curl into fists and I reflexively flinch, but I press on.

"And he hurt me, Emma. He hit me and he knocked me down and he almost strangled me. Ask him about the jewelry he gave me to cover my injuries. He will hurt you, too! He will ruin your life!"

Richard exhales and squeezes his eyes shut.

Can she sense how close he is to the edge? I wonder. *Has she ever seen Richard disappear into anger before?* But perhaps I've said too much. She might've believed some of what I've told her, but how can she reconcile my outlandish accusations with the solid, successful man standing beside her?

"Vanessa, there is something deeply wrong with you." Richard pulls Emma close to him. "You are never to come near her again."

The restraining order means Richard will have an official record of my being a menace to them. If there is ever a violent confrontation between us, the evidence will support his side. He always controls the perception of our narrative.

"You need to leave." Richard walks over and reaches for my elbow. I flinch, but his touch is gentle. He has vanquished his anger for now. "Should I take you downstairs?"

I feel my eyes widen at his words. I shake my head rapidly and try to swallow, but my mouth is too dry.

He wouldn't do anything to me in front of Emma, I assure myself. But I know what he is insinuating.

As I walk past Emma, she folds her arms across her chest and turns away.

CHAPTER

THIRTY-FIVE

I wish I could have given my Moleskine notebook to Emma along with the Raveneau receipt. Maybe if she had the chance to leaf through the pages, she would detect the undercurrent churning together these seemingly disparate events.

But that notebook no longer exists.

By the time I wrote my last entry, my journal contained pages and pages of my recollections and, increasingly, of my fears. After the night when Richard told me he'd gone for the sperm analysis and I vowed to get to the bottom of what had really happened, I could no longer suppress my intuition. My notebook served as a courtroom, with my words arguing both sides of every issue. *Perhaps Richard went to a different clinic to have his semen tested,* I'd written. *But why would he do that when he'd scheduled an appointment at the original one?* I'd hunch over in bed in the guest room, the dim bulb in the nightstand light illuminating my scribblings as I tried to puzzle out other confusing encounters, going back to the very beginning of our marriage: *Why did he tell me the lamb vindaloo I made was delicious, then leave more than half of it on his plate and send me a gift certificate for cooking lessons the following morning? Was it a thoughtful gesture? Was he trying to convey a subtle message about the inadequacy of the meal? Or was it a punishment for my revelation that day at Dr. Hoffman's office that I'd gotten pregnant in college?* And, a few pages before that: *Why would he suddenly appear the night of my bachelorette party when he hadn't been invited to join us? Did love or control propel him?*

As my questions mounted, it became impossible for me to continue to deny it: Something was either deeply wrong with Richard, or deeply wrong with me. Both possibilities were terrifying.

I had been certain Richard sensed the change between us. I couldn't help withdrawing from him— from everyone. I dropped out of all my volunteer work. I rarely went into the city. My friends from Gibson's and the Learning Ladder had moved on with their lives. Even Aunt Charlotte was away; she and a Parisian artist friend had arranged a six-month apartment exchange, something they'd done several times in the past. I had felt steeped in loneliness.

I explained to Richard that I was depressed because we couldn't have a baby. But not being pregnant was a blessing now.

I escaped into alcohol but never around my husband. I needed to be sharp in his presence. When Richard noted the amount of wine I was consuming during the day and asked me to stop drinking, I agreed. Then I began driving a few towns over to buy my Chardonnay. I hid the empty bottles in the garage and sneaked out on early-morning walks to bury the evidence in a neighbor's recycling bin.

The alcohol made me sleepy, and I napped most afternoons, sobering up in time for Richard's return from work. I craved the comfort of soft carbohydrates and soon dressed only in my forgiving yoga pants and loose tops. I didn't need a psychiatrist to tell me that I was trying to add a protective layer to my body. To make me less attractive to my trim, fitness-conscious husband.

Richard didn't directly say a word about my weight gain. I'd shed and put on the same fifteen pounds several times throughout our marriage. Whenever my weight ticked upward, he made a point of requesting that I cook broiled fish for dinner, and when we went to restaurants, he eschewed bread and asked for his salad dressing on the side. I followed his lead, ashamed that I lacked his discipline. On the night of my birthday dinner with Aunt Charlotte at the club, I'd grown agitated, but not because I thought the waiter had made a mistake with my salad. By that birthday my old clothes no longer fit. My husband had refrained from commenting on this.

But the week before the celebratory dinner, he'd bought a new, high-tech scale and had set it up in our bathroom.

One night I woke up in our Westchester house desperately missing Sam. I'd realized the previous afternoon

that it was her birthday. I wondered how she was celebrating. I didn't even know if she still worked at the
Learning Ladder and lived in our old apartment, or
if she'd gotten married. I turned to see the clock announce it was almost three A.M. This wasn't unusual;
I rarely slept through the night anymore. Beside me
in bed, Richard was like a statue. Other women complained about their husbands snoring or hogging the
blankets, but Richard's stillness always camouflaged
whether he was deeply slumbering or on the verge of
waking up. I lay there for a few moments, listening to
his steady exhalations, then I slipped out from beneath
the covers. I padded quietly to the door, then glanced
back. Had my movements awoken him? In the darkness
it was impossible to tell if his eyes were open.

I eased the door closed behind me, then headed to
the guest room. I'd blamed Sam for our rift, but now
that I was reevaluating everything, I'd begun to wonder
where the fault truly lay. After our dinner at Pica, we'd
drifted further apart. Sam had invited me to a going-
away party for Marnie, who was moving back home
to San Francisco, but Richard and I already had dinner plans at Hillary and George's house for the same
evening. When I showed up at the party late, bringing
Richard with me, I recognized disappointment on my
best friend's face. We stayed for less than an hour. For
much of it, Richard stood in the corner on his phone. I
saw him yawn. I knew he had an early meeting the next
morning, so I made our excuses. A few weeks later, I
called Sam to see if she wanted to meet for a drink.

"Richard isn't going to come, is he?"

I lashed back, "Don't worry, Sam, he doesn't want to spend time with you any more than you do with him."

Our argument escalated, and that was the last time we spoke.

As I entered the guest room and reached under the mattress to retrieve my notebook, I wondered if I'd been so hurt and angry because Sam seemed to know something I wouldn't allow myself to accept—that Richard wasn't the perfect husband. That our marriage only looked good on the surface. *The Prince. Too good to be true. You're dressed like you're going to a PTA meeting.* She'd even called me Nellie once in a tone that felt more mocking than joking.

I lifted the mattress with my right hand and stretched out my left arm, sweeping it back and forth on top of the box spring. But I couldn't feel the familiar edges of my journal.

I eased down the mattress and turned on the night-stand lamp. I dropped to my knees and hoisted the mattress even higher. It wasn't there. I checked under the bed, then began to peel back the comforter, then the top sheet.

My hands stopped moving when I felt static rise over my skin. I detected Richard's stare before he spoke a word.

"Is this what you're looking for, Nellie?"

I slowly rose to my feet and turned around.

My husband stood in the doorway, wearing boxers and a T-shirt, holding my notebook. "You haven't been writing this week. Although I guess you've been busy. You went to the grocery store on Tuesday right after I left for work, and yesterday you drove to the wineshop in Katonah. Sneaky, aren't you?"

He knew everything I was doing.

He lifted up the journal. "You believe I'm the one who can't get us pregnant? You think there's something wrong with me?"

He knew everything I was thinking.

He moved closer to me and I cowered. But he merely took an object off the nightstand behind me. A pen.

"You forgot something, Nellie. You left this here. I saw it the other day." His voice was different, more high-pitched than I'd ever before heard it, and the cadence was almost playful. "Where there's a pen, there must be paper."

He riffled through the pages. "This is fucking insane." His sentences tumbled out faster and faster. "Duke! Lamb vindaloo! Turning your picture around! *I* set off the house alarm!" With every accusation, he tore out a new page. "My parents' wedding photo! You snuck into the storage unit! You're wondering about my parents' cake topper? You've been going into the city to talk about our marriage to some stranger? You're psychotic. You're even worse than your mother!"

I didn't realize I was backing up until I felt the nightstand hit the back of my legs.

"You were a pathetic waitress who couldn't even walk down the street without thinking someone was going to come after you." He dragged his hands through his hair, and part of it stood up. His T-shirt was rumpled and stubble coated his jawline. "You ungrateful bitch. How many women would kill to have a man like me? To live in this house, to vacation in Europe and drive a Mercedes."

All the blood seemed to rush out of my head; I felt dizzy with fear. "You're right, you're so good to me," I began to plead. "Didn't you see the other pages? I wrote how generous you were in paying for the animal shelter renovation. How much you helped me when my mom died. And how much I love you."

I wasn't reaching him; he seemed to be looking through me. "Clean up this mess," he ordered.

I dropped to my knees and gathered the pages.

"Tear them up."

I was crying now, but I obeyed, gathering a handful and trying to rip them in half. But my hands were shaking and the stack of pages was too thick for me to shred.

"You're so fucking incompetent."

I sensed a metallic change in the air; it felt swollen with pressure.

"Please, Richard," I sobbed. "I'm so sorry. . . . Please . . ."

His first kick landed near my ribs. The pain was explosive. I curled into a ball and pulled my knees into my chest.

"You want to leave me?" he shouted as he kicked me again.

He climbed on top of me, forcing me onto my back and pinning my arms with his knees. His kneecaps ground into my elbows.

"I'm sorry. I'm sorry. I'm sorry." I tried to twist away

from him, but he was sitting on my abdomen, trapping me in place.

His hands closed around my neck. "You were supposed to love me forever."

I gagged as I thrashed and kicked beneath him, but he was too strong. My vision became spotty. I wrenched one hand free and clawed at his face as I grew light-headed.

"You were supposed to save me." His voice was soft and sad now.

Those were the last words I heard before I blacked out. When I came to, I was still lying on the floor. The pages of my notebook had vanished.

Richard was gone, too.

My throat felt raw and desperately parched. I lay there for a long time. I didn't know where Richard was. I rolled onto my side, my arms encircling my knees, shivering in my thin nightgown. After a while I reached up and pulled the comforter around me. Fear immobilized me; I couldn't leave the room.

Then I smelled fresh coffee.

I heard Richard's footsteps coming up the stairs. There was nowhere to hide. I couldn't run, either; he was between me and the front door.

He walked unhurriedly into the room, holding a mug.

"Forgive me," I blurted. My voice was hoarse. "I didn't realize . . . I've been drinking and I haven't been sleeping. I haven't been thinking clearly. . . ."

He just stared at me. He was capable of killing me. I had to convince him not to.

"I wasn't going to leave you," I lied. "I don't know why I wrote those bad things. You're so good to me."

Richard took a sip of coffee, keeping his eyes on mine over the rim of his mug.

"Sometimes I worry I am becoming like my mother. I need help."

"Of course you wouldn't leave me. I know that." He had regained his composure. I'd said the right words. "I acknowledge I lost my temper, but you pushed me," he said, as if he'd merely snapped at me during a minor spat. "You've been lying to me. You've been deceiving me. You are not acting like the Nellie I married." He paused. He patted the bed and I hesitantly climbed up to sit on its edge, keeping the comforter around me like a shield. He sat down next to me, and I felt the mattress sink beneath his weight, tilting me toward him.

"I've thought about it, and this is partly my fault. I should have recognized the warning signs. I indulged your depression. What you need is structure. A routine. From now on you'll get up with me. We'll work out together in the morning. Then we'll eat breakfast. More protein. You'll get fresh air every day. Rejoin some committees at the club. You used to make an effort with dinner. I'd like for you to do that again."

"Yes. Of course."

"I am committed to our marriage, Nellie. Do not ever make me question whether you are again."

I quickly nodded, even though the motion hurt my neck.

He left for work an hour later, telling me he would phone me when he got to the office and that he expected me to answer. I did exactly as he said. I could only swallow some yogurt for breakfast because of my throat, but it was high in protein. It was early fall, so I took a walk in the cool fresh air, keeping the ringer on my cell phone turned up as high as possible. I put on a turtleneck to cover the red, oval imprints that would turn into bruises, then went to the grocery store and selected filet mignon and white asparagus to serve to my husband.

I was in the checkout lane when I heard the cashier saying, "Ma'am?" I realized she'd been waiting for me to pay for my groceries. I looked up from the bag of food I was staring at, wondering if he already knew what I was buying for his dinner. Somehow Richard was aware of every time I left the house; he'd found out about my secret journey into the city, the liquor store I frequented, the errands I ran.

Even when I'm not there, I'm always with you.

I looked at the woman at the next register over as she appeased a cranky toddler who wanted to be lifted out of the cart. I glanced up at the security camera near the door. I saw the pile of red baskets with gleaming metal handles, the display of tabloid magazines, the candy in bright, crinkly wrappers.

I had no idea how my husband was constantly watching me. But his surveillance was no longer stealth. I could not deviate from the more stringent new rules of our marriage. And I could certainly never try to leave him.

He would know.

He would stop me.

He would hurt me.

He might kill me.

A week or two later, I looked up from the breakfast table and watched Richard select a crispy piece of turkey bacon that I'd prepared along with our scrambled eggs. His face was still slightly flushed from our morning workout. Steam curled from his cup of espresso; *The Wall Street Journal* was folded by his plate.

He bit into the bacon. "This is perfectly cooked."

"Thank you."

"What are your plans for today?"

"I'm going to shower and then head over to the club for the used-book drive. Lots of sorting to do."

He nodded. "Sounds good." He wiped his fingertips on his napkin, then snapped opened the newspaper. "And don't forget Diane's retirement luncheon is next Friday. Can you pick up a nice card and I'll put the cruise tickets inside?"

"Of course."

He bent his head and began to scan the stocks.

I stood up and cleared the table. I loaded the dishwasher and wiped down the counters. As I ran the sponge over the marbled granite, Richard approached me from behind and wrapped his arms around my waist. He kissed my neck.

"I love you," he whispered.

"I love you, too."

He put on his suit jacket, then picked up his briefcase

and walked toward the front door. I followed him, watching as he headed to his Mercedes.

Everything was exactly as Richard wished it to be. When he came home tonight, dinner would be ready. I'd have changed out of my yoga pants into a pretty dress. I'd entertain him with a funny story about what Mindy had said at the club.

Richard looked up at me through the big bay window as he walked toward the driveway.

"Good-bye!" I called, waving.

His smile was wide and genuine. He radiated contentment.

I realized something in that moment. It felt like glimpsing a pinpoint of sunlight in the cottony, suffocating gray pressing in on me.

There was one way my husband would let me go.

It would need to be his idea to end our marriage.

CHAPTER
THIRTY-SIX

I AM UPDATING my résumé on my laptop when my cell phone rings.

Her name flashes across the screen. I hesitate before answering. I worry this could be another of Richard's traps.

"You were right," says the husky voice I've come to know so well.

I remain quiet.

"About the Visa bill." I fear that even my slightest utterance will cause Emma to stop talking, change her mind, hang up. "I called the credit card company. There was no wine charge from Sotheby's. Richard never ordered the Raveneau."

I can hardly believe what I have just heard. Part of me still worries Richard may be behind this, but Emma's tone is different from in the past. She no longer sounds contemptuous of me.

"Vanessa, the way you looked when he said he would escort you downstairs . . . that's what convinced me to check. I thought you were jealous. That you wanted him back. But you don't, do you?"

"No."

"You're terrified of him," Emma says bluntly. "He actually hit you? He tried to strangle you? I can't believe Richard would—but—"

"Where are you? Where is he?"

"I'm home. He's in Chicago on business."

I'm grateful she's not at Richard's apartment. Her place is probably safe. Although her phone may not be. "We need to meet in person." But this time it will be in a public place.

"How about the Starbucks on—"

"No, you have to stick to your routine. What do you have planned today?"

"I was going to take a yoga class this afternoon. And then go pick up my wedding gown."

We won't be able to talk in a yoga studio. "The bridal shop. Where is it?"

Emma gives me the address and time. I tell her I will meet her there.

What she doesn't know is that I'm going to arrive early to make sure I'm not ambushed again.

"What a perfect bride," Brenda, the boutique's owner, exclaims.

Emma's eyes meet mine in the mirror as she stands on the raised platform in a creamy silk sheath. She is unsmiling, but Brenda seems too busy surveying the final fit of the dress to notice Emma's somber mood.

"I don't think it needs a single tweak," Brenda continues. "I'll just steam it and we'll messenger it to you tomorrow."

"Actually, we can wait," I say. "We'd like to take it with us." The dressing area is empty, and in a corner are several armchairs. It's private. Safe.

"Would you care for some champagne, then?"

"We'd love some," I say, and Emma nods in agreement.

As Emma slips out of the dress, I avert my gaze. Still, I see her reflection—smooth skin and lacy pink lingerie—in a half dozen angles in mirrors around the room. It is an oddly intimate moment.

Brenda takes the gown and carefully places it onto a padded hanger while I impatiently wait for her to leave the room. Before Emma can even finish fastening the button on her skirt, I head to the chairs. This bridal shop is one place where I can be certain Richard won't unexpectedly show up. It's practically forbidden for a groom to see his fiancée in a wedding gown before the ceremony.

"I thought you were crazy," Emma says. "When I worked for Richard, I used to hear him on the phone with you, asking what you'd eaten for breakfast and if you'd gotten out for some fresh air. I had access to emails he sent asking where you were. Saying he'd phoned four times that day but you hadn't answered. He was always so worried about you."

"I can see how it seemed that way."

We fall silent as Brenda returns with two flutes of champagne. "Congratulations, again." I'm worried she will linger and chat, but she excuses herself to check on the dress.

"I figured I had you sized up," Emma tells me bluntly once Brenda is gone. She looks at me carefully, and I see an unexpected familiarity in her round blue eyes. Before I can place it, she continues, "You had this perfect life with this great guy. You didn't even work, you just lounged around in the fancy house he paid for. I didn't think you deserved any of it."

I let her continue.

She tilts her head to the side. It's almost as if she is seeing me for the first time. "You're different than I imagined. I've thought about you so much. I wondered what it would feel like for you to know your husband was in love with someone else. It used to keep me up at night."

"It wasn't your fault." She has no idea how true that statement is.

A loud ding emanates from Emma's purse. She freezes with the flute almost touching her lips. We both stare at her bag.

She pulls out her phone. "Richard texted me. He just arrived at his hotel in Chicago. He asked what I'm up to and wrote that he misses me."

"Text him and tell him you miss him, too, and that you love him."

She raises one eyebrow but does what I ask.

"Now give me your phone." I tap on it, then show it to Emma. "It's tracking you." I point to the screen. "Richard bought it for you, right? His name is on the account. He can access your phone's location—*your* location—at any time."

He did the same thing to me after we got engaged. I eventually figured it out after that day in the grocery store when I wondered if he already knew what I'd be serving him for dinner. It was how he discovered my clandestine visit into the city, and to the wine store a few towns over.

Richard was also responsible for the mysterious hang-ups that began after I met him, I've realized. Sometimes they served as punishment, such as during our honeymoon, when Richard thought I'd been flirting with the young scuba instructor. Other times I believe he was trying to keep me off-balance; to unnerve me so that he could subsequently reassure me. But I don't tell this part to Emma.

Emma is staring at her phone. "So he pretends he doesn't know what I'm doing even though he does?" She sips her drink. "God, that's sick."

"I realize it's a lot to take in." I recognize this is an extraordinary understatement.

"Do you know what I keep thinking about? Richard showed up right after you slipped that letter under my door. He immediately tore it up, but I keep remembering this one line you wrote: 'A part of you already knows who he is.'" Emma's eyes grow unfocused and I suspect she is reliving the moment when she began to see her fiancé anew. "Richard wanted to—it was like he wanted to *murder* that letter. He kept ripping it into smaller and smaller bits, then he shoved them in his pocket. And his face—it didn't even look like him."

She lingers in the memory for a long moment, then

shakes it off and stares directly at me. "Will you tell me the truth about something?"

"Of course."

"Right after the cocktail party at your house, he came in with a bad scratch on his cheek. When I asked him what happened, he said a neighbor's cat did it when he tried to pick it up."

Richard could have covered the scratch or come up with a better story for it. But conclusions would be drawn after my sloppy conduct at our party; it was more proof of my instability, my volatility.

Emma is very still now. "I grew up with a cat," she says slowly. "I know that scratch was different."

I nod.

Then I inhale deeply and blink hard. "I was trying to get him off me."

Emma doesn't react initially. Perhaps she instinctively realizes that if she shows me sympathy, I'll crumple into tears. She simply looks at me, then turns away.

"I can't believe I got this so wrong," she finally says. "I thought you were the one . . . He's coming back tomorrow. I'm supposed to spend the night at his place. Then Maureen's coming to town. We're meeting at my apartment so she can see my dress . . . then we're all going to taste wedding cakes!"

Her chatter is the only sign that she's nervous, that our conversation has thrown her.

Maureen is an added complication. I'm not surprised Richard and Emma are including her in the wedding preparations, though; I remember wanting to do the same. Along with the butterfly-clasp necklace I gave her, I sought out her opinion on whether Richard would want black-and-white or color photographs in the album that was my wedding gift to him. Richard also called her and put her on speakerphone while the three of us discussed entrée options for the meal.

I put my arm around Emma. At first her body is rigid, but it softens for a brief moment before she pulls away. She must be holding back a tidal wave of emotions.

Save her. Save her.

I close my eyes and recall the girl I couldn't save. "Don't be scared. I'm going to help you."

When we arrive at Emma's place, she lays her wedding gown across the back of her sofa.

"Can I get you anything to drink?"

I barely touched my champagne; I want my thoughts to remain clear so I can figure out how Emma can safely extract herself from Richard. "I'd love some water."

Emma bustles about her galley kitchen, anxiously chattering again. "Do you take ice? I know my place is a little messy. I was going to do laundry and then all of a sudden I just felt like I had to check on the Visa charge. He added me to that account after we got engaged, so all I had to do was call the number on the back of my card. I've got some grapes and almonds if you want a snack. . . . Usually I reviewed his AmEx statements before submitting them to Accounting for reimbursement, but a couple of times, he told me he'd handle it himself. That's why I never saw the refund." Emma shakes her head.

I absently listen to her as I look around. I know she is grasping for ways to blunt the impact of what she has learned about Richard. The champagne she quickly drank, the frantic energy—I recognize the symptoms too well.

As Emma cracks ice cubes into our glasses, I study her small living room. The couch, the end table, the roses that are now slightly wilted. Nothing else is on the end table, and I suddenly realize what I'm looking for.

"Do you have a landline?"

"What?" She shakes her head and hands me my glass of water. "No, why?"

I am relieved. But all I say is "Just figuring out the best way for us to communicate."

I am not going to tell Emma everything yet. If she learns how much worse the reality could be, she may shut down.

There's no need to explain that I am certain Richard was somehow eavesdropping on calls I made from our house phone during our marriage.

I finally made the connection after I saw the pattern emerge on the pages of my notebook.

When our burglar alarm erupted in the Westchester house and I fled to cower in my closet, I was initially reassured that the video cameras posted by our front and back doors showed no evidence of an intruder. Then I realized Richard had checked the cameras. No one else had verified what they might reveal.

And immediately before the siren had blared, I was on the phone with Sam. I'd made a joke about bringing guys home after a night of barhopping. I now believe Richard had set off the alarm. It was my punishment.

He feasted on my fear; it nurtured his sense of strength. I think of the mysterious cell phone hangups that began shortly after our engagement, how he'd booked a scuba dive for his claustrophobic new bride, how he always reminded me to set the burglar alarm. How he'd enjoyed comforting me, whispering that he alone would keep me safe.

I take a long drink of water. "What time is Richard coming back tomorrow?"

"Late afternoon." Emma looks at her gown. "I should hang this up."

I walk with Emma into her bedroom and watch as she hooks the gown on the back of her closet door. It appears to be floating. I can't pull my gaze away from it.

The bride who was supposed to wear this exquisite dress no longer exists. The gown will remain vacant on her wedding day.

Emma straightens the hanger slightly, her hand lingering on the dress before she slowly pulls it away.

"He seemed so wonderful." Her voice is filled with surprise. "How can a man like that be so brutal?"

I think of my own wedding dress, nestled in a special acid-free box in my old closet in Westchester, preserved for the daughter I never had.

I swallow hard before I can speak. "Parts of Richard *were* wonderful. That's why we stayed married for so long."

"Why didn't you ever leave him?"

"I thought about it. There are so many reasons why I should have. And so many reasons why I couldn't."

Emma nods.

"I needed Richard to leave me."

"But how did you know he ever would?"

I look into her eyes. I have to confess. Emma has already been devastated today. But she deserves to be told the truth. Without it, she will be trapped in a false reality, and I know exactly how destructive that can be.

"There's one more thing." I walk back to the living room and she follows me. I gesture to the couch. "Can we sit down?"

She perches rigidly on the edge of a cushion, as if steeling herself for what is to come.

I reveal everything: The office holiday party when I first spotted her. The gathering at our house when I pretended to be drunk. The night I faked illness and suggested Richard take her to the Philharmonic. The business trip when I encouraged them to stay overnight.

She is holding her head in her hands by the time I finish.

"How could you do this to me?" she cries. She leaps to her feet and glares at me. "I knew it all along. There really is something wrong with you!"

"I am so sorry."

"Do you know how many nights I lay awake wondering if I'd contributed to the demise of your marriage?"

She didn't say she felt guilt, but it's natural that she would have; I am certain their physical relationship began while Richard and I were still married. Now all of Emma's memories with Richard are doubly tainted. She must feel like a pawn in my dysfunctional marriage. Maybe she even thinks we deserved each other.

"I never thought it would go this far. . . . I didn't think he would propose. I thought it would just be an affair."

"*Just* an affair?" Emma shouts. Her cheeks flush with anger; the passion in her voice surprises me. "Like it's some innocuous little thing? Affairs destroy people. Did you ever consider how much I would suffer?"

I feel battered by her words, but then something ignites in me and I find myself pushing back at her.

"I *know* affairs destroy people!" I shout, thinking of how I'd curled up in bed for weeks after learning about Daniel's deception, after seeing his tired-looking wife. It happened almost fifteen years ago, but I can still visualize that little yellow tricycle and pink jump rope behind the oak tree in his yard. I still remember how my pen had trembled across the page when I signed in at the Planned Parenthood clinic.

"I was deceived once by a married man in college," I say, more softly now. This is the first time I've ever revealed this particular piece of my story to anyone. The rush of pain that hits me is so fresh, it's as if I'm that heartbroken twenty-one-year-old all over again. "I thought he loved me. He never told me about his wife. Sometimes I think my life could have been so different if I'd only known."

Emma strides across the room. She yanks open her door.

"Get out." But the venom is gone from her tone. Her lips are trembling and her eyes shine with tears.

"Just let me say one final thing," I plead. "Call Richard tonight and tell him you can't go through with the wedding. Tell him I came over again and it was the last straw."

She doesn't react, so I continue quickly as I begin to walk toward the door. "Ask him to announce to everyone that the engagement is off; that part is really important," I stress. "He won't punish you if he gets to control the message. If he comes out with his dignity."

I pause in front of her so she cannot miss my words. "Just say you can't deal with his psycho ex-wife. Promise me you'll do that. Then you'll be safe."

Emma is silent. But at least she is looking at me, even though it is with a cold, appraising stare. Her eyes rake across my face and down my body, then back up again.

"How am I supposed to believe anything you say?"

"You don't need to. Please go stay with a friend. Leave your cell phone here so he can't find you. Richard's anger always passes quickly. Just protect yourself."

I step over the threshold and hear the door close sharply behind me.

I hover in the hallway, staring down at the dark blue carpet beneath my feet. Emma must be reevaluating everything I've told her. She probably doesn't have any idea who to trust.

If Emma doesn't follow the script I've given her, Richard may unleash his rage on her, especially if he can't find me. Or worse, he may convince her to change her mind and go through with the wedding.

Maybe I should not have told her of my role in this. Her security should have trumped my need to unburden my guilt, to be scrupulously honest. Her faulty perception would have left her less vulnerable than this dangerous truth.

What will be Richard's next step?

I have twenty-four hours until he returns. And I have no idea what to do.

I slowly walk down the hallway. I am so reluctant to leave her. I am about to step into the elevator when I hear a door open. I glance up and see Emma standing in her threshold.

"You want me to tell Richard I'm calling off the wedding because of you."

I nod quickly. "Yes. Blame it all on me."

Her brow furrows. She tilts her head to one side and looks me up and down again.

"It's the safest solution," I say.

"It might be for me. But it isn't safe for you."

CHAPTER
THIRTY-SEVEN

"I'VE MISSED YOU so much, sweetheart," Richard says.

Something in my chest twists at the love and tenderness filling his voice.

My ex-husband stands not nine feet from me. He returned from Chicago a few hours ago and stopped by his place to change into jeans and a polo shirt before arriving here, at Emma's apartment.

I am crouched down, staring through an old-fashioned keyhole in her bedroom closet. It is the only place that gives me both cover and a vantage point into the room.

Emma sits on the edge of her bed in sweatpants and a T-shirt. A package of Sudafed, a box of tissues, and a cup of tea rest on her nightstand. I thought of those touches.

"I brought you chicken soup and fresh-squeezed orange juice from Eli's. And some zinc. My trainer swears by it to kick summer colds."

"Thank you." Emma's voice is feeble and soft. She is convincing.

"Can I get you a sweater?"

My insides clench as Richard's form fills my vision, blotting out the rest of the room. He is approaching my hiding place.

"Actually, I'm too warm. Could you bring me a cool washcloth for my forehead?"

We didn't practice those lines; Emma improvises well.

I don't exhale until I hear his footsteps reverse themselves as he heads to the bathroom.

I shift slightly; I've been kneeling for several minutes and my legs are aching.

Emma hasn't looked my way even once. She is still reeling from my revelation; she doesn't seem to completely trust me. I don't blame her.

"You don't get to orchestrate my life any longer," she'd said to me yesterday as I stood in her hallway, by the elevator. "I'm not going to end things with Richard on the phone just because you told me to do it. I'll decide when to call my wedding off."

But at least she is allowing me to remain close by tonight with my cell phone in hand. Watching him. Protecting her.

We both predicted Richard would insist on visiting when Emma told him she was sick. Faking illness solves a multitude of problems. If Richard is tracking Emma's movements, it would explain why she skipped her yoga class. Why she wants to sleep at her own place. And why she can't even kiss him, let alone have sex with him. I wanted to spare her that.

"Here you go, baby," Richard says, coming back into the room.

I glimpse him bending over the bed, then his back blocks me from seeing his movements. Still, I imagine him holding the damp washcloth to Emma's forehead and smoothing back her hair. Looking at her with so much love.

My kneecaps feel as if they are grinding against the hardwood floor. My thighs are burning; I am desperate to stand up and shake out my legs. But Richard might hear.

"I hate for you to see me like this. I'm a wreck."

If I didn't know the truth, I would be certain she was innocent of any ulterior motives.

"Even when you're sick, you're the most beautiful woman in the world."

I still know Richard so well. He genuinely means every word. If Emma expressed a craving for a strawberry sorbet or cozy cashmere socks, he'd scour Manhattan to get her the best. He'd sleep on the floor next to her if she said it would make her feel better. This is the part of my ex-husband's nature that is the most difficult to expunge from my heart. At this moment, just like his profile through the keyhole, it is all I can see.

I squeeze my eyes shut.

Then I immediately force them open. I've learned the danger of failing to observe the things I don't want to behold.

If Emma didn't live up to Richard's expectations—and it was inevitable that she would fail to—there would be consequences. If she wasn't the wife of his fantasies, he would hurt her, then give her jewelry to smooth it over. If she didn't provide the family or create the kind of home he desired, he would systematically assault her reality and twist it until it became unrecognizable even to her. And worst of all, he would take away whatever or whomever she loved the most.

"I'll tell Maureen you need to cancel tomorrow," Richard says to Emma.

Perfect, I think. This delay could buy us some more time to figure out how to best extract Emma.

But instead of agreeing, Emma says, "No, I'm sure I'll be better if I just get some rest."

"Anything you want, my love, but the most important thing is you."

Even through the closet door I can feel the magnetic pull of his charisma.

I was holding on to the hope that Emma would begin to create distance between her and Richard tonight. But after only a few minutes in his presence, she seems to be wavering.

Through the keyhole, I can see their clasped hands. His thumb is gently stroking her wrist.

I want to leap out of the closet and wrench them apart; he is swaying her. Luring her back to him.

"Besides, Maureen has to come over so I can show her my wedding dress." That dress is now hanging six inches to my left; Emma tucked it in here so Richard wouldn't see it. "Plus we have those fun wedding errands. You don't think I'm going to let you do the cake tasting alone, do you?" she continues in a playful voice.

This is the opposite of what should be happening. The Emma of right now is a completely different woman from the one of twenty-four hours ago who asked me, as we stood in this same room, how Richard could be so wonderful yet so brutal.

I cannot hold my position any longer. I slowly lift my right knee off the floor and plant my foot gently down. I repeat the motion with my left leg. Inch by agonizing inch, I rise. Dresses and shirts engulf me, silky fabrics sliding across my face.

A hanger clinks against the metal rod, the sound as delicate and precise as a wind chime striking a single note.

"What was that?" Richard asks.

I cannot see anything.

His citrus scent surrounds me, or am I imagining it? I suck in a shallow inhalation. My heart pounds violently. I am terrified I will pass out, my body thumping against the closet door.

"Just my creaky old bed." I hear Emma shift, and miraculously, the bed squeaks. "I can't wait until I only sleep in yours."

Again, I am stunned by her lightning-quick subterfuge.

Then Emma says, "But there is one thing I need to tell you."

"What's that, sweetheart?"

She hesitates.

I sink back down to peer through the keyhole again. I wonder why she's drawing out their conversation. She knows how clever Richard is; doesn't she want him out of the apartment before he figures out she isn't really sick?

"Vanessa called me today."

My eyes widen and I barely suppress a gasp. I can't believe she has set me up again.

Richard barks an expletive and violently kicks the wall next to Emma's dresser. I feel the vibrations through the floorboards. I see his fists clench and unclench.

He stands facing the wall for a few moments, then he turns around to look at Emma.

"I'm sorry, baby." His voice is strained. "What bullshit did she tell you this time?"

Emma has chosen to believe Richard. The act she has been putting on was to trick me. I can call 911, but what will the police think if Emma and Richard tell them I broke in here?

Emma's clothes are suffocating me. There's no air in this small closet. I'm trapped. I feel the grip of claustrophobia descend as my throat tightens.

"No, Richard, it wasn't like that. Vanessa apologized. She said she's going to leave me alone."

My head is swimming. Emma is so far off any script I could have anticipated that I can't even guess at her intentions.

"She's said that before." I can hear Richard breathing heavily. "But she keeps calling and coming to my office and writing letters. She won't stop. She's insane—"

"Honey, it's okay. I really believe her. She sounded different."

My legs feel as if they've turned to liquid. I have no idea why Emma created this pretense.

Richard exhales. "Let's not talk about her. I hope we never have to again. Can I get you anything else?"

"All I want to do is sleep. And I don't want you to get sick. You should go. I love you."

"I'll pick you and Maureen up at two tomorrow. I love you, too."

I stay in the closet until Emma opens the door a few minutes later. "He's gone."

I bend and unbend my legs and wince. I want to ask her about the unexpected turn in her conversation, but her face is so expressionless that I know she only wants me out.

"Can I wait a few minutes before I leave?"

She hesitates, then nods. "Let's go into the living room." I catch her sneaking appraising looks at me. She's wary.

"What are we going to do next?"

She frowns. I can tell my use of the word *we* chafes her. "I'll figure it out." She shrugs.

Emma doesn't get it. She doesn't seem to feel any urgency to call off the wedding. If Richard can be this compelling in a brief visit, what will happen when he feeds her bites of cakes, his arm wrapped around her waist, and whispers promises of how happy he'll make her?

"You saw him kick the wall," I say, my voice rising. "Don't you see what he is?"

This is so much bigger than just Emma. Even if Richard lets Emma go—which I'm not convinced he'll do—what about all the many ways in which Richard hurt me? And the woman before both of us, the dark-haired ex who couldn't bear to keep that gift from Tiffany's? I am now certain he hurt her, too.

My ex-husband is a creature of habit, a man ruled by routines. Whatever stunning piece of jewelry that glossy blue bag contained was his apology; his attempt to literally cover up an ugly episode.

Emma does not know that I intend to save any woman who could become Richard's future wife.

"You have to end it soon. The longer it goes on, the worse it will be—"

"I said I'll figure it out."

She walks to the door and opens it. I reluctantly step past her.

"Good-bye," she says. I have the distinct feeling she plans to never see me again.

But she's wrong about that.

Because by now I know I need a plan of my own. The seed of an idea was planted as I watched Richard's explosive flash of anger at the mention of my name, my fictitious call. It takes shape in my mind as I walk down the blue-carpeted hallway, following the path Richard took only minutes ago.

Emma thinks Maureen is coming over to see the wedding gown tomorrow, then they'll go cake tasting with Richard.

She has no idea what will really happen.

CHAPTER
THIRTY-EIGHT

THE PAGES OF MY BRAND-NEW life insurance policy unspool from the printer.

I clip them together, then slide them into a manila envelope. I have made sure to select a plan that covers not only my demise from natural causes, but also death and dismemberment from an accident.

I place it on my desk, beside the note I've penned to Aunt Charlotte. It is the hardest letter I have ever written. In it I've left information about my bank account with my swollen new balance so she can easily access it. She is the sole beneficiary of my life insurance policy as well.

I have three hours left.

I pick up my to-do list and mark off that task. My room is clean, my bed neatly made. All of my belongings are stored in my wardrobe.

Earlier today I also checked off two other items. I telephoned Maggie's parents. And then I called Jason.

At first he didn't recognize my name. It took him a

few moments to remember. I paced during the pause in which he made the mental connection, wondering if he would acknowledge our past encounters.

Instead, he thanked me profusely for the donations to the animal shelter, then caught me up on his life since college. He told me he'd married the girlfriend he'd met on campus. "She stuck by me," Jason said, his voice thickening with emotion. "I was so angry at everyone, but mostly at myself for not being there to help my little sister. When I got arrested for drunk driving and went to rehab—well, my girlfriend was my rock. She never gave up on me. We got married the next year."

Jason's wife was a middle-school teacher, he said. She'd graduated the same year as me. That was why he went to her ceremony at the Piaget Auditorium and stood in the corner. He was there to support her.

My guilt and anxiety had concocted a lie. It was never even about me.

I couldn't help but feel sad for the woman who let all that fear shape so many of her life choices.

I am still very afraid, but it is no longer constricting me.

Only a few items remain on my list now.

I open my laptop and clear my browser history, wiping away evidence of my recent investigations. I double-check to make sure my searches into airline tickets and small, non-chain motels are no longer visible to anyone who might access my computer.

Emma does not understand Richard as I do. She cannot grasp what he is truly capable of. It's impossible to imagine what he becomes in his worst moments.

Richard will simply move on unless I stop him. He'll be more careful, though. He will find a way to rotate the kaleidoscope and sweep away the current reality, forming a bright, distracting new image.

I lay my outfit on my bed and take a long, hot shower, trying to ease the tightness in my muscles. I wrap myself in my bathrobe and clear the fog from the mirror above the sink.

Two and a half hours left.

First my hair. I brush back the damp strands into a tight bun. I carefully apply makeup and select the diamond stud earrings Richard gave me for our second anniversary. I fasten my Cartier Tank watch around my wrist. It's essential that I am able to keep track of every second.

The dress I've selected is one I wore when Richard and I went to Bermuda. A classic snow-white sheath. It could almost serve as a wedding dress for a simple beachside ceremony. It is one of the outfits he sent back to me a few weeks ago.

I've chosen it not only for its history, and for its possibilities, but also because it has pockets.

Two hours remain.

I slip on a pair of flats, then gather the items I will need.

I tear up my list into tiny bits, then flush them down the toilet. I watch as they swirl away, the ink blurring.

A final act I must do remains before I leave. It is the most wrenching item on my list. It will require every bit of strength and all of the acting expertise I have accumulated.

I find Aunt Charlotte in the extra bedroom that serves as her studio. The door is open.

Canvases are stacked three deep throughout the room. Splatters of succulent colors layer the soft wood floor. For a moment, I surrender to the beauty: cerulean skies, clinquant stars, the horizon in the ephemeral moment before dawn. A rhapsody of wildflowers. The weathered grain of an old table. A Parisian bridge spanning the Seine. The curve of a woman's cheek, her skin milky white and creased by age. I know this face so well; it is my aunt's self-portrait.

Aunt Charlotte is lost in the landscape she is creating. Her strokes are looser than they have been in the past; her style more forgiving.

I want to capture her like this in my memory.

After a few moments she looks up and blinks. "Oh, I didn't see you there, honey."

"I don't want to disturb you," I say softly. "I'm heading out for a bit, but I've left lunch for you in the kitchen."

"You look nice. Where are you off to?"

"A job interview. I don't want to jinx it, but I'll tell you about it tonight."

My eyes fall on a canvas across the room: a laundry line hanging outside a building above a Venetian canal, the shirts and pants and skirts billowing in a breeze I can almost feel.

"You have to promise me one thing before I go."

"Bossy today, aren't you?" Aunt Charlotte teases.

"Seriously. It's important. Will you go to Italy before the end of the summer?"

The smile fades from Aunt Charlotte's lips. "Is something wrong?"

I desperately want to cross the room and hold on to her, but I fear if I do, I might not be able to leave.

This is all in my letter, anyway:

Remember that day when you taught me about how sunlight contains all the colors of the rainbow? You were my sunlight. You taught me how to find rainbows. . . . Please go to Italy for us. You will always carry me with you.

I shake my head. "Nothing's wrong. I was planning on taking you as a surprise. But I'm worried if I get this job, we won't be able to go together. That's all."

"Let's not think about that now. You just focus on your interview. When is it?"

I check my watch. "Ninety minutes."

"Good luck."

I blow her a kiss and imagine it landing on her soft cheek.

THIRTY-NINE

FOR THE SECOND TIME in my life, I stand in a white dress at the end of a narrow swath of blue, looking at Richard.

The elevator doors close behind him. But he is motionless.

I feel the intensity of his gaze all the way down at my end of the hallway. I've been deliberately stoking his anger for days, coaxing it from the place where he struggles to keep it buried. It is the opposite of how I taught myself to behave during my marriage.

"Are you surprised, sweetheart? It's me, Nellie."

It is precisely two o'clock. Emma is a dozen yards from where I stand, in her living room, with Maureen. Neither of them knows I am here; I snuck into the building an hour ago by trailing a deliveryman through the door. I knew exactly when the uniformed man carrying the long rectangular box would arrive. It was I who placed the order for a dozen white roses to be sent to Emma this afternoon.

"I thought you were out of town," he says.

"I changed my mind. I wanted to have another chat with your fiancée."

My hands are touching a few different objects in my pockets. Which I pull out first will depend on Richard's reaction. Richard takes a step onto the carpet runner. It is almost impossible for me to avoid shrinking back. Despite the summer heat, his dark suit, white shirt, and gold silk tie appear creaseless and elegant. He isn't unhinged yet, not the way I need him to be.

"Really? And what do you intend to say to her?" His voice is dangerously quiet.

"I'm going to start with this." I pull out a piece of paper. "It's your Visa bill showing you never ordered the Raveneau." He's too far away to see the fine print and realize it's actually one of my own statements.

I need to press on before he demands to see the proof. I smile at Richard, though my stomach is churning. "I'm also going to explain to Emma that you are tracking her through her phone." I keep my voice as low and steady as his. "Just like you did to me."

I can almost feel his body clench. "You've gone over the edge, Vanessa." Another measured step. "This is my fiancée you're messing with. After everything I went through with you, you're trying to ruin this now?"

Out of the corner of my eye, I gauge the distance to Emma's apartment door. I tense my body in preparation.

"You lied about Duke. I know what you did with him, and I'm going to tell Emma." This isn't true—I never found out what happened to my beloved dog, although I truly don't think Richard actually harmed him—but it hits its target. I see Richard's face compress in rage.

"And you lied about the sperm analysis, too." My mouth is so dry it's difficult to form the words. I take a step backward, toward Emma's door. "Thank God you couldn't get me pregnant. You don't deserve to have a child. I took photos after you hurt me. I collected evidence. You didn't think I was smart enough, did you?"

I've carefully chosen words I know will incite my ex-husband.

They are working.

"Emma is going to leave you when I tell her everything." I can no longer keep my voice from shaking. But the truth it contains is undeniable. "Just like the woman before me left you." I take a deep breath and deliver my closing lines. "I wanted to leave you, too. I was never your sweet Nellie. I didn't want to stay married to you, Richard."

He explodes in fury.

This I expected.

But I miscalculated how quickly he would lose all control, how fast he would be.

He is upon me before I have taken more than a few running steps toward Emma's door.

Richard's hands tighten around my throat, cutting off my supply of oxygen.

I thought I'd have time to scream. To bang on the door and summon Emma and Maureen, so they could witness Richard's transformation. Richard would never be able to explain this violence away; it would be the physical proof that couldn't be found in a notebook or a filing cabinet or a storage unit. This was the other insurance policy I needed to save us all—me, Emma, and the women in Richard's future.

I was also counting on Richard to halt his attack when Maureen and Emma appeared—or that, at least, they would be able to stop him. Now there is no reason for him to deny himself his need to extinguish me.

My windpipe feels as if it is being crushed into the back of my neck. The pain is agonizing. My knees buckle.

My left arm helplessly stretches out toward Emma's door, though I know it's futile. She is twirling in her wedding gown for her future sister-in-law. Completely unaware of what is happening on the other side of her living room wall.

Richard's assault is nearly silent; a gurgling noise wrenches free from my throat, but it is not loud enough to reach her or anyone else who may be home on this floor.

He thrusts me back against the wall. His hot breath brushes my cheeks. I see the scar above his eye, a silvery crescent, as he leans closer.

I am engulfed by dizziness.

I fumble for the pepper spray in my pocket, but as I pull it out, Richard bangs my head against the wall and I lose my grip on it. It tumbles to the carpet.

My vision recedes; it is being hemmed in by black

borders. I frantically kick at his shins, but he is unaffected by my blows.

My lungs are burning. I am desperate for air.

His eyes blaze into mine. I claw at his body and my hand hits something hard in his suit jacket pocket. I wrench it free.

Save us.

I summon the last of my strength and smash the object against his face.

Richard releases a cry.

A splash of bright red blood erupts from the wound by his temple.

My limbs grow heavy and my body begins to relax. A calmness I haven't felt in years—perhaps ever—overtakes me. My knees give way.

I am fading into the blackness when the pressure abruptly disappears. I collapse and draw in a ragged breath. I cough violently, then I retch.

"Vanessa," a woman calls from what seems a great distance away.

I am splayed on the carpet, one of my legs bent beneath me, but I feel as if I am floating.

"Vanessa!"

Emma. All I can do is roll my head to one side, bringing broken pieces of porcelain into view. I see jagged pieces of china figurines—a serenely smiling blond bride and her handsome groom. It was our cake topper.

And beside them is Richard on his knees, his expression blank, a rivulet of blood streaming down his face and staining his white shirt.

I suck in a painful breath, then another. All of the menace has leached out of my ex-husband. His hair has fallen forward into his eyes. He is immobile.

Fresh oxygen returns a little strength to my body, though my throat feels so swollen and tender I can't swallow. I manage to edge backward and pull myself into a sitting position, slumping against the hallway wall.

Emma hurries to my side. She is barefoot and, like me, clad in a white sheath. Her wedding gown. "I heard someone yell—I came out to see—but then . . . What happened?"

I can't speak. I can only suck in shallow, greedy breaths.

I see her eyes drift down to my neck. "I'm calling an ambulance."

Richard doesn't react to any of this, not even to the gasp of surprise Maureen gives as she suddenly appears in the doorway.

"What is going on?" Maureen stares at me—the woman she dismissed as unstable, as her brother's cast-off wife. Then she looks at Richard, the man she helped raise and loves unconditionally. She goes to him. She reaches out and touches his back. "Richard?"

He raises a hand to his forehead, then stares at the streak of red on his palm. He seems oddly distant, as if he's in shock.

I hate the sight of blood. That was one of the first things he'd ever said to me. I suddenly realize that in all of the ways Richard hurt me, he never once made me bleed.

Maureen hurries into the apartment and returns with a wad of paper towels. She kneels next to him and presses the towels to his wound. "What's going on?" Her words grow sharper. "Vanessa, why are you here? What did you do to him?"

"He hurt me." My voice is hoarse and every syllable feels as if one of the shards of porcelain is rubbing against the inside of my throat.

I need to finally say these words.

I grimace as I make my voice louder. "He choked me. He nearly killed me. Just like he used to hurt me when we were married."

Maureen gasps. "He wouldn't—no, not—"

Then she falls silent. She is still shaking her head, but her shoulders sag and her face collapses. I am certain that even though she hasn't yet seen the fingerprint-shaped marks that I know are blooming on my neck, she believes me.

Maureen straightens up. She pulls the paper towels away from Richard's face and examines his injury. When she speaks again, her tone is brisk, yet caring.

"It isn't so bad. I don't think you need stitches."

Richard doesn't react to this, either.

"I'll take care of everything, Richard." Maureen gathers up the shattered pieces of porcelain. She cups them in one hand, then wraps her arms around her brother and tilts her head close to his. I can just barely make out her whispered words: "I always took care of you, Richard. I never let anything bad happen to you. You don't have to worry. I'm here. I'm going to fix everything."

Her utterances are bewildering. But what shocks me most is the strange emotion infusing them. Maureen doesn't sound angry or sad or confused.

Her voice is filled with something I can't identify at first, because it is so out of place.

I finally realize what it is: satisfaction.

CHAPTER
FORTY

THE BUILDING BEFORE ME could be a Southern mansion, with its grand columns and wraparound porch lined with a tidy row of rocking chairs. But to gain access to the grounds, I have to pass through a gate manned by a security guard and show photo identification. The guard also searches the cloth bag I'm carrying. He raises his eyebrows when he sees the items inside, but merely nods for me to continue on my way.

A few patients at the New Springs Hospital are gardening or playing cards on the porch. I don't see him among them.

Richard is spending twenty-eight days at this acute mental-health facility, where he is undergoing intensive daily therapy sessions. It is part of the deal he made to avoid being prosecuted for assaulting me.

As I climb the wide wooden steps toward the entrance, a woman unfolds herself from a chaise lounge, her limbs sharp and athletic looking. The bright afternoon sun is in my eyes and I can't immediately identify her.

Then she moves closer, and I see it is Maureen. "I didn't know you'd be here today." I shouldn't be surprised; Maureen is all Richard has left now.

"I'm here every day. I've taken a leave of absence from work."

I look around. "Where is he?"

One of his counselors passed along Richard's request: He wanted to see me. At first I was unsure if I would comply. Then I realized I needed this visit, too.

"Richard is resting. I wanted to talk to you first." Maureen gestures to a pair of rocking chairs. "Shall we?"

Maureen takes a moment to cross her legs and smooth a crease in her beige linen pantsuit. Clearly she has an agenda. I wait for her to reveal it.

"I feel terrible about what happened between you and Richard." I see Maureen glance at the faded yellow discoloration on my neck. But there is a disconnect between her words and the energy she is conveying. Her posture is rigid and her face is devoid of sympathy.

She doesn't care for me. She never has, even though early on I'd hoped we would become close.

"I know you blame him. But it isn't that simple. Vanessa, my brother has been through a lot. More than you ever knew. More than you can ever imagine."

At this, I can't help blinking in surprise. She is casting Richard as the victim.

"He attacked *me*," I almost shout. "He nearly killed me."

Maureen seems unaffected by my outburst; she merely clears her throat and begins again. "When our parents died—"

"In the car accident."

She frowns, as if my remark has irritated her. As if she has planned for this to be less a conversation than a monologue.

"Yes. Our father lost control of their station wagon. It hit a guardrail and flipped. Our parents died instantly. Richard doesn't remember much, but the police said skid marks showed my dad was speeding."

I jerk back. "Richard doesn't remember—you mean he was in the car?" I blurt.

"Yes, yes," Maureen says impatiently. "That's what I'm trying to tell you."

I am stunned; he concealed more of himself than I ever realized.

"It was horrible for him." Maureen's words are almost rushed, as if she wants to hurry through these details before she gets to the important part of her story. "Richard was trapped in the backseat. He hit his forehead. The frame of the car was all twisted and he couldn't get out. It took a while for another driver to pass by and call for paramedics. Richard had a concussion and needed stitches, but it could have been so much worse."

The silvery scar above his eye, I think. The one he said was caused by a bike accident.

I picture Richard as a young teenager—a boy, really—dazed and in pain from the crash. Crying out for his mother. Failing to rouse his parents. Trying to wrench open the upside-down station wagon's doors. Beating his fists against the windows and yelling. And the blood. There must have been so much blood.

"My dad had a temper, and whenever he got mad, he drove fast. I suspect he was arguing with my mother before the crash." Maureen's cadence is slower now. She shakes her head. "Thank God I always told Richard to wear a seat belt. He listened to what I said."

"I had no idea," I finally respond.

Maureen turns to look at me; it's as if I've pulled her from a reverie. "Yes, Richard never talked about the accident with anyone but me. What I want you to know is that it wasn't just when he was driving that my father lost his temper. My father was abusive to my mother."

I inhale sharply.

My dad wasn't always good to my mom, Richard had told me after my mother's funeral as I sat shivering in the bathtub.

I think back to the photograph of his parents Richard hid in the storage unit. I wonder if he needed to literally bury it to suppress the memories of his childhood, so they could yield to the more palatable story he presented.

A shadow falls over me. I instinctively whip my head around. "I'm sorry to interrupt," a nurse in blue scrubs says, smiling. "You wanted me to let you know when your brother woke up."

Maureen nods. "Can you ask him to come down, Angie?" Then Maureen turns to me. "I think it would be better for you two to talk here rather than in his room."

We watch the nurse retreat. When the woman is out of earshot, Maureen's voice turns steely. Her words are clipped. "Look, Vanessa. Richard is fragile right now. Can we agree that you will finally leave him alone?"

"He's the one who wanted me to come here."

"Richard doesn't know what he wants right now. Two weeks ago, he thought he wanted to marry Emma. He believed she was perfect"—Maureen makes a little scoffing sound—"even though he barely knew her. He thought that about you at one time, too. He always wanted his life to look a certain way, like the idealized bride and groom on the cake topper he bought for my parents all those years ago."

I think of the mismatched date on the bottom of the figurines. "Richard bought that for your parents?"

"I see he didn't tell you about that, either. It was for their anniversary. He had this whole plan that we'd cook them a special dinner and bake them a cake. That they'd have a wonderful night and start loving each other again. But then the car crash happened. He never got to give it to them.

"It was hollow inside, you know. The cake topper. That's what I thought when I saw it broken in the hallway that day. . . . I guess he was bringing it to the tasting to show the cake designer. But Richard really has no business being married to anyone. And it's my job now to make sure that it doesn't happen."

She suddenly smiles—a wide, genuine grin—and I'm completely unnerved.

But it isn't for me. It's for her brother, who is approaching us.

Maureen stands up. "I'll give you two a few minutes alone."

I sit beside the man who both is and is no longer a mystery to me.

He wears jeans and a plain cotton shirt. Dark stubble lines his jaw. Despite the fact that he's been sleeping so much, he appears tired and his skin is sallow. He is no longer the man who enthralled me, then subsequently terrorized me.

He appears ordinary to me now, somehow deflated, like a man I wouldn't look at twice as he waited for a bus or bought a cup of coffee at a street kiosk.

My husband kept me off-balance for years. He tried to erase me.

My husband also hugged my waist on a green sled while we sped down a hill in Central Park. He brought me rum raisin ice cream on the anniversary of my father's death and left me love notes for no reason at all.

And he hoped I could save him from himself.

When Richard finally speaks, he says what I have wanted to hear for so long.

"I'm sorry, Vanessa."

He has apologized to me before, but this time I know his words are different.

At last they are real.

"Is there any way you could give me another chance? I'm getting better. We could start over."

I gaze out at the gardens and rolling green lawn. I had envisioned a scene much like this when Richard first showed me our Westchester house: The two of us side by side on a porch swing, but decades into our marriage. Connected by memories we'd constructed together, each of us layering in our favorite details with every retelling, until we'd created a unified recollection.

I'd expected to be angry when I saw him. But I only feel pity.

By way of an answer to his question, I hand Richard my cloth bag. He pulls out the top item, a black jewelry box. In it are my wedding and engagement rings. He opens the box.

"I wanted to give these back to you." I have spent so long mired in our past. It is time to return them to him and truly move on.

"We could adopt a child. We could make it perfect this time."

He wipes his eyes. I have never seen him cry before.

Maureen is between us in an instant. She takes the bag and the rings from Richard. "Vanessa, I think it's time for you to go. I'll see you out."

I stand up. Not because she told me to, but because I am ready to leave. "Good-bye, Richard."

Maureen leads me down the steps toward the parking lot.

I follow at a slower pace.

"You can do whatever you want with the wedding album." I gesture to the bag. "It was my gift to Richard, so it's rightfully his."

"I remember. Terry did a nice job. Lucky that he was able to fit you in that day after all."

I stop short. I'd never told anyone how close we'd come to not having a photographer at our ceremony.

And it has been nearly a decade since our wedding; even I couldn't come up with Terry's name that quickly.

As Maureen meets my stare, I recollect how a woman had phoned to cancel our booking. Maureen knew which photographer we were using; she had suggested I include black-and-white shots when I emailed her a link to Terry's website and sought her opinion about Richard's gift.

Her icy-blue eyes look so much like Richard's in this instant. It is impossible to gauge what she is thinking.

I recall how Maureen came to our house for every holiday, how she spent her birthdays with her brother engaged in an activity she knew I didn't enjoy, how she never married or had children. How I cannot remember her mentioning the name of a single friend.

"I'll take care of the album." She stops at the edge of the parking lot and touches my arm. "Good-bye."

I feel cold, smooth metal against my skin.

When I look down, I see she has slipped my rings onto the fourth finger of her right hand.

She follows my gaze. "For safekeeping."

CHAPTER

FORTY-ONE

"THANK YOU FOR SEEING ME today," I say to Kate as I settle into my usual spot on her couch.

Though I haven't been here in months—since when I was still married—the room is exactly the same, with magazines fanned on the coffee table and a few snow globes on the windowsill. Across from me, in the large aquarium, two angelfish languidly wind around a leafy green plant, while orange-and-white clown fish and neon tetra swim through a rock tunnel.

Kate is unchanged, too. Her eyes are large and sympathetic. Her long dark hair is brushed back behind her shoulders.

Richard caught me the first time I snuck into the city to meet Kate. I didn't return for quite a while. When I did, I made sure to tell him I was going to visit Aunt Charlotte. Then I deliberately left my phone at her place while I rushed the thirty blocks here.

"I'm divorced," I begin.

Kate smiles slightly. She has always been so careful to

avoid letting me know how she feels, but even though we've met only a few times, I've learned to read her.

"He left me for another woman."

The smile disappears from Kate's face.

"But she's not with him anymore, either," I add quickly. "He had a kind of breakdown—he tried to hurt me and there were witnesses. He's getting help."

I watch Kate as she processes all of this.

"Okay," she finally says. "So he is . . . no longer a threat to you?"

"Correct."

Kate cocks her head to the side. "He left you for another woman?"

This time it's me who smiles slightly. "She was the perfect replacement. That's what I thought the first time I saw her. . . . She's safe now, too."

"Richard always did like everything to be perfect." Kate leans back in her chair and crosses her right leg over her left, then absently massages her ankle.

The first time I met Kate, she'd merely asked me a few questions. But the queries helped me untangle the twisting thoughts in my mind: *Can you tell me why you think Richard is trying to keep you off-balance? What would his motivation be for this?*

The second time I came to see Kate, she'd reached over as if to pat my arm. But she didn't touch me; her hand had just hovered there. My gaze had fallen on the thick cuff bracelet on her wrist.

She'd held her arm still, letting me take it in. But she hadn't said a single word.

Seeing that distinctive cuff shouldn't have come as

a surprise. After all, collecting information was part of the reason why I'd sought out Richard's ex, the dark-haired woman he'd been with before me.

It hadn't been difficult to find her; Kate still lived in the city and was listed in the phone book. I was so careful. I never even mentioned her by name when I wrote about our meetings in my Moleskine notebook, and when Richard discovered I'd snuck into the city, I had lied and told him I'd been to see a therapist.

But Kate was even more careful.

She listened to me thoughtfully, but she didn't seem willing to share the story of what had happened during the years she and Richard were together.

I believe I discovered why during my third visit.

During our previous meetings, Kate had moved to one side after letting me into her apartment, gesturing for me to walk ahead of her toward the living room. When she stood up to signal our conversations had concluded, she motioned for me to go first and then followed to see me out.

On our third visit, though, when I wondered aloud if I should simply try to leave Richard and go stay with Aunt Charlotte, Kate abruptly stood and offered me tea.

I nodded, confused.

She walked into the kitchen while I stared after her.

Her right foot dragged along the floor; her body compensating for it by tilting down and up, gathering momentum to propel her forward. Something had happened to her leg, the one she massaged at times during our talk. Something that had left her with a pronounced limp.

When she returned with the tray of tea, she merely said, "What was it you were saying?"

I shook my head when she tried to hand me a cup. I knew my hands were trembling too violently for me to hold it.

I looked at the intricate platinum necklace she was wearing, that cuff bracelet, and the emerald ring on her right hand. Such exquisite, expensive pieces. They stood out against her simple clothing.

"I was saying . . . I can't just leave him." I choked out the words.

I rushed out a few moments later, suddenly terrified that Richard was trying to call my cell phone. That was the last time I'd seen Kate until today.

"There's a police record of the incident. And Maureen has stepped in to watch over Richard," I say now.

Kate closes her eyes briefly. "That's good."

"Your leg . . ."

When Kate speaks, her voice is emotionless. "I fell down some stairs." She hesitates and shifts her gaze to stare at her fish gliding through the aquarium. "Richard and I had argued that night because I was late to an important event." Her voice is much softer now. "After we got home and he went to bed . . . I left the apartment. I was carrying a suitcase." She swallows hard and her hand begins to massage her calf. "I decided to take the stairwell instead of the elevator. I didn't want anyone to hear the chime. But Richard . . . he wasn't asleep."

Her face crumples for an instant, then she recovers. "I never saw him again."

"I'm so sorry. You're safe now, too."

Kate nods.

After a moment, she says, "Be well, Vanessa."

She stands and walks me to the door.

I hear her lock click behind me as I start down the hallway. Then my head snaps back to look toward her apartment, a connection firing in my brain as I recall a long-ago vision.

The woman in the raincoat who'd stood outside the Learning Ladder, staring while I packed up my classroom. She had turned away with an odd jerking motion when I approached the window.

It could have been a limp.

CHAPTER
FORTY-TWO

I AWAKEN TO FEEL RICH sunlight pouring through the slats of the window blinds, warming my body as I lie in bed in Aunt Charlotte's spare room.

My room, I think, spreading out my arms and legs like a starfish so I take up the entire bed. Then I stretch out my left hand and turn off my alarm before it can blare.

Sleep still eludes me on some nights, as I turn over in my mind all that has happened and try to put together the pieces that remain a mystery to me.

But I no longer dread mornings.

I rise and wrap myself in my robe. As I walk toward the bathroom to take a quick shower, I pass my desk, where the itinerary for our trip to Venice and Florence rests. Aunt Charlotte and I leave in ten days. It's still summertime, and I won't begin work teaching pre-K students in the South Bronx until after Labor Day.

An hour later, I step out of the apartment building into the warm air. I'm not in a rush today, so I stroll down the sidewalk, taking care not to smudge the chalk hopscotch squares a child has drawn. New York City is always quieter in August; the pace seems gentler. I pass a cluster of tourists taking photos of the skyline. An elderly man sits on the steps of a brownstone, reading the paper. A vendor fills buckets with clusters of fresh poppies and sunflowers, lilies and asters. I decide I'll buy some on my way home.

I reach the coffee shop and pull open the door, then scan the room.

"Table for one?" a waitress asks as she passes by with a handful of menus.

I shake my head. "Thanks, but I'm meeting someone."

I see her in the corner, lifting a white mug to her lips. Her gold wedding band glints as it catches the light. I pause, staring at it.

Part of me wants to run to her. Part of me wants more time to prepare.

Then she looks up and our eyes meet.

I walk over and she stands up quickly. She reaches out unhesitatingly and hugs me.

When we draw back, we wipe our eyes in unison. Then we burst into laughter.

I slide into the booth across from her.

"It is really good to see you, Sam." I look at her bright, beaded necklace and smile.

"I've missed you, Vanessa."

I've missed me, too, I think.

But instead of speaking, I reach into my bag.

And I pull out my matching happy beads.

EPILOGUE

Vanessa walks down the city sidewalk, her blond hair loose around her shoulders, her arms swinging free at her sides. Her street is quieter than usual in the waning days of summer, but a lone bus lumbers by the spot I've staked out. A few teenagers loiter on the corner, watching as one spins on a skateboard. She passes them and pauses at a flower stand. She bends down, reaching for a generous cluster of poppies in a white bucket. She smiles as the vendor makes change, then continues on toward her apartment.

All the while, my eyes never stray from her.

When I've watched her before, I've tried to gauge her emotional state. Know thy enemy, Sun Tzu wrote in *The Art of War*. I read that book for a college course and the line resonated with me deeply.

Vanessa never realized I was a threat. She only saw what I wanted her to see; she bought into the illusion I created.

She thinks I am Emma Sutton, the innocent woman

who fell into the trap she laid to escape her husband. I'm still stunned by Vanessa's admission that she orchestrated my affair with Richard; I thought I was the one spinning a web.

Apparently we were unwitting coconspirators.

Vanessa has no idea who I really am, though. No one does.

I could walk away now, and she'd never be privy to the truth. She looks completely recovered from all that has happened to her. Maybe it's best for her not to know.

I look down at the photograph I am clutching. The edges are worn from age and frequent handling.

It is a picture of a seemingly happy family: a father, a mother, a little boy with dimples, and a preteen girl with braces. The photo was taken years ago, when I was twelve, back when we lived in Florida. A few months before our family shattered.

It was after ten P.M. and I should have been asleep—it was past my bedtime—but I wasn't. I heard the doorbell ring, then my mother call, "I'll get it."

My father was in his room, probably grading papers. He often did that at night.

I heard the murmur of voices, then my father scrambling down the hallway toward the stairs.

"Vanessa!" he cried. His voice sounded so strained it propelled me out of my room. My socks slid silently along the carpeted floor as I crept past my younger

brother's bedroom, to the top of the stairs, and hud-
dled there. I could see everything unfolding directly
below me. I was a spectator in the shadows.

I witnessed my mother fold her arms and glare
at my father. I witnessed my father gesture with
his hands as he talked. I witnessed my little calico
cat wind between my mother's legs, as if trying to
soothe her.

After my mother slammed the door, she turned to
my dad.

I will never forget how her face looked in that mo-
ment.

"She came on to me," my father insisted, his round
blue eyes, so like mine, widening. "She kept showing
up during my office hours and asking for extra help. I
tried to turn her away, and she kept— It was nothing,
I swear."

But it wasn't nothing. Because a month later, my father
moved out.

My mother blamed my father, but she also blamed
the pretty coed who'd enticed my dad into an affair.
She would throw out the name Vanessa during their
fights, her mouth twisting as if those three syllables
tasted bitter; it became shorthand for everything that
went wrong between them.

I blamed her as well.

After I graduated from college, I came to New York
for a visit. I looked her up, of course; she was Vanessa

Thompson by now. My name was different, too. After my father left, my mother reverted to her maiden name, Sutton. When I became an adult, I changed mine to it also.

Vanessa lived in a big house in an affluent suburb. She was married to a handsome man. She was gliding through a golden life, one she didn't deserve. I wanted to see her close up, but I couldn't find a way to get near her. She rarely left her home. There was no way we could naturally intersect.

I almost cut my trip short. Then I realized something.

I could get close to her husband.

It was easy to find out where Richard worked. I quickly learned that he liked double espressos from the corner coffee shop every afternoon around three. He was a creature of habit. I brought my laptop and camped out at a table. The next time he came in, our eyes met.

I was used to men hitting on me, but this time I was the pursuer. Just as I imagined she had been with my father.

I'd given him my brightest smile. "Hi. I'm Emma."

I'd expected him to want to sleep with me; men usually did. That would have been enough, even if it was just for one night; eventually, his wife would have found out. I'd have made certain of that.

The symmetry of it appealed to me. It felt like justice.

Instead, he suggested I apply for a job as an assistant at his company.

Two months later, I replaced his secretary, Diane.

A few months after that, I replaced his wife.

I look down at the photo in my hand again.

I was so wrong about everything.

About my father.

I was deceived once by a married man when I was in college, Vanessa had said on the day we'd met at the bridal salon. *I thought he loved me. He never told me about his wife.*

I was wrong about Richard.

If you marry Richard, you will regret it, she'd warned me when she confronted me outside my apartment. And later, while Richard stood beside me, she'd tried again, even though she was visibly scared: *He will hurt you.*

I think of how Richard pulled me to his side, wrapping his arm around me, after Vanessa uttered those words. The gesture seemed protective. But his fingertips dug into my flesh, creating a little trail of plum-colored marks. I don't even think he knew he was doing it; he was glaring at Vanessa in that moment. The next day, when I met Vanessa at the bridal salon, I made sure to keep her on my other side.

And most of all, I was wrong about Vanessa.

It is only fair that she knows she was wrong about me, too.

I make myself visible as I cross the street and approach her.

She turns around even before I call her name; she must have sensed my presence.

"Emma! What are you doing here?"

She was honest with me, even though it wasn't easy. If she hadn't fought so hard to save me, I would have married Richard. But she didn't stop there. She risked her life to expose him, preventing him from preying on yet another woman.

"I wanted to say I'm sorry."

Her brow creases. She waits.

"And I wanted to show you a picture." I hand it to her. "This was my family."

Vanessa stares at the photograph as I tell my story, beginning with that long-ago October night when I was supposed to be asleep.

Then her head snaps up and she searches my face. "Your eyes." Her tone is even, measured. "They seemed so familiar."

"I thought you deserved to know."

Vanessa hands back the picture. "I've been wondering about you. You seemed to materialize out of nowhere. When I tried to look you up online, you didn't exist until a few years ago. I couldn't find much more than your address and phone number."

"Would you rather not have known who I really was?"

She considers this for a moment.

Then she shakes her head. "The truth is the only way to move forward."

And then, because there is nothing more for either of us to say, I signal for an approaching cab.

I climb into the taxi and twist around to stare out the back window.

I lift my hand.

Vanessa stares at me for a moment. Then she raises her palm, her movement a mirror image of my own.

She turns and walks away from me at the exact moment the cab begins to move, the distance between us growing greater with each breath.

ACKNOWLEDGMENTS

From Greer and Sarah:

We are grateful every day for our editor and publisher, Jennifer Enderlin at St. Martin's Press, whose brilliant brain has made this a much better book and whose unparalleled energy, vision, and savvy have launched it higher and farther than we ever dreamed.

We are lucky to have an outstanding publishing team behind us, which includes: Katie Bassel, Caitlin Dareff, Rachel Diebel, Marta Fleming, Olga Grlic, Tracey Guest, Jordan Hanley, Brant Janeway, Kim Ludlam, Erica Martirano, Kerry Nordling, Gisela Ramos, Sally Richardson, Lisa Senz, Michael Storrings, Tom Thompson, Dori Weintraub, and Laura Wilson.

Thank you to our amazing, smart, and generous agent, Victoria Sanders, as well as her fabulous crew: Bernadette Baker-Baughman, Jessica Spivey, and Diane Dickensheid at Victoria Sanders and Associates. Our gratitude also to Mary Anne Thompson.

To Benee Knauer: We are so appreciative of your spot-on early edits, most especially teaching us the true meaning of "palpable tension."

Many thanks to our foreign publishers, notably our dreamy dinner partner Wayne Brookes at Pan Macmillan UK. Our deep appreciation also to Shari Smiley at the Gotham Group.

From Greer:

Simply put, this book would not exist without Sarah Pekkanen, my inspiring, talented, and hilarious co-author—and cherished friend. Thank you for being my partner in crime on this wondrous journey.

In my twenty years as an editor, I learned a tremendous amount from the authors I worked with, especially Jennifer Weiner and also her agent, Joanna Pulcini. I also want to thank my former colleagues at Simon & Schuster, many of whom I also regard as dear friends, especially my mentor at Atria Books, Judith Curr; the sublime Peter Borland; and the most talented young editor in the business, Sarah Cantin.

From elementary school through graduate school I was fortunate to have teachers who believed in me, most remarkably Susan Wolman and Sam Freedman.

I am deeply grateful to our early readers, Marla Goodman, Alison Strong, Rebecca Oshins, and Marlene Nosenchuk.

I am gifted with many friends—both in and outside of the publishing industry—who cheered me on from the sidelines. Thank you to Carrie Abramson (and her husband, Leigh, our wine consultant), Gillian Blake, Andrea Clark, Meghan Daum (whose poem to me inspired Sam's), Dorian Fuhrman, Karen Gordon, Cara McCaffrey, Liate Stehlik, Laura van Straaten, Elisabeth Weed, and Theresa Zoro. A special shout-out also to my Nantucket book club.

Thank you to Danny Thompson and Ellen Katz Westrich for keeping me physically and emotionally fit.

And my family:

Bill, Carol, Billy, Debbie, and Victoria Hendricks; Patty, Christopher, and Nicholas Allocca; Julie Fontaine and Raya and Ronen Kessel.

Robert Kessel, who always motivates me to break down walls.

Mark and Elaine Kessel, for passing on their love of books, serving as my earliest readers, and always telling me to "go for it."

Rocky, for keeping me company.

Extra-special gratitude to Paige and Alex, who encouraged their mother to pursue *her* childhood dream.

And finally to John, my True North, who not only told me that I could and should, but held my hand every step of the way.

From Sarah:

Ten years ago, Greer Hendricks became my editor. Then she became my beloved friend. Now we are a writing team. Our creative collaboration has been a singular joy, and I am so grateful for the way she supports, challenges, and inspires me. I cannot wait to see what the next ten years have in store for us.

My appreciation to all of the Smiths for their assistance through this process: Amy and Chris for the encouragement, laughter, and wine; Liz for her early read of the manuscript; and Perry for his thoughtful advice.

Thanks to Kathy Nolan for sharing her expertise on everything from marketing to websites; to Rachel Baker, Joe Dangerfield, and Cathy Hines for always having my back; the Street Team and my Facebook friends and readers who spread the word about my books with fun and flair; and my vibrant, supportive community of fellow authors.

I'm grateful to Sharon Sellers for keeping me strong enough to climb that next mountain, and to the wise, witty Sarah Cantin. My appreciation also to Glenn Reynolds, as well as Jud Ashman and the Gaithersburg Book Festival crew.

Bella, one of the great dogs, sat patiently by my side as I wrote.

Love to the incomparable Pekkanen crew: Nana Lynn, Johnny, Robert, Saadia, Sophia, Ben, Tammi, and Billy.

Always, and most of all, to my sons: Jackson, Will, and Dylan.

Read on for an excerpt from

Greer Hendricks and Sarah Pekkanen's novel

You're Invited: Seeking women aged 18 to 32 to participate in a study on ethics and morality conducted by a preeminent NYC psychiatrist. Generous compensation. Anonymity guaranteed. Call for more details.

It's easy to judge other people's choices. The mother with a grocery cart full of Froot Loops and Double Stuf Oreos who yells at her child. The driver of an expensive convertible who cuts off a slower vehicle. The woman in the quiet coffee shop who yaks on her cell phone. The husband who cheats on his wife.

But what if you knew the mother had lost her job that day?

What if the driver had promised his son he'd make it to his school play, but his boss had insisted he attend a last-minute meeting?

What if the woman in the coffee shop had just

received a phone call from the love of her life, a man who'd broken her heart?

And what if the cheater's wife habitually turned her back on his touch?

Perhaps you would also make a snap judgment about a woman who decides to reveal her innermost secrets to a stranger for money. But suspend your assumptions, at least for now.

We all have reasons for our actions. Even if we hide the reason from those who think they know us best. Even if the reasons are so deeply buried we can't recognize them ourselves.

CHAPTER
ONE

Friday, November 16

A LOT OF WOMEN want the world to see them a certain way. It's my job to create those transformations, one forty-five minute session at a time.

My clients seem different when I've finished helping them. They grow more confident, radiant. Happier, even.

But I can only offer a temporary fix. People invariably revert to their former selves.

True change requires more than the tools I wield.

It's twenty to six on a Friday evening. Rush hour. It's also when someone often wants to look like the best version of themselves, so I consistently block this time out of my personal schedule.

When the subway doors open at Astor Place, I'm the first one out, my right arm aching from the weight of my black makeup case as it always does by the end of a long day.

I swing my case directly behind me so it'll fit through the narrow passageway—it's my fifth trip through the turnstiles today alone, and my routine is automatic—then I hurry up the stairs.

When I reach the street, I dig into the pocket of my leather jacket and pull out my phone. I tap it to open my schedule, which is continually updated by Beauty-Buzz. I provide the hours I can work, and my appointments are texted to me.

My final booking today is near Eighth Street and University Place. It's for two clients, which means it's a double—ninety minutes. I have the address, names, and a contact phone number. But I have no idea who will be waiting for me when I knock on a door.

I don't fear strangers, though. I've learned more harm can come from familiar faces.

I memorize the exact location, then stride down the street, skirting the garbage that has spilled from a toppled bin. A shopkeeper pulls a security-grate over his storefront, the loud metal rattling into place. A trio of students, backpacks slung over their shoulders, jostle each other playfully as I pass them.

I'm two blocks from my destination when my phone rings. Caller ID shows it's my mom.

I let it ring once as I stare at the little circular photo of my smiling mother.

I'll see her in five days, when I go home for Thanksgiving, I tell myself.

But I can't let it go.

Guilt is always the heaviest thing I carry.

"Hey, Mom. Everything okay?" I ask.

"Everything's fine, honey. Just checking in."

I can picture her in the kitchen in the suburban Philadelphia home where I grew up. She's stirring gravy on the stove—they eat early, and Friday's menu is always pot roast and mashed potatoes—then unscrewing the top on a bottle of Zinfandel in preparation for the single glass she indulges in on weekend nights.

There are yellow curtains dressing the small window above the sink, and a dish towel looped through the stove handle with the words *Just roll with it* superimposed over an image of a rolling pin. The flowered wallpaper is peeling at the seams and a dent marks the bottom of the fridge from where my father kicked it after the Eagles lost in the playoffs.

Dinner will be ready when my dad walks through the door from his job as an insurance salesman. My mother will greet him with a quick kiss. They will call my sister, Becky, to the table, and help her cut her meat.

"Becky zipped up her jacket this morning," my mother says. "Without any help."

Becky is twenty-two, six years younger than me.

"That's fantastic," I say.

Sometimes I wish I lived closer so I could help my parents. Other times, I'm ashamed at how grateful I am that I don't.

"Hey, can I call you back?" I continue. "I'm just running in to work."

"Oh, did you get hired for another show?"

I hesitate. Mom's voice is more animated now.

I can't tell her the truth, so I blurt out the words: "Yeah, it's just a little production. There probably won't even be much press about it. But the makeup is super elaborate, really unconventional."

"I'm really proud of you," my mom says. "I can't wait to hear all about it next week."

I feel like she wants to add something more, but even though I haven't quite reached my destination—a student housing complex at NYU—I end the call.

"Give Becky a kiss. I love you."

My rules for any job kick in even before I arrive.

I evaluate my clients the moment I see them—I notice eyebrows that would look better darkened, or a nose that needs shading to appear slimmer—but I know my customers are sizing me up, too.

The first rule: my unofficial uniform. I wear all black, which eliminates the need to coordinate a new outfit every morning. It also sends a message of subtle authority. I choose comfortable, machine-washable layers that will look as fresh at seven P.M. as they do at seven A.M.

Since personal space vanishes when you're doing someone's makeup, my nails are short and buffed, my breath is minty, and my curls are swept up in a low twist. I never deviate from this standard.

I rub Germ-X on my hands and pop an Altoid in my mouth before I ring the buzzer for Apartment 6D. I'm five minutes early. Another rule.

I take the elevator to the sixth floor, then follow the

sound of loud music—Katy Perry's "Roar"—down the hallway and meet my clients. One is in a bathrobe, and the other wears a T-shirt and boxers. I can smell the evidence of their last beauty treatment—the chemicals used to highlight blond streaks into the hair of the girl named Mandy, and the nail varnish drying on the hands Taylor is waving through the air.

"Where are you going tonight?" I ask. A party will likely have stronger lighting than a club; a dinner date will require a subtle touch.

"Lit," Taylor says.

At my blank look, she adds: "It's in the Meatpacking District. Drake was just there last night."

"Cool," I say.

I wind through the items scattered across the floor—an umbrella, a crumpled gray sweater, a backpack—then move aside the Skinny Pop popcorn and half-empty cans of Red Bull on the low coffee table so I can set down my case. I unlatch it and the sides fold out like an accordion to reveal tray upon tray of makeup and brushes.

"What kind of look are we going for?"

Some makeup artists dive in, trying to cram as many clients as possible into a day. I take the extra time I've built into my schedule to ask a few questions. Just because one woman wants a smokey eye and a naked mouth doesn't mean another isn't envisioning a bold red lip and only a swipe of mascara. Investing in those early minutes saves me time on the backend.

But I also trust my instincts and observations. When these girls say they want a sexy, beachy look, I know they really want to resemble Gigi Hadid, who is on the cover of the magazine splayed across the love seat.

"So what are you majoring in?" I ask.

"Communications. We both want to go into PR." Mandy sounds bored, like I'm an annoying adult asking her what she wants to be when she grows up.

"Sounds interesting," I say as I pull a straight-back chair into the strongest light, directly under the ceiling fixture.

I start with Taylor. I have forty-five minutes to create the vision she wants to see in the mirror.

"You have amazing skin," I say. Another rule: Find a feature to compliment on every client. In Taylor's case, this isn't difficult.

"Thanks," she says, not lifting her gaze from her phone. She begins a running commentary on her Instagram feed: "Does anyone really want to see another picture of cupcakes?" "Jules and Brian are so in love, it's gross." "Inspirational sunset, got it . . . glad you're having a rocking Friday night on your balcony."

As I work, the girls' chatter fades into background noise, like the drone of a hair dryer or city traffic. I lose myself in the strokes of different foundations I've applied to Taylor's jawline so I can match her skin tone flawlessly, and in the swirl of copper and sandy hues I blend on my hand to bring out the gold flecks in her eyes.

I'm brushing bronzer onto her cheeks when her cell phone rings.

Taylor stops tapping hearts and holds up her phone: "Private number. Should I get it?"

"Yes!" Mandy says. "It could be Justin."

Taylor wrinkles her nose. "Who answers their phone on a Friday night, though? He can leave a message."

A few moments later, she touches the speakerphone button and a man's voice fills the room:

"This is Ben Quick, Dr. Shields's assistant. I'm confirming your appointments this weekend, for tomorrow and Sunday from eight to ten A.M. The location again is Hunter Hall, Room 214. I'll meet you in the lobby and take you up."

Taylor rolls her eyes and I pull back my mascara wand.

"Can you keep your face still, please?" I ask.

"Sorry. Was I out of my mind, Mandy? I'm going to be way too hungover to get up early tomorrow."

"Just blow it off."

"Yeah. But it's five hundred bucks. That's, like, a couple sweaters from rag & bone."

These words break my concentration; five hundred is what I make for ten jobs.

"Gah. Forget it. I'm not going to set an alarm to go to some dumb questionnaire," Taylor says.

Must be nice, I think, looking at the sweater crumpled in the corner.

Then I can't help myself: "A questionnaire?"

Taylor shrugs. "Some psych professor needs students for a survey."

I wonder what sort of questions are on the survey. Maybe it's like a Myers-Briggs personality test.

I step back and study Taylor's face. She's classically pretty, with an enviable bone structure. She didn't need the full forty-five-minute treatment.

"Since you're going to be out late, I'll line your lips before I apply gloss," I say. "That way the color will last."

I pull out my favorite lip gloss with the BeautyBuzz logo on the tube and smooth it along Taylor's full lips. After I finish, Taylor gets up to go look in the bathroom mirror, trailed by Mandy. "Wow," I hear Taylor say. "She's really good. Let's take a selfie."

"I need my makeup first!"

I begin to put away the cosmetics I used for Taylor and consider what I will need for Mandy when I notice Taylor has left her phone on the chair.

My rocking Friday night will consist of walking my little mixed terrier, Leo, and washing the makeup out of my brushes—after I take the bus across town to my tiny studio on the Lower East Side. I'm so wiped out that I'll probably be in bed before Taylor and Mandy order their first cocktails at the club.

I look down at the phone again.

Then I glance at the bathroom door. It's partly closed.

I bet Taylor won't even bother to return the call to cancel her appointment.

"I need to buy the highlighter she used," Taylor is saying.

Five hundred dollars would help a lot with my rent this month.

I already know my schedule for tomorrow. My first job doesn't begin until noon.

"I'm going to have her do my eyes kind of dramatic," Mandy says. "I wonder if she has false lashes with her."

Hunter Hall from eight to ten A.M.—I remember that

part. But what was the name of the doctor and his assistant?

It's not even like I make a decision to do it; one second I'm staring at the phone and the next, it's in my hand. Less than a minute has passed; it hasn't locked out yet. Still, I need to look down to navigate to the voice mail screen, but that means taking my eyes off the bathroom door.

I jab at the screen to play the most recent message, then press the phone tightly to my ear.

The bathroom door moves and Mandy starts to walk out. I spin around, feeling my heartbeat erupt. I won't be able to replace the phone without her seeing me.

Ben Quick.

I can pretend it fell off the chair, I think wildly. I'll tell Taylor I just picked it up.

"Wait, Mand!"

Dr. Shields's assistant . . . eight to ten A.M. . . .

"Should I make her try a darker lip color?"

Come on, I think, willing the message to play faster.

Hunter Hall, Room 214.

"Maybe," Mandy says.

I'll meet you in the lob—

I hang up and drop the phone back onto the chair just as Taylor takes her first step into the room.

Did she leave it faceup or facedown? But before there's time to try and remember, Taylor is beside me.

She stares down at her phone and my stomach clenches. I've messed up. Now I recall that she left it with the screen facing down on the chair. I put it back the wrong way.

I swallow hard, trying to think of an excuse.

"Hey," she says.

I drag my eyes up to meet hers.

"Love it. But can you try a darker lip gloss?"

She flops back onto the chair and I slowly exhale.

I re-do her lips twice—first making them berry, then reverting to the original shade, all the while steadying my right elbow with my left palm so my shaking fingers don't ruin the lines—and by the time I'm finished, my pulse has returned to normal.

When I leave the apartment with a distracted "Thank you" from the girls instead of a tip, my decision is confirmed.

I set the alarm on my phone for 7:15 A.M.

Saturday, November 17

The next morning, I review my plan carefully.

Sometimes an impulsive decision can change the course of your life.

I don't want that to happen again.

I wait outside Hunter Hall, peering in the direction of Taylor's apartment. It's cloudy and the air is thick and gray, so for a moment I mistake another young woman rushing in my direction for her. But it's just someone out for a jog. When it's five minutes past eight and it appears that Taylor is still asleep, I enter the lobby, where a guy in khakis and a blue button-down shirt is checking his watch.

"Sorry I'm late!" I call.

"Taylor?" he says. "I'm Ben Quick."

I'd correctly gambled on the assumption that Taylor wouldn't phone to cancel.

"Taylor is sick, so she asked me to come and do the questionnaire instead. I'm Jessica. Jessica Farris."

"Oh." Ben blinks. He looks me up and down, examining me more carefully.

I've traded my ankle boots for Converse high tops and slung a black nylon backpack over one shoulder. I figure it won't hurt if I look like a student.

"Can you hang on a second?" he finally says. "I need to check with Dr. Shields."

"Sure." I aim for the slightly bored tone Taylor used last night.

The worst thing that'll happen is he'll tell me I can't participate, I remind myself. No big deal; I'll just grab a bagel and take Leo for a long walk.

Ben steps aside and pulls out his cell phone. I want to listen to his side of the conversation, but his voice is muted.

Then he walks over to me. "How old are you?"

"Twenty-eight," I respond truthfully.

I sneak a glance at the entrance to make sure Taylor isn't going to saunter in at the last minute.

"You currently reside in New York?" Ben asks.

I nod.

Ben has two more questions for me: "Where else have you lived? Anywhere outside the United States?"

I shake my head. "Just Pennsylvania. That's where I grew up."

"Okay," Ben says, putting his phone away. "Dr. Shields says you can participate in the study. First, I need to get your full name and address. Can I see some ID?"

I shift my backpack into my hand and dig through it until I find my wallet, then I hand him my driver's license.

He snaps a picture, then takes down the rest of my information. "I can Venmo you the payment tomorrow at the conclusion of your session if you have an account."

"I do," I say. "Taylor told me it's five hundred dollars, right?"

He nods. "I'm going to text all this to Dr. Shields, then I'll take you upstairs to the room."

Could it possibly be this simple?